Savannah in the Old South

WORMSLOE FOUNDATION PUBLICATIONS

NUMBER TWENTY-THREE

Savannah
in the
Old South

By Walter J. Fraser Jr.

The University of Georgia Press
Athens and London

Paperback edition, 2005

© 2003 by the University of Georgia Press

Athens, Georgia 30602

All rights reserved

Designed by Louise OFarrell

Set in 10.6/13.5 Adobe Garamond by Graphic Composition, Inc.

Printed and bound by Thomson-Shore

The paper in this book meets the guidelines for
permanence and durability of the Committee on
Production Guidelines for Book Longevity of the
, Council on Library Resources.

Printed in the United States of America

09   08   07   06   05   P   5   4   3   2   1

The Library of Congress has cataloged the hardcover edition
of this book as follows:

Library of Congress Cataloging-in-Publication Data

Fraser, Walter J.

Savannah in the Old South / by Walter J. Fraser Jr.

p.   cm. — (Wormsloe Foundation publications ; no. 23)

Includes bibliographical references and index.

ISBN 0-8203-2436-1 (alk. paper)

1. Savannah (Ga.)—History. 2. Savannah (Ga.)—Social conditions.

3. Savannah (Ga.)—Race relations. I. Title. II. Publications

(Wormsloe Foundation) ; no. 23.

F294.S2 F73 2003

975.8'724—dc21

2002007563

ISBN-13 978-0-8203-2776-1 (pbk. : alk. paper)

ISBN-10 0-8203-2776-x (pbk. : alk. paper)

British Library Cataloging-in-Publication Data available

For Jay, Thomas, Erin, Fernanda,
Philippa, and, of course, Lynn

The building of cities is one of man's greatest achievements. The form of his city . . . will be . . . an indicator of the state of his civilization.
—Edmund Bacon

The city . . . remains man's greatest work of art.
—Lewis Mumford, *The Culture of Cities*

Contents

Preface

A book about Savannah, *Midnight in the Garden of Good and Evil,* remained near the top of the nation's best-seller lists for over four years during the 1990s. It focused on a sensational murder case and the city's eccentrics and was referred to, if at all, by some of Savannah's most prominent families as "the book" or "that book." It was made into a major motion picture. This book, *Savannah in the Old South,* unlike "the book," paints with a wider brush and on a broader canvas a history of the city and all its people. And there is a major theme woven throughout: the paradox of the humanizing influences of a city whose economic, political, social, cultural, and intellectual life was built on the institution of slavery.

It is impossible to write a book of this scope without being deeply indebted to a legion of people and many institutions. The staff of the following archives provided invaluable assistance in the collection of public and private documents relating to Savannah's history: the Georgia Historical Society, Savannah; the Hargrett Rare Book and Manuscript Library, University of Georgia; the Georgia Department of Archives and History; the Southern Historical Collection, University of North Carolina; the William R. Perkins Library, Duke University; the National Archives; Emory University; and the Atlanta History Center. I was also fortunate to have the assistance of Lisa Sapp and the ideas of history graduate students at Georgia Southern University like Roger Allen, Linda Awe, and Kevin Creamer. The Georgia Southern University Foundation provided funds to help defray travel expenses, and a stipend from the National Endowment for the Humanities allowed me to participate in a seminar on urban history during the summer of 1989, which was directed by the distinguished professor Oliver Zunz at the University of Virginia, where research began on this book.

I owe thanks to Warren Jones, dean emeritus, Georgia Southern University, for creating an atmosphere conducive to research and writing and to Professor Jerry Steffen, chair of the History Department, who arranged my class schedules so that I had blocks of time to think, synthesize, and write. Karen

Orchard, former director of the University of Georgia Press, and Malcolm Call, former senior editor, are remembered for their patience in waiting for the manuscript, which took ten years to complete. The research and writing was interrupted by another project, which came to fruition as *Portraits of Conflict: A Photographic History of Georgia in the Civil War*. It both delayed and enriched the present book.

Finally, I wish to thank Louis Rubin, professor emeritus, University of North Carolina at Chapel Hill, Bennett Wall, professor emeritus, University of Georgia, and Professor Charles Joyner for their generous words about my first urban history—*Charleston! Charleston! The History of a Southern City*—which encouraged me to undertake another. And I am especially indebted to the following historians who read this book in part or whole and saved me from numerous errors of commission or omission: even though desperately ill, the late professor Phinizy Spalding of the University of Georgia offered sound advice on the early chapters, as did my colleagues Frank Saunders, professor emeritus, Georgia Southern University, and Professor Alan Gallay, Washington State University; Professor Hardy Jackson, Jacksonville State University, and Professor Edward Cashin, director, Center for the Study of Georgia History, Augusta State University, read and commented on the complete manuscript. Any errors remaining in this study are mine alone. And if "the past is prologue," I have no doubt I will hear about them from readers.

Savannah in the Old South

CHAPTER I

The Earliest Years,
1733–1754

THE RIVER

*I*N THE BEGINNING was the river, long before the town and later still the city. Rising in the west and fed by mountain springs and streams, the pristine river flowed southeasterly, falling gradually across piedmont and coastal plain over four hundred miles to the Atlantic Ocean. The river and its tributaries drained more than ten thousand square miles. The composition of the soil in its upper reaches was marl, red clay, and sand, which was poor farm land. But farther to the south the banks and beyond were a yellow sandy loam, good earth for farming. Turning, twisting, slowing in speed as it neared the sea, the river changed dramatically, as did the accompanying countryside. Flanked by thick, lime-green marsh grasses, the widening river cut myriads of tiny channels through the landscape. The rich, dark banks were alive with shell life. Native willow, red cedar, sweet bay, live oak, and cypress hung with gray moss grew along the river's edge; beyond towered palmetto, myrtle, giant pine, gum, and red maple trees that formed great, dense forests. Huge alligators prowled the shore, and deer teemed in the thickets; wild ducks and geese rafted in the river, and beavers and the great horned owl moved about at night. The ivory-billed woodpecker, Carolina paroquet, and passenger pigeon nested deep in the swampy floodplain.

The Indians first called the river Keowee, then Isundiga, which means "blue water," perhaps a misnomer since the river is copper colored. An Indian trail ran parallel to the river to its mouth, and the Natives called the island there Tybee, meaning "salt."

Spanish explorers named the river Rio Dulce.[1] Later, French adventurers planted a colony at Port Royal Sound to the north of the river, which they referred to as the Grande river. The Spanish ousted the French and in 1565 established the first permanent European settlement in North America at St. Augustine. From here northward to Port Royal Sound, across territory they named Guale (much of present-day Georgia), the Spanish built a string of missions for Christianizing and controlling the Native Americans. At these sites and those settled by the English, like Charles Town in Carolina, diseases of the Old World were transmitted to the New World's Indians with devastating effects.

Equally catastrophic for the Indians was the English economic system, which extracted for profit, and by force if necessary, the raw materials of the land. The Carolinians traded guns, balls, and powder for Indian slaves and animal skins with the Westos, a fierce tribe whose fortified settlement was located on a bend of the river about five miles below present-day Augusta. The river was called the Westobu after them.

Anxious to profit from the lucrative trade in flesh and skins, a faction of Carolinians around 1680 armed the Savannahs, a neighboring tribe, who attacked the Westos, killing and enslaving them. Now the Savannahs became the favored tribe of the Charles Town merchants and traders. They built Savannah Town on the Carolina side of the river at the site of the former Westos village, today Beech Island, South Carolina. Once again, and for the last time, the river was named for the conquerors of the region, the Savannah.[2]

Savannah Town became the entrepôt for trade from the west in humans and skins and a boisterous rendezvous for Charles Town traders and their Indian allies. From Savannah Town flatboats started the twenty-day trip to Charles Town piled high with furs and deerskins and carrying manacled Indian slaves to be bartered for rum and calico, scissors and beads. Carolina traders piloted the vessels, which were poled by Indians. They dropped down the Savannah and passed Yamacraw Bluff, named for the small band of Indians living there, and the last high land before the sea. The pilots now headed north by an inland waterway to Port Royal Sound and eventually unloaded their cargoes for shipment abroad at Charles Town's Ashley River wharfs. The Savannah River was a bustling artery of trade connecting Carolina's port westward to the mountains. Hundreds of Indian slaves and over fifty thousand deerskins and beaver pelts were shipped annually from Charles Town in the late seventeenth century.[3]

ALLIES AND ENEMIES

From the Carolina settlement south to St. Augustine the land became a battleground between Protestant Britain and Catholic Spain and France and their Indian allies. In 1702 the Spanish and French joined forces to thwart the aggressive, expansionist-minded English, but the Carolinians soon laid waste to what remained of the Spanish mission system. About the only Indians left in Guale were those allied with the traders of Charles Town, who for years cheated and exploited their Indian allies, and in 1715 the Yamasees and their confederates rose against the Carolinians. But with the aid of the Cherokees, the Charles Town traders drove the Yamasees south into Spanish Florida, which again exposed the southern frontier of the English.

The British government and the lords proprietors of Carolina were keenly aware that the Carolinians feared the new threat of incursions from the Spanish, French, and Indians. For this reason the Carolinians built Fort Moore in 1716 to protect Savannah Town and the lucrative trade with their new allies, the Cherokees.[4]

The following year the proprietors and the London government enthusiastically endorsed a proposal from Sir Robert Montgomery for a buffer settlement south of the Savannah River. He was granted all the land between the Savannah and Altamaha Rivers for the purpose of establishing within three years a province, "the Margravate of Azilia."

"THE MOST AMIABLE COUNTRY"

Montgomery used the hyperbole of promoters to attract investors. In two booklets he touted the region as "the most amiable Country of the Universe," a "*paradise*" . . . whose "gentle Hills are full of . . . *Silver.*" Here "The Air is . . . temperate, and . . . there is no Excess of *Heat,* or *Cold.*" Its fertile soil would produce silk, wine, and olives and make England independent of foreign markets. Citizen-soldiers would raise these crops and defend the province, "one continued Fortress" impregnable to invasion. But Montgomery's appeals did not meet with success, and by 1720 the scheme had failed.[5]

The British government remained interested in building strategic sites south of the Savannah River. Fort King George, named after the English monarch, was constructed at the mouth of the Altamaha River in 1721. Also in the 1720s, the London government agreed to the request of Jean-Pierre Purry, a Swiss native, to plant a colony of European Protestants to the south and west of the Carolina grant, which he would call Georgia. Purry, like Montgomery before him, promoted "the boundless wealth" that could be extracted from the "remarkable . . . fertility of its soil," especially through the production of "SILK." Soon he founded Purrysburg on the north bank of the Savannah River.[6]

Meanwhile, interest remained high in London for planting a colony for strategic and commercial reasons south of the Savannah River. Several new motives emerged in the early 1730s. James Edward Oglethorpe promoted one of them. An educated aristocrat and a soldier of fortune, Oglethorpe first experienced combat as a lieutenant in Europe at the age of twenty. Six years later he was elected to Parliament. Stern, driven, and determined, Oglethorpe was shocked by the cynicism and corruption he observed in London society. Working with the associates of Dr. Thomas Bray—philanthropists who promoted the Anglican Church in America—and on the parliamentary committee on jails, Oglethorpe discovered drunkenness, unemployment, poverty, and widespread imprisonment for debt under gruesome conditions. He was especially moved by the prison death of a young acquaintance, architect, and debtor, Robert Castell. This incident galvanized Oglethorpe. In his work as chairman of the parliamentary committee on jails, he gained the release of thousands of debtors and won national recognition.

By early 1730, the Bray Associates and Oglethorpe were considering how these unfortunates could be resettled in America. Motivated primarily by the philanthropic aim of planting a charity colony, the Bray Associates requested a charter from the Crown. They also stressed the military and commercial advantages of the proposed colony. In 1732 King George II awarded the charter, which created the Trustees for Establishing the Colony of Georgia in America. On the north and on the south the colony was bounded, respectively, by the Savannah and Altamaha Rivers.[7]

Through newspapers and pamphlets, the trustees promoted their scheme. They invited all classes to enlist in the enterprise. Oglethorpe and other Georgia propagandists relied heavily on ideas current in England and Carolina and on the writings of earlier boosters while promoting visionary reasons of their own. Georgia would become a haven for the "worthy poor" of England and "distressed Protestants in *Europe*" where "Thousands starve for want of . . . Sustenance." Oglethorpe pledged that the trustees would "prevent luxury and oppression in the officers, and idleness and vice in the people." In Georgia where "the Winter is . . . short, and the Summer cool'd with refreshing breezes," the land would "produce almost every Thing in wonderful Quantities." Citizen-soldiers on their own small plots without black slaves could produce crops and protect the colony, which would serve as a military buffer between Carolina and Spanish Florida.[8]

The Georgia publicists were so successful in recruiting prospective settlers that a screening committee was created to interview the applicants. Ironically, in view of one of the purported motives of the colony, no former debtors were chosen, and few ever immigrated. Those selected were failed, hard-bitten and sometimes hard-drinking, indigent small merchants, artisans, and unemployed laborers and their families from the London area. They would be transported, supplied for one year by the trustees, and granted fifty acres of land per family. Land could be inherited only in tail male—it would pass to the eldest son. If there was no male heir, the land reverted to the trustees because women were excluded from inheriting or owning land. This policy prohibiting absolute inheritance sparked protest from the beginning. It retarded the growth of the colony and was repealed only near the end of the trusteeship period.[9]

In sum, the trustees planned to resettle a group of unemployed or underemployed citizens from the world's most thickly populated metropolitan area to a rugged, isolated, and desolate frontier where, untrained in farming, they would all become yeoman farmers. At the very least, it was a utopian scheme. The plan succeeded where others had failed, due in part to the vast financial commitments made by both the trustees and the Crown.

THE VOYAGE

Without family obligations after the death of his domineering mother and impatient to launch the colony, Oglethorpe volunteered to lead the expedition to Georgia. A contract was let for the two-hundred-ton ship *Ann,* which was fitted out with supplies including "ten tons of Alderman Parson's 'best beer.'" At a meeting in early November 1732, the trustees agreed to establish a civil government and a court system in Georgia "and a Town on the River Savannah to be call'd by that name."[10]

In mid-November, following the end of the hurricane season in the Atlantic, the *Ann* was readied for departure from Gravesend. Seven trustees met aboard with Oglethorpe and pronounced the ship "Tight & Strong & well Manned." Captain John Thomas called the roll of passengers, and the trustees upon leaving the ship thought that all 114 colonists, including children, appeared "very well satisfied." Oglethorpe, however, observed that some of the youngest were very weak and half-starved. Aboard to tend the physical and spiritual needs was a doctor, William Cox, and a minister, the Reverend Henry Herbert. On Friday, November 17, the ship dropped away from its moorings and down the Thames with the tide. In a few days the vessel was rolling in the swells of the open sea.

The trustees relied on a young former merchant and now recorder for the colony, Thomas Christie, to keep a daily record of the voyage. Christie was later accused of drunkenness, adultery, and dishonesty. During the fifty-eight-day crossing, Oglethorpe comforted seasick colonists, acted as a godfather for a newborn infant, and saw that the colonists were amply supplied with a varied, but heavily salted, diet of pork, peas, fish, and beef. Following a squall, he had the passengers' quarters between decks cleaned with "Vinegar, wch proved very wholesome & refreshing." He drilled the men most skilled with muskets and bayonets. Oglethorpe imposed a moderate discipline—for instance, prohibiting "Smoking unless wth a Cap on the Pipe & then on the Deck." For special occasions he ordered extra wine, liquor, rations, and games. But he was not always accorded the deference he expected. During one misty night a dog belonging to Oglethorpe was apparently "flung Over board by some of the Sailors." Days later when the company assembled for the funeral of an infant, someone tried to "throw water on them." This so angered Oglethorpe that he kicked the culprit in the backsides.[11]

Near the end of the voyage, the passengers were tired and quarrelsome. One incident forecast future trouble: "Some of the people falling out altogether, Mr. Oglethorpe Ordd. 'em to . . . be friends," and he called for rum punch for everyone. A few days later, on January 13, 1733, landfall was made off Charles Town, South Carolina. It was welcome news to the passengers and crew.[12]

Oglethorpe went ashore but ordered the passengers to remain aboard ship lest they might refuse to go on to Georgia. Carolina officials greeted him enthusiastically. For years they had wanted a buffer colony to the south. They promised Oglethorpe food, tools, and military assistance. The following day the colonists sailed south and arrived in Port Royal Sound on January 15; here they went ashore and stood on firm earth for the first time in over eight weeks. Oglethorpe immediately left for the south with Captain Francis Scott and several of his men from the *Ann* "to view the Savannah River." They remained gone for ten days.

SETTLEMENT AT YAMACRAW BLUFF

Carolina traders and scouts may have pointed out to Oglethorpe the high bluff known as Yamacraw and the last high ground along the Savannah River before it reached the sea. It was the site of the trading post of Johnny Musgrove, offspring of the interracial union of a well-to-do South Carolina planter and a Creek woman; Musgrove himself married a mixed-blood woman, Mary, who was in her thirties by the time Oglethorpe met her. She became Oglethorpe's favorite intermediary with the Indians and helped him conclude two major treaties and land cessions with them. Also on the bluff was a small village of Yamacraws, a mixed group of about one hundred Creeks and Yamasees, pitiful survivors of the diseases, liquor, and economic system of the newcomers. These "trader's Indians"—mercenaries and interpreters for the English—were led by Tomochichi, "a white man's Indian."[13]

Oglethorpe visited the site and found that "The River here forms an Half-moon, along the South side of which the Banks are about Forty Feet high . . . and is pretty wide. . . . Ships that draw Twelve Feet Water can ride within Ten Yards of the Bank." He knew that the river for years had been a major artery for the Carolina trade. The location afforded a good view and was easily defensible. John and Mary Musgrove acted as interpreters for Oglethorpe as he conferred with Tomochichi about settling there. The Yamacraw leader welcomed him.

Oglethorpe returned to Carolina and arranged for soldiers and boats to transport the colonists to Yamacraw Bluff. When they arrived there on February 1 (February 12, according to the new style calendar adopted in 1752), Captain Scott and his troops welcomed them with a volley of musket fire. They climbed up the high steep bluff on stairs cut into the escarpment by the soldiers. Almost immediately they were greeted by a singing, dancing Indian wearing a headdress of white feathers and holding a great fan "Set from top to bottom with small Bells." Chief Tomochichi, his queen, and a retinue of followers trailed behind, "making a very uncouth Hollowing." The spectacle must have awed and unnerved the former residents of London.

That night the colonists pitched four large tents (in the vicinity of what is today the Hyatt-Regency Hotel) and slept for the first time on Georgia soil. The long desired buffer between Carolina and Spanish Florida had been founded; Savannah became the first settlement in Georgia, the last of the original thirteen English colonies.[14]

The settlers spent their first few days unloading the boats. They constructed a crane and ramp near the original steps to hoist and slide their boxes, provisions, and belongings up the steep bank. Here also the colonist Peter Gordon noted, "we began to digg trenches for fixing palisadoes . . . in case we should be attacked" by the Spanish or Indians. Atop this sandy bluff along "the riverside in the center of this plain," Oglethorpe felled huge pine trees, and on February 9 he "marked out the town and common" with the assistance of a trained surveyor, Colonel William Bull of South Carolina. It would take several months to lay out the public squares, wards, and streets, which apparently were fashioned after those of London.[15]

Oglethorpe was everywhere supervising and cajoling while dealing with a host of problems. Although he was a strict disciplinarian, some said that he was beloved by the colonists, who reportedly called him "Father." Apparently, they appreciated his sense of fairness and benevolence. During the first days of the settlement a "servant maid" was "accused of a loose disorderly behaviour, and trying to seduce severall other young women." She was sentenced to be tied to a cart and dragged through the settlement by "a negroe." But when several persons interceded with Oglethorpe, he remitted her punishment and sent her to Charles Town.

"I am . . . taken up in looking after a hundred . . . things," Oglethorpe told the trustees. His expenses soared. During Savannah's first fire, when a guard room and a hut near Oglethorpe's tent burned, weapons and tools had to be replaced; provisions had to be bought, and Indians were plied with gifts as "rewards for taking outlaws and spies" of the Spanish. Governor Robert Johnson of South Carolina believed that without Oglethorpe's leadership among settlers "unused to . . . Hardships and fatiques," the colony would have perished.[16]

Each family was issued an iron pot, a frying pan, wooden bowls, a Bible, and a *Book of Common Prayer*. The able-bodied received "a musket and bayonett, cartridge box and belt." On February 11 the settlers assembled under arms for the first time, and Oglethorpe organized them into military units or four tithings of ten men each. A clapboard guardhouse was located on the bluff at the best point "for commanding the river both wayes," and it was from here that sentinels marched to take up their posts for the first time on February 11.[17]

The colonists planted corn, peas, and potatoes; the Indians provided venison and small game; and the government of South Carolina supplied over two hundred head of cattle, hogs, and rice. Oglethorpe allowed the men a pint of

Madeira wine and a pint of "strong beer" daily. Colonel Bull and other Carolinians—John Whitaker, Joseph Bryan, and James St. Julian—brought in foodstuffs and their own African slaves, some of whom were carpenters skilled in fashioning squared lumber and boards. Oglethorpe employed Carolina's Independent Company for heavy labor and building. In March he reported that a battery of cannon and a magazine were completed despite colonists "unused to labour" and others down with the "bloody flux," or dysentery. Nevertheless, "our people still lie in tents," Oglethorpe noted. By late April, a blacksmith's forge, two clapboard or split log huts, and nine framed houses were completed, their sides "covered with feather-edged board" and the roofs shingled. The single-floor timber houses had one large and two smaller rooms below and a loft above for two beds. They sat on logs two feet above the ground with floors one and one-half inches thick. The houses, 16 feet wide by 24 feet long, were centered on town lots measuring 60 feet wide and 90 feet deep. One visitor observed, "Savannah's houses are arranged in mathematical regularity, which will look very pretty after everything has been put in order."[18]

During the warm Georgia spring, the town's fortifications continued to undergo modifications. Two blockhouses went up "at the Angles of the town." One was located on present-day Oglethorpe Avenue just east of Abercorn Street; the location of the second remains a mystery. The battery along the river was augmented and the palisades extended 140 yards along the east side of the town. Apparently, it was decided not to continue the palisades following treaties with the Yamacraw and Creek Indians, who were employed as scouts to prevent surprise attacks. Two companies of Tomochichi's tribe were enlisted, and each man was issued a gun, a bushel of corn per month, and a blanket annually. Also Oglethorpe purchased a sloop mounting six swivel guns for transport, fighting, or service as a pilot boat. Assisted by South Carolina's Company of Southern Rangers under the command of Captain James McPherson, Oglethorpe also began exploring sites for the location of military strong points beyond the town.[19]

TROUBLESOME TIMES

In adjusting to the fauna and flora of their new environment, the colonists tried to reconcile the "paradise" promised to the reality found. Already in March, Thomas Causton noted, "we have some grumbletonians here." The heat, the violent rains that beat through their tents, sand flies and ants, which "bite desperately," pestered the settlers; rattlesnakes and alligators terrified them. To help them overcome their fears, Oglethorpe had a wounded, twelve-foot alligator brought to town, where "the Children pelted and beat him to Death."[20]

In the spring Oglethorpe visited Charles Town for several weeks to seek aid for Georgia. Leaderless and with little to do, the colonists began drinking heavily, as was their custom in England. Upon his return, Oglethorpe "found the people . . . mutinous and impatient of labour and discipline." He believed that "this petulancy" or disobedience was due to heavy rum drinking and the presence of slave artisans who encouraged idleness among the settlers. He immediately sent the Africans back to South Carolina, staved in all the barrels of rum, and prohibited its sale, substituting instead moderate rations of wine. Oglethorpe also blamed the widespread drunkenness for the sickness he found raging in Savannah.

Drinking contaminated water from shallow wells or the Savannah River was the probable cause of death of William Cox in April, the first of the settlers to die. Ironically, he was the town's physician, and his demise "was very much lamented." Oglethorpe ordered a military funeral, and the town bell atop the crane rang during the burial. In the late spring and summer others fell ill with "burning fever," dysentery, and convulsions, probably typhoid fever. A former carpenter, Noble Jones, attempted to aid the sick with Indian root, rhubarb, and laudanum, but most who fell ill succumbed. Shortly, sixty colonists were down with the disease. People "begane to die so fast that the frequent firing of the canon and small arms" and the tolling of the bell "struck such terrour in our sick people," Peter Gordon reported, that Oglethorpe discontinued military funerals.

The lack of a ready supply of fresh water contributed to the high death rate. Over one-quarter of the colonists died during the first year. Oglethorpe had no reason to know that springs dried up and the river became brackish during high tides in the heat of spring and summer, but he had a well dug in the center of town where good water was found at twenty-five feet. It was built with bricks sent by the trustees, and a pump was installed. The location today lies beneath the asphalt at the intersection of Bull and Broughton Streets.[21] Despite all these precautions, typhoid fever continued to menace Savannah for decades.

PUBLIC SQUARES AND PRIVATE DWELLINGS

In the midst of the epidemic, Oglethorpe assembled the colonists along the river on July 7 for prayers of thanksgiving and praise. They then proceeded into the town, where several of the colonists were assigned lots. Homes were already constructed on some.

Since February the town had been laid out on a tract of land of twenty-four square miles, or 15,360 acres, according to Oglethorpe's specifications and plan. He most likely conceived of the layout of the town before he left England, as he had served on a committee of Parliament that supervised the building of Hanover Square in London. Nevertheless, historians still debate the origins of Savannah's unusual design, the most unique in colonial America.

Four public squares had been laid out at regular intervals. They approximated the size of those of London—one was named after St. James' Square there. On each of the squares the surveyors had centered neat, rectangular wards. The wards contained forty town lots and consisted of four blocks, called tithings. Each of the lots were bounded by a street in front and an alley behind. Twenty lots were located to the north of each open square and twenty to the south; to the east and west four larger trustee lots were reserved for public buildings. A tithingman and ten other males were responsible for standing watch in each ward; a constable was the chief official.

This pattern of wards around open squares was envisioned as fostering a sense of community and the social, economic, and religious life of the neighborhood. Over time, subsequent squares and wards would be laid out and modeled on the original. There were other planned cities in colonial America, but none had the carefully designed wards around open public spaces, which then and now account for the special character of Savannah.[22] These squares, later public parks, became adorned with native trees and flowering shrubs. The town was located on a high bluff, initially for defense, and above a graceful winding river, and it was bathed by salubrious southeastern sea breezes; over time the location provided a place pleasing to the senses and a humanizing influence on Savannah's residents.[23]

Oglethorpe named the four wards after trustees—Heathcote, Percival, Decker, and Derby (pronounced Darby). The latter was the first ward laid out and contained lots one through forty, which were subsequently referred to as "the First Forty." Derby was centered on Johnson Square, an open space named in honor of the governor of South Carolina, who had been so helpful to the Georgians. Five of the streets were named after other Carolinians who aided the colonists: Drayton, Whitaker, and Bull Streets ran north to south and intersected Derby Ward and Johnson Square at right angles, as did St. Julian and Bryan Streets, which bisected the ward in an east-west direction. Bay Street at the northern tip of the ward paralleled the river. Abercorn and Barnard Streets, running north to south and named after the colony's English benefactors, and King, Prince, and Duke Streets, running east to west, were named somewhat later and subsequently were renamed.

On July 7 Oglethorpe assigned to families the town lots in Derby Ward. When squabbles erupted over who was to receive the choice lots and those where houses stood already, Oglethorpe exercised his wits and diplomacy. Male heads of households received a five-acre garden plot and a forty-five-acre farm beyond the town's borders.

Following a grand dinner on July 7, perhaps to put the colonists at ease, Oglethorpe established a municipal court to adjudicate all civil and criminal affairs. Following instructions of the trustees, he appointed and took the oaths of the colony's highest officials, the bailiffs or magistrates and the judges, and impaneled a jury. Beyond this, the trustees were silent on a form of government. Apparently, they assumed Oglethorpe could provide the leadership needed without formal title or legislative assistance.

The first court case also was heard on July 7. The accused were expected to defend themselves, since the trustees had forbidden lawyers in Georgia. This trial may have taken place in the courthouse, the first permanent public building constructed. Built at the corner of Bull Street and Bay Lane, the courthouse was thirty-six feet long and twelve feet wide and constructed of split boards; it also served as a house of worship.[24]

ETHNIC AND RELIGIOUS DIVERSITY

During the winter and spring the *Volant,* the *James,* and the *Pearl* touched at Savannah and disembarked a few charity colonists from England. But on July 11 the *William and Sarah,* buffeted at sea by gales for months, dropped anchor off Savannah with forty-two prospective settlers aboard; all were Jewish, including both Sephardic and Ashkenazic Jews, and they comprised the largest single group to arrive since the original settlers. Despite opposition by the trustees, this group of men, women, and children sailed from England to

Georgia for the same reasons as the first settlers. Unlike most of the original colonists, however, several of the Jews were very wealthy.

Oglethorpe consulted lawyers in Charles Town for advice on permitting the Jews to come ashore. They probably advised him that Georgia's charter permitted all persons "liberty of conscience in the worship of God" except Catholics. Upon this advice and aware that there was a physician among the Jews who might assist those colonists afflicted with the "fever," Oglethorpe allowed them to land. Dr. Samuel Nunez was soon prescribing "cold baths, cooling drinks and other . . . applications . . . for the sick." Oglethorpe informed the trustees in August that the colonists "have wonderfully recovered."[25]

When the trustees told Oglethorpe to pay Dr. Nunez but not grant any land to the Jews, he ignored these instructions. He soon awarded lots to them on the same basis as the original settlers, although some of the wealthier Jews may have purchased their lots. Oglethorpe was motivated by very practical considerations: one of the settlers, Abraham De Lyon, was experienced in "cultivating vines and making wine," which the trustees wanted for export; also, most of the Jewish settlers were young, able-bodied men who would make good soldiers. Oglethorpe appointed one of them, Benjamin Sheftall, a lieutenant in his militia.

The new immigrants showed far greater interest in Judaism than did the Protestant settlers in Anglicanism. Although a parsonage house was built during the first year near the trustee lot at the southeastern corner of Johnson Square, it would be seventeen years before a church of any single denomination was erected separately from the dual-purpose courthouse and house of worship. It would be constructed on the trustee lot set aside for the church, today the site of Christ Episcopal Church.

The first Anglican minister arrived on the *Ann,* but he soon became ill and returned to England. The second was the Reverend Samuel Quincy, who observed that "Religion seems to be the least minded of anything in the place." A visiting Lutheran minister confirmed Quincy's observations when he noted that the English settlers did not keep their Sabbath holy: "They drink, play . . . and pursue all worldly amusements" with the Jews. Meanwhile, the Jewish settlers met in their dwellings for religious observances, although the building of a synagogue was delayed due to sharp differences within the Jewish community. From the outset, Quincy was unhappy with the frontier conditions in Savannah, was annoyed by his congregation, and frequently neglected his duties; the trustees removed him from his position.[26]

During August and into the autumn of 1733, Oglethorpe built a ring of military strong points around the town. He employed Captain James McPherson and his company of Southern Rangers to build Fort Argyle on the Ogeechee River about thirty miles west of Savannah; he established a guardhouse and cannon at a place Oglethorpe called Abercorn, fifteen miles north on the Savannah River near Purrysburg in Carolina. To protect the approaches to Savannah, defenses were constructed on Skidaway Island, and forts were built at Thunderbolt on the Wilmington River and on Tybee Island. Here, too, at the mouth of the Savannah River construction began on a beacon or lighthouse of pine and cedar, octagon in shape, ninety feet tall and twenty-five feet wide; outposts were also located at Highgate and Hampstead. Ten families were sent to settle each site. Charity colonists who arrived during the first year on vessels such as the *Georgia Pink* and the *Susannah* were deployed to these military strong points; subsequently, German-speaking colonists also were relocated to these defensive works. Oglethorpe told the trustees that now neither small nor large numbers of Spanish or Indians could approach Savannah "without . . . discovery."[27] As originally projected, Georgia had become a military buffer for South Carolina.

Houses went up quickly in Savannah and on Hutchinson Island. By the end of 1733, some public facilities were completed. Hutchinson Island, adjacent to the town and named for a benefactor of the colony, was "one of the most delightful spots of Ground I ever saw," Oglethorpe wrote. About "three miles in length and one wide," the island was partly covered in tall trees, particularly bays, and the remainder was meadow, which Oglethorpe believed perfect for cattle grazing.

A public pillory or stocks was built within the shadow of the guardhouse near the eastern edge of Savannah. It was used to enforce a strict discipline occasionally tempered by Oglethorpe's paternalism. One passenger aboard the *Georgia Pink* who arrived in August imbibed so heavily the day after he came ashore that he "was put into the Stocks for being drunk." Another passenger, Mary Preston, whose husband had been swept overboard at sea, was accused of picking the "Pockets of . . . [a] Drunken man." She argued "that She was drunk" and unaware of what she was doing. Upon proving that she was pregnant and posting bail, Mary's trial was delayed until "her Delivery."

A "large and commodious" public storehouse was built on the trustee lot next to the church lot at the southeastern corner of Johnson Square. Everything was dispensed from here that the charity colonists needed "for keeping house and tilling the soil," including food such as salted meat, cheese, flour, rice, and Indian corn. A public mill was built at the center of town. Undergoing construction nearby on the trustee lot between Johnson Square and Whitaker Street was a house for strangers, which served as a temporary shelter for immigrants; on the same lot a public oven was built on the east side of Whitaker Street between St. Julian Street and today's Congress Street. It was essential if an attack was ever launched against the fortified town, especially since bricks were not yet available for constructing ovens in the houses. One visitor observed that the "glorious large Oven . . . convinces all Travelers that there is no want of good Bread." These public facilities were especially needed in January 1734 when storms at sea and starvation among the passengers forced a sloop carrying forty Irish servants into the Savannah River.

Oglethorpe purchased the starving Irish men and women as "an act of charity" and assigned them to serve widows and magistrates as indentured servants. On this occasion Oglethorpe may have ignored the provision of the Charter of Georgia banning Catholics, as some of the Irish undoubtedly were Roman Catholics. In England, Catholicism was considered a threat to the state; the nearby colony of Florida and the Catholic Spanish there reinforced the attitude of the trustees and Savannahians toward "papists."[28]

The religion of some and the nativity of all the Irish immigrants probably engendered some hostility toward them locally. Most likely some of the Irish servants were Protestants, probably Presbyterians, since all came from Ulster. Historians have asserted, however, that all were Irish Catholic convicts, some of whom brought murder and mayhem to the colony. The late Rodney Baine, however, offered "overwhelming" evidence that the Irish were neither convicts nor very troublesome but were indentured servants maligned by those colonists who wished to replace white servitude with black slavery. Indeed, some contemporaries, including Oglethorpe, found the Irish "very usefull" to the colony.[29]

By early 1734 there were fifty framed houses standing in Savannah and 259 persons in the town and the nearby settlements of Hampstead and Highgate. In addition to Indians, another 184 colonists receiving the trustees' support were posted at outlying military sites. Late in 1733 and early in 1734, the *Savannah,* the *London Merchant,* and the *James* delivered supplies and English immigrants of varying character sent by the trustees. Ninety Lowland Scots arrived in the colony in 1734. In March the linguistic and cultural diversity of the colony continued to multiply when 78 Salzburg Lutherans, in search of religious asylum and approved by the trustees for settlement, entered the Savannah River aboard the *Purisburgh*. Here, they found, "we . . . were shelter'd . . . from all Dangers . . . of the Sea." They marveled at the river, abundant with oysters and sturgeon, and the woods beyond, which resounded "with the Musick of Birds, who sung the Praise of their Creator." Booming cannons and townspeople shouting "Huzzah!" welcomed them. Lodged in a tent, they worshiped in the temporary church-courthouse and visited the trustees' garden. This ten-acre plot just to the east of the town had recently been established for the encouragement and promotion of agriculture. One of the Salzburgers noted "Horses, Cows, Fowls, etc. in plenty" in the town. Although the Salzburgers remained in Savannah only briefly, the local English officials noted their German enthusiasm for work.

Different in language and customs from the Savannahians, the Salzburgers wished to locate beyond the town. Oglethorpe accommodated them by leading them twenty-five miles northwest to a place that he envisioned as a military outpost. Here they founded Ebenezer, their "Rock of Help," on Ebenezer Creek. Within a few years the Salzburgers moved to the banks of the Savannah River itself and founded New Ebenezer, which prospered. Other vessels subsequently arrived carrying German-speaking Lutherans, Moravians, and Swiss settlers.

A few of the Salzburger immigrants such as Margaretha Bach ended up in Savannah. She was accused of whoredom by her church and continued her lifestyle in the town while British authorities looked the other way. Local officials themselves, William Stephens noted, often had "housekeepers" of their own. A Lutheran congregation began to emerge in Savannah composed mostly of German-speaking Swiss and Palatines of the Reformed faith. A few Moravian pacificists immigrated but did not remain long.[30]

In May 1734 Oglethorpe sailed from Savannah for England carrying with him Tomochichi and his wife, his heir, and five other Yamacraws. Oglethorpe planned to ask the trustees for aid and the enactment of certain laws for the good of the colony. As in Oglethorpe's previous absence, criminality and dissension again surfaced in Savannah.

CRIME AND PUNISHMENT

The murder trial of two Irish indentured servants, Alice Riley and Richard White, was underway in May. They had robbed and murdered an incapacitated charity colonist living on Hutchinson Island, William Wise. Both Riley and White were convicted and sentenced to death by hanging though both maintained their innocence to the end. After the birth of her child, Riley was the first female murderer to die on the gallows in Georgia. White escaped from the crude log jail, but he was soon apprehended and executed.

A visiting merchant in Savannah wrote Oglethorpe in England that the Irish indentured servants caused trouble constantly. They were "Stealing from their Masters and carrying the Goods to Some Others." However, one resident in late 1734 was concerned that the punishments meted out were too "frequent & Shocking." He had witnessed an indentured female servant confined in the stocks for three hours during a rainstorm. Afterward she was dunked in the river and bruised so badly that "she was lame for 2 or 3 Months after." This would not have happened, he believed, if Oglethorpe had been in Georgia.

Rumors swept Savannah in March 1735 that Irish indentures and other aggrieved residents had conspired to burn the town and murder its inhabitants. Chief magistrate and storekeeper Thomas Causton, the official in charge during Oglethorpe's absence, summoned the tithingmen to patrol the frightened town. This Red String Plot, so called because the conspirators identified one another by a red string around their wrist, ended quickly when several alleged plotters were apprehended. If such a plot existed, it may have been caused by anger over the strict disciplinary measures and by the land tenure policy in the colony. Promptly, a grand jury indicted the alleged conspirators and meted out swift and harsh punishments: three men and a woman received at least sixty lashes from the town's hangman. During the spring five Irish indentured servants were whipped for stealing and running away.[31]

The Irish were not the only troublemakers to receive stiff punishments. In the summer a recent immigrant, Elizabeth Malpas, was tried and found guilty of "lyeing between two fellows naked & leading a dissolute life." She was tied to the rear of a cart and given sixty lashes while being pulled up and down Bull Street. When physician William Watkins married a recent settler but then discovered that his first wife was alive in England, he persuaded his new bride to marry someone else. She was indicted for bigamy and Watkins for a misdemeanor, and he was "whipt . . . at the Carts Tail around the Town."

Some punishments were too light for the crime. Evidently, leniency depended upon one's connections. For instance, James Wilson was convicted of "extortion in selling flesh meat" and of "wilfully destroying other mens hoggs" in 1735, but he was only fined; the following year Elizabeth Penrose was merely fined after being convicted of selling liquor without a license and "keeping a bawdy house." Her mild punishment was understandable: one resident observed that Savannah's chief magistrate, Thomas Causton, "upon all occasions carries strangers and other company to . . . Penrose's house."[32]

FACTIONS AND LAWS

While in England, Oglethorpe was informed in letters from Savannah that Causton repeatedly abused his authority. The recorder of the colony, Thomas Christie, was accused of the same offense. The community became deeply divided. Causton was said to charge "extravagant prices" for necessities, imprison people quickly for indebtedness, and use the lash "unmercifully." Causton, Christie, and "some Scotch gentlemen" profited handsomely by selling rum, a liquor banned by Oglethorpe. One recent immigrant, Elizabeth Bland, pleaded with Oglethorpe to arrange for her return because she would rather "serve my betters in England . . . than be a slave to such vile wretches as govern here." Opposition to the local authorities was rising.[33]

Paul Amatis, brought to the colony as an expert in growing silk, also criticized Causton's leadership. He quarreled, too, with Causton's friend Joseph Fitzwalter, the public gardener. Fitzwalter had planted a variety of fruit and olive trees in the trustees' ten-acre garden, which he considered primarily a nursery for vegetables and plants for the colonists. Amatis believed Fitzwalter had neglected the garden. After Amatis planted grape vines and hundreds of mulberry trees there, he threatened Fitzwalter with bodily harm if he entered the garden.

The variety of mulberry trees that flourished best in Georgia was the wrong kind to provide food for the imported silkworms. However, Amatis was able to send the trustees some silk, and they then made Fitzwalter subordinate to him. Amatis soon discovered that the sandy soil was too poor for all sorts of imported plants, and the fruit trees were frequently stripped bare by the colonists. Cold weather killed the orange trees, and summer heat blistered the grapes, which were to have been used in wine making. Amatis was discharged, and eventually Fitzwalter again became the public gardener.

The trustees' interest in silk persisted, and it was one of the first items exported from Savannah. Eventually a filature was built in the town, but production was a mixed success at best. The export of raw silk from Georgia varied annually from a few pounds to a peak year of nearly one ton. Wine production followed a similar course. Abraham De Lyon, the wine expert, left the colony within a few years. The idealistic vision of a garden in Savannah to feed the colonists and of the town and nearby settlements as centers for the production of silk and wine never fully materialized.[34]

Oglethorpe sailed from England in December with a flotilla of three vessels carrying nearly three hundred colonists, including Salzburgers, Moravians, and two young ministers, John and Charles Wesley. He also brought with him additional cash and bills of exchange for the colony provided by the trustees. However, Oglethorpe's free-spending habits had become a concern of the trustees.

Oglethorpe entered the Savannah River in February 1736. Furious that the lighthouse remained unfinished on Tybee Island, Oglethorpe threatened to hang the chief builder. Probably fearing for his life, the contractor, it was noted, now did "in sixteen days . . . more than he did in sixteen months." The colonists disembarked on Peeper (later Cockspur) Island while Oglethorpe went on to Savannah. He was received with celebrations in a town divided by factions. To some, trade in the town was at "a very low ebb." Nevertheless, Oglethorpe continued Thomas Causton as storekeeper and bailiff and dismissed one of Causton's critics, Paul Amatis. Next, he put into effect the three new laws that he had requested of the trustees and that had been enacted by Parliament: regulation of the Indian trade, prohibition of African slavery, and prohibition of "Rum or Brandys . . . [and] any other kind of Spirits or Strong Waters."

Oglethorpe had become convinced that black slavery and drinks stronger than wine and beer led to white idleness and sickness. The slave law also stated that the prohibition of Africans would encourage the settlement of the colony by whites, who would not have to compete with slaves; it also would prevent black "Insurrections," which could lead to the "Ruin and loss" of the colony.

Georgia officials knew that the colonists imbibed heavily in strong drink, especially beer. The latter was permitted. Shortly after the Salzburgers arrived, they began making beer from "sassafras, a little syrup, . . . and some green pine-tops," a substitute for hops. To "make it better," they added "a little Indian corn" and then boiled the concoction in a kettle of water. Some settlers enjoyed strong drink with every meal. When a Charles Town merchant breakfasted with a family near Savannah in the mid-1730s on "a large dish of Cat fish and perch, fried . . . and a good piece of Cold pork," the diners consumed "two bottles of punch."[35]

By banning Africans and strong liquor and by relying on white indentured servants, Oglethorpe and the trustees believed Georgia could become a colony of yeoman farmers. Again they were idealistic. By the late 1730s, some colonists were demanding slaves and rum. With alcoholism rampant and imbibing impossible to prevent, the trustees eventually stopped enforcing the ban against rum. However, Georgia became the only colony in the Western Hemisphere settled by the English and other Europeans that almost from its beginnings prohibited African slavery.

Oglethorpe soon returned to the ship and sailed south to settle about one hundred of the new colonists at Frederica on St. Simons Island and here "traced out a fort." When it was completed, Fort Frederica became the largest British fortification in North America. Then, dressed in his Highlander plaids, Oglethorpe visited the nearby settlement of some 160 Highland Scots at Darien, which dominated the Altamaha River. Pushing further south, Oglethorpe established Fort St. Andrew at the northern end of Cumberland Island, Fort William on the southern end, and Fort St. George on Amelia Island. His intrusion enraged the Spanish at St. Augustine.[36]

In June of 1736, Oglethorpe ordered Noble Jones and Roger Lacy to lay out a town at a site to be called Augusta. Lacy also was appointed to enforce the new act to regulate the Indian trade. It required traders to buy licenses in Savannah, prohibited liquor sales to Indians, and authorized Lacy to arrest anyone breaking the law. Carolinians were infuriated. For years they had traded with Indians along the borders of the two colonies. Although Oglethorpe agreed to delay implementation of the new Indian act, the previous cordial relations between the Carolinians and Georgians came to an end.

Charles Town was the commercial and social hub of the southern colonies. Its merchants provided the credit and commodities that the Indians wanted. The Carolina merchants resented what they perceived as a threat to their trading hegemony as well as an attempt to make Savannah a commercial center. When it was discovered that some Carolina traders were in Georgia without licenses, they were arrested and their goods seized. This outraged officials in Charles Town. Carolina traders ignored the act, continued to barter with Indians along the Savannah River, and armed their vessels to prevent interference by the Georgians.

Georgia remained a frontier and Savannah a satellite for South Carolina's economic expansion throughout the trusteeship period. Savannah's leading merchant at the end of the proprietary period summarized the trading conditions there when he wrote: "We are little better . . . in respect to trade than a province to South Carolina."[37]

Oglethorpe also was angered by Carolinians who shipped rum into Savannah and Tybee. Fourteen died at sea trying to smuggle the liquor. When he seized one boat in the Savannah River and staved in the rum aboard, his action touched off a boundary dispute between South Carolina and Georgia that lasted for two centuries. Oglethorpe also expelled Carolinians who brought slaves onto the Georgia side of the Savannah River to work a plantation.

While Savannah endured a second major epidemic of "augues and fevers" during the summer of 1736, probably typhoid fever, the Spanish at St. Augustine were prepared for war. To avoid a confrontation between Oglethorpe and the Spanish, the trustees urged him to return to England, which he did in November.[38]

RELIGION, EDUCATION, AND SOCIAL LIFE

The Reverend John Wesley was the third of nine Anglican ministers sent to Georgia during the colony's first twelve years. He entered his ministry with great zeal, but his insistence that the ritual and dogma of the Church of England be strictly observed soon turned members of Savannah's Anglican congregation against him. Georgians, like settlers elsewhere, would influence the way in which the Anglican Church and other sects evolved in the colonies. Wesley also became romantically involved with one of his communicants, Sophia Hopkey. But when he did not seem in a hurry to marry, she married someone else. Piqued, Wesley subsequently refused her Communion, and a suit for defamation of character was brought against him. The case was never brought to trial, but Wesley recognized that his usefulness in Savannah was over. Before completing his second year, he departed quietly after nightfall, writing: "I shook off the dust from my feet, and left Georgia, after having preached the Gospel there . . . (not as I ought but as I was able)."

The Reverend William Norris replaced Wesley, but he soon moved south after being accused by religious opponents of loose living—playing "on the Fiddle, and at cards with the Ladies." Settling at Frederica, Norris soon faced charges of bastardy with his German female servant. In Savannah he was succeeded by the Reverend George Whitefield, who in 1738 opened a school for orphaned boys and girls. Whitefield's young confidant, James Habersham, came from England with him.

Habersham had experience as a merchant in England, but he initially became the master of the trustees' school and orphanage in Savannah, which was founded by Charles Delamotte, an associate of the Wesleys. Within several years Habersham's assistant, John Dobell, became the schoolmaster of the Savannah Town School, which was free of charge; another school was founded at the nearby Bethesda Orphanage in 1740, and less than a dozen years later a school for slave children was established in Savannah. When teachers such as Dobell resigned, others, though less competent instructors, were hired. Nevertheless, a network of teachers existed. For instance, the Reverend Johann Martin Boltzius, the Lutheran minister of the Salzburgers at Ebenezer, who wrote antislavery tracts, and the Anglican minister, the Reverend Bartholomew Zouberbuhler, frequently visited and remained vitally interested in the school for slave children in Savannah. Literate adults in Savannah with the leisure to read would borrow books, primarily religious ones, from the library of the Anglican rector.[39]

The Free and Accepted Order of Masons was one of the first fraternal organizations established in Savannah. Although the organization was initially criticized for clannishness and drunken revelry, membership soon became coveted, and prominent Savannahians joined. The St. Andrew's Club, founded in 1737 by a group of Lowland Scots, was another fraternal organization whose members also were accused of raucous celebrations, especially on St. Andrew's Day. Their behavior angered William Stephens when the Scots organized a pony race from the trustees' garden to Johnson Square.

Well-educated and sixty-six years of age, Stephens had been recently appointed secretary to the colony. The trustees had granted him five hundred acres of land located about twelve miles south of Savannah on a bluff dotted with oak trees overlooking the Vernon River. He had the land cleared and planted in a variety of crops, including mulberry and orange trees; Stephen also raised poultry and hogs. Although he choose to live in Savannah, he eventually built a dwelling on the Vernon River, which he called Beaulieu (pronounced "Bewly") after a place of the same name in England.

Stephens served as the eyes and ears of the trustees and for political reasons came to deplore the Lowland Scots. Like Stephens, the Reverend Whitefield also denounced pony or horse racing and may have been thinking about the Scots when he condemned the several persons in Savannah who "lived most scandalous Lives with their Whores."

The usual diversions in Savannah during its earliest years included hunting, gambling, drinking at public houses, weddings, occasional dancing, and commemoration of the founding of Georgia and the king's or Oglethorpe's birthdays, which featured flag raisings, toasts, and the firing of cannons. Christmas was a holiday, and as in England, the celebration of Easter took place over several days and included cricket playing and quoits.

THE ECONOMY

Beginning in 1737 and extending into the following year, Roger Lacy, as directed by Oglethorpe, laid out a town and fort at Augusta over one hundred miles upriver from Savannah. It would defend the colony on the north and sever the trade of the Carolinians with the Creeks at Ft. Moore a few miles downriver. Soon after completion of the fort, Lacy died in Savannah of exhaustion, fever, and alcoholism.

As a new center for the Indian trade, Augusta grew quickly. Its prosperity, however, at first did not fuel Savannah's economy. Since Carolinians controlled the trade with the Indians, most of the skins and furs sent by boat followed the old route: downriver, *past* Savannah, and then by the inland waterway to Charles Town. Savannah merchants had neither the capital nor the knowledge to profit from the Indian trade until somewhat later.

The use of periaguas, flatboats, schooners, and sloops on the waterways and along the coast served as the primary means of transportation between Savannah and nearby settlements until roads began to be cut at the end of the 1730s. One of the first paths connected Savannah with Darien, and another linked Savannah and Augusta. It eventually became known as the river road. Packet boats carried mail between Savannah and Charles Town.

During the 1730s Jewish immigrants Abraham Minis and Colman Solomons kept a tavern on Bull Street and a store that catered to the Indian trade. They engaged in commerce along the coast in their twenty-ton sloop, which they patriotically named *Oglethorpe,* and carried on business with persons in New York, Charles Town, and Frederica. Robert and William Williams attempted to operate an export-import business at Savannah and managed to send several thousand pounds of deerskins annually to London. John Brownfield also opened a mercantile establishment for a brief period of time. But competition from the trustees' store and Charles Town, trade regulations, lack of credit and the poverty of the colonists, and the lack of a wharf until 1739 created nearly insurmountable economic problems for Savannah merchants.

Termination of the trustees' policy of sending charity colonists to Georgia, fear of invasion by the Spanish, and a severe food crisis in the colony in 1737 also hurt commerce. In that year there were about 150 dwellings and public buildings and over 500 inhabitants in Savannah. The number of people living there soon dropped dramatically. During October 1738 a blaze destroyed the houses of Giles Beçcu, a French baker, and Peter Baillou, a French hatter. The fires were precursors of more devastating conflagrations to come.[40]

While in England, Oglethorpe was promised some of the economic aid he requested from the trustees. By this time several trustees had resigned, and those remaining attempted to reduce spending in Georgia. But Oglethorpe got most of the military and financial support he requested from the British government. Indeed, during Oglethorpe's years in Georgia, the London government provided more than 90 percent of the cost for defense; none of the other twelve colonies in British North America received *any* public funds.

During the summer of 1738 the worst heat wave and drought since the founding of Georgia devastated the crops in and around Savannah. Some settlers never adjusted to what William Stephens called the "Violent heat," which rendered him "uncapable of much Action" and obliged him to pass an occasional "day in Indolence." To him "the Sultry nights were no . . . less affecting." The hot weather and the frontier environment led to increased simplicity in dress, which included a sharp decline locally in the wearing of wigs.

Provisions were running short in the colony by the time Oglethorpe returned from England in September 1738. He now bore the title of "General and Commander in Chief of the Forces of South Carolina and Georgia"; he brought with him a regiment of over 625 soldiers. He stationed his troops at Frederica on Georgia's southern border. Oglethorpe now spent most of his time with his soldiers on the frontier, where he waited for an opportunity to attack the Spanish.

In October Oglethorpe went to Savannah for several days and implemented orders from the trustees to cut costs. He closed the trustees' store and fired its manager and Savannah's chief official, Thomas Causton, who had extended large and uncollectible loans to the settlers. Small shopkeepers and artisans who previously obtained public credit from the store to buy and sell goods at a good profit lost their livelihood; planters living near Savannah who received bounties from the store went broke and moved to town, straining local resources. As a further cost-saving measure, Oglethorpe dismissed the public gardener, Joseph Fitzwalter—who had only recently regained the post—and suspended Noble Jones, the public surveyor and constable. Several years passed before another surveyor was appointed, but he disliked working in the summer and fall "for fear of snakes." When Oglethorpe returned to Frederica, he left behind the impression that Savannah faced "a gloomy Prospect" and a colony near bankruptcy.

Causton, Fitzwalter, and Jones all had arrived aboard the *Ann*. Each had both friends and enemies among the first settlers. Some settlers had reported to the trustees that Causton had appropriated the colony's funds for his own use. However, his financial problems stemmed more from mismanagement than fraud. But for seven years after he was fired, Causton experienced harassment and imprisonment in both Savannah and England and personal tragedy. When his health failed in 1740, he and his family left their comfortable home and plantation of 260 acres, Ockstead, at Causton's Bluff, five miles south of Savannah on St. Augustine Creek, and moved to Savannah. Here both his child and wife died within a month of each other. In deep mourning, Causton returned to Ockstead and planted vineyards and farmed until he sailed for England, where he hoped to clear his name. But the charges against him remained unsettled, and on his return voyage Thomas Causton died at sea.

Following his termination as public gardener, Joseph Fitzwalter operated a public house with his second wife, the widow Penelope Wright. His first wife, an Indian woman, "ran away." He was subsequently appointed wharfinger and vendue master and reappointed public gardener, so he was once again able to work with his beloved "baby Nusary of Plants." But Fitzwalter and his family, like others in Savannah, experienced hard times, and he died in a "helpless and distressed state." His wife Penelope outlived two husbands and a daughter. She overcame a serious illness, was also appointed wharfinger, and with remarkable fortitude sustained herself for years on her town and garden lots.

Noble Jones fared the best of these three first settlers. Shortly after Jones was terminated, Oglethorpe asked him to construct a fortification at a site Jones had been developing near Savannah on the Isle of Hope. The property became Jones's Wormsloe Estate. Later as a soldier, planter, and businessman, Jones was one of the colony's first successful entrepreneurs.[41]

RISE OF THE MALCONTENTS

After Oglethorpe terminated Causton and Fitzwalter and suspended Jones, things were never again quite the same in Savannah. Oglethorpe's actions redounded to the opponents of his and trustee policies. The opposition coalesced around Lowland Scots such as physician Patrick Tailfer and the merchant David Douglass, owner of one of Savannah's larger houses; Hugh Anderson also joined the opposition. He was a well-educated Scottish "gentleman" whose knowledge of natural philosophy and natural history led the trustees to appoint him as "Inspector of the Public Garden." But growing personal misfortunes and his increasing doubts over trustee policies led Anderson to join "the Club" of Tailfer and Douglass, which began meeting in Edward Jenkins's tavern. They became known by William Stephens and other enemies as "the Malcontents," somewhat of a misnomer since they advocated change.

All three of these leading malcontents, like other Savannahians, experienced problems with white indentured servants who refused to work and sometimes ran away to South Carolina. Tailfer gave up farming and practiced medicine in Savannah after thirteen of his eighteen servants fled. His alleged cruelty may have caused their flight. He purportedly seduced one young girl, sold her to an Indian trader, and beat another servant to death. Anderson's indentured servants also ran away, became ill, or died. Some claimed that the Irish, English, Welsh, and German servants generally were idlers who spent too much time and "money in the ale houses" of Savannah.[42] Even the leading advocate of trustee policies, William Stephens, concluded that his own servants were "a Sad crew, . . . some whores, others thieves, others Sick, So that their work paid not for their food & cloathes."[43]

By the late 1730s there was no longer a ready market for most indentured servants who disembarked in Savannah; the few purchased there continued to show an aversion to work and a fondness for running away. The failure of white indentured servitude and the lack of a labor supply contributed to the rise of the malcontents. In December 1738 they sent a petition to the trustees signed by 117 Savannahians, including all local officials except William Stephens. The petitioners asked for the right to own slaves and the right to have fee-simple land ownership. Stephens described the petitioners as "the Pest of the place" and was shocked when his own son asserted that Africans were "as essential . . . to the cultivation of Georgia, as axes (and) hoes." Black slaves could withstand the heat better and were cheaper to maintain than white servants—or so it was argued. In Savannah this touched off a fierce debate over slavery and led to petitions and pamphlets filled with vicious charges and countercharges.[44] One antislavery Savannahian said of the malcontents that he "would like to knock them Scotch Sons of Bitches brains out."[45]

Oglethorpe and Stephens advised the trustees against the malcontents' petition, and so it was denied. Within the next year some of these critics, such as Hugh Anderson and Patrick Tailfer, left the colony to continue their opposition from South Carolina. Here Tailfer published *A True and Historical Narrative of the Colony of Georgia.* This exposé of conditions in the colony, one historian observed, occupies "a distinctive place in the literature of early Georgia." In vigorous prose Tailfer blamed the tepid success of the colony on the trustees' hyperbole in recruiting, their ill-conceived land policies, poor planning for the production of silk and wine, Oglethorpe's increasing influence, and the prohibition of African slavery. But many Savannahians believed that the introduction of slavery would threaten the colony with insurrections, especially after the Stono Rebellion in South Carolina and the outbreak of war with Spain in 1739.[46]

On September 8, 1739, a sloop from Rhode Island arrived in Savannah with the alarming news that England had declared war on Spain. The report was inaccurate. But late in September, when Oglethorpe returned from Georgia's western frontier by way of Augusta—where he reaffirmed English friendship with the Creek Indians—he summoned Savannahians to meet at the courthouse under arms. Here on October 3 at high noon, to the beat of drums and in the presence of magistrates wearing their official robes, Oglethorpe assured the people that military preparations were underway to protect them. Next, William Stephens read a declaration of war drafted under orders from Oglethorpe, which warned the people of Georgia to be watchful for enemy spies and runaway slaves from South Carolina. After Oglethorpe departed the courthouse, the militia fired cannons and small arms "in Defiance. . . of any Dread of the Spaniards." Georgia had declared war, but the British government did not officially enter the War of Jenkins' Ear until late October. One of the causes of the war was the dispute over the Georgia-Florida boundary, a matter of enormous interest to Oglethorpe.

Chief Tomochichi died on October 5. He had asked to be buried in Savannah, the town he had helped found. His corpse was brought down the Savannah River, where it was met by Oglethorpe, Stephens, and four military officers who served as pallbearers. Oglethorpe had ordered that his good Indian friend be given an elaborate military funeral. Followed by Indians, townspeople, and officials, Tomochichi's pall was carried to Savannah's principal square, Percival Square (later Wright Square), where an open grave awaited the body.

During the procession and interment, minute guns boomed from the battery. Over forty militiamen fired three volleys from small arms over the burial site. Oglethorpe promised to mark the grave with a giant stone "in testimony of Gratitude" to Tomochichi. But it was not until much later that a monument was erected in Wright Square to the memory of Tomochichi. In 1899 the Georgia Society of Colonial Dames placed a huge granite boulder in the square to honor him. However, the rock is not over his grave. Years earlier a monument to the famous Savannahian William Washington Gordon had been built over Tomochichi's last resting place, the middle of Wright Square.

Preoccupied with the defense of the colony, Oglethorpe summoned the townspeople to assist him and led what was probably the first general cleanup of Savannah. He ordered all rubbish cleared, especially the high weeds in the squares, which if set ablaze could threaten the security of the town. He estimated from the number of persons who turned out that there were nearly two hundred men able to carry arms. Several days later he selected the "proper Officers" for the town's militia.

As Oglethorpe prepared to leave again, his critics fumed. They said that in departing Savannah he was "gratifying his Spleen against the People. . . who had set a-foot the Complaints against him and the trustees by leaving them defenseless." Oglethorpe eventually became so angry with most Savannahians that he stretched the truth when he informed the trustees: "The mutinous temper at Savannah . . . [was] fomented by the Spaniards." In late October Oglethorpe, spoiling for a fight, sailed for Frederica.[47]

OGLETHORPE'S IMPERIALISM

A Spanish-Yamasee war party struck first. In mid-November 1739 Oglethorpe reported that the enemy fell upon Amelia Island and killed two unarmed, "poor sick men, cut off their heads, [and] mangled their bodies . . . barbarously." To repel the invaders, Oglethorpe and his men resolved "to die hard." Oglethorpe retaliated by invading Florida and capturing a Spanish fort on the St. Johns River.

Next Oglethorpe planned an expedition against St. Augustine. He spent two months haggling with the government of South Carolina before the legislature provided the men, arms, and supplies he needed. During early 1740 he assembled an army at Frederica of more than two thousand Indians and regular and provincial troops, which included English, Scottish, Swiss, and German soldiers. However, the German-speaking Moravians—also in Georgia called "Germans"—departed the colony. Standard histories have emphasized that the Moravian pacifists moved on to Pennsylvania rather than take up arms for the colony; recent scholarship, however, stresses that sharp internal Lutheran-Moravian religious disputes were the real reason the Moravians left Georgia.

In the spring of 1740, supported by a fleet of British ships, Oglethorpe and his army attacked St. Augustine by land and sea. The campaign was a disaster. In July, Oglethorpe withdrew to St. Simons Island and Frederica. South Carolinians blamed Oglethorpe's poor generalship for the costly, failed campaign; Oglethorpe blamed their legislature for its tardy and parsimonious support. Scholars have usually agreed with the Carolinians until recently, when one or two have come to agree with Oglethorpe. They have censured South Carolina's Commons House of Assembly for its "biased accusations" against Oglethorpe. Regardless of who was to blame, the military blunder touched off a new and bitter dispute between Georgia and South Carolina. The conflict between the Spanish and the English widened into a general colonial and European war. It became known in America as King George's War.[48]

WAR AND ECONOMIC DEPRESSION

Dissension in Savannah over issues raised by the malcontents and the threat of invasion caused many townspeople and those living nearby to leave. The malcontents informed the trustees in November 1740 that there were seventy-two empty houses and huts in Savannah, and its vacant lots and squares again had become overgrown with tall weeds. Nearby outposts such as Tybee and Skidaway Islands were abandoned. Armed male inhabitants were relocated to the south. During the year the townspeople might have become completely impoverished had not the Reverend George Whitefield employed local artisans and laborers to build an orphanage ten miles beyond Savannah. Bethesda, or the "House of Mercy," was operated by James Habersham, who moved his orphanage and school from Savannah. Here the girls received instruction in homemaking; they learned their duties and responsibilities as future heads of households. Both sexes received a rigorous religious education. Bethesda also became a center of activity for the malcontents.

As one of the leaders of the religious revival, or Great Awakening, sweeping the colonies, Whitefield filled the courthouse in Savannah with his enthusiastic preaching and emotional sermons. Occasionally, both he and his congregation wept together. William Stephens disapproved of such zealotry. Whitefield initially was the leading public opponent of slavery in Georgia and South Carolina, but by the early 1740s he was advocating its legalization in Georgia. He told the trustees that without African slave labor the colony would never prosper. He had changed his views for political reasons: only by sanctioning slavery and its extension from Carolina into Georgia could the Evangelical movement be propagated among slave owners, since they distrusted anyone who questioned the legitimacy of black slavery. In sum, as Alan Gallay has argued, the Reverend Whitefield was more interested in the survival of the Evangelical movement than the reform of slavery. One of his successors, Anglican minister Bartholomew Zouberbuhler, became wealthy in land and slaves.

The winter of 1740–1741 was the most severe that anyone in Savannah remembered. At the beginning of the new year the collector of the port, John Fallowfield, noted that the "town is full of buildings but thin of inhabitants, three houses are empty through the town for one that has a family in it." Many of the poor would risk "contagion by going into Carolina . . . rather than stay in Georgia and . . . starve." With the exception of the Abraham Minis and Benjamin Sheftall families, the Jewish residents of Savannah also packed up and departed because of the threat of war and a stagnant economy. If this was not enough to trouble the remaining townspeople, the first major fire broke out in April 1741. It spread from Bull to Drayton Streets and southward along what is today Congress Street, destroying five houses in the heart of Savannah.

Finally, recognizing the discontent and problems in Georgia, the trustees attempted to create a more effective means of governing the colony by dividing it into two counties. Frederica and the southern part of Georgia constituted one; Savannah and the northern region formed the other. William Stephens was made president of the latter.[49]

In June 1742, the Spanish launched an attack against St. Simons with fifty-two ships carrying nearly two thousand troops. Oglethorpe evacuated the fort there, and the Spanish seized it. When word arrived of the Spanish invasion to the south, confusion and panic swept Savannah. William Stephens could muster only one hundred able-bodied men to repel an enemy invasion. By this time many townspeople had taken refuge in South Carolina. One Savannahian charged that President Stephens, who was also colonel of the militia, not only failed to post guards at "the greatest time of danger" but "kept his horse . . . saddled in his garden" so that he might flee if necessary. John Fallowfield, who himself departed for Charles Town, remarked that few "principal persons" remained in Savannah.

On July 7 the Spanish moved out of Fort St. Simons and along the military road to Frederica. Here Oglethorpe's force struck and repulsed the Spanish in the Battle of Bloody Marsh. When British warships appeared, the Spanish sailed for St. Augustine. By this time, one Savannahian observed, Savannah and the surrounding countryside was "almost deserted due to flight, sickness, and death." Direct trade with other ports by coastal or seagoing vessels came to a virtual halt. Merchant Abraham Minis, however, did manage to do a lively business shuttling supplies from Savannah to the troops at Frederica aboard his patriotically named sloop, *Oglethorpe*. Another daring former merchant profited handsomely during the war. Captain Caleb Davis outfitted a twenty-gun brig as a privateer, boldly preyed on Spanish shipping, and sailed into Savannah with his prizes.[50]

It was primarily the threat of invasion and the dissension, rather than low birth rates or high death rates, that contributed to Savannah's depopulation in its earliest years. Of course, fevers, "augues," and dysentery caused numerous deaths in Savannah from its founding. But unlike the British settlements to the north at Jamestown and Charles Town, whose populations were decimated from the beginning by yellow fever and smallpox, Savannah remained relatively healthy. For several reasons diseases that proved so devastating during the early years in other southern trading centers came later to Savannah.[51]

In March 1743, the militarily ambitious and imperial-minded Oglethorpe made one last, unsuccessful incursion into Spanish Florida. Several months later he departed for England. There he married and settled. Although he never returned to America, Oglethorpe remained interested in the Georgia experiment and its welfare, occasionally attending meetings of the trustees until the colony reverted to the Crown.

President William Stephens became the deputy general of Georgia following Oglethorpe's return to England and the merger of the two counties of Frederica and Savannah into one government. With the threat of a Spanish invasion over, former residents of Savannah, many of them in the malcontents group, began to trickle back. They remained committed to the view, perhaps more than ever, that the labor system and crops of South Carolina must become the model for Georgia.

Ironically, General Oglethorpe's military enthusiasms, supported by the trustees, protected the colony and Savannah from defeat by enemies without but led to a victory for the enemies within. During the war with the Spanish, the population and economy surged at Frederica; it became the largest settlement in Georgia while Savannah's economy collapsed and its population atrophied to one-quarter of its prewar size. Dissension in Savannah played into the hands of the malcontents. The presence of Oglethorpe in Savannah rather than Frederica may have stymied the rise of his enemies. The Georgia colony was saved, but the vision of a province peopled only by white, sober, hardworking citizen-soldiers died during King George's War.[52]

CHURCH AND STATE

In 1743 the trustees appointed Thomas Bosomworth the Anglican rector at Savannah. Shortly afterward he married Mary Musgrove Matthews, a twice-married mixed-blood woman who had outlived her first two husbands. Some whispered that she quickly remarried because of strong sexual desires and because she wished to improve her status by remarriage to a minister. No doubt she wished to elevate her social standing, and the quick remarriages protected her reputation. William Stephens offered the couple the use of the house furnished him by the trustees to celebrate their marriage. Here with a crowd of parishioners on a hot night in August 1744, they feasted, drank, and danced to a fiddle.

Bosomworth became increasingly involved in Mary's business affairs, which diminished his effectiveness as a minister. He and his wife soon left Savannah for Mary's Indian trading post at the forks of the Altamaha River. They soon returned to challenge Georgia's leadership.

The Reverend Bartholomew Zouberbuhler was appointed to fill the vacancy created by Bosomworth's departure. Zouberbuhler was the last rector named under the trustee government. Savannahians appreciated his versatility. Upon request, he preached in English, French, or German, which underscored the local ethnic and linguistic diversity. Unhappy with his salary and lodgings, Zouberbulher complained to the trustees, and they increased his income substantially. He became a wealthy man. Under the leadership of Zouberbuhler and William Stephens, construction on the long-delayed Anglican church got underway. The first Christ Church, a wood-frame structure built on a three-foot-high stone foundation, was completed in 1750.[53]

The vestry of the Anglican church in Charles Town and other colonies in the South heard and acted on appeals for relief from the poor. However, in Savannah such pleas came before President William Stephens and his Board of Assistants. The board was the local governing agency of the colony and was composed of those who passed for the local gentry. Requests for welfare, then as now, came from the same constituency: of fifteen requests for aid in the 1740s, fourteen were from women with dependent children or elderly and infirm widows incapable of supporting themselves. Several were desperately ill or actually starving. If judged "sober and industrious"—the "deserving poor"—they received relief ranging from ten shillings to a barrel of rice. Several cases underscored the depressed economy of the period. For instance, the board, upon providing welfare to one woman, noted that it was without money and granted her relief by providing her credit at local stores. One widow who had successfully managed her husband's business for three years after his death, but who now faced "Business failing and Times growing hard with her for Want of Employment," was granted forty shillings.[54]

COMMERCE AND SLAVERY

By the late 1740s the population of Savannah was growing. The Reverend Zouberbuhler reported to the trustees that there were over 600 inhabitants, 225 of them Anglicans, but only 63 were active communicants. More than 380 persons professed to be Presbyterians, Independents, and "Dissenters of all sorts," which again highlights the religious diversity of early Savannah.

The rising population encouraged James Habersham to leave his post at Bethesda and enter a partnership with Savannah storekeeper Francis Harris. Habersham purchased a town lot at Bull Street near the river and built a large house with storerooms and a trade room. He found the location ideally situated for business and moved his family and the firm of Habersham and Harris there in 1745. Initially the partnership turned a profit by purchasing dry goods and edibles in Charles Town and reselling them in Savannah. But conducting any import-export business through the South Carolina port entailed high costs for insurance, freight, and storage, which cut sharply into profits. To eliminate Charles Town's middlemen, Habersham and Harris in the late 1740s opened direct trade between Savannah and London. The factor for the London firm sold their rice, lumber, and deerskins and in turn provided them with credit for merchandise purchased. Subsequently, Habersham and Harris traded directly with the West Indies in lumber and other goods and purchased a sloop, the *Georgia Merchant*. Where others had failed, Habersham and Harris prospered by business acumen and political connections.

The trustees recognized that the partnership was the most successful mercantile business ever in Savannah and provided support. They granted the partners frontage on the Savannah River for their proposed wharf, permitted them to issue sola bills—a paper medium of exchange previously issued by the trustees only—and appointed Habersham to the Board of Assistants. Habersham was the first to convince the board to survey the river to identify its sandbars and to request that the trustees provide funds to deepen the shipping channels. Ships drawing more than ten to twelve feet of water could not offload or load at Savannah. However, dredging the river was something that did not occur until the following century.

Habersham and Harris initiated the practice of partially loading deep-draft, seagoing ships at Savannah and completing the task with lighters at Cockspur Island nearly seventeen miles below the town. Offloading was accomplished the same way. Habersham, who acquired stores, town lots, and houses, was one of the biggest boosters of Savannah as a commercial port. But he still envied and wished to emulate those Charles Town merchants he knew who became wealthy in rice lands worked by African slaves.[55]

Slaves smuggled in from South Carolina labored for years in remote regions of Georgia. Indeed, one Georgian asserted in 1748 that Africans worked in and around Savannah, and yet local officials "wink at" the violation of the law. About this time William Stephens estimated that enslaved blacks in Georgia totaled 349 men, women, and children. He and his Board of Assistants became convinced that for Georgia to prosper the 1735 slave act needed to be modified. They believed its repeal would attract slaveholding "Men of Substance" from Carolina who would create a new socioeconomic system and provide stimulus to commerce. In May 1748 Stephens and his assistants told the trustees that if slavery were legalized in Georgia, "great numbers of People from divers parts of America Would soon settle in this Colony which would create a considerable Trade to enter here."

In October 1748 any fears or military concerns over a black uprising during wartime evaporated when England and Spain signed a treaty ending more than a decade-long conflict. In May 1749 the trustees acquiesced to the presence of slaves in Georgia and promised to ask for repeal of the law; during the following year, the trustees and the colonists worked out the details of a new policy.[56]

Curiously, there was little mention of Indian enslavement, which was practiced from the beginning of European settlement in Georgia. The colony undertook surveys of the number of African slaves, but never Indian slaves. Owners of Native American slaves included some of the most prominent early Savannahians—Thomas Causton, John and Mary Musgrove, later Mary Bosomworth.[57]

In late July 1749, Mary and Thomas Bosomworth returned from their trading post south of Savannah with three Indian chiefs. The Indians met with local officials and asked for land owed them, part of which they claimed belonged to the Bosomworths. They hinted darkly that some two hundred Creek warriors soon would arrive. Mary Bosomworth was convinced she was inadequately compensated for her services to the colony as an interpreter for Oglethorpe and other English officials. Before Oglethorpe departed, he had given her a diamond ring and some money and had promised more. Now she and her husband hoped, with the help of the Creeks, to compel Savannah authorities to officially recognize that she was the rightful owner of Sapelo, Ossabaw, and St. Catherine's Islands. President Stephens and others feared a crisis, and Noble Jones was ordered to call out the militia.

On August 7 and 9 large groups of Indians came down the river, "Firing their Guns . . . in [a] menacing . . . Manner." Stephens and his assistants, now thoroughly alarmed, entertained the Indians and the Bosomworths the following day. Meanwhile Jones, who had collected a force of about 170 armed men, demanded that the Indians surrender their weapons. Then in a jovial mood Jones and the militia, Thomas Bosomworth, "in his Canonical Habit," and the Indians paraded through the town. Later they smoked pipes and drank glasses of wine and liquor.

Mary saw her plans coming unraveled. At a meeting on August 11 she was excluded. She was outraged. For years she had acted as an ally of and diplomat for the English with the Indians. Unannounced, Mary burst into the meeting, declared that she was the "Queen of the Creeks" and that neither she nor the Creeks would any longer suffer abuse at the hands of the English, and threatened the destruction of the colony if her demands went unmet. Shouting and stamping her feet, Mary told Savannah's officials: "You talk of your White Town, your General and his Treaties . . . [but] you have not a foot of Land in

the Colony"; rather, she asserted, the "very ground was hers." The male officials thought Mary was drunk or a lunatic, and they arrested her. But she was
released after her husband, Thomas, promised to gather the Indians for another meeting the next day.

Oglethorpe was long gone, and Mary now recognized she no longer could
count on his promises of money; she also knew that her long record of success
as an intermediary with the Indians and the prosperity and success she brought
the colony were no longer appreciated; therefore, she was desperate for the
colony to recognize her claim to lands she felt were rightfully hers. Treaties
with the Creeks stripped Mary of her usefulness to the colonists. White male
authorities no longer needed her influence and power with the Indians; to the
contrary, Savannah officials wanted Mary to conform to the appropriate racial
and gender roles expected of a "mixed-blood" female Indian. Mary was useful
to them only when her influence was needed on behalf of the colony. Now she
was threatening the authority of the white male leaders and the patriarchal
society they were putting in place. After Mary's outburst to white authorities
on August 11, Savannahians slept uneasily that night. Horse patrols roamed
through the town, guarding against any sudden uprising.

During discussions over the next several days, Stephens and local officials
again tried to placate and win over the Indian chiefs with gifts, tobacco, and
drinks. On the evening of August 16, Mary interrupted one of these gatherings
by rushing in, "Spirited up with Liquor, [and] Drunk with Passion." This time
she was arrested. That night most of Savannah's men remained armed and on
the streets. Thomas Bosomworth appeared before local officials the next day
to apologize for his and Mary's conduct and "burst into a flood of Tears."
After a dinner for the chiefs on the evening of August 19, most of the Indians
left Savannah. The month-long fear that had gripped the town passed. Mary
Bosomworth continued to seek satisfaction for her claims through the courts
and the London government. In the white male-dominated society, Mary's
tenacity eventually won her legal title to St. Catherines's Island and a cash
settlement.[58]

On July 7, 1750, the anniversary of the Battle of Bloody Marsh, Christ
Church was dedicated. Savannah's Anglicans at last had a place of worship separate from the courthouse. The Reverend Zouberbuhler described the building as "large, beautiful, and comodious." During the day-long celebration he
had "the pleasure to see many Negroes . . . join in our service."[59] The attendance of African Americans at Christ Church apparently was accepted by

whites of all social classes within the congregation. It is unlikely that a racially integrated private institution like Christ Church existed in the countryside. Even at this early date Savannah offered a forum where blacks and whites might interact, if only formally and briefly, get to know each other better, and perhaps round off the sharp edges of white racism. Across time the many and diverse churches that migrated to Savannah served as humanizing agencies.

In August 1750, Parliament legalized slavery in Georgia and the importation of Africans. Slavery was now permitted in all of Britain's thirteen colonies in North America, those in the Caribbean, and the West Indies. The enslavement of Africans and Native Americans also was legal in the nearby colonial outposts of France and Spain. The brief, visionary scheme of prohibiting slavery in Georgia had ended.[60]

The trustees incorporated into the new slave law some of the suggestions made by Savannahians and ignored others. "Four Male Negroes or blacks" were allowed for every white male in the colony. It was illegal to hire out slaves, which was a provision of great importance to Savannah's white artisans who felt threatened by slave labor. There was evidence of class consciousness when these mechanics or artisans declared that "those Folk who wanted to bring in Negroes, . . . would put an End to all White Men's Work." The town's white artisans had recently formed the Union Society and perhaps were flexing their muscles as an organized group. Intermarriage and miscegenation were prohibited. Slave owners could be fined if their slaves were not instructed in the Christian religion on Sundays. Only if a white man murdered a slave was he subject to the same penalty for killing another white man; lesser crimes against slaves were punishable only by fines. This law was not a slave code. It placed few restrictions on blacks and left the treatment of slaves essentially up to the discretion of the slaveholder.

With slavery legalized, wealthy slave owners from South Carolina and the West Indies immediately prepared to move to Georgia to cultivate rice along the fertile banks of its tidal rivers. In 1750 the trustees received 103 applications for land from Carolinians alone. Georgia's land rush was underway.

Also in 1750, the trustees appointed James Habersham to supervise the rejuvenation of silk production in the colony. He was pleased with the appointment and enthusiastic about the project. With Pickering Robinson, a silk expert the trustees sent to the colony, Habersham promoted the rebirth of silk production and built a twenty- by thirty-six-foot filature of two stories in Savannah. It was constructed about two blocks from the Bay, as the harbor was called, just northeast of what is now Reynolds Square. Habersham's firm arranged to buy and deliver the cocoons in hopes of making profits in raw silk. The reelers began to wind quantities of raw silk from the cocoons in May 1751, and Habersham and the colony caught "silk fever." He purchased a five-hundred-acre tract of land and christened it Silk Hope. However, his expectations for silk production never fully reached fruition.

As the population of slaves increased in Savannah and nearby, the Reverend Zouberbuhler of Christ Church and the trustees in London desired to Christianize and catechize these Africans. The two Anglican missionary societies, the Bray Associates and the Society for the Propagation of the Gospel in Foreign Parts, promptly engaged the services of a forty-year-old Italian-born Jew, Joseph Solomon Ottolenghe, who had immigrated to England, converted to Anglicanism, and served time in a debtor's prison. The trustees, pleased with Ottolenghe since he also understood silk making, financed his voyage to Georgia. Ottolenghe and his wife arrived in Savannah in July 1751. Ottolenghe was talented and ambitious, and his remarkable success in Georgia dramatizes the openness of colonial American society.

He soon was educating and evangelizing local slaves three nights a week. By the end of his first year he observed that most had learned the catechism, and "several begin to read tolerably well." Some "have really good voices and having learned the words and tune [of the Psalms] . . . join in the congregation at Church." After the Bray Associates requested that Ottolenghe encourage white children to attended religious instruction, he began conducting biracial classes. Caste differences did not trouble the Bray Associates nor apparently the congregation of Christ Church. This time the town's predominant religious group, the Anglicans, brought together black and white children whose interactions in classes may have mitigated suspicions of one another and even passed on through them to other generations.

In his second year more than sixty Africans participated in the services at Christ Church. Over time, however, as more "new Negroes" arrived, Ottolenghe experienced less success. He bemoaned that the Negroes were "as ignorant of our language as we are of theirs." The Africans had difficulty "understanding what it is that is offer'd to them in order to forsake Paganism and embrace Christianity."[61] Ottolenghe also took charge of the silk reelers at the Savannah filature and soon became superintendent. Eventually he won recognition as an expert in silk production and was elected to membership in the prestigious American Philosophical Society.

Like other local advocates of Christianizing the Africans, Ottolenghe him-self owned slaves. They worked land granted to him by the trustees north of Savannah and along the river. Ottolenghe named his holdings Exon after his previous home in England. He eventually acquired over two thousand acres of land through crown grants and purchase. Some of this land became the origi-nal acreage for the Hermitage, perhaps the best-known plantation in coastal Georgia.

As his work with the filature and civic duties demanded more of his time, Ottolenghe resigned his position as an evangelist and catechist of slaves, and the school closed. However, local Anglicans remained intensely interested in Christianizing the "new Africans." The Reverend Zouberbuhler established a trust fund to be used for evangelizing slaves, and upon his death catechists came from England to teach them.[62]

One of the final acts of the trustees was to issue a call for a meeting of the Georgia Assembly. Its membership was popularly elected, and an Assembly of sixteen members convened in Savannah in 1751. Four represented Savannah, and one of these, Francis Harris, Habersham's partner, was elected speaker.

The first military review took place in Savannah in June while rumors circulated that some colonists in South Carolina wished to annex Georgia. Under the command of Noble Jones, 220 militiamen paraded. The defense of the colony was now in their hands, since Oglethorpe's old regiment was dis-banded.

William Stephens retired in ill health to his plantation Beaulieu in 1751, and in his stead James Habersham was appointed secretary of the colony. Henry Parker, a former critic of the trustees who had advocated legalizing slavery, was appointed president of Georgia. He soon died in office and was replaced by Patrick Graham, one of the most vociferous critics of the trustees. Graham appointed other advocates of change to local offices, and thus the so-called malcontents now controlled the local government. This was reflected in the Assembly's recommendations. For instance, assemblymen made arguments in favor of developing the river and town for trade and against the trustees' rec-ommendations to tax imported Africans. The administration composed of former critics of the trustees also promoted settlement in Georgia, which en-couraged a new wave of immigrants—prosperous planters from Carolina and adventurers from Virginia and even New England. The price of land around Savannah began rising.

In June 1752 the few remaining trustees of the Georgia experiment met for the last time in England. Discouraged, their funds exhausted, they gave up their powers to the king. On November 24, 1752, it was publicly announced in Savannah that Georgia was now a province of the Crown. The trustees had sponsored over 2,000 colonists to Georgia; another 3,500 paid their own way over. About 2,500 died, but by the end of the trustees' period, the colony's population numbered from 2,000 to 3,000 whites and "about 600 Negroes." Within several years the population of whites and blacks more than doubled. Georgia also successfully served as a military buffer for other British colonies. But the trustees, trying to govern the colony from several thousand miles away, remained inflexible with their rules and refused to adapt the regulations to meet the needs of the settlers; they encouraged the growth of agriculture that would best serve the British empire—silk, wines, and hemp—rather than crops that could be best grown in the local soil and climate. Theirs was a mixed record of success and failure. Paradoxically, about the time the trustees surrendered their interest in the colony, an agricultural and economic revolution was beginning in the region around Savannah. It was fostered by the Carolina planters who were migrating in record numbers to Georgia, where cultivation of fertile coastal marshlands offered an opportunity for the rapid accumulation of wealth and social mobility. Jonathan Bryan was one of the first to arrive. He had promoted the Carolina system for Georgia—unrestricted land ownership and slavery.

During 1751 and 1752, Bryan moved his family and 66 slaves to the 500 acres he was granted just east of Savannah. Here he began the first rice plantation operated by slaves on the Savannah River. He called it Walnut Hill. In 1752 he received another 500 acres from the trustees on the Little Ogeechee River and named this plantation Dean Forrest. Within several years Bryan owned more than 100 slaves and 5,000 acres for planting rice and raising cattle along the coast between the Savannah and Altamaha Rivers.

Other Carolinians, bringing their slaves with them, like the Deveaux, Fox, West, and Butler families, settled southwest of Savannah near the tidal marshes of the Little and Big Ogeechee Rivers and carved out rice plantations from the dense forests. Shortly after James Deveaux arrived in Georgia, he became wealthy enough to enjoy a lifestyle that set him apart from most of his fellow planters. He lived in Savannah and left the management of his lands to an overseer.

The Carolinians brought to the Georgia colony wealth, slaves, skill, and experience. They were the forerunners of the agricultural revolution that, for better or worse, established a plantation economy across Georgia built on the political system of African slavery. Ultimately, the success of the planters stimulated the economic life of Savannah, which began attracting Carolina merchants such as James Powell and Matthew Roche by 1752. By 1754, Georgia's exports to England exceeded its imports. As commerce increased, so did Savannah's prosperity.[63]

The new migration and the growth of rice planting near Savannah brought more and more Africans to and near Savannah. One visitor wrote in 1752 that the "rich Carolina Planters . . . came with all their Families and Negroes to settle in Georgia and . . . near 1000 Negroes were brought in."[64] By 1754, the official population of the colony was 4,500 whites and 1,855 Africans.

James Habersham was an advocate of change. He vigorously promoted slavery and unrestricted land ownership and became one of the best-known slave traders in Georgia. He was also one of the custodians of the colony's caretaker government until the first royal governor arrived in 1754.[65]

CHAPTER 2

Royal Government, War, and Economic Boom, 1754–1763

A NEW GOVERNOR

*J*OHN REYNOLDS WAS APPOINTED governor of "His Majesty's Colony of Georgia in America" in August 1754 and soon sailed from England for Savannah. Reynolds was in his early forties and had served as a captain in the British navy. During King George's War he directed naval operations off the Georgia coast. He was used to issuing orders, and he expected to be obeyed.

Reynolds climbed up the steep bluff at Savannah on Tuesday, October 29, to the discharge of guns and the ringing of bells. He symbolized a new beginning for the colony and the end of a perilous era. In the evening the "lower Class of People" joined in the celebration by tearing down the wooden guardhouse for a bonfire.

When Reynolds arrived in the thirteenth and final English colony founded in North America, the machinery of colonial government had been evolving for over 150 years. Reynolds was instructed to establish a legislature and a system of courts and was vested with broad executive powers. The new government began on October 31 when Governor Reynolds and his newly formed Council took the oath of office. Afterward, the militia fired several volleys into the air, and in the evening there was a public dinner.

The governor's Council was a twelve-member advisory body officially appointed by the king. From the first it included prominent local men such as Patrick Graham, James Habersham, and Noble Jones, all former members of the government under the trustees. One original appointee to the Council was the great planter Jonathan Bryan, who was viewed as a man of remarkable skills and who enjoyed close personal connections with major Georgia figures over a period of twenty years. He served on the Council for fifteen years until expelled for revolutionary activities.

The royal governor, the Upper House, and the Commons House of Assembly constituted the legislature. The appointed governor's Council acted as the Upper House when it met without the governor. The Upper House could initiate any legislation except money bills. On most matters the governor sought the advice and consent of his Council. If sitting as a judicial body, the Council constituted the supreme court of Georgia with the governor acting as the chief judge. It heard appeals from such lower courts as the General Court and justice of the peace and chancery courts. A vice-admiralty court specialized in breaches of the law on the high seas and customs violations.

To stand for election to the popularly elected Assembly, a person was required to own five hundred acres of land; free white males who were at least twenty-one years of age could vote if they possessed fifty acres of land. The original nineteen members of the Assembly represented twelve districts.

The Assembly raised money by taxing free blacks, land, stock in trade, and money loaned at interest; it decided on how tax money was spent, initiated other bills, and approved legislation. The Assembly met in the fall, took a Christmas recess, and then resumed from January through March. Unlike most royal governors, Reynolds received an annual salary from the English Parliament rather than the local Assembly. He could convene and dismiss the Assembly, pardon criminals, try sailors for local crimes, and commission ships; he was the commander-in-chief of the colony and chief negotiator with the Indians. The royal governor could declare martial law, issue warrants for the expenditure of funds, and grant lands.[1]

Reynolds met with his councilors for one of the first times in early November in the Council House, which faced Percival Square. It was later renamed Court House and then Market Square; today it is called Wright Square. Diagonally across Percival Square from the Council House was the public jail, near today's location of the Chatham County Courthouse. The Council House was the largest structure in the town at the time, which included about 150 small, old, wooden houses. The meeting began with a discussion of the ruinous condition of the Council House when suddenly one end of it collapsed. The governor and his Council barely escaped. The incident dramatized the condition of the town's buildings and the difficulties facing the new governor.[2]

A portion of the old two-story filature located on the square in Lower New

Ward—later renamed Reynolds Square for the governor—was renovated; a meeting place for the Council was built nearby under the supervision of Noble Jones. The old Council House was torn down, and within a few months the refurbished filature and a new Council House were ready for use.[3]

The same year that Governor Reynolds arrived in Georgia, war erupted in the Ohio Valley between England and France, which was called the French and Indian War in the colonies and the Seven Years War abroad. The London government and the military officers sent to Georgia always viewed the colony as a buffer between England's other colonies and its enemies. The outbreak of war sharply focused the thoughts of Reynolds on security matters.

In the late fall Governor Reynolds informed London that it was most important "to have . . . Troops in this Defenceless . . . Province, which . . . is the South Frontier of His Majesty's Dominions in North America." The Spanish at nearby St. Augustine encouraged slaves to run away, and the Indian tribes on Georgia's frontiers now were under the influence of the Spanish and the French. Reynolds was appalled that locally there were not sufficient soldiers or cannons, forts, or small arms fit for service. Therefore, he asked London for regular English troops since without them the colony is "in Danger of being Destroyed."[4]

On November 30 the eligible voters of Savannah went to the polls to elect four members to the nineteen seats in Georgia's first royal Assembly. After an Augusta politico and adventurer backed several of Savannah's office seekers, the town's first elections became bitterly contested. The initial meeting of the royal Commons House of Assembly in Georgia began in Savannah on January 7, 1755. It was dominated by former malcontents. One of the members representing Savannah was Joseph Ottolenghe, a recent immigrant, catechist to the slaves, and authority on the silk culture in Georgia. His election to the first legislature highlighted his personal meteoric rise in the economic, social, and political life of the colony. With the exception of one session, Ottolenghe sat for Savannah in every legislature for the following ten years.[5]

The nature, number, and speed with which bills passed through the first legislative session reflected the interests of the Georgians and their initial cordial relationship with the new governor. Laws were enacted to defend the colony, to promote its economy, and to protect property owners.[6] On January 24 the legislature passed the Militia Act, which required all males in the colony from age sixteen to sixty to enroll in the militia; it called for the formation of cavalry units consisting of men of "substance" whose captains in an emergency could recruit slaves "recommended as faithful."[7]

Fear of fugitive slaves and the growing number of blacks in the colony moved the legislature to enact a law "For the better Ordering and Governing Negroes and other Slaves." It was the first slave code passed in Georgia and was patterned after South Carolina's. Its purpose was to keep slaves "in due Subjection and Obedience" and to prevent masters "from exercising too great Rigour and Cruelty."

The new code prohibited punishments such as castration and blinding but permitted whipping and imprisonment; it required masters to provide minimal amounts of food and clothing and permitted a sixteen-hour work day, but it encouraged slaveholders to recognize the Sabbath as a day of rest; it did not require masters to provide religious instruction. Many slave owners had reached the conclusion that religious instruction fomented rebellion rather than docility in slaves. Apparently, masters thought that obedience could be better enforced by severe punishments and careful policing.

Slaves were not to leave plantations or towns without written permission unless accompanied by a white person. Any white had the authority to demand to see a slave's permission slip or ticket. If the slave was not forthcoming, the African could be restrained and whipped, and those physically resisting could "be Lawfully killed." Anyone capturing a runaway or pursuing one and returning with the "Scalp with Two Ears of a grown Man Slave" was entitled to a reward. Recaptured runaways were remanded to constables who were required to examine the slaves "for any Mark or brand" and to advertise a description of the runaway in Savannah.

The slave code specified that during weekends and holidays especially, whites should be on the lookout for large assemblies of slaves that might "endanger" them. In the new code teaching slaves to read or write was forbidden; slaves were not permitted to blow horns or beat drums, which might be a signal to other slaves for an insurrection, and they were forbidden to carry any weapon unless specifically authorized by their masters.

Capital crimes by slaves—insurrections, murder, destruction of exports, and striking a white person—were tried by justices of the peace and freeholders. If convicted, slaves could be sentenced to death by hanging or burning. Masters received £50 for each slave they owned who was executed by the colony. For noncapital offenses, corporal punishment short of death could be inflicted.

The new slave code—unlike the wording of the law passed by Parliament in 1750 legalizing slavery in Georgia—permitted owners to hire out their slaves. This concerned Savannah's white artisans, who resented competition from slaves. The code prohibited slaves from keeping boats, raising horses, or bartering, which afforded them opportunities for "receiving . . . Stolen Goods" and for plotting "Conspiracies dangerous to the peace and Safety." Slaves were prohibited from selling any produce in Savannah unless authorized by their masters. If any retailer sold alcohol to slaves without the consent of their masters, the retailer could be fined.[8] This provision reflected the rising concern over Savannah's "little tippling houses."[9]

A MARKET, FORTS, AND A FALL FROM FAVOR

In 1755 the legislature also established a market in Savannah. Here slaves were prohibited from selling anything unless they had the express permission of their owners. Prominent planter or merchant politicians had no interest in denying themselves the privilege of sending goods to be marketed by their own bondpeople; of course, bondmen and bondwomen soon seized the opportunity to sell their own produce in the market. So, over time city authorities found it increasingly difficult to determine which slaves did or did not have permission to sell goods in the market.

The public market was originally located on Percival Square. Here beginning at sunrise daily except Sundays victualers sold meat, poultry, fish, fruit, and fresh vegetables. Retailers paid a fee to sell, and business was strictly regulated. For instance, upon any complaint of the sale of "unwholesome Meats," commissioners of the market could remove, burn, and destroy merchandise.[10] Also during the first legislative session, bills were passed to tax shipping, repair the lighthouse, and regulate interest rates.

The first meeting of the Assembly and Governor Reynolds had been cooperative, friendly, and productive. He adjourned the body on March 7. Reynolds continued to press for increases in taxes for arms and fortifications, but his Council balked at tax increases for defense. They recognized that the tax base was inadequate to support increases for defense. Angry that the councilmen did not act on his demands, Reynolds ignored them. He appointed his crony,

William Little, to positions where he carried out the governor's plans through chicanery. This infuriated influential members of the Council, who asked the governor to fire Little. Governor Reynolds refused, which strained relations with the Savannahians.[11]

Reynolds consulted John Gerar William DeBrahm, a royal surveyor and engineer, who was building defensive works at Charles Town. He asked De-Brahm for a plan to fortify Georgia. DeBrahm's plans called for the construction of forts and bastions mounting numerous cannons and mortars on Cockspur Island, along Georgia's borders and in Savannah. A thousand regulars, militia, and Indians would be garrisoned at the fortifications. Governor Reynolds recommended the scheme to the Board of Trade in London, which balked at the expense. Without funds for plans for defense, Reynolds was left with a militia of just over 750 poorly armed whites organized into eight companies and dispersed across the colony.[12]

Reynolds also urged the Board of Trade to support other projects: he wanted to move the capital of Georgia from Savannah to the town of Hardwicke twelve miles to the south. The governor's desire—some say threat—to abandon Savannah for Hardwicke outraged Savannahians, who believed that Reynolds planned to profit handsomely from his investment in land there.

Facing local opposition and again with no funds forthcoming from London, Reynolds requested money for use at Savannah for things that were "absolutely necessary": repairing the Tybee lighthouse, the courthouse, and Christ Church, building a jail, and clearing the river of obstructions.[13]

There was little spirit for cooperation between the leaders of the colony and the governor when the Assembly convened in February 1756. When the Council insinuated to Reynolds that his aide, William Little, was guilty of misconduct in office, Reynolds capriciously dissolved both legislative bodies. In March the Council asked the Board of Trade to recall the governor, which they did.

The policies and abrasive actions of Governor Reynolds led to his downfall. The taxes he called for angered wealthy Savannahians; the colonists wanted Reynolds to increase commerce, but because of the war, trade collapsed, and more people departed than entered the colony. His dismissal of the Council and the Assembly also soured Savannahians on Governor Reynolds.[14]

Before the governor left the colony in 1757, he admitted that it was difficult to establish a government given the "lawless, anti-monarchial people" with whom he had to deal.[15] But before he departed, Reynolds signed a bill to improve the roads leading to the town and to repair the public wharf.[16] An anonymous rhymester soon published the first extant poem by a Georgia writer. The ode expressed Savannah's relief at the departure of the first royal governor.[17]

GOVERNOR ELLIS TAKES CHARGE

The newly appointed lieutenant-governor for Georgia, Henry Ellis, arrived at Savannah on February 16, 1757, and was cheered from the bluff by the townspeople. The thirty-six-year-old Ellis was born to wealth, but at an early age he ran away to sea and later may have studied law. He joined an expedition to search for the Northwest Passage, wrote a book about the voyage, and was invited to join the Royal Society. A bachelor, he was known among the English gentry as a great wit and party giver. Through influential friends, Ellis received appointment as Georgia's second royal governor.

Savannah must have seemed a desolate place to the new governor. Several hundred people lived there in aging wooden houses, and a vast forest pressed in on three sides. There were probably no more than 4,500 white and 1,800 black inhabitants in the entire colony.[18]

Soon after Ellis arrived, he wrote London officials: "I found the people here exceedingly dissatisfied with each other."[19] Ellis took the oath of office, dismissed the legislature to avoid fights between his supporters and a pro-Reynolds faction, and then watched and listened. He quickly concluded that the colony needed a strong military presence and fortifications. He also discovered that Christ Church was "decayed" and needed repair, and he described the public jail as "shocking to humanity." Barely fifteen feet square, the prison was "filled with Felons [and] Debtors . . . quite exposed to the scorching Sun" and existing in "filth and vermin." He found other public buildings deteriorating or nonexistent. The lighthouse at the mouth of the Savannah River was almost "tumbling down," and Savannah lacked a local magazine to store arms and powder.

Ellis furnished "provisions, . . . promises, [and] a few presents" to the "Gangs of Indians" who came to Savannah almost weekly. He paid the Creeks for the scalps of Spaniards, Frenchmen, or other "enemies."[20] Meanwhile, he established good working relationships with the powerful Council members, restored prerogatives of the governor by appointing militia officers, and reestablished the colony's credit by immediately paying all creditors. By the spring, opposition to Governor Ellis evaporated, and the bitter factionalism ended.[21]

SECURITY MEASURES

In June, when Governor Ellis convened the Assembly in Savannah for the first time, he was convinced that inadequate defenses, too few people, and too little wealth were hindering progress in Georgia. He prepared legislation accordingly. Four major bills were enacted in July that improved fortifications and security throughout the colony, especially in Savannah. The first act funneled the tax money levied for road maintenance into defensive works. Like Governor Reynolds, Ellis also consulted the royal engineer, John Gerar William De-Brahm, and upon his advice employed white laborers and black slaves to build a palisade around Savannah and construct forts to the south during the steamy, dog days of late summer. The palisade was linked with bastions that mounted cannons; the earthwork without and within was fronted by a ditch. If Indians or Europeans attacked the colony, outlying settlers could take refuge within the fortifications.[22]

The legislature also created a night watch that was staffed by Savannah's white males. Five to ten men would patrol the streets nightly and be especially alert for "Slaves . . . lurking and caballing about," which may "prove of dangerous Consequence to the Peace and Security of the . . . Town." The patrol was authorized to arrest and whip slaves found abroad without permission after 10:00 P.M. A substantial guard house was to be constructed on the bluff near the site of the original one, with funds raised from licenses granted "to Taverns & punch house keepers."[23]

The growing number of these retail liquor outlets alarmed Savannahians. They viewed the "tippling houses" as "haunts for lewd idle & disorderly people, runaway Sailors, Servants and Slaves" who threatened "the common good and welfare." Fraternization of poor whites and blacks breached the racial boundaries—the "lines in the sand"—drawn by the slaveholding elite. Ellis also thought that when Indians and Negroes consumed liquor, "great disorders have arisen." He signed a bill into law in July to regulate the taverns and their proprietors: anyone selling liquor was required to purchase a license; it banned liquor sales to Indians and slaves excepting permission of the owners of the latter.[24]

The legislature enacted yet another security measure: a patrol "for the . . . prevention of . . . Insurrections . . . amongst Negroes and slaves." The bill reflected the racial fears of the rising gentry and was intended to protect their property. Seven heavily armed men would patrol Savannah; if necessary, they

would search the homes of African Americans for "Weapons" and would enter "any disorderly tippling-House . . . suspected of harbouring [or] traf-
ficking . . . with Negroes . . . and . . . apprehend and correct all disorderly
Slaves."[25] The matter of regulating liquor sales and the fraternization of poor
whites and blacks in "tippling-houses" remained a hot political topic in Old
South Savannah.

INVASION FEARS AGAIN

Ellis was pleased with the cooperation of the legislature by the time the session
ended in July 1757. But the appearance of several French privateers off the coast
alarmed him, and he put the Savannahians on alert and "constantly under
Arms." A combined attack by the French and their Indian allies could
"overwhelm" the colony "in its present weak & defenceless condition."
These threats offered Ellis the opportunity to renew his requests for a warship
and troops at Savannah. Finally, in September, Colonel Henry Bouquet, the
British commanding officer at Charles Town, sent one hundred provincial
troops from Virginia to be quartered in Savannah. Ellis must have breathed a
sigh of relief.[26]

Concerned over the loyalties of Indians on the frontier, Governor Ellis
staged a meeting in Savannah that made the town appear militarily stronger
than it was. Ellis ordered a company of rangers to escort about 150 Creek and
Cherokee chiefs to Savannah for a conference. Near the town the Indians were
met by Captain Jonathan Bryan and other citizens on horseback. When the
group approached the recently constructed palisades, cannons boomed from
the bastions. The Indians passed through the new town gates, Colonel Noble
Jones greeted them, and his militia escorted the guests to the governor's residence and then the Council chamber, where the Virginia provincials greeted
the Indians with a volley of musketry. Here Governor Ellis welcomed the chiefs
and invited them to dinner. The military demonstrations must have intimidated the Indians. Before the conference ended, an alliance was concluded
against their "mutual enemies," the Spanish and French.[27] Still, Ellis asked London for regular troops. He felt that the colony was threatened from "every quarter," and he needed men who "can shoot on horseback & ride full speed."[28]

In 1758 Ellis traveled southward to oversee the buildup of fortifications. In
March the Assembly acted on projects promoted by Ellis that had been deferred due to a shortfall in tax revenues: the lighthouse at Tybee Island was re-

paired, and the Assembly agreed to build a substantial powder magazine, "highly necessary in this time of public danger."

ESTABLISHMENT

In March Ellis signed an act that divided the colony into eight parishes and made the Church of England the "established" church of Georgia. Christ Church Parish—roughly encompassing the boundaries of present-day Chatham County—included the town of Savannah. No longer was there a District of Savannah; Savannah now was referred to as being located in Christ Church Parish; the Anglican church there officially became known as Christ Church. The act created governing units that could levy taxes. Settlers now elected members to the Assembly from their parishes and filed land claims there. The act was an important part of Ellis's program for encouraging settlement in Georgia.

Since the founding of the colony, the Church of England or Anglican Church had enjoyed "privileged" status, but now public taxes could be used to build churches and the homes of ministers and to pay their salaries. As ecclesiastical, electoral, and taxation units, parishes elected their own vestrymen and churchwardens who selected the parish priests, provided relief to the poor, kept vital statistics, and maintained the roads.

Church officials in Christ Church Parish also served as superintendents of the watch, protected the town from fire by keeping in order the town's "fire engine" and fire-fighting equipment, served as caretakers of the cemetery, and ensured that trash and dung were not dumped around the town. To fund these services, church officials levied taxes on slaves, land, and money earned at interest. In addition to their religious duties, these church officials also performed those of today's civic officers. The Assembly helped subsidize the "established" church by issuing paper money and appropriating income from liquor licenses and taxes on liquor.[29]

Regardless of where the money came from to support Savannah's Anglican Church, the leaders of the congregation vigorously promoted morality and religious observance. An act of the legislature in 1759 permitted churchwardens to arrest "Negroes and other disorderly People" for causing disturbances during Sunday services. If the guilty parties refused to attend church, they could be fined or placed in the town stocks for an hour. Several years later a more severe law was enacted to prevent and punish "Vice, Profaneness, and Immorality." Magistrates could fine persons who did not attend church, could close public houses, and could prohibit persons from all work and sports on Sundays. There is no evidence of how rigorously the law was enforced. Although a substantial sum of money was appropriated to repair Christ Church, Governor Ellis regarded the structure as "dangerous."[30] But years passed before major repairs began.

Presbyterians, Lutherans, and other religious dissenters living in Savannah apparently raised little protest to the "establishment" of the Church of England. However, it is significant that in 1758, when Christ Church became the state-supported church, Savannah's Independent Presbyterians summoned the Reverend John J. Zubly of South Carolina to become its first resident minister. The thirty-four-year-old Zubly was born in Savannah and previously preached there. Well-educated, he enjoyed a reputation as a dynamic public speaker. Wealthy members of the local Independent Presbyterian congregation received permission to build a church in Decker Ward on a trust lot, which is today bounded by St. Julian, Whitaker, Bryan, and Barnard Streets. Apparently, by the time the Reverend Zubly moved from South Carolina to Savannah, there was a structure on the site, which was known as the Independent Presbyterian Church or Meeting House. Several years later, a smaller group of religious dissenters, Savannah's Lutherans, erected a wooden meeting house.[31]

CRAFTSMEN AND FEMALE LANDHOLDERS

Despite what Ellis called "these calamitous times," he wrote London in 1758 that the colony was progressing and that the colonists enjoyed "happiness and tranquillity." Immigrants arrived who were driven by war from their homes on the frontiers of the northern colonies. The migration was encouraged by the land policies promoted by the government at Savannah: debtors who escaped to Georgia received asylum, land was available at a nominal cost, and restrictions on the size of land grants were lifted.[32]

Legislation passed the Assembly in March 1758 that encouraged craftsmen to settle in Georgia. However, Savannah's white artisans asked for protection for themselves from slave craftsmen. Responding to their pressure, the Assembly enacted a measure prohibiting the employment of "Negroes & other Slaves being handicraft Tradesmen." There were exceptions. Slave artisans who worked as "Ship-wrights, caulkers, Sawyers, [and] Coopers" might be employed, but only whites could practice most other crafts and trades. However, the well-to-do planters who dominated the Assembly had a vested interest in renting out their slave artisans for income, and they included wording in the bill allowing this practice. The legislators justified this practice by arguing that otherwise they would only be indulging "the Greediness . . . of a few Tradesmen . . . of Savannah."

The law might not have passed without the support of Governor Ellis. Savannah's craftsmen praised him for his efforts to prevent the migration of Negro artisans into Georgia. Prosperous slave owners controlled the Assembly, and legislation was never enacted that prohibited masters from hiring out their slaves. This remained a source of conflict between wealthy slaveholders and the artisan class.[33]

With the beginnings of royal government, women began acquiring thousands of acres of real estate through grants, inheritances, and purchases. Women now could legally own land. In the late 1750s one of Georgia's first Jewish settlers, Abigail Minis, received a sizeable land grant; she purchased slaves and additional land, became a successful planter, and soon owned lots in Savannah.

Women frequently inherited land. Ann Green, the wife of Thomas Green of Savannah, received a town-garden-farm lot in Savannah from the estate of her brother, Edward Jenkins. Women receiving such lots sometimes became businesswomen: midwives, proprietors of stores and taverns, and seamstresses. The only black woman identified as owning property during this period was Isabella Elliott. She inherited all of the real estate of her father, Andrew Elliott of Savannah, a sailor.

Women received about 70,000 acres in grants during Georgia's royal period. Eighty percent were widows or unmarried. Through prenuptial agreements and dower rights women also received property. Sixteen Georgia women accumulated a thousand or more acres apiece. But royal Georgia's most notable woman, Mary Musgrove Mathews Bosomworth, acquired the largest single grant made to a female in colonial Georgia. She received in compensation for her services to the colony, 6,200 acres, the entirety of St. Catherine's Island[34]

FIRE

In July 1758 a blaze that started by accident "raged . . . with fury" through Savannah's wooden filature, and few cocoons of the silkworms were saved. The fire threatened to engulf the Council House just a hundred feet away. Only the intervention of sailors and their "extraordinary efforts" saved it. Rebuilding the filature was soon underway.

The conflagration most likely moved the Assembly in 1759 to pass an act to prevent "accidents of fire" in Savannah. Wooden chimneys were prohibited, and fifteen persons were to keep Savannah's "fire engine" ready to roll. Church-wardens purchased any fire-fighting equipment needed and each homeowner was required to keep a ladder to reach flames in their domicile.

WAR AND PROSPERITY

Governor Ellis informed London officials during the summer of 1758 that Spanish privateers "infested . . . the Coasts" and seized local vessels. He asked for protection, but receiving none, he outfitted a sailing craft by mounting twenty-eight small guns to protect the coast.[35] The threat of invasion and an unusually hot summer bothered Governor Ellis. Ever the scientist, he sus-pended a thermometer from an umbrella to eye level and strolled along Sa-vannah's sandy streets recording the changes in temperature at various places. Ellis wrote that the "debilitating . . . heats" induce "an inexpressible languor" that "enervates every faculty." He thought it likely that Savannah's inhabitants "breathe a hotter air than any other people on the face of the earth" and that the climate had destroyed his constitution.[36]

Despite the fierce heat, enemy ships off the coast, and the lack of military assistance from London, Ellis remained optimistic. In early 1759 he informed the Board of Trade that 7,000 whites and 2,100 blacks inhabited Georgia, mainly concentrated in the coastal region. Others later estimated that in 1759 the number of black slaves in Georgia exceeded 3,500.

Exports, too, had increased despite the war. The growth in commerce came in part from the construction of new private wharfs and the rebuilding of the public wharf at Savannah. Built under Ellis's supervision, the public wharf probably was located midway between the termini of present-day Bull and Whitaker Streets. Ellis also placed beacons in the river to assist the river pilots in navigating vessels to and from the port. In late 1758 some 25,000 pounds of indigo, 5,500 barrels of rice, and large amounts of corn and lumber were ex-ported. By comparison, 217,000 pounds of indigo were shipped several years earlier through the port at Charles Town.

Even with the threat of war hanging over Savannah, some merchants prospered. In the late 1750s, one of the first Jewish settlers, Benjamin Sheftall, bought a one-third interest in a schooner, which carried cargoes back and fourth between Savannah and New York City. Sheftall, like other white well-to-do Savannahians, also invested in land and slaves. In 1759 his son Mordecai, "short and slim, with a prominent nose and dark piercing eyes," began constructing a wharf and warehouse on the Savannah River for his fast-growing export-import business. James Habersham and his partner Francis Harris both profited handsomely from trade and then in the 1750s turned to planting rice, "Carolina Gold"; they became "silent partners" in the firm Thomas Rasberry & Company, which at that time managed the stores and assumed the credit and connections of Habersham and Harris. In less than a decade Thomas Rasberry became a wealthy man. Thomas Lloyd, who was attracted by Savannah's growing trade, relocated from Charles Town in the winter of 1758–1759. He was a commission merchant who bought and sold cargoes. Habersham, who then lived at his rice plantation, Silk Hope, believed that the handsome new homes he saw going up in Savannah in 1759 reflected the new prosperity.[37]

Defense remained uppermost in the governor's mind, especially after the Cherokees attacked settlers on South Carolina's frontier and threatened Georgia's borders in 1759. Ellis called up the militia and rushed what forces he could to defend the backcountry settlers.

To defend Savannah, the town's militia was reinforced by any "Negroes to be trusted with arms." Governor Ellis continued to consult royal engineer John Gerar William DeBrahm on the construction of the town's fortifications; white laborers were impressed into service, and slaves were employed to repair the works, to build a fort encircling the magazine, and to construct blockhouses within the lines. One of the strong points was built on the eastern edge of town at a site commanding the Savannah River on a corner of the former trustees' garden, now a suburb known by the same name. A road was cut through a large Indian burial mound to link the suburb and the town.

The fraternization of poor whites and black slaves who worked side by side to build the city's fortification must have rounded the sharp edges of racism. Such close working and social relationships between large numbers of blacks and poor whites occurred only in the towns and not in the countryside of the Old South. About the same time another suburb, Yamacraw, was created on the western edge of Savannah. Increasingly over the years large numbers of blacks, both free and slave, and poor whites came to live, socialize, and brawl there. It was one of Savannah's first slums. The defensive works built by poor whites and black slaves that went up in the Trustees' Garden suburb were briefly called Fort Savannah, then Fort Halifax, and eventually Fort Wayne. Its massive brick walls tower above Bay Street today. The original fort was a square of two hundred feet on each side composed of post, planks, and earth. A blockhouse adorned each corner, and there was a powder magazine within. A similar fortification was located at the northwest angle of the town, and eventually two blockhouses went up on the south side of Savannah.

While Savannah's defenses were being built, Governor Ellis used bribery and threats with the Indians. These policies helped save the lives of colonists on Georgia's frontier in 1760 and briefly ended the Indian menace.[38]

DISEASE AND A GOVERNOR'S DEPARTURE

Fearful of smallpox being brought by ship from Charles Town in the spring of 1760, the legislature passed a measure requiring the quarantine of vessels arriving at Savannah from places experiencing epidemics. The governor and customs officials were required to ensure that the quarantine was kept in effect until the ship and passengers became "free of infection." There was no site specified for the quarantine, but for years all slave ships entering the Savannah River anchored near its mouth at Cockspur Island for inspection. If necessary, the crew and human cargo remained quarantined in nearby Tybee Creek until the danger from any disease passed.

The heightened awareness over cleanliness also moved the legislature to enact a measure forbidding Savannahians from leaving any "Offensive thing" in the streets and lanes and prohibiting butchers from slaughtering "beasts" within the town. Before the session of 1760 ended, the legislature and Governor Ellis authorized the purchase of a "commodious House" in Savannah for the use of the royal governors. Ellis became the first chief executive to reside in Government House, which was built on St. James' Square, today called Telfair Square.[39]

Governor Ellis remained frustrated with the failure of the London government to send troops and ships to protect Georgia, and his constitution was "greatly injured" by the "intense heats," he wrote. On May 15, 1760, he pleaded with the Board of Trade "to be speedily relieved." Two days earlier London officials had approved his return to England "for the recovery of his health" and appointed his replacement, but Ellis had to spend another summer in Savannah. He accomplished many of the things he set out to do. Georgia and Savannah, its capital, were better defended, and the number of settlers and the wealth of the colony were increasing.[40]

DEFENDING SAVANNAH

In October 1760 Governor Ellis welcomed the new chief executive of Georgia, Lieutenant Governor James Wright, and soon departed. Wright, was forty-four years of age, had practiced law, acted as attorney general of South Carolina, and amassed a small fortune in land and slaves. In public policy, Wright also focused on improving the colony's defenses and increasing its wealth and population.[41]

Lieutenant Governor Wright immediately asked the Board of Trade for troops and arms and for money to repair Savannah's timber and sand fortifications, which he described as "Continually Rotting" away. The London government sent swivel guns for the fortifications, gifts for the Indians, and additional British Rangers, but local taxes had to be raised to support the repair of the defenses.[42]

Word reached Savannah in early February 1761 that King George II had died, and the townspeople and troops celebrated the accession of George III. Cannons boomed, a proclamation was read celebrating the crowning of the new king, and Lieutenant Governor Wright led a procession through the town. This unique celebration and those on the king's birthday both entertained the people and nourished their patriotism.[43]

In July 1761 a French schooner entered the Savannah River and seized some boats and slaves. Governor Wright dispatched a scout vessel to search for the French, but they had sailed away. Alarmed by the enemy's bold actions, the governor immediately proposed to build a battery on Cockspur Island to protect Savannah. For funds to construct it, the legislature imposed a tax on the export of skins. John Gerar William DeBrahm was engaged to design and build the fortification. Completed in 1762, the small fort on Cockspur Island was constructed of "mud walls faced with Palmetto Trees," mounted with several cannons, and was called Fort George.[44]

In January 1762 Lieutenant Governor Wright was promoted to governor of the colony, and in the spring word reached Savannah that Spain had entered the war against England. English privateers occasionally brought their prizes up the river to Savannah to sell. Young export-import merchant Mordecai

Sheftall also invested in privateering and profited. By age twenty-seven he owned town lots, more than a thousand acres, and nine slaves. He married a young Charles Town woman, Frances Hart, and brought her to Savannah, where they resided on Broughton Street just east of Barnard.

Although the fighting never reached Savannah, there were constant reminders of the war. In July 1762, Spanish deserters reported a buildup of men and ships at St. Augustine, which alarmed the Savannahians. In September a Spanish half-galley intercepted the schooner *Anne* just off Tybee Island and seized its cargo of rice; during December eight Spanish prisoners escaped from Savannah's dilapidated prison. From time to time the scout boat at Savannah was dispatched to prevent illicit trade between Georgians and the enemy. Occasionally, Creek Indians, now allied with the Georgia colonists, turned up in Savannah with a Spanish scalp to sell. Otherwise, the war remained far away; as the threat of invasion waned, some residents who fled the town earlier returned.[45]

WAR'S END

Word arrived in early 1763 that the French and Indian War was over. In the Treaty of Paris, France and Spain relinquished their claims to North America. The war won for the British the eastern half of the continent and at the same time planted the seeds of the American Revolution.

Several months after the cessation of hostilities, Governor Wright signed a treaty with the Indians. It brought peace along Georgia's borders for some years. With the fear of attack from within and without finally over, trade and commerce surged. In the early 1760s a visitor to Savannah observed that "much building has been going on. . . . there are about 200 houses . . . three . . . brick [and] the rest are wood and are painted in shades of blue and red."[46] Governor Wright informed London officials that the colony was "in a very thriving Condition, our Trade considerably increased."[47]

The common goals pursued by Governor Wright and members of the legislature brought them closer together. Wright's vigorous opposition to South Carolina's plans to grant Carolinians land south of Savannah in territory previously claimed by both the British and Spanish cemented the relationship between the governor and legislators. Now population growth fueled an economic takeoff that continued for over a decade.

BOOM TIMES

In 1763 the legislature moved Savannah's public market from Wright Square to Ellis Square, named for the former governor. It was nearer the western edge of town and the increasing traffic on the river. As from the beginning, the economic life of Savannah turned on its export-import trade.

The ringing of a bell for fifteen minutes at sunrise six days a week signaled the opening of the public market for business. It was closed on Sunday except to fishmongers, whose product might otherwise spoil. The bell was first suspended from a pole and later placed in a belfry, but pranksters sometimes rang it in the dead of the night. Eventually, the bell was placed in the middle of the market. The market itself, filled with stalls rented to vendors, enclosed the square; it was entered through passageways on each of the four sides. Blacks were legally forbidden from selling in the market without permission of their owners. But by the mid-1760s local grand juries complained that bondpeople from the countryside were coming to Savannah, especially on Sundays, to sell or trade "corn, wood and other commodities, without tickets [permission] from their masters." The city officials may have imagined that they ran the market, but by now enslaved vendors, plantation bondpeople, and river people were well along in controlling the market. Both slaves with and without permission carried on financial transactions in the market and also met friends, exchanged news and gossip, and found sexual partners. Like the church, the market offered a haven from the institution of slavery. Except for brief periods of time, the public market remained in Ellis Square for nearly two hundred years.[48]

The same year that the French and Indian War ended, James Johnston was appointed public printer, and the first printing press was established with assistance from the legislature. Johnston, a twenty-five-year-old Scottish immigrant, was probably encouraged to come to Savannah by his brother Lewis, a successful physician-planter and member of the Assembly. He saw the need for a press in the economically reviving town. James Johnston located his printing press and office on what is today Broughton Street, just east of Drayton Street. The first issue of his paper, the *Georgia Gazette,* appeared on April 7, 1763. It brought to about nineteen the number of papers published on a regular basis in Britain's North American colonies.

Johnston was required to publish all laws and official publications of the legislature. The weekly paper of four pages, approximately seven by eleven inches in size, also carried local news and reported on events in other colonies and abroad. The arrival and departure of ships were regularly noted, and there were advertisements for goods and property ranging from runaway slaves to the sale of books. Before the publication of the *Gazette,* public notices and messages had been written and posted in Johnson Square, and gossip and news were available only in the town's public taverns. The publication of the *Gazette* enriched the cultural and social life of Savannah. It also stimulated political and economic interests.[49]

In the early 1760s Savannahians owned only 10 ships. In 1761, a total of 42 vessels cleared the port, but several years later, 153 vessels took on goods at Savannah. Over the next decade these figures increased dramatically. There was other evidence, too, of emerging prosperity during the opening years of the 1760s.

TRADERS AND MERCHANTS

South Carolina banned unlicensed private individuals from trading with the Indians during the early 1760s. This encouraged some Charles Town commission merchants who traded with the Indians to move their businesses to Savannah. In Georgia, regulation of the trade had become more difficult as increasing numbers of unlicensed traders infiltrated the Indian country. Meanwhile, Savannah profited as the Indian trade declined at Charles Town.[50]

One of Georgia's first and most prosperous Indian traders, Lachlan McGillivray, always grabbed the main chance. He had become a well-to-do merchant-storekeeper in Augusta and by the early 1760s decided to move his family from Augusta to the coast. He purchased two plantations, Rowcliff and Mulberry, of five hundred acres each along the Savannah River and just beyond Savannah's town limits. He renamed the tract Vale Royal, which was reminiscent of the names of English manor houses. Here he built a home for his family, one for an overseer, and a barn. He planted rice on the low ground and raised racehorses on higher land. McGillivray was now considered a Savannahian by the townspeople, and they honored him by electing him captain of the local militia. He continued to purchase nearby land, acreage on Hutchinson Island, where he planted rice, and he also bought lots and two houses in Savannah. He gave his property distinctive names such as Springfield and Sabine Fields. His total holdings in Georgia soon exceeded ten thousand acres.

With James Habersham and Jonathan Bryan, McGillivray became one of the largest property owners in the colony, and like other members of Georgia's emerging gentry, he moved about Savannah and to his scattered plantations in clothes imported from London and in phaetons pulled by prize horses. He also joined the new elite when he was elected from Christ Church Parish to the Commons House of Assembly. During the 1760s he entered a mercantile partnership with one of Georgia's richest merchants, John Graham, and imported goods on commission. Indian traders were their best customers.[51]

The Georgians cultivated the Indian trade in what was once Spanish Florida, and small centers there became economic satellites of Savannah. The dramatic rise in deerskin exports from Savannah and their drop as a commodity exported from Charles Town dramatized the shift in trade. Savannah shipped only 13,140 pounds of deerskins in 1761, but seven years later it exported 306,510 pounds while a corresponding decline occurred in Charles Town. Savannah's rapidly growing trade with the Indians was nothing short of spectacular. In less than a decade, the Georgia port had supplanted Charles Town as the major exporter of deerskins in Britain's North American colonies.

Savannah's merchants played an enormous role in encouraging the Indian trade. For instance, they paid higher prices for the skins than Charles Town merchants and profited handsomely from the trade. Like Charles Town's merchants before them, Savannah's merchants plowed their profits into land, slaves, and rice cultivation; consequently the export of rice through Savannah also increased dramatically.[52]

THE RICE LORDS

Rice planting was encouraged, too, by an act of Parliament that made it a duty-free export. Previously, rice had to be shipped first to England, where a duty was paid before it was re-exported and sold. This new legislation and the new Crown policy of unlimited land grants led planters to acquire and clear more and more land for rice cultivation along the Savannah, Ogeechee, Altamaha, and Satilla Rivers. In the swamp lands adjacent to these waterways William Bartram observed slaves "daily clearing and improving them into large fruitful plantations."[53] Indeed, imperial policy helped create an exclusive planter elite in Georgia who, like those in coastal South Carolina, grew rich on rice.

These few planters, like feudal lords, accumulated vast acres of rice lands, which they worked with black slaves. Before the end of the colonial period a mere 60 persons, fewer than 5 percent of all landholders, owned 20 percent of the land granted by the government, or 350,000 acres. These few large planters owned on the average 2,500 acres worked by 40 to 45 slaves. About 20 of them owned from 5,000 to 27,000 acres. This slaveholding elite of 60 men included planters, merchants, and royal officials. Governor James Wright alone acquired eleven plantations of 24,578 acres worked by 523 slaves. His friends also acquired huge tracts of land. John Graham, the Scottish immigrant and wealthy Savannah merchant whom Wright befriended, eventually accumulated by grant and purchase 26,578 acres worked by his 277 slaves. Graham owned plantations named Monteith, Mulberry Grove, and New Settlement along the Savannah River. Wealthy Charlestonian Miles Brewton purchased Walnut Hill from Jonathan Bryan in 1765 and came to own 2,500 acres of rice lands in Georgia. By midcentury Walnut Hill was the site on the Georgia side of the lower Savannah River of a major ferry crossing that linked the colony with South Carolina. First known as Rochester Ferry, then Screven's Ferry, it soon became the principal crossing point for nearly the next century. Bryan moved his family west of Savannah to Brampton, a plantation on the Savannah River, and continued to acquire additional plantations.

In the 1760s another wealthy Charles Town merchant, Henry Laurens, received a grant of 3,000 acres on the Altamaha River, where he developed a prosperous rice plantation; he also purchased 2,000 acres on the northern edge of the Savannah River, which he described as "almost opposite the town of Savannah." Another Carolinian, Colonel John Mullryne of Beaufort, developed an 800-acre rice plantation on Hutchinson Island just across the river from Savannah. Hutchinson Island became one of the most valuable pieces of real estate in the entire colony—and all because of rice.

THE EXPORT-IMPORT TRADE

Throughout the colonial period rice remained remarkably steady in price at 2.1 cents per pound. The rice for export was shipped in barrels containing about 230 pounds. The Carolinians who owned rice lands near Savannah sent their rice to Charles Town to sell rather than to nearby Savannah. Nevertheless, the rising exports of rice and other commodities and the import of goods through Savannah fueled its economy and forever changed the face of the town along the waterfront.[54]

The production of indigo in Georgia in the late colonial period actually declined, perhaps due to the rise of intensive rice cultivation. Therefore, export of indigo through Savannah remained only a fraction of Charles Town's export trade in indigo. But Georgia led South Carolina in the export of lumber, which increased substantially after Parliament granted a bounty or price support on lumber. In 1765 the colony exported, primarily through the port of Savannah, 12,224 barrels of rice, 16,019 pounds of indigo, 1,879,454 feet of lumber, 661,416 staves, and 3,722,050 shingles. The West Indies received most of Georgia's timber products. By comparison, at about the same time, Charles Town exported 610,952 feet of lumber, 236,327 staves, and 1,354,500 shingles.

Within a decade of 1765, the export of rice from Savannah doubled. By the end of the colonial period, Georgia ranked about third among the southern colonies in the annual production and export of forest products. The naval stores industry in Georgia never fully matured in the colonial period.

The growing diversity and volume of exports—rice, indigo, and forest products—provided the foundation for Georgia's boom times. The colony's territorial expansion made Savannah more than an economic satellite of Charles Town; by the mid-1760s Savannah was well on its way to developing control over an economic hinterland of its own.

As the economy gained momentum throughout the 1760s, Savannah's merchant community also grew. By 1764 twenty-four merchants served low-country planters. Merchant John Gordon left a partnership in Charles Town for one with Grey Elliott in Beaufort and Savannah. James Read, a Charles Town rope manufacturer, formed a mercantile partnership with James Graham and James Mossman, who had stores at Yamacraw and "on the Bay"— along the riverfront. They developed through Read close business ties with Charles Town's premier merchant, Henry Laurens, one of the wealthiest men in the American colonies. The firm of Graham, Read, and Mossman also opened a shipping business, which transported both freight and passengers. The merchant James Devereux also opened a freight service to New York in the 1760s.[55]

Consumers bought goods either directly from ships tied off Savannah's wharves or from local retailers. The prized wharf lots owned by the merchants ran along the river from the Trustees' Garden suburb to Yamacraw Bluff. The nine most desirable lots just west of Bull Street began to be known as "commerce row." Here long wharves and large warehouses went up for stacking and storing the goods of the export-import trade. By 1765 sixteen warehouses rose four stories in height from the level of the river to the top of the steep bluff.

This wharfage and warehouse area was already beginning to resemble today's River Street.[56]

The merchants imported East and West Indian goods and European-made products. Advertising in both the *Georgia Gazette* and the *South Carolina Gazette,* Savannah's mercantile firms offered a huge assortment of consumer goods, which appealed to the emerging well-to-do families of town and country who bought, bartered, or credited the items to their accounts. Credit was extended frequently by Savannah's merchants, but debts were hard to collect. Like other firms, Morel and Telfair became so frustrated with unsuccessfully seeking payment of bills that they sued to collect the money owed them.

Upon entering the warehouses and stores springing up along the riverfront and on Broughton and Bull Streets, shoppers could be overwhelmed by a vast array of goods and aromas. Morel and Telfair offered for sale silk handkerchiefs, perfumes, petticoats, caps, rugs, silver thimbles, firedogs with tongs, shoe thread, sail and seine twine, pickles, perfumed hair powder, telescopes and magnifying glasses, "negroe cloth," and silver and brass mounted pistols; Inglis and Hall imported clothing, coffins, "mourning buckles," fishhooks, canvas, and "oil cloth umbrellas." Even smaller establishments such as that of Jewish merchant Isaac De Lyon offered for sale a great variety of goods, including deerskins, chocolate, linseed oil, mackerel, gingerbread, cranberries, and apples. Joseph Callender imported Liverpool ale, cheese, salted fish, wooden ware, and Irish linen; in the store of Ann Cunningham and James Brooks, shoppers could purchase liquors and molasses. Button Gwinnett, who arrived in Savannah in 1765, first tried merchandizing and advertised for sale Turlington's "elixir of life" and Dr. James's powders for fevers, as well as cutlery, earthen and Delft ware, and tobacco. When Gwinnett's business failed, he borrowed money to buy St. Catherine's Island, where he became a planter and later entered politics. Gordon and Netherclift sold flour and pork in barrels, ship bread in tierces, oakum, and chariot wheels; William Handley offered for sale ham, wine, cider, chocolate, candles, and iron pots; and Alden Bass imported for sale New England and West Indian rum, blubber, cordials, and potatoes. Only the wealthy could afford the imported Madeira wine and port, but many others bought and enjoyed huge quantities of rum and beer. Savannahians also consumed large quantities of tea and coffee, the latter being the more popular.

Physicians also advertised their services, wares, and cures. Henry Lewis Bourquin, who had a shop in a house near Christ Church and who practiced "physick and surgery," also imported raisins, Jordan almonds, "white and brown sugar-candy," Epsom salts, and Squire's and Daffy's elixir. He specialized in curing "rupture of the gut." Physician Lewis Johnston imported medical instruments for drawing teeth and "glass nipple bottles for drawing women's breasts." He also promoted various panaceas for fits, convulsions, and depression; elixirs for gout and rheumatism; and "beaume de vie" for stomach and bowel disorders. Dr. Andrew Johnston sold instruments for amputation of arms and legs as well as a variety of health items—figs, prunes, rose water, smelling bottles, mortars and pestles, juniper berries, cloves, nutmegs, and preserved citron. Other physicians prescribed and sold remedies like pink root and snakeroot, which the Indians most likely introduced to the colonists.

Savannah's growing commerce attracted men such as Captain Telemon Cuyler, who bought a large house in the 1760s on the southeast corner of Broughton and Bull Streets. Well-connected with prominent New York, Philadelphia, and West Indian mercantile families, Cuyler entered a partnership with Savannah merchants Edward Telfair and Archibald Bulloch. This partnership began the first regular shipping runs to New York City and the West Indies. All correspondence between Savannah and other points was conducted by waterborne transportation until 1765, when a rough postal road was opened from Charles Town through Savannah to St. Augustine to carry communications overland.[57]

THE EMERGING GENTRY

By the 1760s merchant-planter James Habersham had an income of approximately two thousand pounds annually. It was derived from some six thousand acres worked by about two hundred slaves. Habersham was one of the richest men in America. After his wife Mary died in 1763, he turned over the day-to-day operations of Silk Hope and other plantations to overseers and black drivers and spent most of his time in Savannah. The death of Mary Habersham was undoubtedly hastened by the debilitating physical experience of birthing ten children in twenty-three years. It was a premature death common among colonial women. Only three sons survived her. Habersham kept the youngest with him and sent the two older boys to Princeton. On Johnson Square he built a "comfortable Habitation," which for a while became the chic architectural style for the town houses of the well-to-do. Like members of the English gentry, Habersham now owned both a country estate and a house in town.

Habersham was delighted with the growth of Savannah and the goods and services available locally. By now he had acquired the tastes of the wealthy of any time or place. For instance, he complained that his clothes were "miserably spoiled by Bunglers here," those persons who passed for tailors.[58]

Habersham may have been referring to any number of tailors in Savannah by the 1760s. John McFarlein, who immigrated from London, specialized in making uniforms for officers and riding habits for ladies; James Gregory and Alexander Stuart, "Taylors and Habit-Makers from Great Britain," had a shop on the Bay. Roche and Eden had relocated their tailoring business from Charles Town to Savannah. But despite a growing number of apparently qualified tailors, Habersham sometimes placed his orders with London clothiers. On one occasion he requested a dark silk dress coat and black silkwaist and breeches for daily wear.

Hairdressers and peruke makers also catered to the emerging gentry and their bourgeois tastes. Richard Thompson, John Webster, and George Norman all claimed to offer the latest styles in wig making from London. For the women, milliners and mantua makers advertised in the *Georgia Gazette,* offering the latest styles from London and Paris. Mary Hughes specialized in London lace, the newest ribbons, pompons, French trimmings, garnet earrings, necklaces, and ladies' silk ruffs. Joseph Tyrrell, a stay maker from London, made foundations for dresses.[59]

Philemon Kemp maintained the horses of the gentry in Savannah for eight shillings per month. Anyone wishing to breed their mares might contact William Smith. He offered his "high-bred English Horse Valiant" to "cover mares . . . at ten shillings the leap, 30 shillings for the season." Smith guaranteed that should the mare "not hold to the horse, she may be sent gratis next year."[60] To satisfy the equipment needs of the equestrians, Robert Bolton, sold saddlery from London; apparently business was so good by the mid-1760s that Hugh Sym left Charles Town to join Bolton. Frequent advertisements appeared in the *Gazette* announcing the sale of chairs and phaetons for members of the growing carriage trade.

Typical of the wealthy of the age, James Habersham had his portrait painted by the famous Jeremiah Theus of Charles Town and the more renowned John Singleton Copley. He also entertained his guests at elaborate dinners set by his slaves; his Charles Town friend, Henry Laurens, sometimes dined with him.

A grandly successful immigrant, Habersham was so optimistic about the future of Savannah as a trade center that he promoted its prospects to family members. Indeed, he provided advice, cash, credit, buildings, and his good name to his eldest son, James Jr., and his nephew, Joseph Clay, to establish a commercial venture in Savannah. Clay was the son of Ralph Clay, a London merchant who had married Habersham's sister, Elizabeth.[61]

Marriages between the offspring of Savannah's wealthy merchants and planters helped establish their economic, social, and political hegemony. For instance, in the 1760s James Graham, a well-to-do Indian trader, married Sally Stuart, the oldest daughter of John Stuart, superintendent of Indian Affairs for the Southern Department. Alexander Inglis of the Savannah merchant firm of Inglis and Hall married the daughter of Charles Town's prominent merchant David Deas; and Elizabeth Inglis, the first cousin of Alexander, married Thomas Loughton Smith, the son of one of Charles Town's wealthiest merchants. Pregnancies and childbirth soon followed the marriages of these well-to-do couples, and they sometimes advertised for wet nurses. A typical advertisement in the *Georgia Gazette* required "a young, careful and healthy WET NURSE," either black or white.[62]

Although marriages between the offspring of the wealthy of Savannah and Charles Town joined prominent lowcountry families, some citizens of Carolina's principal town questioned the character of Savannah's merchants. Isaac Da Costa, a well-known Charles Town merchant, indicated concern and perhaps even jealously over Savannah's economic boom when he snidely remarked that "there is hardly one man in Savannah whom one can trust . . . most are pirates."[63] By the 1760s Savannah's leading merchants occupied substantial, two-story, wood-frame structures built on brick foundations with outbuildings. The dwellings served also as their places of business. Lewis Johnston owned a home "on the Bay" containing a large dry-goods store, "with a counting room, and one for a clerk adjoining"; two rooms had fireplaces, and the dwelling house contained a parlor, dining room, three bedrooms, and a large cellar. The outbuildings included one with bedchambers and fireplaces, a kitchen, washhouse, stable, and a pigeon house.

At the upper end of Bull Street John Graham offered his large two-story dwelling house—with a "handsome balcony"—for sale in the mid-1760s. On the first floor were a dining room and two bedrooms, and a ten-foot-wide piazza ran the length of the house. The local climate made the piazza or long porch a standard feature in homes like Graham's; it provided a cool place to escape from crowded interiors. There was also a dining room and a bedroom with a fireplace on the second floor; a kitchen adjoined the house, which contained a storeroom and bedroom; other outbuildings included two lodging rooms with lofts, a poultry house, and a lot for a garden with a well.

The furnishings of the homes of Savannah's emerging gentry reflected their tastes and rising wealth. Mahogany and occasionally walnut and cedar furniture predominated; feather beds largely had replaced deer-hair ones; and almost every home had brass or iron candlesticks and snuffers. There was usually a writing desk with a stone inkstand and brass ink holder and inkhorn. Tableware included silver knives, forks, and spoons, and pewter was commonplace; food was served on china, earthenware, tinware, and glassware. Delft ware was especially popular.

There was mostly pine furniture in the modest one-story wood frame or log houses of the "lesser classes" who used pewter in place of silver, and glassware and earthenware instead of china. Here one found few feather beds, and stools predominated in lieu of chairs. Even slaves accumulated a little property: spoons, pewter, iron pots and tongs, pillows and blankets, and occasionally books.[64]

THE ARTISANS

Home building and furniture making attracted painters, carpenters, and cabinetmakers. Gotlieb Long, Gotlieb Grover, and John Telmack formed a partnership in house carpentry; James Morison and George Williams formed one in bricklaying. After he arrived in Savannah from London in 1764, James Bell carried on the business of painting, glazing, gilding, and paper hanging. Savannah cabinetmaker John Farley used the large red bay trees found in the nearby swamps to make tables, chests, bedsteads, chairs, and desks. Cedar occasionally was used, while pine, cypress, and magnolia served as secondary woods. But mahogany was the favorite wood of the cabinetmakers, and by the mid-1760s large quantities of mahogany arrived in Savannah from the West Indies.

James Love, a cabinetmaker working in Savannah in the 1760s, liked to work in mahogany and red bay. He had a shop on the Bay equipped with a vise, benches, and lathes; he used bed screws, casters, chisels, nails, brads, gimlets, hinges, moulds, and glue. When he died he left behind ready for sale mahogany desks, chests of drawers, bedsteads, stools, thirty-two red bay chairs, a bookcase, and two armchairs. In a deferential society his social standing in the community was modest, but he left a large estate, which he accumulated in a short period of time. He owned two town lots, five hundred acres of land, three slaves, seven "pictures," and sixty volumes, a remarkably large library for the time. In addition to his real estate holdings in town and country, he was worth over £500 pounds.

Unfortunately, today the work of James Love and other Savannah cabinet-makers of the time remains unidentified, although several Savannah-made pieces in the Queen Anne style are extant. Because Savannah had neither numerous nor renowned artisans in woodworking, the local emerging planter-merchant elite frequently purchased furniture made elsewhere. Beginning in the mid-1760s vessels regularly brought in desks, chairs, tables, and bureaus from Rhode Island, Charles Town, and occasionally England, most of which were fashioned in the popular Chippendale style. Only a few of these pieces survive.[65]

The growing affluence of some Savannahians in the 1760s attracted silversmiths, jewelers, and watchmakers, who repaired timepieces and produced tea sets, tankards, porringers, mugs, and other practical and ornamental articles. These artisans included Isaac Brabant, James Green, Adrian Loyer, Jacob Moses, Benjamin Dudley, William Sime, and Christopher Syberry. Dudley, for instance, who was from Birmingham, England, opened a shop on Broughton Street, where he planned to "carry on the Business of Silversmith in all its branches." About the same time William Sime and Jacob Moses, "Goldsmiths and Jewelers from London," also opened a shop on Broughton Street. Here "Gentlemen and Ladies . . . may depend on having their work executed in the neatest manner and at the shortest notice." Sime and Moses dissolved their partnership within a year. Moses invested his money in land and went into the retail liquor business in Savannah. Sime continued in the Broughton Street location, where he claimed to make and mend "jewelry . . . superior to any imported." Sime later went into partnership with William Wright. Christopher Syberry left Charles Town to relocate in Savannah apparently because business was so good there. He had a shop on west Broughton Street, where, Syberry advertised, "he cleans and repairs all sorts of clocks and watches and has for sale fancy articles."

Adrian Loyer was something of an entrepreneur. He was the son of a bookkeeper who settled in Savannah from England in 1734. By the early 1760s the younger Loyer had a shop where he offered for sale a "large variety of Gold and Silverware," made or mended "any gold or silver work," and did "clock and watch work." Loyer was paid a salary for two decades "for winding up and keeping in repair the Town Clock." He also hired out "negroes and Canoes . . . by the day" and invested the income he made in land and Africans. Within a few years he owned twelve slaves and a 450-acre plantation on the Savannah River.[66]

Married with two children, Loyer on one occasion entered a curious business transaction with a free Negro, Alexander Lorimore. He gave Loyer £70, "in part [for] a negro wench named Mary, and her two children, Joe and Cumba." Clearly there were now free blacks in Savannah, and at least one owned and traded slaves.[67]

The construction of new public buildings provided work for carpenters and contractors, which indicated that a growing number of wealthy Savannahians were willing and able to pay new taxes on town lots, land, and slaves for public projects. An act of the legislature in 1764 authorized the demolition of the old courthouse, which was in a "decayed . . . condition" and the building of another on the same lot in Percival Square, which was renamed Wright Square that same year. But nearly a decade passed before the money was raised, the old structure demolished, and a new brick courthouse built.[68]

POVERTY, CRIME, AND PUNISHMENT

As Savannah's wealth increased, the crime rate did, too. Like other port cities in British North American, the number of poor people in Savannah also was increasing, and some turned to crime.

In early 1764 Georgia legislators worried that "many Persons" coming into the colony had no property or means of support. In February the legislature passed an act "For the Punishment of Vagabonds and other Idle and Disorderly persons and for Erecting Prisons." Now anyone found loitering or residing in "Tippling Houses . . . shall be deemed Vagabonds and . . . Disorderly persons." Any Savannah resident was authorized to apprehend them and take them before a justice of the peace, who could imprison them for up to ninety days. A "vagabond" resisting arrest could expect sentencing of up to six months in prison or a whipping. The law also encouraged justices of the peace to supervise the building of tax-supported jails.[69]

Savannahians appeared willing to spend money on most public buildings, except adequate jails. The authorities dumped together blacks and whites of both sexes, minor offenders and murderous felons, into the same foulsmelling, poorly ventilated "wooden huts" that passed for jails. Some inmates died of disease, but others routinely escaped. When prisoners broke out of these notoriously inferior prisons, the jailers themselves were punished by confinement.

Savannah's Fort Halifax was used as a prison during the 1760s. Here escape artist and horse thief William Sikes was incarcerated upon sentence of death with eight other horse thieves. Fearing a mass breakout, local authorities posted a heavy guard. This time Sikes met his rendezvous with the hangman. A public executioner paid from the public purse escorted him up the ladder to the scaffold, placed a rope about his neck, and then pulled the ladder away before a crowd of Savannahians. He strangled to death. It was widely held that public executions deterred crime, but often pickpockets worked the spectators while the sentence was being carried out.

Horse stealing and murder, the most common capital offenses committed by whites, received the maximum penalty; so did cattle rustling, sodomy, and theft of the king's supplies. Lesser crimes such as forgery, rioting, disorderly conduct, indebtedness, drunkenness, theft, and flight by an indentured servant could be punished with a hot branding iron, at the whipping post, or by imprisonment in jail or the public stocks.[70]

DOMESTIC MATTERS

Savannah's newfound prosperity may have also affected marital relations. John Oates publicly acknowledged in the *Georgia Gazette* in April 1765 that his wife Elizabeth had gone to town and rented a house and "run herself into" debt, "contrary to my expressed order." Oates warned that he did not intend to reimburse anyone extending her credit. A dispute over "things" apparently strained relations between Henry Frederick Myers and his wife. Myers charged that she had eloped and taken "a gold sleeve button" and other objects; he offered a reward to anyone informing him of her whereabouts. Myers also cautioned that he was not responsible for her debts.[71]

CLUBS, RECREATION, AND EDUCATION

Savannah, like other southern trade centers, provided a social and cultural environment that mitigated the harshness of life on the eighteenth-century southern frontier. By the 1760s the Union Society, founded earlier by artisans, was admitting attorneys, who were once banned in Georgia. The annual and quarterly meetings were held at local taverns. The members adopted St. George, England's patron saint, as their protector; as both a social and charitable organization, the society offered scholarships to private schools for deserving children.

On November 30, 1764, the St. Andrew's Club was reorganized at James Machenry's Tavern in Savannah, where its thirty-odd members entertained the legislature. Patrick Mackay was the first president and Dr. Andrew Johnston the treasurer. This society also served both charitable and social purposes: it provided relief for the poor and suitable places for its members to meet. Well-to-do merchant-planters John Graham and James Habersham sometimes dinned with the St. Andrew's Club at Savannah's taverns and inns such as Machenry's, Mrs. Goffe's, Creighton's, and Lyon's.

Other organizations included the Society of St. Patrick, which observed St. Patrick's Day on March 17; members of the Ugly Club gathered periodically to dine in "harmony and festivity," as did those belonging to the Amicable Club and the Masons; the Georgia Library Society, founded by persons dedicated to reading for pleasure and learning, loaned books to its members in the 1760s; eventually its name was changed to the Savannah Library Society.

Royal engineer John Gerar William DeBrahm observed in the 1760s that there were three libraries in Savannah; the literate read essays on religion, "how to do it" books, and almanacs. James Johnston, editor of the *Gazette,* also operated a bookshop. Savannahians who could afford it indulged in art collecting. Johnson and Wylly at their store on the Bay and Inglis and Hall sold prints made by Hogarth. Horse racing was never as popular as it was in Charles Town; nevertheless, spectators enjoyed races run on a course near Savannah. The patrons of Machenry's Tavern played cards; the proprietor also kept a backgammon table for use by his customers. Savannahians owned violins, lutes, flutes, Jew's harps, and drums in the 1760s, which they played for entertainment. A donor wealthy in slaves and land presented a gift of a pipe organ to Christ Church. John Stevens Jr., a recent immigrant from England with a wife and four children, was appointed the first organist of the church and played the first service on the first organ in Savannah on Sunday, November 17, 1765. Several months later in honor of the king's birthday, Stevens organized a concert in the long room at Lyon's Tavern, perhaps the first concert performed in Georgia. He was most likely Georgia's first professional musician. Stevens soon left Savannah with notices of attachment and judgment against him to become the organist at St. Michael's Church, Charles Town.

The theatrical highlight of the royal period in Savannah came in the 1760s when at the long room in Lyon's Tavern a farce was performed entitled "Lethe, or Aesop in Shades." It featured "entertaining Characters" and vocal and instrumental music between the acts. The price of admission was high, and no one was admitted without a ticket.[72]

Savannah had several dancing schools. Timothy Cronin was the first dancing instructor to advertise in the *Gazette*. He also taught fencing. So did Charles Francis Chevalier, who relocated from Carolina; Chevalier, who probably taught the minuet and the gavotte, offered lessons in a large room in the home of Mrs. Robe. One summer, however, he discontinued classes because it was "too hot for the performances of his scholars." He was regarded as a person of "immaculate" character and died toward the end of the century on Sapelo Island. John Revear offered instruction in fencing and dancing for children, "where all the celebrated dances that are used in polite assemblies will be introduced." He also offered an evening school for "grown persons." The only female to teach dancing was Medley D'Arcy Dawes. She offered instruction for young men at the home of Mrs. Mary Smith and for young women at Mrs. Judith Swinton's home.[73]

On rare occasions balls and masquerades took place; assemblies occurred more frequently. Mrs. Sarah Lyon gave a ball in late 1763, and several years later Mrs. Mary Blake served as the hostess of the only other private ball announced publicly during the royal period in Georgia. James Habersham observed that Savannahians enjoyed some "brilliant" assemblies. The music at these social gatherings of the local elite was often provided by slaves. The slave Joe sometimes played a "good" fiddle at local assemblies; in the evenings the slave Ishmael could be found "playing the fiddle at tippling houses"; and a frequent runaway, Hercules, was fond of "making and blowing a pipe in imitation of a fife." But some of Savannah's gentry, such as Habersham, lamented the local lack of "Plays, Operas, or public Exhibitions, either in point of Literature or Amusements."[74]

Prominent Savannahians sent their male offspring to Charles Town, the northern colonies, and England for an education, but the sons and daughters of some received formal instruction in Savannah in subjects other than music and dance, especially through Savannah's private schools. During the royal era more than twenty immigrant instructors in Savannah from Paris, London, and other European cities offered instruction in writing, English grammar, arithmetic, geometry, trigonometry, navigation and surveying, Latin, Greek,

French, bookkeeping, reading, swordsmanship, military drill, painting, and needlework.[75]

At Bethesda, the orphanage near Savannah founded by George Whitefield, artisans gave instruction in the trades, and Methodist-leaning clergymen offered classes in religion and the classics. Whitefield attempted to convert Bethesda into a college, but he encountered stiff opposition from the Church of England. The new rector of Christ Church, the Reverend Samuel Frink, especially disliked both Whitefield and his orphanage. Reverend Frink was pugnacious and a master of invective; he despised dissenters and was perhaps jealous of Whitefield; and he viewed Bethesda as "a nest for the Enemies of the Church." He ridiculed Whitefield for his "broad bottomed" approach to theology as well as for his "broad bottom."[76] Frink remained an outspoken critic of local dissenters despite the fact that he expressed his views upon a less than solid base of communicants: fewer than 20 percent of the four thousand persons of Christ Church Parish claimed to be adherents of the Church of England, and of these, only 6 to 7 percent actively participated. Nevertheless, Frink was influential. He convinced the Council to defeat a bill passed by the Assembly setting aside a cemetery in Savannah for dissenters.

The Reverend John Joachim Zubly, the equally outspoken minister of the Independent Presbyterian Meeting House of Savannah, also opposed turning Bethesda into a college. He did not believe that Whitefield was a friend of dissenters. This was perhaps one of the few issues upon which Frink and Zubly made common cause, but for different reasons. When the child of the Reverend Zubly died, Frink, the only other clergyman in town, refused to speak at the funeral because Zubly was a Presbyterian. Despite the opposition to Whitefield and his plans, at his death the Georgian government was plunged into mourning, and black cloth draped Christ Church and the Presbyterian church. Both Frink and Zubly preached at Whitefield's funeral.

Whitefield willed the orphanage to a patron of English Methodists, Selina, countess of Huntingdon, and two ministers continued to teach there. Near the end of the colonial period, Bethesda was destroyed by fire. Eventually rebuilt, it continues to function as a home for boys to the present day.[77]

Parliamentary and local public support for education remained meager during the royal era although there was a Board of Commissioners of the School and Market in Savannah. Plans to build a public schoolhouse, however, never came to fruition. Alexander Findlay and James Seymour, both educated at the University of Aberdeen, did open a school in Savannah toward the end of the 1760s and apparently received some public money for their services. Members of the Assembly indicated that they appreciated the instruction offered by Findlay and Seymour, but the received little financial encouragement, and both soon departed Savannah. Peter Gandy received such a paltry salary for teaching in Savannah in the mid-1760s that he had to take clerical jobs to supplement his income. Despite both public and private educational endeavors, white and black Savannahians received little or no formal education during the colonial era.[78]

In Savannah during the 1760s the white members of more than six social clubs met regularly for dinning and conversation at establishments like Machenry's Tavern; lending libraries loaned books to those who could afford to pay; white musicians gathered frequently to play for their own amusement; more than twenty educators offered instruction in a variety of subjects; and the wealthy attended balls, masquerades, and assemblies. Only in towns, not in the rural backcountry, could such a plethora of organizations and activities flourish to invigorate the mind and the spirit, again attesting to the humanity of urban places such as Savannah. But coexisting with such enjoyable intellectual and social activity was disease. And Savannah was "ripe" for an epidemic in the mid-1760s.

SMALLPOX

The first major smallpox epidemic occurred in 1764 and motivated construction of a public lazaretto at Tybee Creek. There were hundreds of new residents—second or third generation born in the Carolinas and Virginia—who relocated to lowcountry Georgia. Unlike earlier immigrants from Britain or other parts of Europe, they had never been exposed to smallpox.

Despite the inspection procedures specified in the new Quarantine Act of the early 1760s, a slaver from the West Indies introduced smallpox into Savannah. After Joseph Butler, a plantation owner, purchased the slaves, the telltale signs of smallpox erupted on the face of one of them. A Savannahian, Joseph Stanley, agreed to conceal the slave at his home so Butler would not have to quarantine his entire parcel of Africans. However, a mulatto slave in the Stanley household contracted the disease and infected other Savannah families. In May 1764 Governor Wright announced that smallpox was present in the town. Terrified Savannahians locked themselves behind their doors or fled to the countryside; those in the country stayed away; business came to a standstill.

Some blamed Dr. James Cuthbert, a Savannah physician, for spreading the disease. Secretly he had variolated several persons—cutting into a vein in the arm and inserting the pus of smallpox victims. This treatment usually produced a less deadly disease than otherwise. Variolation was practiced throughout the colonies, but when Cuthbert's activities came to the attention of Governor Wright, he prohibited further immunizations in Savannah. Cuthbert responded by offering free inoculations outside the town limits.

From May through October about forty persons succumbed. The disease lingered into 1765. To prevent future epidemics, the legislature enacted measures prohibiting variolation and providing for construction of a public lazaretto on the west end of Tybee Island; here newly imported slaves with infectious diseases could be quarantined. Within a short time a forty-by-twenty-foot, two-story, tabby lime brick structure was built here. The low-ceiling, poorly ventilated building resembled a prison more than a "pest house" or quarantine hospital. The maximum capacity of the lazaretto was seventy-eight persons. This allowed each quarantined slave a space of three by six feet. If more than one infected slave ship arrived, the Africans aboard merely exchanged the filth of a packed slaver for that of the filthy lazaretto. Nonetheless, the building of the "pest house" was a significant step in preventing epidemics like that of 1764–1765.

During most of the eighteenth century, Savannah did not experience the periodic epidemics of smallpox, yellow fever, and other "fevers" that ravaged Carolina's principal urban center, Charles Town. This was due in part to the arrival of far fewer slavers in Savannah than Charles Town, which most likely imported the yellow-fever-carrying mosquito, the smaller population of Savannah and its environs, and the limited agricultural development nearby. Savannah remained comparatively free of yellow fever and other "autumnal fevers and agues" until the 1780s. Indeed, for years the view prevailed among wealthy planters and their families that Savannah was a health resort where they could escape their disease-ridden rice plantations, especially those on the Carolina side of the Savannah River. But as the population increased in the 1780s and trees were felled and land cleared for rice cultivation, vast areas around the town became breeding grounds for fever-carrying mosquitoes, and Savannah's reputation as a healthy place declined.[79]

SLAVERY AND ITS DISCONTENTS

In 1761 the black population of Georgia numbered 3,600, and the white population totaled 6,100; over the next several years the black population increased more rapidly than the white population. By the mid-1760s the number of whites in the colony reached 10,000 and the blacks 8,000. Africans now constituted about 44 percent of Georgia's population. The population of Christ Church Parish, which included Savannah, closely tracked this increase. More than 4,000 persons lived in Christ Church Parish by mid-1760, and some 1,800 individuals, or 45 percent of the population, were black.

Many slaves arrived with their owners who migrated from Virginia or the Carolinas to cultivate rice in the rich, dark soil of coastal Georgia. Some of the slaves had extensive experience at growing rice either in Carolina, Africa, or both. Slave ships also brought hundreds of other Africans to Savannah for sale. The rapidly expanding slave trade was another indication of the growing local wealth. During the early 1760s the number of imported slaves increased each year: in 1763 the number totaled 135, in 1764, 255, in 1765, 404; and more than 1,000 came in the following year.

Planters viewed slaves imported from the African Gold Coast, Gambia, and Angola as the most desirable; Eboes from Nigeria were the least desirable since they were believed to be prone to suicide. Some slaves were also brought in from the West Indies. During the 1760s the firms of Clay and Habersham, John Graham and Company, Inglis and Hall, and Telfair, Cowper, and Telfair—founded by three migrants from the West Indies—regularly imported and sold slaves in Savannah. But most of the slaves brought directly from Africa for sale in Savannah came aboard English-owned ships; rarely did Savannah merchants own ocean-going slavers.[80]

The growth of the slave population in Savannah was dramatized in several ways. An act of the legislature in the early 1760s added a plot of one hundred feet to the cemetery "for negroes and other slaves," which was under the care of Christ Church and today is known as the Colonial Cemetery. The number of public notices of runaway slaves increased; during the summer of 1763 robberies committed by runaways around Savannah became so numerous that the governor called out the militia. Two years later a group of fugitives located on the South Carolina side of the Savannah River occasionally robbed and harassed plantations in Georgia.

In 1763 the *Gazette* reported several grisly murders of whites by slaves. That same year the paper carried gruesome accounts of blacks murdering whites during insurrections in Jamaica and Suriname. Such reports reminded Savannahians that the slave code needed rigorous enforcement. Also concern was growing that the 10:00 P.M. curfew in Savannah for blacks was disregarded. Likewise, the white well-to-do townspeople worried over the "frequent meetings of slaves," especially "at night," and their socializing with whites in some of the town's disreputable "tippling houses." Savannah's grand juries repeatedly criticized tavern owners Luke Dean and Peter Johnson, who catered to a racially mixed clientele.[81]

Savannah's white wealthy class believed, and rightly so, that the nightly fraternization of poor whites, black slaves, and free African Americans in dram shops or liquor stores, gambling dens, and even brothels posed a threat to law and order. Repeated attempts to shut down the liquor shops failed. The keepers of the bars located them on the bluff near sailors' haunts or at the western and eastern ends of Savannah near the dwelling places of their black and white customers. In these drinking dens slaves could trade stolen goods for liquor. Occasionally, knives flashed and brawls erupted in these biracial bars. But something else took place, too, and it concerned the elite. The blacks and whites frequenting these taverns came to know each other and developed lasting friendships, which may have led to collaborative criminal acts against property. The friendships also served to mitigate white racism. Such interracial gathering places were unknown in the countryside. Biracial liquor stores became another humanizing factor found only in towns such as Savannah.[82] Concern over the lack of racial control was rising among well-to-do whites. There may even have been an abortive rebellion in Savannah during the 1760s, and the possibility of black insurrectionists haunted the townspeople.[83]

Running away was another form of rebellion, but slaves also ran away for a variety of specific reasons: they disliked their new masters, or they wished to be closer to family and friends; others fled cruel treatment. Many of the hundreds of runaways listed in the extant issues of the *Georgia Gazette* were described as scarred from whippings or brandings. For instance, Billy and Peter, owned by masters living near Savannah, persistently ran away. On one occasion Billy fled with an "iron chain" around his neck, which he tried to conceal by wrapping it in cloth; once Peter escaped with an iron on each leg. Some owners fastened iron caps with bells on the heads of slaves who frequently ran away. Slaveholders occasionally shipped out of Georgia habitual runaways and troublemakers. Some slaves stole canoes in an attempt to return to their native land, Africa; others were enticed away by persons with enslavement in mind or perhaps for carnal reasons. In the early 1760s Elizabeth Deveaux was convinced that sailors had lured away her slave Flora and "harbored" her on the bluff near the waterfront. A "harbored" slave meant that she was well known in Savannah and was most likely hidden by friends, perhaps white friends. Flora eventually escaped slavery on an outward-bound ship.[84]

There also were occasional instances of miscegenation in Savannah. Edward Somerville, a prosperous merchant and owner of two wharf lots in Savannah, died in the early 1760s leaving an estate that included "a woman and two mulatto children," who may have been his offspring. Apparently, the woman and the children were deeply aggrieved with the disruption of their living conditions caused by Somerville's death. When auctioned off as slaves by the town's provost marshal to a new owner, the woman and children immediately ran away.[85]

The growing problem of runaway and rebellious slaves influenced the Assembly in 1763 to enact legislation to build a workhouse in Savannah. The wording of the act began: "Whereas a Law for regulating a Work House for the confinement of Negroes, and punishment of such as are obstinate and disorderly is highly Necessary." After the workhouse was built and recaptured runaways were confined there, the warden advertised their whereabouts in the *Georgia Gazette* until their owners claimed them. If a slave remained unclaimed for eighteen months, the warden sold the slave and applied the funds to the maintenance of the workhouse. While the slaves remained confined, the warden employed them and if necessary punished them by putting them in "Fetters or Shackles . . . and by Moderate whipping." Owners of "stubborn . . . or incorrigible . . . Slaves" who did not wish to administer punishment themselves sent them to the workhouse for correction. Here the warden put the slaves "to hard labour" or corrected them as the owners requested. The owners paid for the punishment and maintenance of their slaves.[86]

The fear of blacks grew as their numbers increased in the colony, and in March 1765 this anxiety was reflected in the passage by the legislature of another "Act For the better Ordering and Governing Negroes and other Slaves." This law and a later one revised the 1755 code and tightened the system. The new, harsher codes deleted prior provisions that specified a sixteen-hour workday and requirements to provide slaves decent clothing and food. Teaching slaves to read was also prohibited, as was carrying arms unless accompanied by a white person. In an attempt to stop the "detestable Crime of Poisoning . . . frequently committed by Slaves," any black person poisoning a person or privy to the act, but failing to provide such information to authorities, would be executed. There is no evidence of an epidemic of poisoning by slaves at the time, but the provision may have been modeled after an addition to the Negro Act of South Carolina over a dozen years before. The law passed the Carolina legislature because it was said that poisonings had reached alarming proportions. Georgia's new codes, like those in South Carolina, reflected the desire to maintain white supremacy and docile slave labor, by physical force if necessary.[87]

The same month that the new slave code was enacted, the British Parliament passed the Stamp Act to raise revenue, legislation that caused a sea change in Great Britain's relationship with its North American colonies.

CHAPTER 3

Savannah in the Revolution, 1763–1782

A NEW COLONIAL POLICY

*T*HE PEACE OF PARIS that ended the Seven Years' War in 1763 made Great Britain the dominant power in Western Europe and North America. France surrendered Canada and the Mississippi Valley, and Spain relinquished Florida. In acquiring this new land, the London government spent a fortune in maintaining warships and soldiers abroad. Since these British soldiers and sailors fought the war for the benefit and protection of the colonists, England expected the Americans to contribute to the past and future costs of keeping troops in the colonies and for other expenses related to a "new colonial policy."

For Savannahians, the treaty brought a peace of mind they had rarely enjoyed: the Spanish for three decades had threatened the very existence of Georgia, but in 1763 East and West Florida became British provinces protecting Georgia's southern flank; with the departure of the Spanish, settlers pushed safely south of the Altamaha River, and for the first time Georgia had a definite southern boundary, the St. Marys River. Among Savannahians there was a new sense of hope and enthusiasm. This soon changed.

In the mid-1760s the London government ended its policy of "salutary neglect" toward the colonies and initiated its new colonial policy, which included taxation. During 1764 and 1765 Parliament passed the Currency Act, Sugar Act, Stamp Act, and Quartering Act to raise revenue and help defray expenses in the colonies. Members of Parliament and the new, young monarch, George III, were astonished at the reaction of the Americans.[1]

The Currency Act was a blow to the great merchants especially. It forbade the use of locally printed paper money for legal tender, thereby devaluing bills of exchange already in circulation. Always facing a chronic shortage of hard currency, Henry Laurens complained to his friend in Savannah, James Habersham: "one of my greatest troubles has been to raise money. Nothing but Cash wou'd procure good Rice or Deer Skins. . . . Bills of Exchange will not command Money." Both Laurens and Habersham also agreed that the commerce of the two colonies would suffer from the Sugar Act. It was an act to raise revenue, but Georgia merchants worried that the act would jeopardize the lumber trade with the Caribbean Islands. Thus to American merchants it became painfully apparent that their interests had been subordinated to those of British merchants.[2]

"NO STAMPS . . . GENTLEMEN"

The colonists reserved their severest criticisms for the Stamp Act. It passed Parliament in March 1765 and was to take effect on November 1. The act required that colonists purchase from agents of the Crown revenue stamps to affix to all printed and legal documents such as newspapers, bonds, licenses, ship clearances, dice, and playing cards. This affected the most educated and articulate colonists. Street protests erupted in several colonies when the act became known in America. The cry of "no taxation without representation" reverberated from Boston to Charles Town in South Carolina.

At first the Georgians moved cautiously. In April 1765 the Council and the Commons House of Assembly sitting in Savannah asked the colony's agent in London, William Knox, to seek repeal of the Stamp Act. However, when Knox defended Parliament's right to tax the colonists, Georgia's Assembly dismissed him and hired South Carolina's agent, Charles Garth, to represent them. But the Council did not concur, and it was several years before Georgia had a fully accredited agent, Benjamin Franklin.

The Council, or Upper House, was the center of the royal faction in the colony. James Habersham, president of the Council, opposed the assumption of power by the Assembly, but he also opposed the Stamp Act; the Assembly, or Lower House, composed of young, wealthy planters and professional men such as the sons of James Habersham and Noble Jones, seized upon the controversy over Knox and the Stamp Act to try and make the Assembly the center of political power. Testing their power, members of the Assembly began to create and fill several new, local executive offices, such as the assistant Crown's comptroller of customs at Savannah. The young planters and professionals were a loosely organized coalition in Christ Church and neighboring parishes linked by economic, social, and political ties. Later they were joined by a country faction composed of planters in the outlying parishes. Differences of opinion over the Knox matter ignited a bitter and protracted quarrel between members of the Assembly and the Council.[3]

The *Georgia Gazette,* edited by James Johnston, took the side of the Christ Church or Whig coalition against the royal or Loyalist faction. During the controversy over the Stamp Act, the *Gazette* published seventy-six articles against the act and thirteen for it.[4]

In the late summer of 1765, during the recess of the legislature, the Speaker of the Assembly, Alexander Wylly, received a circular from Massachusetts inviting Georgians to an intercolonial congress to discuss the Stamp Act. Wylly called together sixteen of the twenty-five members of the Assembly, and they voted to send representatives. But Governor James Wright, observing the rising tensions over the Stamp Act, refused to allow the Assembly to convene to consider sending delegates. Nevertheless, Wylly informed the Massachusetts Assembly that the Georgians supported the "Common Cause of the Colonies," and he sent an observer to the congress.

When the Assembly met in Savannah for its fall term in October 1765, it agreed to publish all documents Speaker Wylly had received pertaining to the Stamp Act. Suddenly rumors were rife that a stamp agent was in town. A group of Savannahians who styled themselves the Sons of Liberty—a name assumed by groups in other colonies—announced their opposition to the Stamp Act.[5]

Friday, October 25, was set aside as a muster day for the local militia and for the public celebration of the fourth anniversary of the accession of King George III. Ironically, it also marked the first appearance of the Savannah mob, which most likely was organized by the Sons of Liberty. At seven o'clock in the evening a body of people assembled to carry an effigy of a stamp officer through the streets. It was then hanged and burned in a square to the cheers of "people of all ranks." Prominent officials, including James Habersham, received threatening letters accusing them of being stamp agents. Governor Wright and his faction were alarmed by the new violent tone of the opposition.

On November 1 of 1765 the Stamp Act went into effect. The day passed quietly for Savannahians. There were neither stamps nor stamp agents in town. But liberty caps appeared. According to tradition, the first Savannahian to wear one was widow Jane Latouche Cuyler. Her home at the corner of Bull and Broughton Streets became the unofficial headquarters of the local radicals, the Sons of Liberty. Governor Wright called them "the Sons of Licentiousness."[6]

On Tuesday, November 4, the Sons of Liberty met publicly for the first time in Savannah's principal pub, Machenry's Tavern. It was a large structure located across from the bustling public market, on the southwest corner of Ellis Square, today the corner of Barnard and West Congress Streets. Machenry's was frequented by a large and mixed clientele of backcountry farmers, sailors, and well-to-do merchants and planters. The tavern, lot, and outbuilding were assessed at £800; by comparison, the governor's home was valued at about £500. The tavern was owned and operated by James Machenry and his wife, Ann, with the labor supplied by their six slaves. The dwelling also served as an inn and had nine or ten beds painted green, yellow, red, white, and blue. Most of them were curtained to protect the guests from mosquitoes. Lodgers must have appreciated the comfortable surroundings: six large china pots were filled with flowers during the season; some thirty-six pictures and maps adorned the walls, and there was a Turkish carpet on the floor; Machenry could seat twenty-four persons in matching Windsor chairs and forty-one persons when every chair in the tavern was used. He owned a corner buffet, two tea boards, and ten tables where guests might play cards or backgammon; the kitchen was equally well furnished, and serving dishes were of china, Delft ware, stoneware, and pewter. Expensive fire implements adorned his hearth, and brass firedogs rested in his large open fireplace.[7]

By the time of their meeting at Machenry's on November 4, the Liberty Boys knew the name of the stamp agent appointed for the colony, George Angus. He was not yet in Georgia. They resolved to ask any stamp agent arriving in the colony to "resign his office so universally disagreeable to his Majesty's American subjects."[8]

One writer has identified leaders of the Sons of Liberty as some of the wealthiest Savannahians, Dr. Noble Wimberly Jones, Edward Telfair, and Archibald Bulloch; working closely with them and to the same end was the Parochial Committee, which, among others, included Mordecai Sheftall, chairman, his half-brother, Levi, and Abraham Minis, which indicated the close working relations of Christians and Jews in Savannah.[9]

Another public holiday and demonstrations against the Stamp Act occurred on November 5. A gang of sailors, some of whom had been drinking, gathered and chose one of their fellows to impersonate a stamp agent. He was placed on a makeshift gallows and hauled about the town with a rope around his neck. Occasionally, he cried out: "No stamps . . . gentlemen." Finally, he was "hanged" in front of Machenry's Tavern before a crowd of revelers.

Now apprehensive, Savannahians watched and waited. Meanwhile, Governor Wright and his Council began planning for armed resistance to the arrival of the stamps and George Angus. When the Liberty Boys discovered that John Parnham, a local resident, had been appointed the interim stamp agent, they threatened him with bodily harm. He resigned on November 12. The same day Governor Wright and his advisers issued a proclamation "forbidding all Riots . . . and tumultuous Assemblies"; they also decided to place any stamps that arrived in the guardhouse at Wright Square. If there was any reappearance of the mob, Wright planned to call in soldiers from their outposts to augment his local forces.[10]

Following the letter of the law in the Stamp Act, Wright curtailed all civil proceedings that required stamps, but he kept the port open by issuing special clearances to outbound ships. This mollified most Savannahians. Both rich and poor alike continued to make money through trade in one of the few ports remaining open in the colonies.

Finally, on November 22 Governor Wright received a copy of the Stamp Act and took the oath to enforce it. James Habersham worried over the rising "Popular Clamour and Passion." On December 4 he told a friend that anyone who attempted to speak for "Moderate Measures is threatened to be mobbed . . . by . . . the Sons of Liberty."[11]

The following day, December 5, H.M.S. *Speedwell* arrived with the stamps. But there were no demonstrations, and prominent citizens assured Wright that no attempt would be made to seize or destroy the stamps. Nevertheless, the governor took the precaution of moving the stamps under guard to Fort Halifax. But still there was no agent to issue them, and according to the wording of the Stamp Act, which Governor Wright had pledged to enforce, ships could not sail without stamped papers.

The number of vessels riding at anchor in the harbor increased, their holds only partially filled with rice. The export trade ceased. As more rice came to town, merchants and planters alike became alarmed that their crop would rot before being shipped abroad. Governor Wright recognized the growing frustration caused by the economic slowdown and the rising possibility of violence. He reported to London that "Cabals were frequently held & Inflamatory letters &c sent from Charles Town" by the Sons of Liberty.[12]

During December the Georgia Assembly approved the work of the Stamp
Act Congress in Philadelphia and joined the twelve other colonies in petition-
ing the London government for repeal of the Stamp Act. Prodded by Charles
Town's radicals, Georgia's Liberty Boys gathered in Savannah on January 2,
1766. About two hundred assembled to storm Fort Halifax and seize and destroy the stamps stored there; a smaller force with drums beating and flags flying marched to Governor Wright's house. The governor recruited some soldiers from the guardhouse and with a musket in his hand met the mob before
his house. He acted "with the haughtiness of a Nero," one of the onlookers observed.[13] Wright lectured the crowd on their ill-mannered behavior, and they
soon dispersed. The governor then gathered a force of rangers, sailors, and
merchants and moved the stamps from Fort Halifax to the guardhouse on
Wright Square. For the remainder of the day the governor and armed troops
patrolled the streets.

The next day, January 3, George Angus, the stamp agent assigned to Georgia, arrived at Tybee Inlet, where he was met by Wright's rangers in the scout
boat *Prince George*. He was rowed quickly to Savannah and escorted to the
governor's home. With the arrival of Angus, Wright reopened the port. He had
the backing of the local merchants and planters who wanted their perishable
cargoes to depart quickly. While a unit of armed rangers stood at the ready,
stamps were sold to ship captains. On January 17, sixty vessels sailed downriver
carrying the proper stamped credentials. Savannah's Sons of Liberty did not
intervene. They subordinated principle to the hope of reviving prosperity by
allowing the departure of cargoes of rapidly rotting rice.

After the initial purchases of stamps, however, it appears that a deal was
struck between Wright, the merchants and planters, and the Sons of Liberty:
stamp sales would be suspended pending Parliament's response to petitions
asking for repeal of the Stamp Act. George Angus also agreed to go "into the
Country, to avoid the resentment of the people."[14] Because he went into hiding, Angus was one of the few stamp agents who was not forced by mobs to resign his commission. He was the *only* agent who retained his post until the end
of the Stamp Act crisis. Georgia was the only one of the thirteen colonies that
complied with the Stamp Act. It infuriated Charles Town's Sons of Liberty that
Savannahians had not followed their example. The Liberty Boys in the Carolina port had forced the resignation of the colony's stamp agent and prevented
the sale of the stamps.

In late January 1766, Governor Wright learned that "Some Incendiaries from Charles Town full [of] . . . Sedition & Rebellion" had inflamed the backcountry people of Georgia. An armed force of some six hundred were marching to Savannah. The news electrified the town. James Habersham was warned that his home might be destroyed if he continued to oppose the Sons of Liberty. He moved in with Governor Wright, agonizing over having his "person and property under the Dominion of a Mob." Governor Wright sent the remaining stamps to Fort George on Cockspur Island under guard of fifty rangers. Later they were transferred to the man-of-war *Speedwell*.[15]

On February 4 an armed mob of some 250 backcountrymen marched into Savannah with colors flying and mustered near the town common. Rumors circulated that they planned to raze the town, demand that Governor Wright relinquish the stamps, and shoot him if he refused. The governor acted quickly. He met them with 100 well-armed rangers and sailors from the *Speedwell*. The two groups traded insults, but intimidated by the show of force, the mob slowly straggled from the field. The governor had won the day. To James Habersham, Governor Wright had acted "with unusual Firmness & Spirit."[16]

Except for an incident about a week later when a crowd of "some of the very Lower Class" burned an effigy of an English official in the sandy streets of Savannah, the immediate threat from the mob was over. But the issue over the stamps left Wright a shaken and changed man. He wrote officials in London that he was greatly mortified "to see the Reins of Government nearly wrested out of my hands, His Majesties authority insulted, & the Civil Power obstructed."[17]

When white Savannahians disagreed, sometimes violently, over social, economic, and political matters such as the Stamp Act, black slaves seized the opportunity. At the height of the confusion over the Stamp Act, a group of slave men, women, and children fled into the swampland along the north side of the Savannah River. Here they formed a maroon stronghold and raided farms near Savannah. The Assembly offered a reward for "the head of every such Slave making Resistance" and sent the militia into the swamps to hunt down the slaves. But it appears that the black runaways eluded the patrols for years.[18] Crises reignited white supremacy among both rich and poor. Friendships between laboring class whites and black slaves nurtured in the town's liquor shops for years sometimes fractured in the face of threats of African American rebelliousness. White Savannahians kept a watchful eye on the African Americans. Near the peak of the crisis over the Stamp Act in 1766 a local grand jury demanded that the Negro Act be enforced to stop slaves from "attending funerals in large bodies in the night, rioting . . . and in a most notorious manner breaking the Lord's day."[19]

In March 1766, when Governor Wright met with leaders of Georgia's Liberty Boys, some of the province's "largest Property" owners, "[they] seemed . . . convinced of . . . the danger and folly . . . of their late rebellious assembling." But Wright told his friends that "a knot of rebellious turbulent Spirits still remain here in Town, kept hot by their continual correspondence & intercourse with Charles Town."[20]

Poor whites or laboring-class Savannahians comprised a significant number of the Sons of Liberty. With the economic slowdown caused by the Stamp Act, the urban poor increased throughout the colonies. At the same time, the middle and upper middle classes saw their wealth grow. By 1766 the vestry of Christ Church spent £100 in providing relief for the local indigent. This was a sizeable sum, about one-quarter of the cost of building Christ Church itself. Indeed, the parish became so burdened with debt that the vestry of the church begged for funds from the legislature "Lest they be under the lamentable necessity of being deaf to the cries of the distressed, and . . . obliged to dismiss them to perish in the streets."[21] The number of poor continued to rise. In the early 1770s, Redmond Burke, a "Professor of Physick," offered Savannah's indigent ill "Advice gratis." He informed the poor that they could find him "every morning from sunrise till night at the Cedar Trees near the Independent's Camp-Ground."[22]

After news of Parliament's repeal of the Stamp Act reached Savannah on June 16, 1766, the town's anti-Parliament faction persisted. Governor Wright himself was dismayed by Parliament's repeal of the act and little heartened by passage at the same time of the Declaratory Act, which asserted Parliament's right to tax colonists in the future.

Essays written by local citizens touting either the Christ Church or the royal faction appeared in the *Gazette* after it resumed publishing following repeal of the Stamp Act. These letters to the editor were personal, sometimes abusive, and polarized the local citizenry. At the end of July Governor Wright told friends that there were Georgians who "still retain the late avowed Sentiments and strange Ideas of Liberty, & insist that no power can . . . subject them to . . . Taxes . . . [except] . . . themselves or [their] Representatives."[23]

Governor Wright's courage and his alliance with the great merchants and shipmasters who feared mob violence brought about a singular victory in the colonies for royal authority in the matter of revenue stamps. In the long run, however, Wright's actions antagonized some local leaders and those in other colonies, increased tensions between local factions and the Assembly and Council, and dramatized the need to protect the rights of the colonists. Like northern radicals, Savannah's Sons of Liberty sought to increase the power of the Assembly to protect their rights and privileges from an arbitrary Parliament.[24] Indeed, the year following repeal of the Stamp Act, the Assembly moved aggressively to assert its rights.

THE QUARTERING ACT AND THE TOWNSHEND ACTS

Under the Quartering Act passed by Parliament in 1765, colonial governments were directed to furnish supplies to British troops stationed in the colonies. Serious opposition erupted in several colonies, and South Carolina refused to comply fully with the letter of the law. This provided a precedent for its neighbor to the south.

In early 1767 the commander of British forces in Georgia asked for "barracks necessities"—candles, salt, bedding, utensils, beer, and other items—from the Assembly in accord with the language of the Quartering Act. After some delay, on February 18, the Assembly refused. The assemblymen argued that to comply would violate the trust of their constituents and set a dangerous example. Two months later, however, when the Assembly asked for troops to replace the rangers who had been recently disbanded, it agreed to pay the soldiers a modest stipend in lieu of barrack's supplies. Therefore, while not obeying the act of Parliament, the Assembly was making a voluntary contribution to maintain the troops. The Assembly also sent the bill to Governor Wright without asking approval by the Council, which only fueled the ongoing dispute between the two legislative bodies. Eventually a tax bill did pass, but the controversy with Parliament was defused when the British withdrew their troops from Georgia.[25]

Into 1767 the Assembly continued to fight for legislative supremacy over the Council and to dispute the right of the British Parliament to raise taxes in the colonies. The Assembly asserted its authority on the matter of free passage for postmen on ferries and on the funding of the quarantine station on Tybee Island. But the news in the *Gazette* on October 14 that Parliament had passed the Townshend Acts, another tax measure, caused great alarm among members of the Assembly. The new legislation levied duties on tea, glass, paint, and paper imported into the colonies.

During the winter of 1767–1768 fierce opposition to the Townshend Acts developed in New England, Pennsylvania, and Virginia. In the spring the Georgia Assembly asked its new agent, Benjamin Franklin, to seek repeal of the acts. Opponents of the Townshend Acts, like opponents of the Stamp Act, argued that only locally elected assemblies could levy taxes, not Parliament. Circular letters arrived in Georgia from Virginia and Massachusetts condemning the Townshend Acts as unconstitutional and urging redress through petitions to the king.

Governor Wright viewed the intercolonial letters as a conspiracy against the king. He warned in November 1768 that he would dismiss the legislature if it approved the letters. A month later the Assembly endorsed the Massachusetts letter, and Wright prorogued the Assembly.[26] The following year rumors circulated in Savannah that Parliament intended to repeal the Townshend Acts. Governor Wright doubted this would alter local attitudes, "for the grievance complained of, whether real or imaginary, will still remain unredressed."[27]

Resolutions and protests against the Townshend Acts in other colonies as well as local letters condemning the Acts appeared in the *Gazette* throughout 1769. In late July, South Carolina began enforcing economic sanctions against the British. Jonathan Bryan, a former Carolinian and now a wealthy Georgia landowner and member of the Governor's Council, prodded Savannahians to take a similar step. But talk of a boycott of British goods alarmed the merchants. It was not good for business. Hoping to gain control over the local patriotic movement, the merchants held a meeting in Savannah on September 16 and adopted a weak nonimportation agreement.

Most Savannahians recognized the hollow patriotic act by the merchants, and three days later another public meeting was convened. Jonathan Bryan presided. Those present agreed to boycott all British goods except such items as guns, shoes, and "goods necessary for the Indian Trade," to end the slave trade, to refuse to buy from local merchants who did not observe the boycott, and to promote American manufacturing. But there was no machinery to enforce the agreement. Thus, unlike in South Carolina and other colonies, trade between Georgia and Great Britain through Savannah continued at a lively pace, especially the slave trade.[28]

When the legislature met in Savannah for the fall session of 1769, Governor

Wright addressed the Assembly but did not mention the local boycott of British goods. Rather, Wright called for passage of certain legislation and mentioned that the king planned to reduce "Taxes . . . on America." Jonathan Bryan served on a committee of the Council that responded to the governor by promising to carry out his wishes and to draft a new law for governing slaves, which was desired by the Crown. The Council hoped that the tax reductions promised by the king would heal the differences between colonies and Crown. In December the king suspended Bryan from the Council when he learned that Bryan had presided at the public meeting that agreed on a policy of nonimportation, the local boycott of British goods.[29]

Without the leadership of Bryan, the Council became a pawn of the governor. Bryan became an overnight hero. The *Georgia Gazette* called him "a Gentleman of Revolution principles"; the road running west to east just two blocks north of Bay Street was named Bryan Street in his honor; and the *South Carolina Gazette* praised Bryan as "a staunch and jealous friend to liberty."[30]

But the Carolinians praised few other Georgians. Charles Town radicals were furious that Savannahians still traded with Great Britain. Even after Parliament in 1770 repealed the Townshend Acts, except for the tax on tea, Carolina merchants trading in slaves especially remained angry with Savannah's merchants. These traders believed that they had lost slave cargoes to Savannah when ships carrying Africans had been turned away at Charles Town. One writer in the *South Carolina Gazette* angrily observed: "is it possible that *any Planter* in *this* Province can be so *destitute* of *public Virtue* as to countenance the unfeeling Merchants of Georgia . . . by *purchasing* SLAVES in THAT *province* and *introducing them over Land into* THIS."[31]

A BOOMING MARKET AND A NEW SLAVE CODE

Georgians also continued to purchase slaves in Carolina or receive them as gifts or in marriage settlements. Also by the mid-1760s, Savannah firms began importing more and more slaves directly from West Africa, especially from Gambia, Angola, Sierra Leone, Senegal, Guinea, and Nigeria. Like Carolinians, Georgians looked on men and women from these regions as "a guaranty of high quality." Beginning in the mid-1760s and continuing for a decade, Georgians imported over 10,800 slaves. About 5,500 came from West Africa, and of these about 44 percent were imported from Sierra Leone and Gambia. During this period the company of Basil Cowper and William and Edward Telfair handled and disposed of fifteen cargoes, the most of any one firm; John Inglis and Nathaniel Hall organized and sold the second largest number of cargoes, nine; James Habersham and the company of John Graham and Joseph Clay did not put their capital at risk by organizing and outfitting cargoes but vended slaves for the usual commission fee of 5 percent.[32]

Savannah's slave dealers and buyers, like those elsewhere in the colonies, were interested especially in the age, health, and comportment of newly imported Africans. These factors had a direct bearing on their capacity for work. The demanding labor that planters required of slaves—the clearing, cultivation, tending, and harvesting of rice and indigo fields or the felling and fashioning of timber for the lumber industry—dictated the composition of slave cargoes. Cowper and Telfair believed that the best cargoes for the Georgia market were "prime Men & Women . . . not exceeding twenty five years of age . . . with a few Boys and Girls."[33]

Slave dealers arranged for their human cargoes to arrive between April and September, the busiest season of the year for planters; demand slackened during the fall and winter, and prices usually fell. Cowper and Telfair also recommended to English firms that no slave ships should arrive in Savannah "after the middle of September as the weather considerably affects the Slaves."[34]

Small shipments of slaves brought in from the West Indies sometimes were taken ashore along the Savannah River at places convenient to the planters; other ships tied off Savannah's wharves and sold slaves directly from the deck; large cargoes of slaves imported directly from Africa by the local slave merchants were landed at Savannah and held in slave yards until public sales were conducted. Sometimes these firms had the responsibility of trying to sell privately or at public auction a shipload of two hundred slaves at short notice. The firms cared for and fed the slaves, and they tried to prevent the outbreak of epidemic diseases. Upon landing, slaves received their best meals in months, usually rice, meat, drink, and limes to prevent scurvy. Sometimes, to enhance a healthy appearance, they were rubbed with oil. The slave traders attempted to sell the Africans quickly; however, if the price of slaves was depressed, they were held off the market until prices rose. Merchants extended credit at interest for buyers, required a partial deposit, and also accepted immediate payment in cash, rice, indigo, live hogs, and barreled pork.[35]

Slaves arriving in poor health increased the costs of the slave merchants. Doctors had to be summoned and paid, and the ships had to be cleaned. Vessels carrying diseased slaves could be quarantined up to four months. To prevent a long and costly quarantine, slave dealers sometimes risked inoculation. John Graham sought permission from Governor Wright in the late 1760s to inoculate a group of slaves for small pox "in Order that the Inconvenience of a long Quarantine and the Danger of spreading the Disorder might . . . be avoided."[36]

Despite precautions taken to preserve the health of slaves, "New Negroes" occasionally died after they were purchased, a financial disaster for the buyer. On one occasion Cowper and Telfair were besieged with complaints from customers about the "Great Mortality" among 211 Africans brought in aboard the *Mary* and sold by the firm. It did not surprise Cowper and Telfair. The merchants had known that "an inveterate Scurvey, in a Great measure owing to the Long [voyage]," swept through the slave ship a few days before the auction. However, they had not informed the public. The firm took the position of caveat emptor.[37]

Often over a short period of time some slaves learned the skills in high demand locally. For slave traders these acculturated, skilled, adult slaves— carpenters, blacksmiths, barrel makers, and other artisans—brought higher prices than common field hands.[38]

Convinced that planters in the West Indies used Georgia as a dumping ground for their most "Rebellious Negroes," Georgians tried to stop the importation of black West Indians who might foment disorder. Therefore, in the 1760s a duty was levied on all slaves brought in from the Caribbean Islands.[39]

In the mid-1760s Savannahians were surprised and alarmed when they learned that the London government had disallowed the slave code of 1765 on a technicality. Governor Wright expressed their sentiments when he wrote London: "The Negro Law is so absolutely Essential . . . that without a Law to keep our Slaves in Order, no Man's life or Property would be safe a Moment. In Short our very existence depends upon it." Wright quickly approved a temporary slave code to "Prevent the province from being thrown into the utmost Confusion & distress."[40]

By 1770 Georgians drafted another slave code. It differed in several ways from the earlier code: now the penalty was death for the rape or attempted rape of a white woman and for the unlawful entry or destruction of a building. The sexual anxieties of Georgia's well-to-do whites were aroused by the growing number of black Africans among them. The provision in the earlier slave code encouraging free blacks to settle in Georgia was omitted. White Savannahians believed that already too many free blacks lived in the town, that free blacks set a bad example for slaves and encouraged disorder. As many as two dozen free blacks may have resided in Savannah by the mid-1760s; some were the offspring of slave women and their owners.[41]

For instance, a Savannah mariner, Andrew Elliott, left his estate to Isabella, "the reputed daughter of me" and a free Negro woman; Francis Harris of Christ Church Parish ordered that upon his death, the son of his slave Betty, a mulatto boy, Jack, be provided for and freed at the age of twenty-one; and in 1770, Daniel Ross, an overseer near Savannah, stipulated in his will that Sally, a mulatto "daughter to my Negro woman Phyllis," be educated and set free at age fifteen. The presence of mulattoes worried some well-to-do townspeople who saw them as troublemakers. One Savannah grand jury complained that "free Negroes are allowed to rent houses, whereby many notorious offenders are . . . screened from publick Justice."[42]

A changing attitude toward free blacks may have been reflected in the dramatic increase in the tax levied on them: from twelve shillings six pence in 1768 to over twenty shillings three years later. By comparison, the tax on slaves in 1770 was fixed at one shilling six pence.[43] Nevertheless, the continued growth of the numbers of free mulattoes in Savannah and other southern urban centers indicated that the close proximity of blacks and whites in Savannah nurtured biracial sexual relations and softened virulent white racism. Humanizing relationships occurred in Savannah and other southern towns and modulated white supremacy, but such interracial relationships were rarer in rural areas.

But as the crises grew between colony and mother country, wealthy white Savannahians remained anxious that slaves were meeting together in groups and frequenting "tippling houses"; it was asserted that there were "cabals and riotous" gatherings "of negroes in . . . Savannah . . . particularly on Sundays." One Georgian reflected the views of many well-to-do Savannahians when he observed that whites must remain vigilant lest slaves "in large bodies in the night" launch insurrections. A grand jury found it "a very great grievance that many negroes in . . . Savannah are allowed to live . . . from under the supervisions of their masters," which was a common complaint throughout Savannah's colonial and antebellum years and one unique to southern cities, not the countryside.[44] And slaves permitted to "live out" most likely also "hired themselves."

The limited prohibition against the hiring out of skilled slaves in Savannah ended in the mid-1760s. Wealthy masters who owned skilled blacks for hire saw to that in light of the great demand for house and ship carpenters, plasterers, and painters. The port also bustled with small boats and bateaux—flat-bottomed skiffs—made of heart pine or live oak. These craft were poled, rowed, and sailed by some slaves who had learned their skills navigating Africa's rivers. When these boats were piloted by black captains through a myriad of creeks, they provided the fastest and easiest means of getting produce to Savannah. Slave owners ranked their skilled "watermen" with their best craftsmen. Some watermen also fished and sold their catches in Savannah with permission from their owners.[45]

The watermen apparently supplied fish, shrimp, oysters, and crabs for bondpeople to sell in the town's market. But as the number of blacks in Savannah climbed sharply, it became impossible to tell who did or did not have their owner's consent to vend goods. Therefore, market vendors "hired out" to sell for their owners in Savannah were now required to "constantly" display a "Publick Badge or Ticket." Nevertheless, bondpeople with or without their owner's consent, as well as fugitive slaves, sold goods to make money, which provided them a modicum of economic independence.

Some slaves who were "hired out" by their owners or who hired themselves also made money and were not required by their owners to return each evening; they found whites willing to let them rooms, although renting to slaves was prohibited by law. A grand jury in 1768 heard the complaint that too "many Negroes . . . are allowed to live so much at large. . . . By which means a door is open to robberies and other bad practices," such as frequenting houses where "spirits are sold." And it was evident on the streets of Savannah that bondpeople were making money for themselves one way or another. In 1775, one grand jury demanded passage of a law "for preventing the excessive and costly apparel of Negroes and other slaves in Savannah."[46]

Unskilled slaves who were porters and carters also were hired out by their owners or hired themselves out; they swarmed through Savannah doing the heavy labor of loading and unloading ships and hauling goods back and forth between the town and the wharves. With the booming economy of the early 1770s and the heavy demand for unskilled bondpeople, Savannahians came to believe that laborers were overcharging, which put cash into black hands to spend on liquor and other "evils." To regulate such high labor costs and black habits, the Assembly passed legislation specifying the wages to be paid for the work of porters and carters. For instance, a town porter was limited to earning one shilling and six pence daily; nine pence was paid for every hogshead of rum or sugar and for a pipe of wine brought to the top of the bluff and delivered

along Bay Street or as far as St. Julian Street; one shilling was paid for deliver-
ing any goods to Broughton Street, and three pence was paid for carting light
bundles and casks from the wharves to any part of town.[47]

The fact that some owners hired out their slaves or permitted them to "live
out" was doubtlessly a "grievance" to the nonslaveholding skilled white artisans who faced competition from bondpeople as well as to some slaveholders
who wished to keep their slaves under close supervision. But the master class
was on the horns of a dilemma: if they permitted slaves to live out, they were
happier and often hired themselves out to work to make money for both their
owners and themselves; however, slaves who lived out also frequently worked,
fraternized, drank, and traded goods for liquor with poorer whites in Savannah's many liquor shops, which nurtured interracial friendships and even
criminal acts such as theft, which was most often aimed at the elite. Slaves continued to live out and to hire themselves out in Savannah, which brought them
some extra money and independence. Rarely did slaves in the countryside gain
such an opportunity. And while living out was a humanizing experience for
Savannah's slaves in the friends they made and the freedom from constant
scrutiny by their owners, it remained a dilemma that skilled upwardly mobile
and prosperous white Savannahians never resolved.[48]

Owners recognized, too, that those slaves allowed to live out and hire out
seemed happier. Slaves who were not allowed some independence became the
most disgruntled and were the most likely to rebel against the system.

SLAVE RESISTANCE

For some slaves flight was a form of resistance and self-assertion, and they ran
away from their masters for a variety of reasons: to avoid punishment or separation from loved ones, to join friends or family, and to seek independence and
permanent freedom. At least 160 owners placed advertisements in the Savannah *Gazette* from the early 1760s through the mid-1770s asking for help in the
return of 453 fugitive slaves. At least one-quarter of these slaves who were concentrated in lowcountry Georgia headed for Savannah; another 41 were "well
known in Savannah" and may even have been "harbored" by nonslaveholding
whites. The owner of Yamow advertised that he "has often been seen in and
near Savannah"; another master remarked that his slave Caesar was "supposed
to be lurking near Savannah." Owners frequently warned readers that runaways used every ruse to escape recapture. They were "artful" and "cunning."[49]

The same pattern prevailed in Savannah as in Charles Town: country slaves fled to the colony's urban center, where they found a measure of anonymity, and where free blacks or whites who needed casual labor would harbor them and ask no questions. The hiring of black fugitives by nonslaveholding whites was a good example of an illegal biracial alliance in the workplace, which permitted runaways to earn money and sustain themselves. It also undercut the authority of the wealthy slaveholders. Hence in Savannah fugitives passed for free blacks or a local slaveholder's bondperson sometimes for months until they could find passage to freedom on an outward-bound vessel. Usually the acculturated slaves headed for Savannah, where their knowledge of English and skills served them well.

But most of the runaways were "New Negroes" or African-born slaves, unskilled men twenty-five years old or younger who ran away alone, in pairs, and in groups. Some formed maroon societies on islands in the Savannah River or in the swamps along its north bank, where they lived by fishing, hunting, and raiding plantations on the Georgia side of the river. In the mid-1760s one group of fugitives killed a white man and an Indian near Savannah.

Runaways often were identified by the marks of earlier whipping or the owner's mark made with a white-hot iron. Some slaves remained at large for long periods of time; Mahomet, a slave owned by John Graham, was gone for over three years. Others soon were caught, or they returned to their owners voluntarily; a few were never taken alive, and fewer still escaped and were never caught.[50]

By the early 1770s Africans constituted about 45 percent of Georgia's population; in the rice-growing parishes of the lowcountry, slaves reached 60 percent of the population. Savannah had a population of 1,175 whites and 821 blacks in 1771. Paradoxically, as white merchants and planters bought more and more Africans to increase their wealth and pleasure, the rising turbulence from the same slaves raised the anxieties of the owners. The rapid increase in the number of blacks, the problem of runaways, the rumors of "night cabals," and possibly a "failed insurrection" in the town in 1768—a story that has persisted among local African Americans—led to the passage of legislation reflecting white fears and their desires for social control.[51]

In 1765 the legislature passed an act requiring all white males to carry weapons to church. Sundays, when most whites were in church, were deemed an especially likely time for black uprisings. The act was renewed by the legislature five years later, and the preamble to the 1770 act was very specific:

"Whereas it is necessary for the security and defense of this province from internal dangers and insurrections," persons attending public worship services "shall . . . carry fire arms." Under penalty of a fine, white males were expected to keep their weapons beside them in their pews.[52] In 1770 the legislature also created the Savannah Watch. The watch was composed of three officers, a drummer, and twenty-one watchmen whose duties were to patrol Savannah's streets. Charles Town had a similar unit. Much like a police force, the watch was organized to keep law and order, especially among the slaves. The Savannah Watch could arrest slaves, chastise them, and incarcerate them in the workhouse without the owner's permission.

Militia companies also were called out occasionally to hunt for runaways. In December 1771 it was reported to the governor that "a great number of fugitive Negroes had committed many robberies and insults" near Savannah and that their numbers "might . . . increase daily." Members of the local militia were dispatched to apprehend them and destroy their swamp encampment just west of Savannah. But six months later the same band of maroons continued to rob, pillage, and set fires in the countryside. Again the government sent troops to search for and capture or destroy these fugitives.[53]

Slaves suspected of committing capital offenses were speedily brought to trial and, if convicted, were executed by hanging or burning within three weeks of their crime. Usually they were decapitated, and their heads were impaled on a pole near the scene of the crime. By speedy execution and public display of the culprits, capital courts hoped to deter future crimes. From the mid-1760s to the early 1770s at least twenty slaves in the colony were executed for murder, arson, robbery, or insurrection. Ironically, skilled and unskilled black slave labor fueled Savannah's economic boom in the early 1770s.[54]

PROBLEMS AND PROSPERITY

Occasionally, the economic boom of the early 1770s was interrupted by natural disasters, human frailties, and tragedies. In early 1771 torrential rains fell along the coast. James Habersham observed that the "terrible Wet Spring hindered our planting our Rice fields in due time"; rivers surged over their banks, and on some plantations "floods damaged a good deal of Rice." Then in December Habersham experienced "the most severe weather I ever knew in Georgia." Freezing rain turned to snow and froze so solidly that for several days "Boys were sliding upon the sandy streets and squares" of Savannah.[55]

Two months later, in early 1772, reports of mad dogs attacking Savannahi-ans in the suburbs of Yamacraw and the Trustees' Garden reached Habersham, now the acting governor. A mulatto boy Habersham had given to his son was bitten on the cheek and contracted "canine Madness." Just prior to the young slave child's death, Habersham wrote: "the dreadful shrieks of the Boy has rung such a Peal in my Ears, that I never can forget." He quickly convened several meetings of the Council to consider how best "to secure the Inhabitants of the Town . . . from so alarming a danger" as rabid dogs. Subsequently, an ordi-nance was issued authorizing white persons "to kill . . . dogs . . . going at large."[56] This may have been disturbing to some Savannahians who had dogs as pets, especially to blacks, who kept large numbers of dogs. White residents who could afford it also kept cats and, like eighteenth-century Englishmen, enjoyed the exotic appeal of parrots, goldfinch, and other birds, which they kept in cages in their homes.[57]

Despite the growing local prosperity, the Savannah jail and the Watch House remained notoriously in disrepair. Repeatedly James Habersham urged the legislature to investigate the conditions there. In the early 1770s a carpen-ter employed to make "repairs to the Gaol" told Habersham that the building was "so rotten and defective that he dare not enter" it lest his weight "should bring down the prison." Habersham asked the legislators to give the matter their immediate attention "as the lives of the unhappy people now confined there are in imminent danger."[58] But the unwillingness of wealthy legislators to raise taxes, the lack of adequate mechanisms to collect revenue, and the avoidance of taxes by many meant that few funds were available to repair the town's jail.

Habersham informed London officials in 1772 that there were frequent jail-breaks by hardened criminals from "the present Wooden Hutt, improperly called a Gaol, [which] was not secure enough to confine an Infant." Further-more, "fugitive and Criminal Slaves" also frequently escaped from the Watch House because it was "in the same Condition with the Gaol."[59] Habersham worried that the lack of adequate places of confinement encouraged criminal-ity. Habersham also pointed out that Fort George on Cockspur Island was also in "Ruin, tho' so necessary for the Protection of this Port and Shipping."[60] Funding from London for Fort George had stopped after 1763 when the threat of invasion by the Spanish or French ended.

Shoaling in the river also had become a real hazard to navigation. John Gerar DeBrahm, surveyor general for the Southern District of the British colonies in North America, noted in the early 1770s that freshets "hurried down" the river a "great Quantity of Ground, Sand and Gravel," which was deposited below Savannah near the mouth of the river. Now "a Man-of-War Sloop with difficulty goes up" to Savannah, whereas only a few years before "a forty-gun Ship found no difficulty to come up and anchor before the Town." The "Eddys" and currents also caused shoaling where the Back and Front Rivers merged into a single channel at the head of Elba Island just below the town.[61] There was extended discussion in the legislature as to how to keep the river free of debris, which threatened shipping. In the early 1770s an act to keep the channels open prohibited persons from throwing ballast, rubbish, or trees into the river and creeks and required captains of vessels to comply with its provisions under penalty of a fine.[62]

Despite the increasing hazards to navigation on the river, Savannah's economy, which depended heavily on river traffic, boomed. In January 1772 James Habersham told a friend in London that there were "near 40 square rigged Vessels before the Town, and this Province is making a rapid progress in her Commerce, Wealth and Population. . . . I am loaded with Business. . . . it increases daily."[63]

Governor Wright observed that between 1756 and 1770 the foreign and coastal trade, primarily from Savannah, had increased in the amount of products shipped "more than 5 times; their Value more than 6 times, and the Number of Vessels more than 3½ times."[64] By 1775 the amount of rice, indigo, skins, timber, and tobacco exported had increased about ten times. Fifty-two vessels were used in the export-import trade in 1755, but 225 vessels were engaged in trade by the early 1770s. Georgians alone owned 36 ocean-going vessels and another 50 smaller craft, which plied the river and coastwise trade. Local shipbuilding was promoted by the Telfair Company, which directed the construction of some of the largest ships listed in Lloyd's Register, including the huge 400-ton ship *Butler,* which could transport eighteen hundred barrels of rice. It was built at Yamacraw by shipwright Robert Watts. Yet Savannah did not become a major shipbuilding center due to the costs of expensive items—iron work, sails, and rope—which had to be purchased abroad.

By the early 1770s Savannah was engaged in a brisk trade rivalry with Charles Town. Georgia's capital and urban center was no longer an economic satellite of Charles Town—a collection point for produce that was then shipped to the Carolina port and abroad. Charles Town remained, however, the principal port and center of wealth and culture for the southern colonies;

it was twice the size of Savannah in the number of houses, and with a population of over 12,000 blacks and whites, it was nearly three times larger. But by the early 1770s Savannah had developed an economic hinterland of its own and had taken over part of the trading territory and the lucrative Indian trade, which was once Charles Town's. Savannah was the only urban center in the South to challenge Charles Town's export monopoly of staple crops.

The growing commercial importance of imperial Georgia's major port and town also reflected the growth of the colony. Savannah's increasing prosperity was noted in its population, its structures, new clothing and jewelry shops, and its public houses.[65]

Approaching Savannah by the river in the autumn of 1774, visitors noticed the forest of ships' masts at wharfside barely reached the heights of stores and warehouses on the bluff, which, a visitor remarked, "put a man out of breath to reach the Top."[66] The noise and bustle of sailors, porters, and merchants was confined to the wharf area; the rest of the town sprawled quietly in the warm sun to the south, west, and east of the bluff till it was hemmed in by towering pine trees. From the northern side looking across the river, fast ripening rice fields could be seen on Hutchinson's Island. Three major roads linked Savannah with the rest of the colony: the Augusta or Ebenezer Road ran west to Zubly's Ferry and here crossed the river to Carolina and then passed through pine barrens into the piedmont region; to the southward was the Ogeechee Road, which followed old Indian trails to Midway and Darien; and to the southeast was the Sea Island Road, which traversed swamps toward Thunderbolt, Beaulieu, and other settlements along the network of sounds, rivers, and creeks.[67]

Savannah's population tripled between 1760 and the early 1770s. By this time about 3,500 black and white inhabitants lived in the town and its three suburbs: Ewenburgh, Yamacraw, and the Trustees' Garden. Savannah was among a dozen towns in the thirteen colonies with populations of 3,000 to 5,000. Some 560 houses lined its wide, sandy streets; on Reynolds Square a large, two-storied Georgian mansion built on a brick foundation was under construction for James Habersham Jr., son of the elder Habersham. Other prosperous merchants owned similar homes constructed of wood with brick chimneys. There were three churches—Christ Church, a Lutheran church, and an Independent Presbyterian congregation. Over half of the population of Savannah was affiliated with the Church of England. By 1772 the Lutheran worshipers were meeting in the old wood-framed courthouse, which they had purchased and moved to the eastern corner of Bull and State Streets. Here Henry Melchior Muhlenberg, "the Father of American Lutheranism," preached in 1774 to a congregation of about two hundred. This same site on Wright Square today is the location of the Lutheran Church of the Ascension. Savannah boasted three libraries, and a post office was operated by Robert Bolton. The old Silk Filature was being renovated for use for concerts, lectures, and dances, and there was a small theater on Broughton Street.[68]

New jewelers, watchmakers, milliners, and clothiers from abroad opened new businesses in Savannah in 1774. Mary Martin, a milliner and manta maker from Paris, advertised that "she dresses ladies hair"; Catherine Clark advertised that "she . . . makes gowns, [and] childrens habits"; and Mary Hughes had just imported from London "lace, newest fashioned ribbons, garnet earrings and necklaces."

In 1774, six men and one woman, Abigail Minis, were issued business licenses to keep taverns in Savannah. Tondee's Tavern, on the northwest corner of Broughton and Whitaker Streets, had replaced Machenry's Tavern as the most popular gathering place to drink, read the *Gazette,* and argue imperial politics.[69] And there was much to debate. Revolution was in the air. In the early 1770s Savannah was in the early stages of a vast economic boom, but as in the past a world war brought it to an end.

ROAD TO REVOLUTION

Repeal of the Townshend Acts did not end the struggle for power between Governor Wright and the Commons House of Assembly. In 1771 the quarrel erupted again when the Assembly won a dispute with Governor Wright over all changes in the election laws except one. That year the London government allowed representation in the legislature from the new parishes south of the Altamaha River but denied the Assembly the prerogative of limiting its sessions. Seizing as a pretext the London government's failure to permit them all their "Rights and Privileges," members of the Assembly resumed their dispute with Governor Wright by refusing to pass a tax bill. He responded by dissolving the Assembly and calling for new elections. The quarrel grew bitter.

Members of the new Assembly convened in Savannah in April and unanimously re-elected as speaker Noble Wimberly Jones, one of the town's leading Sons of Liberty and the son of former public surveyor and constable Noble Jones. Immediately, Wright disallowed his election. Angered by the rejection of their elected officer, the Assembly selected another of Savannah's Sons of Liberty as speaker, Archibald Bulloch, but informed the governor that his veto of Jones should not be viewed as precedent setting.[70] The Assembly also resolved that Wright's rejection of its elected speaker was a "high Breach of the Privilege of the House" and tended "to subvert the most valuable rights and Liberties of the People . . . and their Representatives."[71] In the face of such insolence, Governor Wright dissolved the Assembly, which had been in session only three days. During July Wright departed for a planned visit to England.

His friend and president of the Council, James Habersham, became acting governor. Old, suffering from gout, and without political ambitions, Habersham decided not to call the Assembly until he had the Crown's reaction to the prior session and the people demanded another session. When he did convene the Assembly in April 1772, the membership quickly tested him.

At the opening session, the Assembly once more elected Noble Wimberly Jones as speaker. Habersham informed the House that he was under orders from the king and had to reject Jones. Jones was elected again, and Habersham once more disallowed the vote; when he was elected a *third* time by his colleagues, Jones declined the honor. Once again the Assembly elected Bulloch as speaker but refused to strike the election of Jones from the minutes. Because of this, Habersham dismissed the Assembly on the third day of the session. Once more, important public business remained undone.

The quarrel between the governor and the Assembly raised a constitutional issue, and the local Lutheran minister, John J. Zubly, a religious dissenter and rising planter, sided with Georgia's men of property. Ever a friend of law and order, he attacked the veto power of the governor in a pamphlet published in 1772. By now radicals in colonies to the north were forming committees of correspondence to keep in touch regarding parliamentary encroachments on colonial rights.[72]

Habersham called a meeting of the legislature for December 1772. Most of the men recently elected to the Assembly appeared anxious to attend to the long-neglected public business. Noble Wimberly Jones, Jonathan Bryan, and William LeConte formed the core of the opposition faction in the legislature. But they had neither an issue or a rallying point in early 1773; nor could they command a majority in the new Assembly.

In February 1773 Governor Wright returned; much of the animosity toward him had abated during his two years in England. Wright's scheme to purchase almost two million acres of good farmland from the Creeks and Cherokees was approved in London and acclaimed across Georgia; furthermore, the colony was prosperous. Wright found such "Harmony amongst" the legislators that he kept the Assembly in session until September 1773. The struggle for power between the governor and the Assembly had been put aside temporarily to address long-deferred public business.[73]

THE TEA ACT AND INTOLERABLE ACTS

The Tea Act of May 1773 and subsequent measures passed by Parliament shattered the cordial relations between Georgians and Governor Wright. The Tea Act provided powerful financial interests in England a virtual monopoly on the tea trade with America. Furthermore, the tea would be taxed to raise revenue. The colonists believed that the establishment of a monopoly and passage of a duty without their consent once more threatened their independence, property, and the prerogatives of their assemblies.

In the fall of 1773 at Philadelphia, New York, and Charles Town there was resistance to the landing of English tea. No tea was consigned to Savannah. In December Bostonians held the famous "tea party" by dumping the tea shipped there into the harbor. Members of Parliament and King George III considered this a criminal act and responded by shutting down Boston harbor and placing the government of Massachusetts under royal supervision. Outraged colonists from Boston to Savannah called the legislation the Intolerable Acts. But at this time Georgia's Assembly was about evenly divided between those who eventually sided with the movement for separation from England and those who remained loyal to the king.

Virginians called for an intercolonial congress to consider this new threat to American liberties. In mid-July 1774, Noble Wimberly Jones, Archibald Bulloch, John Houstoun, and George Walton invited Georgians through the *Georgia Gazette* to a public meeting at Tondee's Tavern to consider a response to the acts of Parliament. At the public gathering on July 27, a Committee of Thirty was elected to draft objections to the Intolerable Acts, but it deferred action so that distant parishes could send representatives to a public meeting scheduled for August 10. Governor Wright issued a proclamation calling the past and subsequent meetings "unconstitutional, illegal, and punishable by law"; he told the colonists to "pay due regard to . . . my proclamation, as they will answer the contrary at their peril."[74]

Representatives from all parishes attended the August meeting in Savannah. The two most well-represented and powerful parishes were Christ Church, which included Savannah, and St. John's Parish, located forty miles to the south. Its political center was Midway, Georgia. The delegates from both parishes were predominantly Whigs, opponents of Crown policies, but Christ Church represented the conservative wing while St. John's represented the radical. Both factions included members of the local elite who had prospered under British colonial policies and were closely connected with the governor; both factions wished to limit the power of the executive branch and to expand that of the legislative branch. But the Christ Church Whigs for years had dominated the Assembly; therefore, they wished only to alter the system, not launch a revolution: they wanted the legislative branch rather than the governor to shape policy, which was similar to Parliament's relationship with the Crown. On the other hand, the representatives in the Assembly from St. John's had seen their political goals blocked by both the governor and delegates from Christ Church. Therefore, the growing dissatisfaction with British policies provided the representatives from St. John's with an opportunity to challenge Georgia's entire power structure. With little to lose, they wanted a redistribution of power. For this they earned the sobriquet *radicals*. In Georgia, the American Revolution was, in the words of historian Carl Becker, not only a struggle for home rule, but a struggle over who should rule at home.

At the meeting in Savannah on August 10, 1774, all parishes unanimously supported resolutions defending American rights and condemning the acts of Parliament. But when representatives from St. John's moved to send delegates to the first Continental Congress in Philadelphia, the conservative representatives from Christ Church opposed the motion, and it was defeated. The Christ Church Whigs wanted change, but not outside of the established lines of authority. Otherwise their hegemony within Georgia's political and social world might be compromised.

Calls went out first from the St. John's faction and then the Christ Church coalition for meetings to rally supporters to their side in the debate. But most Georgians had little interest in taking sides in the long-standing dispute between the two parishes. Furthermore, backcountry settlers, angry that the Georgia government had failed to protect them from marauding Indians, declared that any action taken by the parishes at the August 10 meeting did not represent them. When the Continental Congress convened in September 1774 in Philadelphia, no Georgians were represented. Within the colony the conservatives and the radicals remained divided.[75]

The radicals now attempted to convince other Whigs that the views and interests of Savannah differed from those of most Georgians; they argued that to secure the liberties they desired, Georgians had to oppose the arbitrary power of both the English government and the Christ Church faction. The radical coalition would force the conservative Whigs to confront major issues head-on; these radicals moved Georgia faster and further along the road to revolution than any other force.[76] The failure of Governor Wright to prevent depredations by Indians in the backcountry was a factor in radicalizing men and women on Georgia's frontier.

During the fall the Continental Congress adopted the Continental Association, a boycott of British trade, and acrimonious debates between Georgia's two factions appeared in the *Georgia Gazette*. African Americans may have interpreted these quarrels and deep divisions among the elite in the press, public houses, and streets as an opportunity to strike for freedom. It had happened in other colonies.

In the late summer, Jack, a slave owned by Captain William Lyford, the pilot for the port, was convicted of "setting fire to his master's house." He was taken to the Savannah Common on the evening of September 20 and "burnt . . . [but] denied . . . being guilty of the crime . . . to the last."[77] Coincidentally, in the politically tumultuous year of 1774, there were 2,465 slaves imported into Georgia, the largest number ever brought in during one year. About two months after Jack was executed, some of these newly arrived slaves in St. Andrew Parish, about fifty miles south of Savannah, fomented the most violent and extensive insurrection in colonial Georgia.

Ten newly arrived Africans, four of them women, owned by a planter named Captain Morris joined with an American-born slave and murdered their overseer, his wife, and a young boy; they proceeded to the homes of Angus McIntosh and Roderick McLeod, wounded them both, and killed McLeod's son before they were apprehended. The two slaves said to have planned the uprising were burned alive.

The account of the "revolt" published in the *Georgia Gazette* on December 7, 1774, must have sent a chill through Savannahians. It was an event that white Georgians feared the most: a black uprising. It threatened the very foundations of their society. At the same time, Crown officials and British military officers noted with increasing interest the rebelliousness of southern slaves and the anxiety it caused among their owners.[78] And to the conservatives of Savannah, the growing political radicalism seemed equally threatening.

At a gathering in St. John's Parish on December 6, the radicals adopted the recommendations of the Continental Congress to boycott British goods. Three days earlier the conservative Committee of Thirty called for a provincial congress to meet in Savannah in early 1775 when the Commons House of Assembly convened. On January 17 the Assembly opened, and the following day the Provincial Congress began its meeting. The congress was poorly attended. St. John's Parish refused to send representatives because other parishes had not adopted the boycott against England. Christ Church dominated the meeting. Three representatives were elected to the second Continental Congress: Archibald Bulloch, Noble Wimberly Jones, and John Houstoun, all from Savannah or its environs. The boycott of British goods recommended by the Continental Congress was adopted, but with reservations. Before the members of the Provincial Congress adjourned on January 25, they sent their work to the sitting Commons House of Assembly. Approval here would give their actions the appearance of popular support.

A few delegates to the congress also were members of the Assembly. Governor Wright addressed them and conveyed his deep sense of sadness at the recent events. He appealed for calm, clear thought and the rule of law, which was so essential to the enjoyment of liberty. He told the representatives: "I have lived amongst and presided over you upwards of fourteen years, and have . . . a real and affectionate regard for the people, and it grieves me that a Province that I have been so long in, and which I have seen nurtured by the Crown . . . should, by the imprudence and rashness of some inconsiderate people, be plunged into a state of distress and ruin."[79] Ironically, Governor Wright had brought the colony to the point of political and economic maturity where it now challenged royal authority.

Before the Assembly could act on the measure passed by the Provincial Congress, Governor Wright dismissed it. Quickly the Whigs retaliated for the governor's dismissal of the Assembly and again undermined royal authority. On February 15, 1775, Savannah's royal customs collector seized illegally imported sugar and molasses. Lieutenant William Grant, the commanding officer of His Majesty's Schooner *St. John,* sent two sailors ashore to guard the confiscated stores. That evening a mob of Savannahians with blackened faces overpowered the two British seamen, threw them into the river, and carried away the sugar and molasses. One of the sailors drowned.[80]

This act of revolutionary violence failed to impress South Carolinians. They remained angry that Savannahians earlier had not taken sterner extra-legal measures against the Crown. In March Charles Town radical Christopher Gadsden remarked that "we have determin'd to have nothing further to do with [Georgians], as they have not agreed to the American Association [the boycott of British goods]."[81] Nevertheless, Governor Wright's power was ebbing. The Georgia Assembly ignored Wright's call to meet in Savannah in May 1775.

On May 10 Savannahians received the alarming news that blood was spilled during a skirmish between American and British troops at Lexington and Concord, Massachusetts. A meeting was called for the following evening at the home of Noble Wimberly Jones to discuss Georgia's response. At the evening meeting on May 11, it must have been known that South Carolinians had already raided the royal powder magazine in Charles Town; when the Georgians adjourned their meeting, Noble Wimberly Jones and Joseph Habersham—whose fathers served on the Council and enjoyed a close relationship with Governor Wright—along with Edward Telfair, Joseph Clay, John Milledge, William Gibbons, Mordecai Sheftall, and others, led a mob to the king's magazine, smashed in the door, and carried away six hundred pounds of powder. It was later used against British troops.

Henry Laurens, a wealthy Charles Town resident and friend of the Habershams, believed that the theft of the powder was symptomatic of the turmoil in Georgia; he felt that "a large majority of the Inhabitants [of Savannah are] ready to participate in the measures of their American Brethren."[82] Daily more Georgians were joining the "cause." By this time conservatives and radicals had united to strip the governor of his power.

In this new, highly charged atmosphere of early May and as rumors persisted about the British instigating slave uprisings in the South, a black minister named David was invited to speak to a gathering of whites and blacks. Savannahians heard he preached that "'God would send Deliverance to the Negroes, from the power of their Masters, as he freed the Children of Israel from Egyptian Bondage.'" His words spread quickly through Savannah and frightened slaveholders. Some vowed to find David and "hang him." James Habersham probably saved David's life by quietly putting him aboard an outward-bound ship. David's mention of the "exodus motif" sometimes used by Christian slaves to justify their pursuit of liberty touched grave concerns among his white audience. Their response dramatized how defensive they were of the institution of slavery and how deeply they feared their own slaves.[83]

Three days before King George's birthday, on the night of June 2, a battery of twenty-one cannons located near what remained of Fort Halifax were spiked and rolled down the bluff and into the river. It was an attempt to make the weapons permanently inoperable and especially to ensure that they could not be used in the upcoming birthday celebration. The governor's authority again had been challenged. Wright retrieved and repaired some of the cannons, which were used to fire off salutes to the king on June 4. By this time Savannah, like Georgia, was divided into two hostile camps, those who opposed the governor and those loyal to him.

On the evening of the following day, June 5, while the governor and loyalists drank the health of the king, Joseph Habersham, his friends, and a mob of citizens carrying guns and clubs assembled at Peter Tondee's tavern for the ostensible reason of looking for some "Tories" or loyalists who had recently arrived in Savannah. Next the crowd boisterously paraded through the streets to St. James' Square, Telfair Square today, the location of the governor's house. There, in view of Wright's guests, the mob erected Georgia's first "liberty pole."[84] Over a week later Governor Wright was angered that a flag hoisted by the "Liberty folks" was "still flying in contempt and defiance of . . . all law and government, and which here and elsewhere seems now nearly at an end."[85] Wright was being replaced by mob rule.

Royal officials were on the run. John Stuart, the British superintendent of Indian Affairs, was accused of attempting to incite the Cherokees against the colonists. He was forced by Whigs to flee first Charles Town and then Savannah on June 17. He found refuge aboard Lieutenant Grant's schooner, *St. John.* In an effort to prevent the British vessel from leaving, a combined armed force of fifty to eighty men from Carolina and Savannah occupied Tybee Island and its lighthouse and hoisted a liberty flag. They fired on the *St. John* but could not stop it from sailing for St. Augustine with Stuart aboard.[86]

In late June and early July the public storehouse was burglarized by the local Whigs, who carried away military hardware. The governor was powerless to stop them. Royal authority was also challenged in nearby parishes, but leadership of the movement remained in Savannah and in the hands of its merchants. Meetings were held in Savannah throughout June by Whigs who called for a second provincial congress to meet on July 4. A Council of Safety was created to see that boycotts were enforced and to seek ways to resolve the escalating crisis with England. William Ewen was elected president, and Seth John

Cuthbert, secretary. Other members included Joseph Habersham, his cousin Joseph Clay, Edward Telfair, George Walton, John Glen, Francis H. Harris, John Morel, William LeConte, George Houstoun, William Young, John Smith, Samuel Elbert, and Basil Cowper. The Council of Safety assumed the powers of the governor and the legislature.

More Georgians drifted into the Whig camp during June and July, and the terrorizing of Loyalists escalated. The British schooner *St. John* returned to Savannah to take aboard "some Gentlemen and their Servants," who, Lieutenant Grant noted, had escaped "the Violence of the Mob." It departed for the Bahamas in early July.[87]

On July 4, 1775, a total of 102 delegates representing all parishes except two assembled at Tondee's Tavern for the second Provincial Congress. The number of representatives reflected the recent extension of the vote to all free white men "liable to pay towards the General Tax." More than half of the delegates, 64, were from Savannah and its environs. Governor Wright complained that among them were "few Men of real Abilities, Gentlemen or men of Property." Indeed, men of moderate means had seized the opportunity to govern: 67 of the representatives had never served before at the provincial level of government. Such representation was revolutionary; the meeting also was revolutionary in that it was the beginning of the end for royal government and the beginning of state government in Georgia.[88]

Following the election of Archibald Bulloch of Savannah as president and George Walton as secretary of the Provincial Congress, the delegates adjourned to the Independent Presbyterian Church to hear the pastor, the Reverend John J. Zubly, preach a sermon. Zubly was also a member of the Provincial Congress, but he was dismayed at the erosion of British authority. In his speech he blamed a bumbling London government for the present state of affairs and called on the king to end the crisis by respecting American rights. Over the next several days the Provincial Congress adopted a series of resolutions on American rights similar to those endorsed previously by Georgia's sister colonies, petitioned George III to recall his military forces in America, elected five delegates to the Second Continental Congress—Zubly, Bulloch, Lyman Hall, John Houstoun, Noble Wimberly Jones—and informed the Continental Congress that Georgia would help defray the expenses to defend American rights. Despite his early zeal in support of American liberties, Zubly could not sever his loyalty to the king; neither could his son, David Zubly, nor Basil Cowper and George McIntosh, members of Georgia's coastal elite.[89]

On July 10, 1775, as the Provincial Congress met, Joseph Habersham Jr. watched, waited, and sweated in the hot midsummer sun with fifty other Liberty Boys aboard the *Liberty,* an armed schooner near the mouth of the Savannah River. A red-bordered white flag with the words "American Liberty" waved from the schooner's mast. Habersham, who had outfitted the *Liberty,* was expecting the arrival of a British ship laden with powder for the Indian trade. Nearby were two barges carrying forty heavily armed Carolinians.

When the British ship *Philippa,* under Captain Richard Maitland's command, came into sight, the *Liberty* sailed out to intercept it. Maitland was forced to anchor his vessel off Cockspur Island. Here Habersham's Liberty Boys unloaded six tons of gunpowder and seven hundred pounds of bullets, which were used to supply Whig troops in Boston, Charles Town, and Savannah.

That same month the elder Habersham, physically ill and heartsick that his family was divided politically—his sons and his nephew Joseph Clay were leaders of the local revolutionary movement—sailed north to escape Savannah's hot politics and summer. Habersham, one of Savannah's first self-made elite, never reached his destination. He died aboard ship. Noble Jones, another early Savannah colonist who accumulated great wealth and shared the sentiments of the elder Habersham, died that same year; his son, Noble Wimberly Jones, was so active in the movement to limit royal authority that he won the sobriquet "Morning Star of Liberty." The revolutionary movement was dividing families.[90]

Men such as the younger Jones and Habershams and such as Jonathan Bryan willingly parted with the politics of their families and friends who viewed the royal government's armed forces and economic policies as the foundation of Georgia's prosperity and their own. But James Habersham Sr. always urged his sons to become independent thinkers on controversial subjects, and they did: all three, James Jr., Joseph, and John, supported the movement for independence while their father opposed it. In August 1775, when King George III declared that all "rebels" were "traitors" and must be punished, the younger Habershams were more convinced than ever that the British government no longer protected, but instead threatened, their lives, their liberties, and the vast wealth in land and slaves their loving father recently bequeathed them. Jonathan Bryan was willing to support the move for independence for some of the same reasons. Bryan, a planter-capitalist who sought power, prestige, and affluence, amassed plantations totaling ten thousand acres and worked by three hundred slaves. Always land-hungry, Bryan recognized in the

1760s that the British government no longer was willing to assist him in expanding his estates; indeed, the government inhibited his settlement on lands
south of Darien and specifically forbid him from expanding into Florida. In
sum, Bryan saw royal government as thwarting his aggressive capitalism at
every turn and knew that his economic interests would be better served if
Georgia became independent of Great Britain.[91]

When the Provincial Congress adjourned on July 17, the Council of Safety
served as the government of the colony. This body subsequently called for elections, dealt with money matters, reformed the customs service, regulated the
slave trade, appointed committees, enforced resolutions passed by the Continental Congress, seized control of the militia, and purged it of Loyalists. Militia units previously acting on orders from Governor Wright now took their orders from the Council of Safety. Control of a militia sympathetic to the Whig
movement was essential to the dismantling of the royal government at Savannah and across the colony.[92]

Mob violence encouraged by the Sons of Liberty escalated during the late
summer. On the night of July 24 a mariner, John Hopkins, was snatched from
his quarters in Savannah. Accused of acting disrespectfully toward the Liberty
Boys, he was tarred and feathered, paraded through Savannah's streets, and
made to drink to "American Liberty." That same night the mob visited the
home of the rector of Christ Church, the Reverend Haddon Smith, but he was
not in. Smith had referred to the Provincial Congress as "an unlawful authority." By August Smith no longer felt safe in Savannah, and with his family he
departed for England on the brigantine *Joe*. In his haste to leave Savannah,
Smith left behind slaves, horses, and household goods, which soon were auctioned off on the courthouse steps. The Reverend John Rennie was appointed
by Governor Wright to succeed Smith at Christ Church. Within a year, however, Rennie also was prohibited from performing his duties for his refusal to
renounce his allegiance to the king.[93]

With help from local militia and the Sons of Liberty, the political power
of Savannah's revolutionary Council of Safety reached into the backcountry
to enforce the trade boycott with the British. There were many settlers sympathetic to the revolutionary movement. Most of the region's small farmers sided
with the radical Whigs, while the planter-merchant class favored the Christ
Church faction; still others steered another course. The political situation on
the frontier was fluid.

By the summer of 1775 backcountry settlers were angry with the recent policies urged by Governor Wright and passed by the Assembly, which appeared to subordinate the interests of the settlers to those of the Creek Indians. A rumor that agents of the king were planning to encourage an Indian uprising heightened fears and ended forever the loyalty of many settlers to royal authority. Therefore, when a friend of Governor Wright's in Augusta, Thomas Brown, began to rally local support for the Crown, he created an explosive environment. On August 2, Brown was assaulted, stabbed, partially scalped, burned, tarred and feathered, and pulled through the streets of Augusta in a cart. It was surprising that he lived. Brown then left the colony, but he later returned to avenge the brutal attack.[94]

Savannah's Council of Safety continued to nurture its alliance with settlers in the backcountry. On September 17 a Whig vessel intercepted the *Polly* and confiscated the 250 barrels of powder it was carrying for the Indians and 50 muskets for loyalist troops. This again augmented local Whig ordnance stores, but seizure of the powder destined for the Creeks posed a new dilemma for the Whigs: the possibility of a Creek uprising against backcountry settlers. To pacify the Creeks, some of the gunpowder was sent to them.[95]

During the summer the Council of Safety closed the port of Savannah. Authorized to enforce the boycott, the council in September prohibited the captain of a slaver from landing a cargo of two hundred Africans from Senegal, which ended the slave trade in Georgia for a decade. The boycott was taking effect. By October, Savannahians began "to feel the ill effects. . . . Bread being . . . scarce & Flour in Town nearly consumed, Rum & Sugar very scarce and dear."[96] In December, Governor Wright observed that few members of the Council of Safety or other revolutionary bodies were of "the better Sort . . . Merchants and Planters"; rather many were "of the Lowest People Chiefly Carpenters, Shoemakers, Blacksmiths &c." He continued: "It is really Terrible . . . that such People Should be . . . [allowed] to Overturn the Civil Government."[97] The daughter of a local royal official was more succinct: "the scum rose to the top."[98]

THE REVOLUTION BEGINS

In January 1776 news reached Savannah that British warships were sailing toward Georgia. The presence of a formidable British force off the coast raised the fearful specter of invasion and black insurrection. Some believed that if the British invaded the colony and brought enough arms, and if their commander "proclaimed freedom to all the negroes who would join his campaign, twenty thousand would join." The slave network sped intelligence quickly, and news of a nearby British fleet encouraged runaways. Some headed for Tybee Island.[99]

Alarmed that Savannah might be the target of the British, George Walton, a young lawyer and the newly elected president of the Council of Safety, immediately ordered a draft of one-third of Georgia's militia for the defense of the town. The council appointed Samuel Elbert as colonel, Stephen Drayton as lieutenant colonel, and Joseph Habersham as major, to take charge of Savannah's defenses.[100]

Fort George on Cockspur Island was stripped of its cannons to prevent them from falling into British hands; horse patrols searched the dwellings of all "overseers and negroes" on both sides of the Savannah River and confiscated arms and ammunition. A lookout was posted at Causton's Bluff, about four miles below the town. A vessel was sunk in the channel near Fig Island just below Savannah to prevent British sailing craft from coming up river; a battery of cannons was placed in the vicinity of the Trustees' Garden suburb and another on the wharves. Royal Governor Wright felt helpless. He told London officials that he had "no Troops, no Money, no Orders, . . . and a wild Multitude gathering fast."[101]

On January 18 four heavily armed British vessels anchored just off Cockspur Island at the mouth of the Savannah River. The Council of Safety immediately ordered Major Joseph Habersham to arrest Governor Wright. He and other royal officials were taken into custody at the governor's home, where he was meeting with members of his Council. Placed on parole, they were instructed not to contact the British warships.

While the colony's militia arrived in Savannah, the Provincial Congress discussed raising a unit of Continental troops to ease the burden on the citizen soldiers. The Continental Congress had authorized a battalion of 728 officers and men to defend Georgia. The selection process for commander of the battalion disrupted the recent harmony among the Whigs.

The conservatives who dominated the Provincial Congress nominated the commanding officer of the militia, Colonel Samuel Elbert, for the colonelcy of the Georgia Battalion; the radicals nominated Button Gwinnett, who had failed first as a Savannah merchant and then as a planter in St. John's Parish. But he had a "Lofty and commanding appearance" and could be "mild and persuasive" in speech. Politically ambitious, he convinced delegates from the southern and western parishes that it was not in their interest to be governed by the conservatives of Christ Church, and they helped him win the election.

Gwinnett epitomized the radical Whig, for he wanted to wrest home rule both from the British and from the conservative Whigs at home. But Gwinnett and Elbert both turned down the offer to command the Georgia Battalion, perhaps to prevent a crack in the fragile Whig coalition. The compromise candidate was Lachlan McIntosh of Darien, a prominent planter from St. Andrew's Parish. He was a conservative Whig with a good name and maturity, but with little military experience. Elbert was appointed lieutenant colonel and Joseph Habersham major of the Georgia Battalion; most of the appointments below major went to radical Whigs. In this way the radicals became influential among the enlisted ranks. The remainder of the compromise sent Button Gwinnett to the Continental Congress in Philadelphia. But the split between radical and conservative Whigs continued to plague the revolutionary movement in Georgia. In less than a year Gwinnett and McIntosh fought a duel.[102]

Major Joseph Habersham was troubled by the disputes between the factions over who would rule at home. He told a friend in February: "this province is remarkable for a number of parties and I am afraid . . . that a house divided against itself can never stand."[103] The colony was far from unified. On February 3 Governor Wright wrote that "if we had Proper Support and Assistance, I think Numbers would Join the King's Standards."[104] This belief may have led Wright to break his parole nine days later. With his three children and numerous black runaways, he fled to the safety of H.M.S. *Scarborough* riding in the river below Savannah.

Slave stealing accelerated on both sides. Slaves were encouraged to desert to the British, who could use them in labor battalions. Governor Wright's own plantation was raided by Whigs who carried away his remaining slaves to dig fortifications around Savannah. When more laborers were needed, the town's revolutionary government passed a law permitting the impressment of 50 percent of all the slaves hiring out their services and living in Savannah. At the same time African Americans seized the new opportunities to resist slavery.

After Governor Wright fled Savannah, others Loyalists quickly followed. For instance, the editor of the *Georgia Gazette,* James Johnston, published his last newspaper in early February and soon took refuge on His Majesty's armed schooner *Hinchinbrook.* Two of his brothers who were also royalists left Georgia.

BATTLE OF THE RICEBOATS

By mid-February Captain Andrew Barkley of the British navy aboard the *Scarborough* commanded the sloops *Tamar* and *Raven,* the armed schooner *Hinchinbrook,* the armed vessel *Cherokee,* two transports, the *Symmetry* and *Whitby,* some smaller craft, and about six hundred sailors, soldiers, and marines. When Captain Barkley was unable to convince Savannahians that all he wanted was a fresh supply of provisions, he decided to seize the twenty-six merchantmen, or trading ships, loaded with three thousand tierces of rice anchored at the north end of Hutchinson Island. Barkley launched his operation on February 23 when vessels under his command began "working up the River" toward Savannah.[105]

An anxious Colonel Lachlan McIntosh, the Whig commanding officer in Savannah, exaggerated when he told George Washington that the town was "defenceless and deserted." Before the turmoil of recent years, Savannah's population had been estimated to be slightly over three thousand. McIntosh and civilian authorities believed that the British planned to capture and destroy Savannah and seize the riceboats. With several hundred men to defend the town, McIntosh sent units to guard possible British landing sites and to set up ambushes along major roads. Colonel Archibald Bulloch and 150 soldiers were concentrated at Brewton Plantation just opposite the eastern end of Hutchinson Island; smaller units took up positions at Causton's Bluff, Half Moon Bluff, and Thunderbolt.[106]

On the afternoon of March 2 Captain Barkley opened a two-pronged attack to capture the riceboats. The same day the revolutionary Council of Safety warned that it would be considered "a defection from the cause of America" for anyone to desert Savannah and not "defend the metropolis as long as the same shall be tenable." The property of anyone fleeing the town could be confiscated.[107]

Aboard his command vessel, the *Hinchinbrook,* and accompanied by the *St. John,* Barkley sailed behind Hutchinson's Island—up today's Back River— and then swung down the main ship channel. Here he planned to anchor between the town and the riceboats and provide covering fire for British marines to seize the vessels. But the *Hinchinbrook* ran aground on a shoal opposite Rae's Hill Plantation, the location today of the Georgia Ports Authority. Colonel McIntosh rushed troops to Yamacraw to establish a battery of three cannons; Barkley also came under small arms fire from two companies of Whig militiamen commanded by Major Joseph Habersham. A second attack force of three hundred British officers and men was landed on the north bank of Hutchinson Island. They worked their way through heavy undergrowth, mud, sawgrass, and several streams to move the short distance across the island. Around 4:00 A.M. on March 3 and unknown to Savannah's defenders, they secured the riceboats.

Later that morning when a Whig officer, ironically named Joseph Rice, and his crew arrived to strip the riceboats of their rudders, rigging, and sails to prevent them from sailing, they were surprised and captured by the British. Around midmorning Captain John Baker of St. John's Parish and a dozen riflemen rowed out into the channel and fired on the British, which ignited an exchange of cannon fire between the battery at Yamacraw and the British. It was the first major firefight of the rebellion by the Whigs at Savannah, and it lasted into the late afternoon. The Council of Safety then ordered Colonel McIntosh to burn the riceboats rather than let them fall into British hands.

The so-called Battle of the Riceboats began near dark when Whig militiamen cut adrift and set afire the riceboat *Inverness* in hopes that it would drift into others on the incoming tide. But it ran aground. Another was set ablaze, which ignited two more. Some British soldiers panicked and fled onto Hutchinson Island; others towed the burning ships to shore while under fire from Whig militiamen at Yamacraw. Both sides sustained several casualties. During the night Savannahians gathered along the riverfront and watched the burning riceboats pass back and forth with the tide.

The British saved about 1,600 barrels of rice, threw some overboard to lighten the loads, and sailed the vessels down the river behind Hutchinson Island. They joined the British ships off Cockspur Island, where the rice was transferred to two naval transports. The Whigs could not stop them.

With the prices of provisions rising rapidly, Archibald Bulloch warned that anyone found profiteering would be punished. Soaring prices made it difficult for the poor to find food.

By March 7 more than 440 Carolina militiamen under Colonel Stephen Bull reached Savannah to join forces with about 200 Georgia militiamen. Still uncertain of British intentions, Colonel McIntosh kept more than 80 slaves digging entrenchments around the town. Anxious for the safety of their own soldiers captured by the British, Whig militiamen seized and confined prominent Georgia Loyalists—Chief Justice Anthony Stokes, Josiah Tattnall, and Lachlan McGillivray—to use in exchange. When Carolinian Colonel Bull heard that there were about 200 black fugitives on Tybee Island who might join the British, he suggested that they be murdered by a party of Creek and Yuchis Indians. Whether or not the runaways were killed is unknown, but Colonel Archibald Bulloch with several companies of militiamen and some Creeks burned several buildings on Tybee that the British were using. Bulloch also attacked a party of British marines on the island. One was scalped by the Creeks.

The British forces soon sailed north with their transports crammed with rice and several Whig prizes in tow. Two British vessels remained to show the flag at the mouth of the Savannah River. Georgia and Carolina militiamen, a handful of Continental troops, and their inexperienced commander, Colonel McIntosh, lost the rice, but they saved Savannah. Both sides could claim a victory. The Georgia patriots enjoyed few in the future.

While Savannahians led armed revolt against British policies in coastal Georgia, similar events occurred on the frontier. The acting commander of the Royal Rangers in western Georgia wrote in early March that "the Rebels" seized his posts, and many of the former Rangers enlisted with the Whigs. Royal rule ended across Georgia. Late in joining the rebellion, the colony now joined with the other twelve. Georgians were now Whigs or Loyalists.[108]

RAISING MEN AND ARMS

After the British sailed out of the Savannah River, Colonel McIntosh recognized that the town and colony remained a tempting target. Although protected by South Carolina to the north, Georgia's sea islands invited invasion. Georgia Loyalists had organized the Florida Rangers and used the British garrison at St. Augustine as their base; they and their Indian allies harassed settlers in the region between the Altamaha and St. Marys Rivers.

Colonel McIntosh posted lookouts along the coast and improved fortifications around Savannah, and he recruited, trained, and equipped soldiers for the Continental Battalion. Georgia's bounty for joining up was modest, and a soldier knew he and his family could not exist on the pay because of an inflation rate of 200–300 percent.

By late April only 286 men had been recruited for the Continental Battalion, which when added to the 600 militiamen available for duty was a woefully inadequate force to defend Georgia.[109] Finding recruits continued to prove difficult, McIntosh believed, because of "the ease in which the poorest

People generally live . . . and the prejudice they have to any regular service, on account of the restraint that anything of a strict discipline requires."[110] This was a common complaint in the southern colonies.

On April 15 the Provincial Congress issued a temporary constitution, which called for the usual three branches of government and a court system. Archibald Bulloch was elected president and commander-in-chief of Georgia and served until his mysterious death the following year. On June 12 the Provincial Congress declared that the governmental authority now rested in the province rather than the king, which completed the revolutionary movement of separation from England.

Colonel McIntosh required more men, arms, and funds to defend Georgia. In June he presented his needs to Major General Charles Lee at Charles Town, the commanding officer of the Southern Military Department. Lee recognized the vulnerability of the Georgians and wanted to help. He appropriated a modest sum to outfit four galleys for coastal defense and for supplies. Captain Oliver Bowen purchased needed equipment abroad to outfit the vessels while Edward Telfair acquired local pine and live oak for their construction. Ship carpenters were brought from Philadelphia. During the following year and a half, the *Congress, Lee, Washington,* and *Bulloch* were launched. Most likely the galleys were lateen-rigged craft with twenty oars and armed with small guns. Eight row galleys and two sloops were also acquired to defend Georgia's coast. Captain Bowen was given command of Georgia's navy and promoted to commodore, a rank equal to an army colonel.

McIntosh and his men cheered the repulse of a British naval and amphibious attack on Sullivan's Island, South Carolina, in late June, but in July they were alarmed by raids of the British Rangers to the south. With Lee's approval, McIntosh invaded East Florida in early August and terrorized settlements of British Loyalists between the Altamaha and the St. John's Rivers. The Loyalists fled to St. Augustine, and in early August, McIntosh returned triumphant to Savannah.[111] He arrived in time to hear a public reading of the Declaration of Independence and to attend a dinner where toasts were made to the "'United, Free, and Independent State of America.'" During a mock funeral, George III was buried in front of the courthouse.

General Lee, who was in Savannah inspecting its defenses, enthusiastically greeted McIntosh's victories in East Florida. Lee concluded that it was not now necessary to attack St. Augustine. The Savannah government and McIntosh disagreed. The Georgians had a historic concern over the defense of their southern border, and they persisted. They suggested such a variety of military options to defend their province that in frustration Lee observed that he "should not be surpris'd if they were to propose mounting a body of Mermaids on Alligators."[112] Disregarding General Lee's advice, McIntosh ordered a second invasion of Florida in late August. It was ill planned and executed. The expedition was aborted.[113]

In late summer the Savannah government responded to calls from the Continental Congress at Philadelphia to write a permanent constitution for the new *state* of Georgia. Elections were held in September to select delegates to a new Provincial Congress that would draft the document. The fragile consensus between conservative and radical Whigs was over, as both factions hoped to shape a constitution after their own political views.

Button Gwinnett returned from Philadelphia to seize the opportunity to lead the radical or "popular" party. The elections became bitterly contested. When a member of the "populars" voted a proxy ballot for Archibald Bulloch, Major Joseph Habersham challenged him. Lieutenant Nathaniel Hughes, a member of the popular party, objected. Habersham and Hughes exchanged angry words and blows. Falling backward, Habersham drew his sword; Hughes, rushing toward him, was impaled. He died about an hour later.

The radicals demanded that Habersham be tried for murder, but conservative political maneuvering resulted in a mistrial. About a month later the Council of Safety promoted Habersham to lieutenant colonel, and he became the commanding officer of the First Battalion. Although the conservatives had protected Habersham from retribution, the popular party won the elections, and they controlled the Provincial Congress when it met in November.

About the same time, a force of Florida Loyalists and Indians crossed the Altamaha River and overran parishes to Savannah's south. McIntosh, by now a general in the Continental Army and authorized to raise a brigade, mustered his troops and marched toward the enemy, who fled before him. General McIntosh built several forts and observation posts along Georgia's frontier.

Meanwhile, in Savannah, the Provincial Congress wrote a new constitution and adopted it on February 5, 1777. It would take effect in May. The document created a three-branch government but lodged enormous power in a unicameral legislature. This single House of Assembly annually elected the governor, a council, and state officials; there was a system of courts, and white males over twenty-one years of age could vote if they owned some property or practiced a trade. County replaced parish as a governmental unit, and state-supported schools were mandated for each county. Entail was abolished, and property was to be distributed more equitably among heirs. The new constitution provided for freedom of religion, freedom of the press, and jury trials and prohibited excessive fines and bail. Based on Whig principles of natural rights, a division of the powers of government, rule by the consent of the governed, and protection against arbitrary power, Georgia's constitution was perhaps the most democratic of the thirteen new states.

Although Savannah was permitted four representatives under the new constitution, well-to-do Savannahians disliked the document.[114] The conservative Savannah merchant Joseph Clay spoke for them when he observed that Georgia's new constitution was "so very Democratical" because the "Rule and Government has got into the Hands of those whose ability or situation in Life does not intitle [sic] them to it."[115] In the struggle for home rule the radicals had won a victory for the common man, if only temporarily. When the Provincial Congress adjourned in mid-February, the government of the state passed to the Council of Safety. The radicals sought to control this body, too.

On February 17, 1777, some three hundred British regulars, Loyalists, and Indians attacked lightly defended Fort McIntosh about a hundred miles south of Savannah. General McIntosh led a relief expedition, but the fort fell in two days, and he was wounded in the fighting. His line of defense held along the Altamaha.

Once more Savannahians felt threatened. They demanded another expedition against St. Augustine. The new president of the Council of Safety and now commander-in-chief of the armed forces, Button Gwinnett, agreed. On March 4, the council voted to allow him to lead the expedition. General Robert Howe, the new commander of the Southern Department and in Savannah at the time, advised against it. Nevertheless, Gwinnett continued to press him for use of Georgia's Continentals, but without their commander, General McIntosh.

Perhaps angling for control of Georgia's Continentals, Gwinnett, on the advice of the Continental Congress, ordered the arrest for treason of General McIntosh's brother, George. Like many of the well-to-do, he was well connected—his wife was Ann Houstoun, sister of John Houstoun.[116] However, George McIntosh was dragged from his sick bed, fettered with chains, and lodged "with felons" in the Savannah jail, which was described as "the dirtiest and most offensive gaol perhaps in the world."[117] Gwinnett then suggested that General McIntosh be reassigned for the good of the service, but Howe refused. Georgia conservatives described Gwinnett's actions as politically inspired.

Angered by Howe's rebuff, Gwinnett launched a witch-hunt against conservatives. He suggested that some might be receiving support from St. Augustine, which was another reason to destroy it. On March 17 Gwinnett presented his plan for invading Florida, but Howe promptly rejected it and returned to Charles Town.

Despite the opposition of General Howe, President Gwinnett called out the militia and asked General McIntosh and his Continentals to join him in an invasion of Florida. When the expedition stalled just south of Savannah, the Council of Safety asked Colonel Samuel Elbert to lead the several hundred troops, and Gwinnett and McIntosh stepped aside only reluctantly. Elbert's intended invasion of Florida, like those before it, was a disaster, and he soon returned to Savannah.

By this time General McIntosh concluded that Gwinnett and other radicals had questioned his loyalty and sought to oust him. Then in May when the first Assembly met under Georgia's new constitution, Gwinnett was defeated for the governorship by John Adam Treutlen, a moderate. Frustrated, radicals in the Assembly blamed General McIntosh for the recent Florida debacle, while conservatives wanted to censure Gwinnett.[118] During heated exchanges on the floor of the Assembly, General McIntosh denounced Gwinnett as "A Scoundrell & lying Rascal."[119] *Rascal* was then a more pejorative term than it is today, and certainly no gentleman could abide being called a liar. On May 15 Gwinnett sent a written challenge to General McIntosh demanding satisfaction for the public insult and suggested they meet at sunrise the following day in a pasture most likely just south of the location of today's Colonial Cemetery. For honor's sake McIntosh accepted the challenge.

On the morning of May 16 McIntosh appeared at the appointed time and place with his second, Colonel Joseph Habersham, and Gwinnett with his, George Wells. The duelists faced each other at about four paces and fired their pistols almost simultaneously. A ball broke Gwinnett's thigh, and McIntosh took a ball in the fleshy part of his leg. The seconds agreed that honor had been assuaged, and the two adversaries shook hands and left the field. However, Gwinnett's wound was fatal, and he died on May 19. McIntosh was shocked, remarking that he regretted the events that brought the "unfortunate man to his own destruction."

After a brief truce between the factions, the radicals resumed their attempts to discredit McIntosh and to remove him. Most of the fighting in Georgia by this date had been between the two Whig factions. The state was in such turmoil by July that the Continental Congress appointed a committee to make recommendations on the situation in Georgia.

In August the Congressional Committee recommended that money be appropriated to pay the troops and Georgia's bills. Food was in such short supply and the number of needy growing so rapidly that Governor Treutlen prohibited the out-of-state shipment of corn, rice, and flour. Nevertheless, merchants disregarded the injunction. Risking capture by friend or foe, they exported goods both north and south along the coast. Some supplies reached the British in East Florida. However, recognizing that trade was essential to the military and economic life of Georgia, the state did buy several vessels for the export of goods.

To stop the feuding between the Whig factions, the Congressional Committee recommended that General McIntosh be transferred. He was reassigned to General Washington's headquarters in Pennsylvania. However, the acrimony between the two factions had left discipline in the state's armed forces ebbing and morale low. Probing this weakness, raiding parties of Florida Loyalists struck within five miles of Savannah in late 1777.[120]

When robberies in Savannah rose dramatically during January and February 1778, suspects included "persons in disguise" acting in concert with Loyalists in Florida. To prevent such criminals from entering and leaving the town with ease, the Governor's Council placed Savannah under a town major who issued a new countersign each day, which was known only to Savannah's highest authorities. Persons who were apprehended by the town's sentinels from dark to dawn and who failed to give the countersign were detained until morning and then turned over to Savannah officials.[121]

Concern over British sympathizers in Savannah also prompted the Whig Assembly to pass an act in March that accused 117 Loyalists of treason, banished them from Georgia, and made their property subject to confiscation by the state. Any Loyalist who returned to the state or was captured in arms against the United States could be executed. But due to the chaotic social, political, and military situation, the law was never fully implemented.

By April Savannahians thought that an invasion from Florida was imminent. In turn, the Georgians began planning their annual preemptive strike against St. Augustine. The new governor, John Houstoun, called on all "friends of freedom" to rally to the colors for the expedition. By late April about two thousand Continentals, Georgia and South Carolina militiamen, and some naval vessels under Commodore Bowen had gathered near Savannah. But once more disputes between the military officers threatened to disrupt the operation. Governor Houstoun, who led the Georgia militia and who had no military experience, refused to cooperate with General Howe, and Commodore Bowen refused to take orders from either. Furthermore, few state funds were available to pay and supply the troops. Some of the soldiers had no shoes or blankets. Discipline was poor, and severe punishments were dispensed, which did not endear the officers to the enlisted men: deserters were shot, hanged, or given a hundred lashes on the bare back.

With a divided command structure and poorly equipped troops, the expedition blundered toward the St. Marys River in June. When Florida's British Rangers retreated, the Continental and militia officers ended the expedition. This was the third and final failed attempt to capture St. Augustine. The lack of resources, soldiers, and strong leadership from civilian and military officers plagued Georgia's military efforts during the first three years of the war. Little was accomplished in this tragicomic period of military operations. By the end of July 1778, all the invading troops had returned to Savannah. The Continentals were temporarily quartered in the parsonage of the Episcopal rector until barracks were completed in late August near the location of today's De-Soto Hotel.

Because of persistent rumors of an impending British attack, security was tightened around the town. The "horse patrol" remained on alert, and a combined artillery and fire company was created to do duty in Savannah. The unit was supplied with fire-fighting equipment, and two prominent Savannahians became "Directors of Fires." An "artillery park" was established in the yard of the Council House. Since troop strength remained low in Savannah, concerns persisted over the threats posed by prisoners in Savannah's jail. The sheriff of Chatham County was instructed by the Governor's Council to maintain a careful watch over them.[122]

THE FALL OF SAVANNAH

After a fruitless three years of fighting in the North, the British government altered its strategy and decided to invade the South. It was anticipated that this would encourage any remaining Loyalists to rush to support the British. The initial plan was to seize Savannah, which was to serve as a base of operations.

In New York in November 1778 an army of more than three thousand British, German, and Loyalist troops assembled by General Sir Henry Clinton, commander of British forces in North America, boarded transports and set sail for Georgia. Commodore Hyde Parker commanded the ships at sea; Lieutenant Colonel Archibald Campbell, 71st Scottish Regiment, was the officer in charge of the land forces. Clinton also ordered General Augustine Prevost to invade Georgia from Florida.

General Prevost dispatched one army by sea and another by land. Units of his invading force reached Sunbury about fifty miles below Savannah and burned nearby Midway. But when the naval force failed to appear, they returned to Florida by early December 1778.

On December 6 civilian and military officials at Savannah received alarming news from a British deserter: a huge armada was headed for Savannah. The news sent shock waves through the town. Savannah was not prepared to repel a large attacking force. Only one small fort near the Trustees' Garden at the eastern end of the bluff, formerly known as Fort Halifax, defended the town. Some Georgia troops were engaged fighting Indians on the state's borders, and only several hundred ill-equipped Continentals and about a hundred Georgia militiamen were present for duty in Savannah. Furthermore, Governor Houstoun and General Howe barely spoke to each other, and Colonel George Walton, commander of Georgia's militia, only reluctantly cooperated with Howe.[123] Governor Houstoun told General Benjamin Lincoln, who would soon replace Howe as commander of the Southern Department, that "the situation of this state is truly perilous."[124]

In late December the British fleet sailed over the bar at the mouth of the Savannah River carrying Campbell's army, which outnumbered the defenders of Savannah by more than three to one. Unopposed, the transports proceeded up river and on the evening of December 28 anchored just below the town. At first light the next morning British soldiers with artillery began coming ashore in flat boats at Brewton's Hill, also called Giradeau's Landing after John Giradeau's nearby plantation. They met no resistance. From here they marched across a causeway and then on to the Sea Island Road, today the route from Thunderbolt to Wheaton Street, which leads into Savannah. The British operation was visible to those standing along the town's waterfront.

Howe had been surprised. The day before he had reconnoitered the terrain around Brewton's Hill and vetoed the recommendation of militia officers to establish a strong defensive site at Giradeau's Landing. But he did post pickets

there. Howe later claimed that the pickets did not notify him quickly enough
of the British landing. Also, disagreements among the officers hindered a
coordinated defense, and Howe only had some six hundred men ready for
duty whose arms were "a medley of Rifles, old muskets & fowling pieces." Yet,
in an area surrounded by rivers and swamps, better defensive sites could have
been erected.

By midmorning Campbell was forming up his troops along the Sea Island
Road. They were some of Britain's finest soldiers. Along this same road and just
to the southeast of Savannah on the town side of a creek, Howe deployed his
Continentals. At this location—today just east of the intersection of Wheaton
and Randolph Streets—Howe decided to make his stand. Lieutenant Colonel
Campbell thought that the position was well chosen and "advantageous." If
retreat became necessary, Howe and his officers planned to retire by the Spring
Hill pass where the Augusta Road ran west from Savannah, today near the site
of the Savannah Visitors Center.

In the early afternoon Campbell brought his troops to a point that is today
just east of the intersection of Wheaton Street and Waters Avenue. It was
only a thousand yards east of Howe's Continentals. Campbell feinted toward
Howe's left flank; meanwhile he employed Quamino Dolly or Quash, a slave,
to guide a strong force of British soldiers through the swamp to strike Howe's
right flank.

Colonel George Walton, who was holding the Georgia militia in readiness
on the Savannah Common, rode over to the Trustees' Garden, where he could
survey the enemy's movements. He soon spotted the British feint and immediately warned Howe. It was too late. The British light infantry guided
by Quash moved quickly along a path in the swamp in a wide semi-circle to
emerge on the southeast of the town near what is today the intersection of
Gwinnett and East Broad Streets. Suddenly, hundreds of British troops
emerged on Howe's right flank.[125]

Walton rapidly moved up his ninety to a hundred militiamen and ordered
them to attack. But the British "opened a heavy fire of musketry" and rushed
forward "with great shouts." A militia private recalled that "the militia broke
and dispersed"; an officer reported that they "appeared in confusion, and could
not be reduced to order." But Colonel Campbell remembered that Walton's
militia "after Fighting bravely, were compelled to retreat."[126] While trying to
rally the militia, Walton was struck in the right thigh by a musket ball and
knocked from his horse.

About to be overrun, Howe ordered an immediate retreat. It turned into a rout. Some soldiers deserted to care for their families and possessions; Continentals and some militiamen streamed back past what is today's Colonial Cemetery, through the town and westward toward Musgrove Creek in Yamacraw. The British pursued and fired on them; some of the Americans fell and apparently were bayoneted on the spot. When the troops reached Musgrove Creek, it was at flood stage; the Americans were trapped. While some hoisted a white flag, a few attempted to cross the swollen river, and here and in other swamps and rivers around the town, they lost their equipment, their weapons, and their lives.

British vessels under Commodore Hyde Parker ranged far up the Savannah River and seized three American vessels. With the capture of Savannah most of the state's military supplies also fell into British hands: 48 cannon, 23 mortars, 817 small arms, 1,545 cannon shot, and 94 barrels of gunpowder.

The British losses were minimal: 7 killed and 19 wounded. But more than 100 Continentals or militia perished, and about 450 were captured, including Colonel Walton, Colonel Mordecai Sheftall, Jonathan Bryan, and Major John Habersham; his brothers, Joseph and James, as well as General Howe and Governor Houstoun, escaped to Carolina. Some of the captured Americans were imprisoned on British ships anchored in the Savannah River. Here numbers of them died in the heat and pestilence of the spring and summer. Colonel Sheftall survived. He was the highest-ranking Jewish officer in America's Revolutionary army. Sheftall, a zealous patriot, had invested heavily in Georgia currency, which at war's end was worthless, and his own personal fortune was nearly exhausted.[127]

Savannah fell to the British so quickly that there was little damage to the homes and public buildings, but there was some looting. The daughter of a Loyalist observed soldiers under British command "rip . . . open feather beds, destroy . . . public papers and records, and scatter . . . everything about the streets." To a Hessian officer it was "a pity to see the finest furnishings, . . . tables and chairs of mahogany . . . smashed and . . . on the streets."[128] Three days after the battle Governor Houstoun informed the Continental Congress that many Savannahians fled into South Carolina: "Most of the People in and about town . . . lost their all, and the Spirit of Rapine Insolence & Brutality indulged in [by] the soldiery, exceeds Description."[129]

Houstoun, Howe, and Walton blamed one another for their failure to coordinate the defense of Savannah. Savannahians blamed Howe for years for the debacle. Charges brought by the Georgians led to his court-martial, but he was acquitted with "highest honor." The British troops, some of the best in the world, simply had overwhelmed Savannah's ill-supplied, ill-equipped, and bickering defenders in quality, numbers, and arms.

Savannah's capture was a great victory at small cost for the British, but for the Americans it was an enormous loss of men, military stores, and territory: Georgia's Continental unit was eviscerated, and the capital of the state was in enemy hands. Once more General Augustine Prevost marched out of Florida, "mopped up" south Georgia, and joined Campbell in Savannah in January 1779. Within a few weeks much of the state was under British control. On St. Andrew's Day members of the St. Andrew's Society met in Savannah for the first time since 1775. There must have been many Loyalists among them. With the governor and numerous British officers they went from tavern to tavern in Savannah for twenty-four straight hours celebrating the day and no doubt the British victory. But over the following months not everything would go the way the British hoped.[130]

THE BRITISH OCCUPATION

British military leaders anticipated that once their soldiers were on Georgia soil, Indians, Loyalists, and disaffected Whigs would flock to the Union Jack. In early January, Commodore Parker and Colonel Campbell issued a proclamation promising protection to all those swearing loyalty to the king; anyone continuing to oppose royal authority would be punished. A Board of Police was appointed to care for and manage the plantations of all absentees, both "Loyal Subjects or Rebells." In February, the board also issued ten licenses to tavern keepers. When civil government was restored, the board was dissolved and replaced by the Commissioners of Claims.

Some Loyalists quickly returned from East Florida to Savannah, and hundreds of Georgians took the oath of allegiance to the king and joined military companies. Whigs joined militia units and began hit-and-run attacks against small British units. Initially, the British threatened to overrun the state, but within six months they controlled only Savannah and about twenty-five to forty miles around the town.[131]

During early March the British privateer *Vengeance* was in the Savannah River taking on wood and water. Aboard was John Richardson, formerly a New York merchant and now an investor in the vessel. He must have gone ashore, since he noted that Savannah was situated "upon a steep sandy Bank" and it "will put a man out of breath before he can reach the Top of it." He found that the town "is very regularly laid out" and "consists of about 300 houses, built for the most part of Wood." Richardson observed that the "Streets are not paved" and that "the Sand in them . . . [is] near a foot deep." Tongue in cheek, he remarked that "in the summer, what between Sand Flies (of which even now there are Legions) Musquettoes etc *must certainly be a most agreeable place* to reside in." He also discovered that "When it blows, a man runs no small risk of being choked by the clouds of sand and dust."[132]

While Richardson was in Savannah, royal government was restored. A temporary lieutenant governor, a council, and a slate of provincial officials were appointed. Once more Christ Church held regular services after British authorities appointed the Reverend Edward Jenkins as rector. Meanwhile, the Whigs kept alive the appearance of governing the state through a council that met in Augusta. Factionalism persisted among the lowcountry conservatives, but by the summer they controlled the Supreme Executive Council, which claimed to be the government of the state.[133]

Also during the summer Governor Wright and other British officials returned to Savannah from England to assume their old positions. But the governor discovered that there were "Many . . . who if they had an Opportunity" would join the "rebels." The governor and military officials were soon complaining to London that the thousand British troops in Georgia were inadequate to protect Loyalists and to subjugate the state.[134]

Food was scarce to feed the British soldiers and sailors in Savannah. The lands of nearby plantations lay fallow; plundering by Whig militiamen, British regulars, and Loyalist bands had devastated whole areas of the state. Rice was available, but British officers reported that the rank and file refused to eat it. Vessels had to be sent abroad to buy and import food. At the same time, British officials reopened and encouraged the local export trade in lumber and naval stores. During 1779 some one hundred vessels jammed with these products cleared Savannah.

The number of merchants in Savannah declined during the British occupation, but about thirty-six firms were open for business; also there were fewer professional people, artisans, and tradesmen. At least one tavern remained open under both the American and British governments; after Peter Tondee died in 1775, his wife operated the pub throughout the war years.[135]

By the summer of 1779 James Johnston returned to Savannah and was again publishing a newspaper, but with a new name on the masthead, the *Royal Georgia Gazette*. He reported that during the summer there were "very genteel" balls in the town, which were attended by ladies who made "a brilliant appearance." Johnston used the paper to tout the Loyalist cause. Once he reprinted an article from a New York paper that described the Continental Congress as "that truly whimsical and egregiously absurd body of despicable wretches . . . who are responsible for the present horrid rebellion."[136]

When General Lachlan McIntosh returned to the Augusta area in late July 1779 he counted forty-two Continental soldiers present for duty, fewer than six hundred Whig militia available for duty, and many of the state's best officers in British captivity. McIntosh described the military situation as "Deplorable." Whig leaders wanted to retake Savannah but recognized that without soldiers and assistance from their new ally, France, it would be an impossible task.

At the urging of military and civilian leaders, the Continental Congress ordered Polish volunteer Count Casimir Pulaski, his Legion, and other troops to Charles Town to join forces assembling there under the new commander of the Southern Department, General Benjamin Lincoln. Count Charles-Henri d'Estaing, commander of the French fleet operating in American waters, was asked to participate in retaking Savannah. He surprised both the British and Whigs when he arrived with twenty-two vessels and four thousand French soldiers and sailors off Savannah on September 1, 1779. Lincoln and d'Estaing now put together an allied invasion plan.[137]

THE SIEGE OF SAVANNAH

Following Lincoln's orders, General McIntosh quickly raised all the troops he could muster and marched from Augusta to meet General Lincoln's army near Savannah. Lincoln was marching from Charles Town and with him were Joseph and James Habersham, who hoped to retake their hometown and free their brother, John, from British captivity. The two forces rendezvoused on September 11 about thirty miles northwest of Savannah and together moved toward Savannah with some 1,500 men. Already d'Estaing's warships and transports had crossed the bar at Tybee Island unopposed, as the British had burned and evacuated the fort at Cockspur Island and sent their vessels upriver to guard Savannah. The French fleet proceeded a few miles south of Tybee to the mouth of the Vernon River. Then at Beaulieu, about thirteen miles from Savannah, on the night of the September 12, d'Estaing began landing 3,200 well-equipped French, Irish, and Haitian troops. In three days they marched to within four miles of Savannah and encamped to the south of the town, paralleling the streets running east to west. General Lincoln's force arrived on September 16 and camped to the southwest of the town. That same day d'Estaing asked the British to surrender. General Augustine Prevost—an experienced and brave soldier—stalled. He was gaining time for reinforcements to augment his 1,200 soldiers and for his brilliant chief engineer, Captain James Moncrief, to rebuild the town's fortifications. Moncrief needed laborers.

There were "several Thousands" of runaway and captured slaves in Savannah who were under British protection. So many blacks were in Savannah that attendance was good at the African American Baptist Church. Governor Wright impressed about five hundred blacks to assist Captain Moncrief in reconstructing the defenses. Around the town he built a semi-circle of entrenchments, and thirteen redoubts protected to the front by an abatis of cedar and pine. The barracks near the southern end of town were leveled and filled with sand to make a strong point near the center of the British works. Cannons were unloaded from British vessels and used in horseshoe batteries in embrasure. Sailing craft were sunk in the Savannah River, and a boom extended across it to prevent enemy vessels from coming up to the town. Civilian volunteers and militia took up positions in the entrenchments. Aware that some 540 black Haitian volunteers were among the French forces, the English armed about 200 slaves to defend the town. Even the Savannah clergy joined in the defense of the town. The Reverend John Zubly served as a chaplain to the British, and his Independent Presbyterian meetinghouse became a hospital for Hessian soldiers. Zubly died during the British occupation of Savannah, loyal to the last to the king of England.

Prevost delayed answering d'Estaing's demand for his surrender long enough to permit his reinforcements of about eight hundred soldiers to arrive and to rebuild a portion of Savannah's fortifications. He then rejected the demand. The opportunity had passed for an allied frontal assault, and Count d'Estaing ordered siege lines dug around the town. From the new French depot at Thunderbolt, located on St. Augustine Creek about five miles downriver from Savannah, heavy guns and mortars were brought up to the entrenchments on makeshift wagons. Thunderbolt also became the site of the French hospital.

In early October, when the maples in the swamps turned blood red, the French began their bombardment. Beginning on October 3 and for the following five days, cannons fired more than one thousand balls and carcasses, or fire-bombs, into Savannah. Some fell in Broughton Street and near the riverfront, igniting fires and destroying buildings. The cannonading terrified the non-combatants, who were among the first casualties. Within a few days the civilians were transported to Hutchinson Island for their safety.

Count d'Estaing was an impatient man; when the British did not capitulate, he ordered an assault on their right flank, which he believed to be their weakest. This flank was anchored by the Spring Hill redoubt, a high point at the terminus of the Augusta Road on the western edge of the town—today it is the location of the Savannah Visitors Center. The redoubt was partially protected by a low, swampy area on its westernmost side. A surprise attack was crucial to taking the strongpoint.

During the early morning hours of October 9, a Franco-American force pushed through Yamacraw Swamp and concealed themselves; a reserve corps with artillery under General Benjamin Lincoln took up a position at "the little cemetery," which is today the same enclosed Jewish Burial Ground as then, about eight hundred yards southwest of the Savannah Visitors Center. At dawn, during diversionary feints at the British center and left flank, the attack on the redoubt was to begin. But when the skirl of bagpipes sounded from the Spring Hill fortification, it sent shudders through the waiting allied force. Apparently, the allied plan was compromised by spies or deserters. Originally scheduled to jump off at 4:00 A.M., the Franco-American assault force began their attack at 5:30 A.M. The Scottish and British soldiers were waiting behind their redoubt.

Despite fierce resistance, the French grenadiers broke the British line. But when the French were not reinforced, the defenders closed ranks. Count d'Estaing ordered French and American troops forward again and again, but withering volleys of musket fire and cannon—loaded with chains, nails, and canister shot—tore through the massed ranks. Some troops reached the ditch and abatis fronting the redoubt before they fell dead or wounded; others bogged down in the swamp and were easy targets for the British. Casualties were heavy among the younger French and American officers. Canister fire fatally wounded Polish General Casimir Pulaski; Sergeant William Jasper, who had survived the fighting at Fort Moultrie near Charles Town in 1776, was also mortally wounded. Years later monuments were raised in Savannah to both men. Count d'Estaing was twice wounded.

Under the ferocious musket and cannon fire, the Franco-American force fell back. In about fifty-five minutes the French sustained 521 casualties, and the Americans counted 231 killed and wounded. The British had 1 killed and 39 wounded. Except for the Battle of Bunker Hill (Breed's Hill), it was the bloodiest day of the American Revolution for casualties on a single side.

Count d'Estaing lifted the siege immediately. The allies had suffered another calamity at Savannah in casualties and territory. Count d'Estaing failed to seize the opportunity to storm the town immediately after his arrival. The failure to retake the southernmost town of the American revolutionaries meant that it became the staging area for the invasion of South Carolina and the capture in 1780 of the South's major port, Charles Town; subsequently, North Carolina was invaded, and savage civil wars broke out between Whigs and Loyalists in the backcountry.

On October 18 General McIntosh and his troops broke camp to return to Augusta, while General Lincoln headed toward Charles Town with what was left of the American forces. The French soon embarked at Thunderbolt and Causton's Bluff for the open ocean.[138]

THE LAST BRITISH OUTPOST

In looking around Savannah after the siege, one Loyalist observed that "there was hardly a house which had not been shot through and some of them were almost destroyed." Carriages moved about the town carefully through sandy streets pockmarked by craters caused by exploding mortar rounds; a Loyalist woman noted that the town "offered a desolate view . . . and the houses were riddled with the rain of cannon balls." Public buildings and churches had been similarly damaged. Many private homes were uninhabitable; there was such a housing shortage that the British commandeered private dwellings for their troops, who faced a fast approaching winter.[139]

It was the coldest winter on record. A Hessian officer reported that there was "ice in the rooms at night and once it even snowed—unheard of things in this part of the country."[140] A minor outbreak of smallpox added to the misery of the unusual weather.

Governor Wright asked all Savannahians who could have defended the city during the siege but did not to give an account of their behavior. Without a good explanation, they were tried for treason. He promised protection to all

Georgians who did not take up arms against the king; many inhabitants of Savannah took the oath of allegiance.

The town was still filled with runaways, blacks who had fled to British protection, and slaves who had been impressed for work on Savannah's fortifications. The Commission of Claims, successor to the Board of Police, was charged with the duty of reestablishing the rural agricultural system by returning the slaves to the nearby plantations for service as a labor force. Governor Wright wanted to confine slaves who resisted being returned to the land and to build "a strong . . . prison."[141]

While Governor Wright was attempting to send the African Americans back to the fields to grow foodstuffs for the occupying forces at Savannah, he also praised the role of slaves in preventing the allies from taking the town. He wrote that blacks "contributed greatly to our defense and safety."[142] Now, however, the slaves and their numbers were posing special problems for him and the townspeople, especially those slaves who had been armed and who refused to give up their weapons. In late October white Savannahians complained that armed slaves "behave [wi]th great insolence." Together with some whites they "plunder in and about the Town." In December a grand jury warned of "the great number of Negroes" who "stroll about . . . in Town and Country, many with Firearms," who commit "Robberies . . . to the great Terror . . . of the Inhabitants." Savannahians were concerned that the social and economic chaos would lead to "Insurrections, or other wicked Attempts of Slaves."[143] Some blacks were bold enough to occupy shops and abandoned houses in Savannah and to begin "selling and otherwise dealing or trading" much to the "distress" of white Savannahians.[144]

Only the presence and actions of large numbers of British soldiers restored law and order in and around Savannah. The British, who had encouraged slaves to run away, now most likely prevented insurrection. Some slaves were kept on as soldiers under British command, and others were disarmed. A number of other slaves somehow retained their weapons and fled into the nearby swamps to join maroon communities. The social and economic chaos of the war provided African Americans greater opportunities to resist the institution of slavery.[145]

Although the British controlled the lowcountry, the Whigs still controlled the upcountry, and in January 1780 an elected assembly met in Augusta. Here the radicals and conservatives buried their differences to create a unified and constitutional government. The first assembly not dominated by coastal representatives proceeded to elect a governor and name Augusta as the seat of the state government. The new administration implemented a program pushed by the radical Whigs.[146]

In early 1780 Georgia was stripped of British troops for the invasion of South Carolina. Some Savannahians, including the rector of Christ Church, the Reverend Edward Jenkins, left with them. Now with only six hundred soldiers under British command in the entire state, Whig raiders were emboldened to plunder near Savannah. Primarily African American and Hessian soldiers commanded by Lieutenant Colonel Friedrich von Porbeck occupied the town. Porbeck complained repeatedly about Savannah's heat, the lack of a sewage system and drinking water, disease, and "the malignant vapors of this death-trap." Excluding the several hundred troops under Porbeck's command, British census takers counted 742 white inhabitants in Savannah in mid-1780. There were probably an equal number of blacks. At this time 241 habitable houses were standing.[147]

Whig guerrillas around Savannah met resistance from interracial forces. With so few soldiers remaining to defend Savannah, Governor Wright called on his Assembly to empower him to "arm and employ Negroes for our defense." Always concerned over armed Negroes, the Assembly agreed to provide slaves weapons only at the "time of Alarms."[148]

Social, political, and military disorganization within the state spawned partisan bands of both Loyalists and Whigs. After Georgia's capital of Augusta fell to the British in early 1780, the region between Augusta and Savannah became "infested with Partys of Robbers on Horseback," Governor Wright noted in the summer 1780. When the last British warships departed for South Carolina, Wright worried that "a rebel privateer . . . may come up the Savannah River and . . . carry away anything." His fears came true. Whig galleys began moving up and down the rivers and inlets near Savannah with impunity; Whig militiamen plundered the riverside plantations and stole slaves from them. Wright believed there were "even in the Town of Savannah . . . many . . . Rebels and Villainous Incendiaries."[149]

Despite apprehensions about the "rebels," social life went on. In March 1781, Savannah's Ugly Club was revived; the Library Society also resumed meetings, and apparently the freemasons were active. For the benefit of charity, members of the British garrison presented several plays.[150]

In June 1781 Augusta changed hands again following a successful siege by troops under General Nathanael Greene, who used partisan bands, militiamen, and Continentals to attack British outposts in both South Carolina and Georgia. Greene asked Savannah conservative Joseph Clay to reorganize government in the state. An Assembly dominated by lowcountry conservatives sent former Savannah merchant and conservative John Wereat to Congress. The power of the radical Whigs was waning.[151]

During the last half of 1781, the British in Georgia gave up one outpost after another. Savannah became the last British stronghold in the state. In October 1781 Lord General Cornwallis was forced to surrender an army of eight thousand to General George Washington at Yorktown, Virginia. When news of this debacle arrived in London, Parliament resolved to bring the war to an end. It was only a matter of time before officials ordered the withdrawal of the British forces from North America.

In January 1782 General "Mad" Anthony Wayne arrived in the state as Continental commander in the Southern Department with a force of about five hundred troops. Wayne ordered Lieutenant Colonel James Jackson and his dragoons and militia to take up a position around Savannah. Jackson was to constantly keep on the move and to strike the enemy often. Wayne instructed him to prevent "marauding & punish any . . . persons . . . found guilty of that disgraceful & Villanious practice."[152]

British strength in and around Savannah was increased to a thousand soldiers. But with Wayne and Jackson moving ever closer, the British were sealed off in Savannah. The Whig forces intercepted and sometimes killed Indian allies of the British who tried to enter the town.

Governor Wright's communications to London took on the tone of the doomed. In late January he told officials: "We are now Confined almost to our Lines round the Town, & are Expecting a Powerfull attack every day."[153] Whig partisans terrorized the nearby countryside, and Wright informed London that Loyalists "came Crowding in upon us, Stript of every thing . . . , merely on account of their Loyalty." Wright bought rice and "Flour & what Beef & Pork could be got . . . all these Articles being very Scare & Dear."[154]

Loyalists and militia came over to the Whigs, while they encouraged Hessian soldiers to desert. The Hessian commander, Colonel von Porbeck, observed that "The women are the best recruiting agents for the rebels."[155] Governor Wright began to fear for his own safety. He had been informed "*beyond a doubt* that my life is Threatened & that offers have been made to General Wayne, to assassinate me," he wrote in late February.[156] Fear grew apace among the British in Savannah. It was ordered that no one could talk to the prisoners in the town jail without permission from the governor or other high officials, and any discussions were to take place only in the presence of a noncommissioned officer; all incoming mail for the inmates was to be examined; anything suspicious was to be reported immediately. The British were taking every precaution.[157]

Conditions worsened in Savannah. In March, the Reverend James Seymour, the new rector of Christ Church, discovered that provisions and rent were so high that he opened a school to prevent his family from going hungry. In April the British government ordered the withdrawal of British troops from New York, Charles Town, and Savannah. Governor Wright opposed the evacuation, but plans were underway to leave the last British outpost in Georgia.

The Whig government met in Augusta in May and passed an act that banished and confiscated the property of all who assisted the British military. More than one hundred former Savannahians or residents of Chatham County were named. During the first six months after its passage, there were eight auctions of Loyalist property in and near Savannah. But the harshest provisions of the act were never enforced. General Wayne asked that Loyalists be treated leniently.[158]

The British evacuation was carried out quietly. By early summer about 3,000 white Loyalists and approximately 3,500 slaves along with other property were packed aboard sailing craft and canoes. Members of Georgia's Whig Assembly attempted by legal means to prevent the exodus, but they could only watch helplessly as the Loyalists "hurried away with our Negroes" to East Florida, Jamaica, and other points. In all probability two-thirds of Georgia's prewar population of 15,000 African Americans relocated, died of disease, or were stolen. This enormous loss of black laborers affected Georgia's agricultural system for years.

On July 10 General Wayne informed Lieutenant Colonel James Jackson that because of his "severe and fatiguing service" he and his Georgia Legion would have the honor of accepting the transfer of power from the British at Savannah. The following day Jackson and his soldiers, "dressed as respectable as possible for the occasion," entered the town by the western gate and accepted the keys to Savannah. Major John Habersham, his brother James, and his cousin Joseph Clay were among those returning to Savannah. A mounted patrol and guards were posted to prevent looting. State officials entered the city with General Wayne and soon restored government to all of Georgia.

The Assembly met in the old capital on July 13, 1782, and elected James

Habersham as speaker; the Council gathered two days later. Initially the government held its meetings in a church and later in Mrs. Tondee's tavern. Priority was given to restoring law and order to the town and state and to provide food and relief for the white indigents.

The British colonial "establishment" was no more. Conservative Whigs were in control of the affairs of the state, if only tenuously. The handiwork of the radical Whigs, however, the Constitution of 1777, which brought political democracy to the state, remained the foundation of the government of Georgia.

Social and economic disorder plagued the state. During the war many of the well-to-do families lost huge investments in real estate, slaves, and other personal property, and for them the future looked bleak. General Lachlan McIntosh believed that "This Cursed War has ruin'd us all"; he was bitter at the loss of his property and reputation, but he found himself almost alone in seeking revenge on his enemies. The attitude of most resembled that of John Wereat, a formerly wealthy Savannah merchant who lost a fortune estimated at £2,400. On one occasion he complained bitterly that "Those who deserted their country and remained with the Enemy have made money," but at the same time he was willing "to forgive anyone now the war is at an end." In August, Dr. Lewis Johnston, who had been named in the act of confiscation and banishment, was permitted to return to Savannah because there was a critical need for physicians; his brother, newspaperman James Johnston, who was also named in the act, was allowed to return to Savannah in September after agreeing to serve as the public printer. Savannah associations that formed to prevent proscribed Loyalists from returning to the state soon became inactive. At the same time, the old conservative-radical conflict also was waning. Georgians were focusing on rebuilding the state's devastated economy with new alliances.[159]

The preliminary treaty ending the war was signed on November 30, 1782, and Savannahians planned an end-of-the-war celebration.[160]

CHAPTER 4

Recovery to the War of 1812, 1782–1815

AFTERMATH OF THE REVOLUTION

*T*HE REVOLUTIONARY WAR dramatically affected the way all Savannahians lived. In 1782 the population of the city included about eight hundred impoverished whites, several hundred slaves, and a few free blacks. Many of the city's 227 private structures and the public buildings showed the scars of war. In the wake of the conflict came social and economic chaos.[1] A grand jury sitting in Savannah during October 1782 asked the state legislature for immediate assistance to repair the city's streets and wells, for a workhouse to correct "disorderly Negroes," for constables to control "loose and idle persons," and for oversight of the armed vessels in the river "obstructing trade and navigation."[2] Lachlan McIntosh observed: "no man is Safe one Night in his House . . . even in the Town Savannah."[3]

The siege and occupation of Savannah and partisan raids across the low-country left the region in "a ruinous state." The experiences of Savannah merchant and plantation owner Joseph Clay typified those of his class. When he returned to coastal Georgia he found neither "a vestige" of his plantation house nor any livestock—"all was desolate."[4] The plantation economy that fueled Savannah's commercial life had collapsed along with its usual sources of authority. In April 1783 Clay observed that due to the "absence of many of our most valuable inhabitants and the slaves" and the "convulsed state" of government, lowcountry planters and Savannah merchants had "to begin the World again." A year later Clay wrote that rice cultivation had resumed but was not "what it used . . . to be."[5]

The decline in the cultivation and export of rice created grave financial problems for Georgia's coastal planters for years. Clay observed that the "great losses this State has sustained . . . in Slaves, and property of every kind" have contributed to the devastation.[6] Loyalists to the king and the British army carried away about one-third of the slave population of Georgia; other African Americans ran away to hide in the countryside.

The daily concern of the poorer classes was their next meal. Crops had not been planted or harvested, and this created a serious food shortage. The state attempted to find food and distribute it to the indigent. In September 1783 a troupe of traveling actors dedicated a performance for the benefit of Savannah's poor whites.[7]

Savannah merchants and lowcountry planters believed that the local economy depended on new supplies of slaves. Joseph Clay told a business associate in 1784 that "the Negro business . . . is to the Trade of this Country . . . as the Soul to the Body." The slave trade was "a foundation for all other business."[8]

That same year two British merchants came to Savannah and received shipments of slaves from Jamaica and St. Croix. Georgians continued to prefer slaves from the Windward and Gold Coast of Africa rather than seasoned slaves from the Caribbean. Although landowners lacked the capital to purchase slaves in great numbers, Savannah factors extended credit to planters for the purchase of slaves.[9] By the mid-1780s, the Savannah firm of Telfair and Company had restored business relations with its British partners and had begun trading in "planting supplies" and slaves. Other city merchants eagerly looked forward to the arrival of their slave cargoes. Due to the heavy demand, prices of slaves remained high for over a decade. From the mid to late 1780s about eight advertisements for imported boatloads of slaves appeared annually in the local press. Most of those purchased locally ended up laboring in the rice fields along the rivers near Savannah.[10]

By the early 1780s a "land rush" for the confiscated estates of Loyalists was underway in lowcountry Georgia. Savannahians enjoyed the public auctions of valuable Loyalist lots, stores, wharves, and rice plantations. After acquiring Loyalist lands, planters such as Joseph and John Habersham planted sea-island cotton to supplement their income from rice, which declined in price without the prewar trading privileges extended by the British. The great boom in cotton growing came a few years later, after the invention of the cotton gin by Eli Whitney.[11]

GOVERNING THE CITY

Following the war the state government held sessions in both Augusta and Savannah and served also as the government of the two towns. Political conservatives from Savannah and the lowcountry such as Joseph Clay, James Jackson, and Joseph Habersham now dominated the Assembly. The radical faction was in retreat. Nevertheless, they left an indelible mark on the state: the concept of political democracy was well established.[12]

The state government sought to restore law and order, to meet the needs of the citizens, and to stimulate a postwar recovery. Meeting in Savannah in July 1782, the government promised to reward handsomely anyone in the public service who produced the corpse or provided proof of "a bona fide kill" of "notorious characters . . . who infest the roads . . . and are continually murdering and plundering."[13] The government ordered "disorderly persons" arrested and appointed a committee "to take charge of negroes running about loose" in Savannah.[14] In August 1783 a statute was enacted reaffirming an earlier law that regulated the hiring out of slaves and their labor. It required owners to purchase a license to hire out male or female slaves, who were required to wear a badge; slaves hiring out without complying with the act could be whipped at the workhouse, which had been established twenty years earlier for the "custody and punishment of Negroes." Owners who permitted their slaves to "sell fruit, Garden Stuff," or other commodities in Savannah had to obtain a license.[15]

To protect citizens from price gouging by Savannah's merchants, the legislature prohibited "extravagant" prices. Families unable to provide for themselves received government "relief": John Riley, "a cripple," was "allowed two rations a day"; Mrs. Clark and her six children received four rations daily.[16] To provide for "the relief of sick and disabled seamen," the government in February 1784 authorized the use of the barracks of Fort Wayne as a hospital and a lottery to support it. But years passed before there was an adequate facility for ill seamen in Savannah. The government briefly prohibited the export of grain and commodities due to the "scarcity of provisions" and the expected arrival of refugees returning to Savannah.[17] The legislators also turned their attention to the repair and cleaning of the streets and the restoration or construction of public buildings: the jail and city market received a high priority.[18]

Worried that commerce was being "injured and retarded . . . by the Wrecks . . . sunk" in the Savannah River by the British, the legislature required vessels sailing in and out of Savannah to pay a tonnage fee, which was to be used to clear the river of obstructions. To compel vessels to comply, Fort Screven, mounting three guns, was to be built on Tybee Island at the mouth of the Savannah River.[19]

With some semblance of order restored, families trickling back, and the economic life of Savannah quickening by early 1785, the legislature passed an act "For . . . Better Regulating the Town of Savannah." It was the first step toward self-government of the port. The legislation named several commissioners to oversee such matters as keeping the streets clean, the sinking of privies to six feet, and the distribution of leather buckets and ladders to householders to fight fires. To meet expenses, the commissioners were authorized to tax the property holders of Savannah.[20]

RELIGIOUS, INTELLECTUAL, AND SOCIAL LIFE

Most of the Anglican and Lutheran clergy left Savannah with the British. But by 1784 Savannah's Presbyterians and the Episcopalians of Christ Church began meeting again to repair their churches. In the late 1780s Samuel Baas reminded the vestrymen of Christ Church that he had completed repairs on the Parsonage House, "which was promised to be paid [for] imiadeatly . . . but time has elapsed these two Months past." Now, due to my "present want of Clothing & other nesesarys of life . . . I am willing to Receive almost any kind of Payments such . . . an order on a Store where I can get such things as I am in want of."[21] Before the century was out, Baptist, Methodist, and Catholic congregations held regular meetings. When the Methodists expressed antislavery sentiments, they drew howls of protest, and the congregation grew only slowly.

The churches carried on some relief work. For instance, Ann Spring and Lucy Whitehead, two widows with a child each, informed the Church Wardens of Christ Church that they were "in great distress . . . and . . . in want of the necessaries of Life both food and cloathing." Each "humbly begs" for any "relief as you may think most proper being unable to get any Labour to Support us."[22]

Solomon's Masonic Lodge also provided "charity and universal benevolence" for whites. By the 1790s this secret society of about twenty-five members met weekly. Protestants, Catholics, and Jews belonged. Savannah's first nine mayors enjoyed membership in this charitable and social organization.[23]

In addition, the Union Society provided relief to the poor. Organized first in 1750, it was incorporated in 1786 with twenty-one well-to-do Jewish and gentile members. The society supported widows and provided for the primary education of poor children.

For those who could afford the tuition, schools were plentiful in Savannah in the 1780s. Several "academies" held classes in the Filature, which was located between Bryan and St. Julian, Lincoln and Abercorn Streets. Instructors offered rather specialized education: fencing, languages, portraiture, business subjects, and military drill. Young ladies desiring instruction in writing and English grammar applied to Mr. John Cleary, who accepted payment in flour, rice, and liquors! Mr. Godwin offered instruction in dancing.[24]

Captain John Hiwill, inspector of music in the American Army during the Revolution, opened a music school, announcing that he had enough instruments on hand to outfit a band. His school flourished and provided musicians for theatrical performances and concerts. Hiwill enriched Savannah's musical activities until his untimely death in 1788.

Traveling actors presented tragedies, comedies, "tumbling and posturing feats." Savannahians patronized more than ten taverns in the late 1780s, which offered beers, liquors, and sometimes heated debates; here they played such games as shuffleboard, billiards, and "skittle alley." At Burt and Stebbins's Savannah Coffee House patrons could find accommodations for lodging and dining and could read newspapers from neighboring states.[25]

After James Johnston, the former Loyalist editor of the *Royal Georgia Gazette,* was permitted to publish again, Savannahians had the only newspaper in the state until 1785. From his Broughton Street location, Johnston began publishing a weekly in early 1783, the *Gazette of the State of Georgia,* later the *Georgia Gazette.* The paper was filled with notices of runaway slaves, legislative proceedings, and events abroad. But Johnson also printed excerpts from books, poems, and other solid intellectual fare. In the 1790s the biweekly *Columbian Museum* became a successful rival to Johnson's paper. The *Georgia Gazette* continued to be printed until Johnson's retirement in 1802.[26]

Private schools for those white Savannahians able to afford them, fraternal and social societies, musical concerts, newspapers, and taverns where patrons could meet, drink, and gossip—all provided humanizing influences on the local residents.

Although Savannah remained Georgia's largest urban center and most cosmopolitan town for years, the violence of the frontier occasionally exploded in its streets. During the early 1780s, for example, William McIntosh intercepted George Walton, the chief justice of the state, on the streets of Savannah. Angry with Walton for his part in suspending General Lachlan McIntosh from command during the Revolution, McIntosh publicly chastised Walton with a horsewhip "well laid on."[27]

SLAVES AND RESISTANCE

By 1787 the slave population of Georgia was growing rapidly. Some four to nine hundred slaves arrived annually in the state. Representatives from Georgia and South Carolina to the Constitutional Convention in Philadelphia in 1787 vigorously opposed any prohibition of the slave trade, which led to a compromise allowing the international trade in slaves to continue until 1808.

In 1790 the slave population of tidewater Georgia surpassed 13,000—exceeding the number before the war—while the white population was only 5,847. In Savannah alone the African-American population jumped from 1,104 in 1791 to 3,216 in 1800, roughly 40 percent of the city's population. Twenty years later the city's black population numbered about 3,500 and the white 6,000, except during the summer months when about half the whites—those who could afford it—sought cooler climes. Small wonder why whites in Savannah desired social order at any price.[28]

Some Savannah slaves and poor and criminal whites profited from the war and the social disorganization that followed. Slave artisans disregarded local laws and hired themselves out to work where and when they desired, paying a percentage of their earnings to their owners. With the little money they kept, they were able to afford a few luxuries in clothing, vary their diets, and in some cases save enough to purchase their freedom. Several who did attain freedom bought slaves themselves. Jane Habersham, "a free woman of color," owned Hannah and her child, Mary. In late-eighteenth-century Savannah, the number of free blacks was increasing.[29]

Slaves from nearby rice plantations traveled to Savannah both with and without the permission of their owners to socialize and sell their wares, especially on holidays. In the mid-1780s the Chatham County Grand Jury complained about "the number of idle and disorderly Negroes who came to town on Sundays." It remained a common complaint by Savannahians over the next half-century.[30]

Whites convicted of felonies and incarcerated in the dilapidated Savannah jail frequently escaped; so did blacks confined in the local workhouse. Two white prisoners broke out in 1784, and two more the following year; in 1786 the warden of the workhouse, Frederick Long, reported that six male slaves had escaped apparently by tearing away portions of "The floor [which] was . . . rotten."[31] These slaves may have joined other runaways who sometimes hid for years in maroon camps near Savannah.

The experience of slaves who served with the British army and the revolutionary rhetoric about liberty and equality encouraged slave resistance. By 1786 a maroon community on the lower Savannah River included twenty-one houses for male and female slaves. The camp was protected by a breastwork of logs and organized along military lines. It was led by "Captain Lewis," a former slave who had murdered a white South Carolinian, and "Captain Cudjoe." They organized raids by some one hundred armed fugitives on plantations along the Savannah River.[32] In December, General James Jackson, commander of the Georgia militia, warned that if the "marauding" was not stopped and "severe Examples" made, "there is no knowing how far the revolt may lead."[33]

The legislatures of Georgia and South Carolina offered bounties for the fugitive slaves, but they eluded capture. In May 1787, when the fugitives attacked a detachment of Georgia state troops, lowcountry Georgians suddenly felt threatened by open, armed slave rebellion. Savannah officials ordered the maroon village destroyed. During the attack by the Georgians, "Captain Cudjoe" and six other "head men" died defending the community. Many of the remaining fugitives fled and continued their resistance. Fearing "a capital insurrection," General Jackson attacked and destroyed a second maroon camp where "Captain Lewis" was taken prisoner. Subsequently, he was tried and sentenced to be hanged and "his head . . . cut off and stuck upon a pole to be set up on the Island of Marsh . . . in Savannah River."[34]

MUNICIPAL GOVERNMENT

In 1787, the year following the relocation of the state government and capital from Savannah to Augusta, the legislature moved Savannah one step closer to self-government: the town was divided into seven wards, and representatives of each were elected annually; the wardens then elected one of their own to serve as president of the board of wardens. The wardens possessed the power to enact laws for the good government of the town. William Stephens was elected the first president of the board of wardens; a descendant of one of the first Jewish families of Savannah, Sheftall Sheftall, became the first town clerk.

There was no division in Georgia between Federalists who approved the new Constitution of the United States and Anti-Federalists who opposed it, and in early 1788 delegates to a state convention quickly ratified it. Early the following year, Georgians elected their representatives to the first Congress of the United States and also fashioned a new frame of government for the state that was a more balanced document than the previous one. For instance, it provided minimum property qualifications for office and allowed any twenty-one-year-old male taxpayer the right to vote.

With constitutions at the national and state level by 1789, Savannah leaders such as Joseph and John Habersham asked the state legislature for a city charter for Savannah, whose landside approaches were encircled by fields of rice, corn, cotton, and indigo. On December 23, 1789, the state took the final step to provide self-government for Savannah by incorporating the town and providing an aldermanic government for the city. Aldermen were to be elected from each of the city's wards by the qualified male property owners on the first Monday in March 1790 and annually thereafter. Following the elections, the aldermen would elect one of the aldermen as mayor. (Some years later the election day was changed to the first Monday in July, and still later the first Monday in September, and provision was made for electing a slate of aldermen rather than one representative from each ward.) The act extended the city limits to include lots in the suburbs. Provision was made for the appointment by the governor of a health officer for the city. (After 1823 the appointment was made by the City Council.) The health officer's duties included inspecting vessels arriving in port, imposing quarantines, and preventing the spread of contagious diseases.[35]

The first municipal election took place in March 1790, when the population was under 2,500. Savannah's qualified white males selected seven aldermen, among them Joseph Habersham and John Houstoun. The city's first seat of government was the Silk Filature on Reynolds Square at Abercorn and St. Julian Streets. In the first official act of the City Council, the aldermen elected John Houstoun as the first mayor of Savannah; they also created the offices of treasurer, clerk, marshal, scavenger, and clerk of the market. The council adopted Tuesday mornings as a regular meeting time. The city marshal rang a bell to remind the elected officials and all Savannahians of the appointed hour; at the conclusion of the meeting, the marshal was required to march through the streets with a drum to announce ordinances enacted by the government. A seal for the city was devised and used for several years until it was broken. At that time a new seal in the "form of a coat of arms" was adopted, most likely the seal in use today.[36]

The new city officers faced the old problems: maintaining order and protecting the city from fire and epidemic disease. Dr. Ignatius Geoghagan, the first health officer, inspected vessels for signs of disease and required those infected to anchor below the city, to burn sulfur and tar aboard, and to send their sailors' clothing ashore for airing. To enforce regulations, a gunboat was purchased, and a cannon was mounted and manned on the abandoned fortification at Cockspur Island, which was to be fired at "any vessel refusing."[37]

The health officer and council also monitored the activities of the city scavenger, who collected the city's garbage and human waste and dumped it on the commons; in the summer months the scavenger was required to dispose of it beyond the city limits. A burial place for blacks was authorized by the council, and by 1790 an interment site was laid out near the edge of the city's east side. Soon enlarged for the burial of all "Christian people," the cemetery later was closed, and another opened south of the city.

The Savannah government ordered the city's firefighting apparatus, hooks and ladders, placed in convenient locations for emergencies; a firehouse was planned for the city's single engine, and additional wells were to be sunk.

Members of council paid for the costs of the city by taxing slaves and real estate, selling city lots, holding public lotteries, charging fees for badges for blacks who hawked goods, and requiring licensing fees for keeping billiard tables or shuffle boards and for selling liquor. During the first twelve months of the new government thirty-seven persons made applications to sell spirituous liquors in a city of about 2,500 persons. The City Council strictly regulated the retail liquor dealers, even setting the price that taverns charged for drinks. Income came from fines collected for violations of the public peace, such as "shooting" off guns in the city and "galloping through the streets" on horseback. For violating the latter ordinance, Savannahians and visitors received sixty-one summonses in 1790, more than for all other breaches of the law.

Horse racing, held under the auspices of the Jockey Club, was one of the most popular entertainments. But when some Savannahians frowned on the morality of racing horses on the Sabbath, the council quietly appealed to the stewards of the Jockey Club to cease the practice or see the track closed.[38]

The council sometimes imposed special taxes to raise money. When the public market in Ellis Square went up in flames in 1788, it was rebuilt with funds raised by a tax designated for this purpose. Within a few years another market was located near the foot of Drayton Street; another opened opposite the wharf of the Exchange Building, which catered primarily to persons who used boats to bring in meat, poultry, and fish for sale.[39]

Council members—later the mayor's court—sat in judgment on violations of the law. They adjudged vagrants, such as John R. Rust, "a vagabond" and ordered him imprisoned; they dissolved the relationship between Dr. John Love and his white apprentice William Cross upon learning that Love "ill used, and beat [Cross] with a knotted rope."[40]

Sheftall Sheftall, the first clerk in Savannah's city government, and his family played prominent roles in the political, social, and religious life of Savannah. Mordecai and Levi Sheftall bridged the gap between the city's Jewish and gentile communities. Both belonged to the Union Society. In 1790 the Sheftalls successfully applied to Governor Edward Telfair, a wealthy Savannah merchant-planter, for a state charter for the Congregation of Mickve Israel. This act officially established Judaism in Savannah and Georgia. For years the congregation remained small and continued to pray in rented buildings or the homes of members, but they dreamed of building their first synagogue.[41]

President George Washington visited the city in May 1791. The welcoming party included Joseph Habersham, other prominent Federalists, and members of the city government. Within a year Habersham was elected the second mayor of Savannah, and President Washington subsequently appointed him postmaster general of the United States. The president was entertained by a militia parade, concert, and ball. The city paid the expenses.[42]

REVOLTS AND RELIGION

The same year that Washington visited Savannah, a successful slave revolt swept over the French colony of Santo Domingo in the Caribbean in August 1791. The bloody insurrection alarmed white lowcountry Georgians, who feared that word of it might encourage local rebellions. Adding to the anxieties and panic of low country whites was "a Negro alarm" in nearby Bryan County. In 1792 the state legislature enacted a curfew for slaves. It forbid them from being on the streets after 8:00 P.M. in the winter and 9:00 P.M. in the summer.

During the several decades after the American Revolution the fear of slave rebellions made white southerners consider ways of controlling slaves other than by force alone. From the patriarchal ethic of the old world, southerners developed the more benevolent ideology of paternalism, which had a foundation in evangelical Christianity. Paternalism became institutionalized in the law, in the society, and in the culture of the region. It gave the South a complex set of values that set it apart from the rest of the nation.[43]

The Second Great Awakening that swept the South in the post-Revolutionary years and emphasized the equality of all persons before Christ may have inspired organized black resistance to slavery. One form of resistance came with the founding of African American churches by indigenous black leaders.

BLACK AND BIRACIAL CHURCHES

Before he departed Savannah in 1782, black preacher George Leile baptized Andrew Bryan, a slave. Bryan continued the ministry to the city's blacks in Yamacraw Village in Oglethorpe Ward on Savannah's west side, the heart of the black community. Occasionally whites, suspicious of so many blacks congregating in one place, disrupted Bryan's services; Bryan himself was publicly whipped. After the insurrection in Santo Domingo, worshipers at the evening service listened for the sound of the city's curfew bell or a patrol's drum rolls ordering them to be off the streets. Slaves feared arrest for violating the curfew because they faced a night in jail and possibly a flogging.[44]

Andrew Bryan purchased his freedom in the late 1780s. Prominent white Savannahians helped him buy a lot on Bryan Street. Here, eventually, a plain, frame church went up. In 1788 the Reverend Bryan was ordained and officially installed as the minister of the First African Baptist Church. Local lore notwithstanding, it was the second black Baptist church in Georgia and in North America, according to Dr. Edward J. Cashin, director of the Center for the Study of Georgia History, and distinguished black historians Carter Woodson and Walter Brooks. The original First African Baptist Church was demolished in 1873, and a neoclassical brick and stucco building was built in its place. Today it is known as the First Bryan Missionary Baptist Church. By the end of the 1790s Bryan's congregation swelled to more than seven hundred. Whites occasionally attended, and prominent white Savannahians continued to support his ministry. They believed in the Christianizing effects on slave discipline—religion for social control—and the city government made it illegal to interfere with black worship.

As the congregation of Bryan's church increased, skilled artisans and house servants left to form the Second African Baptist Church of Savannah. They elected as pastor Henry Cunningham, a slave who soon received his freedom. The Second Baptist Church is located today on Greene Square on Savannah's east side. Within several decades the First and Second African Baptist churches counted 3,397 members, or about 80 percent of the membership of the five African Baptist churches in and around Savannah.

A small number of male and female slaves worshiped with their masters in Savannah's Episcopal and Lutheran congregations. In the early 1800s, the congregation of the First Baptist Church was biracial, and over half of its white members were nonslaveholders; the Independent Presbyterian Church included both races throughout the antebellum period. Free African Americans and slaves were members of the Methodist and Catholic congregations. Catholic priests occasionally baptized the illegitimate offspring of interracial unions. The environment of these biracial congregations promoted toleration. No other forum offered blacks and whites theoretical equality before God. In these churches humans interacted if only briefly and must have come to know one another somewhat better, which may have mitigated suspicions of each other despite the hierarchies of caste, class, and gender. Such a variety and number of churches could be found only in cities like Savannah, not in the rural countryside; even in a slave society where violence exploded suddenly like a summer thunderstorm, the churches remained humanizing elements found only in an urban environment.[45]

The black churches themselves brought together a unique spiritual and cultural identity by blending African folkways and Christianity, which shaped the outlook of the members. These African Americans believed that goodness was rewarded, evil punished, and the sorrows of this world compensated for in the next, which was a consoling notion. The church also provided a place where the black community reaffirmed their African identity and culture and gained support from one another. The black churches exercised rigorous social control over their members, censoring immorality and expelling those who failed to abide by the rules. For Savannah's blacks, the black church was a place of worship, government, education, and recreation. Their ministers became their leaders.[46]

At his death the Reverend Bryan left a substantial estate. His funeral procession included five thousand black *and* white Georgians. He was interred in the "Negro Cemetery" near the potter's field and later reburied in a section set aside for free blacks and slaves within Laurel Grove Cemetery when it opened in the 1850s. He was succeeded by Andrew Marshall, whose reputation exceeded even that of Bryan.[47]

Like the church, music offered Savannah's free blacks and slaves a way to express themselves as individuals within the repressive institution of slavery. By the early 1800s black bands dressed in the uniforms of Savannah's white militia organizations summoned the militiamen to the parade field on muster days. Sounding the call for the Chatham Troop of Light Dragoons was "Boy Chatham," a young bugler and slave whom the members purchased. With other investors they leased him to other organizations and collected the fees. One of the city's earliest black bands was the Reverend John Deveaux's "Old Hundred," which was organized in 1817.[48]

BLACK RUNAWAYS, WHITE FEARS

Despite the promotion of black churches by whites and a few biracial congregations where the rough edges of white racism may have been smoothed, physical force was employed by white Savannahians to maintain a docile slave population. Nevertheless, lowcountry blacks continued to resist slavery by flight. Between 1782 and the mid-1790s, Savannah's *Georgia Gazette* carried advertisements for the return of 528 adult runaways. Many were suspected of being near or in Savannah, and some were "well known" there.

Georgia's principal city acted as a magnet for black fugitives. Since the black population fluctuated daily, runaways found some anonymity. Notices of fugitives posted by owners cautioned whites that the runaways were "artful," even "impertinent." The fugitives hired their skills to whites as carpenters, barrel makers, bricklayers, and fishermen; female runaways competed with free blacks, bondwomen, and white females for jobs as seamstresses and domestics. Whites usually knew when they hired runaways, but in their desire for quick profits they willingly employed skilled, illicit, cheap labor. Runaways who worked in Savannah constantly faced the threat of capture, but some remained hidden for years. Tom Prunier, a former Savannah slave, passed as a free black for eight years. A handful of runaways even successfully escaped by sea.

Sometimes whites formed close personal friendships with slaves in the workplace and assisted them in escaping, which jeopardized the property interests of the slaveholding elite. At the beginning of 1789 Samuel Iverson advertised in the *Georgia Gazette* for his slave Isaac, a runaway once employed as a barber in Savannah. Iverson thought he might be "harbored by some white person as he has been encouraged in making his escape by Mr. Clark, a waggoner or barber." [49]

The act of running away took great determination, which was dramatized by frequent escapes from the Savannah Work House. For instance, on October 7, 1789, several male and female slaves broke out. One inmate, Tom, managed to flee with "a large iron on one leg," and Charles, a one-legged boy, also successfully escaped. [50]

The frequent breakouts of black slaves and white criminals from the jail or the workhouse located in the heart of Savannah alarmed well-to-do white citizens. Local grand juries and the City Council complained about the jail's "ruinous" state. Little was done to repair the jail or ensure the security of the city until events in Santo Domingo again stirred white anxieties across the South. [51]

Murder, rapine, arson, and pillaging once more swept Santo Domingo in 1793. As blacks and whites fled the island, local authorities in southern ports kept a wary vigil. Rumors reached Savannah that Santo Domingo's black émigrés in Charleston were sowing the "seeds of revolt," as Charleston slaves were becoming "very insolent." The Georgia legislature immediately prohibited the importation of slaves from the Caribbean since they might harbor dangerous ideas. For decades southerners believed that the examples of terrorism by slaves on Santo Domingo encouraged the violence among their own slaves. [52]

The Savannah City Council ordered military officials to make every effort to prevent vessels from landing slaves from the West Indies; in June 1793 the council established a "night watch," consisting of a captain, two sergeants, and twenty-four privates. Citizens enrolled for twelve months and were required to patrol armed "to prevent fires, robberies, [and] murder." Members of the watch were instructed to arrest "all Negroes" on the streets "after ten o'clock, who cannot give a satisfactory account of themselves." Law and order during daylight hours were maintained by the city marshal and constables. [53]

A REVIVING ECONOMY

By the early 1790s lowcountry rice planters had recovered from the economic disaster caused by the American Revolution. But due to a dramatic population shift, the lowcountry became less important politically and economically. After the revolution thousands of Virginians and Carolinians with their slaves poured into Middle Georgia. In 1790 nine-tenths of the whites and one-half of the blacks in Georgia lived in the upcountry. Here they planted and trapped and sent their tobacco, grains, and skins to Savannah, which became the exchange, collection, and distribution point for these goods as well as lowcountry rice, indigo, and sea-island cotton.

Coastal or "green seed" cotton thrived in Georgia's upcountry, but it was too labor intensive to produce as a commercial crop until Eli Whitney's invention. Whitney, a recent Yale graduate visiting Mulberry Grove, a plantation near Savannah, revolutionized the process for removing the cotton fiber from the cottonseed. His easily copied cotton engine, or "gin," slashed the cost of producing cotton for market. It provided the impetus for the spread of coastal cotton and slavery across the Deep South. By the end of the 1790s cotton and rice together became the principle exports from Savannah, amounting to some $2,000,000 annually. The primary imports were sugar, molasses, salt, and wines.[54] Near the end of the decade Savannahians became obsessed with the new economy based on cotton. In lowcountry Georgia huge fortunes would be made in the fiber.[55]

During the 1790s Savannah also emerged as an important port for the export of lumber. Commission agents who owned lumberyards and warehouses boosted Savannah as a lumber center. Firms such as Lawrence and Spencer and Taylor and Miller bought lumber in the upcountry, stored it, and then sold, consigned, and shipped it to domestic or international markets.[56]

About four hundred ocean-going, square-rigged vessels sailed in and out of Savannah's port annually in the 1790s. As the economy revived, demand increased for shipwrights, ship caulkers, and carpenters to build wharfs, warehouses, and shops. Although the port city was the largest urban center south of Charleston, which had a population of 20,000 by 1800, Savannah's population was only slightly more than 5,000. The two major southern port cities, some one hundred miles apart, remained linked only by public water transportation for years. A visitor to Savannah in 1811 groused that it was "an inconvenience . . . felt . . . by . . . the Inhabitants of both places who are extensively connected together in Business."[57] Even after roads linked the ports, coach travel remained hazardous.[58]

Small nonslaveholding upcountry farmers sometimes traveled for days pushing two-wheeled carts filled with their products to barter or sell in Savannah and then purchase "store-goods" for their families. But it was the upwardly mobile, profit-driven, slaveholding rice and cotton planters especially who fueled the local economy. Commission houses run by local merchants furnished the planters with credit and supplies. At harvest time they served as intermediaries by selling and shipping the planters' rice and cotton to Charleston, Liverpool, or Glasgow. The merchants then drew drafts on the consignees, which would be paid from the proceeds of the crop. Finally, after discounting the drafts at the local banks and receiving funds, the merchants deducted their own commission and shipping charges, paid off the planters' notes, and sent them the remaining funds.[59]

Of course, a good portion of the profits made by the planters and the local commission houses went abroad to the bigger firms. This minimized reinvestment locally and limited Savannah's growth as a dynamic urban center. But the large planters used their sometimes handsome incomes to buy clothes, furniture, silver, carriages, and slaves. Savannah's artisans also profited by satisfying the planters' drive for material possessions.[60]

The city's skilled workers produced everything from agricultural tools to silver tankards. They knew what the wealthy planters wanted, and the number of artisans working in luxury products soared. From the 1790s through the 1820s advertisements in Savannah's newspapers increased 7 percent for craftsmen in the construction trades but jumped 40 percent for furniture makers and 54 percent for silversmiths and watchmakers. These artisans also imported ready-made goods from the northern states for sale in Savannah.

About 70 percent of the artisans migrated from Great Britain, other European countries, or states other than Georgia. Many came from urban centers, bringing with them the cosmopolitanism and humanity of cities. Due to the heavy demand for their crafts, most of these artisans remained in Georgia until their deaths.[61]

By the end of the 1790s there were approximately 400 artisans in Savannah—about 40 percent of the adult white male population; some 59 slaves, or about 10 percent of the adult male slave population, and 23 free blacks, or about 50 percent of all adult male free blacks, also worked as craftsmen.

Some free black artisans accumulated extensive property, including slaves. White craftsmen resented the competition of blacks and pushed through the City Council several ordinances restricting their trade. On the surface it appears that the wealthy whites who dominated the city government promoted the interests of the white artisans over the black. But the government did not rigorously enforce the ordinances, and there was a reason for this. By largely ignoring the laws prohibiting skilled slaves from practicing their skills, Savannah's wealthy elite—who hired out their own slave artisans—protected their own economic interests.

Perhaps aware of these motives, artisans had other reasons to distrust the wealthy. They complained, for instance, that the largest planters did not pay them promptly, but these same planters thought nothing of spending recklessly on "negroes" or "a frolic." Some craftsmen sued in court for money owed them, but they found "the courts [are] . . . tedious and will tire the carpenter out before the planter."[62]

But most artisans in the luxury crafts concentrated on accumulating wealth themselves. The ambition of these artisans was the same as the planters or the merchants—to become gentlemen planters by investing in land and slaves. Although they espoused equality and independence in promoting artisanal republicanism, these craftsmen firmly believed in white racial superiority and black subordination.[63]

With the outbreak of the French Revolution and war between England and France in the early 1790s, the city's artisans looked on the French revolutionaries as good republicans, while local British merchants and speculators sympathized with England. These sharp differences led to the formation of two political parties. One, composed of artisans or mechanics, asked the legislature in December 1793 to be incorporated as the Savannah Association of Mechanics and became known as the Savannah Mechanics' Association. Most of the artisans joining the association possessed modest wealth.[64]

Members of the Savannah Mechanics' Association were galvanized into action when it became known in the mid-1790s that Georgia legislators accepted bribes to vote for the Yazoo Land Act, which permitted the sale of millions of acres of land in Georgia by four private companies. Artisans believed that legislators should work for the public good and that those who traded their votes for private gain threatened republicanism. The association came to support candidates for the legislature such as popular local leader General James Jackson, who promised to rescind the Yazoo Act. Jackson was elected, and the act was repealed. The political power of the artisans was growing. The craftsmen had become a potentially significant block of voters.[65]

DEMANDS FOR LAW AND ORDER

With France and England at war in the 1790s, French privateers sailed into Savannah's port. French sailors sometimes thronged the streets near the river, carrying cutlasses, pistols, and daggers. They repeatedly harassed Savannahians and almost killed a constable. A city guard was established "to protect citizens against the insults of these seamen," but occasionally the city guardsmen also threatened law and order. Charges brought against one guardsman included intoxication on duty, smuggling liquor to prisoners, and threatening the life of a fellow sentry.[66] Authorities kept a close watch on the French sailors. When a bell tolled the beginning of the nightly curfew, the sailors had to return to their ships. In 1796 a drummer also "beat the tattoo" to announce the curfew. To prevent disturbances, council required "tippling houses" to close by 9:00 P.M. in the summer; another ordinance prohibited assemblies of blacks at night.[67]

With French sailors and blacks jeopardizing law and order in the city, Savannah's security-minded government advertised in the early 1790s for artisans to build a three-story brick jail. The City Council saved costs to the taxpayers by combining the functions of the workhouse and jail into one building. But seven years passed before events speeded completion of the new jail and workhouse for both white and black offenders.[68]

Security-conscious white Savannahians welcomed the federal government's decision in the early 1790s to build a fort on Cockspur Island, seventeen miles below the city. Here in 1795–1796 an earthen and timber work was constructed to mount six guns and was named after Revolutionary War hero General Nathanael Greene. It was part of a new federal defense policy that called for the construction of a series of fortifications along the Atlantic coast. A small number of troops soon garrisoned Fort Greene, the southernmost fortification in a projected chain of federal works.[69]

At a mass meeting of the inhabitants on July 2, 1795, white Savannahians called on the City Council to prevent the docking of a boat from Jamaica, which was carrying a hundred slaves whose "landing may be dangerous to the Inhabitants of this State." The crowd expressed sympathy for the whites on the French Islands who had experienced such violent "insurrections of their Negroes." A resolution passed and was loudly cheered and applauded. It prevented any boat from entering the Savannah River carrying slaves from the West Indies.[70]

As wild talk of insurrections swirled about, military officials in Savannah reported to the council in September 1795 that Savannah blacks planned to revolt. The mayor purchased most of the powder in the city for the militia and increased patrols. Apparently, the supposed insurrection was just another rumor. But Savannahians became ever more mindful of law and order. In August 1796 authorities arrested two "free Negroes," John Planter and Jerry Fetheree, and a slave named Jack and brought them before the City Council charged with insolent behavior toward the city constables. The council levied fines and jail costs on the free blacks and discharged them; Jack received fifty lashes on the bare back in the public market.[71]

The attempt by city officials to keep out Caribbean blacks was only partially successful. Some "French Negroes" reached Savannah as free black immigrants, while others came as slaves with their white owners when they fled the Caribbean islands. By the late 1790s Oglethorpe Ward, which included the suburb of Yamacraw on the western edge of the city, was populated by more African Americans, both slave and free, than any other ward in Savannah. Here and on the eastern fringe of the city lived one-fourth of the slaves, one-third of the free blacks, and some poor whites. Over time the numbers of both blacks and whites increased.[72]

FREE BLACKS

In the early 1790s the "free colored" in Savannah numbered over three hundred and increased during the decade. Some bought their own freedom and that of their spouses and children; others received their freedom for faithful service or for their blood relationships with their owners. White male Savannahians freed over 80 percent of the adult female slaves; most of the children freed were mulattoes. Peter Levegur manumitted his slave Clarissa because of his "natural love and affection" for her.[73] Francis H. Harris of Savannah stipulated in his will that the son of his slave Betty—Jack, a mulatto boy—be provided for and freed at age twenty-one.[74] Undoubtedly, many of the biracial sexual relations in Savannah were loving, caring ones and eased white racial fears and suspicions. After the beginning of the nineteenth century, manumission of slaves required legislative action.

Color mattered among the city's African Americans. Blacks usually married blacks, and those of lighter skin married one another. The Reverends Andrew Marshall and Henry Cunningham and well-to-do Jack Gibbons and Simon Jackson, all mulattoes, married mulattoes. Pervasive color bias and wealth linked to class appeared to be major marriage considerations for Savannah's free mulattoes. Such was the case in other southern cities.[75]

THE FIRE OF 1796 AND THE UNDECLARED
NAVAL WAR

In the spring 1796 a French duke visited Savannah for a week. He knew the city's reputation for "unhealthiness," but its residents insisted that it was much healthier than Charleston, "for Charleston and Carolina are constant objects of jealousy for Savannah and Georgia." He found the wholesale merchants greedy, wild game and fish inexpensive, but flour $20 a barrel. He saw new houses springing up in a year when a record $900,000 in commodities passed through the port. Imports included more than two thousand slaves. After a week and with a fever, the duke "gladly departed" a city "unpleasant [in] climate and location," where a "spirit of license and anarchy" reigns.[76] A few months later a disaster nearly destroyed Savannah.

On November 26, 1796, a horrific fire raged through the city; a smaller one flared up December 6. For years Savannahians had worried about the outbreak of fires, and volunteer groups met occasionally with city officials to urge them to provide adequate firefighting equipment. Sometimes the government responded positively.[77] But in late 1796 it was reported to the council that the "Fire Engines are much neglected."[78]

As flames leaped from private homes to churches to commercial buildings and their contents, firefighters in blue jackets, overalls, and leather caps fought valiantly but unsuccessfully to control the conflagration. Several black firefighters perished. The blaze burned quickly and fiercely, destroying 229 homes and leaving only 129 standing. Thefts of property became epidemic, and the government directed the militia to patrol around the clock to prevent looting. The conflagration left many townspeople "without shelter . . . or subsistence," and business ceased.[79]

The City Council appointed a committee of three prominent Savannahians to receive donations from cities and individuals and to set prices to prevent price gouging. The government authorized the distribution of funds to victims of the fire to cover up to 10 percent of their losses. This ignited a class dispute between rich and poor whites led by craftsmen who argued that it was economically unfair to reimburse persons based on their wealth in property. The mechanics demanded social justice, which indicated that they had reshaped republicanism to suit their new political and social ideas.

Savannah recovered rapidly. Dozens of brick masons and carpenters rushed to the city to rebuild it. The construction of private dwellings, shops and stores, and churches got underway immediately. A private census conducted two years after the fire counted 618 dwellings, 415 kitchens, 288 outhouses, and a population of 2,772 whites, 3,216 slaves, and 238 free blacks. Within a decade the city's population had doubled. Its booming commerce drew hundreds of people annually.[80]

During July 1798, an undeclared naval war flared up between France and the United States. Savannahians petitioned the federal government for both soldiers and fortifications. The federal government rejected the request because no northern troops wanted to be garrisoned where "the unhealthiness . . . is so well known." The secretary of war did send one thousand muskets, and the Navy Department authorized the building of two galleys to prevent French raids on the coast. The launching of the *Savannah* and the *St. Marys* boosted public morale, and anxieties over a French invasion soon evaporated.[81]

The city government ordered construction of a new Exchange Building at the foot of Bull Street, the site of the old building destroyed by the fire of 1796. It was to be both "useful [and] ornamental" and available for both public and private purposes. The cornerstone was laid on June 5, 1799, and in a few years the 75-by-50-foot, three-story building of brick and stone was completed. Installed in the steeple in 1804 was a clock and bell. The bell chimed the closing of the business day and rang the beginning of the curfew.[82]

By 1800 Savannah was the fourteenth largest city in the nation. Savannah's commercial boom was augmented by the opening of a branch of the Bank of the United States in James Habersham's brick and stucco mansion on Reynolds Square. The bank provided a ready source of capital for Savannah's economic expansion.[83] Cotton now dominated the export trade, and thousands of bales cleared the port annually. One traveler, John Davis, was dinning at Dillon's boarding house and listened to unceasing conversations over "Cotton! Cotton! Cotton!" which affected him like a "dose of opium."[84] At 20 cents per pound until 1810, Savannah offered some of the best prices of any port on the Atlantic coast.

POLITICS AGAIN

Local politics heated up with the approach of the presidential election of 1800. In July claims of voter fraud surfaced following the election of Savannah's ten aldermen. An investigating committee found only one of four contested votes illegal, and the council agreed to seat all the aldermen elected.[85]

In the presidential race, a majority of Savannahians cast their votes for Thomas Jefferson. Responsible for his win locally was a Democratic-Republican coalition of white artisans, shopkeepers, and small merchants who found common cause in protecting their individual rights from powerful low-country and state elites. With Jefferson's election, a "Friend of Equal Rights" proclaimed the "triumph of republicanism over aristocracy" in Savannah.[86]

The *Georgia Republican* became the voice of the artisans. Republicans received appointments to replace Federalists in positions as port collector and U.S. marshal at Savannah. Loyal protégés of Georgia Republican leader James Jackson and Thomas Usher Pulaski Charlton now controlled important city offices. A Republican-dominated City Council wiped out "aristocratic" federalism by changing the city's street names from King, Prince, and Duke to President, State, and Congress.[87]

City leaders and artisans worked together politically. Thomas U. P. Charlton told former governor Edward Telfair: "The people are good, virtuous, & brave, and the principle which delegates to them sovereign power is an holy one." Charlton also confided to Telfair that reforming local aldermanic elections "will be a glorious triumph for republicans, but a knell of death to federalists."[88]

Artisans and slaveholders joined forces on the City Council, and neither group saw a contradiction in their commitment to both slavery and republicanism, which meant equality, virtue, independence, and material gain. In the early years of the nineteenth century, clashes over class issues died as most Georgians became Jeffersonian Republicans.[89]

Racism provided a common bond for all whites, but it did not interfere with the sexual, social, and economic bonds forged between laboring class whites and African Americans. Nonslaveholding whites refused marginalization by the elite. White supremacy helped guarantee social order and promoted an ideology of political and social equality among all whites despite sharp distinctions in wealth and class.[90] But with the emergence of a slave and landholding artisanal elite, any prior feelings of class consciousness evaporated. Occasionally white artisans joined together to attempt to prevent black craftsmen from working, but increasingly the artisans became less interested in such matters and more interested in national politics. Accordingly, membership in the Savannah Mechanics' Association dwindled over time.[91]

THE FRENCH NEGROES

Worried over the number of French Negroes in the city, Savannah authorities ordered a census in 1798 of all "people of color" over age fifteen. The census takers counted 1,061 blacks. Of these, 219 French Negroes lived in different parts of the city, and 20 were free. These free French Negroes plus 34 free males and 45 free females revealed that at least 99 free "persons of color" resided in the city in 1798. That year 57 blacks paid taxes to the local government; the most prosperous was John Gordon. In 1800 only 23 whites in Chatham County paid more taxes than Gordon. The City Council wanted to deport the French Negroes, but in June 1798 the city was unable to enforce a deportation order for lack of funds; another 200 French Negroes living outside the city did not come under the council's jurisdiction.[92]

Savannah-based politicians such as Governor James Jackson continued to oppose the immigration into Georgia of "persons of colour" who witnessed the "horrid scenes of massacre" in the West Indies; in 1798 the Georgia Constitution was revised to prohibit the foreign slave trade to the state. Only occasionally now did ships engaged in the international trade in slaves stop at Savannah.[93]

Concern remained so high over the number of free "people of color" that the City Council passed a law in 1799 requiring all free Negroes residing in Savannah to register with the city. In another effort to control Savannah's free blacks, the city asked the state legislature to require all urban free Negroes to adhere to the same regulations as for slaves. The number of free "persons of color" in Savannah continued to increase, and in a few years their number reached 530.[94]

The sharp rise in the number of French Negroes, an upsurge in local crimes, and Sunday sales of liquor, which well-to-do whites alleged caused "riots," alarmed the Savannah government: aldermen patrolled the streets to help maintain law and order, the council proposed installing oil lamps at every corner and public well, and the jail and workhouse authorized years before was rushed to completion in 1802 on Lafayette Square, today the site of the Andrew Low mansion.[95]

At a council meeting in September 1802, Mayor Charles Harris reported that French vessels might attempt to deport and put ashore in Georgia hundreds of "Brigand Negroes . . . the very refuse of the Island of Guadaloupe and highly criminal during the late insurrection there." The council resolved that such action "would greatly endanger the peace and safety" of the lowcountry. The governor promised that the state intended to resist any attempt to land black rebels in Georgia.[96]

ENTERTAINMENT

Savannahians attended 166 plays performed in the city from the early 1780s through 1808. In the 1790s the newly formed City Council, chronically short of funds, required traveling actors and companies to purchase licenses to perform. In August and September 1794 the city permitted a Charleston company to present comic opera and tragedies in a building in Franklin Ward. One performance was given for the benefit of Savannah.

A few years later Alexander Placide and his Charleston company of players performed in Savannah. The proximity to Charleston regularly provided Savannah with polished entertainers. Most of Savannah's elite enjoyed the theater. Recognizing this, a group of amateur thespians organized the Thalian Association in 1799 and offered Savannahians a series of scholarly tragedies.[97]

Nevertheless, the theater had its critics, led by Baptist preacher Henry Holcombe. The Virginia-born Holcombe saw service in the Revolution, was "converted to God," became a preacher, and received an honorary degree from Brown University. He stood over six feet tall and weighed three hundred pounds. In 1802 Holcombe fulminated that "Satanic . . . forces, . . . 'Stage players'" performed within fifty yards of the Baptist meetinghouse.[98] His fanatical opposition to the touring actors probably accounts for the two attempts on his life.

Under Holcombe's leadership, the First Baptist Church on Franklin Square was completed in 1800. A humble wooden structure lit by oil lamps, it most likely included a gallery for blacks. Completion of the First Baptist Church permitted the city's white Baptists to officially join Savannah's community of churches. Eventually the Methodist, Unitarian, and Mariner churches went up, as did the synagogue for the Mickve Israel congregation.[99]

Traveling or residential musicians continued to enrich the cultural life of Savannah in the 1790s. The Filature Assembly Room, and later the Long Room in the Exchange Building, provided the space for concerts and Savannah's "Dancing Assembly" during the annual season beginning in December. One concert at the Filature featured vocal and instrumental music, including "Drink to me only with thine eyes."

Savannah's musicians purchased instruments, music, and songbooks from local merchants and frequently entertained friends and family members. Concerts by child prodigies added a sensational element to performances. During November 1799, Mr. D. Salter, his nine-year-old daughter, and his thirteen-year-old son gave five concerts.[100]

During the 1790s through the early 1800s Savannahians also turned out to enjoy such lowbrow entertainment as traveling wax works, circuses, elephants, a camel, an African lion, a bison, and a "Royal Tiger, fed with a living pig every evening." Reflecting the worldwide craze for so-called educated animals, Savannahians flocked to see a "Learned Pig" and a "Learned Dog" perform in Gunn's Tavern for a month in 1798. The dog supposedly could distinguish colors, indicate the time of day, and tell the dates on coins. Charles Wilson Peale's traveling exhibit of the fossil skeleton of a mammoth piqued local scientific interest.[101]

For entertainment, visitors and Savannahians alike patronized the city's taverns. By the early 1790s, thirty-seven establishments—one for every ninety-five men, women, and children—sold liquor. Savannahians imbibed heavily, but some complained about it. In 1794 a grand jury and the City Council criticized Savannah shopkeepers who sold spirits after nightfall and on Sundays, which encouraged "the Negroes . . . to steal and pillage." It was the government's almost perennial refrain: Savannah's well-to-do white residents thought that slaves who came to Savannah at night to trade threatened law and order in the city; and they were concerned that promises of liquor in exchange for goods, stolen or otherwise, by keepers of the tippling houses encouraged a "Villainous traffick." That same year, 1794, the Savannah City Council passed an ordinance compelling "due observance of the Sabbath."

But the overriding concern of the council was that shopkeepers, by providing a place for commercial transactions and fraternization between blacks and whites, violated the racial boundaries of slavery, especially by empowering the subjugated and undercutting the authority of slave owners. The shopkeepers, mostly poor whites, willingly overlooked Sunday trading laws for reasons of economic self-interest. Despite the threat of heavy fines by the early 1800s, several hundred male shopkeepers between 1790 and 1840 were charged with "entertaining Negroes" and violating the Sabbath ordinance. John Dillon, an Irish immigrant who owned a grog and trading shop, made a small fortune "entertaining Negroes." Mary Gannett, who repeatedly violated the laws for trading with slaves, acquired eleven slaves herself and property in three counties.[102]

In an attempt to limit the consumption of liquor, Savannah's aldermen authorized one liquor license per ward and required shops to close near dusk. Gambling was prohibited after 11:00 P.M. in all "houses of entertainment." But when opposition surfaced, the city government permitted the retailers to remain open later. Furthermore, the number of liquor or dram shops only increased over time. And the elite had cause for concern. Trading, drinking, and fraternizing among poor whites and African Americans in the informal atmosphere of the liquor shops most likely took the edge off white racism and forged bonds of friendship.[103]

Interracial sex must have lessened suspicions and hatred, too. Biracial sexual contact, especially between white men and black women, was present almost from the founding of Savannah. For instance, minister John Martin Bolzius observed that a common "abomination . . . is that white men live in sin with Negresses and father half-black children."[104] It was evident in the lowcountry's growing mulatto population.

Some of the most frequent interracial sexual encounters took place in Savannah's brothels, where black and white women alike entertained African American and mostly nonslaveholding white males. It was a way for desperately poor females to earn a living despite the stigma attached to the white women. Again and again the city government shut down "disorderly houses" suspected as places for interracial sex. In the early 1800s, four of the five defendants charged with "keeping a riotous and disorderly house" in Savannah were women.[105] In 1808 a local grand jury condemned "houses of ill fame," which "are suffered to be kept in the very center of the city." Here, the jurors complained, "the sacred ties of marriage are forgotten, and the foundation of disease laid."[106] Women, not men, were repeatedly indicted for "keeping a house of ill fame" or "a lewd house or place for fornications." Their time in jail was sometimes extended because of their inability to pay jail fees at the completion of their sentences.

Prostitutes also frequented the dives of sailors and walked the streets. One woman who was "in the habit of . . . holding improper conversations with . . . people of color" was arrested by city officers and ordered to be "kept under close confinement."[107] Widowed women, wives deserted by their husbands, or single women expelled by their churches for physical intimacies probably turned to prostitution for economic survival. Thrice-widowed Priscilla Kirkland and her fifteen-year-old daughter, Diana, were without income and established a "sailor's boarding house," which was actually a brothel. Diana died at age seventeen, followed by her mother eighteen months later.[108]

The informal social encounters of blacks and whites, of prostitutes and their clients, in the brothels and in the streets of Savannah may have fostered biracial tolerance between African Americans and nonslaveholding whites. In such encounters white males and females subordinated their racism; furthermore, their mutual distrust, even hatred perhaps, melted away in the embrace of their sexual partners. Although the city repeatedly tried to put the brothels and prostitutes out of business, interracial sex continued because nonslaveholding white men and women experienced few inhibitions about choosing black sexual partners. Occasionally, the white elite also enjoyed the favors of black prostitutes, which may have been another reason that Savannah's government never permanently suppressed the city's brothels.[109]

The elite horsey set also enjoyed entertainment at the Jockey Club. Anyone interested in joining in the early 1790s signed up at Brown's Coffee House. A Savannah Golf Club was organized as early as 1795. The golfers most likely played on the East Common just beyond the city's limits on the eastern edge of town.[110]

HEALTH OF THE CITY

Fears of infectious diseases led Savannah's government to zealously oversee the city's health regulations. When "fevers" raged in the West Indies, New Orleans, and Charleston during the summers of the 1790s, panic gripped Savannah, and its government prohibited vessels out of these ports from docking off the city. In August 1796 the Savannah government distributed handbills declaring that a "fever prevails" in Charleston that is "fatal to many" there. When visitors attempted to enter Savannah from Charleston, they first had to endure quarantine on Cockspur Island for fifteen days. Subsequently, a letter from Charleston's intendant, or chief city official, vigorously denied the presence of fevers at Charleston.[111]

The government may have been attempting to promote Savannah as healthier than their major trade rival, Charleston. When smallpox broke out in Savannah in the 1790s, the City Council and local merchants attempted to conceal its presence. But as the disease reached epidemic proportions, the city authorized an illegal program of inoculation. Word leaked out, and Georgia's governor threatened Savannah's civic officials that if they ever again resorted to inoculation, he would revoke the city's charter. In 1800 the council purchased a dwelling near the city from Levi Sheftall and converted it to a quarantine house. Dr. Moses Sheftall Sr. was hired to oversee it. Either Dr. Sheftall or Dr. Lemuel Kollock first used cowpox virus locally to inoculate against smallpox.[112]

In 1802 slaves near Savannah contracted smallpox, and the city dispatched armed guards to escort blacks exposed to the disease to a quarantine station on Tybee Island. When smallpox was detected in the city in 1805, the government physically removed infected people beyond the city and posted guards to prevent them from returning. Alarmed that the disease was spreading, city officials authorized physicians to begin inoculations. When it became known that the virulence of the smallpox had been greatly exaggerated, city officials worried that the rumors had harmed local commerce.[113]

Despite the city government's efforts to cover up the extent of disease in the city, smallpox and other diseases persisted. In late September 1805, Edward Telfair wrote: "Sickness prevails throughout the city. We have four weeks yet . . . before it can be said that the danger . . . is expired."[114] When smallpox reappeared later in the decade, the city government made vaccinations, now a more widely accepted practice, mandatory.[115]

In the early 1800s Savannahians dumped the city's filth into the streets and the nearby marsh and rice fields; the effluent from the city's privies percolated through the soil and occasionally into the shallow wells of the city, which provided the local drinking water. The destruction of the trees on Hutchinson Island and south of the city removed the shield that provided some protection from yellow fever and malaria-carrying mosquitoes. Local physicians observed that "malignant" and "billious" fevers—most likely yellow fever, malaria, and typhoid—prevailed in the city during the summer and autumn months. Typhoid became endemic in the city until a new water system was adopted. Cholera also posed a deadly threat; influenza, scarlet fever, dengue fever, and typhus remained less serious infectious diseases.[116]

Few, if any, Savannah "doctors" had medical degrees. The city's leaders tried to recruit trained physicians to serve the needs of the well-to-do whites. One Virginia physician who was solicited to settle in Georgia found few qualified physicians "but numerous . . . empirics who . . . deserve . . . A coat ornamented with three Duck's Heads, and the Motto, Quack! Quack! Quack!"[117]

Savannah attracted several good doctors. In April 1804 the city's eighteen

"doctors" formed the Georgia Medical Society for "Lessening the Fatality Induced by Climate and Incidental Causes, and Improving the Science of Medicine." Three of the members included the city's most respected physicians:
Dr. Lemuel Kollock, a Massachusetts native and Brown University graduate,
and two Virginians, Dr. John Grimes and Dr. James Ewell. Dr. Kollock, unlike most physicians of the age, assembled a good medical library, carried on
an extensive medical correspondence, and was the preceptor for numerous Savannah medical students. Dr. Lemuel Kollock was the first of four physicians
of the same name to serve the city for the next hundred years. Dr. Ewell, interested in better hygienic care for mariners and slaves, published *The Planter's
and Mariner's Medical Companion* (1807).

The physicians influenced the City Council. In 1806 the Medical Society
voiced concern over the unhealthiness of nearby marshes, rice fields, and garbage in the streets. This led the government to ask the Medical Society for
advice on how to use lime to prevent disease and promote health. The Medical Society also offered free vaccinations against smallpox to the poor, made an
epidemiological survey of the city, and maintained a small medical library.

Typhoid fever remained endemic, but other "fevers" increased with the
population of humans and animals, which meant that their waste was con-
taminating the city's drinking water. Fevers remained malignant in the eastern
section of Savannah where the bacterial contamination of wells was highest,
since the city sloped toward the river.[118]

Cynics claimed that Georgia doctors used only one method to cure patients, "the lancet." But Savannah doctors also prescribed snakeroot and Peru-
vian bark for anemia and fever, laudanum and mercury compounds for venereal disease, sugar, lead, and white wax for burns, foxglove for cuts, opium as
a painkiller, and calomel for purgatives. As the patient's disease became more
serious, the treatment became more drastic.[119]

In the early 1800s the mortality rate in Savannah rose and with it the city's
reputation as unhealthy, especially from the summer months to the first frost.
A committee of the City Council studying the matter noted the location of the
cemetery near the city had an unhealthy effect and advised planting trees along
its wall to soak up the impurities in the air. Concerned about the high mortality rates of persons unaccustomed to Savannah's climate, the Georgia legislature prohibited the disembarkation of foreigners in the port city from July
through October.[120]

CHARITY

Interest in caring for orphaned or destitute young white females apparently began with the minister of the First Baptist Church, the Reverend Henry Holcombe, and some prominent women of his church and the Independent Presbyterian Church. Unlike most Baptists, Holcombe believed that Christians
bore a responsibility for society's unfortunates.[121]

Humanitarian concerns did provide some of the motivation for the founding of the Savannah Female Asylum. The asylum was also instituted for benevolent reasons thought to benefit society. Launching and overseeing the asylum
also provided a new and influential role for Savannah's well-to-do women. It
became the first of several institutions organized within Savannah's patriarchal
society to assist "distressed" girls seen as more vulnerable to various pressures
than young boys.[122]

The Savannah Female Asylum formally began at a meeting of "ladies" at the
Independent Presbyterian Church in December 1801. From the beginning a
close relationship existed between religion and charity. The donations of the
"ladies" and others permitted the hiring of a matron, "a virtuous woman," to
supervise and teach reading, writing, sewing, and housekeeping to the residents of the asylum, ages three to ten. At a "suitable age" the youngsters could
be placed in local homes or bound out. Within a year more than two hundred
women had become members and made donations to the asylum. Membership was closed to men, but their contributions were encouraged. Before the
end of the asylum's first decade, it was caring for twenty-six orphans.[123]

Strict rules governed the female asylum. The matron held worship services
morning and evening. The children were required to arise "at six in winter, . . .
breakfast at eight, dine at one, and take tea at six," and be abed by nine o'clock.
In summer the same routine was followed one hour earlier. School was held
daily except weekends; on Sunday the children donned their uniforms to attend Sunday school and afterward to worship in the morning at the Independent Presbyterian Church and in the afternoon at the First Baptist Church.

The strict regimen of the asylum reflected the values, morals, and manners
of the directors, Savannah's female elite.[124] Their intention was to instill
"habits of industry & virtue," which would provide the means of obtaining
"useful and respectable employment." On one occasion the directors provided
the matron with "a whip" and "directions to use it" when some older girls
disobeyed the rules.[125] Obviously, the asylum also was another example of an

institution created by the city and served as an extension of Savannah's humanizing and socializing influences.

The city's women of the upper crust also exerted their control over indigent or ill parents who gave up their children to the institution. Priscilla Kirkland placed her seven-year-old daughter, Diana, in the Female Asylum after the death of her husband. Priscilla remarried, was widowed a second time, and, poised to marry again, petitioned for the return of her daughter, who was now about age twelve. But the directors refused, "the ladies knowing [Priscilla's] . . . character to be very bad."[126] Eventually, Diana escaped the asylum to join her mother in running a brothel after the death of the third husband. As mentioned previously, the daughter died while still in her teens, and the mother died less than two years later.

For years it was recognized that the city needed a hospital and poorhouse. The "city was crowded" with the destitute and sick, city councilmen observed, "seeking charity from door to door."[127] A place of confinement was also needed for the city's numerous debtors because the law required imprisonment for debt. In the early 1800s a large building in Yamacraw was purchased from Dr. Lemuel Kollock for $3,000 to serve as the poorhouse and hospital. It was soon operating at an expense to the city of over $5,000 annually.[128] Institutionalizing charity at the taxpayer's expense was, at least in part, an effort by the elite, and in their own interests, to succor the white poor.

UNREST, A HURRICANE, AND LAW AND ORDER

In 1803 the City Council appropriated long-deferred funds to light the city's streets for the safety of its citizens. Within a few years about 180 lamps illuminated Savannah; one was located near each sentry box and well.[129] But soon after installation of the lamps began, "a Negro boy, James Dickinson," was apprehended for breaking some of them. He was to "receive thirty-nine lashes or his owner . . . pay the costs." But threats of severe punishments did not deter "evil minded persons," the city council noted, from destroying the street lamps.[130]

In April 1804 the city government was informed that an insurrection was planned. The council directed the city marshal to arrest any free black ordering sizeable quantities of gunpowder; if any unknown white person attempted a like purchase, the government was to be alerted.[131] Also in April a prominent jurist made pronouncements that again sparked the white elite's old fears and fantasies. Jabez Bowen Jr., judge of the Superior Court of the Eastern District of Georgia at Savannah, charged the Grand Jury of Chatham County to free all female slaves at the age of ten and all males at twenty-one. If slavery continued, Bowen asserted, Savannahians could expect only "blood, massacre and devastation!" It was rumored that Judge Bowen said that if the legislature failed to free Georgia's slaves immediately, he would lead them to freedom "at the expense of the lives of every white inhabitant of the State." Members of the grand jury refused to act on Bowen's request.[132]

White Savannahians were stunned by Judge Bowen's words and actions and found them inflammatory. A warrant was sworn out against him for inciting servile insurrection, and he was imprisoned. In May 1804 the city government released the judge to the custody of his father on the condition that the younger man leave the state. Once in Rhode Island, he continued to swear "vengeance against the white people" of Savannah. Judge Bowen was a curious anomaly. To Savannah's white slaveholders, slavery and black subordination were the very foundation of their social and economic life.[133]

Rumors of servile revolts and Judge Bowen's words stirred prominent whites to action. The City Council put the militia companies on high alert and instructed constables to disperse all gatherings of blacks after nightfall.[134] In June 1804 a military unit seized twenty-one Caribbean slaves imported illegally into Savannah. The council required their owner, Daniel O'Hara, to post securities totaling $10,000 to guarantee deportation of the slaves within thirty days.[135]

In July security was tightened after the mayor received information that was "highly important to the safety . . . of Savannah."[136] The council warned the city patrols to be especially vigilant during the upcoming Christmas season, and the city government restricted black religious assemblies on Sundays to the hours between 10 A.M. and 5 P.M.[137]

In early September of 1804 well-to-do Savannahians faced another form of anxiety. A hurricane swirled out of the West Indies, crossed the American coastline, and headed directly at Savannah. The storm struck with terrific suddenness on Friday evening, September 8, and for seventeen hours it raged "with dreadful fury." At the mouth of the Savannah River huge waves rolled over Cockspur Island, destroying Fort Greene and drowning some soldiers stationed there. In Savannah a terrified observer huddled in a boarding house "which was blown almost to pieces." The tide rose to "astonishing" heights and surged through houses and stores. Every craft in the harbor was "either sunk, driven over the docks or dismasted." Salt waters swept across Hutchinson Island and plantations along the Savannah River, drowning one hundred slaves and washing away rice fields.[138] Homes collapsed, chimneys fell, and winds damaged public buildings.

Christ Church, only partially rebuilt from the fire of 1796, again was destroyed. The hurricane delayed for years the completion of the white-columned building that today faces Bull Street at Johnson Square, the third Episcopal edifice built there. Christ Church is the oldest Anglican or Episcopal Church in Georgia; its cornerstone was laid in 1744, and it was dedicated six years later. During the hurricane the steeple and bell of the Independent Presbyterian Church collapsed. The storm uprooted trees planted years earlier to beautify the bluff and the city squares.

Money was appropriated to haul away the storm's debris and to plant new trees. High winds during later hurricanes in September 1824 and September 1834 bowled over many of them. It was not until fifty years later that a hurricane slammed into Savannah with the fury of the one of 1804.[139] But by February 1805 things had almost returned to normal. A visitor observed that the "town has the appearance of wealth."[140] Even after a terrible storm, the city's surroundings had a salutary influence on a nonresident. Most likely it was due, in part, to the arrangement of the city and its numerous squares.

During 1805 the City Council took action to control "the daring, alarming and almost nightly robberies." To provide for the security of the city, council members created a new, publicly funded city watch.[141] To pay for it, the city imposed taxes on slaves, vehicles, and produce; white males twenty-one years of age and older without property paid an assessment of $2 annually. Free blacks paid property taxes and an additional $5 fee, which on its face appeared discriminatory.

In 1806, Savannah's watch was organized and included two officers and twenty-four men. James Clark, the first superintendent, was salaried at $60 monthly; the watchmen earned half as much. Any citizen wishing to enlist in the watch had to be certifiably sober and honest. Superintendent Clark carried two pistols, and each watchman was armed with a musket and a rattle to raise an alarm. Peter Shick was elected superintendent in 1807 and served in the post for almost twenty years.[142]

The year the city watch was first established an incident reminded white Savannahians that slave unrest might as easily explode in the countryside as in the city. During the Christmas season of 1806 Robert Mackay and several other

Georgia planters nipped in the bud a plot that was said to be led by "drivers & leading Negroes" on plantations along the Savannah River.[143] In 1806 the Savannah city government complained to the state legislature that the city was experiencing "great injury" from the numbers of "free negroes, mulattoes, and mustezoes, of vicious and loose habits" residing there, and the City Council asked for passage of a state law to comply with a local ordinance requiring all free blacks residing in Savannah to be subject "to the same police regulations and restrictions as slaves."[144] The state promptly agreed.[145]

About the same time two members of the City Council's prison committee visited the new jail and found security lax. For instance, inmates climbed into the rafters to move from one cell to another. The committee's gravest concern was the large number of blacks imprisoned there who might conspire to escape en masse. To prevent this, they recommended that a "strong chain" be used to secure the cell doors. The committeemen also found that conditions in the prison posed a health hazard: "The pipes . . . intended to carry . . . off the filth are . . . useless." To remedy the situation, they recommended that tubs be supplied the prisoners. City Council endorsed the recommendations and contracted for the "repairs and improvements" to the jail.[146]

By 1809 the total population of the city of Savannah was 5,342 persons: 2,702 white, 2,311 black slaves, and 329 "free people of color."[147] The Savannah Gaol Book, April 1809–May 1815, is unique. It is the only prison log surviving for this period in Georgia. It reveals that more than 84 percent of the male slaves and over 92 percent of the female slaves imprisoned there for criminal acts resided in Savannah or had owners living there. At least once during the six-year period some 2,366 men and 682 women served time. Most had been sent to the jail by their owners for "safe keeping" or for running away. Some had been apprehended by the vigilant Savannah Watch and upon the instructions of their owners received floggings or were placed in irons or both. Nancy, who was imprisoned eleven times for running away in the years 1809–1815, held the female and male record for the number of incarcerations. Females such as Nancy continued to resist enslavement despite the beatings, irons, and imprisonment.

Less than 1 percent of those sent to the Savannah jail from 1809 to 1815 served time for having committed capital offenses—murder, arson, assault, or theft. No male slave confined during this period was charged with the rape of a white woman.[148] Nevertheless, the sheer number of slaves apprehended and confined more than once—over 65 percent—must have given Savannahians pause. And even though few slaves committed capital crimes between 1809 and 1815, even one capital offense assumed enormous and enduring significance for both slaves and white southerners.[149]

Sailors made up a significant number of the prison's population in the early 1800s. During these years tensions in Savannah, like those nationwide, escalated as English and French ships preyed on American shipping. The threat of war was ever present. To prevent the search and seizure of American vessels, cargoes, and sailors, Congress passed the Embargo Act (1808), which forbid the sailing of American merchant ships. Now penniless, angry sailors aboard ships at Savannah came ashore and roamed the streets.

The City Council provided some lodging and food for these seamen, but disorder flared up. In March, the council ordered all stores and taverns closed between 7:30 P.M. and 5:00 A.M. Mariners were expected to remain aboard their vessels during these hours. In June 1808 a fire almost roared out of control and damaged the city. The following February, the city government received word that an arsonist was plotting to burn the city. In March another arsonist attempted to burn Savannah. On March 20 the city council offered a reward of $500 for the arrest of persons guilty of this "heinous" act.

Following a mass meeting in Savannah, thirty-five citizens were appointed to assist the city watch in preventing arson; in April an ordinance was passed to prohibit smoking in public places. By now the city maintained twenty-five public wells and pumps, seven fire engines, and one floating fire engine. When there was a cry of fire, the council directed the watchman patrolling nearest the Exchange Building to quickly climb to the steeple and hang his lantern in the direction of the blaze in order to guide firemen to the scene. So that the watchmen remained vigilant throughout the night, the council enacted a law requiring them to cry out the time and weather frequently to ensure that they remained awake and on duty.

Unemployed seamen may have attempted to set fires in the city, but the problem of angry, out-of-work sailors ended with repeal of the Embargo Act in 1809. Both vessels and sailors long detained at Savannah sailed away. Two years later, however, two French privateers anchored off the city and sent a party of sailors ashore to dragoon local seamen. With tensions already high, a fight broke out between the sailors and Savannahians patronizing a brothel, and the conflict soon escalated into a riot, which continued for two days. During one bloody clash French and American sailors went after each other with dirks, or daggers. A French privateer was burned to the water's edge, and an armed mob fired on the sailors. Before order was restored, two Americans and three Frenchmen died, others were injured, and more than one hundred persons were arrested.

The riot became an international incident. The French government ordered its consul to leave Savannah. The City Council released the French sailors from jail, publicly apologized for the incident, and brought indictments against eleven citizens for murder. The incident reflected both local and national hostility toward foreign depredations, which soon brought war.[150]

Concern over the possibility of slave unrest continued. In 1810 the Savannah government reprimanded a local booksellers, Messrs. Maure and Huron, for the "impropriety" of selling a book entitled *An Historical Journal of the Revolution of St. Domingo*. It was feared that the book might be read by free blacks and inspire them to launch insurrections locally.[151] The incident underscored the paranoia of white Savannahians.

SOCIAL AND INTELLECTUAL LIFE

Opportunities for private instruction in various subjects abounded in Savannah. Schools for affluent young women prepared them for both the domestic arts—the three R's and needlework—and such "polite" accomplishments as French, dancing, and music. The wealthy also employed private tutors.[152] For those unable to attend day school, twenty-nine evening schools offered courses for apprentices and older tradesmen from the 1790s to 1812. Many instructors held degrees from British or European universities.[153]

Education in leisure activities was also available to Savannah's well-to-do white males and females. Twenty-four teachers offered vocal music, piano, or flute in the city from 1790 to 1812. Horseback riding, dancing, and fencing were taught.[154] Such courses kept pace with the rising affluence in the city. Indeed, a visitor to Savannah in 1808 from the rural upcountry was shocked to observe that "pleasure and dissipation seems . . . to have engrossed the minds of the young [with] little attention paid to . . . useful acquirements."[155] A year later, a young and studious attorney, Daniel Mulford, remarked sarcastically to his relatives that "to get money-dance-gamble-run horses" were the "amusements" for Savannah gentlemen; "amusements" for the local ladies were to "spend money-play piano-contemplate their own beauty."[156]

Wealthy white Savannahians did enjoy displays of wealth, dances, and parties. The Exchange Building provided space for Bachelors' Balls during the "season," December through March. Thomas Telfair told his brother in January 1806: Savannah "is more gay this winter than it has been for many past. Balls in profusion. I went to three in one week." Some of "those who move in the fashionable sphere of Savannah . . . have no character at all," he observed, while others "unite intelligence of mind with elegance of manners." He detected little difference "in the manners or appearance of Southern girls from the North except that the first are more fond of dress & show."[157]

Ice to preserve food for some of Savannah's fetes was imported from the north by merchants such as William Scarbrough.[158] One of the city's great entrepreneurs and a charter member of the Chamber of Commerce, which was formed on December 13, 1806, Scarbrough was accumulating a fortune in merchandising, land, and slaves. He and his wife, Julia—described as "a beautiful wit and belle"—became Savannah's renowned host and hostess. Some called their parties "blowouts." On one occasion Julia invited five hundred people to a party at their Broughton Street home. One newcomer to the city marveled at the local social whirl: "we hear ladies with families . . . boast of having been out to parties 10 nights in succession . . . until three o'clock in the morning."[159] Another observed that the "ruling characteristic" of the local gentry was "to get money and display it in a fashionable hospitality."[160] A few years later a female guest at a 4:00 P.M. dinner noted a similar emphasis on wealth and ostentatious display: "plates were changed seven times and wine glasses five," and the hostess announced the price "at every new decanter." Another visitor observed: "The luxury of this city, as exhibited at dinners, is very great."[161]

The dances, parties, and dinners given within Savannah's upper crust during the social season and on a regular basis were another socializing and humanizing manifestation of the life of cities and, in particular, Savannah. The social whirl was a way to bring together the "right" young people to meet others of their own wealth and status, and it was a way for the elite to attempt to perpetuate their hegemony in the social, political, and economic circles of Savannah and the region.

The growing wealth and the desire of Savannahians to display it attracted portrait artists such as William and Nicholas Boudet, recently arrived from Europe. Rembrandt Peale visited the city briefly in 1804 and was followed by the highly acclaimed Edward Greene Malbone, who painted, died, and was buried in Savannah.[162] Only several decades later could Savannahians of modest means afford a portraitist such as Peter Laurens, a native of the city and apparently self-taught painter, who painted Gilbert Butler, a builder of middling means, and his wife, Jane.[163]

There was also a life of the mind in Savannah usually not found in the southern countryside. Well-to-do white Savannahians especially enjoyed a vibrant intellectual life through their clubs and societies, their newspapers, and their taverns and churches. The city's first club for poetry and music, the Anacreontic Society, was organized in 1804 and modeled after a London organization of the same name. The Georgia Agricultural Society was founded in the early 1800s, as was an Evening Club for dinning, which brought together prominent gentiles and Jews for socializing and conversation.

By the early 1800s about a dozen Jewish families lived in the city, among them the "first families"—the Cohens, Minises, and Sheftalls. Jewish families from Georgetown and Charleston, South Carolina—such as the Cohens, Hertzs, Levys, Myers, and Solomons—married one another or married into the progeny of Savannah's original Jewish settlers, which over time brought South Carolina Jews to Savannah. Their family lineage and their century-long residence in Savannah, their adoption of southern attitudes and behavior, their slave ownership, which solidified their racial status, and the honor ethic—all accounted for the ready acceptance of Savannah's Jews by the city's gentiles. Most of these Jewish men pursued professional or white-collar business opportunities and aspired to the wealth and status of the urban bourgeoisie, which their Christian neighbors respected. By being actively involved in social, intellectual, and benevolent organizations and politics, Savannah's Jews remained in daily contact with the gentile majority.[164]

The educated and well-to-do such as Dr. Lemuel Kollock and Daniel Mulford collected books on a variety of topics in English, Greek, and Latin. Others—some eighty-one citizens notable in the bar, pulpit, medicine, and politics—who wanted access to more books and a reading room, organized the Savannah Library Society in 1809. Each bought a "share" in the library and agreed to pay $10.00 annually. A librarian was appointed, and within several years the members could choose from over 1,100 volumes in the Library Room above Messrs. Seymour and Williams' Book Stores. The holdings reflected a library for the cultured and learned. The society eventually merged with the Georgia Historical Society, which two prominent Jews, Solomon Cohen and his brother-in-law, Mordecai Myers, helped establish. Both practiced law and served in the state legislature.[165]

By the early 1800s bookstores on Whitaker and Bay Streets offered a wide variety of reading materials. The bookstores most likely offered for sale one of the first plays and first histories written and printed locally, "The Mysterious Father: A Tragedy in Five Acts," by Savannahian William Bulloch Maxwell, and Hugh McCall's *History of Georgia,* published in Savannah in 1811. Several years later a periodical titled the *Ladies' Magazine* appeared, but like most periodicals of the day, it survived only briefly.

A group of young men, led by John M. Berrien, Thomas Young, and J. Bond Read, organized the Savannah Literary Society in the early 1800s for the purpose of "the cultivation of literature." Members presented compositions to encourage "literary excellence" and "scientific research."[166]

The newspapers of Savannah promoted culture by publishing literary and poetical essays. Keepers of Savannah's taverns and inns asked sea captains to donate any foreign newspapers for customers. The Exchange Coffee House provided a collection of the "best public journals" and newspapers for their customers, who gathered there to read, eat, drink, and talk.[167]

Five weekly or semiweekly papers of several pages each circulated in Savannah during the early 1800s; after 1809 only two survived, the *Republican* and the *Columbian Museum.* Sometimes bitter political and personal attacks surfaced in the press. For instance, a writer in the *Republican* in 1812 called the editor of a Philadelphia newspaper "a Schoat," adding that there "is a Negro-Fellow in our city, called Monkey Jack, that has forgotten more than ever you remembered."[168]

In 1810 the New England Society of Georgia was holding meetings in the Exchange Building. Such an organization was not unusual. One visitor to the city noted that almost half of Savannah's white businessmen had immigrated from the North.[169]

A group of public-spirited men who were drama lovers met to form Friends to the Drama in 1810. They attempted to raise funds to build a theater; although they were unsuccessful, interest persisted.[170] Members of a whist club who rented a room in the Exchange Building and met weekly for gaming, discussions, and drinks switched their meeting place to the Georgia Hotel after it opened in 1812. Washington Hall, a larger hotel, opened that same year at the corner of Jefferson and Bay Streets. It came to rival the popular hostelry on the Bay, Gunn's Tavern.

Local ministers contributed to the intellectual life of Savannah through publications and sermons. The Reverend Henry Holcombe briefly edited the first religious periodical published in Savannah and the state. Lutheran pastor John Bergman, a graduate of a German university, studied languages and history. The minister of the Presbyterian Church, Dr. Henry Kollock, who took his degree at Princeton, lectured on topics from manners to doctrinal matters. Despite the eloquence and brilliance of such ministers, however, some churchgoers occasionally dozed in their pews.[171] With the exception of a few other southern cities, Savannah's social and intellectual life was unrivaled in the South.

REVIVALISM AND CATHOLICISM

Revivalism invigorated the Methodist Church. A visitor in Savannah in the early 1800s heard the Methodist preacher, "with furious looks and vehement gesticulations," condemn the congregation as "sinners unless they were born again in faith." Some appeared "on the point of fainting away, or going into hysterics." From some came "groans and screams."[172]

At a cost of $5,000 the Methodists built a church on the northeast corner of Lincoln and South Broad Streets, the latter subsequently renamed Oglethorpe Street. It was named Wesley Chapel, after John Wesley, Savannah's first Anglican priest and a founder of Methodism. Revivalism attracted both whites and African Americans. Within twenty years membership exceeded six hundred, about equally divided between blacks and whites.[173] Apparently, more blacks attended Wesley Chapel than any other white-led church in Savannah.

The Roman Catholic congregation of St. John the Baptist outgrew its small wood-framed structure on Liberty Square and received from the City Council a site in Elbert Ward on which to build a larger church. From the earliest times the congregation included both slave and free "people of color." In the first several decades of the nineteenth century, priests conducted marriage ceremonies for no fewer than sixty-two blacks at St. John's. But during church services, blacks, a minority within a minority, were relegated to the gallery.

In 1812, on the day of the Feast of St. Patrick, March 17, forty-four prosperous gentlemen founded the Hibernian Society. Most of the members immigrated years before from Ulster and included Protestants and Roman Catholics. These bourgeois "gentlemen" had little in common with the hundreds of "Paddys" and "Bridgets" who later immigrated to Savannah. But the celebration of St. Patrick's Day brought them all together. It was an affair that helped shape Irish-American life in Savannah.

The annual celebration usually began with an early morning business meeting and the election of officers for the year, including a committee to aid needy Irish. Members next paraded through the streets, and crowds of onlookers sporting shamrocks cheered. The marchers ended at the St. John's Catholic Church, where they attended Mass and heard a lengthy oration. In the evening the celebrants reassembled for the annual banquet, notorious for its ample supplies of whiskey, food, "wit . . . and song." A banquet speaker usually paid tribute to Ireland's glorious past and raised toasts to Savannah, the state, and the Union. This ritual, a day-long celebration of the Feast of St. Patrick, affirmed Irish life and demonstrated community solidarity. It was one of the ways that the leading Catholic families served as "cultural mediators" between Savannah's Catholics and Protestants and prevented sectarian violence, which erupted in other southern and in northern cities.[174]

Savannah's prominent Catholics also supported benevolent and cultural institutions and participated in local politics. Although many of the Irish poor who later immigrated found lodging on the extreme eastern and western fringes of Savannah, the first- and second-generation Irish-Catholic elite— about fifty-seven families, or 52 percent of the city's Catholics—built homes on Bull Street and nearby thoroughfares. Here the Dillons, Pendergasts, Gaudrys, O'Byrnes, Reillys, Bloises, and Guilmartins resided and became interconnected through business, baptisms, and marriage. The city's well-to-do Protestants held the leading Catholic families in high regard, while the Irish poor remained the butt of demeaning jokes. Some lamented that the average Irish immigrant was hated for his poverty, worn out prematurely by hard work, "and the victim of his own folly."[175]

THE WAR OF 1812

After years of British ships seizing American merchant ships, their crews, and their cargoes on the high seas, feelings for and against war intensified across the country. In 1807 when a British ship fired on the United States frigate *Chesapeake* off Norfolk, Savannah officials angrily denounced the "piratical outrage." Powerful local politician Edward Telfair lobbied for "ten or twelve Gallies [and] five thousand stand of arms" to protect the city; Savannah's council provided funds for gunpowder and additional cannons for Fort Wayne.[176] Savannah's nine militia units and volunteer corps paraded and drilled constantly in preparation, "should the tocsin of war be sounded." Young men joined the units for social reasons, invasion fears, and a desire to intimidate the city's blacks. A local citizen noted that Savannah was "a Garrison Town."[177]

In the face of British insults on the high seas, President James Madison asked Congress for a declaration of war on Great Britain on June 1, 1812. In Savannah the Federalist mouthpiece, *American Patriot,* attacked the "fumbling" foreign policies of Madison, while the *Republican and Savannah Evening Ledger* defended them. As Congress debated, tensions in the city escalated with the war of words between the newspapers. At a public meeting of anti-war Federalists on June 4, pro-war Republicans called for support of President Madison. John S. Mitchell, editor of the *American Patriot,* on June 5 angrily criticized the conduct of the Republicans. Denounced for his views, Mitchell was dragged from his home and into the street where, he recalled, "a large mob, the very filthy dregs of Democracy," beat him. On June 8 Mitchell shut down his newspaper permanently. He had nearly died, and Georgia's Federalist party all but died, too, on June 18 when Congress declared war on Great Britain. Savannah's anti-war minority and freedom of the press succumbed to mob violence.[178]

The war hurt local commerce; British ships cruised off the coast, threatening merchant vessels. In December 1813 a former Savannah mayor, William B. Bulloch, remarked that there was no demand for rice: "I have not sold a barrel." Rice cultivation was curtailed in a most productive area, St. Peter's Parish, South Carolina, on the lower Savannah River and adjacent to the city of Savannah.[179]

A trickle of imports continued. In late 1812 brigs and ships brought in cargoes from Havana and Liverpool consigned to such Savannah merchants as Andrew Low. Hoes, linens and woolens, "segars," sugar and coffee, Madeira wines, hogsheads of fish, flour, barrels of limes and oranges, earthenware, kegs of nails and spikes, boxes of window glass, shot, and lead crammed their holds.[180]

Savannah's defenses could not have thwarted a British invasion because there was no fortification on Cockspur Island after the hurricane of 1804. Savannah's City Council did authorize the use of federal money and slave labor to rebuild Fort Wayne on the eastern fringe of the city; three miles below Savannah, Fort Jackson, named after politician General James Jackson, was hurried to completion, and eight cannons were mounted there. Temporarily, the Chatham Artillery and several free blacks garrisoned the fort. Money was raised to purchase boats to patrol the river.

Word spread in March 1813 that the British planned to seize Savannah. The

City Council asked the governor for more troops, and at a public meeting on June 1 citizens authorized raising $4,000 for defense. A corps of volunteer riflemen arrived from the upcountry, and the old filature was turned into a hospital for soldiers.[181]

On the evening of July 13 an attempt "was made to set fire to the city," and the mayor subsequently offered a reward for the arrest of the arsonists. The City Council created "Committees of Vigilance" to alert officials about any "idle and disorderly persons." The government asked all citizens to be "alert at . . . night to detect . . . the designs of felons and incendiaries." In August, the council ordered the city constable and officers of the guard to arrest and detain all idle slaves until claimed by their owners. The following year the council reorganized the city's firefighting companies.[182]

In October Savannahians celebrated the "glorious" victory of Oliver Hazard Perry on Lake Erie with a parade, cannon blasts, and bell ringing; in early February 1814 parades and cannon fire saluted another American victory.[183] But in May panic replaced the cheering when a British fleet appeared off Georgia's coast. Two hundred soldiers under the command of British Admiral Alexander Cockrane plundered Georgia's sea islands. People fled Savannah. Some white females were especially fearful. Mary Telfair breathlessly told a friend about a rumor that "the British have landed a large force consisting of two thousand blacks on Cumberland Island," some seventy miles south of Savannah. She continued: "it is reasonable to expect that Savannah the emporium of the State will not escape[.] The inhuman . . . [British] commander . . . is dreaded for no doubt a number of slaves will flock to his standard."[184]

Savannah's mayor informed the local militia and the U.S. frigate stationed at Tybee Island to prepare to defend the city. Despite the threat of invasion, however, July 4, 1814, was celebrated locally with the usual military hoopla, a parade, and patriotic orations. Curiously, during the parade black musicians dropped out of the procession.[185] Their refusal to participate was perhaps an attempt to demonstrate the paradox of slavery and the celebration of independence.

In September the City Council called on the patriotism of all citizens to help build Savannah's defenses.[186] The council borrowed $10,000 from the Planter's Bank, and it was expected that nearby planters would furnish slave labor; the council required free blacks to work on the fortifications for fourteen days. Within a few months a line of breastworks was underway to link major strong points near the jail, the Thunderbolt Road, and Spring Hill.

Following an appeal for troops by Savannah's mayor, Georgia's governor dispatched a force to the city headed by General John Floyd; Commodore Hugh G. Campbell commanded the U.S. flotilla there. But work on the defenses lagged, and the city government asked the newspapers to publish the names of all persons who failed to demonstrate their patriotism by working on Savannah's defenses.[187] Mary Telfair also noted that "the fortifications progress slowly . . . there is a great want of public spirit with us." She believed that the war had "altered" Savannah and told a friend: "Once characters of respectability were at the head of affairs, but now [the city] is ruled by a sett of *Yankees* who have come hither for the purpose of *gain*."[188]

In January 1815 the council issued a report stating that "some citizens have contributed liberally, others sparingly, and others nothing at all" to the war effort. Therefore, the council advised General Floyd to enforce "involuntary service"; the city marshal was authorized to impress all horses needed to finish the fortifications.[189]

Unaware that the Treaty of Ghent was signed on Christmas Eve 1814 ending the war, British Admiral Sir George Cockburn sent Royal Marines ashore to seize Georgia's southernmost barrier beach, Cumberland Island, on January 10, 1815. Notorious for ordering the burning of the nation's Capitol the year before, Cockburn was especially feared. In Savannah, William B. Bulloch reasoned that invasion was eminent as "The enemy are now in full possession of St. Mary's." Bulloch also observed that the local economy was moribund. On January 15 he wrote: "I have no means of purchasing [Negroes] . . . and no sale at any price for rice, it will be all I shall be able to do to support my . . . family." [190] That same day Georgia's governor received the news that "Our state is invaded . . . *and the enemy have black troops with them*"; and under these unique "circumstances," he ordered General Floyd at Savannah to march "towards the points invaded"[191] (emphasis added). Savannah's government immediately ordered vessels sunk in the river to prevent the enemy from reaching the city.[192] The business community remained fearful of a British attack in February, by which time local merchants had removed most of their merchandise to Augusta. Mary Shaffer of Savannah was "expecting the enemy every moment. . . . we are on the half-run."[193]

After news of the peace treaty reached Savannah, Mayor Matthew McAllister designated March 4 as a day of recreation, parades, speeches, and music. During the evening celebration the mayor ordered the police "to patrol the streets and be vigilant in keeping order."[194] The city government soon commemorated battles by naming two city squares after America's great victories in the War of 1812, Chippewa and Orleans Squares, and by naming streets after naval heroes, such as Hull, McDonough, and Perry Streets.[195] The war spawned a new, spread-eagle nationalism locally and nationally, and a postbellum, nationwide expansion quickly got underway.

CHAPTER 5

From Boom to Bust,
1815–1840

PUBLIC AND PRIVATE BENEVOLENCE

*B*EFORE THE WAR ENDED, the trustees of Chatham Academy erected a brick schoolhouse on lower Bull Street and in a wing of the building the Union Society helped educate the poor white children of Savannah. The society raised funds to cover the costs of the children's tuition and supplies. In little over a decade two hundred male and female students matriculated at Chatham Academy in segregated rooms; they included the white sons and daughters of the city's "best people." One such student, William Basinger, recalled that an instructor, the Reverend George White, "used to give us terrible whippings . . . deserved or not."[1]

In 1816 Thomas F. Williams left an estate that in 1832 established the Georgia Infirmary "for the relief and protection of aged and afflicted negroes." It was the first public hospital for blacks in the United States. Apparently, the infirmary was not popular with blacks. On the eve of the Civil War, only one elderly black resided there, and the hospital soon closed its doors.[2]

Following the War of 1812, destitute white women without husbands or hope, and clutching the hands of their children, trudged back to Savannah. To provide for these poor females, the Dorcas Society was founded in 1816. It provided food and clothing for indigent white women. Several years later the Widow's Society was established to assist widowed and single white women of "good characters." It was expected that those receiving charity from either society demonstrate piety and humility.[3]

The Savannah Free School Society was established by a group of ladies "to rescue" indigent white children "from ignorance and vice" and make them "useful members of society." The school opened in 1817 with one teacher and about forty students. Instruction emphasized middle-class values.[4]

Within a few years the number of children attending the school increased to almost two hundred. The City Council granted a lot at the southeast corner of Whitaker and Perry Streets to build the Savannah Free School, and in 1820 a Mr. Cooper was in charge of the school. The female directors applauded his ability to preserve "order and decorum" while "instilling the principles of morality and religion."[5] By 1820, one-third of the white female population of Savannah age twenty-one and under received charity from the Free School or the Female Asylum, which reveals the extent of poverty as well as charity within the city.[6] The founding of the Dorcas Society, the Widow's Society, and the Free School Society also reflected the humanizing and socializing influences of city life and demonstrated that Savannah's well-to-do white females found forums for self-expression in addition to the churches.[7]

There was charity for white mariners also. In 1817 Archibald S. Bulloch, the collector of customs at Savannah, began seeking federal funds for "Sick and Disabled Seamen." He did receive some federal money for a marine hospital, but initially he failed to convince the commissioners of the city's poorhouse and hospital to accept "sick sailors."[8]

PUBLIC HEALTH AND CIVIC IMPROVEMENTS

The health of the city continued to decline and contributed to the unwillingness of people to reside or conduct business in Savannah. Savannahians who could afford to left the city during the summer months. But Savannah escaped epidemic disease until "the sickly season" of 1816, when rumors spread that six to ten people died each day. The city government initially denied the reports but soon became alarmed at the "unusual mortality." The aldermen worried that such news might lend credence to the already "unfavorable" opinions of the healthiness of the city.

The following year smallpox spread throughout Savannah, and those diagnosed with the disease spent time quarantined in the city's poorhouse and hospital. Apparently, medical facilities became so jammed during the epidemic that the city authorized the manager of the poorhouse and hospital to raise capital for a new one. Council members boasted that a new hospital and poorhouse would usher in a new era when "such beings as beggars should not be seen in our streets."[9] Councilmen mixed humaneness and charity to serve their own interests.

The new building was erected on Gaston Street, which was distant from the city's center. Costs soared to nearly $30,000 by mid-1819 when it was completed. For years the Savannah Poor House and Hospital—by this time referred to as the Marine Hospital since large numbers of sailors resided there, too—remained underfunded, its meager resources drained by the large number of ill indigents.[10] Many of the inmates had been born abroad or in other states. A register of deaths of thirty-three persons during one month in the 1820s indicates the place of birth of the inmates: British Isles (14), Europe (2), Georgia and other states (12), and Savannah (5).[11]

At a public meeting convened in March 1817 to discuss the unhealthiness of Savannah, a dry culture program was agreed upon. This meant draining the low-lying rice fields and marshes around the city to prevent fever-causing "miasmas," or vapors, arising from decaying vegetation. This contemporary medical theory was propounded by one of Savannah's most respected physicians, Dr. William R. Waring. The City Council decided that the huge sum of $200,000 was needed to implement the program, and it authorized raising the funds through a bond issue; civic leaders who promoted a healthier city also donated money. The government contracted with property owners to drain their lands, and canal digging began across hundreds of acres of land, especially on Hutchinson Island opposite the city. Savannah officials subsidized planters not to grow rice but to plant crops requiring only dry conditions within a mile of the city. This dry-culture program or "sanative cordon" around Savannah was a singularly unique effort in health planning among southern cities. But, of course, fevers and deaths continued, and some citizens criticized the dry-culture program as useless and too expensive.[12]

To eliminate the costs of examinations and drugs for the needy, the city established a dispensary modeled after Charleston's. Local medical opinion also concluded that long-term residence in the city helped to prevent persons from contracting disease during "the sickly season."

Beautification of the city resumed after the war. Saplings were planted along Abercorn Street, trees were trimmed, dead ones were removed, and the squares were fenced and regularly maintained.[13] Visitors repeatedly remarked on the pleasing design of the city.

Savannah's government and its citizens remained committed to new construction in the beginning years of the nineteenth century. In 1816 city authorities set aside two lots on Chippewa Square for a theater to help "beautify and advantage" the city. The congregation of the Independent Presbyterian Church, the oldest Presbyterian Church in Georgia, began the construction of a new large sanctuary on the corner of Bull and South Broad Streets immediately after the war and dedicated it in 1819.[14]

THE CITY'S INFORMAL ECONOMIES

On Sundays the sandy streets of Savannah were crowded with slaves from nearby plantations who came to hawk vegetables, meat, fish, shrimp, and shellfish for their owners and themselves. As had been the case for years, the numbers of slaves and their trading practices troubled some wealthy white Savannahians.[15] Only slaves who displayed a badge purchased by their owners from the city could sell goods legally. But owners, slaves, and Savannahians who wanted fresh meat, fish, and produce often ignored the law. Slaves sold illegally about $100,000 worth of products annually in the early 1800s and monopolized the trade in poultry and eggs.

Poor white vendors, primarily shopkeepers, may have been divided over the illicit trade. Most likely they unanimously opposed any efforts to restrict their own very lucrative trade with slaves in liquor and tobacco. It was a collaboration of poor whites and blacks for their own economic self-interest. These "informal slave economies" provided blacks with a sense of purpose, dignity, and, more practically, money. Nevertheless, some white consumers were angered by the illicit trade and wanted it prohibited.[16]

African American women constituted the majority of the vendors. Beginning in the early 1800s, these black females began to be described as immoral. For instance, it was rumored that the female slaves who hawked goods in the public market dressed well, not because of the money they took in from the sale of vegetables, but from the sale of sex. But descriptions of slave dress varied. One New Yorker, Whitman Mead, who visited Savannah in 1817, saw slaves "half naked and half starved." Another traveler, Emily Burke, observed that slaves, especially on holidays, "dress extravagantly and decorate their persons with . . . costly jewelry." The *Savannah Republican* remarked that female servants appeared almost as well dressed as their mistresses.[17]

A writer in the local press in 1817 who identified himself as "ANTI-MULATTO" criticized black female vendors for monopolizing the sale of market commodities and lashed out at their sexual promiscuity. "ANTI-MULATTO" warned that their sexual appetites are "apt to vitiate the morals and dilapidate the constitutions of young [white] men." He urged whites to avoid sex with black women since it threatened marriage and the family, the very foundations of white society. He urged the city government to prevent such "wenches" from selling in the market and from renting rooms "for the accommodation of the tastey white souls that feed on the fragrance of muskey blankets." Almost since the founding of Savannah, biracial sexual unions existed. Some were exploitive and others loving. Whatever his motives, "ANTI-MULATTO'S" accusations enlivened a continuing debate.[18]

ENFORCING THE LAWS

Efforts to control the growing number of slaves and free blacks in Savannah resulted in the passage of discriminatory ordinances: it was illegal for blacks to own dogs, smoke in public, gamble, or consume alcohol. Blacks appeared more frequently than whites before the mayor's court, which tried cases involving gambling, disorderly conduct, and public drunkenness. The Chatham County Superior Court and the Chatham Country Inferior Court tried major crimes.[19]

Visitors to Savannah noticed heavy drinking among the city's slaves. Influential local slaveholders continued to complain that sales of liquor to blacks by white shopkeepers were "great and growing."[20] The local paper condemned inebriation because it "desecrates the Sabbath," sets a bad example for children, and fills the jail.[21] The Sabbatarians believed that open shops and an open public market on Sunday violated local laws, God's authority, public morality, and the city's reputation. They collected 250 signatures on a petition, which complained of the "public violation of the Holy Sabbath."[22] But these occasional attempts to prevent shopkeepers from selling liquor to blacks failed once again. Prominent white Savannahians especially opposed liquor sales because they believed that the liquor purchased was paid for with items stolen from them by slaves, sometimes their own slaves, which was sometimes the case. One lowcountry visitor characterized the attitude of local bondpeople to the property of their masters as "I belong to massa, all massa has belongs to me."[23]

It was the responsibility of the Savannah Watch to enforce the laws. In 1820 Peter Shields was the superintendent of a watch of thirty-seven who received a dollar a day. The monthly pay was only six dollars each for Will, the drummer, and Tom, the fifer, most likely African Americans.[24] Thefts by slaves were a special problem for Superintendent Shields.

When arrested for stealing, some slaves remarked that they did not steal anything; they simply took an item from their white families because they had that right. About half of the slaves charged with robbery who appeared before the Chatham County Inferior Court from 1813 to 1825 were found guilty. Earlier convicted felons most likely would have been hanged, but by the early 1800s the usual punishment was 39 to 117 lashes on the bare back laid on at the rate of 39 daily. The whippings took place in public until the end of the 1820s, when the punishment was moved to the jail yard and hidden from view. But one visitor to Savannah observed "runaway slaves dragged to" the jail "with their hands tied behind them" by white men "who made free use of the lash."[25]

One mulatto slave, William Grimes, who was confined to the jail for attempting to escape from Savannah and his master, existed on a quart of boiled corn daily. He saw a large slave, himself a prisoner, use a rawhide whip to beat one woman "till blood ran freely"; he saw Reuben, a slave belonging to John Bolton, receive 39 stripes three times a week "till he looked like a ploughed field." After being released from jail, Grimes was bought by Archibald Bulloch, collector of customs at Savannah. His new owner soon accused Grimes of stealing his wine; Bulloch beat him with his fists and sent him back to jail. Upon release, Grimes met some free black sailors, crew members of a brig out of Boston, and talked them into hiding him aboard. This time Grimes escaped to the north, where he became a free man.[26] But such an escape was rare.

In Savannah most of the violent crime was committed by blacks on blacks. Although proven capital offenses—murder, rape, and arson—by blacks against whites occurred only infrequently, the perpetrators paid for the acts with their lives.[27] Despite the many humanizing influences of city life flowing from private and public institutions and interracial relations, violence and brutality were also commonplace in nineteenth-century southern cities.

STEAMBOATS ON THE SAVANNAH

In early 1816, Samuel Howard of Savannah, Georgia's promoter of steam navigation, launched the *Enterprise,* which was built by John Watts at his Savannah shipyard and which had engines designed and installed by a Philadelphian. The vessel weighed 152 tons; it was 90 feet long by 20 feet wide; its engines generated power "equal to . . . 32 horses." When the boat was launched, the press declared "she moved beautifully through the water. . . . Our enter-prising townsmen have our very best wishes." Savannahians were urged to sup-port such business ventures for the prosperity of the city.

Appropriately named, the *Enterprise* became the first steamboat operated as a commercial success.[28] In 1817 Howard received a charter from the state to or-ganize the Steam Boat Company of Georgia. Within three years the company added seven more steam vessels.[29]

To provide docking space for their new boats, the company spent $100,000 buying four wharf lots. The steamboats soon made regularly scheduled runs up the Savannah to Augusta, to Charleston, and along the Altamaha.[30] The wood-burning boats drew only three to four feet of water, and there was always the threat of explosion or collision. One tourist observed: "A prudent man makes his will before he goes on board."[31]

It was usually only in southern cities such as Savannah that the entrepre-neurs, the capital, and the skilled labor were brought together to produce new, successful services for the general population.

FROM GOOD TIMES TO HARD TIMES

The furious pace of steamboat building reflected the postwar economic boom. By 1817, poleboats, soon to be replaced by steamboats, carried to Savannah thousands of bales of cotton from Augusta and timber from sawmills along the river. Timber also arrived by "rickety timber raft[s] floating down river with a man at either end plying a 'large rude oar' to keep it in mid-stream," an Eng-lishman observed.[32]

To rip the timber brought down the river, speculators operated the first steam-powered sawmill on Savannah's waterfront. It was the first of several sawmills that helped make Savannah "the lumber center of the South Atlantic" coast.

One of the largest lumberyards in the city by 1818 was owned by W. H. Gilliand and R. G. Taylor. Two years later, Andrew Low, an Englishman, opened a dry goods store and acted as a lumber factor with a yard near his store. Within a decade some lumber yards regularly stocked up to 1,200,000 feet of lumber.

Postwar Savannah experienced a dramatic upsurge in exports. In mid-December 1818 alone, six vessels jammed with cotton sailed for Liverpool to meet the demands of its looms. The price of cotton was high, and some enjoyed the good life. Exports from Savannah exceeded $14,000,000 in 1818, an increase of 600 percent since 1800; during the first nine months of 1819, lumber exports reached $65,000. The river and the port propelled the city's economic life.[33]

Savannahians, like other Americans during the speculative postwar commercial boom, focused little on culture and much on money grubbing, according to John M. Harney, who in 1818 began selling subscriptions to his fledgling paper, the *Savannah Georgian*. But failing to sell enough to sustain the publication, Harney soon left the city with an angry, poetic blast, "A Farewell to Savannah":

> Farewell, oh, Savannah, forever farewell,
> Thou hot bed of rogues, thou threshold of hell,
> Where Satan has fixed his headquarters on earth,
> And outlaws integrity, wisdom and worth,
> Where villainy thrives and where honesty begs,
> Where folly is purse-proud, and wisdom in rags;
> Where man is worth nothing, except in one sense,
> Which they always compute in pounds, shillings and pence;
> Where the greatest freeholder is a holder of slaves,
> And he that has most, about freedom most raves,
> Where they'd worship a calf, if like Aaron of Old,
> Where the Devil may reign, if his sceptre be gold;
> Where against knavery is constantly bawling,
> For they seldom agree who pursue the same calling.
> With bailiffs he drives every rogue from the town,
> Determined to put all competitors down;
> Where even the churches, subservient to gain,
> Are bought in by stock-jobbers, to sell out again.
> Each pew is a lucrative turnpike to heaven,
> At which an exorbitant toll must be given.
> At fifty percent, you must purchase salvation,
> And the rich have monopolized all that's in fashion.
> When the most approved tests of a gentleman are
> The taste of his wine and his Spanish segar;
> If these recommend, he's a gentleman sure,
> Though a fool, or a rogue, whether Christian or Moor.
> Where your friend must compute, ere he asks you to dine,
> First your value to him, then the cost of his wine,

Then, if it appears he will not be a Winner,
to the Devil you may go—not to him—for a Dinner.
When the girls cannot tell, if they win you they'd wed you
Without pencil and slate to subtract and to add to.
They make a shrewd bargain miscalled matrimony—
'Tis a mercantile business, a matter of money;
For union in wedlock, in friendship, and trade,
Are alike by the rules of arithmetic made.
Each nation is marked by some national crime,
Which is charged as the first of the soil or the clime.
But the soil of Savannah new vigor imparts,
To vices transplanted from all foreign parts.
Cursed be the winds that blew me to your strand;
Yours houses are board, and your alleys are sand!
Oh, still may your beds be the moss from your trees!
Long life to your bed-bugs, the same to your fleas!
May all your free citizens, wealthy or poor,
Be bribed by their votes, as they have heretofore!
May every quack doctor be patronized still,
And his talents be judged by the length of his bill;
May all your quack lawyers find themes for their tongues,
And their brains get the applause that is due to their lungs;
May your miserly merchants still cheat for their pence,
And, with scarce any brains, show a good deal of cents!
Now, to finish my curses upon your ill city,
And express in few words all the sums of my ditty,
I leave you, Savannah—a curse that is far
The worst of all curses—to remain as you are![34]

Mary Telfair also noticed the local scramble for the almighty dollar. She told a friend in June 1818: "I think . . . the South . . . is only fit *for money mak-ing.*" Mary found the "gay . . . winter . . . balls, & card partys" tiresome. She longed to find a group she could "admire for their mental endowments."[35]

New construction in Savannah accompanied the postwar economic boom. The opportunity to build a theater arrived with English architect William Jay in December 1817, and its promoters hired him immediately. Jay's family and business connections with the Boltons and Richardsons probably lured him to Savannah. Jay's theater went up on a corner of what became Chippewa Square. Upon completion, a writer in the *Georgian* described it as belonging "to the

Grecian order of architecture." One thousand seats formed a semicircle around the stage. Theatergoers looked down from two tiers of box seats featuring paintings of nude female figures, which offended some Savannahians.[36]

Prominent men of property served as trustees of the Savannah Theater. The first theatrical season opened on December 4, 1818, under the management of Charles Gilfert, who brought his Charleston Theater Company to Savannah. The plays performed during the next half-century included those written by Shakespeare, but most of the plays produced were written by nineteenth-century English playwrights. For the evening performances, oil lamps illuminated the theater until gaslights replaced them in the 1850s. The cost of admission ranged from $1 for a box seat to 50 cents for the gallery. Initially, all classes and castes attended, although prostitutes were discouraged, and African Americans had to sit in a segregated section in the gallery. Criticisms of blacks attending the theater during the first season led Gilfert to prohibit them the following year, but they were readmitted a few seasons later. If managers wished to have a profitable theater in a city nearly 50 percent black, it made little sense to exclude African Americans.[37] But city ordinances in the late 1820s did exclude blacks from certain public arenas. One law forbid "colored persons [from] the public promenade in South Broad street" to protect white "Citizens . . . from molestation or intrusion of improper persons."[38]

There was no lack of acclaim or criticism of plays presented during the first season. A humorous description of the audience appeared in a letter to the *Savannah Georgian* from a "Bill Driggers," who wrote, "Thar was a monstrous sight of people and mightly likely gals, with powerful elegant dry-goods on." The writer disliked the constant "cracking and chomping" of nuts by the audience, which sounded like "a drove of hogs in the oakey woods in acorn season," and the music was performed by "a heap of fiddlers" who played some "clever jigs" but refused his request for "Possum up a Gum Tree," which led him to believe that "these low country quality knows nothing about good music." The writer was most likely a talented member of the *Georgian* staff with a good sense of humor and an ear for local dialect.[39] Apparently, most of the theatergoers enjoyed the cultural enrichment plays provided, although some disapproved of the effect on "public morals."[40] Jay's magnificent theater was destroyed by fire in 1948.

William Jay designed other public buildings: a customs house, the Bank of the United States, and perhaps the City Hotel. Jay was completing the brick, two-story customs house when the great fire of 1820 destroyed it. His best-known public building was the Savannah Branch of the Bank of the United States. Richard Richardson, a wealthy Savannahian and patron of Jay's, was the first president of the bank, which was built in the Classical Revival style on the eastern corner of Drayton and St. Julian Streets in 1820–1821. The bank was demolished in 1924.[41]

Jay probably assisted Eleazer and Jane Early in building the City Hotel, which began to go up in 1819 on the south side of Bay Street, between Bull and Whitaker Streets. The hotel became one of antebellum Savannah's social and commercial centers. It had thirty-three rooms, a large barroom, and reading, dining, and sitting rooms. When the City Hotel opened, the local press praised it as "magnificent and spacious." It still stands today, unoccupied and run-down, directly across from the modern Hyatt Regency.

When the City Hotel opened in January 1821, guests had an unobstructed view of the Savannah River. The City Hotel attracted ship passengers and officers and prominent Savannahians. It featured good drink and food— Madeira wine, turtle soup, and fins steaks. Fraternal organizations such as the St. Andrews Society met there for its annual fete. Here members raised thirteen toasts—at least one to "The King of Scotland," another to "the Bonny Lassies That Whirl among the Heather," and one to "The Memory of [Robert] Burns"—and ate what they described as "savory Haggis." The hotel's barroom became a popular rendezvous for nattily attired young blades known as the "sporting crowd," some of whom carried fancy knives in their belts.[42]

Jay's patron, Richard Richardson, commissioned him to build a home for the Richardson family. The mansion he designed was built on Oglethorpe Square, today 124 Abercorn Street. It was a two-story brick and stucco home over a basement, which incorporated both cast-iron construction and an advanced plumbing system. Today, the mansion is recognized as the best example of an American home built in the English Regency style and a rare early example of the Classical Revival style of architecture. The mansion was completed in 1819. The Richardsons furnished it with Grecian lamps, Brussels carpets, ottomans, marble baths, and Chinese floor stands. But tragedy stalked the family. Between completion of the mansion and 1822, Richardson lost his wife, his fortune, and his new mansion. Today it is known as the Richardson-Owens-Thomas House.[43]

While building the Richardson home, Jay was designing a showplace for William and Julia Scarbrough, which stands today at 41 Martin Luther King Jr. Boulevard. Scarbrough, a wealthy entrepreneur and planter, owned over

100,000 acres and four hundred slaves. His firm, Scarbrough and McKinne, imported a vast array of goods. Jay began work on the mansion in 1818 and completed it the following year. Soon after he and his family moved to the new home, Scarbrough, like Richard Richardson, encountered severe financial difficulties from which he never recovered.[44]

Alexander Telfair commissioned Jay to build a home for him, which was completed in 1819. As heir to his father's fortune, young Princeton-educated Telfair spent his life administering his father's extensive land holdings, collecting material objects, and serving on "charitable committees." The Telfair mansion was built on St. James' Square, today Telfair Square, at 121 Barnard Street.

The Telfair mansion bears a strong resemblance to features of the Scarbrough and Richardson homes. All three homes reflected both the English Regency and the emerging Classical Revival styles of architecture. Unlike the Scarbrough and Richardson families, the Telfairs increased their wealth and continued to reside in their mansion until 1875, when upon Mary Telfair's bequest it became the Telfair Academy of Arts and Sciences.[45]

Jay's mansions designed for the wealthy of Savannah are the finest concentration of his work anywhere. His architecture influenced Savannah's landscape, which, in turn, influenced both Savannahians and visitors, as did the city's design.[46] The humanizing effects of the architecture of his private mansions as well as his many public buildings, such as Jay's theater, exerted a profoundly civilizing influence on the city. Jay's architectural legacy must have uplifted the spirits and enhanced the senses of all Savannahians down through the years.

While Jay designed buildings in Savannah, at least twelve furniture craftsmen worked there. Many emigrated from England and built mahogany furniture from the design books of Hepplewhite and Sheraton. The firm of Faries and Miller advertised that they executed "orders for . . . Furniture in a style equal to any Northern City" and hoped to satisfy "those . . . disposed to encourage Savannah manufactories."[47] A number of Savannah-made pieces are still extant in the popular Federal Classical style of the age. But many pieces crafted in "the English taste"—tables, secretaries, chairs, and sideboards— came into Savannah from northern cities.[48]

More than two dozen silversmiths, watchmakers, and jewelers also opened businesses in Savannah in the first decades of the nineteenth century. They produced tea sets, porringers, and other practical and ornamental objects and also imported silver and jewelry for their customers. Fires, however, destroyed many of these items. The Savannah-made silver surviving today is primarily flatware and pieces of tea services.[49]

The silversmiths opened shops throughout the business district. Raimond Lenoirs, a jeweler from Paris who located on Broughton Street in 1818, advertised "a new method of Boaring the ears" of ladies. John F. Legoux, a watchmaker from Geneva, Switzerland, opened a watchmaking shop on Drayton Street and also performed "every operation in the Dental Art."[50]

Two of the most successful silversmiths and jewelers were Moses Eastman and Josiah Penfield. Eastman, a silversmith, served on the City Council and was a Unitarian. In 1819 Jared Sparks observed that a "handsome but not elegant Unitarian Church" existed in Savannah. However, funds left by Moses Eastman helped to build a more substantial brick and mortar Unitarian church. Since Unitarianism's stronghold was in New England, it is not surprising that Savannah's Unitarian congregation grew slowly and was composed primarily of transplanted New Englanders.

Connecticut-born Penfield (1785–1828) moved to Savannah and learned silversmithing from his uncle, Isaac Marquand, and soon became proprietor of his shop at Bryan and Whitaker Streets. Penfield served the local Baptist Church as a deacon, donated his time and money to local charitable organizations, and served on the City Council.[51] Marquand and Penfield, like many artisans, used slave apprentices and sometimes freed them. Apparently, they manumitted Shark Marquand, "a jeweler, and free person of color," who opened his own business.[52] Friendships of black slaves and whites in Savannah's workplaces benefited African Americans again and again and often resulted in their freedom.

President James Monroe arrived in Savannah on May 8, 1819, on an inspection tour of southern coastal defenses. The president's entourage, which included John C. Calhoun, secretary of war, was greeted by a twenty-one-gun salute. A formal reception was held at the new home of William and Julia Scarbrough. Monroe also attended the dedication of the newly constructed Independent Church in an area that was once Savannah's southern boundary. A journalist described the church as a "magnificent building."[53]

During Monroe's visit he boarded the steamship *Savannah* and inspected fortifications along the river. Constructed as a sailing packet in New York, the *Savannah,* a 130-foot by 26-foot vessel, was later converted to a steamer following its purchase for $50,000 by William Scarbrough and his newly organized Savannah Steamship Company. On May 12 a grand ball and dinner were given in a pavilion constructed in Johnson Square by William Jay. The following day Monroe departed, another twenty-one-gun salute ringing in his ears. The city spent $13,000 entertaining him.

On May 25 the *Savannah* prepared to depart for Liverpool, England. Entrepreneur and investor William Scarbrough told his wife, Julia, "I must go . . . as there is too much at stake . . . not to try and speedily do something with her to advantage." But Julia considered the trip too dangerous and prevailed. Scarbrough was not aboard for the voyage.[54] The *Savannah* crossed the Atlantic in twenty-seven days, the first steamship to do so. The voyage brought great notoriety to the city but financial disaster to Scarbrough, who had invested heavily in the venture. After the return of the steamship to the United States Scarbrough doubted that the *Savannah* would ever be a good investment since the engine and fuel occupied too much space to carry cargo profitably. The engine was removed, and the vessel then sailed between Savannah and New York until November 1821, when the *Savannah* was blown ashore on Long Island in a gale and pounded to pieces.[55]

During 1819 the speculative boom fueled by easy bank loans ended in the first major bust and panic in American history. During the early part of the year cotton was selling for $.33 a pound, but due to oversupply the price fell to less than half that figure by the fall. The value of adult male slaves plunged from nearly $1,000 to $600; the shares of banks and property values followed. Bankruptcies multiplied. The political and economic effects reverberated throughout the South. The Bank of the United States with a branch in Savannah called in its loans and was vilified by southerners.[56]

THE FIRE OF 1820

Some Savannahians remembered earlier conflagrations and feared they might strike again. To guard against recurrences the City Council periodically updated such ordinances as one "to prevent the pernicious practice of boiling pitch, tar, and turpentine in the city."[57] A rising worry over fire accompanied Savannah's emergence as a major exporter of lumber. So it was with great alarm that Savannahians learned that arsonists tried to set a lumberyard afire in early 1818. The government increased patrols and warned citizens to be alert for arsonists. Arrests came quickly. Nine suspected arsonists stood trial, but no one was convicted.[58]

The worst fears of Savannahians materialized on the evening of January 11,

1820, after a fire started in a livery stable. A brisk northwest wind scattered sparks, igniting one tinder-dry building after another. One witness observed that very quickly the "fire . . . laid the city in ashes."[59] Four days afterward the rector of Christ Church wrote, "today I preached the Funeral Sermon of Savannah."[60]

It was the most devastating fire in the city's history. Walls of fire burned over Bay, Broughton, Jefferson, Drayton, Bryan, and Abercorn Streets, engulfing in flames lumberyards, the Bank of the United States, newspaper offices, mercantile houses, and the public market on Ellis Square. Gunpowder repeatedly exploded, which hampered the firefighters. The business district was nearly obliterated. Across the blackened area swept by the fire, only the Episcopal Church, the State Bank, and the Planters Bank remained standing. A total of 463 tenements burned down. Hundreds of nearly naked and homeless people wandered the streets. As usual, thieves pilfered during and after the fire.

In the days following the fire a baker provided free bread, and planters supplied rice, corn, and beef for distribution. The City Council appropriated a paltry $1,000 for those burned out. Mayor Thomas Charlton and the council appealed for aid for "this once beautiful city" now "IN RUINS." Individuals, organizations, and great and small cities across the United States responded generously. The mayor of New York City collected and donated more than $12,000 and merchandise, with the "proviso" that the money and goods be distributed without regard for skin color. The mayor's "proviso" angered Savannah's City Council, and Mayor Charlton returned the check and goods to New York, noting an "injustice has been done our citizens." Like southerners generally, Savannahians quickly responded to remarks that they believed questioned their honor. To an Englishman visiting Savannah, the incident dramatized "very strongly the sensitive state of feeling on the subject of slavery between the Northern and Southern States." Savannahians lost not only New York City's handsome contribution but also the donations of other northern cities that heard about the returned check and decided against helping.

Final estimates of personal losses during the fire reached a total of $776,000; compensation went to some citizens from over $99,000 in donations that the city accepted. The fire destroyed the public market, which was rebuilt and reopened on Ellis Square in August 1821.[61]

The exact cause of the fire remained unknown, but the mayor was so suspicious of its origins that he ordered the city watch to take into custody all vagrants and especially "black boys and those of colour." The hysteria over fire was rising, and rumors of arson rippled through the city. The year following the fire, a slave by the name of Susan was tried for allegedly setting a house ablaze in Savannah, but she was exonerated; somewhat later a female slave, Molly, was charged, tried, and convicted of setting her owner's house on fire and was sentenced to hang.[62] An Englishman passing through the city in April 1820 observed that Savannah presented "a most desolate appearance, yet the inhabitants are most unwittingly running up *wooden* houses again." Some months later another visitor noted that fire-gutted buildings were being "replaced by ranges of elegant brick buildings, greatly improving . . . [the city's] appearance, as well as safety from similar misfortune."[63] A wooden synagogue was being erected for the Mickve Israel congregation on the northeast corner of Liberty and Whitaker Streets. The Sheftall family had dreamed of building this synagogue for years, and with the help of David Lyon and Jacob De La Motta, who raised the money, they saw the temple completed. When it burned some years later, the city government donated a lot for a new brick synagogue; eventually, a Gothic temple was built on Monterey Square.

Although the Savannah Theater was not damaged in the fire of 1820, its manager deemed it prudent to close the theater for the season. Charles Gilfert's Charleston Theater Company played two other seasons and departed in May 1823. For several years afterward only circuses, magicians, ventriloquists, and lecturers provided the local entertainment. It was unprofitable and unwise for a professional company to play Savannah due to the lingering economic consequences of the fire, the economic depression, and a virulent epidemic.[64]

YELLOW FEVER EPIDEMIC

The *Aedes aegypti,* or yellow-fever-carrying mosquito, most likely caused outbreaks of disease in Savannah during the summers of 1817, 1818, and 1819, but the disease did not become widespread. In the summer of 1820, however, the fire-altered geography of Savannah helped spread of the disease. The many cavities left by collapsed buildings filled quickly during unusually heavy spring and summer rains, and the pools of warm water incubated the larvae of yellow-fever-carrying mosquitoes. Suddenly, Savannah's first catastrophic epidemic of yellow fever erupted. The first deaths occurred in the slums in the northeastern corner of the city. Attending physicians noted the telltale signs of yellow fever: convulsions and black vomit. The mosquitoes then spread across the city, and 119 Savannahians succumbed by the end of July.

Officials knew that yellow fever was present, but they minimized its extent. Mayor Charlton attributed the mortality to "fever and ague." The City Council published false reports that the health of the city was good even as death rates reached epidemic proportions. Only when newspapers in Georgia, South Carolina, and New York charged officials with covering up the truth did Mayor Charlton publicly admit on September 15 that a "fever" was sweeping through Savannah, which made it "prudent for any person . . . to remove beyond the limits of the city's atmosphere."[65]

William B. Bulloch and others with resources left Savannah. Bulloch wrote a friend: "It is a harrowing task to recount the affliction of our deserted and ill-fated city." The "pestilence . . . few escape—old or young, native or stranger." The very "air . . . [is] poison."[66]

After Mayor Charlton's admission of "fever" in the city, the board of health, which had cooperated in the cover-up, published biweekly mortality reports. In late September the board reported that 202 persons succumbed during the past month. A hospital for the poor was established, war was declared on filth in the city, and physicians worked tirelessly against a disease they did not understand. The standard treatment for the sick was bleeding, cathartics, and various salivants. But as yellow fever patients continued dying, physicians abandoned the usual treatment and tried other prescriptions such as "castor oil, . . . acid drinks, and sometimes mercury." Nothing seemed to work. Savannah's doctors became frustrated. Dr. William R. Waring, chairman of the board of health, performed numerous autopsies but was unable to identify how the disease was transmitted.

By early October only 2,500 persons, mostly blacks, remained in Savannah out of a population of more than 7,500 just four months earlier. During the day the city appeared deserted. Occasionally a slave moved along the streets carrying a blackened corpse toward an overcrowded cemetery. At night hundreds of burning tar barrels gave off eerie glows and pungent smells. Other remedies extolled included "Smyth's Specific," which promised also to cure typhus and the plague. The following year Savannah's medical community asked the legislature to "restrict the practice of medicine . . . to regularly qualified practitioners."

Deaths declined with colder weather. But on September 20 Dr. Richard M. Berrien succumbed to the disease; his brother-in-law, Dr. John A. Casey, had died of yellow fever in 1819. Luckier was Dr. Mary Lavinder, who aided and comforted the city's poor during the epidemic and who survived. She was the first woman in Georgia to receive university training in obstetrics, and she practiced in Savannah for over thirty years.

By December the epidemic was over. Approximately 895 persons died, or about 12 percent of the city's population; most of the victims were white; fewer blacks succumbed due to the African's natural immunity from yellow fever. Refugees slowly returned to the city.[67]

Dr. Waring attributed the epidemic disease to a variety of causes: the "extraordinary virulence" in the atmosphere, an unusually warm winter and spring, uncovered privies, and the nearby marshes, which exuded "unwholesome vapor." In Savannah from 1807 to 1820 some four thousand people perished from yellow fever.[68] Waring and his colleagues never recognized that an insect vector transmitted the disease. The severity of the 1820 epidemic refocused the attention of Savannahians and state officials on the conditions of public health in Georgia. Never again did they approach it with the same complacency.

Following the 1820 epidemic, the City Council appointed Dr. James Proctor Screven as health officer. He began rigorously enforcing sanitation laws in concert with the board of health. The board met weekly during the "sickly months" and conscientiously inspected the city for cleanliness. Board members provided the poor with lime for sanitizing their privies; they expected citizens to clean the streets fronting their homes and to place any accumulated "filth" in receptacles for pickup by the city's scavenger. The board recommended that the city government drain low-lying areas in and around Savannah and ordered the owners of slaughter pens to use lime daily from June to September on the "vast effusions of blood . . . and offal." The board believed that there "is no greater cause of disease than the rapid decay of animal matter."[69]

During the 1820s the city government boasted that the atmosphere of the city now "maintained a character of clearness, dryness and elasticity," and that streets once "muddy and dirty are now clean and dry." But the City Council was divided over the issue. To some the streets appeared cleaner, but to others the lanes remained "depositories of filth." The city's mortality rates improved although periodic outbreaks of influenza, yellow fever, and typhoid rippled through Savannah, especially in the slums of Yamacraw.

Some members of the city government promoted the idea of the city's low mortality rates. A publication of the City Council based on only the white population of 5,000 estimated that Savannah's mortalities for the year 1826 would have been about one person in every twenty-five. This was not fact but rather propaganda to promote the city's healthfulness with the aim of attracting commerce. The "study" was based on the inaccurate assumption of the number of whites and excluded blacks, whose mortality rate was likely higher.[70]

High rates of mortality and frequent outbreaks of disease continued. To some it appeared that Savannah needed more physicians. However, when George J. Kollock requested to study under Dr. P. M. Kollock, the doctor accepted him but warned: "Our City is at present filled with physicians . . . too many for the size of the place."[71]

Savannah's government enacted additional ordinances to improve the city's health and to reduce the risk of fire. New volunteer fire companies were organized. In 1821 seventy-five free blacks formed the Franklin Fire Engine and Hose Company and the Union Axe and Fire Company. The city soon required all free blacks between age sixteen and sixty to enroll in fire companies. Each had to have "a cap or hat" with the initials F.C. (Free Colored) to wear while on duty. Failure to comply was punishable by fine or imprisonment. The city also required that all male slaves be issued work permits (badges) from the city to become members of fire companies. They received pay for their services and drilled monthly.[72]

In 1825 the city created the first regularly organized firefighting unit. By the late 1820s the city's all-male fire department included 178 slaves, 96 free blacks, and a 17-member white unit, the Oglethorpe Company. Ironically, the white property owners who had the most to lose turned over firefighting predominantly to Savannah's African Americans, with white officers in command of the segregated, all-black companies. When white firefighters protested the wearing of uniforms by blacks, their superiors overruled them. The fire chief and other officials apparently recognized that if blacks faced the same dangers as whites but were denied uniforms, blacks could become disgruntled firefighters.[73] Apparently, firefighting helped mitigate suspicions of some blacks and whites for one another and promoted interracial male relationships.[74]

New fire engines and equipment were purchased, and a firehouse was built on Franklin Square. Persons who offered information leading to the apprehension of arsonists received rewards, as did the first engine company to arrive to fight a blaze. Despite these expenditures to fight and prevent fires, rapidly spreading, destructive conflagrations occasionally burned portions of the city, such as the late 1820s fire that swept through Yamacraw.[75]

The fire and the yellow fever epidemic of 1820 and the nationwide depression slowed economic activity in Savannah to a crawl in the early 1820s—exports dropped to $6,032,862, less than half their value a few years before. The press observed that Savannah's businessmen had experienced "shipwrecked hopes and broken schemes."[76] Savannah entrepreneur-inventor William Scarbrough went bankrupt. His mansion sold for $20,000 at auction, and its magnificent furnishings also went on the auction block. Scarbrough himself was briefly imprisoned for indebtedness. He and his wife Julia remained active in the city's highest social circles only through the largess of his English-born son-in-law and wealthy cotton factor, Godfrey Barnsley. Scarbrough remained, however, an irrepressible inventor-entrepreneur.[77]

The once vastly wealthy Richard Richardson experienced both financial disaster and personal tragedy. He too was forced to sell his Jay-designed mansion and its furnishings by 1822. That same year his wife and the mother of their six children died. For the remainder of the decade, Richardson faced a blizzard of lawsuits. To satisfy his debts, sheriff's sales auctioned off his extensive land holdings and slaves. Apparently, by the end of the 1820s he no longer resided in Savannah.[78]

Rising crime rates accompanied the economic depression. The collector of the customs at Savannah, Archibald Bulloch, informed national officials that "acts of piracy are prevelent" in Savannah.[79]

CRIME AND PUNISHMENT

Although money was in short supply, the city appropriated $1,600 to build a new guard house in 1822. Perhaps it was not coincidental that this was the same year that a free black, Denmark Vesey, living in nearby Charleston, allegedly planned the largest slave uprising ever conceived of in North America. Tried, convicted, and sentenced, Vesey and thirty-five co-conspirators met their deaths by hanging in June and July.

That September, two slaves, Dick and Shadrack, appeared before the Inferior Court of Chatham County to stand trial for attempting to poison Robert Flournoy and his family. Shadrack allegedly also had conspired with Robin, another slave, in "attempting to excite an insurrection" at the time of the aborted Vesey revolt. The court acquitted the two slaves. Nevertheless, one prominent slaveholding Savannahian who had heard about the Vesey plot remarked: "All confidence is lost in our Servants."[80] The alleged insurrection planned by Denmark Vesey, a free black, stirred old fears of free "persons of color" in a slave society.

Chatham County Court records indicate a sense of judicial fair play in the sentencing of blacks for capital crimes. Obviously, part of the fairness stemmed from the fact that owners did not want to see their slaves hanged. Juries also occasionally recommended leniency for capital offenses. In one instance in the decade of the 1820s, white well-to-do jurors found George Flyming, a slave, guilty of the attempted rape of a fourteen-year-old white girl, "but earnestly recommend him to mercy." Nevertheless, Flyming was sentenced to hang. However, forty-eight prominent citizens petitioned the governor in his behalf since they believed that the "evidence upon which he was convicted is doubtful & uncertain," and they urged "the commutation of his Sentence from Death to transportation [to] . . . save . . . perhaps, an innocent human being." Why did so many prominent citizens seek clemency for Flyming? Perhaps it was because he was well known in the workplace as a skilled carpenter, or perhaps it was a case of gender and class bias, which called into question the character and "evidence offered" by the indigent teenager, Eliza Hand. Male Savannahians also knew that impoverished white teenage girls were sexually active.[81] Interracial mixing fostered by city life also may have led prominent white Savannahians to intercede in his behalf. Nevertheless, the fate of Flyming is unknown.

Perhaps due to persistent fears of insurrection among Savannah's wealthy whites, the city government passed a more humane ordinance the year after the alleged Vesey plot. On August 23, 1823, the City Council recommended that hereafter "corporeal punishment [whipping] . . . be inflicted on persons of color in other places than the streets, lanes, and squares or market of the city."[82] The City Council responded quickly and in a humane manner several years later when slaves employed by the city "refused to return to duty" when treated "cruelly" by John Sykes, their overseer. The council admonished Sykes to "exercise towards [the slaves] humanity and punish with moderation . . . only when necessary."[83] The city guard used the fife and drum to sound the hour and curfew until 1825, when the time and curfew were announced orally; the mayor's court was also abolished and replaced by a Court of Common Pleas.

Concern over security at night was balanced with the costs of lighting the city's lamps, and the council decided to light about half the lamps. Plans for a new courthouse were delayed for years, but finally one was built in Brown

Ward in 1830. The costs of maintaining the city jail became too expensive for the city, and it was turned over to the sheriff and justices of the inferior court of Chatham County for over a decade.[84] When the responsibility for the jail was returned to the city government, council members complained that the building had fallen into "decay." This conclusion was underlined by a mass escape of prisoners who cut through rusted bars or pulled them away from "soft" walls.[85] Interracial breakouts were not uncommon.

Indeed, the Savannah jail was another public institution that fostered close interracial relationships and took the edge off the rougher edges of racism. Black and white inmates alike saw themselves as allies against the social and economic system and its leaders, who confined them. Jailbreaks often were planned by interracial groups, as was criminal activity upon release, which was usually against the interests of Savannah's white wealthy elite.[86]

A BOOM IN RICE

Savannah's economy limped along, and city revenues fell; nevertheless, the government spent some money to beautify the city with trees and plants. Steamboats regularly left Savannah's wharfs piled with consumer goods for Darien and Augusta and for Milledgeville on the Oconee River and returned crammed with cotton bales. Removal of obstructions in the Savannah River had greatly improved navigation.[87]

In 1823 a public meeting was called to consider how to stimulate the economy. For a variety of reasons business was being diverted elsewhere from both Savannah and Charleston.[88] But during the early 1820s St. Peter's Parish, South Carolina, the state's southeasternmost region, experienced a sudden expansion of its rice fields. The booming region was just to the north and across the river from Savannah.

Luring some of Carolina's wealthiest and most influential rice planters to open new rice fields were new technology, the highest prices ever paid for rice in the antebellum South—6.1 cents per pound—and the boosterism in Savannah, which promised to turn the city into the "New York of the South." Rice planter and politician Judge Daniel Huger moved two hundred slaves to work his new rice plantation in St. Peter's Parish on the Back River opposite Hutchinson Island; attorney and politician James Hamilton Jr. purchased three plantations in St. Peter's Parish, where he worked more than three hun-

dred slaves. The largest rice plantation on the lower Savannah, Delta Plantation, was over 2,750 acres and was owned by Carolinian Langdon Cheves, one-
time Speaker of the United States House of Representatives. Another prominent Carolinian, Charles Manigault, bought the 300-acre Gowrie Plantation,
which he worked with fifty slaves.

Prominent Savannahians also invested in the rice boom in St. Peter's Parish.
Major John Screven of Savannah relocated forty slaves there to cultivate rice
fields near a ferry landing, the main crossing of the river below Savannah,
which became known as Screven's Ferry. His son, Dr. James Proctor Screven,
a graduate of the Medical College of the University of Pennsylvania and a
prominent Savannah physician, businessman, and politician, inherited the
rice plantation and gave up his medical practice to manage the 1,700 acres of
rice fields worked by over a hundred slaves. These rice lands became the foundation of his great wealth.

Another prominent Savannah physician, William Coffee Daniell, invested
in a rice plantation in St. Peter's Parish during the 1820s. He was widely known
for his treatise *Observations upon the Autumnal Fevers of Savannah,* but he
gained vast wealth from his rice fields and by marriage first to Martha Screven
and upon her death to her sister, Elizabeth, both sisters of Dr. James Proctor
Screven. By the end of the 1820s Daniell worked about 125 slaves on his seven-
hundred-acre plantation, named Oglethorpe. Like Screven, he was active in
Savannah politics and a booster of local business. Savannahians Benjamin
Guerard and Archibald Smith also owned rice plantations in St. Peter's Parish.
These absentee owners who lived in Savannah could see their plantations from
Savannah's Factor's Walk.

The absentee Carolina owners of plantations in St. Peter's Parish rode over
their properties in planting and harvest seasons and at night stayed in Savannah. A unique practice of their overseers was to leave a slave driver in charge
and commute to and from Savannah.[89]

The wealthy rice planters denounced the Tariff Bill of 1824, for they found
the legislation contrary to their interests. Powerful Savannahians William
Coffee Daniell and Alexander Telfair called a meeting at the Exchange Building in February 1824 to ask Congress to reject the Tariff Bill because it was a
tax that "will be oppressive . . . to the great landed, agricultural, and commercial interest of the country." It was the beginning of the nullification movement in Georgia.[90]

A STORM AND THE ENVIRONMENT

In September 1824, Savannah's nearby rice fields and the city's buildings and trees sustained heavy damage during a late summer storm. The city's free Negroes, who were required to provide twenty days of annual labor on the streets, cleared away the storm debris. A few years later the City Council paid for the planting by Savannahians of five hundred oak, orange, elm, laurel, and sycamore trees.[91] Within a few years these hardwoods along the streets and in the city's squares enhanced the beauty of Savannah's physical environment. Residents and visitors alike commented on and enjoyed the squares of recurring greenery across the city.

LAFAYETTE'S VISIT

A bright spot in the city's history during the 1820s—according to the white gentry—was the visit of a hero of the American Revolution, the Marquis de Lafayette. On March 10, 1825, Maryanne Stiles observed that "the whole town is . . . crazy because General Lafayette is expected here." When he arrived on March 19, a committee of local officials welcomed him, and a band struck up "La Marseillaise." He was entertained regally at taxpayer expense. Lafayette laid the cornerstones for monuments to General Nathanael Greene and Count Casimir Pulaski. A lottery was authorized by the state to raise money for the monuments, and a shaft was erected in the center of Johnson Square, which served for years to honor both revolutionaries.[92]

SOCIAL LIFE IN HARD TIMES

Some wealthy Savannahians appeared economically insulated from the anemic economy. Dr. Lemuel Kollock, a physician born in Massachusetts, educated his sons and his daughter at private schools in the North and at Yale and Harvard. Teenager Mary Kollock in 1820 enjoyed Savannah weddings because, she confided, they are "followed by a great many parties."[93]

The social whirl of the winter social season excited other young women. Anna Matilda Page of Retreat plantation, St. Simons Island, educated and polished, eligible and anxious to marry, visited Savannah in February 1823. She loved the parties, Page wrote, because she could "dance as often as I feel inclined." She also delighted in visits from gentlemen callers and received nine during one Sunday afternoon. Within a year she married Thomas Butler King, an attorney.[94]

During the 1824–1825 social season, Maryanne Stiles told a friend that "we have had two or three dances . . . every week and parties innumerable. I never knew before so much gaiety and dissipation."[95] Other wealthy families enjoyed outings on Skidaway Island, where they "roasted & ate . . . oysters"; some went to Richmond "in style," and others traveled to Charleston for the races.[96] In December 1828 Mary Kollock, then twenty-two years of age, wrote her brother at Yale College: "I never saw Savannah look as gay and fashionable as it does this winter." She thought it might be due to the large number of persons who spent last summer in the North, as "they have all returned in the very '*tip of the mode*,' to use a very *elegant* expression." Kollock thought it "necessary to be dressed tolerably *a la mode*"; however, she hoped "never to . . . think and talk of nothing else but fashion." In May 1829 Kollock served as maid of honor at two weddings of Savannah's wealthy elite: Charlotte Scarbrough's marriage to James Taylor and Jane Stiles's marriage to Beecroft Penny. Kollock enjoyed immensely the "*grand blow Out*" given by Julia Scarbrough for her daughter, Charlotte.[97]

Near the end of the 1820s Savannah's elite introduced extravagant "Fancy Balls" where partygoers came dressed as famous characters from history or fiction. At one ball "Cinderella" appeared in "glass slippers," and Lucy Scarbrough came dressed as a page in "white satin pantaloons . . . and a . . . blue frock . . . trimmed with gold lace"; a "Venetian" lady led her five-year-old about "as Cupid [in] . . . pantaloons, [a] blue spangled jacket, . . . [a] bow and arrow in his hand, [and] wings on his shoulders."[98] One Savannah woman exclaimed to a northern friend that if she visited during the winter season "the *hospitality* of the inhabitants is not exceeded and hardly equaled anywhere."[99] During the summer months it was de rigueur for the wealthy to desert Savannah for cooler climes such as Flat Rock, North Carolina, and Saratoga, New York.[100]

Savannah's wealthy, sophisticated, and educated white females also asserted themselves and found self-expression in arranging and planning numerous weddings, parties, balls, and masquerades during the social season. These occasions were orchestrated by the city's prominent women to encourage the socializing of the city's elite and their marriageable sons and daughters. It was yet another humanizing facet of city life among the elite.

Savannah's well-to-do white women also read, enjoyed exhibitions and the theater, and discussed their interests with men. They founded a Ladies Society "for the purpose of promoting sociableness" and to provide "an opportunity for free and intelligent conversation—Music etc."[101] A Savannah and Chatham County Lyceum was also begun.[102]

The *Savannah Republican* chastised the Charleston Theater Company for not performing in Savannah, as the theater was missed by "lovers of refined amusement."[103] By the mid-1820s the theater company players returned. It became fashionable for well-to-do women to attend the theater only after the performers had proved themselves. On the sixth night of a play during December 1828 the ladies turned out for an actors' benefit performance, and the *Daily Georgian* described the audience as "a . . . brilliant display of youth, beauty, and fashion."[104]

Almost all the "stars" of the period—among them Edwin Booth, Charlotte Cushman, and Edwin Forrest—played Savannah.[105] The actors who performed usually praised the audiences. Tyrone Power played in Savannah many times and found the theatergoers "merry and intelligent" and the playhouse "well designed and well built." Popular young actor Priscilla Cooper attended "five parties" in a week and found Savannahians "charming." Louis Fitzgerald Tasistro described Savannah's audiences as superior to Charleston's "both in character and numbers."[106]

If the parties and weddings were the domain of Savannah's well-to-do white women, the young men of Savannah found their counterparts in their militia and hunt clubs. Englishman James Silk Buckingham noticed a "military spirit" that seemed pervasive: "Men of all classes delight in military titles, and military displays." The leading citizens addressed one another as colonel or major, and captains abounded in nearly every class. Buckingham described the local militia companies as "well-dressed, well-disciplined, and [they] had as perfectly martial an air as the National Guards of Paris." They excelled at marksmanship, Buckingham believed, because "almost every boy of fourteen or fifteen has a horse and rifle."[107] There was much truth in his observation. Young Phineas Kollock, while hunting on St. Catherine's Island, jumped two grown bucks and "*dropped them both in their tracks, one with each barrel.*" By age twelve William Basinger was an expert marksman who hunted near town with his shotgun and his "beautiful setter, Peppo."[108]

The young militiamen drilled, drank, and hunted together both two- and four-legged game. Robert Habersham, a punster, told a friend that when he came to Savannah, "I'll promise you . . . fun, from a Stag-Hunt to a Belle-

Hunt—which indeed are both Deer-Hunts." Robert A. Lewis of Savannah predicted to a friend that in the 1831 social season the ladies' frocks will be "short . . . by which we may . . . see anklebones . . . [and] the shape of their knees."[109]

Soon after he had returned to Savannah to practice medicine, Dr. Richard Dennis Arnold was "kept awake" for hours "by the orgies of some young men plainly just from the brothel on the Common." Several days later he attended a wedding of a member of the Republican Blues, a local militia, where everyone drank "freely," then "marched on the Bay," and later "serenaded" some "whores." Arnold was himself hot-blooded. Ten minutes after seeing the woman of whom he was enamored, "I was engaged professionally viewing a beautiful woman's pudenda. Good heavens thoughts at the time," he confided to a diary. And Arnold imbibed too freely. A friend told him that he could rise "to the top" of his profession except for "his fondness for social life," which to Arnold meant: "I sometimes . . . drank more than I ought to."[110]

Despite the sincere hospitality toward one another, the wealthy elite exhibited a superficial hospitality toward the lesser classes, usually for the sake of white unity. Mary Telfair exhibited the bias of her class when she confided to a friend: "Our overseers wife made us a visit with an *Ayah* beside her—who she immediately called upon for a glass of water—we afterwards learned that she never combed her own hair or washed her feet. The indolence of that class of people in this country is unexampled."[111] Dr. Richard Dennis Arnold, a sophisticate, exhibited his bias when he helped a friend find "his negro wench Betty with whom a man named Palmer is in the habit of sleeping every night. His taste may be judged from the fact of her being a field-hand."[112] Arnold was a graduate of Princeton and the University of Pennsylvania Medical School. A practicing physician and promoter of public health, he subsequently published a local weekly, was active in the Democratic party, and served four terms as mayor of Savannah. A layperson in the Unitarian Church, Arnold sometimes conducted services at Unitarian Hall, a building rented by the church on Court House Square.[113]

Besides church-related social activities, free blacks, slaves, and often poor whites found their entertainment in "tippling houses." They also enjoyed Saturday night "frolics"—dances and music making—required by curfew laws, however, to end by 10:00 P.M. On Sundays, African Americans enjoyed being pulled in wagons and buggies through the city until the City Council banned the joy riding as a nuisance. Blacks and laboring-class whites swam and bathed in the "River opposite the City" throughout the day until prohibited by the City Council during the hours of 7:00 A.M. to sunset. Once more well-to-do Savannahians fretted over interracial fraternization of poor whites and blacks, which the elite perceived as a threat to their property interests at the very least.

Boat races and regattas on the Savannah River became sporting and social events for all citizens. Black oarsmen in colorful costumes from nearby plantations competed in canoes thirty to fifty feet in length, the sides of which were carved to an inch thick. The crowds along the shore wagered and cheered on the brightly painted canoes, which reached speeds up to a mile in six minutes. Winning boats received awards, and their crews, exhausted but exuberant, sang as they paddled back to their plantations through mazes of marsh-banked creeks.

Perhaps the favorite annual social event for Savannah's African Americans was the firemen's parade. Most likely led by white companies, the "colored" firemen, outfitted in their distinctive uniforms, stepped lively through the city. The parade provided black bystanders along the route a rare opportunity to cheer proudly for African Americans and to enjoy a unique and festive event, which nurtured a sense of community; it was an event that could occur only in the city.[114]

BLACK ARSONISTS, BLACK SAILORS

In 1825 arsonists again frightened wealthy property-owning white Savannahians, who remained obsessed with black insurrectionists. Due to recent attempts by "incendiaries" to set "conflagrations," the city government created committees of "vigilance" in each ward to protect the property of "citizens & possibly their lives from the fiend-like assaults of persons within your bosom."[115] White Savannahians also remained anxious over the influence on slaves of free black sailors. In 1826 the City Council told the Georgia legislature that the "colored seamen of the most depraved and dangerous character have enjoyed . . . almost unlimited" shore leave, and it asked the legislature to empower the city government to pass a stricter act confining black sailors to their vessels. The council warned: "the influence of [colored sailors] upon our slaves is . . . great in the depraving of their morals inducing them to desertion and possibly, occasionally, inciting them to insurrectionary attempts."[116]

REVIVING A MORIBUND ECONOMY

There was growing demand across Georgia for a state-controlled and state-financed system of internal improvements, and in the mid-1820s the legislature created the Board of Public Works. The board focused on the problem of expeditiously moving the cotton of upland planters to the coast for export while also meeting their needs for supplies. After a year the board was abolished, but it had pointed the way for the future development of the state: road building, canal construction, improvement of rivers, and making railroads the primary means of transportation in Georgia.[117]

Canal fever was sweeping the country, and wealthy rice planter Dr. William Coffee Daniell, mayor of Savannah from 1826 to 1828, advocated a canal linking the Savannah and Ogeechee Rivers to promote commercial expansion. After extensive discussions, the City Council granted a charter to prominent Savannah merchants and planters for the Savannah, Ogeechee and Altamaha Canal Company, which allowed the company to cut a canal across city lands. Canal company president Alexander Telfair boasted that the canal would "open new sources of profit to enterprising men and . . . add to the . . . wealth of the city."[118]

Over the next few years, individuals, banks, the city, and the state pledged more than $200,000 to build the canal. Labor recruiters brought in Irish workers who along with blacks were "hired out" by their owners and who dug a trench some sixteen miles long connecting the Ogeechee River with the Savannah River at the city's western end, in Yamacraw, near the bridge that today spans the river. Here slaves and Irishmen labored side by side, and most likely interracial friendships developed. Of course, violence occasionally flared between them, especially when they competed locally for jobs as common laborers.[119]

Savannah's indebtedness climbed to over $78,000, and the city was in jeopardy of not meeting its payrolls by the late 1820s. To solve its financial problems and to improve commerce, the city petitioned Congress to appropriate funds to remove vessels sunk in the Savannah River channel; Savannahians also urged Congress to establish a naval shipyard locally. With such federal aid, some boosters believed that the city could become "the New York of the South."

Congress did appropriate $50,000 to deepen and remove obstructions in the Savannah River, but by 1829 federal funds had been exhausted, the channel had not been deepened, and only the most obvious obstructions had been removed. Some questioned Mayor Daniell's management of the project as well as the misappropriation of federal funds.[120]

In 1828 Henry McAlpin, a local businessman, pointed out to the City Council that over a five-year period in the 1820s Savannah exported only 57,862 casks of rice, while 388,888 passed through Charleston. McAlpin claimed that this was due to the steam-powered milling facilities in Charleston, which far surpassed Savannah's water-powered mills. McAlpin, owner of the Hermitage plantation near Savannah, was another city-nurtured architect, entrepreneur, and inventor who operated the Steam Saw Mill and Cast Iron Factory. Another lumber mill powered by a twenty-eight-horsepower engine was built on Hutchinson Island. It employed a large, predominantly black labor force, probably both slave and free, who worked fourteen-hour days to cut 15,000 feet of timber into lumber and load it into waiting vessels.

The first steam-powered rice-pounding mill was built in Savannah by the firm of Hall, Shapter and Tupper. A twenty-horsepower engine drove the mill, which could clean twenty barrels of rice a day. In 1828 wealthy Charleston investor and planter Daniel Blake moved to Savannah and soon built steam-powered rice mills in Yamacraw. By the 1830s planters in St. Peter's Parish operated six steam-powered mills, each belching smoke from their tall iron or brick chimneys at rice harvest time.[121]

The local economy received a little boost when the United States military Board of Engineers for Fortifications selected Cockspur Island as a site for a fortification envisioned to become part of a chain of forts defending America's Atlantic coast. Since the arrival of the first settlers, a lookout or battery had been situated at Cockspur Island. The new work, named Fort Pulaski after the Polish count who died defending Savannah during the American Revolution, took sixteen years to complete. Construction began in 1829 under the supervision of Major Samuel Babcock of the U.S. Corps of Engineers. He was soon joined by a freshly minted graduate of West Point, Lieutenant Robert E. Lee. In 1833 masonry work began on what became a massive timber, brick, and mortar structure. As the fort neared completion, Lieutenant Barton S. Alexander remarked, "[it] is now susceptible of a strong defence."[122]

SLAVE AND FREE BLACK ENTREPRENEURS

The almost moribund local economy heightened black-white competition and tensions. White farmers and Savannah's butchers complained about illicit trade by blacks and asked the City Council "to prevent slaves from . . . selling meats in the [Public] Market . . . for their individual benefit." Whites alleged that slaves stole cattle in "droves . . . with a boldness unprecedented," and then shot, butchered, and sold the meat in the market. The City Council did not respond to the charges at the time.[123]

In 1820 national census takers counted 616 free African Americans in Savannah and Chatham County. Sixty-four were homeowners, which exceeded the number in Petersburg and Richmond. Less than a decade later, a local census listed 875 free blacks living in Chatham County, but the number of homeowners remained the same. Over time the rate of growth of the free black population declined. This was due to new city and state laws and taxes to control free blacks: they were required to choose a white guardian and to register annually with local authorities who could monitor their movements; although not regarded as citizens, free blacks paid property and personal taxes and were required to work twenty days annually on the public roads; by the 1820s all slaves freed in Georgia had to leave the state; free blacks immigrating to Georgia had to pay a tax of $100; and local and state laws limited their earning potential by barring them from such occupations as pharmacist, mason, teacher, boat pilot, and liquor shop owner and from owning real estate and slaves. If they worked as artisans in trades open to them, free blacks, like slaves, had to purchase a badge or license for $10, and most also paid a poll tax of $10. These were costly fees at the time and were a calculated means of control and an attempt to limit competition with whites in the skilled trades.[124]

The black artisans represented a range of skills and a residential persistence exceeding that of skilled white workers. For instance, of the nineteen carpenters who registered as "colored" in the 1820s, fourteen remained in the city a decade later. These blacks were mostly native born, and their continuing residence indicates a stable free black artisan community. Occasionally, free black artisans lived with some of Savannah's best-known white craftsmen, which suggests a high level of skill among the black workers and an interracial work environment. At least one white master builder, Gilbert Butler, was the guardian of a skilled black carpenter.[125]

Slave artisans appeared essential to some operations. The talented owner of the Hermitage, Henry McAlpin, employed skilled slaves as carpenters, brick masons, and ironworkers. Under McAlpin's direction, slaves built the first horse-drawn rail wagon in the United States. Architect William Jay used the ornamental cast iron made at the Hermitage on the buildings he designed;

contractors used the lumber and the famous "Savannah grays," bricks made of gray clay made in the city.[126]

Some white Savannahians bitterly resented slave artisans hiring their own time since it conflicted with the interests of whites. In the early 1820s Mrs. Martha Richardson wrote a Savannah politico demanding that the number of slaves be limited in Savannah and "all useless ones . . . sent into the country—hucksters, day labourers, draymen." She alone owned over sixty slaves.[127] Little was done, however. A visitor to the city observed: "I saw many black men who were slaves, and who yet acted as free men . . . [who] went to work, where and with whom they pleased, received their own wages, and provided their own subsistence, but were obliged to pay a certain sum . . . to their masters."[128] The Savannah Mechanics' Association met frequently to discuss ways to protect themselves from the competition by black artisans. In the 1830s they supported the election of state representatives "who would make it a penal offense to hire a negro in preference to a white man."[129]

Despite the legal prohibitions and complaints from whites, free black artisans and laborers found ample work in Savannah, and initially their numbers increased. In 1800 census takers counted 247 free blacks in the city; forty years later a more careful enumeration listed 370 "free colored" females and 262 males, or a total of 632 free blacks. It was the largest concentration of free men and women in Georgia.[130]

Free black males worked as laborers, artisans, and wagon drivers to serve the local cotton mill industry. Wagoners such as the Reverend Andrew Marshall, Jack Simpson, Evans Grate, and William Pollard, who transported cotton from the railroad depot to the compresses and then to an outward-bound ship at eight cents a bale, became wealthy. A European traveler in the early 1830s witnessed on the walks contiguous to the river cotton bales "piled up . . . at every corner" awaiting shipment. He heard "nothing . . . but conversations about cotton"; on it "alone depends the prosperity of Savannah," he concluded.[131]

The dearth of "free coloured" males meant that some free black females married slaves, remained unmarried, or engaged in biracial sexual contact as mistresses of white males. In any case, most black females faced economic hardships and had to find work. The most popular occupations included seamstress, domestic, cook, hairdresser, and shopkeeper. Several taught school, and some became prostitutes.[132] A few Savannah free blacks, both male and female, acquired wealth in slaves and real estate before the legislature passed a law prohibiting their ownership of real property. The statue coincided with the rising hostility toward free blacks as troublemakers.

Neither slaveholding nor property ownership by free blacks was widespread. Slave and property ownership peaked in the early 1820s when 20 free blacks held 58 slaves and 64 owned their own homes; in 1826, just 67 free black adults in Chatham County owned any property. After this date, slave and property ownership by free "colored" men and women declined. From the early nineteenth century Savannah's free black women owned more slaves and real property than the free men. It reflected the women's drive for economic independence.[133]

Of the dozen or so successful free black women in Savannah, Susan Jackson and Ann H. Gibbons became the most affluent. Jackson lived for most of her adult years in Reynolds Ward, a hub of business activity. She operated a pastry business and accumulated twenty-three brick buildings, some of which she rented. By 1830 she owned six slaves, and only two of the twenty-two free blacks in Savannah owned more. Susan wisely invested her profits. Following her death, Susan's property sold for $15,000, the highest price up to that time received for the holdings of a black Savannahian.[134] Mystery surrounds the life of Ann Gibbons. She had a daughter, Claudia, in 1820 but apparently was propertyless until some years later when she began to acquire real and personal property. Neither the father of her child nor her source of income is known. Eventually, she acquired four slaves and real property valued at $9,000 in Oglethorpe Ward.[135]

Many of Savannah's blacks lived in Oglethorpe Ward, which came to be centered between the Central of Georgia Railroad yards and the river. It was a dirty and disease-ridden area. Tuberculosis and typhoid fever were frequent killers. Hundreds of shops and warehouses dotted the ward. Rent and land were cheap. Here along the river in the notorious Yamacraw section, sailors found low-priced lodgings, saloons, and brothels. The slaves of masters who permitted them to "live out" huddled in filthy hovels of Yamacraw alongside poor white immigrants. Here, too, lived about one-third of Savannah's free blacks.

The proximity of poor whites, black slaves, and free African Americans in the biracial slums on the western and eastern ends of the city may have mitigated white racism. These groups mixed in the easy informality of the tippling houses, gambling dens, and brothels; indeed, such fraternization encouraged interracial friendships and social and economic activities, some of which threatened the interests of the city's white elite. And when disorder erupted in these biracial suburbs, it unnerved the well-to-do and brought an aggressive response from the watch, city patrol, or police.[136]

Some of the city's wealthiest free African Americans lived in Yamacraw. Louis Mirault was one of Savannah's most successful and prosperous free blacks. An immigrant from Santo Domingo, he became a tailor to the city's prominent citizens. By his death he had acquired six slaves and valuable real estate. Prince Candy, a barrel maker, owned seven slaves, and John Gibbon, a carpenter, owned five; both Candy and Gibbon acquired real property also. Anthony Odingsells owned more slaves (thirteen) and land than any free African American living near Savannah. His one-time master bequeathed to him Little Wassaw Island, which was little valued at the time.[137] The city with its vast opportunities for interracial business contacts offered free blacks a unique fast track to success, one rarely experienced in the countryside.

Andrew Marshall, the drayman who became a preacher, was perhaps the wealthiest and most influential black in Savannah during the first half of the nineteenth century. A former slave who bought his freedom, Marshall operated a successful dray business, invested in real estate, and served as the minister of the Bryan Street African Baptist Church. By the 1820s the value of his property exceeded that of any free black in Savannah and that of many whites. He purchased a lot on Franklin Square and began building a church, but a doctrinal dispute split the congregation; 155 members left Marshall's church to establish a rival one, the Third African Baptist Church.[138]

Every visitor to the city made a point to see Marshall's church. Charles Lyell described Marshall as distinguished looking and having "a fine sonorous voice." Frederika Bremer wept during a sermon. On one occasion Marshall preached before the Georgia legislature. When he died in 1856, his funeral was attended by an "immense throng" of blacks and whites. He was interred in the "Colored" section of Laurel Grove Cemetery.[139]

BLACK CHURCHES AND CLANDESTINE INSTRUCTION

Black Baptists remained the single largest denomination in the city, but by the 1820s several hundred Savannah blacks attended Andrew Chapel, a Methodist congregation controlled by whites and a white preacher and located in Yamacraw. Occasionally, black preachers addressed the congregation from the pulpit; one white visitor remarked that it was "worship that has a heart in it, a soul." Blacks also attended other white churches in the city, where they sat in "the colored gallery pews" but mingled formally and briefly with the white congregation.[140]

Beginning in the 1820s, members of the Independent Presbyterian Church conducted Sunday schools for black children at the two African Baptist churches. This was the brainchild of Lowell Mason. Mason came to Savannah in 1813 from Medfield, Massachusetts, and found work as a clerk, but he was really a "musical man," interested in serving the public good. Hired as the organist and superintendent of the Sunday school at the Independent Presbyterian Church, Mason gave concerts and helped Savannahians appreciate good music. While in Savannah he composed perhaps his most famous hymn, "From Greenland's Icy Mountains." After fourteen years in Savannah, Mason relocated to Boston to become a director of music.[141]

After Mason's departure, whites continued to conduct Sunday school classes for about 150 to 200 black children who listened to them preach from *Catechism . . . for the Oral Instruction of Colored Persons* by the Reverend Charles C. Jones, a Presbyterian minister and prominent slaveholder from nearby Liberty County. The *Catechism* was calculated to ensure faithfulness, obedience, and docility in slaves; for good behavior, it promised a heavenly reward; for those who did not "honor and obey their Masters," it promised punishment. The *Catechism* reflected Jones's view that slavery was morally sanctioned. But Jones also believed that masters would be held accountable by God for their treatment of their slaves.[142]

These Sunday schools provided the only legal means for blacks to learn the rudiments of reading and writing. White fears that black literacy and rebellion went hand in hand led to passage of a law in early Georgia and an ordinance by Savannah's City Council in 1817 prohibiting the teaching of slaves *and* free African Americans. Nevertheless, at least six free persons of color offered instruction to blacks in antebellum Savannah. For instance, Julien Fromatin, a black Frenchman born in Santo Domingo, came to Savannah about 1818 and publicly opened a school to teach reading and writing to free African American children. Then in 1829 David Walker published his famous anti-slavery tract, *An Appeal to the Colored Citizens of the World,* copies of which circulated in Savannah. The Georgia legislature, fearful that blacks would read the subversive pamphlet, enacted a law prohibiting the teaching of reading and writing to either slaves *or* free blacks; Savannah's City Council passed an ordinance supplementing the law, which fined anyone teaching slaves $100; if the instructor was black, it imposed a flogging of up to thirty-nine lashes.

Periodically, the City Council instructed the city marshal to report the names of any persons conducting clandestine schools for blacks. Julien Fromatin illegally continued to teach blacks for years. Several free black females also secretly pioneered instruction for young black children. Catherine Deveaux and her daughter Jane, Mary Beasley, and Mary Woodhouse, who taught in her home on Bay Lane between Habersham and Price Streets, all conducted illicit schools. To avoid detection, their pupils took circuitous routes to the schools, pretended to be on errands by carrying empty buckets, and concealed their books. Amazingly, the illegal activities of these female teachers were never discovered. James Porter, a tailor by day and a teacher by night, used a room with a trapdoor to escape through if raided. When police did discover his school, Porter went into hiding temporarily. The Reverend James M. Simms, a carpenter by trade, bought his own freedom for $750 a few years before the outbreak of the Civil War and opened an underground school on Berrien Street. He was apprehended and publicly whipped. Upon release, Simms again began teaching, but once more he was charged with breaking the law and was fined. Angry with local authorities, Simms soon left the state but returned after the Civil War. At least one white, Sister Jane Frances of the Sisters of Mercy, defied the law and opened a small school for African Americans.[143]

Most Savannah slaves could neither read nor write, but for some the instruction nourished a desire for learning. The literate and accomplished Susie King Taylor attended underground schools in Savannah with "books wrapped in paper" to prevent white officials from detecting them. When Emily Burke visited Savannah, she encountered a young slave who could "read, write, cipher, and transact business so correctly" that a major Savannah firm entrusted him with important financial decisions.[144]

BLACK SLAVES AND THEIR WHITE FAMILIES

Savannah's most favored slaves served the city's well-to-do whites. When a visitor asked one black woman if she was owned by a certain local family, she replied: "Yes, I belong to them, and they belong to me."[145]

Occasionally, deep friendship and affection evolved over the years between masters and slaves. Mary Kollock, a member of Savannah's slaveholding elite, wrote to her brother in April 1821: "The servants all send howdy 'do to you and particularly old Margaret and old Jenny who say they do not expect to see you again in this world but hope to in the next."[146] Kindly owners resisted parting with slaves who had been in their families for years, and when "old and faithful" servants died, the white families grieved.[147] But owners could also be demanding. As Harriett Campbell prepared to return to Savannah after an extended trip, she told a relative to tell her servants, "I shall *depend* upon their industry, in having *every* thing in *fine order* on my arrival."[148]

Sometimes slaves had ways of avoiding all the work piled on by a demanding owner. Sarah Gordon reported to her absent husband: "Hetty has been almost good for nothing . . . she has been sick ever since you left." Sarah believed that it was "half pretense, for when I see her without her knowing it, she walks briskly, and before me she appears as if she could hardly get along."[149]

Sometimes owners even treated valued house servants cruelly. One traveler in Savannah in the 1820s, Mrs. Basil Hall, was informed that the chambermaid was not available, as "the mistress had been whipping her and she was not fit to be seen." When the chambermaid did appear the following morning, Mrs. Hall noticed that her face was "marked in several places by cuts of the cowskin and her neck handkerchief covered with spots of blood."[150]

Rarely did slaves spend their entire lives with the same family. Sudden financial reverses or the death of even a well-to-do master sometimes meant the sale of the most devoted slave. The dispersal of a slave family at public or private auctions could be a deeply traumatic event. A visitor to the city who witnessed one auction described it as "shocking." Since slaves could be mortgaged for collateral, they sometimes went on the auction block at sheriff's sales to satisfy indebtedness. Owners who gave slaves as gifts broke up slave families. Martha Richardson informed her nephew: "Sister has given me a very pretty Boy to bring up for you . . . his name is Patrick, old Mary's grandson."[151]

Beginning in the 1820s, the American Colonization Society sponsored the relocation of blacks to Liberia. Over five hundred free African Americans, many of them Savannahians, departed with great hopes on vessels out of Savannah. As one semi-literate black man wrote, they hoped "for deliverence fr[om] the present Bondege an degradation they are labering under."[152]

SABBATARIANS, POLITICIANS, AND ABOLITIONISTS

Concerns escalated among Savannah's Baptists and Methodists during the 1820s over the extent and immorality of the "informal" economic activities between slaves and nonslaveholding white shopkeepers with whom they traded, fraternized, drank, and gambled on Sundays. The Sabbatarians opposed all business on the Lord's day, particularly the sale and consumption of alcohol. This became one of the major issues dividing the local electorate and was a political football during the next thirty years.

Until the 1820s Savannahians elected primarily Episcopalians, lawyers, merchants, and physicians to the City Council. However, the composition of the council changed with pressure by the Sabbatarians to end Sunday sales. Although the city government passed an ordinance in the 1790s and subsequent ones prohibiting the sale of liquor to blacks, many white shopkeepers regularly provided liquor and rooms to blacks to fraternize with laboring-class whites. Prominent white Savannahians alleged that African Americans used the rooms for gambling, prostitution, and hiding or selling stolen goods. When the Sabbatarians raised the question of prohibiting *all* trading on Sunday, Savannah's merchants divided over the issue. A defender of the status quo used the press to denounce the "pious tampering" of a few, an invidious "attempt to unite religion and politics, and revive an influence which has ever been withering to the liberties of the people."[153]

In a move to salve the division among whites, the old guard on the City Council raised the cost of liquor licenses. But George Shick, a Baptist, formed the Grocer's Ticket to challenge the council's new "exorbitant taxes." In the city elections of 1826 the Grocer's Ticket won a major political victory, which changed the historic membership of the City Council and reduced the cost of liquor licenses.

In the aldermanic elections of September 7, 1829, the decade of heated debate between the two factions for and against Sunday sales resulted in two slates of candidates: "the People's Ticket," which opposed sales on the Sabbath, and the "Independent Ticket," which did not. This time the People's Ticket swept the election. The new council included shopkeepers, a brick mason, and a saddler. The council quickly passed an ordinance "for enforcing the observance of the Sabbath," which prohibited most trade or work on Sundays and any "public sports or pastimes" like "singing [or] fiddling . . . for the sake of merriment." Some slave owners praised the act, which "is founded . . . in safety to society."[154] Yet the ordinance failed to achieve its ends. It was almost impossible to enforce: it closed the shops but not the city market, and on Sundays slaves poured in from the country to trade; it was difficult to apprehend lawbreakers; and the fines proved too small to prevent poor whites, who struggled to survive economically, from trading with blacks. Thus, the ordinance did not end the divisive issue over Sunday sales, the illicit sale of commodities by slaves, and the biracial mixing of poor whites and slaves. These remained volatile issues in local politics.[155]

Fueling local politics was the publication in 1829 of David Walker's *An Appeal to the Colored Citizens of the World.* In this famous tract, Walker, a freedman, Bostonian, and abolitionist, called for a black revolution to end slavery. When a fire swept Yamacraw in March 1829 consuming forty houses, Mary Telfair anxiously told a friend, "We have lately gone through a fiery ordeal and narrowly escaped conflagration."[156] Other blazes began mysteriously in April and December. The fires fed rumors that black conspirators familiar with Walker's *Appeal* planned to burn the town.[157]

Mayor William T. Williams learned that Walker's *Appeal* was brought to Savannah by a white seaman and given to black preacher Henry Cunningham, who refused to distribute the pamphlet. Mayor Williams ordered the police to seize the "sixty pamphlets of . . . insurrectionary character" and destroy them. He viewed the incident as one fraught with "dangerous consequences to the peace and . . . lives of the people of the South."[158] Once more upper-crust Savannahians beheld the terrible specter of black insurrectionists.

In response to such anxieties, the state and the city enacted laws prohibiting the teaching of blacks to read and write; further, any vessels with black mariners aboard were subject to a forty-day quarantine, and any black seaman who met with Savannah's slaves was subject to imprisonment; another law specified capital punishment for free blacks convicted of arson.

In early 1831 two events sent tremors of anger and fear across the South. On January 1, William Lloyd Garrison published a newspaper in Boston, the *Liberator,* which called for the immediate end of slavery. During June, Nat Turner, a slave in Southampton County, Virginia, launched the bloodiest slave insurrection in North American history.

Two years later a rumor sped through Savannah that the pamphlets of abolitionists had reached the city and that local slaves planned to revolt. The rumor started when a black Savannah clergyman received through the postal service two issues of a New York–published periodical, *The Anti-Slavery Reporter,* which he turned over to Mayor Williams. The mayor characterized it as a work designed "to excite insurrection and bloodshed." The postmaster promised "to refuse delivery [of] any [such documents] that may be addressed to Negroes."[159]

At the time abolitionism was rising, the federal government decided to re-move troops stationed in Savannah because of the lack of healthy and adequate accommodations. This so alarmed the local government that it asked that at least one hundred troops remain in the city, especially in the summer, be-cause of the "emigration of many of our [wealthy] white population."[160] Nego-tiations went on until the city offered a site to the federal government to build permanent barracks on lots extending from Liberty to Harris and Bull to Drayton Streets and fronting on Bull Street. Here the federal government erected permanent troop facilities, later named Oglethorpe Barracks and oc-cupied by federal or local forces until after the Civil War.[161]

NULLIFIERS VERSUS UNIONISTS

Paradoxically, while Savannahians negotiated with the federal government to keep federal troops in the city, a clique of well-to-do Savannah merchants and planters supported a states' rights movement to nullify a high federal tariff bill, a plan hatched in South Carolina. In Savannah the Nullifiers, led by wealthy Savannah River rice planter and former mayor Dr. William Coffee Daniell, emerged in 1824 while the Union Party, led by Dr. Richard Arnold, counseled moderation and negotiations. Most of the politically active Catholic lead-ers joined the Union Party.[162] They spoke against nullification, which they viewed as a movement led by "a monied aristocracy" who threatened to disrupt the Union.[163] In the fall of 1833 during a race for the state senate between Dr. Daniell and a Union Party candidate, it "was very unsafe to walk at night unarmed," one citizen claimed.[164] Most Georgians looked on nullification or the states' rights movement as reckless. Senator Daniell won election to the Georgia State Senate in 1833, but the following year he was defeated in a race for the U.S. Congress.

The nullification controversy divided white Savannahians. Politics in Sa-vannah now focused less on personalities and more on issues. By the early 1830s politicos standing for election to the City Council ran either on the Union Party or the States' Rights Party ticket. But on February 12, 1833, most Savan-nahians joined together to celebrate the Centennial of Georgia and Savannah. Troops paraded through the streets, orators made speeches, and in the evening a grand ball was held.

Unionists outnumbered members of the States' Rights Party in Savannah, and Catholics became leaders in the local Union Party. When Andrew Jackson, a Democrat and unionist, won reelection and was inaugurated president in March 1833, a "splendid supper" and grand ball were held at Savannah's Exchange Building. By this time the strength of nullifiers was waning across the South. South Carolina was the exception.[165]

Unionists also swept the elections in Savannah and the state in 1834. The *Georgian* crowed: "the adopted citizens of America aided to swell the majority." Irish politicians boasted of "their fervent attachment to freedom."[166] Such sentiments changed over time. When immigrant Catholics amassed great wealth, they became part of the city's "monied aristocracy," and their politics changed. They sounded more and more like extreme states' rights advocates.[167] But although well-to-do Catholics came to reflect the local culture, it appeared that Unitarians did not.

The new Unitarian church at the southwest corner of Bull and York Streets was dedicated in December 1834. Built of brick and wood at a cost of $10,000 and seventy-two feet by forty-seven feet in size, the church was described as "plain, but beautiful . . . being of the Grecian Ionic order." The first minister of the new church, Ezekiel Lysander Bascom, believed that the members of the "orthodox" religions in the city looked on him as "a leper in the camp of the Israelites." Only the support of one layman in particular, Dr. Richard D. Arnold—young politician and newspaper editor, fluent public speaker and physician—and his push to make the church an intellectual center for the city saved the church from extinction. Along with the families of several businessmen in the city, Dr. Arnold gave the Unitarian church "stature and respectability." Nevertheless, the church suffered when it lost the leadership of Reverend Bascom due to illness and the New England–based American Unitarian Association became actively associated with the anti-slavery movement.[168] After learning that William Ellery Channing, the eminent spokesman for Unitarianism in Boston, publicly supported abolitionism, Arnold was aghast. He told northern church leaders that "the Abolitionists . . . have by their intemperance, united the whole South against them." Furthermore, if "the Abolitionists continue their agitation, it will end by an entire dissolution of this Union, and . . . a civil war."[169] Savannah's Unitarians, already viewed locally as religious heretics, became social pariahs if only by association. Church membership fell, and debt mounted. In the late 1830s some person or persons attempted at least twice to burn Savannah's Unitarian church.[170]

HOTELS, HONOR, AND HEALTH

Savannah's population declined from 7,517 to 6,520 during the decade of the 1830s. The city's economy remained sluggish. Due to hard times Savannah's best hostelry, the City Hotel, changed hands several times, although management advertised the "best bedding, best servants" and a bar furnished "with the best liquors and wines." The City Hotel once again changed ownership when auctioned off from the steps of the Exchange Building in May 1829. To promote the hotel in early 1830, the new management charged admission to see a "Lion & Lioness" in "a large new cage"; two years later a ventriloquist was featured. John James Audubon took rooms at the City Hotel in 1832 and obtained several prominent local subscribers for his *Birds of America,* among them William Gaston and Alexander Telfair.

One of the several "affairs of honor" that ended in the barroom of the City Hotel began in another of Savannah's bars on a spring evening in 1832. Drunk and bragging first at Luddington's Bar, James Jones Stark, a "dissipated" young man, referred to a local physician, Dr. Philip Minis, as a "damned Jew" who "was not worth the powder and lead to kill him," and furthermore, Stark stated, "he ought to be pissed upon." Minis heard about Stark's derogatory comments but waited until August to challenge Stark to a duel. Minis also believed in the southern honor ethic. Stark choose rifles at the Screven Ferry landing on the South Carolina side of the river, but Minis declined, claiming his rifle was being repaired. Nevertheless, Stark showed up, fired his weapon in the air, and returned to Savannah, where he wondered about the courage of Minis. His honor questioned, Minis acted quickly. On August 10 he entered the bar of the City Hotel, saw his antagonist, and called him a "coward." It appeared to Minis that Stark reached for his gun; Minis quickly drew his own pistol and fired, killing his antagonist. Minis was charged with murder and detained in the city jail. His trial before the superior court in Savannah began in January 1833, and after six days, the jury found Minis not guilty. No taint lingered over his actions. Subsequently, his surgical and leadership skills won him the rank of major in the U.S. Army, and after retirement Minis returned to Savannah to practice medicine and serve on the boards of benevolent societies.[171]

A year later Dr. William R. Waring was one of the founders of Savannah's Temperance Society. Uppermost in his mind was the Minis-Stark encounter and the bar of the City Hotel. Waring believed that "excessive drinking is the curse of our community." About the same time a Savannah grand jury condemned small "dram shops" and upper-class taverns as equally "prejudicial of morals and obnoxious to sobriety and good order."[172] The Temperance Society sponsored discussions on "the expediency of withholding licenses for the retail of Spiritous Liquors," which to some was a highly charged political question. In 1835 the Chatham County Temperance Society was founded at the Independent Presbyterian Church. Its object was to "suppress . . . particularly the use of all ardent spirits." That same year a letter writer in the *Christian Index* estimated that some two thousand Savannahians belonged to four large temperance societies in the city.[173]

The efforts by Waring and others to bring the northern evangelical temperance crusade to the city surprisingly met with some enthusiasm in Savannah. But in the long run quick tempers and itchy fingers heated by liquor in defense of honor prevailed. Shortly after the founding of the Savannah Temperance Society, two young men argued violently in the bar of the City Hotel. One challenged the other, who quickly accepted, and despite efforts by members of the Savannah Anti-Dueling Society, the young men crossed the Savannah River to the dueling grounds. Here one duelist was shot and killed. As usual, the newspapers ignored the incident, but the secretary of the Anti-Duelling Society referred to them as "deluded young men, with . . . false notions of honor."[174]

One of Savannah's leading citizens, W. B. Bulloch, also recognized in the city what he called "the aristocratical spirit of insulted honor [which] was determined to avenge [any] . . . indignity."[175] The Anti-Dueling Society no longer met after 1838, but dueling to avenge perceived insults persisted for years. Like most well-to-do Southerners, Savannah "gentlemen" believed that "honor is not to be sported with."[176]

In the early 1830s the City Hotel once more changed hands when Peter Wiltberger became the proprietor. Wiltberger was a forty-two-year-old veteran seafarer and venturesome ship's master. Determined to monopolize the hotel trade, he bought the Mansion House on the northwest corner of Broughton and Whitaker Streets for $10,000 and incorporated another nearby competitor's lodging house into his grand hotel, which he named after Count Casimir Pulaski.

The Pulaski Hotel stood at the corner of Bull and Bryan Streets and developed a more flamboyant style than that of the smaller City Hotel. Englishman James Silk Buckingham complained of "extravagant charges" at the Pulaski Hotel. While there he attended "one of the most brilliant parties I had seen," comparing it to those he had attended in London and Paris. "The dancing was good" and accompanied by a band "wholly formed of negroes"; they performed for some four hundred partygoers, including a "great number of very lovely faces, with the peculiarly animated expression of the southern women, in their dark eyes and hair, and soft Italian complexions."[177] Sophistical travelers such as Buckingham found Savannah a very cosmopolitan city.

In the late 1820s and early 1830s the healthiness of the city was again called into question. Miss Harriet Campbell especially "dreaded" cholera "more on account for the coloured people, than ourselves, for I doubt not, it will prove very fatal among them."[178] When smallpox appeared in the city at the beginning of the decade, Dr. Richard Arnold was appointed public vaccinator. In three months he vaccinated 624 persons.

In 1832 Asiatic cholera erupted in Atlantic coast ports. At that time, no physician in Savannah saw the relation between cholera and the local water supply; instead, Savannah officials revived efforts to remove all filth in the city. Dead animals, manure, garbage, and "fetid boggs" all drew hordes of flies and mosquitoes, especially in the city's lanes and alleyways. What Savannah's hundreds of buzzards did not eat was carried off by the city scavengers and burned at the city dumps, one at the west end of today's Gwinnett Street and another on the east side of town. Local authorities urged owners to splash whitewash on their buildings and douse privies with lime.

By September 1832 the threat of disease passed, and the city gave thanks, but in June 1833 cholera returned with a vengeance. The mayor, alarmed that cholera was spreading so rapidly, ordered cholera victims sent to the state's lazaretto on Tybee Island. In the late summer of 1834, cholera swept through plantations along the Savannah River, and slaves living in squalor died by the scores.[179] Reports spread of cases in the city. Miss Campbell's fears had come true.

To cope with the number of victims, inmates at the city's Poor House and Hospital were transferred to Oglethorpe Barracks, and three temporary hospitals were established. In 1835 the Poor House and Hospital was chartered by the state as a private institution. Five years later it remained, as usual, drastically underfunded and supported a large number of indigents: of the 494 admitted, 330 were paupers. Eighty-nine patients died during the year, 77 of them indigents. The well-to-do overseers—like their counterparts elsewhere—attributed the high death rate to the fact that the "paupers admitted are men of decidedly intemperate habits . . . [and] intemperance . . . is the cause of more than one-half of deaths among the class."[180] After years of requests from the city, the state finally appropriated $15,000 to build a city lazaretto for the quarantine of carriers of contagious diseases. However, many years passed before the legislature released the money.[181]

VENTURE CAPITALISTS

During 1834, Gazaway Lamar, a young Savannah banker, cotton merchant, and ship owner, imported the plates and frames for an iron-hulled vessel from England. It was assembled at John Cant's shipyard in Savannah, and an English steam engine was installed. On July 9 the vessel was launched and christened the *John Randolph*. A member of the local press exclaimed that "She . . . sat as lightly on the water as a duck." The vessel was the first iron-hulled steamboat to operate successfully in the waters of the United States. In August the *John Randolph* departed Savannah for Augusta. It towed two barges filled with two hundred tons of salt. The vessel was a great success. It drew less water than a wooden one, and its hull was immune from worms and rot. Two years later another iron-hulled vessel, the *Chatham,* was assembled locally from parts shipped from England and was put to work on the river.[182]

The number of steamboats navigating the Savannah River reached their peak during the 1830s. But early in the decade Savannah's businessmen vigorously explored new opportunities for expanding commerce. They called on the City Council to appropriate funds to build a bridge over the Savannah River into South Carolina, but it appears nothing came of the request. The city joined with Augusta to seek funds from the legislature to deepen the river and improve navigation between the two cities, but with no results.[183] Some businessmen envisioned only a bleak future for Savannah. One observed that for a dozen years the city had been "retrograding," and he saw "no prospect of a return of its former prosperity." Investing money locally "would be the height of folly," he concluded.[184]

The city's businessmen recognized also that for too long they had relied on the Savannah River for their commercial connection with the piedmont, a connection that Charleston lacked until the early 1830s, when the Charleston to Hamburg, South Carolina, railroad began encroaching on Savannah's hinterlands. Savannah businessmen recognized that to compete with Charleston for freight and passenger traffic in the upcountry, they had to build a rail line into the region. Furthermore, as thousands of cotton-planting whites continued spilling over into upland Georgia as cotton moved west, Savannah could seize the opportunity to siphon trade from its historic competitor, Charleston.

Although the city was mired in debt, aggressive businessmen now promoted the building of the Central of Georgia Railroad. John M. Berrien and Mayor William W. Gordon spearheaded the project. Gordon was Georgia's first graduate of the United States Military Academy (1815), after which he married Sarah Anderson Stites, daughter of prominent Savannahians. He practiced law and was elected to political office at the state and local level.

The plan called for the Central of Georgia Railroad to link Savannah with Macon, a distance of 191 miles. In 1834 the city paid for a survey to determine the best route for the line. With pressure from Mayor Gordon, the Savannah City Council, the Macon government, and towns along the proposed route, the legislature chartered the railroad in December 1835 and permitted it banking privileges.[185]

Groundbreaking ceremonies for the Central of Georgia got under way on Monday, December 12, 1835; it was a red-letter day for Savannah. The railroad launched an unprecedented new era of prosperity for the city. Mayor William Gordon was in Milledgeville lobbying the legislature, but Sarah Gordon communicated the excitement to him, observing that she had never "seen such general rejoicing or such happy faces as I met . . . as the people were coming in from the Commons, where they laid the *first rail,* and it was more like Broadway than anything I have seen . . . from Broughton Street all the way to our house both sides of the street were crowded." The "rejoicing" continued into the night when "a band of Music accompanied by *the people,* for I suppose I must not call them the rabble, paraded the streets." At 10:00 P.M. "they came before the door and called out distinctly 9 cheers for the Rail Road and Gordon and they gave the full number, for I counted to see if . . . they did." In conclusion Sarah wrote, "My Dearest Husband," all the townspeople "agree that to you alone is the credit due of the bills passing." And now she urged him to "let politics alone and live more with your family."[186]

But building the Central of Georgia Railroad became Gordon's life. He continued to be away from his family promoting the railroad, and Sarah's days became full looking after the family. She told him that his mother had broken her leg and was in such "agony" that she could not sleep unless she took an "opium pill," and that the younger son, George, had such a bad case of the croup that the doctor had prescribed "calomel" in hope that "bleeding" would not be necessary.[187] Sarah also told her husband that she was becoming "more and more impatient of being alone." And in somewhat bolder tones, full of sexual allusions, she concluded, "on your return I shall convince you of all that I have written, and you will see by actions . . . that you were wrong [in remaining away so long]"; and in another letter she remarked, "I expect I shall dream of you tonight."[188]

The day that the first rail was laid in Savannah, citizens enjoyed parades and celebrations, and city officials gave orations boasting that the railroad promised a new economic dawn for the city. Their vision was perfect. In less than fifty years the Central of Georgia dominated the means of transportation in the southeast.[189]

That same December of 1835 William Scarbrough was in Baltimore buying equipment for some of the steamers he owned and operated on the Savannah River with his business partner and son-in-law, Godfrey Barnsley. By the mid-1830s about twenty steamers ran almost daily between Savannah, Augusta, and Darien, carrying merchandise there and returning with hundreds of bales of cotton, lumber, and other products for shipment abroad. Steamers did a lively trade with Macon, Beaufort, and Charleston, too. Scarbrough, always the visionary, wrote Barnsley that he had designed an elaborate scheme to connect Savannah with New Orleans by railroads, canals, and steamboats, which would tap the trade of the west. It also would attract crowds and enhance materially the "depreciated Value of the Property in Savannah." Scarbrough died in 1838 and with him his visions, but others breathed new life into them. He had nothing to bequeath his family, but he contributed the concept of international steam shipping, enhanced the cultural and architectural life of Savannah, and was remembered as "an entertaining companion."[190]

Despite the visionary ideas of Scarbrough, the railroad alone supplanted steamboats and canals in Georgia within two decades of his death. The railroad was more dependable due to its more precise schedule and speed, and shippers enjoyed cheaper rates, too. State and local agencies and Savannahians poured thousands of borrowed dollars into building the Central of Georgia. The Savannah City Council alone bought half a million dollars worth of stock. By February, 1836 more than a million dollars was available to begin construction.

The thirty-nine-year-old Gordon became the first president of the Central of Georgia. In October the city government provided five acres of land to the railroad near Spring Hill, site of the bloody Revolutionary War clash, where the railroad constructed a depot and machine shops, part of which today serves as Savannah's Visitor's Center.[191]

Unable to find technical personnel in the non-industrialized South, the railroad company hired northern engineers; iron for the rails was imported from England. The engineers contracted with planters along the route for timber and slave labor. But as construction of the railroad began, speculation in land and slaves and easy credit spawned another economic panic and depression. Between 1835 and 1837 the price of cotton dropped from 15 cents a pound to 9 cents; the prices of slaves in some markets plunged by 30 percent.[192]

IRISH LABORERS, BLACK SLAVES, AND THE ECONOMY

Labor contractors for the Central of Georgia Railroad recruiting in the North during 1836–1837 launched the largest mass migration ever of Irish workers to Savannah. They worked for cheap wages and had experience in railroad building. More than 1,400 Irish came to Savannah and moved into the slums already crowded with blacks and earlier Irish immigrants on the western and eastern fringes of the city. Here informal social life revolved around the grocery store–tavern, the grog shops, and the alleyways of Yamacraw. On Saturdays the sounds of drunken brawls punctuated the night air. Once again Savannah's wealthy recoiled at open drunkenness and violence and worried about whether the social order might be coming unglued. At the same time, shopkeepers once more petitioned the City Council to allow shops to open on Sundays.[193]

Responding to such petitions, one slaveholder publicly condemned the shopkeepers for selling liquor to blacks, which "inflamed . . . the passions of slaves"; another Savannahian observed that with nearly one-half the city's population black, "We are in more danger from the intemperance of Slaves than" elsewhere. And a Savannah grand jury in 1836 condemned the liquor retailers "whose intercourse with slaves . . . [is] an inducement to theft and intoxication." The city government vacillated between supporting the shopkeepers and the wealthy slaveholders.[194] It was a divisive issue in a slave society where white unity was paramount. Liquor dealers continued to petition a council dominated by slave owners to permit them to reopen their stores on Sundays. The city government changed hands several times between those supporting the wealthy and those backing the shopkeepers.[195]

Savannah's well-to-do whites now worried over disorder from both blacks and the Irish. It was a "dark, rainy" night in late 1836 when Sarah Gordon told her husband William, now president of the Central of Georgia and away on business, that a "disturbance" at the nearby Telfair home "startled" her. Although the "guard" had been called out, she remained "nervous." Nevertheless, she told her husband not to worry because ever since she learned "the Town was filled with the Irishmen for the Railroad, . . . I have always had the front door latched at dusk and I always examine every place before going to bed."[196]

In 1837, during a wage dispute with the railroad, 150 Irishmen marched on Savannah. City officials hurried militiamen and cannons to intercept them while a Catholic priest, Father Jeremiah F. O'Neill, rushed to defuse the potential for violence. From the 1830s to his death in 1870, Father O'Neill profoundly influenced the lives of all Savannahians. He was one of a number of priests who ministered to local Catholics. Savannah had been part of the Diocese of Charleston since the eighteenth century, but by the end of the 1830s enough Catholics lived in Savannah to finance the building of the Cathedral of St. John the Baptist, which went up in the center of Savannah's business district. Within a decade, the Cathedral became the bishop's seat for the diocese of the state of Georgia.

During the late 1830s, officials of the Central of Georgia Railroad complained of trouble from the Irish laborers building the railroad. They sometimes squabbled among themselves over "sectional differences," but Father O'Neill believed that the disruptions resulted from the liquor supplied by the labor contractors. The need to expedite work and minimize costs led the management of the Central of Georgia to encourage the hiring of slaves whenever possible, and by the end of the decade, the majority of the five hundred construction workers inching the rail line toward Macon were slaves.[197]

By 1840, the Irish exercised political muscle within the Democratic Party. Occasionally during elections a war of words erupted between the local *Republican* newspaper, an organ of the Whig party, and the *Georgian,* the paper of the Democrats. Whigs denounced the Irish for voting before eligible and for trading votes for the right to carry on illegal trade with the city's blacks. When the rhetoric became too hot for the Irish, as it did in the election year of 1840, an armed mob of Irishmen rioted at the polling places.[198]

Savannah and the country's economy worsened in the late 1830s due to overspeculation in canals, railroads, slaves, and, especially, cotton. Panic set in, banks failed, and prices plunged. Some well-to-do families felt the effects of the downturn; others did not. In mid-March, 1837, for instance, Godfrey Barnsley, the vastly wealthy English-born cotton merchant, gave a fancy ball costing over $20,000 at Scarbrough House, where his family lived. Having made his fortune, Barnsley planned to return to England, and this was his "goodbye to Savannah" ball. A forty-six page poem was written about it, which included the line "When wit and beauty held their festal night." The gala was remembered for years as the most elaborate, ornate, and expensive "Fancy Ball" ever given."[199]

In March 1837, Mary Telfair wrote a friend: "The depression here is very great. The planter as well as the merchant feels it—the incomes of the former will be diminished one third of what they have been." Mary's family told her that "Retrenchment is necessary for everyone," and she believed "if I had to retrench carriage and horses would be the 1st thing to put down. It is certainly the only luxury I enjoy." The depression barely made a dent in the vast wealth of the Telfairs. In June, Mary told a friend, "We sail on the 10th of this month."[200]

Within a month of Barnsley's festive and costly ball, he wrote his English partners that the decline in cotton prices affects "the credit of almost every" cotton merchant. Planters who could afford to do so held their cotton off the market in hopes of higher prices, but by late August good cotton sold at only 10 to 11 cents a pound. The effects of the economic panic of 1837 became so severe and Barnsley's financial losses were so heavy that he canceled his planned return to England and retirement there.[201]

FREE BLACKS AND ABOLITIONISTS AGAIN

Anxieties persisted in Savannah over the activities of free blacks and the possibilities of insurrections, even after the legislature passed an act prohibiting free persons of color from entering Georgia.[202] In 1836, when news spread that blacks had joined forces with Indians in Florida to attack whites, Mayor William W. Gordon told the governor that it caused "much apprehension . . . that our black population may become troublesome." Orders by the governor dispatching volunteers from Savannah to Florida increased the local anxiety. Gordon informed the governor that the population of whites to blacks on the seaboard was small and wanted him to know of "the danger in which we are already."[203] Gordon organized a city guard "to be prepared for any emergency."[204] Despite such precautions, Mary Telfair did not feel safe. She fretted to a friend that with the region so unprotected, "I fear there will be an internal enemy to contend with."[205]

The writings of northern abolitionists outraged wealthy white Savannahians. In the summer of 1835 it was rumored that pamphlets by anti-slavery activists Arthur Tappan and William Lloyd Garrison were circulating in the city, with the intended outcome of breeding discontent among blacks. One merchant in the city was so angry that he donated a thousand dollars to begin a drive to raise money for anyone who kidnapped Tappan and brought him to Savannah, where he could "undergo summary punishment." Charles Greene, a cotton merchant and business associate of Godfrey Barnsley's, said that the kidnapping plan reflected the "mob era!"

It appears that it was amid the heated anti-abolitionist sentiment in 1835–1836 when twenty-eight-year-old Reverend Courtlandt Van Rensselaer came to Savannah. A Yale graduate, he was an ordained Presbyterian minister. When it was charged that he was "holding *secret meetings* with the *Negroes* . . . and consulted with them on their means of revolt," local authorities ordered him detained. Before he could be arrested, Van Rensselaer fled. The incident confirmed for Savannah's slaveholders that the hated abolitionists were encouraging black insurrectionists.[206]

John Hopper, a young New Yorker and son of Quaker abolitionist Isaac T. Hopper, ventured into this highly charged atmosphere in January 1837. He came to Savannah from Charleston, where he had visited with Quakers who had given him some literature on slavery. Hopper took a room at the City Hotel and was recognized by Daniel D. Nash, a slave catcher, also from New York. Nash informed the usual barroom habitués that Hopper shared his father's anti-slavery sentiments. Word spread quickly, and Nash and a mob burst into Hopper's room. He was cursed, hit, kicked, and spit upon. Ransacking Hopper's possessions, the mob discovered the pamphlet given to him in Charleston and decided to hang him as an abolitionist. The proprietor of the hotel, Peter Wiltberger, summoned Mayor Nicoll, who took Hopper into custody until he could investigate the matter. The crowd milled around the jail waiting. Around 5:00 A.M. the mayor announced that the tracts in Hopper's possession favored colonization of African Americans, not the abolition of slavery. A cold, driving rain sent many of the mob scurrying for cover, and city authorities quickly hustled Hopper aboard a ship bound for Rhode Island. Some weeks later Hopper's father wrote Mayor Nicoll to thank him for saving his son "from the violence of unreasonable and wicked men."[207]

Savannahians once more had used violence and threats toward someone suspected of opposing slavery. They had tried to arrest Van Rensselaer for questioning; years before, in 1804, they jailed and ran out of town Judge Jabez Bowen Jr.; and they abused Hopper, whose life most likely was saved by his quick departure. In 1837, Dr. Richard Arnold summed up the matter when he told a Bostonian, "our domestic concerns are for us to manage."[208]

Visitors to the city in the 1830s frequently were informed of the attitudes of Savannahians toward abolitionists. Distinguished scientist Charles Lyell was told that extra precautions had to be taken with slaves "after an insurrection brought on by abolitionists missionaries." The latter, Lyell noted, "were spoken of . . . in the same tone as incendiaries or beasts of prey whom it would be meritorious to shoot or hang." Visiting Englishman James Silk Buckingham was told by white Savannahians that "an abolitionist was more terrible than . . . a murderer."[209]

Wealthy white Savannahians continued to worry over the presence of free blacks in the city, especially those arriving by vessels. In the mid-1830s the government was informed that free blacks visiting Savannah planned to kidnap local slaves. This led to adoption of an ordinance requiring the arrest and confinement of all "free persons of color" arriving by sea in Savannah.[210] The City Council appeared vindicated a few years later when a free black sailor, Bill Owens, came ashore from his vessel and was arrested for attempting to kidnap two black girls. During his imprisonment he received fifty lashes "well laid on" and then was sent back to his ship upon its departure.[211]

Near the end of the 1830s, the City Council enacted laws prohibiting free blacks from keeping or managing "a common ill-governed or disorderly house" and from gambling at cards, dice, checkers, dominoes, or billiards. An ordinance of the same year prohibited more than seven blacks from meeting together at one time aside from church or funerals unless a white person was present; to assemble for dancing or other socializing required written permission.[212]

Near the very end of the decade yet another scare from arsonists unnerved Savannah's well-to-do whites. The city government observed that since Savannah "has been repeatedly fired by incendiary acts," additional measures needed to be adopted to protect the city. Therefore, it was resolved that the mayor use all the police power of the city and that at night citizens of each ward practice extra "vigilance" to guard against arsonists.[213]

FIRMIN CERVEAU'S *SAVANNAH*

There is no hint of the racism, apprehensions of insurrection, the scarlet fever epidemic, or the economic recession gripping Savannah in Firmin Cerveau's painting of the city in 1837, the one work for which he is known. A native of Smyrna, Asia Minor, "He . . . painted a convincing fantasy, a fulfillment of promoters' dreams," one scholar noted.[214]

Savannah appears in the painting as a compact city, running about a mile wide along the river and some three-quarters of a mile deep from Bay Street south to Liberty Street. Cerveau made the city even smaller by leaving out a northern portion, or about a fifth of the whole city; furthermore, by 1837 the city had opened three new wards, Pulaski, Jackson, and Lafayette—all south of Liberty Street to Jones Street. On the clean streets and walks surprisingly bereft of debris are what appear to be contented African Americans and prosperous whites; two members of the Georgia Hussars, in plumed helmets and on horseback, dash by; elegant carriages and a few buggies roll along Bay and up Bull Streets. No laboring-class whites or even those of modest means are seen; nothing is seen of brawling sailors along the waterfront or the brothels of Yamacraw to the west or those to the east. This was purposefully done. Cerveau worked with his back to the river, the very lifeblood of the city. By painting the bright, prosperous, cheerful scene from atop the tower of the Exchange Building on the Bay, Cerveau looked directly down on Bay Street, the business district, and south down the length of Bull Street past the unfinished monument to General Greene. It was indeed "Cerveau's Savannah," a tranquil, happy, quiet city.[215]

Visitors from London, New York, Philadelphia, and other larger cities remarked on the symmetry of the tree-lined streets, the numerous squares filled with live oak and Pride of India trees, the hospitality, and the tranquility of the city—a surface tranquility, however. These well-to-do visitors associated only with their Savannah peers. Miss Henrietta Maria Thomas of Maryland, who arrived in Savannah in November of 1835, described her host and hostess "as sociable as acquaintances of much longer date." Their garden was "a little Paradise, overgrown with jessamine and cluster roses, the air perfumed with the sweets." The parlor was "handsomely furnished," and "every thing looked very sweet."[216]

To the well-off visitors, Savannah was quiet, without crowds and noisy traffic. Some attributed it to "the sand, through which a pedestrian wades in navigating the streets . . . a considerable annoyance to a stranger, who fears every step of sinking to his waist."[217] A young female visitor from New York declared that "Here even the carriages we rode in gave out no sound for their wheels sank down in the sand." She liked the pace: "Southern people . . . always move slowly. No one is ever in a hurry, white or black." She found the ladies "have . . . the highest type of breeding." As for the gentlemen, "they are . . . courteous and chivalrous in their bearing." She also loved the "chinaberry" trees that lined South Broad Street, "which are beautiful in shape. . . and in the spring . . . have the fragrance of lilac."[218]

But like Cerveau's impression, visitors' insights into Savannah could be superficial. The chinaberry trees, growing thick in the city, gloomy and odorous to some, were short-lived and were soon replaced with oak and other hardwoods. As for the streets, which remained unpaved for years, the "dust" from them, Savannahians complained, "is loaded with . . . impurities" and likely causes "throat and lung troubles."[219]

In 1837, the same year that Cerveau painted a portion of the city, the German Friendly Society was chartered on December 23. With the number of German immigrants entering the city, Savannah's German Americans felt the need for an organization to promote fellowship and to provide relief for indigent members of the society and their widows and orphans.[220]

RECESSION AND HOPE

In the spring of 1838 the Lower Creek Boat Club of Savannah was organized and purchased the *Star,* a New York–built boat. They immediately challenged the Aquatic Club of Camden, Georgia, owners of the *Lizard.* The date of the contest was set for Saturday, April 28, and it was agreed that the vanquished would lose their boat to the winners.

On the day of the race a huge crowd milled around the starting point at the foot of West Broad Street, today's Martin Luther King Jr. Boulevard. Some placed bets. The *Star* was a plank-built boat that measured thirty feet in length by three feet, ten inches in width and weighed only 140 pounds; the *Lizard,* called a log or canoe boat, was of like dimensions but most likely heavier. The racecourse was a measured mile marked by a buoy.

The *Star,* black with a gilt stripe, approached the starting point, as did the

Lizard, painted green with a white bottom. Four young oarsmen in each boat, members of the white gentry in loose but bright clothing, readied themselves. A starter gave the signal, and sixteen oars splashed as one, pulling toward the buoy. The race was over in less than seven minutes. The *Lizard* won by 105 feet. The *Daily Georgian,* bursting with regional pride, boasted that the Lizard, a southern boat hewn from trees along the banks of the warm Satilla River, had bested the *Star,* "formed and fashioned in the icy bound regions of the Hudson." The era of club regattas at Savannah, Charleston, and Brunswick was well underway.[221] However, a few weeks after this festive occasion, a naval disaster just off Savannah plunged the city into mourning. In June 1838 the steamship *Pulaski* exploded, carrying to their deaths many well-off white Savannahians.

For some Savannah residents, the persisting recession was also an economic disaster. Savannah's business leaders met once more to consider more direct communication with South Carolina via a bridge or boat ferry. By 1838 the original stock of the Central of Georgia Railroad had plunged from $100 a share to $20; the cotton crisis made tight money even tighter, and contractors building the railroad had to be paid one-quarter of their fee in cash and three-quarters in stock. "Swamp fever" broke out among the laborers and slowed work; the following spring torrential rains unleashed freshets along the rail route, sweeping away over $65,000 worth of bridges and culverts and damaging embankments. In the fall, mosquitoes carrying yellow fever once more swarmed over Savannah, and Irish laborers died in the slums along the river.

Despite the crisis in cotton prices, disease, and floods, by 1839 eighty miles of track had been laid between Savannah and Macon. Dr. Richard Arnold enjoyed a "delightful . . . excursion" on the railroad with a group of young women. And though by now he was married and a father, he confided, "from mere animal spirits I certainly drank more than I might to have done."[222]

On May 24, 1839, Dr. Arnold, northern-born Israel K. Tefft, a collector of historical documents, Dr. William Bacon Stevens, a historian, and twenty-three others founded the Georgia Historical Society. Arnold was one of the fifteen physicians among the 112 charter members of the society. Medical doctors remained some of the foremost leaders of the city's intellectual and political life. Four physicians, Arnold among them, served as mayors in antebellum Savannah.[223]

When cotton was harvested in the fall, the Central of Georgia was "overrun with freight." The railroad needed to add more rolling stock to its seven engines, five passenger cars, and sixty-seven freight cars.[224] However, a victim of the depression was the Savannah, Ogeechee and Altamaha Canal Company, which was nearing bankruptcy in the late 1830s. Only a loan of $25,000 from the city saved it. Irish contract laborers found work on this project, too. By 1840 the canal had been renovated with four lift locks and two tidal locks. Now for the first time the company began to make a profit. Flatboats used the canal to transport rice, bricks, farm products, naval stores, and, especially, hewn lumber to and from Savannah.

The canal basin abutted the black and Irish neighborhoods of Yamacraw in Oglethorpe Ward on the western edge of the city, the freight yards of the Central of Georgia Railroad, and the nearby Savannah River wharfs. The city was becoming a major Atlantic coast ocean export center. For the next two decades the canal added great wealth to the city.[225]

Even so, the recession persisted in Savannah. James Louis Rossignol, owner of a Savannah brickyard, wrote to a friend in Massachusetts: "my situation is pretty bad as I can save no money it all has to go out as fast as it is made." But he told his friend that there is an "immense field a man has open . . . in these parts to make a fortune."[226]

James Rossignol was an astute observer, as were other Savannah promoters and entrepreneurs, both black and white: Samuel Howard, Richard Richardson, William Scarbrough, Andrew Marshall, William Gordon, Godfrey Barnsley, Andrew Low, Gazaway Lamar, John Dillon, and Edward O'Byrne. The spirit of boosterism and enterprise flourished in the port city and among businessmen, not the planters of the countryside. This elite band of civic promoters of Savannah's economic progress—like those identified in other antebellum southern cities by historians Don H. Doyle, James M. Russell, David R. Goldfield, and Harold W. Hurst—also served as chief officers in local and state political, social, and benevolent organizations. And with the labor of black slaves, unskilled white Georgians, and recent Irish and German immigrants, a dramatic transformation was underway, destined to bring economic good times to Savannah.

At the end of the 1830s, the Macon *Telegraph* praised Savannah's recent awakening: "After a long and almost fatal slumber old Yamacraw has . . . determined to go ahead. Had she shown the same spirit, possessed the same enterprise, twenty years ago she would now have been at the very head of Southern cities."[227] In 1839 English traveler James Silk Buckingham described

Savannah's many private residences as "handsome . . . brick buildings . . . of sumptuous interior. . . [which] combine as much of elegance and luxury as are to be found" in the United States.[228]

That same year at the annual Hibernian banquet, Edward O'Byrne raised a toast to Savannah: "Her commerce is increasing, her private and public works are fast progressing," and he hoped she might become "the Queen of the South."[229] In 1840, the Savannah *Republican* remarked: "Savannah is looking up—her Rail Road is looking up—her Schools—her Promenades—her Politics—every thing is improving. Nothing can stop her onward course."[230]

Between 1830 and 1840 the population of Savannah jumped nearly 54 percent, from 7,303 to 11,214 inhabitants. The white population increased from 3,620 to 5,888. The black population rose from 3,683 to 5,326—the number of slaves increased from 3,279 to 4,694, with the number of "free colored" males increasing from 169 to 262 and the "free colored" females rising from 235 to 370. The increasing wealth in slaves manifested itself in the rising number of slave owners: 87 Savannahians owned 10 or more slaves in 1830, whereas a decade later 133 owned 10 or more slaves; 16 Savannahians owned 20 or more slaves in 1830, whereas a decade later 31 owned 20 or more slaves. Only 2 Savannahians owned more than 30 slaves in 1830: J. B. Read held 33 slaves, and Eliza Willing owned 61; however, 11 Savannahians had more than 30 slaves by 1840, including E. E. Pynchen with 43 and Robert Habersham with 55. A few Savannahians had become rich especially in slave property.[231]

In sum, about half of Savannah's white population owned no slaves; in the other half of white households that did own slaves, bondpeople usually outnumbered their masters. This meant that far more individuals inhabited much less space in the slave quarters than in the main house. Furthermore, in every neighborhood, slaves comprised from a quarter to a half of the population, and free blacks lived in every section of the city. Savannah's population of blacks and whites remained thoroughly integrated during the antebellum period, as it did in other southern urban centers.[232]

By 1840 Savannah had survived hurricanes, catastrophic fires, yellow fever epidemics, and a prolonged economic depression. Soon the economic doldrums ended. The canal and especially the railroad linked Savannah to its hinterlands and abroad; they resuscitated commerce and launched a boom in the financial life of the city. Savannah's wealthy amassed more and more assets in the decade of the 1840s, which increased the widening gap between the very rich and the poor.

The founder of Georgia at Savannah, General James Oglethorpe. This romantic image nevertheless conveys Oglethorpe's determination as a military leader. He was also a creative city planner whose design for Savannah was sui generis in Britain's American colonies. Courtesy of Georgia Historical Society, Savannah, Georgia.

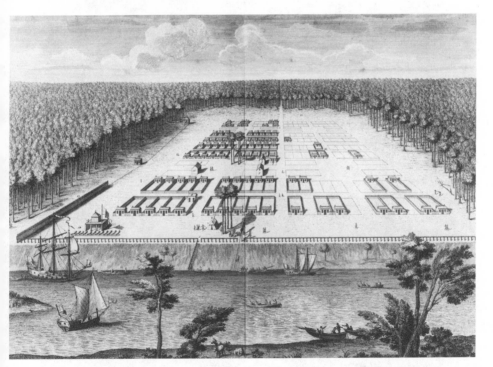

Town of Savannah. In this engraving attributed to Peter Gordon and done in March 1734, about a year after Savannah was founded, General Oglethorpe's unique design for the settlement is taking shape. Courtesy of Hargrett Rare Book and Manuscript Library, University of Georgia Libraries.

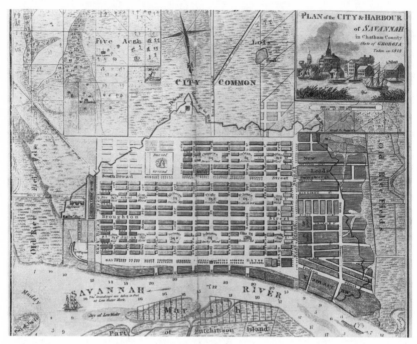

"Plan of the City & Harbour of Savannah" done in 1818 in the midst of one of the city's periodic economic booms. Oglethorpe's remarkable early design for a city of green squares fronted by dwellings is now dramatically evident as the city sprawls southward from the river. Drawn and published by I. Stouf, April 9, 1818. Courtesy of Hargrett Rare Book and Manuscript Library, University of Georgia Libraries.

The Savannah Theater built by William Jay. The theater hosted hundreds of plays and concerts beginning in 1818 and served as a civilizing venue unknown in the countryside. The structure, one of numerous architectural gems throughout Savannah, contributes to both the built and humanizing environment. Courtesy of Hargrett Rare Book and Manuscript Library, University of Georgia Libraries.

The Bulloch mansion. This magnificent home was built (ca. 1818–1820) on Orleans Square by the English-born architect William Jay for the wealthy Savannah merchant Archibald S. Bulloch. Jay designed and constructed other grand dwellings and public buildings that provided an environment quite different from the countryside. Bulloch lost his fortune and his mansion, as did other wealthy local businessmen, in the economic depression beginning in the 1820s. The Bulloch mansion was razed in the early twentieth century. Courtesy of Georgia Historical Society, Savannah, Georgia.

The Savannah Poor House and Hospital. This structure was established by the city's civic elite to provide a place of refuge for the ill and indigent among the white population—usually the aged and single women with children. The facility was also designed to remove the growing number of poor whites from the city's streets so that visitors would envision a prosperous Savannah and so that blacks would not develop any feelings of superiority to whites, even indigent ones. Engraving in George White, *Historical Recollections of Georgia* (New York: Pudney and Russell, 1855).

Cerveau's Savannah. This is an idealized view of the city by Fermin Cerveau. He painted this panorama from atop the Exchange Building in 1837, but with his back to the busy river. He perhaps purposely left out the east and west ends of the city along the waterfront where several thousand blacks and whites crowded together in hovels, sailors brawled, and brothels flourished. Courtesy of Hargrett Rare Book and Manuscript Library, University of Georgia Libraries.

Savannah in 1855. The view of Savannah in this lithograph is north down Bull Street from the Pulaski Monument and Monterey Square, one of many such squares in the city by this date. The squares surrounded by greenery and by private and public buildings such as Mickve Israel Synagogue immediately right of the square, the magnificent St. John's Episcopal Church in the left background, and the Independent Presbyterian Church in the distance provided a humanizing environment for residents and visitors alike. Courtesy of Georgia Historical Society, Savannah, Georgia.

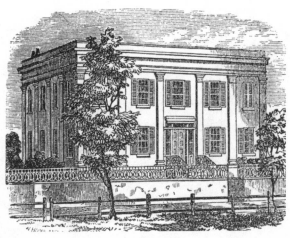

The Female Asylum. This facility for orphaned or abandoned white girls was founded by Savannah's well-to-do women and was evidence of their self-expression, which they also exhibited in their churches and in the many parties and weddings they planned within a patriarchal society. The wives of Savannah's white male elite hoped to ensure that the girls in the asylum became disciplined, moral, and Christian young women, and that they went on to make their way in the world and lead productive lives, to the extent possible. Engraving in George White, *Historical Recollections of Georgia* (New York: Pudney and Russell, 1855).

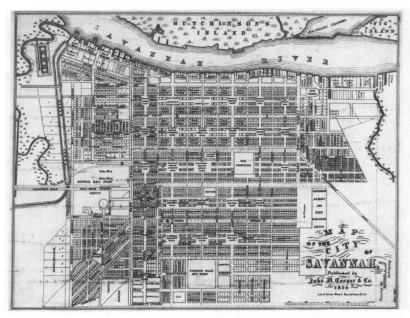

"Map of the City of Savannah, published by John M. Cooper & Co., 1856." The map shows that Savannah has sprawled just beyond Forsyth Place, and that the last squares have been established, which created tranquil spaces within a booming commercial city. Courtesy of Hargrett Rare Book and Manuscript Library, University of Georgia Libraries.

Wright Square after the Civil War. The photograph conveys the parklike setting of Savannah's many squares, which had such a civilizing effect on residents and visitors alike. Courtesy of Georgia Historical Society, Savannah, Georgia.

Distributing Reservoir. In late antebellum Savannah a desire for good water and a burgeoning population led civic leaders to construct a waterworks, which began operation in the winter of 1852–1853. This reservoir rose about eighty feet above street level. Atop the masonry circular tower was the iron reservoir, which stored water and distributed it through cast-iron pipes to businesses, dwellings, and fire hydrants throughout much of the city. Courtesy of Hargrett Rare Book and Manuscript Library, University of Georgia Libraries.

The Chatham County and Savannah city jail, which was located on Hall Street in the 1850s. Here in poorly ventilated cells and generally unhealthy conditions blacks and whites were incarcerated together, sometimes planned future criminal acts together, and occasionally escaped together. Such close association of poor whites and blacks must have contributed to feelings of friendship for one another and mitigated racism. Courtesy of Hargrett Rare Book and Manuscript Library, University of Georgia Libraries.

Savannah's waterfront and the river, the city's artery to the world. This undated waterfront scene, filled with incoming and outgoing vessels, is reminiscent of commercial activity on the river for much of the nineteenth century. Courtesy of Georgia Department of Archives and History.

Bales of cotton awaiting shipment from Savannah. The photograph, taken about a decade after the Civil War, accurately depicts an aspect of the city's economy that depended on the Central of Georgia Railroad to carry cotton from the upcountry to the lowcountry port. The image is a reliable reflection of the booming export trade in cotton from the 1840s forward. Courtesy of Georgia Department of Archives and History.

A forest of masts pointing skyward from the decks of coastal and ocean-going vessels tied off Savannah's wharves and loading lumber. This scene could have been photographed almost any time from the mid-1800s to the end of the nineteenth century. It testifies to the city's bustling port and economic boom, which was interrupted by the Civil War. Courtesy of Georgia Department of Archives and History.

Pulaski Hotel,
Savannah, Ga.

The Pulaski Hotel. This example of the many structures of Savannah's splendid built environment was located at the corner of Bull and Bryan Streets. The hotel was named after Casimir Pulaski, a Polish count who was killed in action in Savannah in 1779 while fighting with American and French forces to retake the town from the British. By the 1850s the hotel was Savannah's premier hostelry and looked much like it did in this photograph taken some years later. In the twentieth century, the hotel was demolished to make room for a cafeteria. Courtesy of Georgia Department of Archives and History.

City Market in the late nineteenth century. The market was located on the corner of Congress and Barnard Streets for over 140 years. African American vendors can be seen still dominating the market trade as they had done for generations. The building was demolished in 1954 to make way for a parking garage. Courtesy of Georgia Department of Archives and History.

Unidentified bondwoman who belonged to Charles C. Jones Jr., mayor of Savannah, 1860–1861. The woman is remarkably well dressed and most likely was a house servant who, like so many slaves, enjoyed the relative freedom and opportunity to earn money in the city. Jones himself believed that the city exerted a pernicious influence on slaves. Courtesy of Hargrett Rare Book and Manuscript Library, University of Georgia Libraries.

Two slaves plowing rice fields near Savannah, ca. 1855. This rare image of African Americans illustrates the dramatic differences between the lives of most bondpeople in the countryside and those residing in the city. Courtesy of Georgia Historical Society, Savannah, Georgia.

A rare photograph of one of Savannah's many African American firemen in uniform. This unidentified firefighter, whose dress and countenance reflect great pride in his work, was most likely a free black. However, he might have been a slave since several hundred free and bond blacks were required to combat Savannah's frequent blazes. Black and white firemen worked closely during monthly drills and while fighting fires. Courtesy of Special Collections Department, Robert W. Woodruff Library, Emory University.

Israel K. Tefft from Rhode Island, one of the Savannah literati. Tefft edited a local paper and became nationally known for his collection of 25,000 autographs, primarily from the colonial and Revolutionary War eras. In 1839 the Georgia Historical Society was founded in his home on St. Julian Street. He was a lifelong friend of a circle of the city's intellectuals, George Wymberley Jones, William Bacon Stevens, Richard Dennis Arnold, William B. Hodgson, and Alexander S. Smets. Courtesy of Georgia Historical Society, Savannah, Georgia.

The Reverend Stephen Elliott, Episcopal bishop of the diocese of Georgia. Elliott was one of Savannah's several intellectual leaders who exerted a humanizing influence on life in the city in the antebellum years, but like others of his privileged class, he supported the status quo and the Confederacy. Courtesy of Georgia Historical Society, Savannah, Georgia.

Mrs. Alexander R. Lawton in the 1880s. Like other white women of the privileged class, Sarah Lawton found self-expression in the patriarchal society of antebellum and Civil War Savannah in the church, in her work for charities, and in manipulating social life among the elite, all of which served as civilizing influences on life in the city. Courtesy of Georgia Historical Society, Savannah, Georgia.

Julia Schwartz, née Barnsley, the vivacious daughter of wealthy cotton merchant Godfrey Barnsley, in a photograph taken a decade after the Civil War. She and other women in Savannah found self-expression through the church, charities, and the whirl of social life. During the prewar years, Julia and her sister Adelaide lived with their father in New Orleans part of the year and traveled to Savannah for the social season. Courtesy of Georgia Historical Society, Savannah, Georgia.

The first flag of independence raised in the South. Following word of Lincoln's election, white Savannahians on November 8, 1860, gathered in Johnson Square, one of the oldest green, leafy squares surrounded by private and public buildings, as depicted in this lithograph. There they unfurled a banner with a coiled rattlesnake and the words "Southern Rights . . . Don't Tread on Me." Courtesy of Special Collections and Archives, Robert W. Woodruff Library, Emory University.

Exodus from Savannah. This scene from *Frank Leslie's Illustrated Newspaper* depicts the hurried evacuation of Savannah by the well-to-do in December 1861 following the landing of Union troops at Tybee Island, just seventeen miles southeast of the city. Once again the action takes place in one of the city's many squares, which indicates the association of northerners, as well as southerners, with the city's design and its squares. Courtesy of Georgia Historical Society, Savannah, Georgia.

Charles C. Jones Jr., a member of the Georgia lowcountry's privileged class. This image was made about 1860, when Jones was twenty-nine years of age. He wears the uniform of a first lieutenant, Chatham Artillery, the oldest and most prestigious of Savannah's nine volunteer companies. Jones was also the city's mayor, 1860–61. He was the son of the Reverend Dr. Charles C. Jones, a wealthy slaveholding planter and Presbyterian clergyman. He spent his youth on his father's three plantations near Savannah in Liberty County and graduated from the College of New Jersey (Princeton) in 1852 and Harvard Law School in 1855. He returned to Savannah to practice law and enter politics. In August 1861 Jones left public office for military service in the Confederate Army. Courtesy of Hargrett Rare Book and Manuscript Library, University of Georgia Libraries.

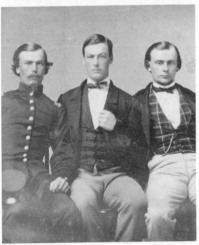

Left: A remarkable and clear photograph of the Branch brothers, one of the few middle-class Savannah families with extant images. From left to right John, Hamilton, and Sanford Branch. Lieutenant John Branch was killed at First Manassas in 1861, Hamilton was slightly wounded, and Sanford was captured. The latter two brothers survived the war. Courtesy of the Atlanta History Center. *Right:* A member of the Irish Jasper Greens, a Savannah volunteer company, poses in uniform and holds a muzzle-loading rifle. Organized by Irishmen, the unit saw service in several conflicts, including the Civil War. This photograph was taken several years after the conflict. Savannah's numerous militia companies were organized before the war for both social and military reasons. Courtesy of Georgia Department of Archives and History.

Two views of Savannah's waterfront and namesake river at the end of the Civil War. Courtesy of the National Archives.

CHAPTER 6

Prosperity to Civil War, 1840–1865

*T*HE ECONOMIC RECESSION gripping Savannah during the 1820s and
1830s slowly loosened its grip before the gathering commercial boom in
the two decades before the Civil War. The railroad and the river fueled
the economic expansion. Attracted by new jobs spawned in expanding and
new industries, foreign immigrants and northerners streamed into the city.
The rapidly growing population strained municipal services, and the government created new facilities—a waterworks and the initial sewerage system for
the city, a gasworks, and public schools—to meet the demand. To maintain
law and order, a professional, uniformed police force was organized, a new jail
designed, and better streetlights installed.

BUILDING THE CENTRAL OF GEORGIA RAILROAD

In the face of the persistent economic downturn and natural disasters that continued to plague the building of the Central of Georgia Railroad, some wondered if the line would ever be completed. Worried Savannah merchants and
factors met in 1841 and resolved it was "necessary and expedient that a *Chamber of Commerce* be organized" to promote commerce. About the same time
the city government appealed to federal officials for assistance to combat shoaling and for assistance in removing "obstructions" in the Savannah River so as
to "improve . . . navigation" and trade.[1] Over a decade elapsed before the federal government responded.

By March 1841 some 125 miles of track of the Central of Georgia Railroad
were laid north and westward of Savannah. Trains carried goods and passen-

gers profitably to and from Savannah that year until heavy downpours of rain caused streams to boil over and sweep away small bridges and culverts, causing $56,000 in damages. In 1842 an epidemic of "swamp fever" felled both laborers and engineers building a railroad bridge across the Oconee River. The chief engineer remarked that it was "almost impossible to employ others" to take the place of the disabled and dead. Even the young founder and first president of the railroad, William W. Gordon, succumbed from the "fever" in March 1842.

Richard R. Cuyler, also a major promoter of the Central of Georgia, succeeded President Gordon. Cuyler's energy and his experience with the Central's Railroad Bank helped him meet the financial crisis facing the railroad and to complete its last miles. The stock of the Central, which was first offered at $100 per share, had plunged to $20 per share. With few assets remaining and the directors' desire to complete the line quickly, Cuyler offered two contractors a deal that they could not refuse: to speedily finish the railroad for an extra $21,000 in bonds. Cuyler's special incentive worked. On October 13, 1843, the first train puffed to the east bank of the Ocmulgee River just opposite the city of Macon. A barbecue and toasts by city and railroad officials celebrated the completion of the 191-mile railroad after seven years and at a cost of $2,581,273. Savannah was now directly linked with the piedmont cotton country. Despite such an achievement, low cotton prices into the mid-1840s resulted in reduced traffic to Savannah and modest earnings for the railroad. It was a temporary phenomenon.[2]

Savannah's economy remained sluggish and its debt high. When privates of the city watch asked for a modest pay increase in 1841, the City Council replied that it was impossible because of the city's strained financial resources. For the same reasons, construction of a new jail was deferred again despite the current jail's "dilapidated state."[3] Finally, five years later, a new county jail was built near the corner of Hall and Whitaker Streets and placed under the control and management of Savannah's city government. In 1841 the city's bonded indebtedness reached $547,075, and to maintain the debt cost $35,000 annually. Twice during 1843 the city treasury lacked the money to meet the semiannual interest payments on its bonds due to Georgia and New York banks. The city's young mayor, Dr. Richard D. Arnold, appealed to the state government for assistance, telling the governor that the city is "very much embarrassed for funds." Councilmen investigated ways to reduce the city's debt and decided to levy a tax on the least taxed residents but those most able to pay—professional men and brokers of rice, cotton, and lumber. The City Council estimated that in 1841 Savannah brokers in the cotton and rice trade alone pocketed $350,000. An income tax of 2½ percent was imposed on the incomes of brokers and professional men and was collected for ten years despite rising opposition by influential white citizens who called the tax "cruel" and "unjust." To preserve harmony among Savannah's most prominent white men, the city government eventually repealed the 2½ percent tax on income; subsequently, a 1 percent income tax was instituted.[4]

A cotton factor in Savannah wrote in December 1845 that he had "done very little in cotton & prospects are far from cheering." The following year a dispute over Oregon's boundary strained U.S. relations with Great Britain, and the United States went to war with Mexico. These international events cast a pall over the cotton trade. There was little demand in Liverpool, and the return on cotton remained so low that ships at Savannah loaded lumber instead. In September 1846 one Savannahian wrote: "There is nothing of interest in our . . . city beyond some excitement about a railroad." In 1847 the Central Railroad line was completed between Savannah and Atlanta, and citizens of both cities celebrated the event on August 19. The following year telegraph lines went up in Savannah.[5] Without this means to communicate down the line, expansion of the Central of Georgia Railroad would have been difficult to imagine.

Despite the poor market in cotton, the Central of Georgia Railroad, under its energetic president, Richard Cuyler, promoted the building of feeder railroads, spurs, branches, and a steamship line to connect with northern ports. Beginning in 1845 and for more than a decade, the Central encouraged, subsidized, and eventually controlled lines linking Macon to Atlanta and to the booming cotton centers of the western and southwestern counties. One carrier subsidized by the state connected Atlanta and Chattanooga, and another provided Savannah with a direct line into southwest Georgia. The rail line, Charleston and Savannah, provided a link to the northeast. President Cuyler, who exerted powerful influence over the Georgia legislature, successfully opposed most appeals for state aid from other railroads, which, if funded, would have cut into the profits of the Central.[6] It was Cuyler, Savannah's *Daily Morning News* observed, who shaped "all the roads in Georgia to suit the interest of the Central Road."[7]

These many subsidiary lines of the Central of Georgia Railroad pushed deep into Georgia's hinterlands, and when the recession in cotton prices lifted in the late 1840s, the Central's trains brought thousands of bales to Savannah.

For instance, in 1844 the railroad transported only 77,437 bales of cotton to Savannah and earned a net income of $180,000. Four years later, the Central, then supplied by some feeder lines, carried 168,718 bales to Savannah and earned almost $250,000; then in 1849 it hauled 391,000 cotton bales to the port city for a net return of $330,755. By the following year 35 percent of the country's entire cotton crop was hauled to and shipped from Charleston and Savannah, while the receipts at New Orleans dropped. From this time on, the Central of Georgia Railroad became "serenely prosperous." Beginning in the early 1850s, the Central's net earnings climbed steadily from $507,625 to $764,574 in 1860, when the rail line carried over 500,000 bales of cotton to Savannah for shipment to domestic and foreign ports. In the 1850s cotton counted for four-fifths the value of all exports from Savannah. In the last year before the outbreak of the Civil War, Savannah edged out Charleston to become the third largest port behind New Orleans and Mobile in the export of cotton.[8] The number of railway cars and locomotives the Central operated on its line indicated the soaring volume of business: in 1847 the Central had 20 locomotives and 249 cars; in 1852, 46 engines and 449 cars; and by 1860, the Central's rolling stock reached 59 locomotives and 729 cars.[9]

Increased cotton production, the Central of Georgia Railroad, its entrepreneurs and financiers, Savannah's government particularly, and supportive legislators and governors were responsible for the city's extraordinary commercial expansion and Georgia's transportation revolution. The state's rail network of 1,420 miles in 1860 was exceeded by one state in the South, Virginia, and by only five others within the Union. Well-to-do white Savannahians invested heavily in railroad stocks and bonds. Savannah's government from the 1830s to 1860 invested $2,744,560 in railroads; this was two-thirds the investment of the government of Charleston, with twice the population of Savannah. The city's investments in rail lines almost equaled the combined investments in railroads of Alabama's four major cities. Savannah's City Council also subsidized the Central Railroad by depositing city tax revenues—which surged with the expanding economy—in the Central of Georgia Railroad Bank; the local government also granted the railroad thirty-five acres of land for its major facilities on the western edge of the city. As in Charleston, prominent Savannahians eagerly promoted the railroad but did not want the clacking, steam-hissing, and cinder-belching locomotives in their urban center or near their residences. So, they ensured that the railroad was located near Yamacraw in Oglethorpe Ward, a poorer section of the city.[10]

The Central of Georgia Railroad Freight Department was built just north of the Augusta road, and its depot went up nearby. New Street (later Hull) bounded the project on the north, Jones Street on the south, Boundary Street on the west, and West Broad Street (today Martin Luther King Jr. Boulevard) on the east. The depot, built on the property in the 1840s, was soon insufficient to accommodate the burgeoning passenger and freight traffic; likewise, the Central needed additional facilities built by skilled engineers, who were in short supply locally and elsewhere in the South. It was not surprising, then, that one of the hundreds of northerners and foreign immigrants who flocked to Georgia to seize economic opportunities, William M. Wadley, was selected to launch the Central's massive building project.

Wadley, a native of New Hampshire and a blacksmith, arrived in Savannah as a young man and assisted in the construction of Fort Pulaski. A self-taught engineer and a sober and industrious worker, Wadley was promoted to superintendent of public works at the fort; he subsequently built bridges in Savannah. His skills came to the attention of President Cuyler, who appointed him road master of the Central and in 1849 superintendent of the entire railroad line. Soon after Wadley began the building of the new $500,000 depot.[11] When he departed for more prestigious positions, the Central hired Augustus Schwaab and Martin P. Mueller, architect-engineers and recent German immigrants, to design and oversee the largest building project ever constructed in Savannah. Under the direction of Schwaab and Mueller, an army of managers and laborers—recent immigrants, resident Irishmen, slaves, and free blacks—erected in the 1850s about a dozen remarkable buildings, some in the Romanesque and Gothic styles: an 800-by-63-foot brick freight warehouse went up next to the new depot in 1853, and within seven years two others nearly as large were built nearby; the main office building for the Central of Georgia Railroad and Banking Company was completed in 1856 at 227 West Broad Street; a roundhouse 250 feet in diameter with a brick floor and forty stalls for locomotives and with an iron, center-vented roof supported by cast iron columns was built; an engine house with a corrugated roof made in Europe and shipped from Philadelphia went up, as did a boiler and patten room and a carpentry shop. New York native Alvin N. Miller, owner of an iron foundry on Savannah's wharves, and David and William Rose, immigrants from Preston, England, provided some of the building materials.[12] In the mid-1850s a reporter for the *Savannah Daily Morning News* toured the Central's grounds and enthusiastically described what he saw: "the well-lighted, well ventilated, and . . . arranged buildings . . . form a complete symmetrical whole." He doubted "if *any* other" railway facility in the nation "can equal this."[13]

Thousands of bricks, vast numbers of timber trusses and iron supports, and numerous stone lintels and window sills, most likely of granite, were used in construction. Untold gallons of mastic—a paste-like substance of blended powdered lime or brick and tar—was mixed and used like cement as mortar or to spread over the finished brick buildings. An army of skilled and unskilled laborers, black and white, sweated, strained, argued, and died constructing the Central of Georgia's main depot, passenger station, warehouses, and repair shops. The company hired skilled workers to retrofit and later build locomotives and to construct freight and passenger cars.

The boilers of the Central's locomotives hissed steam as they pulled cars into the rail depot jammed with cotton from the upcountry. In the early 1850s, C. G. Parsons, a visitor from the north, counted nine locomotives arriving daily, each pulling "twenty to thirty cars . . . loaded mountain high with [cotton]." Scores of laborers worked in shifts around the clock to unload the trains. They heaved, rolled, and pushed the heavy bales into the waiting drays pulled by "long trains of horse teams." When the wagons filled, the black drivers turned their horses toward the river; day and night the wagon wheels clattered over the plank road—the city's only paved street—linking the railroad yard with the wharves and warehouses where the cotton was stored until sold. Then the cotton was moved again to the compresses and eventually to shipside, where it was hoisted by black stevedores aboard waiting vessels.[14] Black dray or wagon drivers made money because they moved the same bale at least three times. African Americans, slave and free, enjoyed prosperity unequaled in many southern cities. This led one Savannahian to observe, "Cotton was . . . in evidence everywhere, and at all times of the day" and night, "from the first of October until the first of May."[15]

THE BOOM IN EXPORTS: COTTON, RICE, LUMBER

It was Savannah's development as a rail and shipping center for cotton, rice, lumber, and other commodities as well as being Georgia's major port for imported goods that stimulated the city's economic boom. The railroad linked Georgia's cotton fields to a national economy, and the building of a rail system into the interior and the local demand for housing stimulated an economic expansion in lumber and building construction. Supporting industries sprang up. The number of banks increased, and the price of real estate soared. Between the mid-1840s and 1861 Savannah became a boomtown. The City Council scrambled to expand the city's infrastructure to keep up with the burgeoning population. The prevailing sentiment among Savannah's citizens became one of optimism, which was reflected in Savannah's *Daily Morning News* in 1850 when it announced that the city was destined to become "the great commercial emporium and seaport of Georgia and the adjoining interior States."[16]

Large rafts of timber were floated to Savannah, and timber also came in on the freight cars of the Central of Georgia rail line along with upcountry cotton; barges of the Savannah and Ogeechee Canal Company brought in timber, rough rice, and bricks to the canal basin on Savannah's booming west side, which had become a center for sawmills, brickyards, and foundries; the prized staples of sea-island cotton, rice, rosin, lumber, and turpentine, as well as molasses and corn, came in on coastal sailing sloops and steamers from sea-island and river plantations. Charles Stevens, a beefy, broad-shouldered, ham-handed immigrant born in Denmark in 1816, was one of the boat captains in this coastal trade. For nearly twenty years, beginning in the early 1840s, Captain Stevens transported plantation produce to Savannah in three different sailing vessels and returned with foodstuffs, cloth, "seegars," doors, coal, and whiskey. Frequently his cargoes were consigned to one of the oldest and most prestigious commission merchants or factors, Robert Habersham & Son, which served as the banker, buyer, and merchant for plantation owners. On some trips Stevens carried loads exceeding thirty-three tons.[17]

Local pressure for more than a decade finally moved Congress to appropriate $201,000 in the 1850s to remove the "wrecks" below the city and the "bars, shoals, banks, and other impediments . . . caused by said obstructions" in the Savannah River channel; the city government itself issued $63,000 in bonds to improve the river. By 1857 the main channel had been cleared and dredged by the U.S. Corps of Engineers to permit vessels drawing over seventeen feet of water—previously only those of fourteen-foot draft—to proceed at high tide directly to the city's wharves without the extra expense of using lighters, and vessels of twenty-one feet of water now could anchor at Venus Point seven and a half miles below Savannah. Doubtless, this in part accounted for the 91.5 percent increase in the number and a 142 percent increase in the tonnage of ships clearing Savannah for foreign ports.[18]

In the final decade before the Civil War 4,091,038 cotton bales, 335,725 casks of rice, and 353,112,618 feet of timber and lumber left Savannah's wharves, which accounted for more than 90 percent of the value of all exports. Other commodities exported included grains, fruits and vegetables, pork and beef, hides and skins, wool, cooper ore, and naval stores. A variety of imports flowed principally from New York, Boston, Philadelphia, and the West Indies and included primarily barrels of ale and whiskey, fabrics, iron, salt, tea, fruit, molasses, sugar, and coffee. But the value of imports was modest in comparison to the exports—the imports amounting to $782,061 in 1859–1860 while that same year the exports reached $18,351,554. Attesting to the economic boom, Savannah's exports exceeded those of Boston and San Francisco.[19]

MILLS AND MANUFACTURING

Savannah's industrial development was linked to the port's three major exports: cotton, rice, and lumber. The final processing of cotton before being hoisted onto waiting ships included compressing the bales. Five steam-powered cotton presses operated on the riverfront by 1850. Likewise, at wharfside two steam rice mills pounded and polished "rough rice" into clean white rice, which was then packed into Savannah-made casks weighing about seven hundred pounds and loaded aboard waiting vessels.[20]

William W. Gordon II was overseeing such rice processing on a cool day in January 1855. The son of the founder of the Central of Georgia Railroad, Gordon was a recent graduate of Yale and employed as a clerk for Tison and McKay, factors or commission merchants. The following year he became a partner in the firm, renamed Tison and Gordon. At the time he was engaged to Chicagoan Nellie Kinzie, whom he met while at Yale through his sister, Eliza. Immediately "Willie" was charmed by the vivacious Nellie, and she, too, fell in love with him, though she thought him retiring, serious, and like a "Methodist parson" in appearance. He described the rice processing and his role in it to his fiancée. Gordon's words are almost lyrical:

> I play . . . a veritable 'Slave-Driver' to a gang of hands. Amid clouds of dust & chaff, a confusion of tongues, and a trampling of . . . heels . . . , I keep an account of the no. of sacks as the crew . . . bring in and empty them upon the floor of the mill, and an account of the no. of bushels as the women of the mill measure them out and bear them into some . . . receptacle within. The measurers sing out the tally and the bearers, their burthens on their heads & hands gracefully outstretched to preserve balance, shuffle along now and then breaking into a wild but musical cry by way of chorus. The thick

cloud of yellow rice dust soften down the harsher features of the scene and give a rich and mellow tint even to the uncouth forms of the negroes. The whole, combined with the almost twilight in the mill—its machinery incessantly at work around us—has a strange effect and could the noises—musical, hilarious, exhortatory, expostulatory and the rest—be for a moment checked, would seem more like the dusky phantasms of a vision than forms and actions in real life.[21]

As more and more timber was floated into Savannah in rafts of 30,000 broad feet of timber, additional sawmills and wood finishers set up operations on the wharves on Hutchinson Island, Fig Island, and along the Savannah and Ogeechee Canal. By the late 1840s seven sawmills with a total capability of 80,000 feet daily cut the timber into boards. Two "Steam Works" manufactured doors, blinds, and sashes. By the 1850s six other makers of wood products or sawmills were operating.[22] The E. Jenck's Steam Mill, located near the Central Railroad's depot, employed twenty-five laborers and produced 15,000 pine casks for rice each year.[23]

  The largest lumber business in the port city and one of the nation's largest by 1850 was the Royal Vale Steam Saw & Planing Mill, which was located on the Savannah River and close to Musgrove Creek. It was built by William B. Giles and a group of venture capitalists. A 1,200-foot-long wharf constructed on posts driven 28 feet into the mud by steam power jutted into the river far enough to permit 100-ton burthen vessels to take on lumber. At one end of the wharf a 131-by-47-foot mill housed a planing machine and three steam engines that powered sash and circular saws for cutting shingles, tongued and grooved boards, and ship planks; the mill's towering 62-foot-high chimney was made of 70,000 bricks. At the rear of the wharf was an enormous water-storage basin capable of holding over 2,000,000 feet in timber. Giles and his associates invited friends and city officials to celebrate the opening of the mill with fine wines and champagne. Capitalized at $70,000, the mill in 1850 produced over $100,000 in lumber and wood products. It employed about twenty skilled white men and forty black laborers in the mill yard on fourteen-hour shifts.[24]

Savannah's lumber industry employed large numbers of workers, black and white, whose jobs included hewing, rafting, sawing, milling, draying, loading, stacking, and marketing Georgia pine and cypress. Many were neighbors in the city who fraternized on and off the job, which most likely softened racism's rough edges.

But for owners it was difficult to find qualified white applicants for the best-paying jobs, sawyers and engineers, to either build or supervise the mills.[25] Luckily for the owners, as in other local industries, migrants or recent immigrants provided a small pool of skilled workers. For instance, William Harris Garland, who was born in England about 1812, migrated with his parents to South Carolina. By the late 1830s and into the early 1840s Garland went from one job to another during the depression gripping Georgia and the nation. He worked as an engineer aboard steamboats and at sawmills in Savannah, Macon, Darien, and Beaufort. But when the economic expansion of the late 1840s began to unfold, Garland opened a machine shop in Savannah. He received orders for repairing local sawmills and other machinery, and he purchased, repaired, and resold boilers. He built machinery from the roughest sketches and enjoyed a growing reputation as an engineer. But for various reasons his prosperity did not last.[26]

Slaves and free blacks performed most of the heavy labor—the unskilled and semi-skilled jobs—in the lumberyards and mills of Savannah. The mills employed their own slave labor force and also hired slaves from masters. Owners trained some blacks for skilled jobs in the mills because of the scarcity of white sawyers and engineers. Free blacks received a wage of about $20 monthly, which was the sum paid to unskilled white lumber mill workers. Most of the more than two hundred people working in Savannah's lumber mills in 1850 were black laborers.[27] A decade later, the industries involved in the preparation for export of cotton, rice, and lumber and wood products accounted for nearly 70 percent of Savannah's total industrial productivity.[28] Savannah's other major industries included those building or repairing the means of transportation for these commodities.

Four different shipyards built thirty-four vessels and two floating dry docks between 1849 and 1860. The total tonnage built exceeded Charleston's but remained modest. Many owners simply preferred to buy their boats elsewhere. The manufacturing record of the Central of Georgia Railroad was better than the shipyards. At its shops in Savannah, the Central, near the end of the 1850s, constructed five locomotives and eventually built all of its rail cars there, turning out eighty-five alone in 1860. Four other foundries operated in the city; the best known was owned by Alvin N. Miller, a New York transplant who supplied machinery for the Central and for most of the steamboats built locally. Other small machine shops and blacksmith firms did a lively business. By the late 1850s the city also supported three manufacturers of carriages and wagons, two cooperage firms, three sash, door, and blind businesses, five flour mills, and several producers of boots and shoes, saddles and harnesses, stoves and tin-ware, guns, sails, awnings and tarpaulins, umbrellas, and cigars.

Capital investment in manufacturing and productivity jumped dramati-cally in Savannah in the decade before the Civil War: in 1850 some $130,550 was invested in manufacturing firms that produced $254,750 in goods yearly; by 1860 the capital invested totaled at least $902,300, and industrial produc-tion soared to more than $1,907,300. In sum, Savannah, Georgia's largest city, had about 8 percent of the industrial capital and 11 percent of its productivity and led all Georgia cities in these categories, but only slightly. Furthermore, Savannah's industrial production surpassed that of Memphis, Mobile, and Charleston, but compared to cities of the upper South and the North, its in-dustrial productivity was modest.[29]

COMMISSION HOUSES AND COMMERCE

The enormous increase in the number of commission houses kept pace with the rapid rise in the exports of cotton, rice, and lumber. In the 1840s Irish-born architect Charles B. Cluskey and in the 1850s New York architect John S. Nor-ris and local merchant John Stoddard designed and built along the riverfront and at the edge of Savannah's famous forty-foot-high bluff long rows of con-nected mercantile houses. Some rose five or six stories on their waterfront sides, but just two or three stories above the bluff or Bay Street on the city side. Ground floors served as warehouses, with access provided by alleyways of bal-last stones behind them; on the riverside, factors, clerks, and managers looked down from their desks on a quay of ballast stones (River Street), wharves, cot-ton presses, rice mills, and a forest of ship masts. Wooden or cast iron bridges on the city side of the mercantile houses provided employees access to and from Bay Street as well as vantage points for factors or their agents to view and grade the bales of cotton stacked below in the alleyways during high season. The bluff was faced with ballast stones to prevent erosion, as were the numer-ous dray ways or ramps, which cut through the bluff at steep angles from Bay Street to permit wagons jammed with cotton or other products to reach the warehouses of the mercantile houses or the wharves.[30]

Here along the river people observed the city's flourishing commercial life. Strolling past the wharves in the early 1850s, a local newspaperman saw "our fine marine of 1 steamship, 15 ships, 16 barques, 5 brigs, 6 schooners, and many steamboats"; he could have noted the "bustle . . . among sailors, stevedores, laborers . . . and clerks employed in receiving and shipping immense freights, and draymen loading and unloading their vehicles—all vigorously bending to work." More than five oceangoing vessels flying the colors of various shipping companies and countries entered or cleared the river daily by the mid-1850s, and coasters—barks, brigs, steamers, schooners, and skiffs—that transported cargoes up and down the coast from Charleston to Key West constantly moved to and fro along the waterfront.[31]

William Gordon of Tison and McCay was one of dozens of new clerks hired in the 1850s to handle the burgeoning paperwork and assorted duties in the rapidly expanding number of mercantile houses. When the owners traveled during the summer months, Gordon had to be there. He suffered in what one called "a state of torpid existence."[32] Gordon told his fiancée that the company had to be "open all the year around to meet the orders of their patrons [planters] and also to furnish them a convenient *loafing place* when they came to town."[33] Gordon's office and duties were similar to those of other clerks. Frequently, he could be found "sitting at an old secretary" whose "dusty shelves and holes . . . are filled with letters, bills, Notes, and Drafts." The room itself was twenty by twelve feet; behind him on the opposite side of the room "are the Partners and every where else . . . little bundles of [cotton] Samples." Entering from the street, Gordon passed "thro' a defile, narrow & dangerous, of cotton-bags, standing upon end and reaching to the ceiling. . . . Our windows are upon a level with the masts of the tallest [ships]."[34]

From the windows a cacophony of sounds and smells swept through the open windows of the mercantile houses during the business season, which sprang to life in September and October and continued through May. There were the sounds of masts creaking, the wind in the sails and rigging, the slap of water against the hulls of dozens of oceangoing vessels, and the shouts of captains to deck hands, who in turn called out to others as they tied or cast off dozens of ships. Smaller vessels bringing in rice banged and rubbed against the wharfs, drays pilled high with cotton clattered across the wooden planking along Bay Street, and the machinery of cotton presses, rice mills, and lumber mills roared into the night. When the wind came from the southeast, the smells of the distant sea, of tar and rosin, of food cooking and of horse droppings, mingled and wafted through the open windows. A Yankee visitor saw "bales of cotton . . . passing into vessels from the wharves as fast . . . as ripe blossoms from the trees in the spring-time, when shaken with a strong east wind." A local reporter watched cotton loaded aboard a steamer by sixty men and heard the "shrill creaking ropes, the bass thump of bales striking the iron work, [and] the musical, if nonsensical, cries of the men." The clerks of the commission houses, their hands jammed with bills of lading, hurried around corners "running into each other."

By October most of the 246 merchants who ran the ninety-eight commission houses in Savannah at the beginning of the 1850s had returned to Savannah from pleasure trips north to escape the heat. The majority were northern or foreign born: 71 migrated from the northeastern states, 29 hailed from other states, 60 had immigrated from abroad, and 86 were native Georgians. Many of these merchants enjoyed substantial profits and invested in real estate and personal property. A few left "handsome estates" exceeding $300,000. But the greatest profits were made by northern and European dealers.[35]

By the mid-1850s 27 steamboats operated out of Savannah—only 11 out of Charleston—although the halcyon days of the steamer had passed, as much of its business was absorbed by the railroads. New ships and ship firms appeared. Seven packet lines in Savannah operated about 60 vessels, which regularly sailed or steamed to Boston, New York, Philadelphia, and New Orleans. The Central of Georgia Railroad alone invested over $300,000 in steamship transportation. Retail establishments, banks, and insurance companies multiplied. More people with more money than ever before pushed into Savannah's new stores in the late 1850s to buy clothes at more than 30 stores, to buy foodstuffs at 150 groceries, and to shop at new jewelry and piano stores. There was ample capital locally to lend to new merchants and to businesses. Five additional banking institutions opened their doors in Savannah between 1848 and the mid-1850s, bringing the number of banks in the city to 10, which held half the banking capital in the state. Bank profits and dividends soared. During the same years the number of insurance companies jumped from 11 to 59. Since most had their headquarters in northern states or abroad, local agents acted in their behalf by insuring ships and their cargoes and for coverage for fire and loss of life. In this way, too, capital flowed to the north and investors abroad.

Savannah's prosperity depended primarily on the flow of cotton from the interior to its wharves, on ships for transport, and on agencies to insure the ships and their cargoes, all of which depended on northern and European manufacturers, merchants, and economic conditions. In sum, Savannah was a halfway house, an intermediate agency.[36] Nevertheless, while new, fertile lands in the southwest lured thousands, depopulating and economically ruining some towns in the South Atlantic states, Savannah's population and commerce surged. While land values declined elsewhere, the taxable value of land and its improvement jumped nearly threefold, increasing from $3,600,000 to $10,000,00 between 1848 and 1860.[37] For an almost uninterrupted period from the late 1840s to 1860, Georgia's largest city enjoyed boom times. Most of the commission merchants, clerks, managers, engineers, blacksmiths, and the skilled and unskilled workers who flocked to Savannah in search of economic opportunity found it.

POPULATION AND BUILDING BOOMS

Savannah's midcentury economic boom brought a population explosion. By 1860 Savannah was the sixth largest city in the South. Between 1840 and 1860 the port city nearly doubled its population, increasing from 11,214 to 22,292 white and black adults and children. Between 1850 and 1860 the number of slaves in the city increased from 6,231 to 7,712, while their numbers declined in other southern urban centers. The city's greatest growth spurt came between 1848 and 1852, when the population jumped 51 percent. Attracted by opportunities, white foreign-born immigrants and migrants from the northern states poured into Savannah, whose residents at the time were predominantly of British or African heritage and Protestant. First came a trickle and then a mighty flood of immigrants, most of whom were not British, African American, or of the Protestant faith. Savannah changed them, and they changed Savannah. On the eve of the Civil War, 66 percent of Savannah's adult white males were born abroad or in the North. Many of the foreign born included Irish-Catholics, Germans, and German Jews.[38]

By 1860 the birthplaces of the 4,400 migrant white males in Savannah eighteen years of age and older included 2,581 foreigners (58.1 percent), the majority of whom, 1,605, came from Ireland; 484 immigrated from Germany, 291 from Britain, and another 201 from France and other countries. Migrants from the north totaled 775 (17.5 percent), and 1,084 (24.4 percent) came from elsewhere in Georgia and the South. Almost all of the migrants spent some time in urban centers before settling in the port city. For instance, Felix McKenna and his wife, Margaret, age thirty, emigrated from Ireland to Boston in 1847 and spent time in Troy, New York, before moving to Savannah in 1857; German-born shoemaker Christopher Haas at age thirty immigrated to New York City in 1850 and with his wife, Harriet, settled in Savannah by 1856. Furthermore, 602 white males and a vast majority of 725 black males aged eighteen and older were born in Savannah. By 1860 Savannah had an ethnically diverse population that came primarily from urban centers, and four out of every five white males aged eighteen and older were born elsewhere than the rural South.[39]

Many of the migrants successfully seized the opportunity to accumulate wealth and status and to gain the public's trust during Savannah's commercial boom. By 1860 some fifty-seven northern migrants amassed wealth ranging from $20,000 to $480,000; though not quite as successful, fifty-nine of the foreign-born accumulated at least $20,000, while the wealth of twenty of these exceeded $50,000, and several owned property worth between $80,000 and $136,000. The migrants, especially the Irish, involved themselves in the city's political life. By 1860 the foreign-born population accounted for 51.2 percent and the northern-born 15.4 percent of the white adult males in Savannah, while the former numbered 48.8 percent of the city's registered voters and the latter 12.8 percent. Two Philadelphians, William T. Williams and Thomas M. Turner, were elected mayors of Savannah; of the 78 councilmen elected by 1860, 10 were northerners and 6 were foreign-born; and many other migrants served in positions of public trust, from school commissioners and teachers to judges. Despite the success of many migrants, the seasonal nature of unskilled labor and fluctuations in the economy left hundreds of migrants penniless, especially Irish laborers.

This vast migration of foreigners and northerners changed the culture of Savannah. The city became more cosmopolitan, and the migrants eroded any tenuous foothold that evangelical Protestantism may have established in the city. Non-evangelicals, Episcopalians, Catholics, Lutherans, and Jews grew in numbers. The new Irish-Catholic immigrants became so numerous that in 1850 the city's Catholic Church separated from the Diocese of Charleston and became the Diocese of Savannah. New German immigrants formed a Lutheran congregation and hired a teacher-minister, the Reverend Wilhelm Eppings, to conduct services for them in the German language. At ceremonies during the laying of the cornerstone for the new German Lutheran Church on Drayton and Wayne Streets, with a capacity of three hundred persons, the Reverend Epping delivered his address in German. Jews from Germany arrived in the city about the same time, but only reluctantly did the congregation of Mickve Israel admit them to membership. The congregation was long controlled by Sephardic Jews, and admission of the German Jews led to changes in rules governing the congregation and a growth in members, and it also gave the synagogue a firmer financial footing. In 1852 the synagogue employed its first full-time rabbi, German-born Jacob Rosenfeld.

At the end of the 1850s, white Savannahians attended two synagogues, a Catholic cathedral, and the following churches: three Episcopal, two Presbyterian, two Methodist, one Baptist, one Lutheran, and one Unitarian. More than a third of Savannah's African Americans attended church; some sat in the galleries of their master's churches, but most worshiped in nurturing communities of their own at the city's three African Baptist churches and one Negro Methodist church.

Prominent politicians worried that the southern cities, Savannah among them, might waver from the proslavery cause due to the dramatic differences in population between the countryside and the city. A South Carolinian commented that "northern influence is very potent in Savannah; the Yankees exert themselves to the utmost to carry the elections their way."[40]

To accommodate the new immigrants and migrants, the city spread southward. In the twenty years before the Civil War, the city expanded from its southernmost east-west boundary, Liberty Street, to Gaston Street, which became the city's new east-west boundary on the south side. City workers felled trees, extended streets, and carved new avenues, and contractors built new houses and private and public structures. Although many of the newcomers poured into the older, fringe areas of the city along the river, Savannah's government created new wards and squares. In 1840 the city consisted of twenty wards; over the next twenty years Savannah added sixteen more wards and numerous squares. Just south of Gaston Street, the City Council created Forsyth Place in 1851 as a municipal park in honor of William B. Hodgson, a local scholar of Near Eastern languages. The park marked the southward advance of the city. The building boom created some three hundred dwellings and stores between 1848 and 1851; nevertheless, a housing shortage developed. Hotels and boarding houses filled to overflowing, which resulted in exorbitant rents. Public buildings erected in the 1850s included the United States Customhouse (1848–1852) on Bay Street, which was designed by John S. Norris of New York in the Classical Revival style for the federal government and which was an indication of Savannah's growing importance as a major port.

The talented Norris designed twenty-three other buildings in Savannah, several on the south side of the city where numerous brick private residences were going up. Here along the new streets south of Liberty Street—on Harris, Macon, Charlton, Jones, Taylor, Gordon, and Gaston Streets—and on the new squares—Pulaski, Madison, Lafayette, Troup, Chatham, Monterey, Calhoun, and Whitfield—homes went up. Visitors saw splendid mansions, row houses, and townhouses under construction mainly in the Greek Revival style, but also in the neo-Gothic and the Italian villa styles. If erected with Savannah gray bricks, the buildings gave off a pinkish cast.[41] The squares laid out in the 1840s and 1850s provided the wealthy with unparalleled sites for their mansions, which provided vistas of lush, verdant tropical settings and monuments. This city's environs had a humanizing influence on well-to-do visitors and residents.

John Norris built a Greek Revival mansion for Andrew Low, a wealthy English cotton merchant, on Lafayette Square (named for the Marquis de Lafayette). Low was born in Scotland and inherited a Savannah cotton brokerage firm from his uncle. When he employed Norris to build his mansion, Low could well afford it, with an income of about $250,000 a year, the highest in the city. Low, his wife—the daughter of an Irish-born Savannah merchant—and children moved into the mansion in the fall 1848. Tragically, his wife and son died the following spring, but Low later remarried.

Charles Greene, apparently impressed with the mansion built for his partner, Andrew Low, commissioned Norris to design one for him. Greene, an Englishman, arrived in Savannah virtually penniless at age seventeen and took a job as a clerk. But he soon amassed a fortune in the cotton-exporting business and went into partnership with Low. Greene was second only to his partner in Savannah in annual income, which was about $80,000 when he asked Norris to build his mansion at 14 Macon Street on Madison Square. Norris began construction in 1850 of what became the most costly private home built in Savannah in the nineteenth century. Greene's home took eleven years to complete and cost $93,000. Known as the Green-Meldrim house today, it is rated as the foremost example of the Gothic style of architecture in the United States. It serves as the rectory of St. John's Episcopal Church, whose architect, Calvin Otis, a New Yorker like Norris, presided over the construction of the church at 329 Bull Street from 1851 to 1853. For his work, he received a miserly $500. Built in the neo-Gothic style, St. John's was one of the few architectural gems built in the 1840s and 1850s that matched the buildings designed years before by William Jay. Attesting to the versatility of Norris, he designed a mansion in the Italianate style for Hugh W. Mercer on Monterey Square (named to commemorate the American capture of the Mexican city in 1846 during the Mexican War). In 1855 a monument was erected in the square to honor Polish

Count Casimir Pulaski, who died defending Savannah in 1779. Construction of the Mercer home was interrupted by the Civil War.[42]

Visitors to the city in the 1840s and 1850s almost invariably commented on Savannah's wide streets lined with chinaberry trees and live oaks hung with Spanish moss, its lush, tropical-like appearance, and the many squares. Emily Burke observed that each square is "surrounded by a beautiful growth of ornamental trees." Savannah, she observed, "looks like a city built in a forest." Another northern woman visiting in February marveled at the private gardens "brilliant with . . . Japonicas" and thought the many "Palmettos . . . and Cabbage trees, a species of palm, . . . very handsome." A writer observed that the squares in the city were "laid out with grass plats and walks" and "interspersed with trees . . . give the city . . . a cool, airy, and rural appearance."[43]

This romantic view of Savannah among visitors—its quiet forested squares, the elegant mansions and townhouses rapidly going up for Savannah's white nouveaux riches along its wide new streets—generally prevailed because most travelers did not mention the conditions of its thoroughfares and avoided the slums. These were located along the river on the western and eastern fringes of the city. On the west was Oglethorpe Ward, which embraced Yamacraw, a swampy, poorly drained, unsanitary area of cheap boarding houses where prostitution flourished; on the eastern fringe in the Old Fort and Trustees Garden area was an equally disreputable slum. But even in the finer residential districts of the city, the sandy, mostly unpaved streets, alleys, and lanes were filthy partly due to Savannah's exploding population. Such conditions were commonplace in mid-nineteenth-century American cities. Dogs, cows, goats, and pigs wandered through the city, and streets were strewn with litter and horse droppings, "dirty water and kitchen slops." The aromas enhanced by the city's semitropical climate assaulted the olfactory senses, especially when combined with the smells arising from the dirty stalls of the public market and hundreds of privies. Such odors—"with more of earth than of heaven about them," a wag wrote—elicited complaints from Savannah's residents, its newspapers, and the Board of Health.[44]

One northern traveler, C. G. Parsons, did see the city's stinking slums, either those on the city's eastern fringe near the Old Fort and Trustees Garden or those in Oglethorpe Ward on the western fringe where the Savannah and Ogeechee Canal terminated. The ward was growing rapidly in population and in sawmills, rice mills, and manufacturers. No friend of slavery, Parsons compared the dwellings and surroundings of the poor with the well-to-do: "In the heart of the city every thing imparts to . . . the stranger an idea of comfort; but in the suburbs the . . . negro huts, remind the . . . visitor of the fearful price paid by one class to support another."[45]

THE LIVES, SOCIETY, AND CULTURE OF THE ELITE

A handful of wealthy, slaveholding, educated families dominated the business, social, and political life of Savannah during the 1840s and 1850s. This elite hierarchy included about eighty to a hundred families who owned some twenty or more slaves, possessed real estate or personal property between $100,000 and $460,000, and belonged to the exclusive Savannah Club. They had enough leisure time and income by the 1840s and 1850s to give and attend extravagant parties and weddings, to send their sons and daughters to preparatory schools and colleges, to travel, and to provide the impetus and support for cultural organizations such as the theater and libraries, open to them alone. This "tangled cousinry" of families visited, dined, played together, and intermarried. They enjoyed seeing one another, drinking and eating together at their clubs, such as the Chatham Hunting Club, the Savannah Jockey Club, the Quoit Club, the Whist Club, the Cricket Club, and the Savannah Club, which opened in 1853 and four years later enrolled ninety members who had avoided two blackballs and paid the initiation fee of $50; they went together on swimming and fishing retreats to the nearby Isle of Hope, Wilmington Island, and Skidaway Island; they competed with one another in sailboats and vessels hollowed out of logs, which they steered while their slaves pulled the oars on the Savannah and nearby rivers. They read Shakespeare and Lord Byron, but the novels of Charles Dickens and Sir Walter Scott were among their favorites. Next to novels they enjoyed biographies of men such as William Pitt and Patrick Henry, histories of Greece, Rome, and the United States, and controversial works such as *Uncle Tom's Cabin.* The elite turned out for lectures by nationally known scientists and writers such as Louis Agassiz, William Makepeace Thackeray, and Edward Everett, but when little-known speakers lectured, audiences were slim. Magazines published in the city endured only briefly. Only Ohio-born humorist William Tappan Thompson, the cofounder and editor of the *Savannah Morning News,* won a national reputation as a writer. The city's contribution to literature paled by comparison with its neighbor Charleston, whose literate white population was twice Savannah's. But in a booming economy, the drive and time allotted to making money sometimes did not permit even the educated elite all the energy and hours they desired for intellectual pursuits. On one occasion William W. Gordon regretted he was too tired from work even to read.[46]

Some churchmen and poets, however, believed Savannahians spent too much time pursuing wealth and too little time pursuing culture. The rector of Christ Church, later Bishop Stephen Elliott, observed that the elite's drive for material gain exceeded their interests in "intellectual culture." Likewise, Savannah poet Samuel Jones Cassels wrote:

> Oh, Savannah, I would have thee
> All thou art and greater still;
> Yet above thy trade would see thee
> Learning's pure and classic hill.

On the other hand, upcountry Georgians looked on Savannah as a Sodom and Gomorrah. The rural populace condemned card playing, dancing, the theater, and reading novels, all commonplace entertainments for well-to-do white Savannahians. Dr. Richard Arnold observed that his kind had always been looked upon "by the upcountry as Swelled Heads." There was little doubt that a cultural and social divide existed between urban and rural society. In the city the private schools were better, and books, newspapers, and the theater were easily accessible. One bookish Savannah wag put it: "a life in the country is a voluntary exile."[47] On the other hand, life in the city invigorated the mind and cultivated the senses, especially those of the white upper crust.

William Norwood, a transplanted North Carolinian working as a clerk in Savannah in the 1850s, observed that "if a man is reported to be wealthy he can get into society with all ease." Another resident, Mary Baber, remarked that "wealth is the 'open sesame' here."[48] And as economic opportunities in the city exploded during the 1840s and 1850s, vast wealth was accumulated. As in other urban centers, a disproportionate share of wealth was concentrated in the hands of a few families. By the end of the 1850s about 6 percent of the population owned 90 percent of Savannah's real estate.

Slaveholding was equally concentrated. About a thousand people owned the 7,712 slaves in the city, but 20 percent of the masters held 58 percent of the slaves. At the top of this hierarchy of wealth were the large planters, wealthy merchants, bankers, lawyers, and physicians. These rich few included affluent foreigners and northerners, such as French native and wealthy lumber dealer Alexander Smets and Massachusetts native and commission merchant Edward

Padelford, worth $480,000 and the wealthiest Savannahian in 1860. This privileged class embraced men of diverse ethnic and religious backgrounds, such as Jewish attorney Solomon Cohen, and occasionally professional men of more modest means, such as physician and three-time mayor Dr. Richard D. Arnold.

This elite of wealth, education, and talent occupied the choice property in the central city. Here their new mansions went up on the squares along the three principal streets running south from the river: Bull, Barnard, and Abercorn. By the end of the 1850s several hundred white families living between Barnard and Abercorn streets held about 50 percent of the value of the city's real estate and almost 60 percent of its personal property.[49] The Protestant elite intermarried for reasons of land, slaves, and politics; most easily socialized with wealthy Catholics and Jews.

The Protestant elite's inclusiveness toward Jews more so than toward Irish Catholics was due in part to the long history in the city of such civic-minded and wealthy Jewish families as the Minis, Sheftall, Levy, Cohen, Solomon, and Myers families. The acceptance of Jews by local Christians also came from their adoption of such southern traits as the honor ethic, their willingness to defend it by duels, their ownership of slaves and belief in black racial subordination, and their purchase of slaves, all of which identified them with the region's dominant class. Hundreds of unskilled Irish Catholic immigrants, however, remained impoverished, unable to afford slaves. And like prosperous white Protestants and Catholics, slave-owning Jews "hired out" their bondmen and bondwomen to make money. Attorney Solomon Cohen, with twenty-three slaves, and Dinah Minis, who owned eighteen, rented their blacks to individuals and local industries. And finally, these Jewish families vigorously defended states' rights, the South, and its institutions in the 1850s when northern abolitionists escalated their crusade against slavery.

Christians readily accepted Jews in political, fraternal, cultural, and social organizations such as the freemasons; Solomon Cohen and Mordecai Myers helped to found the Georgia Historical Society; Philip Minis, Octavius Cohen, and Moses A. Cohen were members of the Savannah Jockey Club; and though they were fewer than the Irish in numbers, Jews won numerous elections to local, state, and national political offices. The number of Jews in the city reached about 350, or only 2.5 percent of the white immigrant population, whereas the Irish Catholic population reached 23 percent in 1860; therefore, in population alone, the Irish appeared to pose serious economic, religious, and political challenges to the Protestant elite, whereas the Jews did not.[50] The privileged class viewed the Catholic masses as drinkers, brawlers, and a destabilizing element to the foundation of society, which was slavery. Their religion posed a special problem. The Reverend Charles C. Jones, for instance, told his son that the Catholic religion "takes away the key of both worldly and heavenly knowledge from the people, rules them by superstition and brute force, sanctifies them in sin."[51]

Among the elite, grand dinner parties, weddings, and balls reflected the rising prosperity, as did the grand homes of the nouveaux riches being built southward across the city. Beginning slowly in the depression years of the 1840s, the social whirl accelerated in the 1850s. Dr. Richard D. Arnold attended a "pleasant and well got-up dinner" party in the 1840s during which was served "a most capacious dish of real green turtle stew . . . [with] spice . . . and madeira and claret enough to mingle with its own juices and form a rich gravy"; this dish was followed by "a calf's heads stews in white sauce . . . the brains in the sauce"; next came veal cutlets, cold roast lamb, and pâté de fois gras, followed by "ice cream, then nuts and olives."[52] Such a formal dinner differed from other entertainment explained Alexander R. Lawton, a member of the city's upper crust in the 1840s: "when we have friends 'to tea', they are usually more intimate friends, & there is not the same call for style as at the dinner table where more formal company is entertained." Born in St. Peter's Parish, Beaufort District, South Carolina, Lawton graduated from West Point, studied law at Harvard, and practiced in Savannah. Married to Sarah Gilbert of Washington, Georgia, he became president of a local railroad, a member of the state legislature, and active in the local militia.[53]

During the early 1840s "old money" dominated the winter social season. In January 1841, Mrs. Henrietta J. Wayne informed her sister, Mary Harden, that "Savannah has been as usual very dull." She added that Mrs. James Wayne, Mrs. McAllister, and Mrs. Williamson have had "soirees every week," but "*only the elite* are invited." She concluded with a bit of gossip—the death of Mrs. Williamson's husband during the social season barely interrupted her party going and party giving; he left her "an immense estate," which included "four hundred and fifty negroes." A few years later Mrs. Wayne told her sister that Savannah was "unusually gay" for April. Parties and soirees for two brides provided "splendid entertainment"; one supper cost $300.[54]

Intermarriage was commonplace among Savannah's "old money." For instance, Dr. George Jones, offspring of one of Savannah's founding families and heir to one of its greatest fortunes, was related by marriage or social connections to some of the most prominent families of South Carolina and Savannah, including the Cuthbert, Campbell, Tattnall, Fenwick, Drayton, Gibbons, Telfair, Bulloch, Kollock, Cumming, Hunter, Habersham, and Glen families, among others. Dr. J. J. Waring of Savannah married Mary Brewton Alston of South Carolina; the Wayne family of Savannah was related by marriage to the prominent Stites, Anderson, Clifford, Gordon, and Campbell families; and the well-known Anderson, Mercer, and Gordon families were related. Marriages among the elite assured the preservation of property and aided political ambitions. For these same reasons, some marriages reflected the historic pattern of intermarriage between the elite families of lowcountry South Carolina and Georgia. The offspring of the wealthy frequently said their wedding vows in Savannah's Episcopal church, Christ Church.

Privileged families indulged their kin with gifts of slaves, especially when they married. Sarah Mackay gave Henry Stites an entire family of slaves including seven prime hands and two children. In 1846 Alexander R. Lawton's father presented him with ten slaves for the sum of one dollar. Henrietta J. Wayne informed her sister that a relative's daughter, Mary Wayne, "not yet sixteen," planned to marry "a Mr. Mitchell of Edisto Island," South Carolina, who had been given "a very pretty property, . . . a plantation and negroes."[55] When John Screven married Mary White Footman, daughter of Dr. Richard Hunter Footman, the groom's father, Dr. James Proctor Screven, a South Carolina planter-millionaire and Savannah politico, was so "very much pleased with the match" that he gave his "son a plantation and negroes."[56] The lowcountry of Georgia and South Carolina was becoming "one tangled cousinry." On Christmas day in the early 1850s, the patriarch of Savannah's wealthy Habersham family sat down to dinner with seventy-one cousins and other relatives.[57]

During the winter social season of 1850, Henrietta Wayne observed that "Savannah is very gay at present." As usual, weddings dominated the social calendar. Henrietta's relative, Elisabeth Wayne, who was marrying George Owens, was entertained on numerous occasions. The family of the groom invited several hundred persons to "a splendid party" for the newlyweds. "The gayety, however, will shortly be over," Henrietta wrote, "as the Episcopalians rarely ever go out much to dances during Lent." During the social season a few years later, Sarah Anderson Stiles Gordon told her son, William, that his cousin Caro Lamar "gave a large party," and "all the world was there." Most likely Sarah meant that only Savannah's privileged residents, such as herself, were there—the city's older elite, wealthy in land and slaves.[58] By the early 1850s "new money" was competing with "old money" in entertaining, but not very well according to Julia Barnsley, daughter of wealthy cotton merchant Godfrey Barnsley, who by this time lived in New Orleans. Julia and her sister Adelaide lived with their father part of the year and sometimes traveled to Savannah for the social season. Barnsley's business partner, William Duncan, met Julia and Adelaide at the train depot and informed their father that while in Savannah, "They will be very safe." A month after they arrived, in late November, and following a nearly continuous round of parties and teas given by the city's upper crust, Duncan reported that the two "young ladies are quite contented & . . . will do much more than think of N[ew] O[rleans] this winter." Julia informed her father that she and her sister attended "delightful" parties given by the old-money families such as the Bradleys, Warings, and Stoddards. She enjoyed telling him that a party "given by one of the Savannah parvenus . . . did not succeed." But times appeared to be changing. Julia wrote to her father that the vastly wealthy Mrs. Williamson "intends leaving here. . . . She thinks there is some difference between the society here now and what it was in your time," the 1830s and 1840s. Adelaide noted changes, too, in the fashions, remarking that "Wearing beards seemed to be as fashionable as hoops in Savannah." Their escort, William Duncan, sported a "most marvelous" one. When Adelaide and Julia commented on its dark and white streaks, Duncan replied, "Oh girls, 'I took a gin toddy last night that was the cause I suppose of its turning.'"[59]

Duncan escorted them to the "Bachelors Ball," where Mrs. George Kollock attended them. As Christmas approached, the girls accepted an invitation from the wealthy Barnwell family of Beaufort, South Carolina, and Julia, Adelaide, and their brother, George, spent part of the holidays on a rice plantation. Here they enjoyed "candy-pulling, firecrackers and played 'Smut' with cards, and on the whole had a great deal of fun."[60]

William Gordon explained to his northern-born fiancée that "Christmas is the great event of the year at the South." Family gatherings take place and "are accompanied by the 'fatted calf' and the . . . consumption of huge quantities of eggnog. Santa Claus visits the children too" and, among other gifts, "bestows . . . [fire] crackers much to the annoyance of quiet peace-loving *citizens*" of Savannah. On Christmas Day 1854, Gordon sat down to an "excellent" dinner with the family of his "guardian" and wealthy president of the Planters' Bank of Savannah, Edward Anderson. Black slaves served twenty-eight adults and eleven children, all cousins of Gordon, including his contemporary, Edward Clifford Anderson Jr., who soon matriculated at the University of Virginia. In the course of the meal, Gordon enjoyed "five varieties of Madeira and three of Sherry," all aged from ten to thirty years.[61]

Wealthy white Savannahians enjoyed a variety of entertainments during the Christmas holidays and the winter social season. George Barnsley hunted deer on Christmas Day at the Barnwell's rice plantation. Other guests of Savannah's well-to-do traveled to nearby plantations, where they climbed aboard springless wagons driven by slaves and pulled by mules into the fields. Here they shot "splendid bags of snipes, quail, duck, doves, lark & rabbit," which were cooked over open fires by "old negroes" who "delighted in pleasing" the visitors. George Smith wrote excitedly about watching six- and eight-oar boat races just opposite the city on the Savannah River. Wealthy South Carolina and Georgia rice planters and Savannah residents such as John Screven, Randolph Spaulding, and J. Hamilton Couper entered boats named respectively the *Ella Brooke,* the *Mary Halsey,* and the *Sunny South.* Smith counted himself lucky in December 1853 that he was not watching the regattas from a bridge at the lower end of the city. It collapsed from the weight of spectators, dumping them into the river and drowning "a negro man . . . and a mason."[62]

During the spring the city's elite entertained themselves with more weddings, picnics, fishing in nearby waters, and militia parades and parties; by early summer the wealthiest went to the mountains, the north, or abroad to escape the heat. In late April the water was warm enough for Henrietta Wayne to enjoy outings to catch "plenty of fine crabs, shrimp and fish." Invited to his uncle's home near Savannah, one visitor in late April "caught about 50 pike in two hours" and "about 75" on another day. "It was beautiful sport. They would bite so fast," he wrote.[63]

In May militia units assembled in the city. The Savannah Volunteer Guards commanded by Captain James P. Screven, the wealthy rice planter, assembled in the city on May 1, 1852, to celebrate the fiftieth anniversary of their founding. A member of the guards and son of the commander, Private John Screven, was chosen to deliver an oration to the gathering. With great gusto and enthusiasm he told his "fellow soldiers" that they served both as "guardians" of their "liberties and . . . honor" as well as their "country and . . . homes. Keep your steel burnished and sharp. The war-storm afrights not them that are prepared to meet its coming!"[64] Such oratory flourished in the South by the 1850s and most likely was lost neither on northerners or Savannah's African Americans.

Blacks also observed the frequent parades and displays of arms. William Gordon, too, was impressed. On parade days the "city swarms with dashing Dragoons—Handsome Hussars" who "made a splendid appearance," Gordon noted. He thought the Hussars to be "some of the finest riders in the world," especially "the troops from the country . . . men . . . born on horseback [who] . . . have lived there ever since."[65]

The upper crust and their children celebrated May Day. In 1854 "five hundred" well-to-do "young people" held a "May Party" in Oglethorpe Barracks. Miss Bradley was "crowned" queen, and she in turn "chose Potter Williamson, King." The Bradleys and the Williamsons were old acquaintances and among the city's wealthiest families. The celebrants did not go home until three o'clock in the morning.[66]

Those among the wealthy elite whose work did not demand that they swelter in Savannah's summer heat or endure its insects left the city. In early July 1849 Henrietta Wayne described the city as "almost deserted . . . , so many persons going north and to the upper part of the state. Two elegant steam ships . . . leave here every week for New York and are generally crowded with passengers."[67] A decade later when "every one" of Henrietta's relatives left Savannah "for the summer," she felt "lonely" and decided to spend the season in Saratoga, New York. There were numerous Savannahians staying at Saratoga's hotels or private boarding houses, "so we had a fine society," Henrietta remarked. She found the "mineral waters . . . very beneficial," and "we remained until the weather got very cold."[68]

Savannah's wealthiest families also summered at Newport, Rhode Island, with Charlestonians and other affluent southerners. The George Noble Jones family, perhaps Savannah's wealthiest, built a rambling Gothic "cottage" in Newport in the 1840s and entertained others like themselves. William Gordon's mother, Sarah, spent the summer in New Haven, Connecticut, and others went abroad. As a junior member of the firm Tison and McKay in the early 1850s, William Gordon left the city only briefly in the summer. In July 1855 he did escape for brief a "holiday" to nearby plantations owned by associates and relatives, and there he delighted in rifle and pistol shooting; Gordon also swam in the Ogeechee River, where he encountered an alligator.[69] Likewise, Charles H. Olmstead, son of a wealthy banker, also remembered that as a young man he "learned to ride . . . , to swim with ease, . . . to use a gun safely, . . . and to find my way through the woods."[70] The bishop of the Diocese of Georgia and former Episcopal rector of Savannah's Christ Church observed that for the privileged class, field and water sports were "as much parts of their education as Latin or Mathematics."[71]

Savannah's well-to-do valued education, attended preparatory schools and colleges, and earned college degrees. George Frederick Tilghman Jones, scion of one of Savannah's founding families, was educated at St. Paul's College and School, near New York City, and the University of Pennsylvania. Here he developed a fascination with history and developed a "bibliomania"—a rage to collect the finest books, which became his lifelong passion. Jones graduated in the mid-1840s and subsequently took a medical degree, but his vast inheritance allowed him the luxury of not having to practice medicine. In the late 1840s he returned to the ancestral location of the Jones family home, Wormsloe Plantation on the Isle of Hope near Savannah, and at age twenty changed his name to George Wymberley Jones of Wormsloe. He soon became active among the literati of Savannah and the Georgia Historical Society.[72]

Jones's career was exceptional; nonetheless, other members of Savannah's privileged class took prestigious degrees, such as William Gordon, whose mother sent him first to Russell's Preparatory School in New Haven, Connecticut, and then to nearby Yale. Here he graduated in the early 1850s. Gordon kept a large library, appreciated classical music, and was an authority on the contemporary American theater. During the social and theater season of the 1850s he saw one of his favorite actresses, Miss Lyons, perform as Bianca in the *Tragedy of Fazio*. Gordon told his fiancée that he was "perfectly enraptured. I never before was so completely carried away by acting, tho' I have seen nearly all of the fine actors and actresses." He thought Miss Lyons "consumately graceful and natural" and "her voice . . . unsurpassable"; he concluded, she "is a very great favorite here." When a concert was canceled at the playhouse, Gordon wrote that it was "greatly disappointing [to] all lovers of good music in Savannah."[73]

Savannah's theater revived with the city's economic and population boom. The interior of the playhouse on Chippewa Square was painted, renovated to seat 1,200, lit with gas, and heated in the 1850s through the largess of its public-spirited theater lovers and wealthy proprietors such as Edward Padleford and Dr. Richard Arnold. In February 1853 a Savannah paper editorialized that a recent concert drew a "Fashionable and numerous assemblage" and reflected the "changing fortunes . . . [and] onward progress" of the city. The "best" Savannahians "handsomely . . . treated" such "stars" as Eliza Logan, who was given $500 worth of diamonds by her admirers following her appearance in

1853. When she and other "stars"—Edwin Booth, Charlotte Cushman, and Julia Dean—performed, "all the world that [was] the fashionable world of Savannah" attended, William Gordon noticed. Likewise, the theater filled for prima donnas who sang in popular operas or for renowned minstrel shows. However, unknown actors played before "thin houses."[74] The pampered daughters of wealthy Godfrey Barnsley, Julia and Adelaide, attended the theater in Savannah, but sniffed that it as "on a small scale compared to the St. Charles Theatre" of New Orleans.[75]

Like Gordon, other members of the city's privileged class enjoyed the theater, music, and books. George Anderson Mercer, son of West Point graduate and Planters' Bank executive Hugh W. Mercer and Mary Anderson, who was the daughter of prominent local merchant George Anderson, was born in Savannah in 1835. Mercer's family, like Gordon's, sent him to the well-known Russell's Preparatory School in New Haven, Connecticut. In 1856 he graduated from Princeton University, studied law at the University of Virginia, and traveled in Europe; in 1859 he passed the Georgia bar exam and began the practice of law in Savannah. Mercer read widely. By the late 1850s, he had read the works of Alexis De Tocqueville, Edmund Burke, and Lord Kames, all of which, he believed, were "permeated with a strong philosophic spirit, and cannot . . . be too often or attentively studied." Mercer reserved a "portion of each week for historical reading" and nearly always spent time with his "especial favorites, Montesquieu and Shakespeare."[76]

Charles C. Jones Jr. was born in Savannah in 1831, where his father was pastor of the First Presbyterian Church, author of books on the religious instruction of slaves, and a wealthy planter. The younger Jones was reared on his father's plantations in nearby Liberty County. Here he learned to hunt with guns and dogs, fish, ride horses, swim, sail, and row. His primary education came from private tutors, and at age seventeen he matriculated first at South Carolina College and then at Princeton, where he graduated with distinction in 1852; he received a law degree from Harvard two years later. He became a junior partner in the Savannah firm of Ward, Owens, and Jones and in 1860 was elected mayor at the age of twenty-nine.

The son of William Ward and Sarah Ann McAllister of Savannah, John Elliott Ward was born in 1814. He attended Amherst College, studied law at Harvard, and in 1836 commenced practicing law in Savannah. Within twenty years he headed one of the city's most prestigious and lucrative law firms, accumulated a fortune, was elected president of the Georgia Historical Society, mayor of Savannah, and to the Georgia house and senate, and became the first U.S. minister to China.

John Screven, the son of James P. Screven, a physician and wealthy planter, and Hannah Georgia Bryan, was born in Savannah in 1827, attended Franklin College in Athens—soon thereafter named the University of Georgia—and practiced law in Savannah, but he soon retired to manage his father's rice plantations. His father was delighted with his marriage to Mary White Footman, daughter of Dr. Richard Hunter Footman and Mary Constance Maxwell. Young Screven was steeped in the military history of the Roman Empire, knew well the life of the Athenian dramatist Aeschylus, and occasionally quoted Latin to make a point.[77]

The family of Charles Olmstead appreciated education. They sent Charles and his sister to boarding schools. He first attended a school near Savannah conducted by the Reverend Benjamin Burroughs, a Princeton graduate, and later the Georgia Military Institute in Marietta, Georgia, where he met other cadets from Savannah: Alexander Butler, Tom Carmody, George Turner, and Theodore McFarland. In 1856 Olmstead graduated as adjutant of the corps. His education gave him a lifelong interest in books, the theater, and opera. He especially enjoyed hearing sung Mozart's *Twelfth Mass* and Schubert's *Barcarole*. Olmstead's sister first attended the Montpelier School for Girls near Macon, Georgia, and then "a finishing school for young ladies" in New Haven, Connecticut. Here she frequently enjoyed the company of Yale professors and lived in a heady "literary atmosphere."[78]

Savannah's privileged class wanted their daughters educated. Henrietta Jane Harden Wayne and her husband, physician Richard Wayne, employed tutors for their daughter, Henrietta, her mother's namesake. Mrs. Wayne told her sister that the local "schools are very inferior and I feel I am doing the child injustice keeping her" in Savannah "when I have an opportunity of having her properly educated." Henrietta enrolled her daughter at age fourteen in an exclusive boarding school in Charleston, Madam Ann Marsan Talvande's French School for Young Ladies, where "she will make a good French scholar."[79] Edward Harden was equally concerned with the education of his younger daughter, Mary. On one occasion he counseled Mary on her "course of reading" and to "take up without delay, Middleton's *Life of Cicero*," which "gives an account of . . . the heroes and statesmen of Rome . . . their domestic manners & habits in the finest style." Harden advised her to read *Caesar's Commentaries* and Tacitus after first reading the "prefaces and introductions."[80]

Godfrey Barnsley, the English cotton broker who first made a fortune in Savannah and later moved to New Orleans, wanted only the best education for his five children but wondered if he could afford it. When his son, George, wanted to study in England, Barnsley told him that a college education in Georgia would be "far less expensive than at Cambridge"; he concluded: "providing my children with education in a respectable manner . . . has not been without great sacrifice of my own ease."[81]

In the 1840s and 1850s, Savannah's literati included bibliophiles such as Israel Tefft, Alexander S. Smets, George Wymberley Jones, physician-historian William Bacon Stevens, and the many-faceted intellectual Dr. Richard Arnold. Tefft, from Rhode Island, was coeditor of the local paper, the *Savannah Georgian*. He assembled a vast library in his home and was nationally known for his collection of 25,000 autographs, especially from the colonial and Revolutionary eras. After making a fortune in the lumber business, French-born Smets devoted himself to collecting the world's classics and was recognized nationally for his library of more than two thousand volumes. Jones was more selective than Smets, buying only books that he planned to read. While in his twenties he assembled at Wormsloe Plantation a remarkable library of British and Latin classics and the finest collection of works in private hands relating to Georgia. Jones became lifelong friends with Tefft, Arnold, and William B. Hodgson, who was also a member of the local literati and one of Savannah's elite by marriage into the Telfair family, one of Savannah's wealthiest.

The Georgia Historical Society was founded in 1839 at Tefft's home on St. Julian Street, and its founding fathers included Tefft, Arnold, and Dr. William Bacon Stevens. The society was first located in a second-story room at Whitaker Street and Bay Lane. Dr. Stevens had migrated from Maine to Savannah for his health. He married the daughter of a prominent physician, became a practicing and affluent doctor himself and later an Episcopal minister, and, after being judged "sound" on slavery—sharing the view of the local privileged class—was admitted to the circles of the city's elite.[82] William Gordon, among others, shared the prevailing sentiment. Apparently, while he was studying at Yale he was influenced by antislavery views, but after he returned from the North and began working as a cotton and rice broker, he told his fiancée, Nellie Kinzie: "I see so much of Negroes in my business, I know so much more of them than I ever did before that I feel vexed at ever having doubted the system [of slavery] as much as I often did in the past."[83] Other members of the local elite profoundly believed in vast racial differences between black and white. For instance, one prominent Savannahian wrote regarding a marriage proposal: "I have not the least objection to our girl Liby marrying Mrs. Cable's boy provided he supports an unblemished character for she is indeed more like a white person . . . than a negro."[84]

The officers of the Georgia Historical Society tapped William Bacon Stevens to deliver an oration to celebrate the founding of the colony of Georgia by General James Oglethorpe. On February 12, 1841, Stevens, accompanied by uniformed military escorts, paraded from the Exchange Building up Bull Street to the Unitarian Church—Dr. Arnold's church—and delivered his speech. He was soon at work on a history of Georgia subsidized by the society. When published in the late 1840s, Stevens's *History of Georgia* was both praised and bitterly criticized, especially by George Wymberley Jones, for both personal and professional reasons. By this time Jones was writing *Theory Concerning the Nature of Insanity* and publishing rare documents. In late 1848 Jones was elected to membership in the Georgia Historical Society. By November of the year following, many of the society's nearly 250 members met in their new quarters, a two-story building in the popular Gothic architectural style just off Monument Square. The society was called to order by its president, Savannah native James Moore Wayne, now an associate justice of the United States Supreme Court. Present were Tefft, Dr. Arnold, William B. Hodgson, and Alexander R. Lawton. These Savannah literati, like George Wymberley Jones, were of a like mind with other southerners. They believed that "intellectual progress" was possible and would be led by intellectuals such as themselves who had the leisure to do so because of the wealth created by their slaves.[85]

They met periodically throughout the 1840s and 1850s to hear and discuss lectures on a variety of topics—religion, education, the law, and the early Indians of southern Georgia. Although largely unknown and far fewer in number than Charleston's nationally recognized and sizeable circle of writers and scientists, Savannah's conservative literati appeared to enjoy a vibrant life of the mind. Savannah's small band of intellectuals and their activities support the contention of historian Michael O'Brien that the leading thinkers of the Old South resided in the cities and towns, not in the countryside. Although staunch advocates of slavery, the literati nonetheless provided a humanizing influence in Savannah.[86]

The mansions of Andrew Low and Charles Greene became centers of the city's cultural and intellectual life. These wealthy cotton brokers invited visiting literary men to dine and sometimes included the local literati. Celebrated British novelist William Makepeace Thackeray came to Savannah twice to give lectures during the 1850s. On both occasions Andrew Low invited Thackeray to stay with his family. Thackeray enjoyed his visit and later recalled that during his stay with Low, "There was endless talk between us." On one occasion Greene gave a dinner party for a visiting newspaperman, William Howard Russell, which included a local editor, the former mayor and now minister to China, John Elliott Ward, Brigadier General Alexander R. Lawton, and William B. Hodgson, a former U.S. consul and an expert on the Far East. Russell later recorded in his diary that Hodgson now spent his leisure time "reading monographs on the language of divers barbarous tribes in Numidia and Mauritania."[87]

THE LIVES, SOCIETY, AND CULTURE OF THE
MIDDLE CLASS

Savannah's middle class lived in a different world from that of the city's elite. Long hours, hard work, sometimes inadequate income, and little job security made life for Savannah's middle class uncertain and allowed little time for social and cultural activities.

Savannah's middle class by the 1840s and 1850s included a handful of professionals but consisted mainly of clerks, bookkeepers, owners of small businesses, and mechanics or artisans. The majority had migrated from northern states, and another one-third were foreign-born immigrants. They found skilled jobs in the commission houses, in the booming construction businesses, and with the Central of Georgia Railroad as bookkeepers, carpenters, bricklayers, painters, plasterers, and mechanics; others found employment with the city's mills and manufacturers. They managed and owned most of the retail establishments such as groceries, clothing stores, bars, and bakeries. The small shopkeepers lived above their businesses in the city's retail district between Broughton Street and the river; other small businessmen and artisans were scattered throughout the city between West and East Broad Streets, while still others resided in Oglethorpe Ward.

By the 1850s overcrowding in the lower city pushed immigrants into new suburbs such as Robertsville in the southwest corner of Savannah. Here a "mostly industrial" population lived in "neat houses, generally small." A labor shortage in Savannah's booming economy by the early 1850s meant that most skilled artisans earned good wages, over $2 daily while the national average for carpenters was $1.85 in 1860. A few acquired considerable wealth in land and slaves. But only 5 percent of the artisans owned real estate and 64 percent owned less than $500 in personal property. None ever accumulated anything approaching the vast wealth of the large slaveholding merchant-planters.

Carpentry was the specialty of most of the successful middle-class artisans. Joseph Gammon, a carpenter, increased his real and personal property between 1850 and 1860 by $11,000 to $26,000 and owned 11 slaves; Francis Blair, carpenter, increased his holdings by $8,000 to $18,000 and owned 13 slaves; Gilbert Butler, carpenter, increased his holdings by $29,000 to $31,000 and owned 7 slaves. Perhaps the four most successful artisans in the city, George M. Willet, John Scudder, Mathew Luftburrow, and Frederick Henry Willink, amassed enough wealth in real and personal property to move into the city's upper middle class. Willet was a native of New Jersey and a master builder, and by age 42 he owned real estate and personal property worth $98,000 and 18 slaves. Scudder, also a native of New Jersey and a master builder, had worked in Savannah with his father and brother for about twenty years; by 1860 at age 45 he had accumulated $87,000 and owned 5 slaves. Luftburrow, also a native of New Jersey and a master mason, built streets and fortifications for the city, public buildings, and private homes. After working for some two decades in the city, Luftburrow by the late 1850s owned over $60,000 in real estate and personal property and 15 slaves. Willink was born locally and named after his father, a German immigrant and merchant, who by 1860 at age 75 had amassed wealth of $59,000 and owned 23 slaves. The younger Willink began work in the city as a ship carpenter, but over a twenty-year period he became a master ship builder and owner of a shipyard, 5 slaves, and $10,000 in property by 1860.

For the middle class, the hours were long and the work hard. In 1852 commission house clerk William S. Norwood worked from first light until early evening for $800.00 annually and could not marry until he found "food for wife self & horse"; currently, he wrote, he could only support the latter two. By the end of the decade however, he married, purchased four slaves, and owned $3,000 in real estate.[88]

Norwood was an exception in that he accumulated significant wealth in a short period of time; otherwise, he was typical of the middle class since he apparently had no time or interest for cultural activities. For example, the demands of work on foreign-born Captain Charles Stevens, who for over twenty years piloted vessels in and out of Savannah in the coastal carrying trade, left him little time, even if he had the inclination, for the Savannah theater or library societies. In his carrying business between plantation owners and Savannah merchant houses, Stevens always faced the possibility of economic hard times when, as did occur, merchants purchased their own coast-wise vessels.

Competition or lessening demand for their skills also threatened middle-class engineers such as Englishman William Garland, who had opened a machine shop in Savannah in the 1840s. The business prospered, and by 1850 three apprentices worked with him until for unknown reasons the business failed, most likely from the competition of local skilled blacks and white immigrants who came to Savannah looking for work. Once again Garland was on the road in Georgia and South Carolina seeking employment. Like his skilled middle-class friends—artisans, clerks, teachers, and shopkeepers—Garland faced chronic unemployment, financial insecurity, and impoverishment. Often he was barely able to support himself and his wife and child.[89]

As a middle-class artisan, Garland was not alone. Apparently, because they could not find work in their specialties, more than eighty-five of the city's white artisans (more than half) changed their occupations between 1850 and 1860. The city's prosperity forced Savannah's middle-class craftsmen to change jobs. Merchants knew that the local elite and the upwardly mobile preferred cheaper, imported, mass-produced silver, furniture, and clothing. As more wealth accumulated in fewer hands in the early 1850s, the merchants imported crafted products from firms in New York and London. This displaced Savannah's white artisans. Of the twenty-four cabinetmakers in the city in 1850, only five resided there in 1860. It is assumed that many of these craftsmen, such as engineer William Garland, became itinerant workers seeking opportunities elsewhere to support themselves and their families.[90] Undoubtedly, free skilled African Americans and slaves assumed some of the work of many of these white craftsmen.

When their jobs were threatened or living costs outpaced incomes, skilled artisans and laborers sometimes attempted to organize for better wages. New life was breathed into the old Mechanics' Association, stevedores organized, and the Savannah Typographical Society was formed in the 1850s. But due to several factors, however, the labor movement never gained momentum. Those white artisans who had achieved the status of gentlemen through ownership of land and slaves did not share the white nonslaveholders opposition to the labor of skilled free blacks and slaves. Furthermore, too many white businesses depended on skilled free black and slave labor for their opponents to make much headway. And few of the many new Irish immigrants in the city had skills. In 1856 immigrant stevedores organized a work stoppage. It was not their first, but it was their last. Management fired the white workers and hired black slaves to do the work. In sum, many free white artisans identified themselves first as white men, which made it remote that vigorous efforts would be made to organize. This "shared social identity" of all white men set Savannah's skilled workers apart from the class-conscious, skilled working men of the north.[91] Indeed, race pervaded all facets of the city's life.

In 1850 about 900 youngsters, mostly middle or upper middle class, attended the combined elementary and secondary schools in the city. Chatham Academy educated more than any other school. About 180 of the students attended schools for indigents or orphans, such as the Savannah Female Asylum, the Institute of the Sisters of Mercy, the Free School Society, and the Catholic and Episcopal Church schools. This meant that only 35 percent of all white Savannahians between the ages of five and twenty attended any school. Most Savannah children lacked the money or motivation. A handful of prominent Savannahians calling themselves the "Friends of Education" did promote the establishment of public schools for poor white children, and by the late 1850s two schools opened with funding from the city and private sources. With money bequeathed by Peter Massie of Glynn County and public funds, the Massie School was erected at the corner of Gordon and Abercorn Streets. By 1858 the city had expended over $14,000 in building costs, teachers' salaries, and furniture for the Massie School. Mayor James P. Screven, a millionaire planter-politician, recommended that the City Council annually provide public funds to the school. He explained to Savannahians that in commercial cities like Savannah numerous citizens are unable to pay for education for their children from "the small earnings of their labor"; therefore, to "keep these children from the evils incident to idleness, and to make them useful members of society . . . should be the object of the rulers of the city, and no means are so well calculated to effect these objects as well regulated public schools." During the 1859–60 school year, 59 paying and 211 charity students attended the school. That same year enrollments in the city reached 1,340, which represented approximately 40 percent of Savannah's white children between ages six and eighteen.

The white upper crust had reached out to the offspring of the city's lower middle class and poor whites through publicly funded schools. Perhaps, in the face of the growing antislavery movement in the North and the likelihood of Civil War, the elite believed it was in their interest to cultivate the poor whites. But for whatever reasons the schools were launched, Savannah's public schools provided a humanizing experience for some of the city's poorest white children. Such well-staffed and well-equipped schools were unavailable in the countryside.

There was no free library available to most white middle- and lower-class children in the 1850s. The city's elite had ready access to books through their private clubs or organizations, and for those who paid a fee of $5 annually, Savannahians could peruse books at the Exchange Reading Room or the Savannah Circulating Library. Books may have been available to the offspring of skilled laborers at the library of the Mechanics' Association. The price of local newspapers permitted even the literate poor to buy and read them.[92]

At least one middle-class family believed so profoundly in education that Charlotte Branch, a widow, willingly sacrificed to educate her three young boys, John, Sanford, and Hamilton. Her husband, a Rhode Island native, died in 1847, and three years later Charlotte resided with her mother and three sons above her dressmaker's shop at what is today 212 Broughton Street, the heart of the business district. The family belonged to the Independent Presbyterian Church at the corner of South Broad Street (today Oglethorpe) and Bull Street and most likely Charlotte enrolled the boys at Chatham Academy. The family pinned their hopes on John, the eldest, who was a good student; they most likely scrimped to send him first to a school in Wilmington, Delaware, and then to the Georgia Military Institute in Marietta from 1853 to 1855. Here he studied math and engineering. Charlotte told her son to take "advantage . . . of study . . . apply your heart unto wisdom, get Knowledge, get understanding; be obedient to your teachers . . . [and] Be particular in the company you chose."

At seventeen, John returned to Savannah and became the main breadwinner for his family. He took a position as bookkeeper for the prestigious and wealthy commission merchant firm Padelford, Fay & Company. He joined the Oglethorpe Light Infantry, which was formed by graduates of the Georgia Military Institute to maintain their military readiness. In the late 1850s, John was commissioned a lieutenant, and his brother, Sanford, drilled under him; Hamilton was yet too young to join. On the eve of the Civil War, Charlotte Branch, who had struggled to rear her sons as a single parent, most likely brimmed with pride over them. But soon after the war commenced, tragedy engulfed the family.[93]

Preoccupied with earning a living, many middle-class men and women had little time or money for parties, dances, reading, or other cultural activities. Many hunted, fished, and crabbed, and they swam off the docks in the Savannah River despite laws prohibiting it. They attended public balls usually sponsored by their militia units, lodges, fire companies, or the Mechanics' Association. They joined the Alhambra Club, the Phoenix House, and the Oak Lodge at Thunderbolt, where the upper middle class enjoyed seafood and liquor while bowling, pistol shooting, and playing shuffleboard. William Foster Parker, a middle-class Savannahian who was a slave dealer and auctioneer, liked to attend Trinity Methodist Church and hear a good sermon, go to a wedding party, join friends at the Odd Fellows Live Oak Lodge #3, visit with friends, and walk in the cemetery, although he was frequently ill with dyspepsia and took quantities of quinine for his headaches. Some middle-class citizens found entertainment in the bars, gaming houses, and brothels; others enjoyed the performances of the magicians and jugglers who came to town. Entertainment also arrived with the circus, which erected tents on vacant lots in the city. White and black laborers also flocked to see them.[94]

THE LIVES, SOCIETY, AND CULTURE OF
WHITE LABORERS

Common white laborers ranked at the bottom of Savannah's white hierarchy in the 1840s and 1850s. In general, their lives can be likened to the lives of some of the city's African Americans: short, nasty, and brutish. The elite made little distinction between slaves and poor whites. Most of the white common laborers were first-generation Irish men and women, "Paddys" and "Brigetts" in the slang of the day. Census takers in 1850 identified 499 males who described themselves as laborers. Of these, 442 came from abroad, and 416 named Ireland as their place of nativity. Irish males found employment loading and unloading vessels, working for the Central of Georgia Railroad, and driving horse-drawn wagons from the railroad depot to the wharves, warehouses, and stores; the women worked as seamstresses, laundry workers, and household servants. These common laborers, along with sailors, free Negroes, and slaves, crowded into Oglethorpe Ward and the wards east of Habersham Street—described in the mid-1850s as "rapidly increasing" with the "worst elements."[95]

Oglethorpe Ward included all of the city west of West Broad Street and the area from the Central of Georgia Railroad Depot to the river. By 1850 it was the city's largest ward, rapidly growing in numbers, and a bustling, gritty, industrial center. One northerner visiting the city described dwellings likely to have been seen in Oglethorpe Ward as "wooden tenements, of one or two stories . . . [with] a very dingy and somber appearance." Another visitor, C. G. Parsons, characterized hovels he saw in the city's slums as "dingy, dirty, squalid, cheerless." The city's press was alarmed at the health hazard of "crowding four, six, and even eight families into little cribs of brick and mortar . . . and sticking [them] upon a patch of ground 100 feet in length by sixty feet wide."[96] It was the city's only ward that lacked open squares and numerous trees.

The population of Oglethorpe was more than triple that of the city's next largest ward. Some 1,000 whites, many of Irish extraction, 1,046 slaves, and 281 free "people of colour" jammed into 451 dwelling places of wood and 5 of brick. When and if they worked as common laborers, most earned only $1.25 a day, which by the late 1850s did not meet living costs for those with families. If white laborers demanded higher wages, employers replaced them with blacks. Hence, many white laborers became destitute, lived in squalor, faced starvation, and often succumbed to disease. Some turned to charity, others to prostitution.[97]

In the 1840s and 1850s the number of charity cases increased with the flood of immigrants, mostly Irish. As usual they included the very young and the very old, widowed and single women, the ill and alcoholics, and a floating population of the unemployed and sailors. Many lived in shanties or boardinghouses on the eastern and western fringes of the city along the waterfront. Prominent, well-meaning men and women who provided assistance to the white poor nevertheless divided them into the virtuous and vicious, but they looked on most as degraded, immoral, and irresponsible individuals who themselves brought on their illnesses. Motivated by paternalism, a desire to exercise control over the indigents, to improve the morals of the city, and particularly to foster the bonds of race and white supremacy, wealthy, civic-minded Savannahians willingly gave of their time and money for relief of the poor. They saw no inconsistency in providing assistance only to the white poor since they wanted them to have at the very least the same level of care provided slaves, which they believed was cradle-to-grave security. In this way they also offered a defense of what they believed to be their own morally superior society in the face of a growing chorus of northern critics.[98] Well-off Savannahians believed that slaves enjoyed cradle-to-grave security, so they were little moved when northern visitor Emily Burke wrote that she saw old, black men "bent to the ground by hard labor . . . begging a potato [or]. . . a morsel of hominy."[99]

Unlike the northerners, the southern and Savannah elite, men and women, sought in a modest way to feed and care for the white poor's physical needs but formed no organizations to bring about social change. The factor of race and class, especially among the wealthy men and women, permeated every relationship in Savannah and the South.[100]

Members of the Board of Health who inspected property in the city for cleanliness observed those white families most in need of assistance and frequently intervened to relieve the most desperate cases, which were many in the 1850s. It was reported that some faced starvation. The board repeatedly appealed to the City Council or the justices of the inferior court for funds to relieve "the sick and destitute," and they readily responded. Over a period of several years the board handed out small sums amounting to more than $3,000 for the immediate relief of several hundred indigents.[101]

Savannah's elite aspired for the city to become commercially "the New York of the South" and to appear prosperous, so a committee in each ward monitored those in "destitute circumstances." The number of abandoned and orphaned children multiplied in the city. Notified of the growing number of homeless children, the Union Society—the city's oldest continuing charitable organization—in 1855 reopened Bethesda Orphanage for boys at the original site ten miles from Savannah. The distance of the asylum from the city made it more difficult for parents to see or lure their sons away. Nevertheless, the Union Society required that anyone visiting Bethesda had to do so in the presence of the superintendent or have his permission. The mothers and fathers of these youngsters were regarded as paupers, which included both the virtuous poor and the vicious poor in the language of nineteenth-century reformers. Applications for accommodations at the new private home for orphaned boys always exceeded its capacity.

The civic-minded men of the Union Society wanted the young orphans to adopt their manners, morals, and ambitions and become orderly, industrious members of the community. They called on their charges to "Be docile, obedient, and teachable." The society touted the benefits of removing the vagabond boys from the bad influences of city life and their questionable friends to an agricultural environment where each boy was to spend at least a year laboring on the 125-acre farm of the orphanage. This would help transform them into "obedient and steady boys." In the face of this theory, work in the fields around Bethesda Orphanage had only begun when a youngster by the name of Owen Brittles, influenced by "some of his nomadic friends," exchanged the ordered, agricultural life of the asylum for a more exciting and carefree life along the Savannah riverfront, in its grog shops, and with the city's prostitutes.

When the city's ward committees identified the hungry, poor, and ill, they were escorted to the Savannah Poor House and Hospital, a commodious structure at Huntingdon and Drayton Streets, which remained the agency for the relief, control, and warehousing of the city's homeless men, women, and children. Here they came under the control of a group of prominent men who paid a fee of $5 annually to oversee them. They also received token tax revenues from the city. The board occasionally was criticized for reelecting themselves or men like themselves, but most were civic-minded businessmen and physicians. Two long-term board members had impeccable credentials: the ubiquitous Dr. Richard Arnold and William Duncan, the business partner of Godfrey Barnsley.

The indigent, the ill, and pregnant women occupied about one-half of the beds in the hospital infirmary; sick or maimed sailors and paying inmates occupied the rest. If the poor recovered, they were obliged to remain until they had paid their bill through work at the Poor House and Hospital. Board members and the city also kept expenses low by minimizing relief and apparently shipping healthy paupers to other cities. In 1853 the managers bragged that only $8 was expended on patients during the year. By the end of the 1850s a total of only $1,290.50 was allocated to send paupers elsewhere and to maintain the ninety white men, thirteen women, and eight indigent children in the poorhouse, most of whom were Irish immigrants. This sum was estimated to be only slightly higher than the cost of entertaining and lodging visiting dignitaries from Charleston. Independent of the Poor House and Hospital, the City Dispensary provided medicine free of cost to the white poor.

Board members of the Savannah Poor House and Hospital in cooperation with the city ensured that the streets remained free of white beggars, which helped elevate homeless whites over indigent blacks; furthermore, the Poor House and Hospital admitted whites only, which dignified the poorest white over the wealthiest black. Private and public funds kept poor whites out of view and helped maintain the image of white superiority; furthermore, the care for the white poor polished the image of a morally superior slave society by comparison with the image slaveholders had of the ill-treated, dispirited white hireling in the North.[102]

As new immigrants streamed into Savannah in the 1850s, the city's well-to-do women, who found self expression as overseers of the city's benevolence, continued to assist the white adult poor and their children by providing them lodging in frame houses on South Broad Street (Oglethorpe Avenue today). Many of the same women supported the Needle Woman's Friend Society, whose members earned their daily bread by sewing for the privileged class.[103] Women and men with the same aims joined together in a nonsectarian movement to remove white "idle and immoral seamen" from Savannah's mean streets and to provide for them a "pious life" at the Savannah Port Society, where preachers of the Gospel ministered to them. Of course, this was a way to ensure social order, keep white drunken sailors off the streets, and promote the idea of white superiority.

Savannah's well-to-do women also worked with their churches to establish boardinghouses for sailors, which would detract them from the lure of brothels. Matrons in the boardinghouses who enforced rules forbidding gambling, cards, foul language, and liquor also offered to hold the money of the seamen to save them from "dissipation and drunkenness" while ashore. Savannah's well-to-do white women also organized the Female Seamen's Friend Society, which cooperated with the Port Society to provide rooms for sailors in a house at Bay and Jefferson Streets. By 1850 it was accommodating hundreds of sailors yearly.[104]

The rising number of immigrants did not deter women of the privileged class from working diligently to provide an education for poor children of the city, "snatching [them] away as it were from ignorance and vice." Perhaps due to the changing nature of the ethnicity of the young female inmates—now primarily Irish—the director of the Female Asylum came under criticism in the late 1850s for failing to emphasize the "domestic duties of Housekeeping." Since the destiny of the inmates was domestic service, critics objected to the daughters of the poor being taught reading, writing, and arithmetic, subjects they would never use. Critics also charged that upon leaving the asylum, the girls embarked on a life of immorality. The Board of Managers of the Asylum investigated the allegations and concluded that most enjoyed productive lives after leaving the asylum, which was amazing considering "*who* they often are, and the *haunts* from whence these children are rescued." The board did admit that some of the former inmates had disgraced the asylum's good name.[105] Without a doubt, some turned to prostitution.

THE LIVES, SOCIETY, AND CULTURE OF FREE
BLACKS AND SLAVES

Free blacks ranked next to last, behind white laborers, in a social hierarchy where caste trumped class. By the 1850s some 705 free blacks lived in Savannah despite discriminatory ordinances that sought to discourage them. Free blacks relocating to Savannah were required to pay a $100 fee—until Georgia's high court annulled the law in 1848—to have a white guardian, to annually register with the city, to serve with a fire company, and to obey the same laws that governed the movement of slaves within the city; a state law required free blacks to work on public projects twenty days each year. Sometimes they faced prosecution for minor incidents of commission or omission, which required their white guardians to come to their defense. Of course, they could enjoy a family and, if they could afford it, own their home. Many worked as skilled carpenters and bricklayers; the unskilled became porters, draymen, and house servants. Free black women worked as domestics, cooks, laundry workers, and, especially, seamstresses.

The free Negroes lived in almost every ward and in the suburbs, but over one-third resided in Oglethorpe Ward. Many accumulated a modest sum in real estate—half held less than $1,000—and a few owned one or two slaves. By the end of the 1850s about 180 free blacks paid city taxes, usually on real estate.[106]

In 1848 there were 62 free "persons of color" in Savannah identified as craftsmen; in 1860 at least 179 free Negroes called themselves craftsmen. These black artisans did not experience the prosperity that some white artisans enjoyed, and they remained poorer than most white craftsmen. Nearly 60 percent of the black artisans who owned personal property held less than $100; two owned more that $500; of the five who owned real estate, only one held as much as $1,500 worth.[107] But some free blacks found routes to success, which was remarkable.

For free black males in the 1850s, as earlier, the most financially rewarding careers included those of drayman, carpenter, tailor, and baker and in diversified businesses. Joseph Marshall, a drayman like his father, Andrew Marshall, by age 30 had accumulated real estate valued at $3,000, bank and railroad stock, and substantial personal property by 1853. Joshua Bourke, a carpenter, owned real estate in Oglethorpe Ward assessed at $1,000 in 1854. By 1850, Andrew Morel, a tailor from St. Domingue, owned 3 slaves and real estate valued at $1,600. William Claghorn, renowned as a master baker, operated a bakery shop at the corner of Liberty and Habersham Streets. By the late 1850s, at the age of 36, he owned real estate valued at $4,000 and personal property of $2,000. Simon Mirault, the 37-year-old son of tailor Louis Mirault, operated a confectionary on the west side of Broughton Street near Whitaker Street, just two blocks from the city market. In 1854 Mirault and his wife, Mary Jane, owned a slave and $1,500 in real estate. James Hanscomb also owned a confectionary business in Savannah and near the end of the decade of the 1850s, at age 32, he held real estate valued at $4,000. Anthony Odingsells, a mulatto, was Savannah's most successful African American landowner and operator of diversified businesses, which was partly due to the largess of his one-time owner and most likely his father, Charles Odingsells. He freed Anthony and bequeathed to him as a young boy Wassaw Island, just off the Georgia coast. Anthony became the owner of a slaughterhouse and marketed in the city and its environs pork, beef, hides, wool, milk, and also fresh fish. At the end of the 1850s, Odingsells owned 35 milk cows, 50 sheep, 75 swine, 2,000 acres of pine land in the countryside, and 13 slaves. He was Savannah's premier African American businessman.[108]

The best job opportunities for the free black female, like the black male, remained the same over time—seamstress, dressmaker, washerwoman, domestic, and pastry cook. Louisa Marshall, widow of successful drayman Joseph Marshall, supplemented her income by becoming a seamstress; in the late 1850s the value of her home was $1,500. Other successful seamstresses included Hannah Cohen, Georgiana Guard, and Estelle Savage. In the late 1850s Savage owned $2,600 in real estate and permitted her sister and brother to live rent free in houses she owned. Sarah Black earned enough as a seamstress to purchase a lot on Gaston Street, between Jefferson and Montgomery Streets, and to build on it two "good houses" and two "shanties," and although prohibited by city ordinance, she most likely became a landlord. She also kept cows on her property and supplemented her income by selling milk, and she shared her habitation in a common-law marriage with a traveling white cotton broker.

Ann Gibbons, a free woman and mulatto with the same surname as a prominent white family, owned the most highly valued property of any African American in the city in 1860. In 1820, when she was nineteen, her daughter, Claudia, was born, but the father is unknown; how she came by the money to buy her property is also a mystery. Propertyless in 1833, she owned two lots with dwellings on them and four slaves in 1850; a decade later, Gibbons at sixty-one years of age owned three slaves and real estate in Oglethorpe Ward valued at $9,200.

The opportunity to accumulate wealth came to those free African Americans, male or female, who possessed skills and a determination to succeed, willingly worked long hours, were lucky, had a supportive white guardian, and were mulattoes. The latter owned the bulk of the real and personal property owned by blacks in Savannah. Almost 70 percent of Savannah's 725 free African Americans were mulattoes, whereas less than 20 percent of the city's slaves, or 1,378, were mulattoes.[109]

Slaves ranked at the very bottom of the white-black hierarchy. Due primarily to the rapid growth of the white population, the percentage of the slaves in the total population of Savannah shrank from 45 percent in 1830 to 35 percent in 1860, although their numbers more than doubled—from 3,279 to 7,712 in the same period. And as the number of whites increased in the city, the number of slaveholders declined. By the end of the 1850s those owning slaves numbered 1,020; of these, 190 owned one slave, 789 held fewer than 10 slaves, 159 owned 10 to 20 slaves, and 72 held 20 or more.

Many slaves in the city, male or female, worked for their owners as domestics in the household, cooking, washing, and cleaning, and as butlers, gardeners, and carriage drivers. The Central of Georgia Railroad, mills, manufacturers, steamboat companies, and the city's largest hostelry, the Pulaski Hotel, owned large numbers of slaves. For income, some owners hired out their slaves; skilled and unskilled slaves frequently hired "their own time." With the extra money they kept from hiring out, some slaves markedly improved their wardrobes. The older black women wore brightly colored turbans, ankle-length skirts, white aprons that they tied in back with bows, and golden hoop earrings; the local press claimed that some male slaves dressed better than their masters.[110]

Christmas for the slaves meant a gift, perhaps, and "no work until New Years and [they] are in a constant state of hilarious excitement," William Gordon observed. On Christmas evening of 1854, Gordon heard noises in the basement and discovered about "40 downtrodden serfs dancing around a huge icing cake . . . to the music of a wild sort of tune accompanied by clapping of the hands and shuffling of the feet." Twisting their bodies they danced "round and round . . . the chant rising with the excitement." Gordon knew that the "dance is one peculiar to Christmas night and is kept up until morning." He observed that the "scene . . . reminded one more of Savage than Civilized life, yet the perfect freedom from all care, the abandonment to pleasure was so different from the harassed look or drunken carousal of the same class elsewhere." Gordon apparently was influenced by the prevailing notion among southerners that their slaves were happier than "serfs," white laborers in the northern states. Savannahians were well acquainted with the notion.

As early as 1848 the *Savannah Georgian* editorialized that the institution of slavery was "a blessing to both races . . . our slaves are better treated, better clothed, better fed, [and] . . . happ[ier] than the laboring classes of any part of the World." Emily Burke, a northern abolitionist and teacher, must have wondered just how much joy was in the lives of the young black chimney sweeps she saw who appeared "half-starved [and] emaciated."[111] Another northerner shared the same view. Philo Tower, a zealous abolitionist and clergyman from New York, watched a vessel disgorging grain in Savannah in the early 1850s. Sixteen women and girls unloaded it by carrying "about half a bushel" at a time on their heads. They were "dressed in a coarse sort of woolen skirt" and forbidden to speak. They appeared to range in age from thirteen to sixty; "all looked mournfully dejected, sad and gloomy . . . and . . . performed their degrading unwomanly task under the crack of the driver's whip and sneers of gaping men and boys," Tower observed.[112]

Escape from such physical labor, long hours, and personal cares through drunkenness was commonplace in Savannah. The local press observed it "was the crying evil of all holidays." Excessive drinking appeared to be widespread among the privileged class as well as other classes and castes. For instance, on August 2, 1855, Mayor Edward C. Anderson found the city treasurer, Joseph W. Robarts, "intoxicated . . . while in discharge of his official duties." He was "immediately" suspended, and the following day the City Council accepted his resignation. Occasionally, young men of the privileged class became inebriated, quarreled, drew knives, and cut or killed one another. For instance, a neighbor of the prominent Kollock family, Jimmy Burroughs, "got into a fight with a young man named Carmody, & stabbed him" to death. The Kollock family learned that "Both were drunk at the time."[113]

The annual black firemen's parade was a day of entertainment for the city's African Americans. It fell on the last Monday in May, and during the 1850s more than seven hundred free blacks and slaves served with the Savannah Fire Company and turned out to march. Others lined the streets with white spectators. For African Americans it was a day equivalent to the annual white militia musters and parades. Savannah's ubiquitous letter writer, William W. Gordon, watched the parade: "They have no band nor instrumental music of any kind, but march to the time of their own songs. . . . Their uniforms were quite tasteful, though each seemed determined to appropriate as many, and as widely contrasted, glaring hues as possible." The firemen wore "white pants and loose, white blouse shirts, gathered in at the waist with broad patent leather belts." The editor of the *Savannah Daily Morning News* saw the parade in the 1850s and noted that the line of march "presented a very handsome and imposing appearance," and "perfect order and discipline were preserved."[114]

Due to the prevalence of disease in the city, slave owners such as William Bulloch, Alexander R. Lawton, Hugh Mercer, Sarah Alexander, and William W. Gordon worried for economic reasons that the most frequent killers of blacks—pneumonia, consumption, typhoid fever, and dysentery—might fell their own slaves. The black mortality rate of 3 to 4 percent annually was slightly lower than the rate for whites; once past childhood, blacks in the city enjoyed a longer life expectancy than whites.

In the 1850s slaves numbered from one-quarter to one-half of the population of every ward. About one-half lived in outbuildings behind their owner's house while others who hired their own time were permitted to rent rooms on the fringes of the city. Owners who hired out their slaves, such as Dr. Richard Arnold, decided that it brought "a better interest than the amount of their value would bring in any other investment." One Savannahian owned 59 slaves who worked in the city. By the late 1850s some 19 white masters hired out 5 or more slaves. James Sullivan hired out a twenty-one-year-old slave for $10 weekly; William Henry Stiles rented slaves at the rate of $1 a day. Slave masters frequently hired out their slaves to the Central of Georgia Railroad and to saw and rice mills, steamboat companies, and hotels.[115]

By 1850 slaves comprised almost 50 percent of the 3,376 renters in western Oglethorpe Ward, which had the largest number of slaves in any ward. By this time about 60 percent of the city's slaves lived away from their owners, which permitted these urban slaves far more control over their own lives than those in the countryside. City blacks, like city whites, were usually more sophisticated than their counterparts elsewhere; William W. Gordon noted that city slaves felt "only pity and contempt for *country* negroes."

Charles C. Jones Jr. told his father that "hundreds of negroes in [Savannah] . . . never see their masters except at pay day." Mary Ann Couper received most of her income by the late 1840s from the ten slaves whom she permitted to hire their own time. Her male slaves paid her about $10 to $12 monthly. Savannah's slaves bought badges from the city government annually, which allowed them to legally hire their own time and to move about the city freely. Like free African Americans, most of the slaves made their money as draymen, carpenters, tailors, and barbers. One of the most successful draymen was Straffon Herb, who paid $4 monthly in rent for a house at the corner of Anderson and Montgomery Streets and $10 monthly to his master for the privilege of hiring out. To meet these expenses, Herb had a more than sufficient income. He earned $25 to $40 monthly from his dray business and the livery stable he operated on the waterfront. Sandy Small was one of several slave butchers who hired out his time. He lived outside the city on South Anderson Street and paid his master $12 to $15 per month over twenty years for the privilege of hiring out. He used the time to slaughter hogs and make sausages for his customers. Likewise, carpenter Edward Hornsby paid his owner $16 per month to hire his own time. He leased a lot at the corner of Williams and West Boundary Streets from a white man and with his permission built a six-room house on it. All parties involved knew of Hornsby's venture and the illegality of a slave owning such a tenement, but no proceedings were brought by his owner, his landlord, or city authorities. Although most slaves who hired their time earned modest incomes and saved little, Dolly Reed was an exception. Working as a laundry worker and domestic, she rented a wagon every few months and hauled tobacco and sugar to the countryside, which she traded for eggs and chickens to sell in the city market. She managed to buy a few comforts with this money and saved $3,000 by the late 1850s.[116]

The African American slaves permitted to hire their own time occupied a twilight zone between servitude and freedom and have been called "nominal" slaves by one historian. Nevertheless, if they wanted time for their own enterprises, they had to remit money to their masters. And even after years of paying their owners and scrimping and saving to buy their own freedom, their owners sometime refused. Such was the case of William Anderson, who paid his owner $10 monthly for a quarter century, but when he asked to purchase his own freedom from his owner, George S. Cope, he was refused. Anderson enjoyed only those rights bestowed by his owner. He was chattel property. William Anderson was no "nominal" slave. He was unfree.[117]

Masters repeatedly acted in their own interest and contrary to that of their slaves. In June 1852, for example, John Couper Fraser informed his mother that "Negroes are selling at an enormous price" and that hers "may not always bring us good wages as . . . at present." Therefore, he proposed selling some and investing the money even it meant "parting" a young slave, "Richard," from his family. Remember, Fraser concluded, "my object is *your* interest."[118]

Some white Savannahians regularly complained about owners hiring out slaves or allowing slaves to hire their own time. In the 1840s a grand jury at Savannah insisted that slave hiring was "an evil of a magnitude" that threatened "directly . . . the existence of our institutions." Slaves who hired out drifted throughout the city and were rarely supervised. Slave owner and prominent Savannahian John Stoddard wrote in 1859 that from "Jan'y to Decr. Many owners cannot tell where their servants are, or what they are doing." Some prominent whites believed that lack of supervision by their masters gave some slaves the "opportunity to brew mischief."[119]

Skilled slaves hired themselves out. Some worked side by side with whites and developed close personal relationships. For instance, Henry Forsyth, a white journeyman, and George, a slave, were employed by cabinetmaker Isaac Morrell; they plotted together to steal $118 from Morrell's cashbox and fled, but they were captured in Augusta. That George stayed with Forsyth, rather than fleeing northward to freedom, and that he took two-thirds of the money perhaps indicated that their work and experiences nurtured a deep friendship despite the racial hierarchal society in which they lived. The rough edges of racism were rounded in the workplace.

Sometimes friendship, love, or master-servant relations between prominent white males and their female slaves resulted in sexual intercourse. The nearly two thousand mulattoes in the city by 1860 testified to that. Eminent jurist James Wayne Moore may have been the father of a child born to his slave, Anna, whom he accepted as his daughter, Elizabeth Isabel Clifford; wealthy mulatto Anthony Odingsells was probably the son of Charles Odingsells, a well-to-do white businessman; and city alderman Levi D'Lyon and African American Margaret Dobson produced two children who were baptized at St. John's Catholic Church, the only church in Savannah that baptized the offspring of biracial unions. Another City Council member, Frederic Densler, over a period of several years was charged by a member of his church, the Independent Presbyterian church, with "visiting houses of ill fame, kept by women of color." He denied the charges and was suspended only briefly after corroborating evidence showed that someone had stolen his trousers while at one house of prostitution. However, when he continued his behavior, he was dismissed from all church privileges indefinitely. These relationships between elite white men and their female slaves or free black women were accepted by Savannahians as an expression of male dominance in white-black relations. But this was not the case with affairs between female slaves or free black women and poor white males.[120]

Many prominent whites feared that fraternization of poor white males and black slaves or free black men in the streets, grog shops, and houses of prostitution might lead to the breakdown of racial barriers and might promote their recognition as a single class at the bottom of society. It was also for this reason that Savannah's privileged class distrusted biracial relations and brothels. Never mind that some owners permitted their bondwomen to hire out as prostitutes as long as they returned to the owners some of the profits.

In the 1850s city officials acknowledged that Savannah counted one prostitute for every thirty-nine men, whereas the ratio in New York City was one prostitute for every fifty-seven men. Brothels outnumbered churches. Nine large brothels flourished in Yamacraw, west of West Broad Street, and in the area of the Old Fort and the Trustees Garden, east of East Broad Street; prostitutes also did a lively business in the dark alleyways of Factor's Walk leading to the wharves just off Bay Street. Here, too, in the grog houses drunkenness, brawling, and gambling occurred almost nightly, and laboring men and prostitutes of both races mixed. Fornication between whites was condemned by evangelical churches, and biracial sex was viewed by the elite as a threat to the very foundations of society. To prevent such carnal contact, city officials issued higher fines for women than men: in 1853 prostitute Sarah Hart was fined $5 for "indecent conduct in the streets" with Patrick O'Halligan, who was fined only $2. Three years later a white woman, Sarah Hoyt, was sent to the Chatham County Jail for nearly three months for "drunkenness and adultery with a Negro." No free black or slave was imprisoned at the time for this offense, which most likely meant that Sarah Hoyt was well known to the police and that the fault was with her and not her lover.

The white women prostitutes who challenged local racial mores most likely were young, foreign, or from out-of-state and did not grow up with the social taboo of miscegenation. In 1860 the four prostitutes in the city jail ranged from the age of 17 to 38; one was from Georgia, one was from New York, and the other two were from Ireland. That same year, Fannie Fall, a 29-year-old woman from Ireland, was indicted locally for keeping a brothel. The ten women she employed ranged in age from 16 to 29; seven came to Savannah from the northern states, one was from Georgia, and two were from nearby states.[121]

It is well known that slaves and free blacks drank and caroused with white males and females in the city's streets and houses of prostitution and in the grog shops whose owners sold liquor to blacks despite city ordinances prohibiting it. However, since slave owners were unwilling to permit any dilution of their authority to use slaves as they wished, city ordinances regulating grog shops always allowed owners to send their slaves to obtain liquor for them. This, of course, allowed slaves to mingle with poor whites at the liquor stores, which was frowned on by the elite. This type of biracial association diminished racial distinctions, the elite believed; furthermore, they knew that the non-slaveholding keepers of liquor stores called the elite "unjust oppressors," which diminished their status before whites and blacks; Savannah's well-to-do also knew that slaves stole their property to trade for liquor. And members of the privileged class repeatedly attempted by-laws or extra-legal methods to prevent this biracial fraternization. In 1846, for instance, they organized the Savannah River Anti-Slave Traffic Association to prevent trade in stolen goods.[122] It was not successful.

Persistently troubled by cross-racial fraternization and the likelihood of the development of class-consciousness between blacks and whites, the city's elite moved in other ways to undercut black-white relationships and to promote white racial supremacy in all aspects of city life. For instance, it took a well-educated person, most likely a member of the white privileged class, to use the local press to reiterate white superiority over black. The remarks appeared in the *Savannah Daily Morning News* on June 30, 1851: "What respectable parent wishes to place his son at a trade (however profitable) working with or alongside an apprentice who is a slave?" It was degrading, the writer alleged. Prominent white Savannahians always lifted up their lowliest white citizens, even if they thought them vicious or unworthy and whether institutionalized or at work, over all blacks. In white-black relations, the white elite emphasized that race trumped class.[123]

POLITICS AND MUNICIPAL SERVICES

The clash between Whigs and Democrats, who splintered into factions occasionally over national issues such as the extension of slavery westward, and the city's indebtedness created obstacles in governing the city. Prominent Democrats who switched from one faction to another and then back included John E.

Ward, Dr. Richard Arnold, Francis Bartow, a young attorney, and Richard R. Cuyler, the president of the Central of Georgia Railroad.

Major improvements in the city's infrastructure, continuous dredging of the river, and investments in six railroads burdened the city financially. The government continued to plow money into railroads into the late 1850s. Multimillionaire-politician Dr. James P. Screven promoted the city's investment in the Savannah, Albany, and Gulf Railroad, which began operating in 1857 from a depot fronting East Broad and Liberty Streets on the southeastern edge of the city, and whose president was his son, John P. Screven. Bond issues to cover all the city's financing exceeded $1.8 million, and of this, $1 million was invested in the Savannah, Albany, and Gulf Railroad. By the late 1850s interest on Savannah's bonded indebtedness soared to over $130,000 annually, which nearly equaled the city's annual expenses. To service the debt and pay the bills, the government sold city licenses and slave badges, rented market stalls, and taxed slaves, dogs and horses, peddlers, locomotives crossing the city, billiard tables, and bowling alleys; additionally, new taxes were levied in the late 1850s on real estate, personal property, income, and sales of goods and services, and poll taxes were increased. Still, the additional revenue was not enough for the city to reduce its indebtedness. In November 1860 a third major rail line, the Charleston and Savannah Railroad Company, opened its road linking the "sister cities."

By the mid-1850s Savannah was controlled by the Democratic Party led by a local clique of about fifty civic-minded young professionals and middle-aged, wealthy merchants, physicians, and attorneys, most of them natives of the city or the region and all of them part of the movers and shakers, the "interlocking directorate" supporting Savannah's commercial progress. Some occasionally profited from their close ties to the powerful.

The Irish-Catholic immigrants formed the base of the party. These Irishmen, with their bullying tactics and votes, helped win elections for the Democrats, who rewarded Irish loyalty by putting them on the city's payroll. Democrats usually had the support of two newspapers, the *Georgian* and the *News*. The papers and the party championed southern rights, local progress, and major expenditures for the city's infrastructure, which was needed in the face of the city's burgeoning population. Between 1850 and 1860, the city spent furiously, opening a new cemetery, a gasworks, and a waterworks, upgrading firefighting equipment, building a drainage system, seeking to improve health conditions, spending big sums to dredge and remove obstacles from the river, and creating a new uniformed police force to enforce law and order among poor blacks and whites.[124] By the late 1850s the city's leadership tried to point out that the city was spending more than it was receiving. There was minor tinkering with the tax system, but resistance continued to any increase in taxes on incomes. Hence, by the end of the 1850s, the cost of running the police department alone reached almost $45,000, or 25 percent of the city's annual revenues. Recognizing that the city was headed toward bankruptcy, Mayor Charles C. Jones Jr. told Savannah's citizens: "the elevation of taxes with a view to the liquidation of the present floating debt and the defraying of annual wants of the City appears to be the proper . . . course to be pursued."[125] It was too late by then for tax reform. The city was on the verge of the Civil War.

By the late 1840s only sixteen street lamps lit by whale oil remained fit for use in the city, and these were maintained by private citizens. The City Council concluded in 1848 that these lamps provided inadequate lighting, an inducement to crime, and that gas provided a better method of illumination. Two years later, the government subscribed $25,000 in the stock of the Savannah Gas Light Company, which undertook construction of a gas system with underground pipes. By 1851 lines were laid and gas flowing. The city purchased 330 lamps and posts and paid the gas company $33 annually for each ornamental lamp to light the city between Bay and Taylor Streets and East and West Broad Streets, a good portion of the affluent neighborhoods. But city officials complained that the western edge of the city needed lighting, too, since in Yamacraw, Oglethorpe Ward, "the total darkness at night . . . renders an increase of watchmen there absolutely necessary." Within four years the city administration laid underground gas lines to lamp posts in an area Mayor Edward C. Anderson called "that pandemonium of darkness after sunset, the river front . . . [which] made [it] passable and safe."[126]

In the early 1850s black and white fire companies rushed to a rash of fires. The old fears returned of "incendiaries" prowling across Savannah. Some blazes originated in the lumberyards, and businessmen offered rewards for the capture of arsonists. One prominent Savannahian wrote in June 1852 that "Fires have become very numerous here & the volunteer companies have been out every night for some time trying to detect the rascals who are amusing themselves at the expense of the city." As he completed his letter, he observed that two "brick buildings . . . are now burning" that had been set afire in the early morning hours.[127]

With new fires springing up in the crowded city, the government built a new brick firehouse in the late 1840s and 1850s in Liberty Square, Washington Square, and Pulaski Square. Another firehouse, the Central Station, was constructed on the southwest corner of Oglethorpe Avenue and Abercorn Street, and another in Lafayette Square. The growing numbers of immigrants and blacks crowded together in "decayed houses" also alarmed Savannahians, and in 1854 the council passed an ordinance authorizing the city to raze any building deemed a fire hazard. After the waterworks began pumping that year, fire hydrants were installed; they were painted black at the bottom and white on top, making them highly visible to the firefighters. When the Savannah Fire Company permitted black firefighters to wear uniforms, white fire companies complained that it was "degrading to white firemen," and the City Council supported them. It appeared once again that in white-black relations race trumped class. However, council members recognized that they needed satisfied black firefighters and backed away from their position. The Savannah Fire Company promptly allowed uniformed black firemen. New companies organized, among them the German Fire Company and the Young Americans Company, which one writer recalled was composed of "the rough element of the community." At nearly every conflagration, the Young Americans "engaged in a fight with some one." Finally, in 1856 the officers of the Savannah Fire Company charged the Young Americans with "insubordination and disorderly conduct" and seized the company's engine, which put them out of operation, much to the relief of the public and other firefighters. By 1860 ten colored and four white companies operated under the direction of the Savannah Fire Company.[128]

Savannah's climate was subtropical. Drenching rains came in the spring and summer along with scorching heat. The discovery of the germ theory of disease was years away, as was the realization that mosquito vectors carried yellow fever. As the population soared, the local press called Savannah's streets "the dirtiest and most unwholesome . . . in the South." Sanitation facilities were minimal, and the numbers of privies increased, with the population fouling the air and the city's shallow wells with typhoid bacteria, which made typhoid fever endemic in Savannah until a new water system was adopted. Further, the diet of both poor blacks and whites was low in nutritional value. Savannahians lived in a more unhealthy environment than the residents of other southeastern coastal cities. And as the numbers of migrants and immigrants swelled the population, the number of deaths spiked upward into the hundreds almost yearly during the late 1840s and 1850s. Most deaths of whites occurred from yellow fever and malaria; blacks died of tuberculosis, cholera, and smallpox; and both perished from pneumonia, bronchitis, scarlet fever, measles, whooping cough, and venereal disease.[129]

The exploding population made the job of the city's Board of Health even more difficult. The pace of deaths and burials increased, and in 1849 health officials called for a new burial ground since graveyards within the city limits were "prejudicial to the health of the citizens," for the "nauseous and noxious" gases of decaying bodies infect the air and lessen "the duration of human life . . . living around them."[130] Therefore, the city cemeteries were to be closed. The council acted quickly by floating a bond issue in 1850 for $27,840 for the purchase of Springfield Plantation beyond the city limits to the southwest. For some years Savannah's government had viewed the plantation's marsh and rice lands as a threat to the health of the city. The government acted promptly, using the dry-culture method to drain the low-lying lands. The higher land of the plantation was divided into lots and sold. In 1851 the city government named the new cemetery Laurel Grove. Subsequently, nineteen acres were set aside for black burials and another portion reserved for Jewish burials. Bodies buried in the old potter's field and Negro cemetery were exhumed and reburied in Laurel Grove.[131]

Filth multiplied as the population surged. The city's Board of Health faced an uphill battle but was diligent in its fight against filth in the streets. If citizens ignored their citations to use deodorizing powder or lime in their privies, or to remove carcasses from their yards, the board called on the city marshal or City Council to enforce the regulations. The board members occasionally complained that the marshal was not carrying out their orders. They asked for the power themselves, since without it, they declared, "the health of our fellow citizens [is] endangered."

The board ordered rich and poor, black and white, to practice cleanliness. A recently installed sewer pipe in the affluent neighborhood bisected by Perry Street had become "a great nuisance" in 1850 in the vicinity of the home of wealthy slaveholder and former Savannah mayor Dr. William C. Daniell. The board found that his "servants" were "throwing offal & dirty water in [the] sewer" and "served notice upon Dr. Danniell . . . to prevent" it. Likewise, a member of one of Savannah's oldest families, Mordecai Sheftall, was cited for "putrid water" standing on his lot after rains. Owners were notified that their "privies [were] full . . . [and] must be cleaned," that houses were "decayed," and that the city scavenger's job was made more difficult by persons "throwing dead animals or birds or other filth in the streets and lanes." In August 1851 the board ordered the city scavenger to clean up "every morning the lanes and alleys between the Bluff and the river."[132]

Streets and sidewalks began to be paved in the early 1850s, and dissatisfaction with the city scavenger's department led the mayor and council to institute a new system in 1853, which contracted out the work of cleaning the streets and lanes. For about $9,000 annually a "Superintendent" was hired who was expected to supply the carts, mules, and manpower and to ensure his force was working six days a week, holidays excepted. Within three years the superintendent was using sixteen carts and mules and black drivers. Under the new system, city officials found the "general cleanliness of the city . . . satisfactory" but more costly than the previous system.[133]

Historically, city water was drawn from public and private surface wells equipped with wooden pumps. With increased use by a rapidly rising population, the pumps broke repeatedly and the wells failed, and complaints flooded the mayor's office. The proximity of privies to these wells was recognized as a threat to the health of Savannahians. One physician declared that the citizens were "in reality drinking filtered sewage more or less diluted."

The city government quickly acted to replace the wells with a modern waterworks and sent council members to visit northern cities to examine works there. Subsequently, Mayor Richard D. Arnold arranged a contract with the New York firm of Worthington, Baker, and Morse to build a modern water supply system, and the chief engineer of the water supply for New York City was hired to oversee the construction. Land was purchased for $22,000 from wealthy Savannahians who owned property just west of Oglethorpe Ward and the Ogeechee Canal Basin, among them Alexander Smets and Robert Lachlison, who served on the committee that authorized building the works. Bonds were issued to pay for the land; an additional bond issue of $122,055 followed to pay for building the waterworks exclusive of laying the water mains. Water from the Savannah River above the city was determined pure enough to be pumped into the new reservoirs built west of the Canal Basin, where it was treated and filtered prior to sending it though water mains to a forty-foot-high distributing tank built in Franklin Square. The water began flowing to residents on March 1, 1854. Consumers paid their water bills semiannually, based on the value of the property, and each house was assessed at least $5 by the tax office. Soon after operations began, the water was determined unfit for consumption, and experiments were begun to improve the filtration process. Initially facing some criticism, commissioners of the waterworks asserted, "The value of the waterworks should not be estimated in dollars and cents only but in the security they give to property and the comfort they bestow upon the citizens."[134]

Savannah was somewhat ahead of other communities in providing potable water to many of its citizens. But in providing services first to well-to-do residents, it was much like other cities. Over three years after it first provided water to affluent neighborhoods and only after strong protests did the government lay water mains and begin pumping water into Oglethorpe Ward, which was densely populated with poor whites and blacks.[135]

MEDICINE AND DISEASE

For years a handful of Savannah physicians who trained in first-rate medical schools abroad or in the North attempted to launch a college to train more doctors; other physicians in the city opposed the enterprise. It seemed appropriate to locate a medical school in Georgia's most sophisticated and cosmopolitan city, where a cadre of well-trained physicians were already present; and with the incidence of disease growing with the population, Savannah seemed a good training ground for doctors in a city needing more trained physicians. By the early 1850s a group of physicians led by J. Gordon Howard, Phinias M. Kollock, Richard D. Arnold, and William G. Bullock formed the Savannah Medical Institute and provided funds to construct a building at the corner of Habersham and Taylor Streets, which was known as the Savannah Medical College. A well-qualified faculty of eight professors, who for years practiced medicine locally, began offering classes in the fall of 1853.[136] The Reverend Stephen Elliott, bishop of the Diocese of Georgia, delivered the opening address. He told the assembled faculty, students, and friends that the college "shall exert a beneficial influence . . . it may become the nucleus of science for an hitherto apathetic city." He believed that the college would stimulate an "intellectual culture . . . the collision of mind with mind" and "the development of science and literature. . . . We have already at the South, too long neglected these things." He hoped that the establishment of the college might lead to the development of "a taste and a cultivation for those pursuits which add so much . . . to life . . . popular lectures upon science and art [and] museums." In conclusion, Bishop Elliott challenged his audience to remember that Savannah's archrival, Charleston, under the scientists Ravenel, Bachman, Gibbes, and Holmes, had become "one of the centers of science for the Union."[137] Indeed, Charleston was recognized as the cultural capital of the South.

Dissension among the faculty over policy and opposition among physicians in the community to the Savannah Medical College soon led to the formation of a second school, the Oglethorpe Medical College. Both colleges provided instruction by lectures, bedside observation of patients, and dissection, for which a recently interred body was provided illegally. But the costs of supporting two medical schools, the lack of a sufficient number of qualified white applicants locally, and the bitter competition between the two institutions minimized their effectiveness and growth. Dr. Richard D. Arnold was elected president of the Savannah Medical College, but even he was unable to salve the large egos and prevent personal quarrels between the faculty of the two schools. When the Civil War drew away many faculty and students, the two colleges closed. The Savannah Medical College reopened after the war, but financial difficulties plagued the institution, and in 1881 it closed its doors forever, ending any possibility of a medical school in coastal Georgia.[138] Unfortunately, Bishop Elliott's high hopes that the Medical College would invigorate the cultural and intellectual life of the city never had time to materialize.

Diseases such as cholera, typhoid fever, and pneumonia continued to plague Savannah, but the city escaped for years an epidemic of the dreaded yellow fever. Only by the end of the nineteenth century did the medical world and most Savannahians realize that yellow fever was caused by the bite of the *Aedes aegypti* mosquito. Perhaps they never thought of mosquitoes as transmitters of disease since they were so commonplace. For instance, William Gordon described the pesky insects one June evening when he wrote his northern-born bride-to-be: "Sitting in a room with a light is nearly impossible at night, unless your windows are protected by mosquito bars and in sleeping even these will not protect you without the addition of a mosquito net to your bedstead. This should truly be called the land of insects, for they are the more numerous than all the other living creatures combined." William Duncan's only way to fight "off the mosquitos" on nights while "panting for a breath of air" was to sit on a "piazza fortified with a good cigar & coat buttoned to the neck." On one torrid August night, Mrs. Alexander R. Lawton told her children: "It is so hot I can't write anymore & I have to see about putting up . . . mosquito netts in my room."[139]

At a meeting of the Savannah Board of Health on August 9, 1854, it was confirmed that there was "much sickness and distress in the Eastern part of the city." A discussion followed about the wisdom of publishing a report citing local deaths from "yellow fever" since it "would give an unnecessary alarm to the citizens and cause a stagnation of business." The following day, a special meeting of the board was convened, and Mayor John E. Ward addressed the members. He told them that release of specifics about disease in the city would do "injury . . . to the reputation and interest of the city." When Dr. Fish was asked how he would characterize the disease, he replied that it was "a very virulent form" of yellow fever. Dr. Richard Arnold agreed it was "black vomit"—yellow fever— but "of a mild & easily managed type." The board then voted to continue to release to the press reports citing the malady as "Yellow Fever," come what may. Obviously, a majority of the Board of Health was more concerned in alerting Savannahians that yellow fever was abroad in the city than in the effects of such knowledge on local commerce.[140]

Soon after the first deaths from yellow fever became public knowledge, Savannahians were outraged at reports in a Charleston paper calling the "sickness" in Savannah "an unusually malignant type"; the *Savannah Georgian* charged that the story did the Georgia city a great "injustice."[141] Such widespread reportage was something the mayor and others had wished to avoid. At about the same time an epidemic of yellow fever raged in Charleston.

As late as August 14, Dr. Phinias M. Kollock informed his son that in the scorching summer heat, yellow fever had developed among the Irish population in the eastern part of the city, where it was confined; only ten to twelve cases occurred. "I do not feel apprehensive of its extending its ravages very much," Kollock concluded. But at the time Dr. Kollock was writing, *Aedes aegypti* mosquitoes were carrying the disease across the city. Eight days later, on August 22, George Gordon, a Yale graduate and Savannah attorney, told his younger brother, William Gordon, that yellow fever was spreading "so rapidly that everybody that can is leaving" the city. "Panic" was developing. On August 29, a drug salesman arrived in Savannah and informed a friend that he had "found a most afflicted city." No carriages were available to transport him; the major hotels and "a great many" boarding houses had closed; "Congress Street looks like Sunday and that's a busy street," he wrote. The city itself "is filled with smoke every night from the tar fires they are burning to purify the air, but it's no go. Pine wood fires during the day—the talk is nothing but yellow fever." Within the previous four days, 35 deaths had occurred, the visitor wrote, and "that is awful for there is hardly any one left to die . . . about one half or more are gone." They fled to Philadelphia, Macon, and Augusta. By the date of his letter, 105 persons had died of yellow fever. He closed saying: "don't let mother know . . . how bad it is here." Whether or not the visiting drug salesman survived is unknown.[142]

On August 27, one of the city's most prominent businessmen, Richard R. Cuyler, president of the Central Railroad and Banking Company, addressed an open letter to the public declaring: "there is not just cause for such excessive alarm as exists . . . and . . . there is . . . no epidemic raging generally throughout this city." Obviously, in speaking for the commercial interests of Savannah, Cuyler was attempting to dispel any images of a chronically unhealthy city. But beginning several days after his letter, deaths in Savannah escalated. By the end of August, 22 blacks and 255 whites had succumbed. Deaths reached epidemic proportions even after a destructive hurricane blowing from the northeast flooded neighboring islands, drowned many, and slammed into the city on September 8, scattering debris throughout Savannah.

On September 16, President Cuyler began donating coffins to the city made in workshops of the Central of Georgia Railroad to bury those succumbing to yellow fever. When the first cool weather arrived in October, deaths dropped sharply and then ceased. By this time 954 whites and 106 blacks had perished from yellow fever. Unlike western Europeans, blacks over time had developed a genetic resistance to yellow fever, which was native to Africa.[143]

In October, Bishop Stephen Elliott wrote from the city: "Our fever here is abating I think both in the number & violence of the cases. But the carnage has been dreadful, especially among the physicians & clergy." Three medical students, ten physicians, the Roman Catholic bishop, two Sisters of Mercy, and two Methodist clergymen perished. "Nearly everybody has had fever in some shape or other," Bishop Elliott concluded. Charles Olmstead, away from the city, was heartsick to learn by telegram that his "dear sister" was stricken and quickly "passed away"; a week later he received a dispatch informing him that his father also had died.[144]

The Young Men's Benevolent Association was founded on September 12, 1854, at the home of the city's wealthiest individual, Edward Padelford, located at the corner of Liberty and Bull Streets. The founding members recognized that in the midst of the epidemic and following the destructive hurricane, the city's poor whites faced "famine and destitution . . . disease and death" and desperately needed assistance. First they canvassed the city to identify the white "sick and needy" only, since they assumed the "colored population" would be cared for by their owners. Next, the association appealed for money and received almost immediately over $24,000 as well as food and clothing; they established depots across the city and distributed soup, bread, and medicines. Association members, mostly well-to-do residents, perhaps for the first time came face to face with the filthy and desperate living conditions of Savannah's poorest white families. The threat of disease and death to both the privileged and the poor linked the two classes as nothing else could.[145]

Following in the wake of the epidemic, speculations as to its cause abounded. Some declared that the disease came into the city aboard the *Charlotte Hague,* a Danish brig from Copenhagen by way of Havana; another theory was that the disease erupted due to "the extremely hot weather"; another attributed it to the mud dredged from the Savannah River; a fourth theory blamed decaying vegetation in the rice fields adjacent to the city. Mayor Ward found no evidence to back these claims; he ascribed the cause of the yellow fever to Providence and stated that "the great Lawgiver may . . . again command the Pestilence to desolate our City."

The Board of Health members, who continued making inspections during and after the epidemic, found in Oglethorpe Ward, at the western end of the city, "privies . . . almost universally in so ruinous & filthy a state, that it is surprising that there is so much health among the residents generally." Likewise, at the eastern end, south of Liberty and east of Price Streets, were acres of "dead animals . . . filth of all kinds, deposits from the Scavengers carts . . . and old clothing . . . of the unfortunate victims to the late Epidemic," as well as clogged drains and ditches throughout the city. The board members concluded that whatever the causes of the epidemic, they believed the "filth about domiciles," especially in the eastern end of the city, "to have been a fruitful source of disease" and asked the government to consider laying sewer lines throughout the city. Four years later yellow fever appeared again. This time it broke out in and was largely confined to the southwestern part of the city "among the Irish" in Robertsville, a contemporary wrote in October 1858. This outbreak claimed the lives of 109 white and no black Savannahians. In response, the city government reorganized the scavenger department, drained nearby lowlands, and finally took the first steps toward installing a citywide sewage disposal system, which took nearly twenty years to complete.[146]

Of course, none of these efforts prevented yellow fever epidemics, and the government remained frustrated. Most likely the 1854 and 1858 epidemics were caused by *Aedes aegypti* mosquitoes brought into Savannah in the holds of ships from tropical ports. Upon arrival the mosquitoes took flight and continued breeding in the water barrels and drainage ditches of the city.

DISORDER, CRIME, AND POLICING THE CITY

Growing disorder and crime troubled well-to-do whites. They reacted nervously wherever and whenever slaves or free Negroes gathered, played, and socialized. African Americans knew that white officials and citizens were watching, but they disregarded city ordinances and the punishments prescribed. For instance, "unlawful assemblage" of blacks was common and especially worrisome to whites because of imagined results. In May 1849 when the ship *Huma* carrying free blacks and slaves prepared to sail for Liberia under auspices of the American Colonization Society, hundreds of well-meaning blacks celebrated their departure at wharfside in speeches and music. But the *Savannah Republican* described the spectacle as "[T]wo thousand negro idlers huzzaing . . . and shouting . . . from a band of music . . . and . . . presenting . . . opportunities for negro excitement and idleness." The paper called on the City Council to prevent "a repetition of such a scene," and something akin to hysteria rippled through the white community. A local grand jury called the event "a serious evil," deplored any "assemblage of Negroes" except for religious reason, and recommended that departures for Liberia be prohibited. City officials acted in 1856. As a ship bound for Africa loaded at dockside, reports circulated that the American Colonization Society was recruiting local slaves for the journey; furthermore, it was rumored that some three hundred hidden runaways around the city waited to board the Liberia-bound vessel. "Such a state of things was dangerous," a city councilman declared. The City Council agreed unanimously that embarkations for Liberia "ought not to be tolerated in a community having interests like this" and acted to prohibit any future departures.[147] Fear of blacks gathering in crowds persisted. In the 1850s when about two dozen blacks held a dance in a local sawmill and a riot erupted, city officials arrested them.

Prominent white citizens complained about what appeared to be trivial matters: Negroes strolling "on the side walks frequented by our wives and daughters" or blacks "wrestling" or "playing ball" and being "boisterous" in the streets; or they objected to having "the dust whirled into your face by some fast mulatto buck driving out his yellow wench, at the fastest rate . . . a hired horse can travel." Although such actions did not violate specific ordinances, blacks occasionally were punished for them. In the early 1850s, two slaves, Jeffrey and Sam, were flogged for "obstructing the side walk"; another slave, Adam, used "vulgar language in a public place" and was "sentenced to receive thirty-nine lashes in jail." Prominent Savannahian John Stoddard was upset that blacks in the late 1850s "walk on Bull St." and that "mulatto women, richly dressed" ride in open carriages. His "love of order" prompted him to condemn such "bold and arrogant behavior" and to tell Savannah's mayor that "unless checkd. . . . [it] will cause great damage to us & our children." Wealthy physician, rice planter, slave owner, and one-time Savannah mayor William Coffee Daniell was so angered at disrespectful and law-breaking blacks that he believed a company of "flying artillery" should be established in the city. Such a military unit, Daniell wrote, "will have a very desirable influence on our slave population . . . which . . . give occasional indications of insubordination which tell badly of the future."[148]

Nevertheless, blacks continued to enjoy liquor served in white-owned grog shops and to socialize and gamble in spite of the laws. It was in the financial interests of the white owners as well as their black customers. Dr. Richard Arnold remarked that the owners of grog shops "often acquire large fortunes" bartering liquor or produce grown for goods stolen by blacks. One owner had opened a shop with less than $50 and in about a dozen years paid $19,000 for a piece of valuable city real estate. "These men [liquor dealers] are pests and corrupt our negroes terribly," Arnold concluded.[149]

The growing numbers of blacks without supervision who hired out and slave runaways contributed to the rising level of crime. Charles C. Jones Jr. was very concerned that slaves running "at large" in the city would learn "idle, vagrant habits." His father's own slave, Jane, fled the plantation, took the name Sarah, and for a month hired herself out "without a ticket" before she was found and apprehended. When discovered, Jones noted, Jane wore "fine ear and finger rings." He believed that "Savannah is the last place in the world for servants inclined to evil." Jones suggested selling Jane, fearing that if she were returned to the plantation, "Her tales of . . . high life in the city would probably not have the most beneficial effect upon her compeers." Likewise, unsupervised slaves remained a problem for their masters. The slaves owned by Hugh Mercer's friend "gave her much trouble . . . Sancho gets drunk and Affy gets drunk & that girl Ellen is a perfect she tiger."[150]

Savannah remained a major urban area where runaways could find anonymity and the best opportunity of flight by sea. Like others before him who had safely fled Savannah, Thomas Sims, a young bricklayer, stowed away aboard a vessel sailing for Boston and landed there safely in 1851. But his owner, James Potter, empowered an agent, an attorney, to find him. Unfortunately for Sims, the Fugitive Slave Law had recently passed Congress. Authorities in Boston surrendered Sims, and he was brought back to Savannah under heavy guard. The usual punishment was whippings, a jail sentence, or both. Potter had Sims lashed publicly thirty-nine times, the maximum for any one day.

Alley dwellers in the city befriended runaways who sometimes formed camps on the edge of the city. In the early 1850s Savannah police raided a runaway camp east of the city opposite Fort Jackson, which was well stocked with food stolen from nearby plantations. The police arrested four runaways and held them in the city jail until their owners came for them. Ever vigilant for plots of slave flight, Savannah police entered a church on the city's fringe that female slave entrepreneur Dolly Reed was attending and arrested her and members of the congregation for singing the words "Yes we shall be free when the Lord shall appear." The officers claimed that the slaves were plotting to run and that the word "Lord" really was a substitute for "Yankee" and was used to confuse white people who might overhear the singing.[151]

As the numbers of young and penniless immigrants and the ubiquitous sailors increased, so did crime. Local officials called the seamen a "floating and often lawless class." They lived in boarding houses clustered at the eastern and western ends of the city; brothels were conveniently clustered nearby, as well as liquor shops. Bay Street running east-west connected the two fringe areas of the city. By the late 1840s Bay Street was becoming crowded. "This street is always so thronged by sailors, slaves and rowdies of all grades and color that it is not safe for ladies to walk there alone," remarked visiting New England schoolmistress Emily Burke. A Savannah resident recalled that in the 1850s a "disgusting sight" to him was sailors "lying in the squares nearest the waterfront in a state of insobriety . . . all of them acting more like swine than human beings." This meant that the privileged class that clustered in the center of the city was cut off from easy access to the riverfront.[152]

On the east side alone a hundred liquor stores did a lively business; an equal number operated on the western fringe. The number of grog shops outnumbered the cotton merchants, and the barkeepers sold liquor to anyone who paid for it. White purveyors of liquor were punished only occasionally. Some prominent whites continued to demand an end to the sale of intoxicants to African Americans. The issue dividing candidates in the 1850 mayoralty race, like prior political campaigns, revolved around permitting or restricting the sale of liquor to blacks. The ubiquitous Dr. Richard D. Arnold campaigned as a reformer to prohibit its sale and ran against the incumbent mayor, Dr. Richard Wayne, who had the support of the liquor retailers. Arnold charged that Mayor Wayne and the city marshal were in cahoots with the liquor dealers and refused to regulate sales. Dr. Wayne's supporters apparently told the liquor dealers that if Arnold were elected, he planned to "fine every shopkeeper a hundred dollars who might be convicted of breaking the ordinances." Then, on election day, Irish gangs brandishing "shillalahs" turned some of Dr. Arnold's supporters away at the polls, and he was defeated by three hundred votes. Arnold declared that "Dr. Wayne's shopkeepers were too strong."

Illicit trading between white, mostly immigrant, liquor shopkeepers was never stopped in old south Savannah. Some of the elite refused to prevent the trading practices of their slaves while other members of the privileged class wanted to close down the grog shops on the Sabbath since sales of liquor to blacks on that day was specifically prohibited by city ordinance and thus illegal. Furthermore, well-to-do whites knew that blacks stole from their residencies or warehouses everything from jewelry to cotton bales and traded it at the grog shops for "the most villainously-poisonous compounds, fit only to excite [blacks] . . . to deeds of blood and violence." [153]

Minor and major lawbreakers of both races, prostitutes, runaway slaves, sailors and laborers, the insane, paupers, and debtors all ended up in Savannah's jail, which was described in the 1850s as "inhuman and demoralizing." Of the more than 800 persons incarcerated in the decade of the 1850s, about 43 percent were confined for crimes of violence; property crime was the second most numerous offense. Thieves committed two-thirds of their offenses where the city's businesses operated: the city market area and along Bay, Broughton, and St. Julian Streets, which was the borderline area between where the criminals resided and where most property was concentrated. More than 230 persons in the 1850s eventually went before the petite jury for a trial by their peers; all were white men except four slaves and four white women. Of those white males tried by a jury, about 47 percent of the white males were foreign born, the majority in Ireland, and were in their twenties or thirties. One city official proposed building police surveillance outposts on the east and west ends of the town to protect the propertied classes near the city center from the city's thieves.[154]

Occasional breakouts from the notoriously dilapidated city jail alarmed well-to-do whites. Charles F. Hamilton informed his wife, Isabella, who herself owned fourteen slaves, that seven prisoners had "gagged" the jailor and escaped. Four had been recaptured, but, Hamilton added, not Flannigan—"that notorious villain is still at large."[155] While confined together, black and white thieves often plotted their next assault on the property of the elite.

As drunkenness, prostitution, and brawls came closer to the homes of the well-to-do, who occasionally fell victim to thieves, prominent Savannahians recognized that the city's commercial boom had both an upside and a downside: while the wealth of the privileged class had increased dramatically, so had disorder. Poor Irish immigrants—"niggers turned inside out" in the phrase of the day—poured into the city looking for work; here they lived and socialized with blacks who enjoyed the freedom of the city as their owners permitted them to hire and live out. After a number of early-evening thefts in January 1851, the *Savannah Republican* editorialized that the city was "infested by a set of bold adventurers, and *guarded* by a set of sleepy watchmen." To some, the night watchmen had become a joke. Gangs of young blacks had become so bold as to enter dwellings in daylight and to take what they fancied. Occasionally, a slave violently struck his owner, an act that may have been provoked initially by the owner or other white males for their own sport. In such cases the slave was turned over to the jailer for punishment. In the 1850s the *Savannah Daily Georgian* commented that the city known for its "enterprise" was bidding to become equally "as notorious in character for crime." In 1852, Mayor Richard Arnold told the City Council that an increase in the number of watchmen was needed because "the great extension of our city limits renders it impossible to get along with the present number." The council responded by increasing the number of watchmen to patrol the growing city from sixty-six to eighty-six. The City Council successfully petitioned the United States government to turn over to the city the site of the old Oglethorpe Barracks, arguing that with the "rapid increase of the city," grounds were needed for "training . . . those volunteer corps which are the pride of Savannah in peace as they would be her security in time of danger."

The city's blue laws prohibited recreation or work on the Sabbath and the sale of most goods, especially liquor. But a reporter strolling through Savannah on a Sunday in January 1853 saw grog "shops open and negroes in them, buying, selling drinking, and talking." At the same time he witnessed "plenty of watchmen walking leisurely about," seemly unconcerned. He concluded by wondering in print: "Where is the Marshal—where the Captain of the City

Watch." He predicted correctly that "public indignation" would soon end their tenure. The city watch finally had lost the support of Savannah's wealthy white elite who saw the need for a large uniformed force to protect their property, enforce the laws, and keep order among both the white immigrants and African American slaves who continued to fraternize at work, in liquor shops, in brothels, and who sometimes planned criminal activities.

Within eighteen months Mayor John Elliott Ward, upon the unanimous approval of the City Council, dismissed half of the hundred-member city watch and replaced them with twenty mounted men. The remaining members of the city watch patrolled the wards near the river while the mounted police in their newly authorized gray pants, blue coats with silver buttons, and caps sporting a badge engraved with the letters *M.P.* patrolled the rest of the city. A uniformed police force was a recent innovation in the country. Savannah's new force became the model for some southern cities, such as Charleston, and was years ahead of northern urban centers in organizing a professional police force.

Mayor Ward appointed as chief of police Joseph Bryan, who was born in Chatham County. His great-grandfather was a plantation owner, and his father served as a member of the United States Congress from Georgia. Young Bryan joined the U.S. Navy and rose to the rank of lieutenant; after eighteen years of naval service, he returned to Savannah, where he became the city's police chief and, subsequently, a slave trader. Like some men of small stature, he was fiercely aggressive and held his subordinates to a "rigid accountability," the local press noted approvingly. Bryan organized his force around a military model with himself as "captain" and under him two lieutenants, four sergeants, and twenty privates. After federal troops moved to Fort Pulaski from Oglethorpe Barracks, site of today's DeSoto Hilton, the barracks became the headquarters for the new police force from 1854 to 1861. When the police held one of the first parades under their new chief, the *Savannah Republican* applauded their "efficiency," which inspired citizens "with confidence and respect."[156]

Chief Bryan planned to focus on the city's "bad spots" with its "very mixed" populations, its brothels, liquor stores, grog shops, and boarding houses for sailors, which he believed fostered the breakdown in law and order. Here violence occasionally flared. Two blacks quarreled and fought; the next day one "waylaid his antaagonist . . . with a clasp knife and killed him," William Gordon wrote. Chief Bryan authorized his men to vigorously enforce the city ordinances, especially the one that prohibited liquor sales on Sundays, and they did. On one occasion, Gordon told his fiancée, "a policeman in attempting to arrest a drunken man struck him so severe a blow with his club as to kill him instantly."[157]

When police arrested white foreign-born grog shop owners for serving liquor on the Sabbath, the practice met with angry opposition from the owners. Chief Bryan also believed that the many policemen living in laboring-class neighborhoods where crime was thickest provided a "habitual presence," which helped curb disorder; he also encouraged his police to infiltrate criminal gangs and to see that informers received one-half of the fines levied on perpetrators caught in criminal endeavors. Chief Bryan's efforts to reform the methods of apprehending criminals were popular among many police officials in America and abroad. But the honeymoon with Chief Bryan was brief, as local political opposition quickly surfaced. The City Council took a dim view of what it called the police's "abuse of . . . power"—the use of paid spies who themselves might "succumb to the power of the almighty dollar." Virtue would be sacrificed to greed, which could undermine a republican form of government. Now in all mayoral elections between 1854 and the Civil War the foreign-born keepers of grog shops supported the Democratic Party and opposed the police reforms, while the nativists—so-called Know-Nothings who championed America for Americans—and the privileged class supported candidates wishing to extend police reforms. Differences among laboring-class and propertied whites, however, threatened white supremacy, which especially worried the wealthy.

In 1854 Edward Clifford Anderson, a Know-Nothing party member and supporter of Chief Bryan and his reforms, was elected to succeed Mayor Ward. Anderson was born in Savannah and was related to the Clifford and Wayne families. Educated in the North, he served in the United States Navy, after which he returned to Savannah and became prominent in business and financial circles. As mayor, Anderson sought to enforce the city's blue laws, especially the ordinance prohibiting the sale of liquor on the Sabbath. Wrangling began immediately between the Democratic-controlled City Council and Mayor Anderson. Liquor shop owners accused city officials of "derelictions," wrote letters to the press, and brought suit against the administration and police. But little was accomplished. In 1855 a Democratic majority was elected to the City Council, and the following year the Democrats elected Dr. James P. Screven as mayor. Now open hostility erupted against Chief Bryan. On election eve Democrats celebrated with liquor and song; they paraded through the city's streets and stopped to serenade the mayor-elect and the new Democratic aldermen. When the noisy crowd passed Chief Bryan's house, a glass bottle was thrown and a pistol fired; in turn, other celebrants responded by throwing stones and firing weapons at Bryan's home. Chief Bryan soon resigned, saying that he could no longer run a police force in the face of "the fang of party venom." Bryan went into the slave-trading business.

In 1859 some members of the elite again launched a council and mayoral campaign to restore Chief Bryan's reforms and to prevent grog shop owners from selling liquor to blacks on the Sabbath. Charles C. Jones Jr., son of a scholarly Presbyterian minister, believed that the Sunday ordinance had become "almost a dead letter" since the police were not enforcing the law. This "affect[s] . . . public peace and order," as the "rum shops are filled with Negroes drinking at all hours of the day and night. Gambling is rampant." Hence, Jones concluded, the "condition of the city is anything but desirable." This time Dr. Richard Dennis Arnold was elected mayor with his slate of councilmen. As the candidate of the propertied classes who desired reform, he immediately initiated changes to return the police department to the era of Chief Bryan. The City Council also passed a new ordinance that permitted the police to levy a substantial fine of $150 per offense for persons dispensing liquor illegally to blacks.

Little was accomplished by the new ordinances, and again the police came under attack, in a step perhaps led by the shopkeepers. A letter in the *Savannah Morning News* in June 1860 complained that "It takes about a half dozen policemen to convey one poor drunk to the Barracks; everyone must show his authority by striking the poor fellow with his club." And that same year, a grand jury concluded that drinking and gambling continued among slaves because of "culpable indifference . . . or collusion" of the police. The writer condemned violent police tactics, while others criticized their ineffectualness. In sum, the police were charged with the difficult task of ensuring uniformity and republican values in a rapidly changing and diverse city.[158]

An economic depression swept through American cities in the late 1850s, and with it came a crime wave. Near the end of 1857 the export of cotton from Savannah fell 82 percent below that of the year before. Because there was no work for stevedores, draymen, and common laborers, many became destitute by the winter of 1857 and turned to stealing to eat. In December the *Savannah Republican* urged the police "to keep a sharp lookout as Savannah seems to be infested with a set of persons who live by thieving." The following year, 1858, the Superior Court of Chatham County prosecuted more people for theft than any other year in the decade. Prosperity returned briefly before another downturn came in 1860, when prosecutions for theft by the Superior Court exceeded those of 1858.

Despite the wave of thefts, the majority from all classes and occupations who appeared before the Superior Court in the 1850s were charged with violent acts. Visitors and commentators on Savannah believed that violence was triggered by excessive drinking. This factor, combined with an exaggerated sense of honor, led to frequent duels, which raised the level of violence in Savannah. William Gordon wrote on February 17, 1855, that there was a duel locally between "two young bloods . . . honorable men . . . of respectable" families, and as a result, both men lay "near" death; "the papers make no mention of it."[159] During the 1850s the city jailer threw down a challenge to the city judge, and a constable and a policeman dueled, as did two male church members. The pugnacious son of a prominent Savannah family, Charles Augustus Lafayette Lamar, argued with his good friend Henry Dubignon over a personal matter at the Savannah racetrack. Lamar told his sister, Caro, that when Dubignon tried to attack him, he shot his friend. The ball struck Dubignon "just beneath the right eye." He fell saying, "I am done. I am satisfied." Amazingly, Dubignon survived but apparently lost his eye.

The floggings meted out to slaves also contributed to the level of brutality and violence in the city. Masters frequently sent their slaves to the jail for corporal punishment. Northern visitor Emily Burke knew that the daily "flagellation" of slaves at the jailhouse had begun when she heard the "dreadful groans and shrieks . . . pour . . . forth from the iron grated windows." But it was not just the institution of slavery or a frontier society that spawned violence in Savannah—the city was hardly a frontier by the 1850s. The young Irish immigrants who swarmed into Savannah imported a Celtic culture of violence; untethered by family ties, these young Irishmen drank and brawled, and they were introduced to and adopted some of the most lethal and traditional local weaponry—"Bowie Knives, Revolvers, and Clubs." Twice the number of whites, mostly immigrants, as blacks usually spent extended periods of time in the city jail. Some were there for "too great indulgence in liquid" and others for such crimes as larceny, fraud, assault and battery, and murder. At the end of the 1850s prominent citizens urged the building of a new jail with a workhouse attached. Mayor Richard D. Arnold told Savannahians that "the necessities of a Work House is deeply felt; our city is increasing, and the number of loungers, both whites and blacks, necessarily augumenting." Loiterers could be removed from the streets, arrested, and lodged in the work house, where they could pursue useful work such as breaking rocks or other tasks before they threatened the status quo. For a variety of reasons, Savannah appeared to be as violent a city in the late 1850s as contemporaries privately admitted.[160]

Slave brokers hired out, bought, and sold slaves in the city in the 1850s. It could be a brutal and violent business. Some communities characterized slave traders as vulgar and loathsome, but Savannah apparently regarded its major brokers in slaves as upstanding, civic-minded men of property. The principal dealers in slaves included Joseph Bryan, a 48-year-old Georgia native and the former police chief; William Wright, a 44-year-old Georgia native, who was a banker and a City Council member; and George Wylly, a 43-year-old. Respectively, they owned real and personal property of $75,534, $53,500, and $105,000. There were other slave brokers, including N. C. Trowbridge and William Foster Parker, who did a booming business in slaves in the late 1850s. Parker was buying young adult slaves for about $700 in neighboring counties and selling them in Savannah for around $1,100.[161]

Savannah was the state's largest slave-trading center. Slave traders bringing slaves to the city for sale kept them in "slave pens" at Habersham and Bryan Streets or in a pen beneath the Pulaski Hotel. It was no longer the finest hostelry in the city, however, having been replaced by the Screven House on the southeast corner of Congress and Bull Streets. Savannah's slave mart was located in a building on Bryan Street opposite the city market where slave brokers presided over the sale of slaves. Joseph Bryan had his own slave pen on Johnson Square, which was frequently crowded with men, women, and children since he was the largest slave broker in coastal Georgia and monopolized the trade. During one day he was known to have offered six separate "gangs" of blacks for sale. Outsiders who attended saw handcuffed slaves brought to the auction block. Jeremiah Evarts found the whole process "a humiliating spectacle." Daniel Nason was moved by the serious looks of the slaves and "the falling tear and the submissive will."[162]

It was a cold, dreary day punctuated by furious downpours of rain on March 2, 1859, when Joseph Bryan, with the assistance of slave auctioneer T. J. Walsh, opened the largest and most famous, or infamous, slave auction in Savannah at the city's Ten Broeck racecourse three miles west of the city along the Central of Georgia Railroad tracks. With the case of the local slave ship

Wanderer before the courts, the auction focused the attention of abolitionists everywhere on Savannah, and the city's white elite became increasingly angry with the hostile press they received.

The slaves offered for sale had been lodged for five days or more in the racetrack's horse stables, where they could be inspected by some two hundred prospective buyers who had arrived from throughout Georgia and neighboring states. Like many other slave auctions, the sale was to satisfy the creditors of Georgia's wealthiest absentee slaveholder, Pierce Butler. He intended to sell the men, women, and children from his plantation near Darien, Georgia, to reduce his indebtedness, which resulted from his extravagant lifestyle in Philadelphia, playing at cards, and speculation in the stock market.

Bryan opened the slave sale, and auctioneer Walsh conducted the bidding in a room adjoining the grandstands of the racetrack. The auctioneer stood next to the slaves on a platform. Drenching rains blew into the room from one open side. Bryan, Walsh, and the prospective buyers and spectators, including Pierce Butler, did not recognize the ace reporter of the *New York Herald Tribune,* Mortimer Neal Thomson, standing in the crowd. With a pencil and a catalogue of the slaves for sale, Thomson posed as a buyer, mingled with the spectators, and talked to the black men and women awaiting auction. He made careful mental and most likely written notes of the two-day auction and was well clear of Savannah when he began preparing his story for publication.

Thomson described Joseph Bryan, "the Negro Broker," as "a dapper little man, wearing spectacles and a yachting hat, sharp and sudden in his movements" and a "bit . . . officious." Thomson's description was somewhat at odds with white Savannah's characterization of Bryan as "a man . . . of honor . . . [and] one whom a large number of the young selected as their . . . example in life." In sharp contrast to Bryan, auctioneer T. J. Walsh was "careless in his dress . . . a large . . . fat, and good-natured man instead of a fierce one. He is a rollicking old boy . . . [with] . . . a hearty word for every bidder." Walsh had a "florid complexion . . . natural in a whiskey country," and "he looks . . . as if he had been boiled in the same pot with a red cabbage."

As to the buyers, Thomson found them "a rough breed, slangy, profane and bearish," and most of them carried "revolvers and kindred delicacies." One he called a "fast young man" who carried both a knife and a revolver and wore his "velvet cap jauntily dragged over to one side, his cheek full of tobacco." He also saw older men with silver hair, white neck cloths, and gold eyeglasses, who may have passed for sanctimonious church deacons; they inspected only the women for sale and asked them about their most personal matters. Other prospective buyers examined the "negroes" as "if they had been brutes . . . pulling their mouths open to see their teeth, pinching their limbs" to test their muscles, and "making them stoop and bend" to ensure there was "no concealed rupture or wound. All these humiliations were submitted to without a murmur," Thomson observed.

The slaves themselves were "dressed in every possible variety of uncouth and fantastic garb . . . the texture of the garments . . . coarse . . . [and] there was every variety of hats." Most of the women "had made . . . some attempt at finery. All wore gorgeous turbans. . . . Their dresses were mostly coarse stuff." The small children "were always better and more carefully dressed than the older ones, the parental pride coming out. . . . The babies were generally good-natured." The average price of $716 per slave sold was less than expected. The sale grossed nearly $300,000. Bryan himself cleared $8,000. Dealing in slaves was a hugely profitable business.

Thomson's article about the slave sale first appeared in the *New York Daily Tribune,* March 9, 1859, and was reprinted two days later in the semiweekly *Tribune* and in Philadelphia's *Sunday Dispatch* on March 13; the London *Times* carried a brief version a month later. When the staff of Savannah's papers read the story, they angrily condemned it. The Ohio-born editor of the *Savannah Daily Morning News* and a vehement champion of southern rights, William Thompson, blasted Thomson as a "libeler" whose article was a "tissue of misrepresentation and falsehood," which only excited "the abolition fanatics of the North" and induced "in the minds of Southern readers only feelings of scorn and contempt." The editor of the *Savannah Republican* called Thomson a "spy" sent by the *New York Tribune* and warned darkly that if he returned, those he labeled "fast young men . . . will straighten" up almost "everything" about him.[163] The wide circulation of the article by Mortimer Thomson and the saga of the slave ship *Wanderer* fueled strong secessionist sentiments in Savannah and the South and equally hot antislavery opposition in the North.

While the spreading notoriety of the sale of Pierce Butler's slaves was being hotly debated, so too was the approaching trial of Charles Augustus Lafayette Lamar in late 1859. Lamar was born into Savannah's privileged class in 1824; his father owned a vast fortune, and his mother was a Creswell. He managed the family's many enterprises in Savannah, became something of an entrepreneur, raised thoroughbred racehorses, was elected to the City Council and captain of the Georgia Hussars, and was an arrogant and ruthless young man. In 1858 he had shot his friend Henry Dubignon and nearly killed him. By this time some members of Lamar's family worried that he might end up in "the penitentiary . . . or . . . a lunatic asylum." Lamar was also an ardent secessionist and a proponent of reopening the slave trade. As one of the owners of the ship *Wanderer,* which landed 409 African slaves at Jekyll Island, Georgia, who were sold across the lower South, Lamar was jailed for violating federal law. The editor of the *Savannah Morning News* defended Lamar and nourished local proslavery sentiment with editorials in which he condemned the North for the "continuing aggression upon our rights . . . [and] these insults and irritations," asserting that this "lawless crusade against the institution of slavery must and shall end, be the consequences what they may."

In April, Charley Lamar stood trial before a U.S. Supreme Court justice appointed to hear the case, James Moore Wayne, a distinguished Savannah jurist and an anomaly among Savannahians. Wayne was an ardent Unionist who had owned slaves until 1856; he had a son and one daughter, Elizabeth Isabel Clifford, who was born to Anna, his slave. In his charge to the jury, Judge Wayne provided a lengthy and stinging indictment of the slave trade. Nevertheless, the jury freed Lamar and the *Wanderer's* crew. Most white Savannahians applauded the jury's decision, but it angered northern abolitionists. Soon after his release from jail, the unrepentant Lamar knocked down his jailer.[164] Charles C. Jones Jr. characterized Lamar as "a dangerous man." Jones believed that the "tone of feeling in the city . . . is extremely at fault" as Lamar and his ilk "run riot without . . . hindrance."[165]

ABOLITIONISM, JOHN BROWN, AND SECESSION

The northern criticism of Savannahians over the sale of Pierce Butler's slaves and the episode of the slave ship *Wanderer* angered the local press and extremists. So did the rising chorus of antislavery zealots, the raid of John Brown, and the election of the first Republican president, Abraham Lincoln. These events became a prelude to a Civil War, a war waged by the citizens of the South and North.

For several decades prominent Savannahians had expressed occasional antinorthern and even disunionist sentiments. Eleanor Baker, a northern woman, observed while visiting Savannah that "Southerners look upon all northerners as their enemies in all that regards slavery . . . but found them courteous . . . towards those who differed from them . . . and did not offensively obtrude their opinions upon them." On the other hand, George Lewis, a Scotch Presbyterian minister, visited Savannah in the 1840s and remarked: "Slavery is a dangerous topic in Savannah." A local resident wished to know if Lewis had "come to be a spy here." While in the city, Lewis discovered "the extraordinary jealously which is had of any intercourse between strangers and the coloured population, free or enslaved. . . . I got more advices here to be prudent on the subject of slavery than in all other parts of the Union." When the new sectional, anti-southern Republican Party, opposed to the extension of slavery, nominated John C. Fremont in 1856, Savannah's wealthy Democratic politician Charles C. Jones Jr. privately called Fremont "a miserable offspring of fanaticism." He told his father that in Savannah "disunion sentiments are already entertained to a very general extent." The following year Sarah Gordon wrote her son William that his fiancée, Nellie Kinzie, in Chicago "is so depressed in spirits" because her "horrid abolitionist Uncle" is determined to "break off her engagement with that *Southerner.* I wish I could just *choke him,*" she concluded.[166]

Near the end of the 1850s a northern teacher named Miss Mason, who taught in the Massie School and openly espoused "abolition sentiments," was discharged; in 1859 a man was tarred and feathered when suspected of anti-slavery sentiments. Nor was Savannah's Unitarian Church able to shake its ties to northern abolitionism. John Pierpont Jr., son of a famous New England abolitionist, served as minister of the Savannah church during most of the 1850s, but his congregation dwindled throughout the decade. By January 1859 there were too few members to pay his salary; Pierpont departed, the church closed its doors, and the property was sold.

Anti-abolitionist sentiment was now widespread in Savannah. Scholarly young attorney George A. Mercer shared the view of many prominent Savannahians. He believed that the northern abolitionists based their opposition to slavery on words from the "Declaration of Independence": that "all men are created equal." But, Mercer argued, the same document prohibits the stirring up of "domestic insurrections among us." Therefore, "If all men are equal, the same arguments which justified our resistance to British rule, support the right of our slaves to assert their liberties," which to Mercer meant that "the Declaration is therefore either very inconsistent, or not susceptible of the Abolition interpretations." In sum, he believed that "Northern aggression is making [the South] a unit; her divisions are being healed by external pressure."[167]

An event that electrified white Savannahians, stirring old feelings of hate, anger, and fear, was John Brown's raid on the federal arsenal at Harper's Ferry, Virginia, in October 1859. Brown felt that God had spoken to him. With the four thousand pikes he carried and the weapons he seized at the arsenal, he planned to arm slaves across the South and "purge this land with blood." The possibility of slave insurrections within Savannah had always worried prominent white Savannahians, and now this feared event seemed to be coming true.

No matter that some of Brown's followers had been killed and that Brown himself was captured and awaiting trial—the most feared genie, insurrection, was out of the bottle. The *Savannah Daily Morning News* received the news by telegraph, and on October 18 its headlines blared: "Terrible Insurrection at Harper's Ferry." Several days later the paper blamed northern abolitionists and leaders of the Republican party for Brown's raid and called for quick action to protect slavery: "What these insane abolitionists have accomplished . . . the frightful scheme of insurrection, murder, and rapine which they have developed will . . . convince the people of the South of the necessity of greater watchfulness, and of some concerted and effective means of protecting themselves." Most white Savannahians, and southerners in general, agreed.[168]

George Mercer again reflected local opinion: Brown's "insurrection . . . is now the absorbing question," he wrote. "It is scarcely credible that a mad, fanatical fellow . . . with sixteen equally mad followers should take Harpers Ferry. . . . If anything could justify lynch law, it would be the conduct of these assassins." To Mercer and other Savannahians it was "the first organized attempt upon the social structure of the Southern States."

John Brown was tried and sentenced to death. On the day he was scheduled to hang, December 2, 1859, William F. Parker, a Savannah slave trader, entered in his diary: "Old John Brown hangs today. I wish I was there to see it." When northern abolitionists publicly pronounced Brown a martyr, George Mercer was aghast that these "northern people are preparing to canonize the monster" after "convicted of murder, treason against the state, and attempts to excite insurrection. . . . northern society has run mad." Mercer believed the time may have come "for the South to calculate . . . her safety in this Union. The South never has been so thoroughly aroused as at present: military companies and vigilance committees are forming throughout her borders." They were forming in Savannah. One "Vigilance Committee," Sarah Lawton explained to a general officer, for "some time before the Northern mail was stopped, examined all matter transmitted through it—unless from persons above suspicion."[169] Vigilante committees also organized.

Anxieties aroused by John Brown's raid persisted even after his death. Rumors fueled by newspaper accounts of conspiracies stirred racial fears of an army of black insurrectionists and arsonists burning their way across the South. White fears of perceived plots by slaves and free blacks spawned racial violence in some counties and cities in Georgia. The Savannah City Council passed a more repressive city ordinance forbidding blacks to gather in crowds for parades or other public events; when some disregarded the law, police apprehended and flogged them. In September 1860, the *Savannah Republican* refused to publish rumors of insurrections in the South because they caused "undue public excitement" and might only encourage local blacks. By this time two sectional candidates represented the Democratic Party in the upcoming presidential election: Stephen A. Douglas, who was primarily supported by northerners, and John C. Breckinridge, who was nominated by southerners. Savannahians now recognized that with the Democratic Party split and with John Bell of Tennessee running on the Constitutional Union Party ticket, the most likely winners would be abolitionists, Republicans, and their candidate, Abraham Lincoln. At that time in Savannah vigilante action focused both on black insurrectionists and northern abolitionists thought to be in the city.[170]

Outdoor meetings kept Savannahians aroused. At a rally on September 17 for the city and county's favorite candidate, radical Democrat John C. Breckinridge, the outspoken local orator for secession, Francis S. Bartow, told the crowd that he was ready to "peril life, fortune and honor in defense of our rights . . . before I will . . . submit to be governed by an unprincipled majority." It was not surprising that Charles A. L. Lamar was even more intemperate. He *wanted* Lincoln elected because, he declared, "I want dissolution" of the Union.

The campaign of repression aimed at slaves and free African Americans continued. In October, a free mulatto carpenter, Joseph W. Ribero, was alleged to have told local slaves that if elected, Lincoln planned to set them free. Vigilantes seized Ribero and took him to a remote section of the city. Here "twelve quiet gentlemen [and] property holders" acted as "jurors," gave him twenty-eight lashes, shaved a side of his head, and hustled him aboard a Boston-bound steamer. Dr. Richard Arnold believed that Ribero "was actually concocting an insurrection and got off well when he took his life with him." Subsequently, the state legislature unsuccessfully attempted to pass laws re-enslaving free blacks; Savannah's City Council did enact ordinances making it more difficult for slaves to live out and to hire out. In late October 1860, Savannah's twenty-nine-year-old mayor, Charles C. Jones Jr., continued to get reports of "scoundrels . . . and suspicious persons . . . tampering with our Negroes." He promptly ordered the arrest and imprisonment of several free black sailors charged just "with this offense [of] attempting to induce [slaves] to leave the state." Jones also planned "to bring to justice those offenders of foreign birth, the rum-sellers, who at the corners of our streets in their shops are demoralizing our servants and ruining them in every point of view."[171] The elite were stepping up the pace of their long crusade against the fraternization of the city's African Americans and poor whites. It was in the elite's interest to do so as disunion approached.

Lincoln's election in November threatened the South's "peculiar institution" of slavery and white supremacy. On November 7, telegraph dispatches arrived in Savannah announcing the results of the presidential election. "South Carolina has today virtually seceded" from the Union, Mayor Charles C. Jones told his family. "We are on the verge of Heaven only knows what." The following day a mass meeting was held to inform the legislature of the views of well-to-do white Savannahians. Thousands turned out, thronging the streets. To encourage attendance and unity of all whites, bands played, bonfires were lit, and rockets exploded into the air. The "town seemed to have gone crazy," Charles Olmstead said. Francis Bartow told the crowd that Lincoln's election "ought not to be submitted to"; hundreds grew hoarse from yelling their approval of this sentiment. In Johnson Square Savannahians unfurled Georgia's first flag of southern independence, featuring a coiled rattlesnake and the words "Our Motto Southern Rights . . . Don't Tread on Me." Henrietta Wayne agreed: "if we are . . . to be injured and oppressed by the North, we had better separate from them." A newspaperman for the *New York Times,* who associated with well-to-do whites, observed that with few exceptions "all are in favor of secession" here. Savannah's clergy used their pulpits to support secession. Bishop Stephen Elliott told the congregation of Christ Church that the South's "cause is just." At masses in the Catholic Church of Saint John the Baptist, church members were encouraged to "offer their fervent prayers" for the South "in repelling the . . . Northern barbarians."[172]

The violent rhetoric of extremists encouraged violence in the streets. Local vigilantes tarred and feathered the captain of a British ship for inviting a black stevedore aboard to dine with him. On December 3, Henrietta Wayne told her mother, "There has been several men tarred and feathered, then sent away who were detected tampering with the Negroes, one was even persuading them to rise and kill the whites." Apparently, a local grocer and liquor dealer who was a native of New York, John Blyler, told blacks "that as soon as Lincoln was President, they would all be free." The educated and kindly Henrietta uncharacteristically remarked: "I think such men should be hung, instead of being sent North to inflame abolitionists by . . . infamous stories." Blyler died of injuries received at the hands of the vigilantes, most likely a group of toughs calling themselves the Rattlesnake Club. Its president was named Grand Rattle. On December 7, Dr. Richard Arnold, politician and intellectual, defended the mob actions to a northern friend: "Those men who have been molested in and near Savannah were notorious receivers of stolen goods from negroes, negro liquor sellers and gamblers. Such was Blyler." Furthermore, Dr. Arnold asserted, using extremist and violent language himself: "to the fanatics who rule you and would rule us . . . we are ready for war to the knife and the knife to the handle." The Republican leaders who "are pulling down . . . our Constitution . . . and . . . ready to cry 'let slip the dogs of war' on the country . . . ought to be shot down in their tracks." Arnold believed that "blind fanaticism" was abroad in the North. He declared, "The very state . . . of the buffoon Lincoln . . . refuses the free negro a habitation within its limits. Glorious consistency!" In sum, Arnold averred: "We here are strictly on the defensive. We are fighting for our very hearthstones. The Southern man who falters now is a wretch" to be scorned. Edward Harden told his mother: "If a fight must come *I for one will not dishonor my proud lineage.*" Honor was much on the mind of Savannah's elite. When the family of Nellie Kinzie of Chicago, who had married William W. Gordon, suggested she come North if war came, Gordon told her, "I would feel disgraced as a husband if you chose any other protector & disgraced as a man & as a citizen if you sought safety with the enemies of my country."[173]

Sarah Lawton agreed. She sounded like the white males of her privileged class, especially her husband, Colonel Alexander R. Lawton. In late December she told a friend, "I can coldly look anything in the face but dishonor." She wrote that she enjoyed "the company of gentlemen *now,* for I am so anxious to hear their discussion of public affairs." She had learned that Savannah "is under the best & strictest police now that it ever had. The best citizens are formed into a Home Guard & they have almost broken up the low shops & those haunts where negroes went to dissipate & to enrich white men more degraded than themselves."[174]

Charles Lamar got his wish. When Lincoln was elected, secessionists in the lower South exploited this by moving for the dissolution of the Union. Georgia's legislature, on the advice of Governor Joseph E. Brown, appropriated $1 million for military supplies and called for an election of representatives to a state convention to decide the state's fate. Georgia's neighbor, South Carolina, seceded on December 20. Savannahian Colonel Alexander R. Lawton told Governor Brown: "Carolina has done all that we could desire; and we are now left without excuse. I pray that Georgia may not disappoint . . . the South!" On December 28, Dr. Richard Arnold explained to a friend: "the . . . North has been subversive of our rights, destructive of our property. . . . The dissolution of this Union is inevitable." The wife of local physician George Kollock agreed. She wrote her son, a student at Virginia Military Institute, "I hope Georgia will be out of this disgraceful Union, and free of the Yankee Constitution."

On January 2, 1861, disunionists swarmed the polling places in Savannah and Chatham County and elected three ardent secessionists to the state convention: Francis Bartow, John W. Anderson, and Augustus S. Jones. Each was a member of a local military organization and quickly rose in rank. Jones was by far the wealthiest of the three. He ranked as the seventeenth wealthiest person in Savannah in 1860, with personal and real estate holdings of $182,000. He was a great planter and owned ninety-seven slaves.[175]

Governor Joseph Brown, a determined secessionist, was in Savannah on election day and took the provocative act of ordering the seizure of the United States fortification Fort Pulaski. This brick pentagon was surrounded by a moat on Cockspur Island, located seventeen miles from the city, and commanded the entrance to the Savannah River. Under command of Colonel Alexander R. Lawton, the First Regiment of Georgia Volunteers seized the fort without a fight. Lawton's command also occupied Fort Jackson, which was even closer to the city. Now the two major forts controlling access to the city by water were in the hands of Georgians and garrisoned by Savannah militia units such as the Republican Blues, Jasper Greens, Phoenix Riflemen, and Chatham Artillery. Members of these units also established an outpost on Tybee Island opposite Fort Pulaski. Here the soldiers fought only "mosquitoes . . . in swarms . . . and fleas."[176]

On January 19, delegates to the state convention met in Georgia's capital, Milledgeville, and voted to secede and join South Carolina, Alabama, Mississippi, and Florida, all already out of the Union. In Savannah the Chatham Artillery unit saluted the news with cannon fire. On Governor Brown's orders

Colonel Lawton seized and threatened to sell to the highest bidder the New York–registered ships at Savannah unless New York authorities released weapons purchased by Georgians. The weapons were promptly shipped to Georgia. Next, Colonel Lawton occupied Oglethorpe Barracks, the quarters of federal troops in Savannah, and seized the United States steamer *Ida*. Meanwhile, Georgia's secession convention authorized Governor Brown to raise and equip two regiments. Radical Savannah disunionist Francis Bartow was one of the ten delegates Georgia sent to the Montgomery, Alabama, meeting in February of 1861, which created the Confederate States of America.

Georgia's secession convention reconvened in Savannah on March 7, adopted a new state constitution, and sent representatives to the border states to encourage secession. The delegates also permitted the newly created Confederate government to oversee military operations in the state. On March 21 Alexander H. Stephens, a brilliant and eccentric Georgian and now vice-president of the Confederate government, gave a speech in Savannah. He lauded the new Confederate government and denounced the government in Washington, D.C., as one committed to racial equality. Stephens said, "Our new government is founded upon exactly the opposite idea; . . . its cornerstone rests upon the great truth, that the negro is not equal to the white man; that slavery—subordination to the superior race—is his natural and normal condition."[177]

Such rhetoric from politicians encouraged an atmosphere of white suspicion and hostility toward blacks and feelings of fear among blacks. It led some blacks to take matters into their own hands and flee to runaway camps near Savannah; in response, Savannahians waged a battle against these black runaways in the spring and summer of 1861. Some blacks were killed, wounded, or captured. Events surrounding the fugitive slave Paul dramatize this campaign. In March, Paul, the slave of wealthy planter and former Savannah mayor Edward C. Anderson, was lured into the dwelling of a white man, Patrick Brady, who thought he was a fugitive. Brady then attempted to seize him, but in a struggle Brady was killed, and Paul ran. He soon was pursued by a local constable and his pack of "Negro dogs." For three days Paul hid out in the house of a slave couple, Palmer and Dolly, until he was discovered. Patrollers battered in the door and discovered Paul hiding in a brick oven. In a scuffle, Paul was shot in the leg and foot and had to be rushed to the jail to save him from being lynched by a mob of whites. The patrollers also apprehended Dolly and Palmer, gave them thirty-nine lashes each, and confined them to jail until "further orders."

A mob of whites gathered before the Chatham County jail, and a lynching was likely averted by an armed force sent there by Mayor Charles C. Jones Jr. But it was too late for Paul. He died the following morning from the gunshot wounds he suffered during capture. Paul, who was innocent, could have sought aid from his well-to-do owner; Palmer and Dolly risked their home and lives by concealing him. Some whites saw the actions of Paul, Palmer, and Dolly as black solidarity at a most anxious time for white Savannahians, who faced the prospect of war with the North.

Toney, who was characterized by the press as a "desperate runaway" and the gang leader of black fugitives hiding in swamps near Savannah, repeatedly eluded captors until "Negro dogs" trailed and cornered him near the Augusta road. When the dogs attacked him, he killed two and wounded others in the pack with his bowie knife. He refused to surrender until one of his pursuers fired on him with a double-barreled gun, injuring him grievously in the shoulder and back.[178]

Such defiant acts by blacks also defied the perceptions of a paternalistic society, which viewed African Americans as happy, childlike "sambos." To whites it was a troubling sign. A few months later, Savannahians again had to rethink their image of blacks as loyal and always returning the affection of their white owners.

Following the Confederate bombardment of Fort Sumter in Charleston Harbor on April 12, Lincoln called for troops to stop the rebellion, and Texas and the Upper South seceded. Governor Brown called for volunteers, and thousands rushed to join the Confederate troops. Despite shortages of weapons and other war materials, some 17,000 Georgians stood ready and armed for combat.

CIVIL WAR SAVANNAH

Excitement and enthusiasm for the war united most of Savannah's white population during the opening months; it also united most of the free blacks and slaves, but in a different way. Whites wanted to preserve slavery, the social, economic, and psychological foundation of their society, while African Americans hoped to see it end.

Soldiers poured into Savannah, and fortifications began going up around the city. But as the Union army and navy approached to within easy striking distance, well-to-do Savannahians took refuge inland to safer locations; meanwhile, slaves in increasing numbers ran to freedom within Yankee lines. Some enlisted to fight their former masters. Firefights between Confederate soldiers and federal troops broke out sporadically on nearby islands. Harsh discipline, dwindling food and military supplies, and mounting casualties for local troops and those in other theaters of the war affected morale, and opposition to the war surfaced. It was manifested first in a trickle of desertions by Confederates stationed in and around Savannah.

But military fervor was running high in Savannah in the spring and summer of 1861. Young George Mercer, a volunteer in the local militia unit, the Republican Blues, was part of the growing military presence in Savannah. Companies, battalions, and three corps drilled and paraded afternoons and "by moonlight." Mercer observed, "Many of our men are burning to fly to the assistance of old Virginia."[179]

In April, Jefferson Davis, president of the Confederacy, appointed Alexander R. Lawton to the rank of brigadier-general in the Confederate Army and charged him with the defense of the coastal region of Georgia and Florida. After the aging Josiah Tattnall resigned his commission in the United States Navy, President Davis appointed him commodore. He was to defend Georgia's coast with a "mosquito fleet" of five vessels: a river steamer and four tugs. Tattnall, born near Savannah at the family home of Bonaventure, followed his native state out of the Union, though he had served in the United States Navy with distinction since the War of 1812, and his friends and wife's family lived in the North. Savannahians, however, remained "anxious" that neither the Confederate nor state governments were moving quickly enough to prevent an invasion. Some of Savannah's white privileged classes shipped their valuables inland by rail.

In early May the *Savannah Morning News* announced that "the patriotic youth of Savannah," aged fourteen to seventeen, had organized as the "Savannah Cadets" to be trained for garrison duty or "the field of battle." The unit was soon drilling under a former West Pointer. Meanwhile, soldiers quartered in Savannah were mustered into Confederate service in May and June and then moved by train to Virginia. On May 21 William Duncan told a friend that a company of the Oglethorpe Light Infantry departed for Virginia "today . . . a hundred strong." He prophetically remarked: "they are anxious for a fight poor fellows." Others remained to garrison and build the growing ring of fortifications around Savannah.[180]

Women of the privileged class were asked to furnish military necessities for the soldiers massing in Savannah and for the recently formed Savannah Cadets. As one Savannahian reminded them publicly, "You may soon require protection. . . . Remember our patriotic ladies during the Revolution!" The local elite frequently compared the Revolution of their forefathers against Great Britain to their own "revolution" against the North. Mayor Charles C. Jones Jr. in his annual report of 1861 declared, "The heroic days of 1779 are come again." The next year Mayor Thomas Purse told Savannahians, "we are now engaged" in a "revolutionary struggle . . . to secure our independence."

George A. Mercer observed that the ladies of Savannah "Continue their patriotic efforts. They make haversacks, mosquito bars, shirts, &c. &c." The women held a fair, raised over $6,000, and "presented flags to most of the companies." Sarah Lawton, the general's wife, told her father in mid-April that "The emergency called me out of my sick room," and now "my house is full of ladies who have been coming here every day to work for the troops & all my time is occupied in that way." Newspaperman William Howard Russell noted the women's work when he was entertained at the Lawton's home. He found the entrance hall and parlor filled with small round rolls of flannel, which General Lawton explained "are cartridges for cannon . . . made by the ladies of Mrs. Lawton's 'cartridge class.'" Russell quickly concluded that "the house was not quite a safe place to smoke a cigar in!" Henrietta Wayne wrote that her daughters worked "all the time" with other ladies "making cartridges and clothing . . . bandages and lint . . . for the soldiers." During the summer, Sarah Lawton again was very "busy" with other women of the privileged class in organizing a "great Tableaux" of a hundred young girls at the Atheneum, which raised $400 for the soldiers. But Sarah also observed that there was criticism in the city of "the poor (rich) ladies [who] were so stingy as to have shut their purses to all the appeals of their struggling country."[181]

A few free African American women and men assisted the Confederacy. Even in the best of times they sometimes feared for their liberties. Now, as the whirlwind of a coming war stirred up anxiety and fear among the white privileged classes, African Americans sought self-preservation from extremists. In the spring of 1861, several free blacks contributed money to aid volunteers for the Confederacy; some raised funds to benefit Georgia's ill or wounded soldiers. Free mulatto Anthony Odingsells, who held more slaves than any black in Savannah, made money selling fish and meat to Confederates and offered his slaves to improve the defenses at Fort McAllister. Free mulatto Jackson B. Sheftall and free black John Laurence made money by slaughtering animals for the Confederate army and at best could be called opportunists. At least two local slaves, conditioned to be servile and to identify with their masters, accompanied their owners to the front lines. Economically well-off free black women, such as the mysterious mulattoes Ann Gibbons and Estelle Savage, who either owned slaves themselves or had close ties with white slaveholders, made uniforms for Confederate soldiers and offered to nurse the sick. They also were opportunists, acting in their own self-interest. A group of about fifty free black men asked General Lawton, the commanding officer in Savannah, "to be employed in the defense of the State, at any place or point." Their offer was accepted, and they were sent to Fort Pulaski to construct defensive works. Moses Dallas, the most skilled pilot on the Savannah River, first served the Union, switched to aid the Confederates, and then switched loyalties again to assist the Union. But over time some of the slaves in Savannah became increasingly restive.[182]

In the late spring of 1861, Henrietta Wayne was unable to accept an invitation because "If there is war I may be obliged to remain [in Savannah] . . . to see after my negroes for there may be danger of their being stolen away." By the end of June, Captain William Gordon, on duty at Skidaway Island near Savannah, had lost confidence that slaves would remain docile if an invasion came: "We believe our Negroes as reliable as the mobs of the Northern cities." A few months later, when William Duncan was warned that his slave Woodson might be planning an insurrection, Duncan agreed that "eternal vigilance . . . should be our watch word."[183]

As Confederate and Union troops massed in northern Virginia in July 1861, Henrietta Wayne in Savannah hoped that "if the vile creatures [Yankees] could only be well whipped they might let us alone." A few days later, Savannahians were in the thick of the fighting close to Washington, D.C., at a rail junction southerners called Manassas and northerners called Bull Run after the nearby creek. Here thousands of young Americans North and South came together to kill each other. It was the first major clash of Confederate and Union forces.

Commanded by West Pointers, the rank and file were more like "armed mobs," a foreign officer remarked. Yet the weapons they fired were the most lethal ever taken into combat—true rifles and accurate field guns firing solid or exploding shells or canister, which when discharged at close range riddled the enemy like giant shotguns. Contemporary medical knowledge or technology was unable to match the carnage wrought by such new weaponry.

When the fight got underway, Union forces initially pushed the southerners backward, but then the Confederates were reinforced and surged forward. Colonel Francis S. Bartow, Savannah attorney, orator, and ardent secessionist, led Savannah's young men of the Oglethorpe Light Infantry Brigade, now Company B, 8th Georgia Infantry, into the fray. The Union troops wavered and then retreated during the Confederate counterattack, but during the fight Colonel Bartow and his adjutant, Lieutenant John Branch, were killed; others in the unit fell dead or wounded. Twenty-one-year-old Sanford Branch, a corporal, saw his brother John fall and ran to his side. Sanford remained by John until he died, and he himself was captured. The youngest of the three brothers, eighteen-year-old Hamilton, sustained only a superficial wound during the fighting. Sanford told his mother, Charlotte Branch, that John had lived about three-quarters of an hour: "He died in my arms. His last words were about you and Hamilton." Charlotte was crushed by the news of the death of her beloved eldest son for whom she had sacrificed so much. She contacted both Confederate and Union officials in a vain attempt to retrieve John's body immediately. Hamilton continued to serve with the 8th Georgia, and during the Peninsula Campaign he was severely wounded and returned to Savannah to recover. In 1862 he was elected second lieutenant of the Savannah Cadets. George Barnsley, also in the fight in Virginia, wrote his father: "I killed one Yankee & found him afterwards. I marked the spot."[184]

The battle of First Manassas or First Bull Run was indecisive, and both sides sustained heavy losses. The fierce fighting with the improved weapons suggested that the war might be a protracted one. When news of the battle and the local casualties was telegraphed to the city, William Duncan remarked that "many a heart must be surely lacerated" over the deaths already reported "in our Savannah Oglethorpe Light Infantry . . . that company is said to have been cut to pieces. I fear we shall hear of others. O' how many anxious faces & beating hearts we have" here as "the Oglethorpes were all of the flower of our young men."

On July 28 the Savannah Cadets assembled with other units to pay their last respects to Colonel Bartow, whose body was returned to Savannah within a week from the battlefield. Bishop Stephen Elliott performed the funeral service, and a procession accompanied the body to Laurel Grove Cemetery. Here, a scribe for the Savannah Cadets wrote, "the last sad rites were paid to the memory of this patriotic and most noble son of Georgia soil." Several months

later the remains of several other members of the Oglethorpe Light Infantry
were returned, including those of Lieutenant John Branch. Local military
units accompanied them first to the Independent Presbyterian Church and
then to the cemeteries.[185]

While some Savannahians died in battle, others profited. An arsenal was established in the city by the Confederacy; the government awarded contracts to
shipbuilders Henry F. Willink Jr. and the firm of Krenson & Hawkes to construct vessels for the Confederate navy. However, less than a year into the war,
George Mercer observed that "carpenters & mechanics to build gun boats are
not to be procured; everybody is in the service." Clothier Henry Lathrop
sought and received a contract from the Quartermaster Bureau and hired
dozens of seamstresses to manufacture Confederate uniforms. City merchants
formed blockade-running companies and made quick and handsome profits
from sales of contraband goods to the Confederate government. Blockade-
running, however, slowed dramatically as the Union blockade off the coast
tightened.[186]

At dawn on September 17, 1861, the steamer *Bermuda* ran the blockade and
pushed up the Savannah River. Owned by John Fraser & Company, it brought
from Liverpool to Savannah's wharfsides rifles, cannons, blankets, shoes,
woolens, and ammunition. It was reloaded with 2,000 bales of cotton and on
a dark night in October ran up the river, into the open ocean, and past the
blockade. William Duncan calculated that John Fraser & Company "by their
ventures are coining money." For months Duncan had been speculating for
himself and his business partner, Godfrey Barnsley. He wrote checks on his
New York bank before any of his money was confiscated and invested it in ster-
ling for a return of 12 to 12.75 percent. In his partnership with Godfrey Barnsley, Duncan ordered 1,000 coils of rope to be brought in by train to sell as "a
good speculation" and bags of java and mocha coffee; in the late spring he
bought "4–500 sacks" of salt for 70 cents a pound and later sold it for $1.50 per
pound. In October he noted that salt then sold locally for $9.00 a sack and was
"in demand," and he moaned, "what a profit I would have made on 10,000
sacks." Like others of the privileged class in the port city, Duncan was an aggressive speculator and capitalist looking for the main chance, very unlike the
so-called pre-industrial capitalists, which some historians have labeled antebellum southern businessmen. George A. Mercer, young and idealistic, had
another name for them. He characterized men such as Duncan as "greedy
speculators and extortioners" who "monopolize everything and resell at enor-

mous profit." The "desire to get rich seems to pervade all." He worried that the "nefarious practices" of the "speculators" may "inflict more injury upon us than the Yankees."[187]

For some months Savannahians had expected an invasion. Fortifications went up, and soldiers poured into the city and its environs. "Tents rise in various parts of the" city, Sarah Lawton wrote; "the drum sounds constantly and many uniforms are visible, here and there along the roads that lead from the city."[188] The white elite prepared to move to the upcountry if the port city was attacked. In mid-October 1861, Henrietta Wayne prepared to leave quickly "with her Negroes and a few valuables, such as silver, table linens and clothing." Likewise Mrs. Edward Anderson packed all her "silver & handsome table linen." Men like William Duncan kept an eye on the slave Woodson, who was accused of plotting an insurrection. Then, on November 4, it became known in Savannah that observers at Fort Pulaski had spotted a large Union fleet lying off South Carolina's coast. Savannahians expected an attack, and the thousands of soldiers stationed in and around Savannah prepared for an invasion. William Duncan had "two rifles . . . all in order." He planned to watch the "servants," for "a break out might happen . . . tonight . . . if Tybee is attacked." On the morning of November 7 distant firing was heard in the city, and the following day the newspapers carried the story of the federal invasion of Hilton Head, South Carolina. Now residents of the port city reckoned they were to be invaded in twelve hours. "We are all in confusion, everybody running 'hither & yon,'" William Duncan wrote. He was "making arrangement to move" his family, and within a week he had sent his valuables and family to Macon. "We are in troublesome times," Duncan wrote. "The panic. . . . cannot be described," Mrs. Anderson wrote, "& the [rail] cars twice a day are loaded down with women & children bound to the Interior." Well-to-do Savannahians were leaving for the upcountry.[189] Banks sent their gold and silver out of the city, and merchants anxiously sold what goods they could and sent the remainder out by rail. Cotton and rice followed to keep these commodities from falling into the hands of the invaders. The city government ordered the paving stones along the Bay torn out, loaded on barges, and towed down the river to be sunk to prevent Yankee gunboats from coming up to the city. Batteries were erected nearby.

In November, General Robert E. Lee, a staff officer in Richmond, was sent by the Confederate government to coordinate the coastal defenses of Georgia and Florida. He conferred with the new commandant of Savannah, Brigadier

General William H. T. Walker, a former commandant of West Point. For several months General Lee remained in the Savannah area. He ordered additional vessels constructed, more obstructions placed in the Savannah River, an increase in the garrisons of Fort Jackson and Fort Pulaski, and the building of additional earthworks and batteries and the reinforcement of others to command the water approaches to the city. Fort Bartow was constructed on Causton's Bluff above St. Augustine Creek four miles southeast of Savannah and just below Fort Jackson; another fort was built four miles southeast of the city on the Wilmington River at Thunderbolt; others included Fort Beaulieu on the Vernon River, Fort Rose Dhu on the Little Ogeechee River, and Fort McAllister on the Ogeechee River about fourteen miles from the city and anchoring the southeastern flank. On the western or landward side of the city, defenses began about one mile east of Savannah at Fort Boggs and ran south and west and then north to Laurel Grove Cemetery, forming a semicircle around Savannah. This interior defensive line extended from one to a little over two miles from the city. Both free blacks and slaves built this semicircular ring of earthworks. Lee evacuated all the soldiers from Tybee, Wassaw, and St. Simons Islands and concentrated them around and within the city. Now unopposed, federal forces occupied Georgia's sea islands, which sent local planters "refugeeing" inland with their slaves. Federal troops held islands in both South Carolina and Georgia just a few miles from Savannah.[190]

Knowing that federal troops were nearby created excitement, and pro-Union sentiments swept through Savannah's slave community. Some slaves became "insubordinate" to whites and their law. This decline of discipline among the slave population may have likely resulted from the actions of the vast number of slaves brought from neighboring counties to build Savannah's fortifications. During the first years of the 1860s there was a 400 percent increase in the number of blacks appearing before the Savannah Mayor's Court and a 50 percent rise in the number of blacks incarcerated in the local jail. African Americans now more frequently than before cursed whites, attacked policemen and resisted arrest, and ran away, first in a trickle and then in a stream, to Union lines and freedom. Neither jail time nor stories circulated by white Savannahians that Yankees sold fugitive slaves in Cuba deterred the runaways. In the early 1860s the *Savannah Morning News* complained, "It is time that efficient measures . . . be taken to stop these desertions."[191]

In late 1861, William Duncan now prepared to move his slaves inland for safety. He purchased two thousand acres of pine forest ninety miles from Savannah as a refuge for his slaves and those of friends and family. Apparently, Duncan's strong-willed slave Woodson, accused of hatching an uprising, never ended up there. He may have been one of Savannah's first slaves to head for the sea islands and Union lines. Isaac Tatnall, a black coastal pilot who escaped from a vessel in the Savannah River in December 1861, surely was one of the first blacks to reach Union lines; other river pilots who fled to the occupied sea islands included Brutus and Cassius. All three men provided Union officers with information about navigating local rivers and creeks and served aboard Union naval vessels operating in nearby coastal waters. Admiral Samuel Francis Du Pont wrote, "These men risk their lives to serve us." The flight of these coastal navigators weakened the effectiveness of the Confederate Navy operating in the myriad of rivers and creeks around Savannah. Other runaways provided Union forces with information about fortifications, shipbuilding, and morale in the city.[192]

A former Savannah slave, stevedore, and river pilot in Savannah, March Haynes, smuggled slaves out of the city to Union lines. He was described as a "shrewd, brave efficient man." When he was suspected of helping slaves escape the city, he and his wife fled to the Union-held sea islands. From here Haynes continued a "commando" type operation by shepherding slaves out of Savannah to freedom by boat after nightfall. Another Savannah runaway, Abraham (or Abram) Murchison, a literate slave and Baptist who had preached in the city, was among the first to recruit black refugees on Hilton Head Island for the Union's armed forces. Subsequently, he served as a Union army chaplain and may have baptized more than a thousand freed slaves in Port Royal, South Carolina, during the war years.

Most slaves risked death by fleeing in boats to the sea islands, and some drowned en route. Woodson, Isaac, Brutus, Cassius, and other runaways acted on the "survival strategies" slaves had used for years.[193] Moreover, these blacks and others seized the opportunity offered by a war between white men. They used the chaos of the war to flee to freedom, as they did in the colonial-era conflicts between British colonists and the Spanish in Florida, during the Revolution, and in the War of 1812; some enlisted in the Union forces to fight their former masters. And they ran early in the war when it was a conflict to save the Union. They did not wait until it became a war to free the slaves.

Many Savannah blacks publicly demonstrated their overwhelming loyalty to the Union and freedom following President Lincoln's initial Emancipation Proclamation in 1862. The local free black church leaders prevailed on Mayor

Thomas Holcombe to permit them to hold a dinner to commemorate the proclamation. Curiously, Holcombe allowed it despite his condemnation of the Emancipation Proclamation as an "infamous attempt to incite flight, murder, and rapine on the part of our slave population"; furthermore, to the mayor it was an attempt to undermine the social system, to raze the homes of whites, and to "convert the quiet, ignorant dependent black son of toil into a savage incendiary and brutal murderer." The dinner was held without interruption from white police or hooligans. Prayers were offered "that God would permit nothing to hinder Mr. Lincoln from Issuing his proclamation." For the first time Savannah's black leaders took the initial step in making their private thoughts known by publicly supporting black freedom.[194]

Besides untrustworthy African Americans, some white Savannahians also suspected that there were white Union sympathizers in the city. One Confederate soldier stationed there told his wife that he had talked with several citizens who informed him that there were "a great many Yankees in Savannah that would aid the Lincolnites if they were to attack the city. . . . many think that half of the city are disloyal." He concluded: "If it were not . . . for the loss of property to a few loyal citizens it would be little matter if the Yankees would burn to the ground."[195] And Union forces moved closer to the city.

During amphibious landings in late November and December 1861, over a thousand federal troops came ashore on Tybee Island, which was earlier evacuated by Confederates. Under the direction of a brilliant Union officer and engineer, Captain Quincy A. Gillmore, new, rifled long-range weapons were wrestled ashore and gun batteries erected under cover of darkness. They were aimed at Fort Pulaski, only two to three thousand yards away and the key to the defense of Savannah. Before the war, Gillmore had overseen the completion of Fort Pulaski for the United States government. General Robert E. Lee called the fort's seven-and-a-half-feet-thick walls "impregnable" before "the heaviest cannon." In February 1862, federal gunboats maneuvered between the fort and Savannah, which cut off resupply of the fort by Commodore Tattnall's "mosquito fleet." Twenty-five-year-old Charles H. Olmstead, now Colonel Olmstead, commanded 365 Confederate soldiers and some 20 officers within the fort, which mounted forty-eight guns and began sporadic exchanges of cannon fire with the Union forces on Tybee Island.

On April 10, Major General David Hunter, commander of the Union forces, asked Colonel Olmstead to surrender. In one of those oddities of war, Hunter was the uncle of Nellie Gordon, wife of Savannah's Captain William W.

Gordon. When Olmstead refused to surrender, Union forces on Tybee Island commenced firing thirty-six mortars, smoothbore, and rifled cannon, and the Confederates returned the fire. The bombardments rattled windows in Savannah. The newly developed rifled Union guns firing the James projectile had a devastating effect, blasting gaping holes in the masonry of Fort Pulaski; by the afternoon of April 11, many of Pulaski's guns were out of commission, and the powder magazine was in danger of exploding. Rather than risk the destruction of his garrison, Colonel Olmstead surrendered. He was criticized, and he questioned his own decision and his code of honor. Captain Gillmore was promoted to brigadier general and later major general. His belief in the new rifled guns and his siege plan resulted in the capitulation of the Confederates and forever changed defensive strategy.

The occupation of Fort Pulaski by Union troops, only seventeen miles below Savannah, alarmed Georgians, especially well-to-do white Savannahians. Governor Brown rushed troops to the coast from the interior, the legislature appropriated money to obstruct the state's major rivers, slaves arrived from the upcountry to dig more fortifications, and one Savannahian relieved another to command the city's defenses: Brigadier General Hugh W. Mercer replaced Brigadier General Alexander R. Lawton. Union gunboats now probed up nearby rivers, and in April a skirmish erupted between Confederate and Union soldiers on Whitemarsh Island. Rumors of a full-scale Union invasion continued to circulate.[196]

The fall of Fort Pulaski sent waves of panic through Savannah. Many more of the affluent whites fled the city. With the exception of shipbuilding, the arsenal and other war-related industries were moved inland. Savannah's trade and commerce dropped off sharply. The trickle of goods brought into the city by blockade-runners ended abruptly because Union forces now controlled the mouth of the river below the city. Visitors noted now "the strange, mysterious . . . quietude" hanging over Savannah.[197]

Military officials remained wary of any foreigners or northerners. Confederate Captain George A. Mercer said: "The enemy derives many advantages from northern born men in our midst; a large proportion of them are hostile. . . . These men become guides, spies and informers." The editor of the *Savannah Daily Morning News* believed that "Traitorous parties in Savannah have been holding communications with the enemy." Internal security was tightened; no one was allowed to enter or leave the city without a pass. Police and military authorities made "terribly unnerving taps upon the shoulder" of civilians "without . . . law or authority," one Savannahian complained. "Our citizens (the few that remain) have been arrested on the street, dragged to camp, shown a tent, and informed that there their habitation should be."[198]

Prices for everything spiked up in Savannah after secession. They continued rising throughout the war. Prices for sugar, salt, flour, butter, fowl, shad, beefsteaks, and lamb climbed so rapidly that Henrietta Wayne was "afraid to buy any thing but what is really requisite." She correctly predicted that "the poor must suffer." Only a few months after Georgia's secession, Charles C. Jones Jr. told his family that in Savannah "the most ordinary necessaries of life are sold for amounts beyond the reach of any but the rich." Provisions became so dear that the local government borrowed $75,000 in early 1863 to establish the City Store and to buy bacon, rice, flour, molasses, meal, sugar, and peas. These "articles of prime necessity" were sold at cost to help "mitigate the sufferings of the indigent and those in more moderate circumstances." By selling such necessities to the needy below their market cost, Mayor Thomas Holcombe was "assured that some suffering has been relieved." It appeared that Savannah's government was simply carrying on the tradition for various reasons of caring for its white indigents. It is significant, however, that the City Store was established in April, precisely the month that hungry women with children to feed and facing soaring inflation led bread riots in several of Georgia's towns and cities. The riots resulted in public efforts to provide free or inexpensive food to the poor.[199] Thus action by Savannah's government to feed the white indigent may, in part, have been taken to head off any similar riots locally. Sometimes soldiers appeared hungry, too.

Savannahians wanted troops in the city to defend it, but as upcountry soldiers poured in, some citizens complained about them. A female member of the upper crust told her daughter in late 1861: "There are too many rowdy soldiers now adays in the [rail] cars to make it safe for a lady to travel without a protector." The newspapers frequently reported altercations between soldiers and civilians. In March 1862 the Savannah News reported a fight between soldiers and civilians, all "under the influence of liquor," near the corner of South Broad (Oglethorpe Avenue today) and East Broad Streets. Two civilians received stab wounds, and the soldiers suffered severe injuries.

Within the month it was forbidden for enlisted men to come into the city without a pass. Twenty-seven-year-old Benjamin S. Garrett, an army private stationed in Savannah in 1862, was from far southwestern Georgia and barely literate. He wrote his family in November telling them that "wee have hard times her[e] to under Go with. wee do not have half a nuf to eat only as wee by it." The following year four hungry soldiers robbed "a hen roost" in the city. When the soldiers were caught, they "had in their possession about a dozen fine fowls, with their heads wrung off." Private Garrett was like so many of the "plain folk" of the Confederate army who owned no slaves but enlisted enthusiastically in what became a slaveholder's war to preserve the southern way of life. Many of these soldiers remained mute on why they joined up. But the master class knew why they fought, or thought they did. Mayor Thomas Holcombe of Savannah made it plain in his annual report for the year 1862–1863 when he averred that Unionists hoped for "our subjugation, and the equality of the negro and the white race. Are we prepared for such. . . . Let patriotic devotion to the South respond, Never! No, never! Annihilation rather than submit to such an alternative."[200]

Obviously, early in the war neither the state nor the Confederacy was able to supply its troops in and around Savannah with sufficient food as well as thread, salt, cloth, and shoe leather. A correspondent for the *Savannah Republican,* Peter W. Alexander, was quick to point this out. In December 1861, he published a report in the *Republican* that chided high Confederate officials for failing to provide for their soldiers: "Men may fight with clubs, with bows, with stones, with their hands; but they cannot fight and march without shoes." A native Georgian, graduate of the University of Georgia, an attorney and editor of the *Savannah Republican,* and correspondent for the paper during the war, Alexander was the forerunner of the modern correspondent who, while remaining loyal to the side of the government or military, was quick to criticize its failures during a time of war. Among some ninety Civil War correspondents, Alexander is ranked in the top three reporters. His credo was that "every heroic act, every daring adventure" of the war should be remembered, but never substitute for the "history of these stern times the exaggerations of thoughtless scribblers, nor the weak inventions of sentimental chroniclers."[201]

Soldiers dispatched from the countryside to defend Savannah sometimes resented civilians they saw there. One soldier complained that in Savannah "there are . . . *hundreds* of pusillanimous whiners, swindlers and extortioners." A visiting correspondent in March 1862, Felix DeFontaine of the *Charleston Daily Courier,* wrote of the upcoming draft or conscription in Savannah. He believed many willingly would enter the service, "provided the burden can be equally distributed among all capable of bearing arms." But, he added, when men "look around them . . . they see able, hearty, vigorous men clinging to their homes, worshiping at the shrine of Mammon, and intent on their own gain." And they "rightly reason that it is unfair" to draft some and not others.[202] To some it appeared to be a "rich man's war, but a poor man's fight."

The war brought class tensions to the surface. Captain George A. Mercer, a member of Savannah's privileged class, characterized the "country troops" defending the city as "reckless and imprudent" men who "seldom wash their bodies or change their close [sic]." General Lafayette McLaws described them as a "mob" of "undisciplined . . . men . . . as ignorant of the art of war . . . as . . . children."[203]

The attitude of the officer class toward the enlisted men, the punishments meted out, the lack of adequate food, medicine, and basic military equipment, the nearness of Union forces, and the hostility some poor whites held for the elite all contributed to the declining morale of enlisted personnel and a growing desertion rate. At a court-martial in September 1861, Savannahian Jakie Read, the commanding officer of an enlisted man charged with "sleeping on post," wanted him shot. The same month another private found guilty of stealing blankets and selling them to "a Negro" in the city was punished with a "ball and chain" for thirty days and then "drummed out" of the service. In January 1862, wealthy Savannahian Major Edward C. Anderson, in charge of the river batteries around the city, found his men on Skidaway Island "disheartened" at the failure of the government to supply the tools needed to mount their cannons, which then permitted Union gunboats to approach and fire unopposed. In July "three more men . . . deserted" Anderson's command, and others were being watched closely. His nephew and namesake, Captain Edward C. Anderson Jr., who served in Major Anderson's command, told his wife: "There is a spirit of disaffection & mutiny among all the troops of this district, which if not promptly checked by some severe examples, will become the means of ruining us all if not of the loss of this part of the state." In August three more men deserted from Major Anderson's command. Another departed for the third time with a seven-pound "iron bar attached to his leg."[204]

During 1863–1864 food, fodder, and equipment shortages drove some soldiers to theft, and desertions around the city increased, especially among soldiers of Irish descent, the most recent immigrants. Captain George A. Mercer worried that "the brave soldier gets poorer and his family starves"; and in a burst of anti-Semitic rhetoric, he blamed the shortages and high prices on "the Jews . . . and their natural avarice." On once occasion, eight members of the Irish Jasper Greens raided a plantation and butchered hogs and sheep for food.

Major Anderson paid $160 for the animals, writing that the owner "made no allowance for the poverty of the men who robbed him and the hard times they suffer under." By this time four shad, which once would have been 30 cents, now cost $30, salt now sold for $25 a bushel, and the price of flour was $125 a sack. The supply of fodder for the horses of cavalry units declined so sharply that officers doubted their mounts could perform in combat; about half the members of most cavalry companies were without arms, and some lacked saddles; the men's clothing was old and not of uniform material, and the tents of the cavalrymen were described as "too old and ragged to be of much service."[205]

Men now began deserting in numbers of five, seven, ten, and, on one occasion, nearly one-third of a company. General Hugh Mercer admonished Major Anderson not to allow the members of the deserters' companies to pursue them as they may not vigorously attempt arrests, and he told Anderson that force should be used "against a deserter who resisted arrest or drew a weapon upon the party seeking to arrest him." Guards may "fire upon soldiers deserting to the enemy." General Mercer also was of the opinion that the desertion of some men "was caused by dissatisfaction with their officers." At least on one documented occasion an officer at Savannah was warned "of the impropriety of striking the men under his command." Examples were made. Henrietta Wayne coldly informed her mother in 1863 that "three men are to be shot in a few days for deserting, it is now time to make some example altho' dreadful to think of as it is becoming too common a crime." A few months later, Ordinary Seaman John Connolly of the Confederate States Navy was sentenced by a court-martial in Savannah to be taken to a place of execution and in the presence of his fellow enlisted men be "shot to death with musketry." Another deserter was sentenced to death by a firing squad, but his sentence was suspended by President Jefferson Davis upon appeal of Savannah's Catholic priests. Jacob Lovette, a deserter from an engineer company, was captured when Confederates seized a Yankee gunboat. Lovette, who was serving as a navigator for the Yankees, was sentenced to die. He was executed along the Ogeechee Plank Road near Laurel Grove Cemetery. Major, later Colonel, Anderson was present along with a large crowd, which he regretted included "very many women." One can only speculate why they attended.[206]

Faced with dozens of desertions and sagging morale, the elite officer class around Savannah publicly praised the common soldiers and urged them to reenlist. In August 1863, Lieutenant Colonel Charles C. Jones Jr. waxed poetic in reminding an audience at Masonic Hall in Savannah that "the private soldiers of the present Revolution . . . are the representatives of the true manhood, the patriotism, and the courage of our country." Brigadier General R. E. Colston distributed a circular to the soldiers of his brigade in Savannah in March 1864 asking them to show to the "foe whose cowardly legions are about to disband that you never intend to lay down your arms until your country is triumphant and free"; he concluded by asking them "in the name of your own noble state to . . . resolve to re-enlist for the war" and promised to send to President Jefferson Davis "this proof of your self devotion and patriotism."[207] But by this time morale among even the privileged class was declining.

For some time Mrs. Edward Anderson wondered "when will this dreadful war come to an end?" After the fall of Fort Pulaski, Major Edward R. Harden wrote his mother: "This war will ruin us all. The prospects are indeed melancholy." In late 1862, William Duncan told his friends, "we are getting whipped at every point." The Catholic bishop of Savannah and vicar apostolic of Florida, Augustin Verot, informed his friend Patrick N. Lynch, bishop of Charleston, that the "sufferings of the people have reached such a height, that there is . . . good & urgent cause for the clergy to do what they can to stop the awful bloodshed that has now stained the land for 3 long years." In Savannah in late 1864, the privileged daughter of Godfrey Barnsley, Julia, remarked: "I have forgotten how to laugh."[208]

To relieve the horrendous overcrowding at Andersonville prison in southwest Georgia, by July 1864 Union prisoners of war were being sent by train to Savannah. Edward C. Anderson, who was a colonel by this time and who commanded the river batteries around the city, was charged with responsibility for the Union prisoners. Warned that hundreds could be sent at any time, Anderson rushed to complete a stockade for 4,500 men. It was located in the rear of the Chatham County jail at the corner of Hall and Whitaker Streets. Trains brought 1,500 prisoners from Andersonville on September 8, and the following day 1,800 more arrived. Colonel Anderson called up troops from the river batteries to guard the prisoners. He lodged 900 in the stockade, and another 900 he sent under guard to Charleston by rail. Anderson was "shocked to see the pitiable condition of the prisoners . . . dirty & half clad & . . . filled with vermin . . . the most squalid gathering of humanity" he had ever seen. Those in the stockade, "The sun bakes . . . from daylight to dark," Anderson observed, and "respectfully dressed women . . . were throwing bread to the Yankees."

On the evening of September 11–12, eleven prisoners escaped through a tunnel they dug under the stockade. Anderson ordered a "gang of Negroes" put to work digging a ditch twelve feet wide and six feet deep to prevent further tunneling. Carpenters completed the stockade, and Colonel Anderson's guards moved 500–600 sick Yankees into the enclosure. Dead soldiers, without "shroud or service," were buried along the Ogeechee Road, just beyond the land-side fortifications. Between September 25 and October 6, trains from Andersonville brought in more than 3,300 additional prisoners; in a makeshift "hospital," 600 ill Yankees were attended by 80–90 of their healthy comrades. Colonel Anderson sent a dispatch to Brigadier General John H. Winder, commander of Andersonville, telling him "that no more [prisoners] must be sent down"; the Savannah stockade was "filled to capacity," and his prisoners lacked shade or shelter.

In early October, the weather turned cold, "which has been fatal to all those cases of diarrhea," Colonel Anderson wrote. More than 50 ill prisoners died on October 9 and 10. "I . . . pitied them from the bottom of my heart," Anderson confided to his diary. "It is pitiable to think that it is not in our power to succor them better." Some were dying of "homesickness." But, Anderson noted, "their government refuses to exchange them." By now President Lincoln and his military officers had concluded that exchanges of prisoners would only prolong the war.

Then, suddenly, Colonel Anderson was notified that the new stockade at Millen, Georgia, some seventy-five miles northwest of Savannah, was completed. Within three days, October 11–13, trains carried away all the prisoners able to travel, and Anderson's burden was lifted: "the stockade is empty," he wrote. Over 100 Union troops died during their imprisonment in Savannah and were buried along the Ogeechee Road; some 400 sick troops remained in the city. Anderson sent the stockade guards back to the river fortifications around Savannah; about 60 Union prisoners were paroled to work as mechanics in the city. In late October, the stockade was dismantled.[209]

Colonel Anderson returned to his duties of inspecting fortifications around the city. By October hundreds of troops had been pulled out of Savannah and rushed to other theaters of the war. Anderson wrote, "Everything looked desolate & unoccupied. The few troops guarding the Batteries had new faces among them—there was wanting that soldierlike neatness which was part and parcel of the old command." He found some batteries manned by "raw reserves just mustered into service," and the "men . . . not drilled & the whole concern . . . is at the mercy of the enemy."[210]

Union officers hesitated to move their gunboats and army up the Savannah River; furthermore, the river was blocked by obstructions in places, and there was no coordinated plan of attack—that is, not until Atlanta fell to General William Tecumseh Sherman in November 1864. Now highly placed United States officers and civilians agreed to Sherman's battle plan to march 285 miles to the sea. In mid-November General Sherman and his 62,000 battle-hardened soldiers marched southward out of Atlanta.

His plan was to take the fight to the enemy soldiers and civilians, to obliterate the countryside, demoralize the population, and destroy the will of Georgians to fight. He hoped this strategy would bring a quick end to years of bloody conflict. It was a tactic the army used successfully against the Indians for years. Sherman's tough veterans of many battles shared their leader's desire to "make Georgia howl." None realized that they faced only some cavalry, Georgia militia, and irregular units with a combined strength of about 8,500 soldiers.

Sherman followed the Central of Georgia Railroad to the southeast toward Savannah. His army tore up the steel rails, burned the wooden ties, and destroyed the rolling stock, the depots, and machine shops of the railroad, which had brought a boom economy over the past twenty years to Savannah. Living off the land as they traveled, Sherman's army—along with deserters from both sides, runaway slaves, and Confederate cavalrymen—looted, vandalized, and terrorized civilians. Several thousand Georgia militia, mainly boys and old men, tried to stop Sherman's juggernaut at Griswoldville near Macon and were slaughtered. The army marched into Milledgeville on November 22 and continued on its way two days later, leaving mostly unscathed the state capitol, where secession was declared four years earlier. The army passed through Sandersville, Tennille, and then Millen, where Central of Georgia Railroad property was destroyed. By this time the Union prisoners of war recently transferred from Savannah to Millen had been moved. The final stage of the campaign began on December 4 when Sherman's army marched directly for Savannah.

Meanwhile, the commander of Savannah, Confederate General William J. Hardee, waited with about 10,000 poorly trained and equipped troops. Hardee concentrated his main defenses about two and one-half miles west of Savannah on a peninsula about thirteen miles wide. The Savannah River was to the north, and the Little Ogeechee River was to the south. Along this line Hardee erected a series of earthworks and batteries to guard the western approach to the city and flooded the rice fields before them.

On December 10 Union troops began probing the Confederate defenses, and on the following day the two armies exchanged fierce bombardments. On December 13, General Sherman ordered an attack on Fort McAllister, seventeen miles to the south of Savannah, which guarded the city's "rear door." Near sunset 4,000 Union soldiers suffered heavy casualties, but in fifteen minutes they captured the fortification defended by only 150 combat effectives.

When General Hardee learned that Fort McAllister had fallen, he hurried ahead with his plans to retreat into South Carolina. Engineers laid pontoon bridges from the foot of West Broad Street—Martin Luther King Jr. Boulevard today—one thousand feet across the Savannah River to Hutchinson Island and then across the Middle and Back Rivers to reach the South Carolina shore. Hardee rejected Sherman's request on December 17 to surrender Savannah or face bombardment, and Sherman ordered his officers to prepare for an assault.

Federal gunboats began moving up the Savannah River, Union troops started marching overland from Hilton Head, and three of Sherman's divisions secured a foothold across the Savannah River on South Carolina soil. Hardee's cavalry protected his line of retreat, and the evacuation of the city began on December 20. After nightfall, Hardee's forces spiked their heavy guns, destroyed other military equipment, and, as silently as possible, moved over the pontoon bridges into South Carolina. One Confederate soldier remarked: "it seemed like an immense funeral procession stealing out of the city." The Union forces knew the Confederates were leaving. Near daylight Union troops cautiously moved forward. When it was confirmed that Hardee's army was gone, there was in the Union ranks "much shouting and hurrahing." City officials surrendered to federal officers around 4:30 A.M., after assurance that private property would be protected. Mayor Richard D. Arnold then escorted a cheering brigade of Union troops into the city, where they raised the Stars and Stripes at the City Exchange. Federal troops patrolled the town to prevent looting. On December 22, General Sherman wired President Lincoln: "I beg to present you as a Christmas gift the city of Savannah."

It was a day of jubilee for African Americans. But for the handful of wealthy white Savannahians remaining in the city, the war was over—their feelings were a mixture of anger, resignation, and loss. Many Savannahians, scattered around the South in military units, began trickling home after Lee surrendered in April 1865. About the same time, a native Georgian and newspaperman reflected the thoughts of many well-do-do white Savannahians when he editorialized: "Well Sherman has marched through Georgia . . . hardly receiving a scratch. . . . We . . . feel deeply mortified—humbled, chagrined—even degraded. It is a bitter draught we have had to quaff." Such sentiments persisted for generations.[211]

Conclusion

*S*AVANNAH WAS FOUNDED in 1733 by General James Oglethorpe as a defensive site on a high bluff above a river of the same name. For fifty years it served as the capital of Georgia, the thirteenth and last of Britain's North American colonies. The settlement was ideally suited for the headquarters for Oglethorpe and other British officials who fortified the colony as a military buffer to protect South Carolina and its port city, Charles Town, against the Spanish, French, and hostile Native Americans.

From the beginning the river was Savannah's commercial artery, and the town was Georgia's major port. The growing export trade in skins, indigo, rice, and lumber and the import trade in everything from nails to muskets were interrupted by King George's war and the French and Indian War. Fearing invasion, hundreds of Savannahians fled elsewhere, and commercial life virtually ceased.

Georgia was the only British colony where slavery was initially prohibited, which some believed stymied commerce and trade. Persistent complaints by Savannahians that they could not compete with South Carolina without slave labor led to permission from the trustees and Crown to allow the importation of Africans, which increased with each passing year after 1750. The introduction of slavery brought a boom in rice cultivation and a reinvigorated export trade through Savannah.

Savannah was ethnically and religiously cosmopolitan and diverse almost from the beginning. Besides English men and women, the earliest settlers included Salzbergers, European Jews, and Irish Catholics. By the mid-1730s there was a babble of languages spoken among the five hundred residents who trod Savannah's sandy paths, including English, German, French, Spanish, and various African and Native American dialects.

After the end of the French and Indian War in 1763, the export-import trade resumed and resuscitated Savannah's commercial life. The town prospered as the capital of the British colony of Georgia, and its population grew rapidly to around four thousand. The good times were evident in new houses and public buildings, jewelry and clothing shops. Prosperity brought the theater, lec-

341

tures, concerts, and dances. But a sea change in British foreign policy slowly moved Savannah's elite—who had grown rich in land and slaves—to challenge the mother country's economic and political policies. Savannah's "reluctant revolutionaries" eventually galvanized the backcountry of Georgia to join them, and the other colonies along the Atlantic coast, in declaring independence from Great Britain.

But independence was not won easily. Savannah itself was invaded and seized by the British in 1778. The next year a counterattack by American and French forces suffered heavy casualities and failed to retake the town. The British occupying force evacuated Savannah only near the end of the American Revolution.

Savannah was heavily damaged by the fighting in and around the town. Its inhabitants and nearby planters suffered severe losses in slaves and other property carried away by the British. Following the Revolution, the capital of the state of Georgia was moved from Savannah to the upcountry, where the population was growing more rapidly. Since the legislature had overseen and enacted laws for Savannah, a new body was created to govern the city—a mayor and council of aldermen.

Savannah's export-import trade soon quickened, more slaves were imported, and rice, lumber, and upland cotton flowed out of Savannah's port. By 1800 Savannah, with a population of some five thousand, evenly divided between blacks and whites, was the fourteenth largest city in the United States. But the postwar economic boom was again cut short by conflict with Great Britain. During the War of 1812, commerce slowed; residents, fearing invasion, fled the city.

With peace, the export-import boom resumed until about 1820, when an economic panic and depression swept the country, and a horrific fire and yellow fever epidemic devastated Savannah. For years low cotton prices depressed the local economy. Savannah's economic depression ended when civic boosters and entrepreneurs established the Central of Georgia Railroad, which by the 1840s dominated rail traffic in the southeast and funneled vast quantities of cotton and lumber by rail to Savannah, where it was shipped north and abroad. The new jobs created by the railroad, the burgeoning steamship lines that carried goods into and out of the port, and a building boom brought a flood of immigrants to the city seeking work. The population of Savannah doubled between 1840 and 1860, growing from 11,000 to 22,000, which made Savannah the sixth largest city in the Old South.

The economic boom and exploding population placed enormous pressure on the city's infrastructure. A gasworks, waterworks, a better street-lighting system, an enlarged scavenger force, and a professional police organization were created to meet the demands.

While the economic boom concentrated more and more wealth in the hands of fewer and fewer Savannahians, hundreds of poor whites and blacks—both slave and free—poured into the slums on the eastern and western edges of the city. Here some diseases remained endemic. Occasionally, an epidemic of yellow fever swept out of these slums and across the city, as it did in 1854. Duels, stabbings, brawls, and other forms of violence occasionally flared in the slums and elsewhere in the city.

Although life was short, nasty, and brutish for many Savannahians, the city itself offered opportunities for interracial relationships mostly unknown in the countryside. Blacks and poor whites lived side by side in the hovels on the eastern and western sides of the city. They worked together at the sawmills, rice mills, and lumber mills and in the yards of the Central of Georgia Railroad; they amused themselves in brothels staffed by black and white women; and they drank and sometimes brawled in the liquor shops of the city. Such close interracial associations most likely rounded the rough edges of racism.

Some of the white elite failed in their persistent efforts to prevent the fraternization of blacks and poor whites in the city's liquor shops. The whole issue of outlawing liquor sales was for years a political football. The city's wealthy whites worried that goods stolen from them were fenced in the grog shops for liquor; they worried, too, about interracial fraternization, which violated racial proprieties. Furthermore, close black-white relations fed the fantasies of some that such associations might lead to arson or insurrections. Indeed, the age-old paranoia of wealthy white Savannahians over the activities of abolitionists—which sometimes led to violence against visitors—was exacerbated by John Brown's Raid. Fearful that Brown's ideas might ignite uprisings, white vigilantes roamed Savannah's streets, occasionally beating whites and free mulattoes suspected of antislavery sentiments. Southern cities such as Savannah differed markedly from northern urban centers in the enormous energies exerted, the time spent, and the ordinances enacted by the white elite to regulate the behavior of African Americans and their perceived accomplices.

Mitigating the violence and brutality that sometimes flashed like summer lighting across Savannah were the city's private and public structures and spaces, which acted as humanizing influences. Black churches provided a nurturing, homogeneous community and a temporary refuge for slaves from the oversight of their masters. Such institutions were unavailable to plantation bondpeople. The scale and design of Savannah's public squares created by Oglethorpe were unknown elsewhere; the squares became forests of greenery, which were admired and enjoyed by visitors and residents. The magnificent private and public buildings of Jay, Norris, Stoddard, and Clusky also must have stimulated the spirits and senses of Savannahians and visitors to the city. Likewise, such public institutions as the Female Asylum, established by local well-to-do women, became a home for orphaned or abandoned white girls who, it was hoped, would be transformed into useful citizens. The Poor House and Hospital offered shelter to the indigent, and a public school system was begun to educate the poor whites. The aesthetics of the buildings and public spaces, the city's charities, the housing arrangements and fraternization of poor blacks and whites, and the social and intellectual life of the well-to-do and middle-class exerted a civilizing influence not present in the countryside.

For Savannah's white elite, historical, literary, and social organizations, unique to southern cities, as well as a flourishing theater and concert season, served as humanizing elements. The Protestant elite readily welcomed prominent Jews and Catholics into civic and social clubs as both ethnic groups embraced southern traditions. Such diversity and social acceptance was a hallmark of a cosmopolitan city. And there was a vibrant social life among wealthy Savannahians in good times and in bad. An annual social season was filled with parties, masquerades, dances, and weddings, which were orchestrated by the female elite. These gatherings of the intermarried "best people" certainly served as a socializing factor in city life.

The Civil War was a disaster for the South, for Georgia, and for Savannah in terms of property and human losses. When slaves from Savannah fled to join nearby Union armed forces, their masters were surprised and angered by their lack of loyalty. At the same time, massive desertions by poor white soldiers defending the city dramatized the fragile relations existing between poor whites and the wealthy elite, which finally fractured and cracked in the crucible of war. Nor did poor white and black relations ever recover from the effects of the war. The once desegregated city became more and more segregated over time, and the interracial relationships once enjoyed by the white poor and African Americans slowly evaporated. Likewise, the white Savannah elite, who lost a fortune in slaves, felt less and less that ever so slight sense of paternalism they once exhibited in Old South Savannah.

Notes

CHAPTER I. *The Earliest Years, 1733–1754*

1. Stokes, *Savannah,* 5–19; J. F. Smith, "Savannah River," 82–83; Bell, "Isundiga"; Rahn, *Savannah,* 1–2.

2. Hudson, "Genesis," 34–39; Crane, *Southern Frontier,* 19–22, 29, 46; Spalding, "Colonial Period," 9–14. There remains some dispute on the origin of the word *Savannah.* See Utley and Hemperley, *Placenames of Georgia,* 277, note 34.

3. Stokes, *Savannah,* 45–56; Crane, *Southern Frontier,* 29, 44, 108, 124.

4. Fraser, *Charleston! Charleston!* 11, 26–27, 32–33; Hudson, "Genesis," 39–40; Crane, *Southern Frontier,* 167–183; De Vorsey, "Colonial Georgia Backcountry," 7, 27; Stokes, *Savannah,* 56–68; Spalding, "Colonial Period," 14–15.

5. Montgomery, *Discourse Concerning the design'd Establishment* and *Description of the Golden Islands,* viii–ix, 7–10, 34–52; Coleman, "Founding of Georgia," 4–5.

6. Coleman, "Founding of Georgia," 4–6; Reese, *Most Delightful Country,* ix–xii, 55–65.

7. Spalding, "Oglethorpe's Quest," 60–69; Baine and Williams, "Oglethorpe in Europe," 112–116; Coleman, "Southern Frontier," 169–173; Baine, "Prison Death of Castell," 67, 71–72; Saye, "Genesis of Georgia," 155–160; Ver Steeg, *Southern Mosaic,* 69–102; Rabac, "Economy and Society," 6–8, 22, 29, 73. There is a lively debate on the reasons behind the founding of the Georgia colony. The last two authors believe that the trustees were motivated primarily by military considerations.

8. Reese, *Most Delightful Country,* xiii–xix, 69, 123; Oglethorpe, *Design of the Trustees,* xi–xxix, 11–49; Bartley, *Modern Georgia,* 1–2.

9. Spalding, "Colonial Period," 16–18; Coleman, *Colonial Georgia,* 20–22; Spalding, "Oglethorpe's Quest," 69; Coulter, "List of First Shipload," 282–287; Saye, "Genesis of Georgia," 160; Caldwell, "Women Landholders," 183–195.

10. McPherson, *Journal of Earl of Egmont,* 7; Lane, *General Oglethorpe's Georgia* 1:xix; Spalding, *Oglethorpe in America,* 7.

11. The name of the ship has been spelled as both *Ann* and *Anne.* Coleman, "Founding of Georgia," 12; Spalding, *Oglethorpe in America,* 7; Coleman, *Colonial Georgia,* 22–23; Spalding, "Colonial Period," 18; Spalding and Jackson, *Oglethorpe in Perspective,* 8, 48, 80; Temple and Coleman, *Georgia Journeys,* 4–7; McPherson,

"Voyage of the *Anne,*" 220, 222; Coulter, *Journal of Gordon,* 28; James Oglethorpe to the Trustees, January 13, 1733, in Lane, *General Oglethorpe's Georgia,* 1:4.

12. McPherson, "Voyage of the *Anne,*" 229–230; Coulter, *Journal of Gordon,* 31.

13. James Oglethorpe to the Trustees, February 10, 1733, in Lane, *General Oglethorpe's Georgia,* 1:4; Coleman, *Colonial Georgia,* 25; Hudson, "Genesis," 40–42; Clinton and Gillespie, *Devil's Lane,* 188, 190.

14. Oglethorpe to the Trustees, February 10, 1733, in Lane, *General Oglethorpe's Georgia,* 1:4; Spalding, *Oglethorpe in America,* 9–11; Coulter, *Journal of Gordon,* 33–36; Thomas Causton to his wife, March 12, 1733, in *Colonial Records,* ed. Coleman and Ready, 20:16; Baine and De Vorsey, "Provenance and Historical Accuracy," 795. The old style, or Julian, calendar was used until the adoption of the new style in 1752.

15. Baine and De Vorsey, "Provenance and Historical Accuracy," 799–800; Oglethorpe to the Trustees, February 10, 1733, in Lane, *Oglethorpe's Georgia,* 1:5; Coulter, *Journal of Gordon,* 37; Levy, "Savannah's Bull Street," 292.

16. Oglethorpe to the Trustees, February 10, 1733, March 12, 1733; Thomas Causton to his Wife, March 12, 1733; Samuel Eveleigh to the Trustees, April 6, 1733, all in Lane, *Oglethorpe's Georgia,* 1:5, 7, 8, 10, 13; Governor Robert Johnson to Benjamin Martyn, July 28, 1733, in *Colonial Records,* ed. Coleman and Ready, 20:26; Coulter, *Journal of Gordon,* 37–38, 40–41; Spalding, *Oglethorpe in America,* 12–13.

17. Coulter, *Journal of Gordon,* 38.

18. William Kilbury to Francis Harbin, February 6, 1733; Oglethorpe to the Trustees, February 10, March 12, 1733; Thomas Causton to the Trustees, March 12, 1733; Eveleigh to the Trustees, April 6, 1733, all in Lane, *Oglethorpe's Georgia,* 1:5–8, 10; Jackson, "Carolina Connection," 152–153. Coulter, *Journal of Gordon,* 38, 39, 48–49; Baine and De Vorsey, "Provenance and Historical Accuracy," 812; *Colonial Records,* ed. Coleman and Ready, 20:1–2, 4. Most likely St. Julian was Carolina surveyor and official James St. Julian.

19. James Oglethorpe to the Trustees, June 9, 1733, in Lane, *Oglethorpe's Georgia,* 1:16–17; McPherson, *Journal of Earl of Egmont,* 44; Baine and De Vorsey, "Provenance and Historical Accuracy," 808–809; Ivers, "Rangers, Scouts, and Tythingmen," 157–158.

20. Coulter, *Journal of Gordon,* 39; Causton to his Wife, March 12, 1733, in Lane, *Oglethorpe's Georgia,* 1:8–11; Reese, *Our First Visit,* 121–122.

21. Cates, "Medical History," 97–98; Baine and De Vorsey, "Provenance and Historical Accuracy," 804–805; Coulter, *Journal of Gordon,* 45–46; Oglethorpe to the Trustees, August 12, 1733, in Lane, *Oglethorpe's Georgia,* 1:19–21; Coleman, *Colonial Georgia,* 34–35; Temple and Coleman, *Georgia Journeys,* 26.

22. Reps, "C2 + L2 = S2?" 101, 109, 131, 138; Coleman, *Colonial Georgia,* 27–33;

for the most recent article on the origins of Oglethorpe's plan for Savannah, see Reinberger, "Oglethorpe's Plan," 339–382.

23. The existence of the many humanizing effects of cities—environment, human interactions, public and private institutions—and in this particular case, Savannah, is a primary theme repeated throughout this book. The theme was suggested by the profoundly important works of John Gulick, *The Humanity of Cities,* and Lewis Mumford, *The Culture of Cities* and *The City in History.* Of course, eighteenth- and nineteenth-century cities such as Savannah, especially those built on the social, economic, and political system of slavery, also were racked by inhumanity, violence, disease, poverty, and death.

24. Reps, "C2 + L2 = S2?" 101, 109, 131, 138; Cadle, *Georgia Land Surveying,* 8–9, 12; Spalding, "Colonial Period," 19–21; Lee and Agnew, *Historical Record,* 7–8; Gamble, *History,* 28–29; Harden, *History of Savannah,* 1:62–63; Leopold Adler, *Historic Savannah,* 61.

25. Levy, "Early History," 163–169; Oglethorpe to the Trustees, August 12, 1733, in Lane, *Oglethorpe's Georgia,* 1:21; Stern, "Jewish Settlement," 169–181.

26. Stern, "Jewish Settlement," 169–181; Morgan, "Judaism in Georgia," 41–43; G. F. Jones, "John Martin Bolzius," 218; Temple and Coleman, *Georgia Journeys,* 28–31; H. E. Davis, *Fledgling Province,* 197.

27. Oglethorpe to the Trustees, August 12, September 17, December [?], 1733, in Lane, *Oglethorpe's Georgia,* 1:xxi–xxii, 22–24, 28–30; Ivers, "Rangers, Scouts, and Tythingmen," 158; Temple and Coleman, *Georgia Journeys,* 34–37, 41.

28. Baine and De Vorsey, "Provenance and Historical Accuracy," 801–813; James Oglethorpe to the Trustees, September 17, 1733, in *Colonial Records,* ed. Coleman and Ready, 20:34; Temple and Coleman, *Georgia Journeys,* 34–37, 41, 76; Strickland, *Religion and State,* 80–81; Baine, "Oglethorpe's Forty Irish 'Convicts,'" 326–338.

29. Baine, "Oglethorpe's Forty Irish 'Convicts,'" 326–338.

30. "An Extract of the Journals of Mr. Commissary Von Reck and the Reverend Mr. Bolzius," in Reese, *Our First Visit,* 46, 57–58, 62; Lane, *Oglethorpe's Georgia,* 1:xxii; G. F. Jones, *Salzburger Saga,* 14–36, 65, 71, 82–83; Coleman, *Colonial Georgia,* 48–49; G. F. Jones, "Bringing Moravians," 847–849.

31. Temple and Coleman, *Georgia Journeys,* 66–67, 77–79, 80–82; Samuel Eveleigh to James Oglethorpe, October 19, 1734, and May 16, 1735; Robert Parker to the Trustees, January 4, 1735; Thomas Causton to the Trustees, March 10, 1735; and Thomas Christie to the Trustees, March 19, 1735, all in *Colonial Records,* ed. Coleman and Ready, 20:87, 141, 169, 256, 258–261, 269, 271–273.

32. Thomas Christie to James Oglethorpe, July 31, 1735, and Peter Gordon to the Trustees, May 7, 1735, in *Colonial Records,* ed. Coleman and Ready, 20:336–337,

456; Temple and Coleman, *Georgia Journeys,* 119; Coulter, "List of First Shipload," 287, 288.

33. Peter Gordon to the Trustees, May 7, 1735; Paul Amatis to the Trustees, June 6 and June 30, 1735; Elizabeth Bland to James Oglethorpe, June 14, 1735; Thomas Gapen to the Trustees, June 13, 1735; John Brownfield to the Trustees, March 6, 1736, all in Lane, *Oglethorpe's Georgia,* 1:165, 182–183, 187, 189, 199, 248.

34. Thomas Christie to James Oglethorpe, December 14, 1734; Joseph Fitzwalter to James Oglethorpe, January 16, 1735; Paul Amatis to James Oglethorpe, January (n.d.); Paul Amatis to the Trustees, June 30, July 5, 1735, all in Lane, *Oglethorpe's Georgia,* 1:xxvii, 70, 87–88, 103–105, 199–200, 212–213; Temple and Coleman, *Georgia Journeys,* 128–144, 208–210; Spalding, "Colonial Period," 23, 52; Coleman, *Colonial Georgia,* 114–117; Spalding, *Oglethorpe in America,* 42–44; Ready, "Economic History," 94–97.

35. Lane, "Some Foods."

36. James Oglethorpe to the Trustees, February 27, May 18, 1736; John Brownfield to the Trustees, March 6, 1736; Samuel Eveleigh to Harman Verelst, March 24, 1736, all in Lane, *Oglethorpe's Georgia,* 1:239, 247, 254–255, 265; Spalding, "Colonial Period," 24–27; H. E. Davis, *Fledgling Province,* 74; Byrne, "Burden and Heat," 1–9; Wood, *Slavery,* 21–29; Temple and Coleman, *Georgia Journeys,* 72, 138; Rabac, "Economy and Society," 68–69.

37. Quoted in Ready, "Economic History," 194.

38. Spalding, "Colonial Period," 28; Samuel Eveleigh to Harman Verelst, March 24, 1736; James Oglethorpe to the Trustees, May 18, June (n.d.) 1736; Thomas Causton to the Trustees, November 26, 1736, all in Lane, *Oglethorpe's Georgia,* 1:256, 267, 275; Temple and Coleman, *Georgia Journeys,* 274–275; Harrold, "Colonial Siblings," 708; Wilkins, "Commercial Rivalry," 38–39, 70, 101–103; Spalding, "Georgia and South Carolina," 50, 83–86, 135–136; Sirmans, *Colonial South Carolina,* 188–191; Chesnutt, "South Carolina's Expansion," 61–62; Cates, "'Seasoning,'" 152.

39. Warlick, *Grain Once Scattered,* 14–19; W. C. Smith, "Georgia Gentlemen," 1–6, 14–17, 24–35; George Whitefield, *A Journal of a Voyage from London to Savannah in Georgia and its continuations [1739–1740],* in Reese, *Our First Visit,* 291; Spalding, "Colonial Period," 38–39; H. E. Davis, *Fledgling Province,* 234–237; Coleman, *Colonial Georgia,* 148–149, 152, 160–161, 169; Arthur, "Schooling and Literacy," 573–579.

40. Temple and Coleman, *Georgia Journeys,* 164–169; H. E. Davis, *Fledgling Province,* 172–174; E. J. Cashin, "Oglethorpe's Contest," 102–106; H. Robertson and T. H. Robertson, "Town and Fort," 60–62; Spalding, *Oglethorpe in America,* 59; Groves, "Beaulieu Plantation," 200–203; Coleman, *Colonial Georgia,* 34, 50–51, 53, 97, 131–135, 170–171; Spalding, "Colonial Period," 40–42; Ready, "Economic

History," 159–161, 323; E. B. Greene and Harrington, *American Population,* 185; Sholes, *Chronological History,* 46; Maguire, *Historical Souvenir,* 6.

41. Temple and Coleman, *Georgia Journeys,* 108–112, 139–143, 208–211; Spalding, "Colonial Period," 35–36; Coleman, *Colonial Georgia,* 61–63, 96–98, 139–140; H. E. Davis, *Fledgling Province,* 65; Rabac, "Economy and Society," 45–46, 144; Coulter, *Journal of Stephens,* 2:136; Spalding, "Oglethorpe, Stephens, and Politics" 89; Cadle, *Georgia Land Surveying,* 25; A. O. Young, "Thomas Causton," 181–182; Spalding, "Noble Jones," 553–554; Granger, *Savannah River Plantations,* 1–8.

42. Byrne, "Burden and Heat," 21–30.

43. Quoted in Byrne, "Burden and Heat," 31.

44. *Ibid.,* 37–38, 49, 51–56; Wood, "Thomas Stephens," 24–28; Reese, *Clamorous Malcontents,* vii–xiii; J. I. Waring, "Colonial Medicine," 147; M. A. Stewart, "'Policies,'" 474–483, 493–496.

45. Quoted in Byrne, "Burden and Heat," 52.

46. *Ibid.,* 21–25, 27–33, 37–38, 49, 51–56; Wood, "Thomas Stephens," 24–28; Reese, *Clamorous Malcontents,* vii–xiii; J. I. Waring, "Colonial Medicine," 147.

47. *Colonial Records,* comp. Candler, 4:284–285, 406–407, 412, 427, 433–435; Temple and Coleman, *Georgia Journeys,* 153–154; Coleman, *Colonial Georgia,* 63–65, 82; Spalding, *Oglethorpe in America,* 90–92, 104–105; Thomas Stephens as quoted in Rabac, "Economy and Society," 148; James Oglethorpe to the Trustees, May 28, 1742, in Lane, *Oglethorpe's Letters,* 2:37, 612; Harden, *History of Savannah,* 102–104; Leopold Adler, *Historic Savannah,* 68.

48. James Oglethorpe to the Trustees, November 16, 1739; James Oglethorpe to the Duke of Newcastle, January 22, 1740; James Oglethorpe to the Trustees, July 19, 1740, all in Lane, *Oglethorpe's Georgia,* 2:420–421, 441–444, 463–465; Coleman, *Colonial Georgia,* 65–69; Wright, *Anglo-Spanish Rivalry,* 95–98; Sirmans, *Colonial South Carolina,* 210–214; G. F. Jones, "'Dutch' Participation," 771–776; Fogleman, "Shadow Boxing," 629, 657–659; Baine, "General James Oglethorpe," 197–200, 229.

49. The Inhabitants of Savannah to the Trustees, November 22, 1740; Hugh Anderson and Others to the Trustees, December 2, 1740; John Fallowfield to the Trustees, January 1, 1741, all in Lane, *Oglethorpe's Georgia,* 1:488–489, 494–495, 527; Warlick, *Grain Once Scattered,* 21–22; W. C. Smith, "Georgia Gentlemen," 24–35; Morgan, "Judaism in Georgia," 41–43, 53; Sholes, *Chronological History,* 47; H. E. Davis, *Fledgling Province,* 76, 159, 243; Gallay, "Great Sellout," 17–27.

50. Coleman, *Colonial Georgia,* 69–71; Coulter, *Journal of Stephens,* 106–109; Spalding, *Oglethorpe in America,* 110–117; Francis Moore to the Trustees, September 11, 1742; John Fallowfield to the Trustees, July 27, September 7, 1742; John Dobell to the Trustees, August 8, 1742; Joseph Avery to Harman Verelst, January 31, 1743, all in Lane, *Oglethorpe's Georgia,* 2:625, 639, 647, 646, 653; Wright, *Anglo-Spanish Rivalry,* 99; Ready, "Economic History," 186, 190–191.

51. Rabac, "Economy and Society," 133–139; Cates, "Medical History," 28–30, 99; Cates, "'Seasoning,'" 154–156.

52. Rabac, "Economy and Society," 155–156; Jackson, "Behind the Lines," 487–492.

53. Coulter, *Journal of Stephens,* 136–137; Coleman, *Colonial Georgia,* 152–153, 158; Clinton and Gillespie, *Devil's Lane,* 196; Ettinger, *James Edward Oglethorpe,* 253–254; Warlick, *Grain Once Scattered,* 27–32.

54. *Colonial Records,* comp. Candler, 6:21, 64, 105, 129, 141–142, 166, 176–179, 184, 193, 230, 301, 309, 314, 343, 361.

55. Warlick, *Grain Once Scattered,* 28; W. C. Smith, "Habershams," 198–204; H. E. Davis, *Fledgling Province,* 52–53; W. C. Smith, "Georgia Gentlemen," 78–106.

56. Byrne, "Burden and Heat," 57–61; Wax, "'New Negroes,'" 195–197; Jackson, "Carolina Connection," 166–167.

57. Baine, "Indian Slavery," 418–424.

58. Coulter, "Mary Musgrove," 13–27; Spalding, "Colonial Period," 43; myths continued to swirl around Mary—see Baine, "Myths of Mary Musgrove," 228–235; Clinton and Gillespie, *Devil's Lane,* 194–199.

59. Warlick, *Grain Once Scattered,* 33.

60. Byrne, "Burden and Heat," 61; Lockley, *Lines in the Sand,* 132.

61. R. M. Miller and J. D. Smith, *Dictionary of Slavery,* 295; Warlick, *Grain Once Scattered,* 35; Strickland, *Religion and State,* 97; Van Horne, "Joseph Solomon Ottolenghe," 398–404; Lockley, *Lines in the Sand,* 133.

62. Strickland, *Religion and State,* 131–132; Warlick, *Grain Once Scattered,* 35; H. E. Davis, "Bartholomew Zouberbuhler," 1106–1107; Levy, "Joseph Solomon Ottolenghe," 135–136.

63. Byrne, "Burden and Heat," 62–69; Jackson, "Carolina Connection," 170–172; Wax, "Georgia and the Negro," 73–74; Rabac, "Economy and Society," 178–190; W. C. Smith, "Georgia Gentlemen," 109–128; Spalding, "Colonial Period," 43–44; Ready, "Economic History," 191; Rowland, "'Alone on the River.'" 123–125; Chesnutt, "South Carolina's Expansion," 51, 67, 136–163; Wood, *Slavery,* 90–92; Coleman, *Colonial Georgia,* 171, 174–175; Bartley, *Modern Georgia,* 4; H. E. Davis, *Fledgling Province,* 97, 169, 253; Temple and Coleman, *Georgia Journeys,* 289–290; Lee and Agnew, *Historical Record,* 25; Levy, *Mordecai Sheftall,* 28; Wood, *Women's Work,* 80.

64. Quoted in Rabac, "Economy and Society," 185.

65. W. C. Smith, "Georgia Gentlemen," 109–128; Rabac, "Economy and Society," 187–188.

CHAPTER 2. *Royal Government, War, and Economic Boom, 1754–1763*

1. W. C. Smith, "Georgia Gentlemen," 132; Abbot, *Royal Governors,* 34; Coleman, *Colonial Georgia,* 179–180; Rabac, "Economy and Society," 193; Lee and Agnew, *Historical Record,* 27; Leopold Adler, *Historic Savannah,* 83; Spalding, "Colonial Period," 45–46; Gallay, "Bryan's Plantation Empire," 256–257.

2. C. C. Jones, *History of Savannah;* Abbot, *Royal Governors,* 34–35.

3. Harden, *Savannah and South Georgia,* 125–128; Leopold Adler, *Historic Savannah,* 83–85; Coulter, *Wormsloe,* 92–93; Stevens, *History of Georgia,* 1:390.

4. Governor John Reynolds to the Board of Trade, December 5, 1754, in *Colonial Records,* ed. Coleman and Ready, 27:32–35.

5. Abbot, *Royal Governors,* 38–43; J. M. Grant, "Legislative Factions," 64–68; Gallay, *Planter Elite,* 216; Van Horne, "Joseph Solomon Ottolenghe," 406–407.

6. Gallay, *Planter Elite,* 215.

7. J. M. Johnson, "'Single Soldier,'" 41–45; Wood, *Slavery,* 117–118.

8. *Colonial Records,* comp. Candler, 18:102–144; Wood, *Slavery,* 112–123; Byrne, "Burden and Heat," 61–77.

9. Quoted in Byrne, "Burden and Heat," 257.

10. *Colonial Records,* comp. Candler, 18:80–85; Wood, *Women's Work,* 82.

11. Coleman, *Colonial Georgia,* 181–183; Rabac, "Economy and Society," 195–198; W. C. Smith, "Georgia Gentlemen," 136–142; Gallay, *Planter Elite,* 215–216; Abbot, *Royal Governors,* 45–46.

12. John Reynolds to the Board of Trade, January 5, 1756, in *Colonial Records,* ed. Coleman and Ready, 27:103–104; C. C. Jones, *History of Savannah,* 156–158; De Vorsey, *DeBrahm's Report,* 15, 25.

13. John Reynolds to the Board of Trade, May 1, 1755, January 5, 1756, in *Colonial Records,* ed. Coleman and Ready, 27:63, 104; Rabac, "Economy and Society," 207–208.

14. Rabac, "Economy and Society," 206–212; W. C. Smith, "Georgia Gentlemen," 148–151; Abbot, *Royal Governors,* 51; Henry Ellis to the Board of Trade, March 11, 1757, in *Colonial Records,* ed. Coleman and Ready, 28, pt. 1:6.

15. Quoted in Rabac, "Economy and Society," 212.

16. *Colonial Records,* comp. Candler, 18:182–188.

17. Quoted in Gallay, *Planter Elite,* 73; see also Waller, "Henry Ellis," 370–371.

18. Waller, "Henry Ellis," 364–369; Shy, *People Numerous,* 38; Abbot, *Royal Governors,* 1, 17, 59–60.

19. Henry Ellis to the Board of Trade, March 11, 1757, in *Colonial Records,* ed. Coleman and Ready, 28, pt. 1:3.

20. Henry Ellis to the Board of Trade, March 11, March 20, May 5, May 25, 1757, in *Colonial Records,* comp. Candler, 28, pt. 1:9–30.

21. Abbot, *Royal Governors*, 60–66.

22. *Colonial Records*, comp. Candler, 18:202–211; Henry Ellis to the Board of Trade, August 1, September 20, 1757, in *Colonial Records*, ed. Coleman and Ready, 28, pt. 1:40, 69; De Vorsey, *DeBrahm's Report*, 25–27, 153–154.

23. *Colonial Records*, comp. Candler, 18:212–217; Wood, *Slavery*, 123–124.

24. *Colonial Records*, comp. Candler, 18:218–224; Henry Ellis to Board of Trade, July 8, 1757, in *Colonial Records*, ed. Coleman and Ready, 28, pt. 1:33.

25. *Colonial Records*, comp. Candler, 18:225–235; Wood, *Slavery*, 124.

26. Henry Ellis to the Board of Trade, August 1, September 20, 1757, in *Colonial Records*, ed. Coleman and Ready, 28, pt. 1:38, 43, 45. 69.

27. *Colonial Records*, comp. Candler, 7:644–648; Waller, "Henry Ellis," 372–373; Gallay, *Planter Elite*, 75–76.

28. Quoted in Johnson, "'Not a Single Soldier,'" 56.

29. Henry Ellis to the Board of Trade, January 1, May 20, 1758, in *Colonial Records*, ed. Coleman and Ready, 27:102, 155–156; Spalding, "Colonial Period," 46; Rabac, "Economy and Society," 223–224; Warlick, *Grain Once Scattered*, 36; Strickland, *Religion and State*, 106, 109–110, 113; *Colonial Records*, comp. Candler, 18:308–313, 316–318.

30. Henry Ellis to the Board of Trade, April 24, 1759, in *Colonial Records*, comp. Candler, 18: 308–313, 327–335; Strickland, *Religion and State*, 128–129.

31. Martin, "John Joachim Zubly," 2:1107; Coleman, *Colonial Georgia*, 233; Harden, *History of Savannah*, 1:136–138; Strickland, *Religion and State*, 113; Shriver, *Historical Pilgrimage*, 8–9.

32. Henry Ellis to the Board of Trade, January 1, 1758, in *Colonial Records*, ed. Coleman and Ready, 28, pt. 1:101–104; Rabac, "Economy and Society," 226–227.

33. *Colonial Records*, comp. Candler, 18:277–282; Wood, *Slavery*, 131–133; H. E. Davis, *Fledgling Province*, 97–98.

34. Caldwell, "Women Landholders," 187–195; *Colonial Records*, ed. Candler, 8:42, 210.

35. Henry Ellis to the Board of Trade, July 20, 1758, in *Colonial Records*, ed. Coleman and Ready, 28, pt. 1:161–164; *Colonial Records*, comp. Candler, 17:313–318.

36. Waller, "Henry Ellis," 374–375.

37. Henry Ellis to the Board of Trade, January 28, 1759, in *Colonial Records*, ed. Coleman and Ready, 28, pt. 1:174–178; *Colonial Records*, comp. Candler, 13:406; Rabac, "Economy and Society," 228–229; Levy, *Mordecai Sheftall*, 21, 32; Gallay, *Planter Elite*, 100; Wilkins, "Commercial Rivalry," 88, 92; Hawes, "Letter Book of Rasberry," 281–282; W. C. Smith, "Georgia Gentlemen," 156; Coleman, *Colonial Georgia*, 214, 219; W. C. Smith, "Habershams," 204.

38. Abbot, *Royal Governors*, 79–81; *Colonial Records*, comp. Candler, 18:408–

417, 433–434; *Colonial Records,* comp. Candler, 8:250–251, 324; Ready, "Economic History," 97; Leopold Adler, *Historic Savannah,* 130.

39. *Colonial Records,* comp. Candler, 18:388–392, 365–371, 455–460; Cates, "Medical History," 46–49; Leopold Adler, *Historic Savannah,* 79–80.

40. Henry Ellis to the Board of Trade, November 25, 1759, May 15, 1760, copy of an Order in Council, May 13, 1760, in *Colonial Records,* ed. Coleman and Ready, 28, pt. 1:218–219, 249–250; Abbot, *Royal Governors,* 81–82.

41. Coleman, "James Wright," 1097; Abbot, *Royal Governors,* 82–87.

42. James Wright to the Board of Trade, October 23, December 23, 1760, May 17, 1761, in *Colonial Records,* ed. Coleman and Ready, 28, pt. 1:291–299, 335; J. M. Johnson, "'Not a Single Soldier,'" 48, 54–56.

43. James Wright to the Board of Trade, February 20, 1761, in *Colonial Records,* ed. Coleman and Ready, 28, pt. 1:301–302; H. E. Davis, *Fledgling Province,* 167.

44. *Colonial Records,* comp. Candler, 8:540–541, 18:472–479; James Wright to the Board of Trade, February 20, 1762, in *Colonial Records,* ed. Coleman and Ready, 28, pt. 1:354–357; Coleman, *Colonial Georgia,* 205; De Vorsey, *DeBrahm's Report,* 160; J. M. Johnson, "'Not a Single Soldier,'" 76.

45. Sholes, *Chronological History,* 50; Siebert, "Spanish and French Privateering," 165–173; Wright, *Anglo-Spanish Rivalry,* 107–108; Levy, *Mordecai Sheftall,* 33–36; Morgan, "Judaism in Georgia," 46; Levy, "Savannah's Jewish Cemeteries," 2.

46. Leopold Adler, *Historic Savannah,* 5; Abbot, *Royal Governors,* 92–94.

47. James Wright to the Board of Trade, February 22, 1763, in *Colonial Records,* ed. Coleman and Ready, 28, pt. 1:405–406.

48. Abbot, *Royal Governors,* 96–101; Wood, *Women's Work,* 81–82; H. E. Davis, *Fledgling Province,* 69–70; Leopold Adler, *Historic Savannah,* 67, 73.

49. Lawrence, *James Johnston,* 3–7; Ready, "Economic History," 329.

50. Wilkins, "Commercial Rivalry," 115–116, 133–140.

51. E. J. Cashin, *Lachlan McGillivray,* 209–211, 252, 256, 260.

52. Wilkins, "Commercial Rivalry," 133–140.

53. Quoted in J. F. Smith, *Slavery and Rice Culture,* 21.

54. *Ibid.,* 20–29; Rowland, "'Alone on the River,'" 125–127.

55. Wilkins, "Commercial Rivalry," 159–162, 167–170, 184, 188, 194, 201–203; Rabac, "Economy and Society," 249–250; Dismukes, "Colonial Newspaper Notices"; Herndon, "Naval Stores," 426–433; Herndon, "Timber Products," 56–62; E. J. Cashin, *Lachlan McGillivray,* 256, 260; Hamer et al., *Papers of Laurens,* 3:136, n. 8, 232–233; 4:73, n. 6.

56. Coleman, *Colonial Georgia,* 215–219; Spalding, "Colonial Period," 51.

57. Dismukes, "Colonial Newspaper Notices"; H. E. Davis, *Fledgling Province,* 72–73; Wilkins, "Colonial Rivalry," 197–198; Ready, "Economic History," 328.

58. W. C. Smith, "Georgia Gentlemen," 174–180; W. C. Smith, "Habershams," 204–206; H. E. Davis, *Fledgling Province,* 40.

59. Dismukes, "Colonial Newspaper Notices."

60. *Georgia Gazette,* March 22, 1764.

61. W. C. Smith, "Georgia Gentlemen," 174–180; W. C. Smith, "Habershams," 204–206; Dismukes, "Colonial Newspaper Notices"; James Habersham to Ralph Clay, September 26, 1764, in *Collections of the Georgia Historical Society,* 6:26.

62. Dismukes, "Colonial Newspaper Notices"; Wilkins, "Commercial Rivalry," 196–199.

63. Quoted in Wilkins, "Commercial Rivalry," 199.

64. Corry, "Houses of Colonial Georgia," 181–201; H. E. Davis, *Fledgling Province,* 37–39.

65. Mrs. Charlton M. Theus, *Savannah Furniture,* 9–11, 29–31, 63, 73–74; Dismukes, "Colonial Newspaper Notices"; H. E. Davis, *Fledgling Province,* 100–101.

66. Cutten, *Silversmiths of Georgia,* 70, 73, 83–84, 92, 102, 108. 118.

67. *Ibid.,* 85.

68. *Colonial Records,* comp. Candler, 14, pt. 1:129–132, 337; 18:577–580; 19, pt. 1:161–163, 193, 496–497.

69. *Colonial Records,* comp. Candler, 18:588–598.

70. H. E. Davis, *Fledgling Province,* 80–84; *Colonial Records,* comp. Candler, 12:155.

71. Dismukes, "Colonial Newspaper Notices."

72. H. E. Davis, *Fledgling Province,* 169–178, 181, 184, 186, 189–192; Dismukes, "Colonial Newspaper Notices"; Broucek, "Eighteenth Century Music," 150–151, 198, 201–202.

73. *Georgia Gazette,* May 18, 1768, June 21, 1769; Broucek, "Eighteenth Century Music," 88, 96–98.

74. James Habersham to James Wright Jr., February 17, 1772, in *Collections of the Georgia Historical Society,* vol. 6: *The Letters of Hon. James Habersham, 1756–1775* (1904), 166–167; see also Broucek, "Eighteenth Century Music," 78–80, 88–89.

75. Coleman, *Colonial Georgia,* 237–242; McCaul, "Education in Georgia," 103–112.

76. Quoted in H. E. Davis, *Fledgling Province,* 78.

77. Warlick, *Grain Once Scattered,* 39–42; H. E. Davis, *Fledgling Province,* 78; M. C. Davis, "Whitefield's Attempt," 469; Morgan, "Judaism in Georgia," 47.

78. Coleman, *Colonial Georgia,* 237–242; McCaul, "Education in Georgia," 103–112.

79. Cates, "Medical History," 49–59, 99–101.

80. Statom, "Negro Slavery," 24–28, 58, 151–156; H. E. Davis, *Fledgling Province,* 131–132; Wood, *Slavery,* 98–99; Byrne, "'Burden and Heat,'" 213–214.

81. Warlick, *Grain Once Scattered,* 37; Johnson, "'Not A Single Soldier,'" 51; H. E. Davis, *Fledgling Province,* 139; Wood, *Slavery,* 125–126, 166–167.

82. Lockley, *Lines in the Sand,* 44, 82, 108.

83. Byrne, "'Burden and Heat,'" 83 n. 4.

84. *Colonial Records,* comp. Candler, 18:558–566; H. E. Davis, *Fledgling Province,* 136–140; Lockley, *Lines in the Sand,* 119.

85. Hamer et al., *Papers of Laurens,* 3:130, n. 4, 4:360, n. 1.

86. *Colonial Records,* comp. Candler, 18:558–566; H. E. Davis, *Fledgling Province,* 136–140.

87. Byrne, "'Burden and Heat,'" 77–80; Wood, *Slavery,* 124–127; Wood, "'Dead, Dead, Dead,'" 377–398.

CHAPTER 3. *Savannah in the Revolution, 1763–1782*

1. Spalding, "Colonial Period," 57–58; Coleman, *American Revolution,* 16–17.

2. Harrold, "Colonial Siblings," 723–724; Ellefson, "James Habersham," 361–362.

3. Miller, "Stamp Act," 318–322; Bartley, *Modern Georgia,* 7–8; J. P. Greene, "Georgia Commons House," 153–154; Coleman, *American Revolution,* 25.

4. Roach, "*Georgia Gazette* and Stamp Act," 479.

5. Spindel, "Stamp Act Riots," 207–209; Miller, "Stamp Act," 321.

6. Miller, "Stamp Act," 321; Killion and Waller, *Georgia and Revolution,* 9–12.

7. H. E. Davis, *Fledgling Province,* 120.

8. *Georgia Gazette,* November 7, 1765.

9. Levy, *Mordecai Sheftall,* 50–51.

10. *Georgia Gazette,* October 31, November 7, 1765; Coleman, *American Revolution,* 19–20; Spindel, "Stamp Act Riots," 209; Spalding, "Colonial Period," 58; Miller, "Stamp Act," 323; Killion and Waller, *Georgia and Revolution,* 10–11; J. M. Johnson, "'Not a Single Soldier,'" 85–86.

11. James Habersham to William Knox, December 4, 1765, in *Collections of the Georgia Historical Society,* 6:49–50.

12. Quoted in J. M. Johnson, "'Not a Single Soldier,'" 86; see also Spindel, "Stamp Act Riots," 211–212.

13. Quoted in Spindel, "Stamp Act Riots," 211.

14. Quoted in ibid., 212; see also Miller, "Stamp Act," 324–325; J. M. Johnson, "'Not a Single Soldier,'" 88–90.

15. Spindel, "Stamp Act Riots," 213–214; Abbot, *Royal Governors,* 116–117; Smith, "Georgia Gentlemen," 195–196.

16. James Habersham to Reverend Mr. George Whitefield, February 7, 1766, *Collections of the Georgia Historical Society,* 6:57; see also J. M. Johnson, "'Not a Single Soldier,'" 91–96; Spindel, "Stamp Act Riots," 214–215.

17. Quoted in Abbot, *Royal Governors,* 119, and J. M. Johnson, "'Not a Single Soldier,'" 94.

18. Frey, *Water from the Rock,* 51–52.

19. Ibid., 41.

20. Quoted in J. M. Johnson, "'Not a Single Soldier,'" 93–94.

21. Warlick, *Grain Once Scattered,* 37, 191 n. 202; see also Fraser, "City Elite," 167–179; Nash, "Urban Wealth," 545–584; Rabac, "Economy and Society," 251.

22. *Georgia Gazette,* November 30, 1774.

23. Quoted in Miller, "Stamp Act," 329; see also Sublett, "Georgia Whigs," 34–35.

24. Abbot, *Royal Governors,* 121–125; Spindel, "Stamp Act Riots," 219; Miller, "Stamp Act," 329; Killion and Waller, *Georgia and Revolution,* 14; Gallay, *Planter Elite,* 114–115.

25. Harrold, "Colonial Siblings," 734–735; Coleman, *Colonial Georgia,* 26–27.

26. Coleman, *American Revolution,* 27–29; Harrold, "Colonial Siblings," 734–735; Coleman, *Colonial Georgia,* 252–255; Gallay, *Planter Elite,* 115–116.

27. Quoted in Gallay, *Planter Elite,* 117.

28. Ibid., 117–118; Harrold, "Colonial Siblings," 735.

29. Gallay, *Planter Elite,* 118–119.

30. *Ibid.,* 119.

31. Quoted in Harrold, "Colonial Siblings," 735.

32. Wood, *Slavery,* 99–100, 103; Wax, "'New Negroes,'" 200–201, 206–207.

33. Quoted in Wood, *Slavery,* 101; see also Wax, "'New Negroes,'" 207–208.

34. Wax, "'New Negroes,'" 209.

35. Ibid., 209–211.

36. *Ibid.,* 210.

37. Wood, *Slavery,* 102–103.

38. Statom, "Negro Slavery," 122–123.

39. Wood, *Slavery,* 104.

40. Ibid., 128–129.

41. Ibid., 128–129; see also Wood, "'Dead, Dead, Dead,'" 378.

42. Washington, "Aspects of Emancipation," 105.

43. R. B. Flanders, *Slavery,* 35.

44. Wood, *Slavery,* 189–190.

45. Statom, "Negro Slavery," 111–120; Fleetwood, *Tidecraft,* 63, 65, 74, 75.

46. Wood, *Women's Work,* 83, 95, 107, 129, 134.

47. Statom, "Negro Slavery," 111–120; Wood, *Women's Work,* 108.

48. Lockley, *Lines in the Sand,* 64–66, 70, 98.

49. Wood, *Slavery in Colonial Georgia,* 177; Statom, "Negro Slavery," 54.

50. Lockley, *Lines in the Sand,* 66, 70; Wood, *Slavery,* 170–187; Byrne, "'Burden and Heat,'" 83.

51. Statom, "Negro Slavery," 36, 38, 168; Federal Writers Project, *Savannah,* 50. African American writers who researched and wrote the section on "Negro Life and History" in *Savannah* stated that an attempt "for physical freedom" was made "in the insurrection of 1768," which failed "due to some misunderstanding"; see also Byrne, "'Burden and Heat,'" 83 n. 4.

52. *Colonial Records,* comp. Candler, 17:210, 218–219, 19, pt. 1: 137–139; Statom, "Negro Slavery," 60.

53. J. M. Johnson, "'Not a Single Soldier,'" 124–125; J. F. Smith, *Slavery and Rice Culture,* 188.

54. Wood, "'Dead, Dead, Dead'" 381–384; Wax, "'New Negroes,'" 212.

55. James Habersham to Mr. John Nutt, August 1, 1771, Habersham Family Papers, Duke University; James Habersham to James Wright, December 29, 1771, *Collections of the Georgia Historical Society,* 6:159.

56. James Habersham to William Knox, February 11, 1772, *Collections of the Georgia Historical Society,* 6:163–164; *Colonial Records,* comp. Candler, 12:217–218.

57. H. E. Davis, *Fledgling Province,* 66–67.

58. *Colonial Records,* comp. Candler, 15:386.

59. James Habersham to the Earl of Hillsborough, April 30, 1772, *Collections of the Georgia Historical Society,* 6:174–180.

60. Ibid., 178.

61. Granger, *Savannah Harbor,* 7–8.

62. *Colonial Records,* comp. Candler, 15:231, 435; Cushing, *First Laws,* 194, 198.

63. James Habersham to Henry Ellis, January 27 1772, *Collections of the Georgia Historical Society,* 7:162.

64. Ibid.; Coleman, *Colonial Georgia,* 221.

65. Coleman, *Colonial Georgia,* 220–222; Fleetwood, *Tidecraft,* 66; *Georgia Gazette,* May 17, 1775; B. Wilkins, "View of Savannah," 577, 582; H. E. Davis, *Fledgling Province,* 104; G. B. Wilkins, "Commercial Rivalry," 170, 184, 200, 201, 214, 222, 227–229, 231–232.

66. Quoted in Lawrence, *Storm over Savannah,* l.

67. Ibid., 1–3.

68. B. Wilkins, "View of Savannah," 578–580; Daniel, "Anglicans and Dissenters," 251; Shriver, *Historical Pilgrimage,* 9–10; Harden, *History of Savannah,* 138.

69. *Georgia Gazette,* January 14, May 18, July 27, September 14, 1774; Dismukes, "Colonial Newspaper Notices," 15, 20, 23.

70. Abbot, *Royal Governors,* 154–156; Spalding, "Colonial Period," 61, 63.

71. Quoted in Ellefson, "James Habersham," 372.

72. Spalding, "Colonial Period," 61, 63; Abbot, *Royal Governors,* 155–157; Miller, *"Warm and Zealous Spirit,"* 17–18.

73. Abbot, *Royal Governors,* 158–159, 162; Gallay, *Planter Elite,* 122–123.

74. Quoted in Killion and Waller, *Georgia and Revolution,* 104; see also Coleman, *American Revolution,* 39–41; Coleman, *Colonial Georgia,* 263–264; Gallay, *Planter Elite,* 124.

75. Jackson, "Consensus and Conflict," 388–392; Jackson, *Lachlan McIntosh,* 23–24; Coleman, *American Revolution,* 43–45.

76. Jackson, "Georgia Whiggery," 251–253, 260.

77. *Georgia Gazette,* September 21, 1774; Wood, "'Dead, Dead, Dead'" 387.

78. Wood, "Female Resistance," 611; *Georgia Gazette,* December 7, 1774; Frey, *Water from the Rock,* 54–56; Statom, "Negro Slavery," 208–209.

79. Quoted in Spalding, "Colonial Period," 64–65.

80. J. M. Johnson, "'Not a Single Soldier,'" 159.

81. Quoted in Harrold, "Colonial Siblings," 740.

82. Quoted in J. M. Johnson, "'Not a Single Soldier,'" 159–160; see also Spalding, "Colonial Period," 65–67.

83. Frey, *Water from the Rock,* 62–63 and n. 69.

84. Spalding, "Colonial Period," 65–67; Coleman, *Colonial Georgia,* 264–268; Mebane, "Joseph Habersham," 76–77; Jackson, *Lachlan McIntosh,* 23–26; Jackson, "Consensus and Conflict," 392–393.

85. Quoted in Harden, "Sir James Wright," 28–29.

86. J. M. Johnson, "'Not a Single Soldier,'" 162.

87. Ibid., 162–163; Spalding, "Colonial Period," 65–67.

88. Jackson, "Georgia Whiggery," 265.

89. Jackson, *Lachlan McIntosh,* 27; Coleman, *Colonial Georgia,* 273–275; Coleman, *American Revolution,* 255–260; Miller, *"Warm and Zealous Spirit",* 20; Kenneth Coleman, "1775–1820," in Coleman, *History of Georgia,* 71–72; Gallay, *Planter Elite,* 124–125.

90. Mebane, "Joseph Habersham," 77–80; W. C. Smith, "Habershams," 209; Spalding, "Colonial Period," 67; Giffen, "Living with Antiques," 370.

91. F. Lambert, "'Father against Son,'" 3–4, 27–28; Gallay, "Bryan's Plantation Empire," 278–279.

92. Jackson, *Lachlan McIntosh,* 27–28; J. M. Johnson, "'Not a Single Soldier,'" 164, 185–186; Coleman, *Colonial Georgia,* 274–276.

93. Warlick, *Grain Once Scattered,* 46–47; Coleman, *American Revolution,* 65.

94. E. J. Cashin, "Sowing the Wind," 242–246; Coleman, *American Revolution,* 65–66; Jackson, "Georgia Whiggery," 253, 262–263.

95. Coleman, *Colonial Georgia,* 275–276; J. M. Johnson, "'Not a Single Soldier,'" 164–165.

96. Quoted in J. M. Johnson, "'Not a Single Soldier,'" 164; Wax, "'New Negroes,'" 214.

97. Quoted in Jackson, "Georgia Whiggery," 266.

98. Quoted in Bridges, "George Walton," 17–18.

99. Frey, *Water from the Rock,* 50, 61–65.

100. Bridges, "George Walton," 31–32, 48–49.

101. J. M. Johnson, "'Not a Single Soldier,'" 188–193, 202; see also Bridges, "George Walton," 49.

102. Jackson, *Lachlan McIntosh,* 29–34; Jackson, "Rise of Western Members," 285–292; J. M. Johnson, "'Not a Single Soldier,'" 197–199, 203.

103. Quoted in Jackson, "Georgia Whiggery," 251.

104. Quoted in J. M. Johnson, "'Not a Single Soldier,'" 204.

105. Ibid., 207–210; Byrne, "'Burden and Heat,'" 84–86; Lawrence, *James Johnston,* 16–18.

106. J. M. Johnson, "'Not a Single Soldier,'" 192–193, 213–214; Jackson, *Lachlan McIntosh,* 33.

107. Quoted in King, *Georgia Voices.*

108. J. M. Johnson, "'Not a Single Soldier,'" 213–230; Jackson, "Battle of Riceboats," 229–243; King, *Georgia Voices,* 64; Jackson, *Lachland McIntosh,* 35–39; Frey, *Water from the Rock,* 65–66.

109. Jackson, *Lachlan McIntosh,* 40–41; Smith, "Georgia Gentlemen," 269–270.

110. Quoted in Jackson, *Lachlan McIntosh,* 40.

111. Ibid., 41–43; Fleetwood, *Tidecraft,* 68; Coleman, *American Revolution,* 111.

112. Quoted in Jackson, *Lachlan McIntosh,* 44.

113. Coleman, *American Revolution,* 78–79; Jackson, *Lachlan McIntosh,* 43–46.

114. W. C. Smith, "Georgia Gentlemen," 274–278; E. J. Cashin, "'Famous Colonel Wells,'" 139–140; Coleman, "1775–1820," in *History of Georgia,* 74–76; Jackson, *Lachlan McIntosh,* 45–52.

115. Jackson, *Lachlan McIntosh,* 45–52.

116. Ibid., 50–57.

117. Quoted in Bridges, "George Walton," 103.

118. Jackson, *Lachlan McIntosh,* 57–64.

119. Quoted in ibid., 64.

120. Ibid., 65–70; Gamble, *Savannah Duels,* 14–16; Coleman, *American Revolution,* 169; Bridges, "George Walton," 112–115; Candler, *Revolutionary Records,* 1:310.

121. Candler, *Revolutionary Records,* 2:41–42, 53–54.

122. Coleman, *American Revolution,* 87, 93, 105, 107–112; R. S. Lambert, "Confiscation of Property," 80–94; Gallay, *Planter Elite,* 156; Candler, *Revolutionary Records,* 2:84–93.

123. Coleman, *American Revolution,* 116–120; Lawrence, "General Robert Howe," 304–314. Curiously, the well-to-do Howe, who was forty-seven years of age and had extensive service in the North Carolina militia, has been described as convivial and well-liked by both men and women.

124. Governor John Houstoun to Major General Benjamin Lincoln, December 19, 1778, in John Houstoun Collection, Georgia Historical Society, Savannah, Georgia.

125. Coleman, *American Revolution,* 119–121; Lawrence, "General Robert Howe," 309–320; Bridges, "George Walton," 132–140.

126. Quoted in Bridges, "George Walton," 141–142, and Lawrence, "General Robert Howe," 320.

127. Coleman, *American Revolution,* 120–121; Lawrence, "General Robert Howe," 320–324; Bridges, "George Walton," 146; C. C. Jones, *History of Savannah,* 243–248; Levy, *Mordecai Sheftall,* 66–67,75–76.

128. Quoted in Lawrence, "General Robert Howe," 324.

129. Governor John Houstoun to the Continental Congress, January 2, 1779, copy in Georgia Historical Society, Savannah.

130. Lawrence, "General Robert Howe," 303–304, 325–327; Searcy, "1779," 170–171; C. C. Jones, *History of Savannah,* 250; Sowell, "Social and Economic History," 101.

131. Coleman, *American Revolution,* 121–125; Hawes, "Minute Book," 245.

132. John Richardson to John Porteous, March 15, 1779, in Howland, "British Privateer," 293–294.

133. Coleman, *American Revolution,* 147; Jackson, *Lachlan McIntosh,* 96; Warlick, *Grain Once Scattered,* 47–48.

134. Governor James Wright to Secretary Lord G. Germain, July 31, 1779, in *Collections of the Georgia Historical Society,* 3:254–255.

135. Coleman, *American Revolution,* 121–127, 169–172; Searcy, "1779," 168–188.

136. Lawrence, *James Johnston,* 19–21.

137. Jackson, *Lachlan McIntosh,* 94–96, 112–114; Searcy, "1779," 171–177.

138. Jackson, *Lachlan McIntosh,* 96–101; Lawrence, *Storm over Savannah,* 31, 35–45, 51, 55, 76–83, 91–92, 103–108, 116, 129–130, 156–161; C. C. Jones, *History of Savannah,* 258–294; Kennedy, *Muskets,* 89, 109, 128; Byrne, "'Burden and Heat,'"

92–94; Murphy, "Irish Brigade," 307–321; Clark, "Role of the Haitian Volunteers," 356–366.

139. Killion and Waller, *Georgia and the Revolution,* 200, 208.

140. Ludlum, *Early American Winters,* 150.

141. C. C. Jones, *History of Savannah,* 296; Frey, *Water from the Rock,* 90, 95, 98.

142. Quoted in Frey, *Water from the Rock,* 98.

143. Quoted in Byrne, "'Burden and Heat,'" 92–95; see also *Colonial Records,* comp. Candler, 12:452.

144. Quoted in Frey, *Water from the Rock,* 102.

145. Ibid., 86–89.

146. Coleman, "Georgia in the American Revolution, 1775-1782," in Coleman, *History of Georgia,* 83; Bridges, "George Walton," 177–180.

147. G. F. Jones, "Victor at Springhill," 377–379; Coleman, *American Revolution,* 136; Warlick, *Grain Once Scattered,* 48; *Colonial Records,* comp. Candler, 15:621.

148. Governor James Wright to Secretary Lord G. Germain, October 27, December 1, 1780, in *Collections of the Georgia Historical Society,* 3:321–323; Frey, *Water from the Rock,* 102.

149. Frey, *Water from the Rock,* 102–103; *Colonial Records,* comp. Candler, 12:488–489; Governor James Wright to Secretary Lord G. Germain, January 25, 1781, in *Collections of the Georgia Historical Society,* 3:332–333.

150. Sowell, "Social and Economic History," 101; Frey, *Water from the Rock,* 103–104.

151. E. J. Cashin, "'Famous Colonel Wells,'" 152–153.

152. General Anthony Wayne to Lieutenant Colonel James Jackson, February 12, 1782, James Jackson Papers, William R. Perkins Library, Duke University.

153. James Wright to the Board of Trade, January 23, 1782, in *Colonial Records,* ed. Coleman and Ready, 28, pt. 2: 408; Coleman, *American Revolution,* 141–142.

154. James Wright to Secretary Lord G. Germain, June 14, 1781, February 15, 1782, in *Collections of the Georgia Historical Society,* 3:358–359, 367–369.

155. Quoted in Coleman, *American Revolution,* 143.

156. James Wright to Under Secretary Knox, February 23, 1782, in *Collections of the Georgia Historical Society,* 3:372–373.

157. Walter Cliffe, Major of Brigade, to Non-Commissioned Officers of the Provost Guard, Savannah, March 21, 1782, Walter Cliffe Paper, Georgia Historical Society.

158. Coleman, *American Revolution,* 183–185; Candler, *Revolutionary Records,* 1:373–411; R. S. Lambert, "Confiscation of Property," 82–83.

159. Coleman, *American Revolution,* 143–146, 179–180, 189; Frey, *Water from the Rock,* 173–174; Lamplugh, "'Check and Discourage,'" 225–304; W. C. Smith,

"Georgia Gentlemen," 300–302; Lawrence, *James Johnston*, 24–25; Jackson, *Lachlan McIntosh*, 124–126; E. J. Cashin, "'Famous Colonel Wells,'" 152–154.

160. Killion and Waller, *Georgia and Revolution*, 224–225.

CHAPTER 4. *Recovery to the War of 1812, 1782–1815*

1. C. C. Jones, *History of Savannah*, 313.

2. "Presentments of the Grand Jurors for the County of Chatham . . . October 3, 1782," John V. Bevan Papers, Georgia Historical Society.

3. Frey, *Water from the Rock*, 208.

4. Ibid., 207 n. 6.

5. Ibid., 208.

6. Byrne, "Burden and Heat," 90.

7. Wilson, *Historic Savannah*, 98; W. C. Smith, "Georgia Gentlemen," 306; Coleman, "Social Life," 226.

8. Wax, "New Negroes," 216.

9. Ibid., 215–220.

10. Telfair & Company to Cooper & Telfair, London, December 1, 1783, Edward Telfair Papers, Duke University; Smith, "Georgia Gentlemen," 307; Statom, "Negro Slavery," 44–46.

11. R. S. Lambert, "Confiscation of Property," 83; W. C. Smith, "Georgia Gentlemen," 308–309.

12. E. J. Cashin, "'Famous Colonel Wells,'" 152–153.

13. Candler, *Revolutionary Records*, 2:321, 348, 384–385; 3:126, 571.

14. Ibid., 2:341, 630–631, 857.

15. *Colonial Records*, comp. Candler, 19, pt. 2: 256–262.

16. Candler, *Revolutionary Records*, 2:317, 321, 373–374, 389, 742.

17. Ibid., 2:389–390, 443–444, 464; 3:534.

18. Ibid., 2:478; 3:571.

19. *Colonial Records*, comp. Candler, 19, pt. 2: 245–246, 476–482.

20. Ibid., 19, pt. 2: 419–433.

21. Samuel Baas to the Honorable Gentlemen of the Vestry for Christ Church, August 7, 1788, Christ Church Records, Georgia Historical Society.

22. Ann Spring and Lucy Whitehead to Church Wardens of Christ Church, January 17, 1789, Christ Church Records; Wilson, *Historic Savannah*, 125.

23. Harris, "Education," 248–250.

24. Coleman, "Social Life," 218–219, 221, 224–225; W. C. Smith, "Georgia Gentlemen," 370; M. G. Waring, "Savannah's Schools," 324–325.

25. Broucek, "Eighteenth Century Music," 153, 172–176; Lamplugh, "Farewell to Revolution," 391–392.

26. Lawrence, *James Johnston,* 25–35.

27. Lamplugh, "George Walton," 82–84.

28. Frey, *Water from the Rock,* 212–214; Wax, "New Negroes," 215–220; Byrne, "Burden and Heat," 222; C. C. Jones, *History of Savannah,* 465; Statom, "Negro Slavery," 45–50, 162–163; Wood, *Women's Work,* 131, 181, 211– 212 n. 6.

29. Frey, *Water from the Rock,* 224; Washington, "Dollys," 101–103; "Jane Habersham" in Wayne-Stites-Anderson Papers, Georgia Historical Society.

30. Byrne, "Burden and Heat," 113.

31. Wood, "Prisons, Workhouses," 258.

32. Frey, *Water from the Rock,* 226–227.

33. General James Jackson to the [Governor of S. C.], December 2, 1786, James Jackson Papers.

34. Wood, "Female Resistance," 612; Wood, "Dead, Dead, Dead," 392; "Chatham Artillery," May 2, 1970, Chatham Artillery Papers, Georgia Historical Society; Frey, *Water from the Rock,* 226–227, 328.

35. *Colonial Records,* comp. Candler, 14, pt. 2: 563–568; Gamble, *History,* 45–47,146; W. C. Smith, "Georgia Gentlemen," 319–324.

36. W. C. Smith, "Georgia Gentlemen," 325–329; Gamble, *History,* 47–49, 60, 132.

37. Gamble, *History,* 60–61.

38. Ibid., 50–56, 61–65; City Council Minutes, March 3, 1793, October 4, 1802, June 2, 1806, Savannah City Archives.

39. Gamble, *History,* 120–121.

40. City Council Minutes, November 25, December 24, 1794, June 4, 1807, December 8, 1806.

41. Morgan, "Judaism in Georgia," 47–51; Greenberg, "Creating Ethnic," 181.

42. W. C. Smith, "Georgia Gentlemen," 331–332 335; Gamble, *History,* 88, 90–91.

43. Frey, *Water from the Rock,* 228–233, 328; Wood, *Women's Work,* 164.

44. O. S. Johnson, "Social Welfare Role," 90–94; Gamble, *History,* 55; Wood, *Women's Work,* 164; W. B. Johnson, *Black Savannah,* 134.

45. W. B. Johnson, *Black Savannah,* 5–14; J. F. Smith, *Slavery and Rice Culture,* 143–149; Dr. Edward J. Cashin to the author, June 4, 2001; Wood, *Women's Work,* 163–165, 169–171; Lockley, *Lines in the Sand,* 140–148.

46. Frey, *Water from the Rock,* 287–290, 298, 305, 325, 328–329; O. S. Johnson, "Social Welfare Role," 94–95; Byrne, "Burden and Heat," 139, 143–146; W. B. Johnson, "Andrew C. Marshall," 175; W. B. Johnson, *Black Savannah,* 27, 34.

47. Byrne, "Burden and Heat," 146–147; W. B. Johnson, *Black Savannah,* 141.

48. Byrne, "Burden and Heat," 138; G. N. Jones, "Boy Chatham," 184–185.

49. Lockley, *Lines in the Sand,* 121.

50. Wood, "Female Resistance," 613–617, 622; Wood, "Prisons, Workhouses," 258; *Georgia Gazette*, October 8, 1789; Statom, "Negro Slavery," 246–250; Wood, *Women's Work*, 95, 112–121; Harris, "Education," 713.

51. Wood, "Prisons, Workhouses," 258.

52. Scott, "Common Wind," 273–290; Hunt, *Haiti's Influence*, 20–24, 115–117.

53. Wood, "Prisons, Workhouses," 259, 261, 271 n. 44; Byrne, "Burden and Heat," 223; Gamble, *History*, 65.

54. Bonner, *Georgia Agriculture*, 47–60; Harden, *History of Savannah*, 472; Gillespie, *Free Labor*, 10–11.

55. Chaplin, "Creating a Cotton South," 171–200.

56. Eisterhold, "Savannah," 526–527.

57. Mohl, "Scotsman Visits Georgia," 260.

58. J. K. Williams, "Travel," 196.

59. Govan, "Banking and Credit," 166, 179, 164–183; W. C. Smith, "Georgia Gentlemen," 378.

60. Frey, *Water from the Rock*, 220–221; Gillespie, "Artisans and Mechanics," 7–19.

61. Gillespie, "Artisans and Mechanics," 7–19, 39.

62. Ibid., 25–34,39, 43, 47–49; Gillespie, *Free Labor*, 12, 28–29.

63. Gillespie, "Artisans and Mechanics," 52–53, 56; Gillespie, *Free Labor*, 63–64.

64. V. Green, "Black Construction Artisans," 46; Harris, "Education of the Southern Urban Adult," 1:282; Gillespie, *Free Labor in an Unfree World*, 10–11.

65. Gillespie, "Artisans and Mechanics," 60–61, 87–98; Gillespie, *Free Labor in an Unfree World*, 49–53.

66. City Council Minutes, August 12, 19, 1796; Gamble, *History*, 58.

67. City Council Minutes, November 5, 1793, April 4, November 6, 1794, June 6, 1796.

68. Wood, "Prisons, Workhouses," 259 n. 45, 271; Wilson, *Historic Savannah*, 97, 158, 162, 169.

69. A. P. Wade, "Artillerists and Engineers," 22, 148.

70. Byrne, "Burden and Heat," 223; City Council Minutes, July 2, 1795.

71. Gamble, *History*, 59; City Council Minutes, August 1, 6, 1796.

72. Byrne, "Burden and Heat," 119–120, 222–224.

73. Ibid., 100–103.

74. Washington, "Aspects of Emancipation."

75. Johnson, *Black Savannah*, 111–113, 130–131.

76. "La Rochefoucauld-Liancourt 1796" in Lane, *Rambler in Georgia*, 1–15.

77. City Council Minutes, April 13, May 4, October 26, 1790, June 27, 1794, June 20, 1796.

78. City Council Minutes, August 1, 1796.

79. *Columbia Museum and Savannah Advertiser,* November 29, 1796.

80. Byrne, "Burden and Heat," 193–195; Gillespie, "Artisans and Mechanics," 98–100; Gamble, *History,* 51–52.

81. W. R. Wells, "Naval Protection," 737–758.

82. Gamble, *History,* 131–138; E. M. Green, "Theatre," 25.

83. W. C. Smith, "Georgia Gentlemen," 364–369.

84. Lane, *Rambler in Georgia,* xxiv.

85. "City Council Records," July 14, 21, 1800.

86. Gillespie, "Artisans and Mechanics," 101–113.

87. Ibid., 112–113; W. C. Smith, "Georgia Gentlemen," 365, 372–376.

88. Thomas U. P. Charlton to Edward Telfair, November 16, 1806, Edward Telfair Papers, Georgia Historical Society.

89. Gillespie, "Artisans and Mechanics," 101–113.

90. Cooper, *Liberty and Slavery,* 248–249; Lockley, *Lines in the Sand,* 28, 30, 63, 70, 76, 84, 130, 164–165.

91. Gillespie, *Free Labor,* 56–59.

92. Gamble, *History,* 78; "Negroes—Census, 1798," Chatham County File, Georgia Department of Archives and History (hereafter GDAH); "Negro File," GDAH; Scarborough, *Opposition to Slavery,* 109; Bryne, "Burden and Heat," 193–195.

93. Bryne, "Burden and Heat," 270.

94. Berlin, *Slaves without Masters,* 54–55, 93–94.

95. Gamble, *History,* 65–66.

96. "Negro File," GDAH; Wax, "New Negroes," 219–220.

97. E. M. Green, "Theatre," 9; Harris, "Education," 298–304, 318–322; Patrick, *Savannah's Pioneer Theater,* 18–21, 31–32.

98. LaFar, "Henry Holcombe," 157–159.

99. Boles, "Henry Holcombe," 385–387; Shriver, *Pilgrims,* 18–20.

100. Shriver, *Pilgrims,* 32, 67; Harris, "Education," 342, 344–345, 353–359, 361–362; Broucek, "Eighteenth Century Music," 155–156, 163–164, 176–177.

101. Harris, "Education," 298–304; Gamble, *History,* 54, 70–73; Patrick, *Savannah's Pioneer Theater,* 31.

102. Gamble, *History,* 54; Lockley, "Trading Encounters," 25–36; Lockley, *Lines in the Sand,* 76–82.

103. Harris, "Education," 241, 297–299; Gamble, *History,* 54–56; Lockley, *Lines in the Sand,* 84–87.

104. Quoted in Lockley, *Lines in the Sand,* 54.

105. Lockley, "Struggle for Survival," 31, 33; see also City Council Minutes, October 5, 1801, June 18, 1804.

106. Quoted in Lockley, "Struggle for Survival," 33.

107. City Council Minutes, May 13, 1814; Lockley, *Lines in the Sand,* 55.

108. Lockley, "Struggle for Survival," 33–38.

109. Lockley, *Lines in the Sand,* 55–56.

110. Kelley, "Fore Lore."

111. City Council Minutes, October 29, 1793, May 23, October 4, 1794, May 23, July 18, August 3, 1796.

112. Cates, "Medical History," 61–62, 79; "Page from the Journal Account Book of Dr. Moses Sheftall, Sr.," manuscript, Special Collections, Duke University; Judge W. Gibbons to Dr. Moses Sheftall Sr., May 27, 1800, Victor H. Bassett Papers, Special Collections, Duke University.

113. J. I. Waring, "Yellow Fever," 398–404; Gamble, *History,* 79–80; City Council Minutes, May 21, 1804, January 25, February 11, 12, March 4, 1805.

114. Edward Telfair to Alexander [Telfair], September 20, 1805, Telfair Papers, Special Collections, Duke University.

115. Harris, "Education," 13–14.

116. Cates, "Medical History," 79, 101–102, 105, 108.

117. Victor H. Bassett, "Southern Medical Student," manuscript in Victor H. Bassett Papers, Georgia Historical Society, Savannah, Georgia.

118. Cates, "Medical History," 79, 101–102, 105, 108; Gurr, "Social Leadership," 69–70, 202–204; Bassett, "Plantation Medicine," 112–122; Bassett, "Early History," 343–349; City Council Minutes, August 26, 1805, June 24, 1807; Harris, "Education," 625–626.

119. Cates, "Medical History," 159–175.

120. Gurr, "Social Leadership," 92–93; Cates, "Medical History," 107; Gamble, *History,* 81.

121. Boles, "Henry Holcombe," 387–389.

122. Lockley, "Struggle for Survival," 28–29.

123. Harris, "Education," 271–272.

124. "27 Rules for the Government of the Asylum," Savannah Home for Girls [Female Asylum], vol. 1, Minutes of the Board, 1810–1843, manuscript, Georgia Historical Society; B. F. Bullard, "The Savannah Female Asylum," manuscript, Savannah Home for Girls, Georgia Historical Society; Lockley, "Struggle for Survival," 31.

125. Lockley, "Struggle for Survival," 29.

126. Ibid., 36.

127. City Council Minutes, June 29, 1818.

128. Gamble, *History,* 82–83, 146; "Minutes of the Inferior Court, Chatham County, 1801–1807," manuscript, Special Collections, University of Georgia.

129. City Council Minutes, October 4, 1802, November 14, 1803, February 6, 1804; Gamble, *History,* 76–77.

130. City Council Minutes, June 18, 1804, March 10, 1806.

131. Gamble, *History,* 68.

132. Byrne, "Burden and Heat," 246; Scarborough, *Opposition to Slavery,* 183–184; Aptheker, "Militant Abolitionism," 442–443.

133. Aptheker, "Militant Abolitionism," 443.

134. City Council Minutes, April 27, 1804.

135. City Council Minutes, June 18, 1804.

136. City Council Minutes, July 4, 1804; Gamble, *History,* 68.

137. City Council Minutes, December 6, 1804.

138. Ludlum, *Early American Hurricanes,* 53–54; Wade, "Artillerists and Engineers," 168–183.

139. Bell, "Isundiga," 11; Gamble, *History,* 83–84; Warlick, *Grain Once Scattered,* 118,181; Collins, "Episcopal Church," 3–4; Wilson, *Historic Savannah,* 108–109; Ludlum, *Early American Hurricanes,* 116–123.

140. Quoted in Lerski, *William Jay,* 41.

141. City Council Minutes, September 9, 1805, March 10, 1806.

142. City Council Minutes, December 14, 1807; Gamble, *History,* 66–68.

143. Chaplin, "Tidal Rice Cultivation," 57.

144. Scarborough, *Opposition to Slavery,* 176–177.

145. Berlin, *Slaves without Masters,* 93–94.

146. Wood, "Prisons, Workhouses," 259–260, 271 n. 48; City Council Minutes, October 7, 1805.

147. Gamble, *History,* 88.

148. Wood, "Prisons, Workhouses," 260–268; Wood, "Female Resistance," 618–622.

149. Wood, "Prisons, Workhouses," 267.

150. Egan, "Fracas in Savannah," 79–86; Gamble, *History,* 75–76, 94–95, 119; City Council Minutes, December 16, 1812.

151. Gamble, *History,* 68–69.

152. Harris, "Education," 456–458, 488–489.

153. Ibid., 463–470, 480–483, 492, 528.

154. Ibid., 536–537, 547, 550, 552, 566, 582, 569.

155. Ibid., 535.

156. Ibid., 535.

157. Thomas Telfair to "My Dear Brother," January 10, 1806, Telfair Family Papers, Duke University.

158. "Ice House," Wayne-Stites-Anderson Papers, Georgia Historical Society.

159. Bell, *Savannah, Ahoy!* 23–25; see also Coleman and Gurr, *Dictionary,* 2:868–869.

160. Harris, "Education," 14.

161. Lane, "Some Foods."

162. Harris, "Education," 333–334.

163. Talbott, *Classical Savannah,* 117–118, 122–123.

164. "Receipt for Arrearages due to the Anacreontic Society, 1805," Wayne-Stites-Anderson Papers, Georgia Historical Society; "Evening Club" Membership List, Habersham Family Papers, Duke University; W. C. Smith, "Georgia Gentlemen," 370; Greenberg, "Creating Ethnic," 86, 89–90, 162, 181, 245–246, 251–254, 258, 261.

165. "Description," Savannah Library Society Papers, Georgia Historical Society; Talbott, *Classical Savannah,* 44–45; Coleman, "Savannah," 323; Harris, "Education," 409–417, 446–447; Greenberg, "Creating Ethnic," 60, 243, 250.

166. Malcolm Maclean Young, "A Few Notes On An Old Minute Book" in Savannah History Research Association Papers, Georgia Historical Society; Harris, "Education," 47–48; Coleman, *History of Georgia,* 123; B. H. Flanders, *Early Georgia Magazines,* 13–14.

167. Harris, "Education," 237–238.

168. Ibid., 118, 122–125, 129–130, 141.

169. Ibid., 14, 247.

170. E. M. Green, "Theatre," 9–10, 37–39.

171. Harris, "Education," 182–183, 195–196; B. H. Flanders, *Early Georgia Magazines,* 6–7.

172. Lane, *Rambler in Georgia,* 46.

173. *Wesley Bi-Centenary Celebration in Savannah, Ga.,* 8–13.

174. Shoemaker, "Strangers and Citizens," 163–168, 175–176; Thigpen, "Aristocracy," 9–17, 37–38, 91–93, 570–572; Gamble, *History,* 84–86; Wilson, *Historic Savannah,* 117–118, 125; Harris, "Education," 235.

175. Thigpen, "Aristocracy," 127, 137, 142–146, 217, 241–243, 247, 251, 255, 418.

176. "Resolution," July 7, 1807, Edward Telfair Papers, Georgia Historical Society; Edward Telfair to General David B. Mitchell, August 16, 1807, Telfair Family Papers, William R. Perkins Library, Duke University; City Council Minutes, July 13, 16, 1807, January 12, 1808, September 24, 1812.

177. Harris, "Education," 749.

178. Talmadge, "Georgia's Federalist Press," 488–500; W. C. Smith, "Georgia Gentlemen," 379–381; Gamble, *Savannah Duels,* 84–88.

179. William B. Bulloch to Governor Davis B. Mitchell, December 6, 1813, Bulloch Family Papers, Southern Historical Collection, University of North Carolina; Rowland, "'Alone on the River,'" 122, 129, 150.

180. "Custom House Collectors Office [Ledger], 1812–1813," Georgia Department of Archives and History.

181. Gamble, *History,* 96–103, 118; Wade, "Artillerists and Engineers," 239, 275.

182. Gamble, *History,* 118; City Council Minutes, July 14, August 16, 1813.

183. Gamble, *History*, 102.

184. Mary Telfair to Mary Few, January [17], 1814, October 19, [1814], William Few Papers, Georgia Department of Archives and History.

185. Gamble, *History*, 103; City Council Minutes, May 14, 1814.

186. City Council Minutes, September 2, 5, 26, 1814.

187. Gamble, *History*, 105–110.

188. Mary Telfair to Mary Few, November 26, 1814, Georgia Historical Society.

189. Gamble, *History*, 105–110.

190. W. B. Bulloch to William Stephens, January 19, 1815, Bulloch Family Papers, University of North Carolina; Bell, *Major Butler's Legacy*, 170–172.

191. Governor Peter Early to Brigadier General John Floyd, January 19, 1815, Governor's Letterbooks, Georgia Department of Archives and History.

192. City Council Minutes, January 21, 1815.

193. Rowland, "'Alone on the River,'" 129.

194. City Council Minutes, February 28, 1815.

195. Gamble, *History*, 105–110; Wilson, *Historic Savannah*, 125.

CHAPTER 5. *From Boom to Bust, 1815–1840*

1. "Personal Reminiscences," vol. 1, William Starr Basinger Collection, University of Georgia.

2. Bryne, "Burden and Heat," 135–136; J. F. Smith, *Slavery and Rice Culture*, 133.

3. Lockley, "Struggle for Survival," 37.

4. December 9, 1816, November 3, December 1, 1817, December 8, 1818, in Savannah Free School Society, Minutes of the Board of Managers, vol. 1, 1816–1838, Georgia Historical Society.

5. Free School Society Minutes, vol. 1, January 14, 1822; Hartridge, "Architectural Trends," 324–330; Gamble, *History*, 86–87.

6. Lockley, "Struggle for Survival," 30–31.

7. Lockley, *Lines in the Sand*, 149.

8. A. S. Bulloch to [?] May 26, 1817, to William H. Crawford, June 1, 1820, January 27, March 21, 1821, A. S. Bullock Letterbook, 1817–1826, William R. Perkins Library, Duke University; *Georgia*, July 31, 1819.

9. Gamble, *History*, 146–149; City Council Minutes, February 7, 1816, January 22, 1817.

10. Gamble, *History*, 148–149; Ceryanec, *History of Candler General Hospital*, 7–8.

11. "Board of Health Minutes [Savannah]," Vol. 1, August 29, 1827, Georgia Historical Society.

12. Cates, "Medical History," 107–112; Gamble, *History*, 142–143; Goldfield, "Business of Health Planning," 561.

13. Gamble, *History*, 111–113, 123, 128–130.

14. Ibid., 86–87.

15. R. B. Flanders, "Free Negro," 261.

16. Wood, "'White Society,'" 316–317, 320; Byrne, "Burden and Heat," 124.

17. Byrne, "Burden and Heat," 125–126.

18. Wood, "'White Society,'" 320–323; Wood, *Women's Work*, 144–145.

19. Byrne, "Burden and Heat," 257–258; Gamble, *History*, 119.

20. Byrne, "Burden and Heat," 255–257, 264, Gamble, *History*, 119.

21. Savannah *Republican* as quoted in Byrne, "Burden and Heat," 257–258.

22. Warlick, *Grain Once Scattered*, 63.

23. Lockley, *Lines in the Sand*, 108.

24. Keith Read Collection, Box 22, Special Collections, University of Georgia.

25. Byrne, "Burden and Heat," 280.

26. Grimes, *Life of Grimes*, 35–37, 44, 50–52, 66–67.

27. Gamble, *History*, 65; Byrne, "Burden and Heat," 258–260, 280.

28. Rahn, *Savannah*, 19–20.

29. Ibid., 22, 31; Goff, "Steamboat Period," 238–243.

30. "Deeds" [1818], Telamon Cuyler Collection, University of Georgia; White, *Statistics*, 156.

31. J. K. Williams, "Travel in Ante-Bellum Georgia," 194–195.

32. Rahn, *Savannah*, 18–19, 41.

33. Gamble, *History*, 123, 128–130; Eisterhold, "Savannah," 526–527, 538–539; Lerski, *William Jay*, 46.

34. Quoted in Harden, *History of Savannah*, 344–345.

35. Mary Telfair to Mary Few, June 1, 1818, in Mary and Frances Few Papers, Georgia Historical Society.

36. E. M. Green, "Theatre," 26–28; Talbott, *Classical Savannah*, 50.

37. E. M. Green, "Theatre," 10, 29–30, 40–41, 47, 63, 67, 72–73, 82–84, 88–90, 97–99, 101.

38. R. C. Wade, *Slavery*, 267.

39. Dormon, *Theater*, 35–36.

40. E. M. Green, "Theatre," 78.

41. Talbott, *Classical Savannah*, 74–76.

42. Bell, "Ease and Elegance," 551–556, 576; Henderson, "Saint Andrew's Society," 10, 9–13; Talbott, *Classical Savannah*, 76; Lerski, *William Jay*, 162–165.

43. Talbott, *Classical Savannah*, 53–60; Lerski, *William Jay*, 56–78; Toledano, *Savannah*, 80–82.

44. Talbott, *Classical Savannah*, 65, 67; Lerski, *William Jay*, 83–88, 94–107.

45. Talbott, *Classical Savannah,* 70; Lerski, *William Jay,* 117–126.

46. Talbott, *Classical Savannah,* 50.

47. Quoted in ibid., 160.

48. Theus, *Savannah Furniture,* 38–39, 52–55, 64–69, 91; Talbott, *Classical Savannah,* 126.

49. Cutten, *Silversmiths of Georgia,* 68; J. A. Williams, "Savannah Silver," 347–349.

50. Cutten, *Silversmiths of Georgia,* 81, 68–119.

51. Ibid., 73, 88–89,98–100; Shryock, *Letters of Arnold,* 17 n. 2.

52. Cutten, *Silversmiths of Georgia,* 73.

53. Coulter, "Presidential Visits," 339–340.

54. Quoted in Lerski, *William Jay,* 89.

55. Gamble, *History,* 123, 128–130; Eisterhold, "Savannah," 539; Harden, *Savannah,* 472, C. C. Jones, *History of Savannah,* 468; Coulter, "Presidential Visits," 342–343; J. Caldwell Jenkins, "Steamship *Savannah,*" 212–216; Dailey, "Vessels," 146–148.

56. Cooper, *Liberty and Slavery,* 142–147.

57. City Council Minutes, December 8, 1806.

58. Byrne, "Burden and Heat," 257–258; Gamble, *History,* 119; Eisterhold, "Savannah," 538.

59. A. S. Bulloch to William H. Crawford, January 20, 1820, A. S. Bulloch Letterbook, 1817–1826, Special Collections, Duke University.

60. Quoted in Warlick, *Grain Once Scattered,* 59.

61. Coulter, "Great Savannah Fire," 1–27; Gamble, *History,* 114–116, 122–123; Eisterhold, "Savannah," 538.

62. Scarborough, *Opposition to Slavery,* 117; Byrne, "Burden and Heat," 261–263; Coulter, "Great Savannah Fire," 3–4; City Council Records, September 24, 1821.

63. Quoted in Coulter, "Great Savannah Fire," 6.

64. Morgan, "Judaism in Georgia," 51; Green, "Theatre," 10–14; Dormon, *Theater,* 137–138; Wilson, *Historic Savannah,* 137.

65. Cates, "Medical History," 80–83.

66. [W. B. Bulloch] to Dear General, September 30, 1820, Bulloch Papers, Southern Historical Collection, University of North Carolina.

67. Cates, "Medical History," 84–89; Coleman, "Savannah," 322; Gamble, *History,* 179; "Index to Registers of Death [in the city of Savannah], 1803–1853", 168, manuscript, Georgia Historical Society; "Resolution by the Mayor and Aldermen of the City of Savannah [1936], Victor H. Bassett Papers, Duke University.

68. J. I. Waring, "Yellow Fever," 398–404; Gamble, *History,* 114–115; Farley, "Mighty Monarch," 57–58.

69. May 26, June 2, 16, August 4, 1824; May 25, 1825; August 2, 1826; August 15, 1827; all Savannah Board of Health Minute Book, vol. 1, 1822–1827, manuscript, Georgia Historical Society.

70. Cates, "Medical History," 86–91, 114–116; Gamble, *History,* 144–146, 179; August 24, 1824; August 29, 1827; all Savannah Board of Health Minute Book, vol. 1, 1822–1827, manuscript, Georgia Historical Society; Thomas Shelman to Edwin Starr, September 26, 1829, Savannah Board of Health Minute Book, vol. 2, 1828–1834, manuscript, Georgia Historical Society; October 14, 1835, Savannah Board of Health Minute Book, vol. 3, 1834–1838, manuscript, Georgia Historical Society.

71. Quoted in Cates, "Medical History," 156.

72. Sweat, "Free Negro," 129; Hoskins, *Trouble They Seen,* 7, 20; Byrne, "Burden and Heat," 194–195.

73. Maguire, *Historical Souvenir,* 19–21; W. B. Johnson, *Black Savannah,* 137–138.

74. Lockley, *Lines in the Sand,* 39–40.

75. Gamble, *History,* 149–153.

76. Lerski, *William Jay,* 160.

77. Bell, *Savannah, Ahoy!* 54; Barton, "Savannah Parties," 17–19; C. C. Jones, *History of Savannah,* 469–470; Lerski, *William Jay,* 86–89; Hoffman, "Godfrey Barnsley," 74.

78. Lerski, *William Jay,* 59–62.

79. A. S. Bulloch Letterbook.

80. Quoted in Byrne, "Burden and Heat," 271.

81. Byrne, "Burden and Heat," 268; Lockley, "Strange Case," 230–253.

82. City Council Minutes, April 17, August 7, 1823.

83. City Council Minutes, May 27, June 2, 1831.

84. Gamble, *History,* 155–156.

85. City Council Minutes, July 23, 1835, August 20, 1838.

86. Lockley, *Lines in the Sand,* 126–128.

87. Samuel Howard to Governor John Clark, April 17, 24, 1821; C. C. Dunning to Governor John Clark, May 5, November 3, 1823, Telamon Cuyler Collection, University of Georgia.

88. Gamble, *History,* 141.

89. Rowland, "'Alone on the River,'" 131–138, 142, 145, 146; Rowland et al., *History of Beaufort County,* 313–321.

90. "Memorial of George Jones, and Others, Praying that No Addition May be Made to the Existing Tariff, March 3, 1824," Georgia Historical Society.

91. Gamble, *History,* 181.

92. Maryanne Stiles to [?], March 10, 1825, Maryanne Stiles Papers, Georgia

Historical Society; Gamble, *History,* 161–165; *Account of the Reception of General Lafayette,* 14–15.

93. Mary F. Kollock to P. M. Kollock, March 2, 1820, Mary Fenwick Kollock to P. M. Kollock, March 13, 1822, in Johnston, "Kollock Letters," 221, 227, 233.

94. Berry, "More Alluring," 866.

95. Maryanne Stiles to [?], March 10, 1825, Maryanne Stiles Papers.

96. M. M. Bulloch to W. B. Bulloch, December 2, 1826, Bulloch Family Papers, University of North Carolina Library, Chapel Hill; S. F. Jones to Mr. G. I. Kollock, February 10, 1830, Kollock Family Papers, Georgia Historical Society.

97. Mary F. Kollock to George J. Kollock, December 22, 1828, Harriett T. Campbell to Dr. Kollock, May 15, 1829, in Johnston, "Kollock Letters," 341–342, 349.

98. A[?] [Kollock?] to Susan M. Johnston, March 13, 1831, Kollock-Johnston Papers, Robert W. Woodruff Library, Emory University.

99. E.B.B. to Harriet Allen, February 2, 1831, Mrs. E. H. Allen Paper, Georgia Historical Society.

100. Rowland, "'Alone on the River,'" 142–146; W. B. Bulloch to My Dear Lou, July 29, 1837, Bulloch Papers, Southern Historical Collection.

101. Habersham to Kollock, July 27, 1832, in Johnston, "Kollock Letters," 121–122.

102. "Membership Card," Keith Read Collection, University of Georgia.

103. Quoted in E. M. Green, "Theatre," 14–15.

104. Quoted in ibid., 97.

105. Ibid., 54, 60.

106. Quoted in Dorman, *Theater,* 139–140.

107. Lane, *Rambler in Georgia,* 140.

108. Robert Habersham to George J. Kollock, July 27, 1832, in Johnston, "Kollock Letters," 141; Robert A. Lewis to Edward [Harden], October 18, 1831, Edward Harden Papers, Duke University.

109. Robert Habersham to George J. Kollock, July 27, 1832, in Johnston, "Kollock Letters," 141; Robert A. Lewis to Edward [Harden], October 18, 1831, Edward Harden Papers, Duke University.

110. Richard Dennis Arnold Diary (1832–1838), July 9, 26, December 7, 1832, September 13, 1838, Duke University.

111. Mary Telfair to Mary Few, February 5, 1833, William Few Papers, Georgia Department of Archives and History.

112. Arnold Diary (1832–1838), August 17, 1832.

113. Gurr, "Social Leadership," 113–127; Gibson, "Unitarian Congregations," 155.

114. Johnson, *Black Savannah,* 119–120, 135–136; J. F. Smith, *Slavery and Rice Culture,* 167–168.

115. Joseph W. Jackson to Sir, December 14, 1825, Letter Books, Mayor's Office, 1817–1851, vol. 1, Georgia Historical Society.

116. City Council Minutes, July 26, November 10, 1826.

117. F. M. Green, "Board of Public Works," 117–137.

118. Gamble, *History,* 167–168; Rowland, "'Alone on the River,'" 138.

119. *Savannah Morning News,* May 21, 1992; Gamble, *History,* 168–170; Lockley, *Lines in the Sand,* 36–38.

120. Gamble, *History,* 157–158; Rowland, "'Alone on the River,'" 132.

121. Gamble, *History,* 141; Rowland, "'Alone on the River,'" 139–140; Eisterhold, "Savannah," 527, 533; Gordon B. Smith, "Daniel Blake: Georgia's First Patron of the Arts," in Daniel Blake Papers, Georgia Historical Society.

122. Quoted in R. W. Young, "Fort Pulaski," 41–51; see also Granger, *Savannah Harbor,* 16–19.

123. Wood, "Informal Slave Economies," 318.

124. Sweat, "Free Negro," 200–201; Wood, "Prisons, Workhouses," 267; W. B. Johnson, "Free Blacks," 418–420; Byrne, "Burden and Heat," 202; R. C. Wade, *Slavery,* 40–41, 274.

125. V. Green, "Black Construction Artisans," 18–32.

126. Ibid., 29–37.

127. Byrne, "Burden and Heat," 201, 240.

128. Lane, *Neither More nor Less,* xxxii.

129. V. Green, "Black Construction Artisans," 46–47.

130. U.S. Bureau of the Census, *Second Census of the United States,* 80–81, *Sixth Census of the United States, 1840,* 232; W. B. Johnson, "Free African-American Women," 261.

131. Lane, *Rambler in Georgia,* 95.

132. W. B. Johnson, "Free African-American Women," 263–265; W. B. Johnson, *Black Savannah,* 58–60.

133. W. B. Johnson, "Free African-American Women," 267, 275–276; Schweninger, *Black Property Owners,* 69–70, 80.

134. W. B. Johnson, "Free Blacks," 423; W. B. Johnson, "Free African-American Women," 273–275; Frasier, "Free Negroes," 33.

135. W. B. Johnson, "Free African-American Women," 275; J. F. Smith, *Slavery and Rice Culture,* 195.

136. D. L. Grant, *Way It Was,* 69–70; W. B. Johnson, *Black Savannah,* 121–122; J. F. Waring, *Cerveau's Savannah,* 45; Lockley, *Lines in the Sand,* 49–50.

137. W. B. Johnson, "Free Blacks," 422–423; W. B. Johnson, *Black Savannah,* 65.

138. W. B. Johnson, "Free Blacks," 424; Yancey, "First African Baptist Church," 42–43.

139. Byrne, "Burden and Heat," 147–150, 153, 155; W. B. Johnson, *Black Savannah,* 141.

140. Byrne, "Burden and Heat," 151–152.

141. J. F. Smith, *Slavery and Rice Culture,* 154; Moore, "Activities of Mason," 5–6, 8, 26, 35–39.

142. J. F. Smith, *Slavery and Rice Culture,* 154–156; Byrne, "Burden and Heat," 159–160.

143. W. B. Johnson, "Free Blacks," 425; Byrne, "Burden and Heat," 160–162; W. B. Johnson, "Free African American Women," 277–278, 283; W. B. Johnson, *Black Savannah,* 126–129; Grant, *Way It Was,* 49–50, 62–63; J. F. Smith, *Slavery and Rice Culture,* 196.

144. Byrne, "Burden and Heat," 163–164.

145. Quoted in ibid., 166.

146. Quoted in ibid., 168.

147. Ibid., 169–175

148. Quoted in ibid., 178.

149. Sarah A. Gordon to William W. Gordon, November 18 [1836?], Gordon Family Papers, Georgia Historical Society.

150. Pope-Hennessy, *Aristocratic Journey,* 227–228.

151. Byrne, "Burden and Heat," 233– 239.

152. Ibid., 283–285.

153. Wood, "Informal Slave Economies," 322–326; Wood, *Women's Work,* 148–149.

154. Wood, *Women's Work,* 158–159; Lockley, "Trading Encounters," 43.

155. Wood, "Informal Slave Economies," 326; Wood, *Women's Work,* 159; Lockley, "Trading Encounters," 39–44.

156. Mary Telfair to Mary Few, March 5, 1829, Mary and Francis Few Papers, Georgia Historical Society.

157. City Council Minutes, April 23, 1829.

158. Mayor W. T. Williams to Mayor Harrison G. Otis, December 12, Governor George W. Gilmer, December 16, 1829, Mayor's Office Letter Books, vol. 1, 1817–1851, Georgia Historical Society.

159. Sweat, "Free Negro," 8, 98; Mayor J. W. Jackson to Justices of Inferior Courts of Chatham Co., November 3, 1826, [Mayor William T. Williams] to Governor Wilson Lumkin, December 7, 1833, in Mayor's Office Letter Books, vol. 1, 1817–1851, Georgia Historical Society; Rowland, "'Alone on the River,'" 144; Aptheker, "Militant Abolitionism," 446, Byrne, "Burden and Heat," 271; Bolster, *Black Jacks,* 198.

160. City Council Minutes, January 26, 1832.

161. Gamble, *History,* 154–155; C. C. Jones, *History of Savannah,* 347–348.

162. Gurr, "Social Leadership," 135–136; Thigpen, "Aristocracy," 586–587.

163. Thigpen, "Aristocracy," 588.

164. Ibid.; see also Robert A. Lewis to Edward [Harden], October 18, 1831, Edward Harden Papers, Duke University.

165. Rowland, "'Alone on the River,'" 139; Coleman, "Savannah," 322; Bell, "Ease and Elegance," 564; Rowland, *History of Beaufort County,* 321.

166. Quoted in Thigpen, "Aristocracy," 588.

167. Ibid., 589–590.

168. Gibson, "Unitarian Congregations," 155–158.

169. Shryock, *Letters of Arnold,* 17–18.

170. Gibson, "Unitarian Congregations," 159.

171. Bell, "Ease and Elegance," 557–560.

172. Quoted in Thigpen, "Aristocracy," 513–514.

173. Cory, "Temperance and Prohibition," 31–33; Greenberg, "Creating Ethnic," 256.

174. Bell, "Ease and Elegance," 560–566.

175. W. B. Bulloch to My Dear Lou, July 29, 1837, Bulloch Papers.

176. Gamble, *Savannah Duels,* 182, 302; for an extended discussion of honor, see Wyatt-Brown, *Southern Honor.*

177. J. F. Waring, *Cerveau's Savannah,* 12; Bell, "Ease and Elegance," 563–567, 570–571; Lane, *Rambler in Georgia,* 140.

178. Miss H[arriet] Campbell to My Dear George, September 16, 1832, Kollock Family Papers, Georgia Historical Society.

179. Cates, "Medical History," 133, 135, 138; J. F. Waring, *Cerveau's Savannah,* 23–24; Mayor George W. Owens to A. B. Fannin, Collector of the Port of Savannah, June 28, 1833, Mayor William T. Williams to Governor Wilson Lumpkin, July 18, 1833, Mayor Williams to "Sir," September 2, 1834, Mayor's Office, Letter Books, vol. 1, 1817–1851, manuscript, Georgia Historical Society.

180. Ceryanec, "History of Candler General Hospital," 9–10.

181. Gamble, *History,* 179–180.

182. Rahn, *Savannah,* 37–38; Fleetwood, *Tidecraft,* 93–94.

183. Rahn, *Savannah,* 37; Gamble, *History,* 158–160.

184. As quoted in J. F. Waring, *Cerveau's Savannah,* 22.

185. Phillips, *History of Transportation,* 253–254; Gamble, *History,* 172–177; M. Dixon, "Building the Central Railroad," 1–2; W. W. Gordon to A. Beale, Mayor of Macon, January 12, 1835, Mayor's Office Letter Books, vol. 1, 1817–1851, Georgia Historical Society.

186. Sarah Gordon to William W. Gordon, December 16, [1835], Gordon Family Papers, Georgia Historical Society.

187. Sarah Gordon to William W. Gordon, November 23, December 5, [1835], Gordon Family Papers, Georgia Historical Society.

188. Sarah Gordon to William W. Gordon, November 23, December 20, 1838, Gordon Family Papers, Georgia Historical Society.

189. Phillips, *History of Transportation,* 253–254.

190. William Scarbrough to Godfrey Barnsley, December 1, 1835, in Godfrey Barnsley Papers, University of Georgia; Goff, "Steamboat Period," 243–251; Coleman and Gurr, "Scarbrough," 870.

191. J. M. Dixon, "Central Railroad," 6, 9, 30, Gamble, *History,* 172–177; W. W. Gordon to Dr. A. Baker, June 9, 1835, Mayor's Office Letter Books, vol. 1, 1817–1851, Georgia Historical Society; J. F. Waring, *Cerveau's Savannah,* 50.

192. Cooper, *Liberty and Slavery,* 192–193; M. Dixon, "Building the Central Railroad," 12–14.

193. Shoemaker, "Strangers and Citizens", 16–18, 75, 244; Lockley, "Trading Encounters," 44.

194. Quoted in R. C. Wade, *Slavery,* 86, 87, 156.

195. Lockley, "Trading Encounters," 46.

196. Cooper, *Liberty and Slavery,* 192–193; M. Dixon, "Building the Central Railroad," 12–14.

197. Shoemaker, "Invasion of the Green," 1–7; Shoemaker, "Irish Immigrants," 4.

198. Weaver, "Foreigners," 8–9.

199. Godfrey Barnsley to John MacSellars, April 17, 1837, Godfrey Barnsley Papers, Emory University; William Scarbrough to G. Barnsley, August [?] 1837, Godfrey Barnsley Papers, Duke University.

200. Mary Telfair to Mary Few, June 1, 1837, Mary and Frances Few Papers, Georgia Historical Society.

201. Barnsley to MacSellars, April 17, 1837, Barnsley Papers, Emory University; Scarbrough to Barnsley, August [?], 1837, Barnsley Papers, Duke University.

202. Mayor John C. Nicoll to Dr. William Fraser [?], Mayor's Office Letter Books, 1817–1851.

203. William W. Gordon to Governor William Schley, January 21, 1836, Mayor's Office Letter Books, 1817–1851.

204. Mayor W. W. Gordon to Governor William Schley(?), January 27, 1836, Mayor's Office Letter Books,1817–1851.

205. Mary Telfair to Mary Few, January 30, 1836, Mary and Frances Few Papers, Georgia Historical Society.

206. [? to ?], letter fragment, written between April 1835 and August 1836, in Courtlandt Van Rensselaer Paper, Southern Historical Collection, University of North Carolina.

207. Bell, "Ease and Elegance," 567–569.

208. Quoted in Gurr, "Social Leadership," 132.

209. J. F. Waring, *Cerveau's Savannah;* Lane, *Rambler in Georgia,* 141.

210. City Council Minutes, August 20, 1835.

211. Frasier, "Free Negroes," 27.

212. Sweat, "Free Negro," 219; Frasier, "Free Negroes," 27.

213. City Council Minutes, April 4, 1839.

214. J. F. Waring, *Cerveau's Savannah,* 1–7.

215. Ibid., 1–7, 26.

216. Miss Henrietta [Maria Thomas] to Julia [Thomas], November 17, 1835, Henrietta Thomas Collection, Georgia Historical Society.

217. J. F. Waring, *Cerveau's Savannah,* 26–27.

218. Ibid., 21–22.

219. Ibid., 21–22, 25.

220. John R. Reiter, "The Germans in Savannah," manuscript, Georgia Historical Society.

221. Fleetwood, *Tidecraft,* 108–110.

222. M. Dixon, "Building the Central Railroad," 12–14; September 13, 1838, Arnold Diary; P. M. Kollock to George J. Kollock, October 14, 1839, in Johnston, "Kollock Letters," 218, 220.

223. Gurr, "Social Leadership," 54; Shryock, "Letters of Arnold", 20–21.

224. M. Dixon, "Building the Central Railroad," 12–14.

225. *Savannah Morning News,* May 21, 1992; Rahn, *Savannah,* 36; Shoemaker, "Strangers and Citizens," 247–250.

226. James Louis Rossignol to John R. Williams, September 3, 1839, Georgia Historical Society.

227. Quoted in Gamble, *History,* 177.

228. Quoted in Lerski, *William Jay,* 50.

229. Quoted in Thigpen, "Aristocracy," 454.

230. Quoted in Shoemaker, "Invasion of the Green," 1.

231. U.S. Bureau of the Census, *Slave Schedule of Savannah* (1830, 1840).

232. R. C. Wade, *Slavery,* 20, 58, 76.

CHAPTER 6. *Prosperity to Civil War, 1840–1865*

1. Charles Greene to Godfrey Barnsley, November 9, 1841, Godfrey Barnsley Papers, University of Georgia; W. Thorne Williams to Senator J. M. Berrian, March 17, 1842, Richard D. Arnold to Hon. John C. Spencer, Secretary of the Treasury, May 11, 1843, and to the Commissioners of Pilotage, June 12, 1843, Mayor's Letter Books, vol. 1, 1817–1851, Georgia Historical Society.

2. M. Dixon, "Building the Central Railroad," 12–16, 21.

3. City Council Minutes, November 18, 1841, February 10, 1842, August 25, 1842, Georgia Historical Society.

4. Griffin, "Savannah's City Income Tax," 173–176; Richard D. Arnold to President of Planters Bank of Georgia and Marine and Fire Insurance Bank of Georgia, January 11, July [?] 1843, Richard D. Arnold to Alfonson M. Horton, January 20, 1843, Mayor's Letter Books; *Facts and Figures,* 4–6.

5. Hoffman, "Godfrey Barnsley," 166, 168–169; John Day to Godfrey Barnsley, January 23, 1846, William Duncan to Godfrey Barnsley, September 6, 1846, Barnsley Papers, Duke University; Gamble, *History,* 193–194.

6. Phillips, *History of Transportation,* 252, 291; Black, "Railroads of Georgia," 513; Haunton, "Savannah in the 1850s," 163, 158–174.

7. *Savannah Daily Morning News,* March 14, 1857, as quoted in Haunton, "Savannah in the 1850s," 162.

8. Haunton, "Savannah in the 1850s," 8–9, 140, 155–158; Phillips, *History of Transportation,* 264.

9. J. M. Dixon, "Central Railroad," 156–157.

10. Griffin, "Savannah during the Civil War," 39; Haunton, "Savannah in the 1850s," 174–176; D. H. Stewart, "Survival," 42 n. 3.

11. Stewart, "Survival," 41–42.

12. Lee Adler, "Right Way."

13. *Savannah Daily Morning News,* July 17, 1855, as quoted in Lee Adler, "Right Way."

14. Lee Adler, "Right Way"; Honerkamp et al., *Reality,* 27; Parsons, *Inside View,* 23.

15. Charles Hardee as quoted in Griffin, "Savannah during the Civil War," 24–25.

16. Quoted in Haunton, "Savannah in the 1850s," 9; see also Honerkamp, *Reality,* 27–28.

17. Pearson, "Captain Charles Stevens," 485–504; Haunton, "Savannah in the 1850s," 129–135.

18. Granger, *Savannah Harbor,* 20–34; "Speech of Congressman William Henry Stiles, 1855," Stiles Collection, Special Collections, Emory University; Haunton, "Savannah in the 1850s," 183–186.

19. Haunton, "Savannah in the 1850s," 144–154; Ayers, *Vengeance and Justice,* 77; M. Hunt, "Savannah's Longshoremen," 6; Eisterhold, "Savannah," 539–540.

20. Haunton, "Savannah in the 1850s," 132.

21. Will [W. W. Gordon] to [Nellie], January 28, 1855, Gordon Papers, Southern Historical Collection, University of North Carolina; M. D. Robertson, "Northern Rebel," 477–479.

22. Haunton, "Savannah in the 1850s," 132–133.

23. Eisterhold, "Savannah," 531.

24. J. Bancroft, *Census of Savannah,* 35; Haunton, "Savannah in the 1850s," 131–133.

25. Eisterhold, "Savannah," 525, 532–533.

26. D. S. Johnson, "William Harris Garland," 41–48.

27. Eisterhold, "Savannah," 533–534.

28. Haunton, "Savannah in the 1850s," 133.

29. Ibid., 129–131, 134–136.

30. Toledano, *Savannah,* 63–65; Hunter, "Bay," 332; Haunton, "Savannah in the 1850s," 97; Hartridge, "Architectural Trends," 327.

31. Ayers, *Vengeance and Justice,* 77; M. Hunt, "Savannah's Longshoremen," 4.

32. Quoted in Haunton, "Savannah in the 1850s," 139.

33. W. W. Gordon to [Nellie] March 25, 1855, Gordon Papers, University of North Carolina.

34. William W. Gordon as quoted in Haunton, "Savannah in the 1850s," 98.

35. Ibid., 100–102, 120–121 n. 105; M. Hunt, "Savannah's Longshoremen," 14; Parsons, *Inside View,* 24.

36. Bancroft, *Census of Savannah,* 24–30; Griffin, "Savannah during the Civil War," 33, 35; Haunton, "Savannah in the 1850s," 121–124, 137–138, 177 n. 81, 178–179.

37. Eisterhold, "Savannah," 526; Honerkamp et al., *Reality,* 26–27; Haunton, "Savannah in the 1850s," 22–23.

38. Rousey, "From Whence They Came," 327; Haunton, "Savannah in the 1850s," 11–18; Byrne, "Burden and Heat," 203–204; Weaver, "Foreigners," 1–2.

39. Rousey, "From Whence They Came," 310–311, 316–319, 323–327.

40. Ibid., 332–336; Haunton, "Savannah in the 1850s," 371–372; Weaver, "Foreigners," 5; Mildred Gartelmann, "A Compiled Chronological History of the Evangelical Lutheran Church of the Ascension, Savannah, Georgia," 64 pages, manuscript, Savannah Public Library, Savannah, Georgia.

41. Toledano, *Savannah,* 82, 123, 145–147; Haunton, "Savannah in the 1850s," 18–26; 28–31; Hartridge, "Architectural Trends," 328.

42. Hartridge, *Green-Meldrim House;* Hartridge, "Andrew Low's House," 350–351; Toledano, *Savannah,* 34, 65–66, 144; Leopold Adler, *Historic Savannah,* 28, 187.

43. Burke, *Pleasure and Pain,* 7; Eleanor J. W. Baker, Journal, February 2, 1848, Eleanor J. W. Baker Papers, Duke University; *Ballou's Pictorial Drawing Room Companion,* 13 (September 5, 1857), n/p, Gamble Collection, Savannah Public Library; Haunton, "Savannah in the 1850s," 26–27.

44. Weaver, "Foreigners," 2; Haunton, "Savannah in the 1850s," 31–33, 283–284.

45. Parsons, *Inside View,* 23.

46. Haunton, "Savannah in the 1850s," 346–347, 352, 355, 360–363; U.S. Bureau of the Census, *Eighth Census;* Myers, *Children of Pride,* 1701.

47. Haunton, "Savannah in the 1850s," 325, 338.

48. Quoted in ibid., 34.

49. Ayers, *Vengeance and Justice,* 78–79; Haunton, "Savannah in the 1850s," 34–48.

50. Greenberg, "Becoming Southern," 55–75; Greenberg, "Savannah's Jewish Women," 752–755.

51. Reverend C. C. Jones to Charles C. Jones Jr., September 24, 1859, in Myers, *Children of Pride,* 519.

52. Lane, "Some Foods."

53. Alexander R. Lawton to "My Dear Cousin," October 2, 1845, Alexander R. Lawton Papers, University of North Carolina; Myers, *Children of Pride,* 1591.

54. H[enrietta] J. Wayne to "My Dear Sister" [Mary Harden], January 11, 1841, April 26, 1844, Edward Harden Papers, Duke University.

55. Bragg, *De Renne,* 10, 447; Myers, *Children of Pride,* 1591; H[enrietta] J. Wayne to "My Dear Sister" [Mary Harden], February 2, 1844, October 28, 1844, Edward Harden Papers, Duke University.

56. H[enrietta] J. Wayne to "My Dear Sister," July 3, 1849, Harden Papers; Myers, *Children of Pride,* 1672–1673.

57. Will [W. W. Gordon] to [Nellie Kinzie], December 26, 1854, Gordon Papers, University of North Carolina; for the reasons cousins married cousins in the South, see J. E. Cashin, "Antebellum Planter Families," 55–70.

58. Henrietta J. Wayne to "My Dear Mother," February 4, 1850, Harden Papers; Sarah A. Gordon to [My Dear Son], February 3, 1854, Gordon Papers, University of North Carolina.

59. William Duncan to Godfrey Barnsley, October 24, November 24, 1855, Julia Barnsley to [Godfrey Barnsley], February 4, 1856, Adelaide Barnsley to "My Dear Father," February 21, 1856, Godfrey Barnsley Papers, University of Georgia.

60. William Duncan to Godfrey Barnsley, February 5, 1856; George Barnsley to Godfrey Barnsley, January 9, 1856, Barnsley Papers, University of Georgia.

61. [William W. Gordon] to [Nellie Kinzie], December 22, December 26, 1854, Gordon Papers, University of North Carolina.

62. George Barnsley to Godfrey Barnsley, January 9, 1856, Barnsley Papers, University of Georgia; Entry of November 25, 1851, Henry Cathell Diary, 1851–1852, 1856, University of North Carolina; George E. Smith to "Dear Cousin" [Marian Baber], December 8, 1853, William J. Blackshear Papers, Duke University.

63. Henrietta J. Wayne to "My Dear Sister," April 26, 1844, Harden Papers;

E. J. C. Wood to N. S. Tyler, April 27, 1847, N. S. Tyler Papers, Georgia Historical Society.

64. G. Robertson, *Savannah Volunteer Guards*, 1–30.

65. [William W. Gordon] to [Nellie], February 20, 1855, Gordon Papers, University of North Carolina.

66. H[enrietta] J. Wayne to "My Dear Sister," May 7, 1854, Harden Papers.

67. H[enrietta] J. Wayne to "My Dear Sister," July 3, 1849, Harden Papers.

68. H[enrietta] J. Wayne to "My Dear Mama H.," December 3, 1860, Harden Papers.

69. Bragg, *De Renne,* 85–86; Will [William W. Gordon] to Nellie, July 31, 1855, Sarah A. Gordon to [My Dear Son], September 24, [1855], Gordon Papers, University of North Carolina.

70. Hawes, "Memoirs of Olmstead," *Georgia Historical Quarterly,* 43 (June 1959): 173.

71. Quoted in Haunton, "Savannah in the 1850s," 47–48.

72. Bragg, *De Renne,* 10–58.

73. [William W. Gordon] to [Nellie Kinzie], January 21, 1855, Will [Gordon] to [?], February 17, 1855 Gordon Papers, University of North Carolina.

74. E. M. Green, "Theatre," 17–21, 32–34, 43–44, 78–79; Dormon, *Theater,* 168–169 n. 73; William W. Gordon as quoted in Haunton, "Savannah in the 1850s," 357, 359.

75. Adelaide Barnsley to "My Dear Father," April 5, 1856, Barnsley Papers.

76. C. C. Jones, *History of Savannah,* 567–568; George Anderson Mercer Diary, [?] 1858, December 3, 1859, University of North Carolina.

77. G. Robertson, *Savannah Volunteer Guards,* 12–15, 27; Hartridge, *Green-Meldrim House;* Myers, *Children of Pride,* 1568, 1672–1673, 1713–1714; C. C. Jones, *History of Savannah,* 585–586.

78. Hawes, "Memoirs of Olmstead," *Georgia Historical Quarterly,* 43 (March 1959) 60–74; 43 (June 1959): 181–182; 43 (September 1959): 263; 43 (December 1959): 379.

79. H[enrietta] J. Wayne to "My Dear Sister," March 9, 1843, October 28, 18[44], Harden Papers.

80. Edward Harden to "My Dear Daughter," November 20, 1844, Harden Papers.

81. [Godfrey Barnsley] to "My Dear George," February 26, 1854, Barnsley Papers.

82. Bragg, *De Renne,* 17–21, 33–35.

83. Willie [William Gordon] to [Nellie Kinzie], December 26, 1854, Gordon Papers, University of North Carolina.

84. Notation of W[illiam] H[arden] to Mr. Rutherford [n/d] on letter of

Henrietta Wayne to "My Dear Sister," January 13, 1850, Harden Papers, Duke University.

85. Bragg, *De Renne,* 49–55, 61.

86. *Georgia Historical Society Addresses* (n/p, n/d bound gift of Charles C. Jones Jr.), University of Georgia Library; see also O'Brien, *All Clever Men.*

87. Quoted in Hartridge, "Andrew Low's House," 352; Hartridge, "*Green-Meldrim House.*

88. V. Green, "Black Construction Artisans," 31–32, 61, 65, 84; Haunton, "Savannah in the 1850s," 49–53, 56 n. 54; Bureau of the Census, *Seventh Census, 1850,* and *Eighth Census, 1860.*

89. Pearson, "Captain Charles Stevens," 498–503; D. S. Johnson, "William Harris Garland," 48–49; Gillespie, *Free Labor,* 163.

90. Gillespie, *Free Labor,* 162–164, 167; V. Green, "Black Construction Artisans," 60.

91. Haunton, "Savannah in the 1850s," 53–55; Byrne, "Burden and Heat," 203–204; Gillespie, *Free Labor,* 57, 167–171.

92. Haunton, "Savannah in the 1850s," 333–339, 342–350; City Council Minutes, July 22, 1852, January 1, 1853; Gamble, *History,* 230–231.

93. Charlotte Branch to "My Dearly Beloved Son," January 8, 1851, Branch Family Papers, University of Georgia; Joslyn, *Charlotte's Boys,* xiv–xvii.

94. Haunton, "Savannah in the 1850s," 359, 364–365; William Foster Parker Diary, 1859–1860, February 13, July 4, August 21, September 23, October 1, December 25, 1859, University of Georgia.

95. Haunton, "Savannah in the 1850s," 56–59; Lockley, *Lines in the Sand,* 28.

96. Quoted in Haunton, "Savannah in the 1850s," 22, 31; Parsons, *Inside View,* 23.

97. Bancroft, *Census of Savannah,* 20; Haunton, "Savannah in the 1850s," 58–59.

98. Bellows, "Tempering the Wind, 14, 29–30, 38–41, 252; J. R. Young, *Domesticating Slavery,* 183, 186–187, 192.

99. Burke, *Pleasure and Pain,* 25.

100. Murray, "Charity," 68–69.

101. Savannah Board of Health Minute Book, vol. 4, 1850–1855, Georgia Historical Society, Savannah, August 7, September 25, October 30, 1850; July 23, September 24, October 8, December 3, 1851; August 4, September 8, April 27, 1853; April 26, 1854.

102. Bellows, "Tempering the Wind," 5, 17, 93, 96–97, 111–112, 122–127,192–193, 220–226, 250–252; Lee and Agnew, *Historical Record,* 163; Ayers, *Vengeance and Justice,* 82; J. R. Young, *Domesticating Slavery,* 186–187; Gamble, *History,* 235.

103. Bellows, "Tempering the Wind," 205; Lee and Agnew, *Historical Record,* 163–164.

104. Bellows, "Tempering the Wind," 85–87; Minutes of the Board of Man-

agers, 1843–1873, Savannah Port Society Papers, Georgia Historical Society, Savannah; *Savannah News Press,* November 20, 1993.

105. M. M. Wilman to William Duncan, September 19, 1860, William Duncan Papers, Georgia Historical Society; Bellows, "Tempering the Wind," 152–153.

106. Haunton, "Savannah in the 1850s," 60–63; Byrne, "Burden and Heat," 193.

107. Gillespie, *Free Labor,* 165; V. Green, "Black Construction Artisans," 62.

108. Hoskins, *Trouble They Seen,* 9; W. B. Johnson, *Black Savannah,* 60–62, 65, 67–68; Sweat, "Social Status," 30.

109. W. B. Johnson, *Black Savannah,* 68–69, 73–76, 78; Sweat, "Free Negro," 157, 159; Haunton, "Savannah in the 1850s," 63.

110. Haunton, "Savannah in the 1850s," 63–72; Byrne, "Burden and Heat," 126; Burke, *Pleasure and Pain,* 24.

111. [W. W. Gordon] to [Nellie Kinzie], December 22, 26, 1854, Gordon Papers, University of North Carolina; Byrne, "Burden and Heat," 211–212; Burke, *Pleasure and Pain,* 25.

112. Philo Tower as quoted in Lane, *Neither More nor Less,* 174.

113. [William W. Gordon] to [Nellie Kinzie], December 26, 1854, Gordon Papers, University of North Carolina; Haunton, "Savannah in the 1850s," 370; City Council Minutes, August 3, 1855; A. J. Kollock to "My Dear Brother," January 22, 1861, Kollock-Johnston Papers, Emory University.

114. Byrne, "Burden and Heat," 195–196; Sweat, "Free Negro," 220.

115. Byrne, "Burden and Heat," 128–129, 184–186; Haunton, "Savannah in the 1850s," 78–79; W. B. Johnson, *Black Savannah,* 96–97.

116. Byrne, "Burden and Heat," 111, 184–185, 188–190, 192; W. B. Johnson, *Black Savannah,* 99–103; Haunton, "Savannah in the 1850s," 78–79 n. 142.

117. W. B. Johnson, *Black Savannah,* 101, 105–106.

118. J. Couper Fraser to "Mother [Mrs. John Fraser]," June 14, 1852, Fraser-Couper Papers, Georgia Historical Society.

119. Byrne, "Burden and Heat," 110–120, 200–202; Haunton, "Savannah in the 1850s," 76–78.

120. Bell, *Major Butler's Legacy,* 548; Sweat, "Social Status," 30; Lockley, "Crossing the Race Divide," 163.

121. Ayers, *Vengeance and Justice,* 79; W. B. Johnson, *Black Savannah,* 49; Lockley, "Crossing the Race Divide," 166–170.

122. Gillespie, *Free Labor,* 165–166; Lockley, "Crossing the Race Divide," 164.

123. Haunton, "Savannah in the 1850s," 55; Bellows, "Tempering the Wind," 193–198.

124. Haunton, "Savannah in the 1850s," 201–210, 216–222, 228, 234–238; Lee and Agnew, *Historical Record,* 145; Goldfield, "Business of Health Planning," 557. Goldfield uses the term "interlocking directorate," by which he means those

prominent citizens linked by religious, social, economic, and political ties who promoted the city's development.

125. C. C. Jones, *Report of Jones,* 14, 20; Mayor Jones as quoted in Gamble, *History,* 243.

126. Gamble, *History,* 214, 240; Lee and Agnew, *Historical Record,* 74; City Council Minutes, January 15, 1852; Anderson, *Report of Anderson,* 6.

127. Eisterhold, "Savannah," 537; J. Couper Fraser to "Mother" [Mrs. John Fraser], June 14, 1852, Fraser-Couper Papers.

128. Maguire, *Historical Souvenir,* 22–26; Farley, "John Elliott Ward," 72; Gamble, *History,* 236–238.

129. Cates, "Medical History," 203; Haunton, "Savannah in the 1850s," 281–287.

130. City Council Minutes, June 16, 1850.

131. Gamble, *History,* 205–207.

132. Savannah Board of Health Minute Book, vol. 4, May 22, June 5, October 23, 1850; July 23, 1851; July 28, 1852; April 27, July 13, August 3, October 5, 1853; July 19, October 4, 1854.

133. City Council Minutes, August 28, 1851; Farley, "John Elliott Ward," 70; Anderson, *Report of Anderson,* 4.

134. City Council Minutes, January 15, 1852; Gamble, *History,* 216–217; Farley, "John Elliott Ward," 71.

135. Honerkamp et al., *Reality,* 28; Goldfield, "Business of Health Planning," 561–562.

136. Cates, "Medical Schools," 49–57.

137. Elliott, *Address,* 11–12.

138. Cates, "Medical Schools," 58–62; Quattlebaum, "Medicine in Early Georgia," 832.

139. W. W. Gordon to [Nellie], June 9, 1855, Gordon Papers; William Duncan to Godfrey Barnsley, September 19, 1843, Barnsley Papers, University of Georgia; [Mrs. Alexander R. Lawton] to "My Dear Children," August 7, 1853, Alexander R. Lawton Papers, University of North Carolina.

140. Minutes of the Board of Health, vol. 4, August 9, 10, 1854.

141. Farley, "Mighty Monarch," 58.

142. P. M. Kollock to George [Kollock], August 14, 1854, Kollock Family Papers, Georgia Historical Society, Savannah; George A. Gordon to William W. Gordon, August 22, 1854, Gordon Papers, University of North Carolina; Edmond [Hacker?] to Francis B. Hacker, August 29, 1854, "Letter—Yellow Fever," University of Georgia.

143. [John Screven], *Savannah Benevolent Association* (Savannah: Morning News Print, 1896), 5–25; Gamble, *History,* 232–233; Farley, "Mighty Monarch," 59–60; Farley, "John Elliott Ward," 68–77.

144. E. H. Campbell to George [Kollock], October 1, 1854, Kollock Family Papers; Gamble, *History*, 232; Hawes, "Memoirs of Olmstead," *Georgia Historical Quarterly*, 43 (September 1959): 269.

145. [Screven], *Savannah Benevolent Association*, 6, 8–12; Bellows, "Tempering the Wind," 178–179.

146. Ward, *Report of Ward*, 11–12; Farley, "John Elliott Ward," 72–75; Gamble, *History*, 233–236; Board of Health Minute Book, vol. 4, August 26, 1854, April 4, 1855; H. Campbell to George [Kollock], October 5, 1858, Kollock Family Papers, Georgia Historical Society, Savannah.

147. W. B. Johnson, *Black Savannah*, 150–153; Byrne, "Burden and Heat," 283–286; City Council Minutes, June 26, 1856.

148. Haunton, "Law and Order," 3–6; Haunton, "Savannah in the 1850s," 365–366; John Stoddard to Thos. M. Turner, January 8, 1859, in Copy and Day book, John F. Hamilton Papers, Duke University.

149. Richard D. Arnold to Col. John W. Forney, December 18, 1850, in Shryock, *Letters of Arnold*, 44–45.

150. Byrne, "Burden and Heat," 253–254; Charles C. Jones Jr. to "My Dear Father," October 1, 1856, Charles C. Jones Papers, University of Georgia.

151. W. B. Johnson, *Black Savannah*, 92–93; Byrne, "Burden and Heat," 253, 279–280.

152. Burke, *Pleasure and Pain*, 17; Ayers, *Vengeance and Justice*, 79, 81.

153. W. B. Johnson, *Black Savannah*, 49–50; Byrne, "Burden and Heat," 257–261; Lockley, "Crossing the Race Divide," 170; Lockley, "Trading Encounters," 46–47.

154. W. B. Johnson, *Black Savannah*, 49; Ayers, *Vengeance and Justice*, 73–75, 79–81.

155. Charles F. Hamilton to [Isabella C. Hamilton], June 19, 1859, Isabella C. Hamilton Papers, Georgia Historical Society, Savannah.

156. Ayers, *Vengeance and Justice*, 82–84, 302–303 n. 28; Bell, *Major Butler's Legacy*, 510–511; Myers, *Children of Pride*, 1475; City Council Minutes, January 15, December 2, 1852; R. H. Haunton, "Law and Order," 2, 8–9, 13, 15.

157. William W. Gordon to [Nellie], June 9, 1855, Gordon Papers; Haunton, "Law and Order," 2–3.

158. Ayers, *Vengeance and Justice*, 84–90; Haunton, "Law and Order," 13–15; Lockley, "Trading Encounters," 47–48; Myers, *Children of Pride*, 1452.

159. Will [Gordon] to [?], February 17, 1855, Gordon Papers; Ayers, *Vengeance and Justice*, 99–100.

160. Ayers, *Vengeance and Justice*, 93–105; Haunton, "Law and Order," 10–11, 18; Charles L. A. Lamar to "My Dearest Caro," January 10, 1858, to James Gardner, January 18, 1858, James Gardner Papers, Georgia Department of Archives and His-

tory; T. H. Wells, "Charles Augustus Lafayette Lamar," 162; McWhiney, "Ethnic Roots," 115–116 and n. 7; Arnold, *Report of Arnold*, 33.

161. Haunton, "Savannah in the 1850s," 73–76; Byrne, "Burden and Heat," 228–230; Myers, *Children of Pride*, 1475; Bell, *Major Butler's Legacy*, 511; William Foster Parker Diary, July 2, September 13, 26, October 20, 24, November 4, 1859, University of North Carolina; N. C. Trowbridge to [James] Gardner, February 20, 1857, James Gardner Papers.

162. Byrne, "Burden and Heat," 233; W. B. Johnson, *Black Savannah*, 88; Bell, *Major Butler's Legacy*, 511.

163. Bell, *Major Butler's Legacy*, 312, 327–340, 511, 546–547.

164. Ibid., 323–324, 340, 352–353, 548–549; Myers, *Children of Pride*, 1588.

165. Bell, *Major Butler's Legacy*, 548; Charles C. Jones Jr. to Rev. and Mrs. C. C. Jones, January 3, 1859 in Myers, *Children of Pride*, 469–470; Wells, "Charles Augustus Lafayette Lamar," 158–164; F. Bancroft, *Slave Trading*, 222–236.

166. Mrs. Eleanor J. W. Baker Diary, February 17, 1848, Eleanor J. W. Baker Papers, Duke University; Lane, *Rambler in Georgia*, 179–181; Charles C. Jones Jr. to "My Dear Father and Mother," October 8, 1856, Charles C. Jones Papers, University of Georgia; Sarah A. Gordon to [William W. Gordon], August 31 [1857], Gordon Family Papers, Georgia Historical Society, Savannah.

167. Gibson, "Unitarian Congregations," 164–166; George Anderson Mercer Diary, December 2, 1858, University of North Carolina; Byrne, "Burden and Heat," 296; Richard D. Arnold to John Stoddard, July [?], 1858 in Shryock, *Letters of Arnold*, 91 n. 2 and 6.

168. Mohr, *Threshold of Freedom*, 3–6.

169. Mercer Diary, October [18?], November 5, December 6, 15, 1859; Parker Diary, December 2, 1859; Sarah Lawton to Brig.-Gen. Henry R. Jackson, September 9, 1861, Sarah A. Lawton Letter, Georgia Department of Archives and History, Atlanta.

170. Mohr, *Threshold of Freedom*, 7–10, 26–27, 34, 37–38, 40.

171. Lawrence, *Present for Mr. Lincoln*, 3; Byrne, "Burden and Heat," 297; Richard D. Arnold to Wm. C. Lowber, December 7, 1860, in Shryock, *Letters of Arnold*, 98 n. 1; Mohr, *Threshold of Freedom*, 43, 46, 48; Charles C. Jones Jr. to Mrs. Mary Jones, October 27, 1860 in Myers, *Children of Pride*, 623–624.

172. Charles C. Jones Jr. to Rev. and Mrs. C. C. Jones, November 7, 1860, in Myers, *Children of Pride*; Lawrence, *Present for Mr. Lincoln*, 5–6; Bailey and Fraser, *Portraits of Conflict*, 28; Henrietta Wayne to "My Dear Mama," December 3, 1860, Harden Papers; Lawrence, *Present for Mr. Lincoln*, 9; Bryan, "Churches of Georgia," 284–287.

173. Henrietta Wayne to "My Dear Mama," December 3, 1860, Harden Papers; Byrne, "Burden and Heat," 296; Richard D. Arnold to Wm C. Lowber, December 7, 1860, in Shryock, *Letters of Arnold*, 98–99; Edward Harden to "My Dear

Mother," April 21, 1861, Harden Papers, Duke University; W. W. Gordon to "My Dear Nellie," June 25, 1861, Gordon Papers, University of North Carolina.

174. [Sarah Lawton] to "My Dear Friend," December 30, 1860, Alexander R. Lawton Papers, University of North Carolina.

175. Bailey and Fraser, *Portraits of Conflict*, 30; Lawrence, *Present for Mr. Lincoln*, 8, 10; Richard D. Arnold to James J. Waring, December 28, 1860 in Shryock, *Letters of Arnold*, 99–100; Mrs. S. M. Kollock to "My Dear Son," January 6, 1861, Kollock Papers, Georgia Historical Society, Savannah; Bureau of the Census, *Eighth Census*, 1860.

176. Quoted in Lane, *Times That Prove*, 18; Bryan, *Confederate Georgia*, 1–6, 70.

177. Bailey and Fraser, *Portraits of Conflict*, 30–32; F. N. Boney, "War and Defeat," in Coleman, *History of Georgia*, 187–189, 194–192; Thomas, *Confederate Nation*, 53–54; Bryan, *Confederate Georgia*, 7–9, 18–21, 28; Alexander H. Stephens as quoted in Boney, *Rebel Georgia*, 20.

178. Mohr, *Threshold of Freedom*, 53–55.

179. George A. Mercer as quoted in Lane, *Times That Prove*, 17–18.

180. Fornell, "Civil War," 245–254; Myers, *Children of Pride*, 1697–1698; William Duncan to Godfrey Barnsley, May 21, 1861, Barnsley Papers, Emory University; May 9, May 28, July 11, 19, 1861, in Savannah Cadets Minute Book, 1861–1873, Georgia Historical Society, Savannah.

181. George A. Mercer and William Howard Russell as quoted in Lane, *Times That Prove*, 17–18, 35, 36; C. C. Jones, *Report of Jones*, 3; Thomas Purse, *Report of Purse*, 3; Sarah [Lawton] to "My Dear Father," April 19, 1861, Lawton Papers, University of North Carolina; Henrietta J. Wayne to "My Dear Mama," May 6, 1861, Harden Papers, Duke University; [Sarah Lawton] to "Dear Sister," September 18, 1861, Alexander R. Lawton Papers, Duke University.

182. Mohr, *Threshold of Freedom*, 65–67, 84, 289–291; Byrne, "Burden and Heat," 300–302; W. B. Johnson, *Black Savannah*, 155–166.

183. Henrietta Wayne to "My Dear Mama," May 6, 1861, Harden Papers, Duke University; W. W. Gordon to "My Dear Nellie," June 25, 1861, Gordon Papers, University of North Carolina; William Duncan, as quoted in Byrne, "Hiring of Woodson," 260–261.

184. Henrietta Wayne to "My Dear Mama," July 15, 1861, Harden Papers, Duke University; Boney, *Rebel Georgia*, 25–27; Bailey and Fraser, *Portraits of Conflict*, 76, 220, 353; Longacre, "Three Brothers," 156–168; George Barnsley to "Dear Father," July 24, 1861, Barnsley Papers, Emory University.

185. William Duncan to Godfrey Barnsley, July 23, 1861, Barnsley Papers, Emory University; Savannah Cadet Minute Book, July 28, 1861, February 3, 1862.

186. Bailey and Fraser, *Portraits of Conflict*, 278; DeCredico, *Patriotism for Profit*, 39; DeCredico, "'War Is Good Business,'" 231–249; Mercer Diary, March 27, 1862.

187. William Duncan to Godfrey Barnsley, May 22, May 27, May 31, September 18, October 30, 1861, Barnsley Papers, Emory University; George A. Mercer as quoted in Lane, *Times That Prove,* 68–69.

188. Sarah A. Lawton to Brig.-Gen. Henry R. Jackson, September 9, 1861, Sarah A. Lawton Letter, Georgia Department of Archives and History, Atlanta.

189. Henrietta Wayne to "My Dear Mama," October 14, 1861, Harden Papers, Duke; William Duncan to Godfrey Barnsley, November 2, 4, 8, 16, 1861, Barnsley Papers, Emory; Mrs. Edward Anderson to "My Dear Daughter," November 5, 9, 1861, Wayne-Stites-Anderson Papers, Georgia Historical Society, Savannah.

190. Griffin, "Savannah during the Civil War," 113–114, 117, 121–122; Bailey and Fraser, *Portraits of Conflict,* 32–33.

191. Byrne, "Burden and Heat," 308–312; Mohr, *Threshold of Freedom,* 207.

192. Byrne, "Hiring of Woodson," 261–263; Byrne, "Burden and Heat," 314–315; Mohr, *Threshold of Freedom,* 84–85; Mohr, "Before Sherman," 348.

193. Mohr, "Before Sherman," 340–342, 349–351.

194. W. B. Johnson, *Black Savannah,* 170–171.

195. Willis to "My Dear Darling Wife," December 1, 1861, Confederate States Army Archives, Army Miscellany, Officers and Soldiers Miscellaneous Letters, Duke University.

196. Bailey and Fraser, *Portraits of Conflict,* 32–34; Fornell, "Civil War," 254–255; Lattimore, *Fort Pulaski,* 24–26, 29–36; F. N. Boney, "War and Defeat," in Coleman, *History of Georgia,* 672; Bryan, *Confederate Georgia,* 67–74.

197. DeCredico, *Patriotism for Profit,* 40; Bailey and Fraser, *Portraits of Conflict,* 278.

198. Quoted in Fornell, "Civil War," 256, 258.

199. Henrietta Wayne to "My Dear Mama," March 10, May 6, 1861, Harden Papers, Duke; Charles C. Jones Jr. to "My Dear Father & Mother," April 24, 1861, Charles C. Jones Jr. Papers, Duke; Holcombe, *Report of Holcombe,* 4–5, 7–8; Mohr, "Slavery and Class Tensions," 64–65.

200. [Mrs. Edward Anderson] to "My Dear Daughter," November 22, 1861, Wayne-Stites-Anderson Papers, Georgia Historical Society, Savannah; Griffin, "Savannah during the Civil War," 127–128; Benjamin S. Garrett to "de[a]r brother or cister," November 11, 1862, in Wynne and Harrison, "'Plain Folk,'" 103–107; Holcombe, *Report of Holcombe,* 3.

201. Risley, "Peter W. Alexander," 35, 37, 39.

202. Griffin, "Savannah during the Civil War," 129; Merrill, "Personne Goes to Georgia," 203–205.

203. Quoted in Griffin, "Savannah during the Civil War," 127–128.

204. General Order #27, Savannah, September 23, 1861, by order of General A. R. Lawton in Confederate Miscellany, Duke University; [Sarah Lawton] to "My

Dear Sister," September 18, 1861, Alexander R. Lawton Papers, University of North Carolina; Edward Anderson to "My Darling Wife," July 26, 1862, Capt. Geo. A. Mercer to Capt. E. C. Anderson, August 23, 1862, Wayne-Stites-Anderson Papers, Georgia Historical Society; M. F. Neufville to John J. Kollock, September 2, 1862, Kollock Papers, Georgia Historical Society; Edward Clifford Anderson Diary, January 18, 26, 27, 1862, University of North Carolina.

205. Mercer Diary, [1863], University of North Carolina; Edward Clifford Anderson Diary, February 2, September 1, 28, 1864, Anderson Papers, University of North Carolina; Capt. Edward C. Anderson Jr. to Maj. H. Bryan, January 25, to Capt. George A. Mercer, February 4, 1863, Captain Robert Grant to Capt. George A. Mercer, Wayne-Stites-Anderson Papers, Georgia Historical Society.

206. Edward Clifford Anderson Diary, November 12, 1863, January 12, March 17, April 15, May 13, 16, June 12, August 9, September 24, 1864, University of North Carolina; Henrietta Wayne to "My Dear Mama," February 24, 1863, Harden Papers, Duke; Capt. George A. Mercer to Maj. E. C. Anderson, Jr., May 22, 27, 1863, W. W. Gordon to Major E. C. Anderson, May 29, 1863, Wayne-Stites-Anderson Papers, Georgia Historical Society; Capt. S. S. Lee to Commodore William W. Hunter, September 14, 1864, October 19, 1864, William W. Hunter Papers, Duke University.

207. Lieut. Col. Charles C. Jones Jr., "The Private Soldier of the Present Revolution" [August 13, 1863] in Charles C. Jones Jr. Papers, Duke University; "Circular" to "Soldiers of this Brigade," March 2, 1864, Wayne-Stites-Anderson Papers, Georgia Historical Society, Savannah.

208. Mrs. [Edward Anderson] to "My Dear Daughter," November 22, 1861, Wayne-Stites-Anderson Papers, Georgia Historical Society; Major Edward Harden to "My Dear Mother," April 17, 1862, Harden Papers, Duke University; William Duncan to Godfrey Barnsley, February 14, 1862, Barnsley Papers, Emory University; Bishop of Savannah, Augustin Verot to Patrick N. Lynch, Bishop of Charleston, March 22, 1864 in Wight, "Letters of Bishop of Savannah," 104–105; Julia Barnsley to Godfrey Barnsley, December 8, 1864, Barnsley Papers, Duke University.

209. Edward Clifford Anderson Diary, July 30, August 8, September 8, 9, 10, 11, 12, 13, 15, 25, 28, 29, October 2, 5, 6, 8, 9, 10, 11, 12, 13, 17, 19, 20, 1864.

210. Anderson Diary, October 4, 14, 1864.

211. Bailey and Fraser, *Portraits of Conflict,* 239–248.

Bibliography

MANUSCRIPT COLLECTIONS

Duke University: Richard Dennis Arnold Diary (1832–1838). Eleanor J. W. Baker Papers. Godfrey Barnsley Papers. Victor W. Bassett Papers. William J. Blackshear Papers. A. S. Bulloch Letterbook, 1817–1826. Charles C. Jones Jr. Papers. CSA (Confederate States Army) Archives, Army, Miscellany, Officers and Soldiers Miscellaneous Letters. Habersham Family Papers. Edward Harden Papers. John F. Hamilton Papers. William W. Hunter Papers. James Jackson Papers. Telfair Family Papers.

Emory University: Godfrey Barnsley Papers. Kollock-Johnston Papers. Stiles Collection.

Georgia Department of Archives and History: Chatham County File—GDAH, "Negroes—Census, 1798." Custom House Collectors Office [Ledger], 1812–1813. William Few Papers. James Gardner Papers. Governor's Letterbooks. Sarah A. Lawton Letter. "Negro File."

Georgia Historical Society: Mrs. E. H. Allen Letter. John V. Bevan Papers. Daniel Blake Papers. Chatham Artillery Papers. Christ Church Records. Walter Cliffe Paper. William Duncan Papers. Mary and Frances Few Papers. Fraser-Couper Papers. Gordon Family Papers. Isabella C. Hamilton Papers. John Houston Papers. Index to Registers of Death [in the City of Savannah], 1803–1853. Kollock Family Papers. Letter Books, Mayor's Office, Vol. 1, 1817–1851. Madeira Club Papers. Maryanne Stiles Papers. Savannah Board of Health Minute Book. Savannah Cadets Minute Book, 1861–1873. Savannah Home for Girls [Female Asylum] Minutes of the Board. Savannah Free School Society Minutes of the Board of Managers. Savannah History Research Association Papers. Savannah Library Society Papers. Savannah Port Society Papers, Minutes of the Board of Managers, 1843–1873. Edward Telfair Papers. N. S. Tyler Papers. Wayne-Stites-Anderson Papers.

Savannah City Archives, City Hall: City Council Minutes, 1789–1865.

University of Georgia, Special Collections: Godfrey Barnsley Papers. William Starr Bassinger Collection. Branch Family Papers. Telamon Cuyler Collection. Charles C. Jones Papers. Minutes of the Inferior Court, Chatham County,

1801–1807. Keith Read Collection. "Letter-Yellow Fever." William Foster Parker Diary, 1859–1860.

University of North Carolina, Southern Historical Collection: Edward Clifford Anderson Diary. Courtlandt Van Rensselaer Paper. Bulloch Family Papers. Henry Cathell Diary, 1851–1852. Gordon Papers. Alexander R. Lawton Papers. George Anderson Mercer Diary.

OTHER SOURCES

Abbot, William W. *The Royal Governors of Georgia, 1754–1775.* Chapel Hill: University of North Carolina Press, 1959.

An Account of the Reception of General Lafayette in Savannah on Saturday March 19th, 1825 and of the Entertainments Given Him. . . . Savannah: W. Williams, 1825.

Adler, Lee. "The Right Way." Madeira Club presentation, Savannah, January 27, 1976, Madeira Club Papers, Georgia Historical Society.

Adler, Leopold, II, et al., eds. *Historic Savannah.* Savannah: Historic Savannah Foundation, 1968.

Aldridge, Alfred O. "George Whitefield's Georgia Controversies." *Journal of Southern History* 9 (August 1943): 357–379.

Anderson, Edward C. *Report of Edward C. Anderson, Mayor of the City of Savannah, for the Year Ending October 31, 1855.* Savannah: Power Press of George N. Nichols, 1855.

———. *Report of Edward C. Anderson, Mayor of the City of Savannah, for the Year Ending October 31, 1856.* Savannah: Power Press of George N. Nichols, 1856.

Aptheker, Herbert. "Militant Abolitionism." *Journal of Negro History* 26 (October 1941): 438–484.

Arnold, Richard D. *Report of R. D. Arnold, Mayor of the City of Savannah, for the Year Ending September 30, 1860.* Savannah: Power Press of John M. Cooper, 1860.

Arthur, Linda L. "A New Look at Schooling and Literacy: The Colony of Georgia." *Georgia Historical Quarterly* 84 (winter 2000): 563–588.

Ayers, Edward L. *Vengeance and Justice: Crime and Punishment in the Nineteenth-Century South.* New York: Oxford University Press, 1984.

Bailey, Anne J., and Walter J. Fraser Jr. *Portraits of Conflict: A Photographic History of Georgia in the Civil War.* Fayetteville: University of Arkansas Press, 1997.

Baine, Rodney M. "General James Oglethorpe and the Expedition against St. Augustine." *Georgia Historical Quarterly* 84 (summer 2000): 197–229.

———. "Indian Slavery in Colonial Georgia." *Georgia Historical Quarterly* 79 (summer 1995): 418–424.

———. "Myths of Mary Musgrove." *Georgia Historical Quarterly* 76 (summer 1992): 428–435.

———. "Oglethorpe's Forty Irish 'Convicts.'" *Georgia Historical Quarterly* 77 (summer 1994): 326–338.

———. "The Prison Death of Robert Castell and Its Effect on the Founding of Georgia." *Georgia Historical Quarterly* 73 (spring 1989): 67–78.

Baine, Rodney M., and Louis De Vorsey Jr. "The Provenance and Historical Accuracy of 'A View of Savannah as It Stood the 29th of March, 1734.'" *Georgia Historical Quarterly* 73 (winter 1989): 784–813.

Baine, Rodney M., and Mary E. Williams. "James Oglethorpe in Europe: Recent Findings in His Military Life." In *Oglethorpe in Perspective: Georgia's Founder after Two Hundred Years,* ed. Phinizy Spalding and Harvey H. Jackson, 112–121. Tuscaloosa: University of Alabama Press, 1989.

Bancroft, Frederic. *Slave Trading in the Old South.* Reprint, New York: Frederick Ungar, 1931.

Bancroft, Joseph. *Census of the City of Savannah.* Savannah: Edward C. Councell, 1848.

Bartley, Numan V. *The Creation of Modern Georgia.* Athens: University of Georgia Press, 1990.

Barton, Tom. "Savannah Parties: Always in Season." *Savannah Magazine* (November\December 1995): 17–19.

Bassett, Victor H. "The Early History of Vaccinations against Smallpox in the Southeastern Part of the United States." *Journal of the Florida Medical Association* 21 (February 1935): 343–349.

———. "Plantation Medicine." *Medical Association of Georgia* 29 (March 1940): 112–122.

Bell, Malcolm. "Isundiga." Madeira Club presentation, Savannah, November 25, 1975, Madiera Club Papers, Georgia Historical Society.

Bell, Malcolm, Jr. "Ease and Elegance, Madeira and Murder: The Social Life of Savannah's City Hotel." *Georgia Historical Quarterly* 76 (fall 1992): 551–576.

———. *Major Butler's Legacy: Five Generations of a Slaveholding Family.* Athens: University of Georgia Press, 1987.

———. *Savannah, Ahoy!* Savannah: Pigeonhole Press, 1959.

Bellows, Barbara L. "Tempering the Wind: The Southern Response to Urban Poverty, 1850–1865." Ph.D. diss., University of South Carolina, 1983.

Berlin, Ira. *Slaves without Masters: The Free Negro in the Antebellum South.* New York: Vintage Press, 1976.

Berry, Stephen. "More Alluring at a Distance: Absentee Patriarchy and the Thomas Butler King Family." *Georgia Historical Quarterly* 81 (winter 1997): 863–896.

Black, Robert C., III. "The Railroads of Georgia in the Confederate War Effort." *Journal of Southern History* 13 (November 1947): 511–534.

Boles, John B. "Henry Holcombe: Minister, Humanitarian, and Man of Letters." *Georgia Historical Quarterly* 54 (fall 1970): 381–407.

Bolster, Jeffrey. *Black Jacks: African American Seamen in the Age of Sail.* Cambridge: Harvard University Press, 1997.

Boney, F. N. *Rebel Georgia.* Macon: Mercer University Press, 1997.

Bonner, James C. *A History of Georgia Agriculture, 1732–1860.* Athens: University of Georgia Press, 1964.

Bragg, William Harris. *De Renne: Three Generations of a Georgia Family.* Athens: University of Georgia Press, 1999.

Bridges, Edwin C. "George Walton: A Political Biography." Ph.D. diss., University of Chicago, 1981.

Broucek, Jack W. "Eighteenth Century Music in Savannah, Georgia." Ph.D. diss., Florida State University, 1975.

Brownell, Blaine A., and David R. Goldfield, eds. *The City in Southern History: The Growth of Urban Civilization in the South.* Port Washington, N.Y.: Kennikat Press, 1977.

Bryan, T. Conn. "The Churches of Georgia during the Civil War." *Georgia Historical Quarterly* 33 (December 1949): 283–302.

———. *Confederate Georgia.* Athens: University of Georgia Press, 1953.

Burke, Emily P. *Pleasure and Pain: Reminiscences of Georgia in the 1840s.* Reprint, Savannah: Bee Hive Press, 1978.

Byrne, William A. "The Hiring of Woodson, Slave Carpenter of Savannah." *Georgia Historical Quarterly* 77 (summer 1993): 245–263.

Byrne, William Andrew. "The Burden and Heat of the Day: Slavery and Servitude in Savannah, 1733–1865." Ph.D. diss., Florida State University, 1979.

Cadle, Farris W. *Georgia Land Surveying History and Law.* Athens: University of Georgia Press, 1991.

Caldwell, Lee Ann. "Women Landholders of Colonial Georgia." In *Forty Years of Diversity: Essays on Colonial Georgia,* ed. Harvey H. Jackson and Phinizy Spalding, 183–195. Athens: University of Georgia Press, 1984.

Candler, Allen D. *The Revolutionary Records of Georgia, 1769–1782.* 3 vols. Atlanta: Franklin-Turner, 1908.

Cashin, Edward J., ed. *Colonial Augusta: "Key of the Indian Countrey."* Macon: Mercer University Press, 1986.

———. "'The Famous Colonel Wells': Factionalism in Revolutionary Georgia." *Georgia Historical Quarterly* 58 (supplement 1974): 137–156.

———. *Lachlan McGillivray, Indian Trader: The Shaping of the Southern Colonial Frontier.* Athens: University of Georgia Press, 1992.

————. "Oglethorpe's Contest for the Backcountry, 1733–1749." In *Oglethorpe in Perspective: Georgia's Founder after Two Hundred Years,* ed. Phinizy Spalding and Harvey H. Jackson, 99–111. Tuscaloosa: University of Alabama Press, 1989.

————. "Sowing the Wind: Governor Wright and the Georgia Backcountry on the Eve of the Revolution." In *Forty Years of Diversity: Essays on Colonial Georgia,* ed. Harvey H. Jackson and Phinizy Spalding, 233–250. Athens: University of Georgia Press, 1984.

Cashin, Joan E. "The Structure of Antebellum Planter Families: 'The Ties That Bound Us Was Strong.'" *Journal of Southern History* 56 (February 1990): 55–70.

Cates, Gerald L. "'The Seasoning': Disease and Death among the First Colonists of Georgia." *Georgia Historical Quarterly* 64 (summer 1980): 146–158.

Cates, Gerald Lee. "A Medical History of Georgia: The First Hundred Years, 1733–1833." Ph.D. diss., University of Georgia, 1976.

————. "Medical Schools in Ante-Bellum Georgia." Master's thesis, University of Georgia, 1968.

Ceryanec, Victor J. The History of Candler General Hospital. N.p., n.d.

Chaplin, Joyce E. "Creating a Cotton South in Georgia and South Carolina, 1760–1815." *Journal of Southern History* 55 (May 1991): 171–200.

————. "Tidal Rice Cultivation and the Problem of Slavery in South Carolina and Georgia, 1760–1815." *William and Mary Quarterly* 49 (January 1992): 29–61.

Chesnutt, David Rogers. "South Carolina's Expansion into Colonial Georgia, 1720–1765." Ph.D. diss., University of Georgia, 1973.

Clark, George P. "The Role of Haitian Volunteers at Savannah in 1779: An Attempt at an Objective View." *Phylon* 41 (December 1980): 356–366.

Clinton, Catherine, and Michele Gillespie, eds. *The Devil's Lane: Sex and Race in the Early South.* New York: Oxford University Press, 1997.

Cochrane, Hortense S. "Early Treatment of the Mentally Ill in Georgia." *Georgia Historical Quarterly* 32 (June 1948): 105–118.

Coleman, Kenneth. *The American Revolution in Georgia.* Athens: University of Georgia Press, 1958.

————. *Colonial Georgia: A History.* New York: Scribner's Sons, 1976.

————. "The Founding of Georgia." In *Forty Years of Diversity: Essays on Colonial Georgia,* ed. Harvey H. Jackson and Phinizy Spalding, 4–20. Athens: University of Georgia Press, 1984.

————. *A History of Georgia.* 2nd ed. Athens: University of Georgia Press, 1991.

————. "James Wright." In *Dictionary of Georgia Biography,* ed. Kenneth Coleman and Charles Stephen Gurr, 2:1097–1098. Athens: University of Georgia Press, 1982.

————. "Savannah—Georgia's Port City." *Antiques* 91 (March 1967): 322–323.

———. "Social Life in Georgia in the 1780s." *Georgia Review* 9 (summer 1955): 217–228.

———. "The Southern Frontier: Georgia's Founding and the Expansion of South Carolina." *Georgia Historical Quarterly* 56 (summer 1972): 163–174.

Coleman, Kenneth, and Charles Stephen Gurr, eds. *Dictionary of Georgia Biography.* 2 vols. Athens: University of Georgia Press, 1982.

Collections of the Georgia Historical Society. 11 vols. Savannah: Georgia Historical Society, 1840–1955.

Collins, Doris Kirk. "The Episcopal Church in Georgia from the Revolutionary War to 1860." Master's thesis, Emory University, 1957.

Colonial Records of the State of Georgia. Comp. Allen D. Candler. Vols. 1–19, 21–26. Vol. 4: A Journal of the Proceedings in Georgia Beginning October 20, 1737 (By William Stephens, Esq.) to Which Is Added a State of That Province as Attested upon Oath in the Court of Savannah, November 10, 1740. Atlanta: Franklin Printing, 1906. Vol. 6: Proceedings of the President and Assistants from October 12, 1741, to October 30, 1754. Atlanta: Franklin Printing, 1906. Vol. 7: Proceedings and Minutes of the Governor and Council of His Majesty's Province of Georgia [October 30, 1754–March 6, 1759]. Atlanta: Franklin-Turner, 1906. Vol. 8: Journal of the Proceedings of the Governor and Council [March 8, 1759–December 31. 1762]. Atlanta: Franklin-Turner, 1907. Vol. 12: Proceedings and Minutes of the Governor and Council [August 6, 1771–February 13, 1782]. Atlanta: Franklin-Turner, 1907. Vol. 13: Journal of the Commons House of Assembly [January 7, 1755–December 16, 1762]. Atlanta: Franklin-Turner, 1907. Vol. 14, pt. 1: Journal of the Commons House of Assembly [January 17, 1763–December 24, 1768]. Atlanta: Franklin-Turner, 1907. Vol. 15: Journal of the Commons House of Assembly [October 30, 1769–June 16, 1782]. Atlanta: Franklin-Turner, 1907. Vol. 17: Journal of the Upper House of Assembly [January 17, 1763–March 12, 1774]. Atlanta: Franklin-Turner, 1908. Vol. 18: Statutes Enacted by the Royal Legislature of Georgia from Its First Session in 1754 to 1768. Atlanta: Chas. P. Byrd, State Printer, 1910. Vol. 19, pt. 1: Statutes, Colonial and Revolutionary, 1768 to 1773. Atlanta: Chas. P. Byrd, State Printer, 1911. Vol. 19, pt. 2: Statutes, Colonial and Revolutionary, 1774 to 1805. Atlanta: Chas. P. Byrd, State Printer, 1911. Vol. 28, pt. 1: Original Papers. Governors Reynolds, Ellis, Wright and Others. 1757–1763. [Typed: WPA Project #3750], 1937. Vol. 28, pt. 2: Original Papers. Governors Reynolds, Ellis, Wright and Others. 1764–1782. [Typed: WPA Project #3750], 1937.

Colonial Records of the State of Georgia. Ed. Kenneth Coleman and Milton Ready. Vols. 20, 27–32. Athens: University of Georgia Press, 1977–1989. Vol. 20: Original Papers, Correspondence to the Trustees, James Oglethorpe, and Others, 1732–1735. 1982. Vol. 27: Original Papers of Governor John Reynolds, 1754–1756. 1977. Vol. 28, pt. 1: Original Papers of Governors Reynolds, Ellis, Wright, and Others, 1757–1763. 1976. Vol. 28, pt. 2: Original Papers of Governors Reynolds, Ellis, Wright and Others, 1764–1782. 1979.

———. *The Colony of Georgia, 1717–1734*. Savannah: Beehive Press, 1972.

Cooper, William J., Jr. *Liberty and Slavery: Southern Politics to 1860*. New York: Knopf, 1983.

Corry, John P. "The Houses of Colonial Georgia." *Georgia Historical Quarterly* 14 (September 1930): 181–201.

Cory, Earl Wallace. "Temperance and Prohibition in Ante-Bellum Georgia." Master's thesis, University of Georgia, 1957.

Coulter, E. Merton. "The Acadians in Georgia." *Georgia Historical Quarterly* 47 (March 1963): 68–75.

———. "The Great Savannah Fire of 1820." *Georgia Historical Quarterly* 23 (March 1939): 1–27.

———, ed. *The Journal of Peter Gordon, 1732–1735*. Athens: University of Georgia Press, 1963.

———, ed. *The Journal of William Stephens, 1743–1745*. Athens: University of Georgia Press, 1959.

———, ed. "A List of the First Shipload of Georgia Settlers." *Georgia Historical Quarterly* 31 (December 1947): 282–288.

———. "Mary Musgrove, 'Queen of the Creeks': A Chapter of Early Georgia Troubles." *Georgia Historical Quarterly* 11 (March 1921): 13–29.

———. "Presidential Visits to Georgia during Ante-Bellum Times." *Georgia Historical Quarterly* 55 (fall 1971): 329–364.

———. *Wormsloe: Two Centuries of a Georgia Family*. Athens: University of Georgia Press, 1955.

Coulter, E. Merton, and Albert B. Saye, eds. *A List of the Early Settlers of Georgia*. Athens: University of Georgia Press, 1949.

Crane, Verner W. *The Southern Frontier*. Ann Arbor: University of Michigan Press, 1959.

Cushing, John D., ed. *The First Laws of the State of Georgia, Part 1*. Wilmington, Del.: Michael Glazier, 1981.

Cutten, George Barton. *The Silversmiths of Georgia: Together with Watchmakers and Jewelers, 1733–1850*. Savannah: Pigeonhole Press, 1958.

Dailey, R. P. "Vessels That Have Borne the Name *Savannah*." *Georgia Historical Quarterly* 18 (June 1934): 147–175.

Daniel, Marjorie. "Anglicans and Dissenters in Georgia, 1758–1777." *Church History* 7 (September 1938): 247–262.

Davis, Harold E. "Bartholomew Zouberbuhler." In *Dictionary of Georgia Biography*, ed. Kenneth Coleman and Charles S. Gurr, 2:1106–1108. Athens: University of Georgia Press, 1983.

———. *The Fledgling Province: Social and Cultural Life in Colonial Georgia, 1733–1776.* Chapel Hill: University of North Carolina Press, 1976.

Davis, Mollie C. "Whitefield's Attempt to Establish a College in Georgia. *Georgia Historical Quarterly* 55 (winter 1971): 459–469.

DeCredico, Mary A. *Patriotism for Profit: Georgia's Urban Entrepreneurs and the Confederate War Effort.* Chapel Hill: University of North Carolina Press, 1990.

———. "'War Is Good Business': Georgia's Urban Entrepreneurs and the Confederate War Effort." *Georgia Historical Quarterly* 83 (summer 1989): 231–249.

De Vorsey, Louis, Jr. "The Colonial Georgia Backcountry." In *Colonial Augusta: "Key of the Indian Countrey,"* ed. Edward J. Cashin, 3–28. Macon: Mercer University Press, 1986.

———. *DeBrahm's Report of the General Survey in the Southern District of North America.* Columbia: University of South Carolina Press, 1971.

Dismukes, Camillus J., ed. "Colonial Georgia Newspaper Notices: Commercial Advertisers in the *Georgia Gazette,* 1763–1776." Manuscript, University of Georgia Library.

Dixon, Jefferson Max. "The Central of Georgia Railroad, 1833–1892." Ph.D. diss., George Peabody College for Teachers, 1953.

Dixon, Max. "Building the Central of Georgia Railroad." *Georgia Historical Quarterly* 45 (March 1961): 1–21.

Dormon, James H., Jr. *Theater in the Antebellum South, 1815–1861.* Chapel Hill: University of North Carolina Press, 1967.

Drago, Edmund L. "How Sherman's March through Georgia Affected the Slaves." *Georgia Historical Quarterly* 57 (fall 1973): 361–375.

Egan, Clifford L. "Fracas in Savannah: National Exasperation in Microcosm, 1811." *Georgia Historical Quarterly* 54 (March 1970): 79–86.

Eisterhold, John A. "Savannah: Lumber Center of the South Atlantic." *Georgia Historical Quarterly* 57 (December 1973): 526–543.

Ellefson, C. Ashley. "James Habersham and Georgia Loyalism, 1764–1775." *Georgia Historical Quarterly* 44 (December 1960): 359–380.

Elliott, Stephen. *An Address Delivered at the Opening of the First Session of the Savannah Medical College, on November 7, 1853.* Savannah: George N. Nichols, 1853.

Ettinger, Amos A. *James Edward Oglethorpe: Imperial Idealist.* Oxford: Clarendon Press, 1936.

Facts and Figures in Connection with the Chatham County Jail. Savannah: George N. Nichols, 1881.

Farley, Foster M. "John Elliott Ward, Mayor of Savannah, 1853–1854." *Georgia Historical Quarterly* 53 (March 1969): 68–77.

———. "The Mighty Monarch of the South: Yellow Fever in Charleston and Savannah." *Georgia Review* 27 (1973): 56–70.

Federal Writers Project in Georgia. *Savannah.* Savannah: Review Printing, 1937.

Flanders, Bertram H. *Early Georgia Magazines: Literary Periodicals to 1865.* Athens: University of Georgia Press, 1944.

Flanders, Ralph B. "The Free Negro in Ante-Bellum Georgia." *North Carolina Historical Review* 9 (July 1932): 250–272.

Flanders, Ralph Betts. *Slavery in Plantation Georgia.* Cos Cob, Conn.: John E. Edwards, 1967.

Fleetwood, Rusty. *Tidecraft: An Introductory Look at the Boats of Lower South Carolina, Georgia, and Northeastern Florida: 1650–1950.* Savannah: Coastal Heritage Society, 1982.

Fogleman, Aaron Spencer. "Shadow Boxing in Georgia: The Beginnings of the Moravian-Lutheran Conflict in British North America." *Georgia Historical Quarterly* 83 (winter 1999): 629–659.

Fornell, Earl W. "The Civil War Comes to Savannah." *Georgia Historical Quarterly* 43 (September 1959): 248–260.

Fraser, Walter J., Jr. *Charleston! Charleston! The History of a Southern City.* Columbia: University of South Carolina Press, 1989.

———. "The City Elite, 'Disorder,' and the Poor Children of Pre-Revolutionary Charleston." *South Carolina Historical Magazine* 84 (July 1983): 167–179.

Frasier, Alfonso. "Free Negroes in Chatham County, Georgia, prior to the Civil War." Master's thesis, Atlanta University, 1965.

Frey, Sylvia R. *Water from the Rock: Black Resistance in a Revolutionary Age.* Princeton: Princeton University Press, 1991.

Gallay, Alan. *The Formation of a Planter Elite: Jonathan Bryan and the Southern Colonial Frontier.* Athens: University of Georgia Press, 1989.

———. "The Great Sellout: George Whitefield on Slavery." In *Looking South: Chapters in the Story of an American Region,* ed. Winfred B. Moore and Joseph F. Tripp, 17–27. Westport, Conn.: Greenwood Press, 1989.

———. "Jonathan Bryan's Plantation Empire: Land, Politics, and the Formation of a Ruling Class in Colonial Georgia." *William and Mary Quarterly* 45 (April 1988): 253–279.

———. "The Origins of Slaveholders' Paternalism: George Whitefield, the Bryan Family, and the Great Awakening in the South." *Journal of Southern History* 53 (August 1987): 369–394.

Gamble, Thomas, Jr. *A History of the City Government of Savannah, Ga., from 1790–1901.* Savannah: City Council, 1901.

————. *Savannah Duels and Duelists, 1733–1877.* Savannah: Review Publishing & Printing, 1923.

Gibson, George H. "Unitarian Congregations in Ante-Bellum Georgia." *Georgia Historical Quarterly* 54 (Summer 1970): 147–168.

Giffen, Lee. "Living with Antiques: Wormsloe, the Home of Mrs. Craig Barrow." *Antiques* 91 (March 1967): 370–373.

Gillespie, Michele. "Artisans and Mechanics in the Political Economy of Georgia, 1790–1860." Ph.D. diss., Princeton University, 1990.

————. *Free Labor in an Unfree World: White Artisans in Slaveholding Georgia, 1789–1860.* Athens: University of Georgia Press, 2000.

Goff, John H. "The Steamboat Period in Georgia." *Georgia Historical Quarterly* 12 (September 1928): 236–254.

Goldfield, David R. "The Business of Health Planning: Disease Prevention in the Old South." *Journal of Southern History* 42 (November 1976): 557–570.

————. *Religion, Race, and Cities: Interpreting the Urban South.* Baton Rouge: Louisiana State University Press, 1997.

Govan, Thomas P. "Banking and the Credit System in Georgia, 1810–1860." *Journal of Southern History* 4 (May 1938): 164–184.

Granger, Mary L. *Savannah Harbor: Its Origins and Development, 1733–1890.* Savannah: U.S. Army Corps of Engineers, 1968.

————. *Savannah River Plantations.* Spartanburg, S.C.: Reprint Company, 1972.

Grant, Donald L. *The Way It Was in the South: The Black Experience in Georgia.* New York: Carol Publishing Group, 1993.

Grant, James Martin. "Legislative Factions in Georgia, 1754–1798: A Socio-Political Study." Ph.D. diss., University of Georgia, 1975.

Green, Elvena M. "Theatre and Other Entertainments in Savannah, Georgia, from 1810 to 1865." Ph.D. diss., University of Iowa, 1971.

Green, Fletcher M. "Georgia's Board of Public Works, 1817–1826." *Georgia Historical Quarterly* 22 (June 1938): 117–137.

Green, Venus. "A Preliminary Investigation of Black Construction Artisans in Savannah from 1820 to 1860." Master's thesis, Columbia University, 1982.

Greenberg, Mark I. "Becoming Southern: The Jews of Savannah, Georgia, 1830–1870." *American Jewish History* 86 (1998): 55–75.

————. "Creating Ethnic, Class, and Southern Identity in Nineteenth-Century America: The Jews of Savannah, Georgia, 1830–1880." Ph.D. diss., University of Florida, 1997.

————. "Savannah's Jewish Women and the Shaping of Ethnic and Gender Identity, 1830–1900." *Georgia Historical Quarterly* 82 (winter 1998): 751–774.

Greene, Evarts B., and Virginia D. Harrington. *American Population before the Federal Census of 1790.* Reprint, Gloucester, Mass.: Peter Smith, 1966.

Greene, Jack P. "The Georgia Commons House of Assembly and the Power of Appointment to Executive Offices, 1765–1775." *Georgia Historical Quarterly* 46 (March 1962): 151–161.

Griffin, J. David. "Savannah's City Income Tax." *Georgia Historical Quarterly* 50 (June 1966): 173–176.

Griffin, James David. "Savannah, Georgia, during the Civil War." Ph.D. diss. University of Georgia, 1963.

Grimes, William. *Life of William Grimes.* New York: Horace Banks Books, 1825.

Groves, Robert Walker. "Beaulieu Plantation." *Georgia Historical Quarterly* 37 (September 1953): 200–209.

Gulick, John. *The Humanity of Cities: An Introduction to Urban Societies.* Granby, Mass.: Bergin & Garvey, 1989.

Gurr, Charles S. "Social Leadership and the Medical Profession in Antebellum Georgia." Ph.D. diss., University of Georgia, 1973.

Hamer, Philip M., et al., eds. *The Papers of Henry Laurens.* 13 vols. Columbia: University of South Carolina Press, 1972–.

Harden, William. *A History of Savannah and South Georgia.* 2 vols. Reprint, Atlanta: Cherokee, 1981.

———. "Sir James Wright: Governor of Georgia by Royal Commission, 1760–1782." *Georgia Historical Quarterly* 2 (March 1918): 22–36.

Harris, Woodrow Wilson, Jr. "The Education of the Southern Urban Adult: Charleston, South Carolina, and Savannah, Georgia, 1790–1812." Ph.D. diss., University of Georgia, 1979.

Harrold, Frances. "Colonial Siblings: Georgia's Relationship with South Carolina during the Pre-Revolutionary Period." *Georgia Historical Quarterly* 73 (winter 1989): 707–744.

Hartridge, Walter C. "Andrew Low's House." *Antiques* 91 (March 1967): 350–352.

———. "Architectural Trends in Savannah." *Antiques* 91 (March 1967): 324–330.

———. *The Green-Meldrim House.* Savannah: Society for the Preservation of Savannah Landmarks, 1943.

Haunton, Richard H. "Law and Order in Savannah, 1850–1860." *Georgia Historical Quarterly* 56 (March 1972): 1–24.

———. "Savannah in the 1850s." Ph.D. diss., Emory University, 1968.

Hawes, Lilla M., ed. "The Letter Book of Thomas Raspberry, 1758–1761." *Georgia Historical Quarterly* 40 (September 1956): 281–309.

———, ed. "The Memoirs of Charles H. Olmstead." Parts 1–4. *Georgia Historical Quarterly* 43 (March 1959): 60–74; 43 (June 1959): 170–186; 43 (September 1959): 261–280; 43 (December 1959): 378–390.

———, ed. "Minute Book, Savannah Board of Police, 1779." *Georgia Historical Quarterly* 45 (September 1961): 245–257.

Henderson, Robert T. "Saint Andrew's Society: 225 Years." *Savannah Magazine* 7 (November 1975): 9–13.

Herndon, G. Melvin. "Naval Stores in Colonial Georgia." *Georgia Historical Quarterly* 52 (December 1968): 426–433.

———. "Timber Products of Colonial Georgia." *Georgia Historical Quarterly* 57 (Spring 1973): 56–62.

Hoffman, Nelson Miles, Jr. "Godfrey Barnsley, 1805–1873: British Cotton Factor in the South." Ph.D. diss., University of Kansas, 1964.

Holcombe, Thomas. *Report of Thomas Holcombe, Mayor of the City of Savannah.* Savannah: E. J. Purse, 1863.

Honerkamp, Nicholas, et al. *The Reality of the City: Urban Archaeology at the Telfair Site, Savannah, Georgia.* Atlanta: National Park Service, 1983.

Hoskins, Charles L. *The Trouble They Seen: Profiles in the Life of Col. John H. Deveaux, 1848–1909.* Savannah: Charles L. Hoskins, 1989.

Howland, Henry R., ed. "A British Privateer in the American Revolution." *American Historical Review* 7 (January 1902): 286–303.

Hudson, Charles M. "The Genesis of Georgia's Indians." In *Forty Years of Diversity: Essays on Colonial Georgia,* ed. Harvey H. Jackson and Phinizy Spalding, 25–45. Athens: University of Georgia Press, 1984.

Hunt, Alfred N. *Haiti's Influence on Antebellum America: Slumbering Volcano in the Caribbean.* Baton Rouge: Louisiana State University Press, 1988.

Hunt, Monica. "Savannah's Black and White Longshoremen, 1856–1897." Master's thesis, Georgia Southern University and Armstrong State College, 1993.

Hunter, Anna C. "The Bay: Savannah's Water Front." *Antiques* 91 (March 1967): 332–333.

Ivers, Larry E. "Rangers, Scouts, and Tythingmen." In *Forty Years of Diversity: Essays on Colonial Georgia,* ed. Harvey H. Jackson and Phinizy Spalding, 152–162. Athens: University of Georgia Press, 1984.

Jackson, Harvey H. "The Battle of the Riceboats: Georgia Joins the Revolution." *Georgia Historical Quarterly* 58 (June 1974): 229–243.

———. "Behind the Lines: Savannah during the War of Jenkins' Ear." *Georgia Historical Quarterly* 77 (fall 1994): 471–492.

———. "The Carolina Connection: Jonathan Bryan, His Brothers, and the Founding of Georgia, 1733–1752." *Georgia Historical Quarterly* 68 (summer 1984): 147–172.

———. "Consensus and Conflict: Factional Politics in Revolutionary Georgia, 1774–1777." *Georgia Historical Quarterly* 59 (fall 1975): 388–401.

———. "Georgia Whiggery: The Origins and Effects of a Many-Faceted Movement." In *Forty Years of Diversity: Essays on Colonial Georgia,* ed. Harvey H.

Jackson and Phinizy Spalding, 251–273. Athens: University of Georgia Press, 1984.

———. *Lachlan McIntosh and the Politics of Revolutionary Georgia.* Athens: University of Georgia Press, 1979.

———. "The Rise of the Western Members: Revolutionary Politics and the Georgia Backcountry." In *An Uncivil War: The Southern Backcountry during the American Revolution,* ed. Ronald Hoffman et al., 276–320. Charlottesville: University Press of Virginia, 1985.

Jenkins, J. Caldwell. "The Steamship *Savannah.*" *Georgia Historical Quarterly* 17 (September 1933): 212–216.

Johnson, Dudley S. "William Harris Garland: Mechanic of the Old South." *Georgia Historical Quarterly* 53 (March 1969): 41–56.

Johnson, James Michael. "'Not a Single Soldier in the Province': The Military Establishment of Georgia and the Coming of the American Revolution." Ph.D. diss., Duke University, 1980.

Johnson, Otis Samuel. "The Social Welfare Role of the Black Church." Ph.D. diss., Brandeis University, 1980.

Johnson, Whittington B. "Andrew C. Marshall: A Black Religious Leader of Antebellum Savannah." *Georgia Historical Quarterly* 69 (summer 1985): 173–192.

———. *Black Savannah, 1788–1864.* Fayetteville: University of Arkansas Press, 1996.

———. "Free African-American Women in Savannah, 1800–1860: Affluence and Autonomy amid Adversity." *Georgia Historical Quarterly* 76 (summer 1992): 160–183.

———. "Free Blacks in Antebellum Savannah: An Economic Profile." *Georgia Historical Quarterly* 64 (winter 1980): 418–431.

Johnston, Edith Duncan, ed. "The Kollock Letters, 1799–1850." *Georgia Historical Quarterly* 30 (September 1946): 218–258; 31 (June 1947): 121–163.

Jones, Charles C., Jr. *History of Savannah, Ga. From its Settlement to the Close of the Eighteenth Century.* Syracuse, N.Y.: D. Mason, 1890.

———. *Report of Charles C. Jones, Jr., Mayor of the City of Savannah.* Savannah: Steam Power Press of John M. Cooper, 1861.

Jones, G. Noble. "Boy Chatham, Bugler." *Georgia Historical Quarterly* 24 (June 1941): 184.

Jones, George Fenwick, ed. "Bringing Moravians to Georgia: Three Latin Letters from James Oglethorpe to Count Nicholas von Zinzendorf." *Georgia Historical Quarterly* 80 (winter 1996): 847–858.

———. "The 'Dutch' Participation in Georgia's Colonial Wars." *Georgia Historical Quarterly* 75 (winter 1991): 771–783.

————, ed. "John Martin Bolzius Reports on Georgia." *Georgia Historical Quarterly* 47 (June 1963): 216–219.

————. "A Note on the Victor at Springhill Redoubt." *Georgia Historical Quarterly* 63 (fall 1979): 377–379.

————. *The Salzburger Saga: Religious Exiles and Other Germans along the Savannah.* Athens: University of Georgia Press, 1984.

Joslyn, Mauriel Phillips. *Charlotte's Boys: Civil War Letters of the Branch Family of Savannah.* Berryville, Va.: Rockbridge, 1996.

Kelley, Verner E. "Fore Lore of Yore." Madeira Club presentation, Savannah, [n.d.], Madeira Club Papers, Georgia Historical Society.

Kennedy, Benjamin, ed. *Muskets, Cannon Balls and Bombs: Nine Narratives of the Siege of Savannah in 1779.* Savannah: Beehive Press, 1974.

Killion, Ronald G., and Charles T. Waller. *Georgia and the Revolution.* Atlanta: Cherokee, 1975.

King, Spencer B., Jr. *Georgia Voices: A Documentary History to 1872.* Athens: University of Georgia Press, 1966.

Kole, Kaye. *The Minis Family of Georgia, 1733–1992.* Savannah: Georgia Historical Society & Abram Minis Jr., 1992.

LaFar, Mabel F. "Henry Holcombe: Minister, Humanitarian, and Man of Letters." *Georgia Historical Quarterly* 28 (September 1944): 113–137.

Lambert, Frank. "'Father against Son, and Son against Father': The Habershams of Georgia and the American Revolution." *Georgia Historical Quarterly 84 (spring 2000): 1–28.*

Lambert, Robert S. "The Confiscation of Loyalist Property in Georgia, 1782–1786." *William and Mary Quarterly* 20 (January 1963): 80–94.

Lamplugh, George R. "Farewell to the Revolution: Georgia in 1785." *Georgia Historical Quarterly* 56 (fall 1972): 387–403.

————. "George Walton, Chief Justice of Georgia, 1783–1785." *Georgia Historical Quarterly* 45 (summer 1981): 82–91.

————. "'To Check and Discourage the Wicked and Designing': John Wereat and the Revolution in Georgia." *Georgia Historical Quarterly* 61 (winter 1977): 295–307.

Lane, Mills, ed. *General Oglethorpe's Georgia: Colonial Letters, 1733–1743.* 2 vols. Savannah: Beehive Press, 1975.

————, ed. *Neither More nor Less Than Men: Slavery in Georgia: A Documentary History.* Savannah: Beehive Press, 1993.

————, ed. *The Rambler in Georgia.* Savannah: Beehive Press, 1973.

————, ed. *Times That Prove People's Principles: Civil War in Georgia: A Documentary History.* Savannah: Beehive Press, 1993.

Lane, Mills, IV. "Some Foods for Thought." Madeira Club presentation, Savannah, October 17, 1990, Madeira Club Papers, Georgia Historical Society, Savannah.

"La Rochefoucauld–Liancourt 1796." In *The Rambler in Georgia, ed.* Mills Lane. Savannah: Beehive Press, 1973.

Lattimore, Ralston B. *Fort Pulaski: National Monument.* Washington, D.C.: National Park Service, 1954.

Lawrence, Alexander A. "General Robert Howe and the British Capture of Savannah in 1778." *Georgia Historical Quarterly* 36 (December 1952): 303–327.

————. *James Johnston: Georgia's First Printer.* Savannah: Pigeonhole Press, 1956.

————. *A Present for Mr. Lincoln: The Story of Savannah from Secession to Sherman.* Macon: Ardivan Press, 1961.

————. *Storm over Savannah: The Story of Count d'Estaing and the Siege of the Town in 1779.* Athens: University of Georgia Press, 1951.

Lee, F. D., and J. L. Agnew. *Historical Record of the City of Savannah.* Savannah: Morning News Steam Power Press, 1869.

Lerski, Hanna H. *William Jay: Itinerant English Architect, 1792–1837.* Lanham, Md.: University Press of America, 1983.

Levy, B. H. "The Early History of Georgia's Jews." In *Forty Years of Diversity: Essays on Colonial Georgia,* ed. Harvey H. Jackson and Phinizy Spalding, 163–178. Athens: University of Georgia Press, 1984.

————. "Joseph Solomon Ottolenghe: Kosher Butcher in Italy—Christian Missionary in Georgia." *Georgia Historical Quarterly* 66 (summer 1982): 117–144.

————. *Mordecai Sheftall: Jewish Revolutionary Patriot.* Savannah: Press Works, 1999.

————. "Savannah's Bull Street: The Man behind Its Name." *Georgia Historical Quarterly* 71 (summer 1987): 286–296.

————. "Savannah's Old Jewish Community Cemeteries." *Georgia Historical Quarterly* 66 (spring 1982): 2–19.

Lockley, Timothy J. "Crossing the Race Divide: Interracial Sex in Antebellum Savannah." *Slavery and Abolition.* 18 (December 1997): 159-173.

————. *Lines in the Sand: Race and Class in Lowcountry Georgia, 1750–1860.* Athens: University of Georgia Press, 2001.

————. "The Strange Case of George Flyming: Justice and Gender in Antebellum Savannah." *Georgia Historical Quarterly* 74 (summer 2000): 230–253.

————. "A Struggle for Survival: Non-Elite White Women in Lowcountry Georgia, 1790–1830." In *Women of the American South: A Multicultural Reader,* ed. Christie Anne Farnham, 26–42. New York: New York University Press, 1997.

————. "Trading Encounters between Non-Elite Whites and African Americans in Savannah, 1790–1860." *Journal of Southern History* 66 (February 2000): 25–48.

Longacre, Edward G., ed. "Three Brothers Face Their Baptism of Battle, July 1861." *Georgia Historical Quarterly* 61 (summer 1977): 156–168.

Ludlum, David M. *Early American Hurricanes, 1492–1870*. Boston: American Meteorological Society, 1963.

———. *Early American Winters, 1604–1820*. Boston: American Meteorological Society, 1966.

Maguire, John E., comp. *Historical Souvenir: Savannah Fire Department*. Savannah: Presses of M. S. & D. A. Byck, 1906.

Martin, Roger A. "John Joachim Zubly." In *Dictionary of Georgia Biography*, ed. Kenneth Coleman and Charles S. Gurr, 1107. Athens: University of Georgia Press, 1983.

McCaul, Robert L. "Education in Georgia during the Period of Royal Control, 1752–1776: Financial Support of Schools and Schoolmasters." *Georgia Historical Quarterly* 40 (June 1956): 103–112.

McPherson, Robert G., ed. *The Journal of the Earl of Egmont: Abstract of the Trustees Proceedings for Establishing the Colony of Georgia, 1732–1738*. Athens: University of Georgia Press, 1962.

———, ed. "The Voyage of the *Anne*—A Daily Record." *Georgia Historical Quarterly* 44 (March 1960): 220–230.

McWhiney, Grady. "Ethnic Roots of Southern Violence." In *Master's Due: Essays in Honor of David Herbert Donald*, ed. William J. Cooper Jr. et al., 112–137. Baton Rouge: Louisiana State University Press, 1985.

Mebane, John. "Joseph Habersham in the Revolutionary War." *Georgia Historical Quarterly* 47 (March 1963): 76–83.

Merrill, James M. "Personne Goes to Georgia: Five Civil War Letters." *Georgia Historical Quarterly* 43 (June 1959): 202–211.

Miller, Randall M. "The Stamp Act in Colonial Georgia." *Georgia Historical Quarterly* 56 (fall 1972): 318–331.

———, ed. *"A Warm and Zealous Spirit": John J. Zubly and the American Revolution: A Selection of His Writings*. Macon: Mercer University Press, 1982.

Miller, Randall M., and John David Smith, eds. *Dictionary of Afro-American Slavery*. New York: Greenwood Press, 1988.

Mohl, Raymond A. "A Scotsman Visits Georgia in 1811." *Georgia Historical Quarterly* 55 (summer 1971): 259–274.

Mohr, Clarence L. "Before Sherman: Georgia Blacks and the Union War Effort, 1861–1864." *Journal of Southern History* 45 (August 1979): 331–352.

———. *On the Threshold of Freedom: Masters and Slaves in Civil War Georgia*. Athens: University of Georgia Press, 1986.

———. "Slavery and Class Tensions in Confederate Georgia." *Gulf Coast Historical Review* 4 (spring 1989): 58–72.

Montgomery, Sir Robert. *A Discourse Concerning the design'd Establishment of a New Colony to the South of Carolina, in the Most delightful Country of the Universe, 1717,* and *A Description of the Golden Islands, 1720.* In *The Most Delightful Country of the Universe: Promotional Literature of the Colony of Georgia, 1717–1734,* ed. Trevor R. Reese. Savannah: Beehive Press, 1972.

Moore, Raymond Douglas. "The Activities of Lowell Mason in Savannah, Georgia, 1813–1827." Master's thesis, University of Georgia, 1967.

Morgan, David T. "Judaism in Eighteenth-Century Georgia." *Georgia Historical Quarterly* 58 (spring 1974): 41–54.

Mumford, Lewis. *The City in History: Its Origins, Its Transformations, and Its Prospects.* New York: Harcourt, Brace & World, 1961.

———. *The Culture of Cities.* New York: Harcourt, Brace, 1938.

Murphy, W. S. "The Irish Brigade of France at the Siege of Savannah, 1779." *Georgia Historical Quarterly* 38 (December 1974): 307–321.

Murray, Gail S. "Charity within the Bounds of Race and Class: Female Benevolence in the Old South." *South Carolina Historical Magazine* 96 (January 1995): 54–70.

Myers, Robert Manson, ed. *The Children of Pride: A True Story of Georgia and the Civil War.* New Haven: Yale University Press, 1972.

Nash, Gary B. "Urban Wealth and Poverty in Pre-Revolutionary America." *Journal of Interdisciplinary History* 6 (spring 1976): 545–584.

O'Brien, Michael, ed. *All Clever Men Who Make Their Way: Critical Discourse in the Old South.* Fayetteville: University of Arkansas Press, 1982.

Oglethorpe, James Edward. *Some Account of the Design of the Trustees for Establishing Colonys in America.* Ed. Rodney M. Baine and Phinizy Spalding. Athens: University of Georgia Press, 1990.

Parsons, C. G. *Inside View of Slavery.* Boston: John P. Jewett, 1855.

Patrick, J. Max. *Savannah's Pioneer Theater from Its Origins to 1810.* Athens: University of Georgia Press, 1953.

Pearson, Charles E. "Captain Charles Stevens and the Antebellum Georgia Coasting Trade." *Georgia Historical Quarterly* 75 (fall 1991): 485–506.

Phillips, Ulrich B. *A History of Transportation in the Eastern Cotton Belt to 1860.* New York: Columbia University Press, 1908.

Pope-Hennessy, Una, ed. *The Aristocratic Journey: Being the Outspoken Letters of Mrs. Basil Hall Written during a Fourteen Months' Sojourn in America, 1827–1828.* New York: G. P. Putnam's Sons, 1931.

Purse, Thomas. *Report of Thomas Purse, Mayor of the City of Savannah.* Savannah: E. J. Purse, 1862.

Quattlebaum, Julian K., Sr. "Medicine in Early Georgia." *Journal of the Medical Association of Georgia,* 72 (December 1983): 832.

Rabac, Donna Marie. "Economy and Society in Early Georgia: A Functional Analysis of the Colony's Origins and Evolution." Ph.D. diss., University of Michigan, 1978.

Rahn, Ruby A. *The Savannah: Canoes, Indian Tradeboats, Flatboats, Steamers, Packets, and Barges.* Savannah: U.S. Army Corps of Engineers, 1968.

Ready, Milton La Verne. "An Economic History of Colonial Georgia, 1732–1754." Ph.D. diss., University of Georgia, 1970.

Reese, Trevor R., ed. *The Clamorous Malcontents: Criticisms and Defenses of the Colony of Georgia, 1741–1743* Savannah: Beehive Press, 1973.

———, ed. *The Most Delightful Country of the Universe: Promotional Literature of the Colony of Georgia, 1717–1734.* Savannah: Beehive Press, 1972.

———, ed. *Our First Visit in America: Early Reports from Colonial Georgia, 1732–1740.* Savannah: Beehive Press, 1974.

Reinberger, Mark. "Oglethorpe's Plan of Savannah: Urban Design, Speculative Freemasonry, and Enlightenment Charity." *Georgia Historical Quarterly* 81 (winter 1997): 339–382.

Reps, John W. "C2 + L2 = S2? Another Look at the Origins of Savannah's Town Plan." In *Forty Years of Diversity: Essays on Colonial Georgia,* ed. Harvey H. Jackson and Phinizy Spalding, 101–151. Athens: University of Georgia Press, 1984.

Risley, Ford. "Peter W. Alexander: Confederate Chronicler and Conscience." *American Journalism* 15 (winter 1998): 35–50.

Roach, S. F., Jr. "The *Georgia Gazette* and the Stamp Act: A Reconsideration." *Georgia Historical Quarterly* 55 (winter 1971): 471–491.

Robertson, George, Jr., ed. *Celebration of the Semi-Centennial Anniversary of the Savannah Volunteer Guards, May 1st, 1852.* Savannah: John M. Cooper & Co., 1952.

Robertson, Heard, and Thomas H. Robertson. "The Town and Fort of Augusta." In *Colonial Augusta: "Key of the Indian Countrey,"* ed. Edward J. Cashin, 59–74. Macon: Mercer University Press, 1986.

Robertson, Mary D. "Northern Rebel: The Journal of Nellie Kinzie Gordon, Savannah, 1862." *Georgia Historical Quarterly* 70 (fall 1986): 477–517.

Rousey, Dennis C. "From Whence They Came to Savannah: The Origins of an Urban Population in the Old South." *Georgia Historical Quarterly* 89 (summer 1995): 305–336.

Rowland, Lawrence S. "'Alone on the River': The Rise and Fall of the Savannah River Rice Plantations of St. Peter's Parish, South Carolina." *South Carolina Historical Magazine* 88 (July 1987): 121–150.

Rowland, Lawrence S., et al. *The History of Beaufort County, South Carolina.* Vol. 1, *1514–1861.* Columbia: University of South Carolina Press, 1996.

Russell, Preston, and Barbara Hines. *Savannah: A History of Her People since 1733.* Savannah: Frederic C. Beil, 1992.

Saye, Albert B. "The Genesis of Georgia Reviewed." *Georgia Historical Quarterly* 50 (June 1966): 127–161.

Scarborough, Ruth. *The Opposition to Slavery in Georgia prior to 1860.* Reprint, New York: Negro Universities Press, 1968.

Schweninger, Loren. *Black Property Owners in the South, 1790–1915.* Urbana: University of Illinois Press, 1990.

Scott, Julius Sherrard, III. "The Common Wind: Elements of Afro-American Communication in the Era of the Haitian Revolution." Ph.D. diss., Duke University, 1986.

[Screven, John]. *The Savannah Benevolent Association.* Savannah: Morning News Print, 1896.

Searcy, Martha Condray. "1779: The First Year of the British Occupation of Georgia." *Georgia Historical Quarterly* 67 (summer 1983): 168–188.

Shoemaker, Edward M. "Invasion of the Green: Irish Immigrants in the Growth of Savannah, 1837–1861." N.d. Paper in possession of Walter J. Fraser Jr.

———. "Irish Immigrants and Community Values in Savannah, 1837–1861." N.d. Paper in possession of Walter J. Fraser Jr.

———. "Strangers and Citizens: The Irish Immigrant Community of Savannah, 1837–1861." Ph.D. diss., Emory University, 1990.

Sholes, A. E., comp. *Chronological History of Savannah from Its Settlement by Oglethorpe down to December 31, 1899.* Savannah: Morning News Press, 1900.

Shriver, George H. *The Historical Pilgrimage of the Evangelical Lutheran Church of the Ascension, Savannah, Georgia.* [Savannah: Lutheran Church of the Ascension, 1991.]

———. *Pilgrims through the Years: A Bicentennial History of First Baptist Church, Savannah, Georgia.* Franklin, Tenn.: Providence House, 1999.

Shryock, Richard H., ed. *Letters of Richard D. Arnold, M.D., 1808–1876.* New York: AMS Press, 1929.

Shy, John. *A People Numerous and Armed: Reflections on the Military Struggle for American Independence.* New York: Oxford University Press, 1976.

Siebert, W. H. "Spanish and French Privateering in Southern Waters, July 1762 to March 1763." *Georgia Historical Quarterly* 16 (September 1932): 165–173.

Sirmans, Eugene. *Colonial South Carolina, A Political History, 1663–1763.* Chapel Hill: University of North Carolina Press, 1966.

Smith, Derek. *Civil War Savannah.* Savannah: Frederic C. Beil, 1997.

Smith, Julia F. "The Savannah River." In *Rolling Rivers: An Encyclopedia of America's Rivers,* ed. Richard A. Bartlett, 83–86. New York: McGraw-Hill, 1984.

Smith, Julia Floyd. *Slavery and Rice Culture in Low Country Georgia, 1750–1860.* Knoxville: University of Tennessee Press, 1985.

Smith, W. Calvin. "Georgia Gentlemen: The Habershams of Eighteenth-Century Savannah." Ph.D. diss., University of North Carolina, 1971.

———. "The Habershams: The Merchant Experience in Georgia." In *Forty Years of Diversity: Essays on Colonial Georgia,* ed. Harvey H. Jackson and Phinizy Spalding, 198–204. Athens: University of Georgia Press, 1984.

Sowell, Mary. "A Social and Economic History of Savannah, Georgia, during the Revolutionary War." Master's thesis, University of Georgia, 1952.

Spalding, Phinizy. "Colonial Period." In *A History of Georgia,* ed. Kenneth Coleman, 9–67. Athens: University of Georgia Press, 1991.

———. "James Edward Oglethorpe's Quest for an American Zion." In *Forty Years of Diversity: Essays on Colonial Georgia,* ed. Harvey H. Jackson and Phinizy Spalding, 60–79. Athens: University of Georgia Press, 1984.

———. "Noble W. Jones." In *Dictionary of Georgia Biography,* ed. Kenneth Coleman and Charles S. Gurr, 553–554. Athens: University of Georgia Press, 1983.

———. *Oglethorpe in America.* Chicago: University of Chicago Press, 1977.

———. "Oglethorpe, William Stephens, and the Origin of Georgia Politics." In *Oglethorpe in Perspective: Georgia's Founder after Two Hundred Years,* ed. Phinizy Spalding and Harvey H. Jackson, 80–98. Tuscaloosa: University of Alabama Press, 1989.

Spalding, Phinizy, and Harvey H. Jackson, eds. *Oglethorpe in Perspective: Georgia's Founder after Two Hundred Years.* Tuscaloosa: University of Alabama Press, 1989.

Spalding, Phinizy Billups. "Georgia and South Carolina during the Oglethorpe Period, 1732–1743." Ph.D. diss., University of North Carolina, 1963.

Spindel, Daniel J. "The Stamp Act Riots." Ph.D. diss., Duke University, 1975.

Statom, Thomas R., Jr. "Negro Slavery in Eighteenth-Century Georgia." Ph.D. diss., University of Alabama, 1982.

Stern, Malcolm H. "New Light on the Jewish Settlement of Savannah." *Publication of the American Jewish Historical Society* 52 (March 1963): 169–199.

Stevens, William Bacon. *A History of Georgia, from its First Discovery by Europeans to the Adoption of the Present Constitution.* 2 vols. Savannah: Beehive Press, 1972.

Stewart, Dorothy H. "Survival of the Fittest: William Morrill Wadley and the Central of Georgia Railroad's Coming of Age, 1866–1882." *Georgia Historical Quarterly* 88 (spring 1994): 39–65.

Stewart, Mart A. "'Policies of Nature and Vegetables': Hugh Anderson, the Georgia Experiment, and the Political Use of Natural Philosophy." *Georgia Historical Quarterly* 77 (fall 1993): 474–496.

Stokes, Thomas L. *The Savannah.* Athens: University of Georgia Press, 1951.

Strickland, Reba Carolyn. *Religion and the State in Georgia in the Eighteenth Century.* New York: Columbia University Press, 1939.

Sublett, Roger Harley. "The Georgia Whigs in the Revolutionary Crisis." Ph.D. diss., Tulane University, 1978.

Sweat, Edward F. "The Free Negro in Ante-Bellum Georgia." Ph.D. diss., Indiana University, 1957.

———. "Social Status of the Free Negro in Antebellum Georgia." *Negro History Bulletin,* 11 (1958): 30.

Talbott, Page. *Classical Savannah: Fine and Decorative Arts, 1800–1840.* Athens: University of Georgia Press, 1995.

Talmadge, John E. "Georgia's Federalist Press and the War of 1812." *Journal of Southern History* 19 (November 1953): 488–500.

Temple, Sarah B. Gober, and Kenneth Coleman. *Georgia Journeys.* Athens: University of Georgia Press, 1961.

Theus, Charlton M. *Savannah Furniture, 1735–1825.* N.p., n.d.

Thigpen, Thomas Paul. "Aristocracy of the Heart: Catholic Lay Leadership in Savannah, 1820–1870." Ph.D. diss., Emory University, 1995.

Thomas, Emory M. *The Confederate Nation: 1861–1865.* New York: Harper & Row, 1979.

Toledano, Roulhac. *Savannah: Architectural and Cultural Treasures.* New York: Wiley & Sons,, 1997.

U.S. Bureau of the Census. *Eighth Census of the United States, 1860.* Washington, D.C., 1861.

———. *Second Census of the United States, 1800.* Washington, D.C.: 1801.

———. *Seventh Census of the United States, 1850.* Washington, D.C., 1851.

———. *Sixth Census of the United States, 1840.* Washington, D.C., 1841.

———. *Slave Schedule of Savannah.* Washington, D.C., 1830, 1840.

Utley, Francis L., and Marion R. Hemperley, eds. *Placenames of Georgia: Essays of John H. Goff.* Athens: University of Georgia Press, 1975.

Van Horne, John C. "Joseph Solomon Ottolenghe (ca. 1711–1775): Catechist to the Negroes, Superintendent of the Silk Culture, and Public Servant in Colonial Georgia." *Proceedings of the American Philosophical Society* 125 (October 1981): 398–409.

Ver Steeg, Clarence. *Origins of a Southern Mosaic.* Athens: University of Georgia Press, 1975.

Wade, Arthur P. "Artillerists and Engineers: The Beginnings of American Seacoast Fortifications, 1794–1815." Ph.D. diss., Kansas State University, 1977.

Wade, Richard C. *Slavery in the Cities: The South, 1820–1860.* New York: Oxford University Press, 1967.

Waller, Tom. "Henry Ellis, Enlightenment Gentleman." *Georgia Historical Quarterly* 63 (fall 1979): 364–376.

Ward, John E. *Report of John E. Ward, Mayor of the city of Savannah for the year ending 31st October 1854 to which is added the treasurer's annual report, and an appendix.* Savannah: Purse's Printing, 1854.

Waring, Joseph Frederick. *Cerveau's Savannah.* Savannah: Georgia Historical Society, 1973.

Waring, Joseph Ioor. "Colonial Medicine in Georgia and South Carolina." *Georgia Historical Quarterly* 59 (July 1975): 140–153.

———. "The Yellow Fever Epidemic of Savannah in 1820 with a Sketch of Dr. William Coffee Daniell." *Georgia Historical Quarterly* 52 (December 1968): 398–404.

Waring, Martha G. "Savannah's Earliest Private Schools." *Georgia Historical Quarterly* 14 (December 1930): 324–334.

Warlick, Roger K. *As Grain Once Scattered: The History of Christ Church, Savannah, Georgia, 1733–1983.* Columbia, S.C.: State Printing, 1987.

Washington, Austin D. "The Dollys: An Antebellum Black Family of Savannah, Georgia." *Faculty Research Bulletin, Savannah State College* 26 (December 1972): 101–103.

———. "Some Aspects of Emancipation in Eighteenth Century Savannah, Georgia." *Faculty Research Bulletin, Savannah State College* 26 (December 1972): 104–106.

Wax, Darold D. "Georgia and the Negro before the American Revolution." *Georgia Historical Quarterly* 51 (March 1967): 63–77.

———. "'New Negroes Are Always in Demand': The Slave Trade in Eighteenth-Century Georgia." *Georgia Historical Quarterly* 68 (summer 1984): 193–220.

Weaver, Herbert. "Foreigners in Ante-Bellum Savannah." *Georgia Historical Quarterly* 37 (March 1953): 1–17.

Wells, Tom Henderson. "Charles Augustus Lafayette Lamar: Gentleman Slave Trader." *Georgia Historical Quarterly* 47 (June 1963): 158–168.

Wells, William R. "The Perception of Naval Protection: The Southern Galleys, 1798–1800." *Georgia Historical Quarterly* 80 (winter 1996): 737–758.

The Wesley Bi-Centenary Celebration in Savannah, Ga.: Wesley's Only American Home, June 25–29, 1903. Savannah: Savannah Morning News Print, 1903.

White, George. *Statistics of the State of Georgia.* Savannah: W. Thorne Williams, 1849.

Wight, Willard E., ed. "Letters of the Bishop of Savannah, 1861–1865." *Georgia Historical Quarterly* 42 (March 1958): 93–106.

Wilkins, Barratt. "A View of Savannah on the Eve of the Revolution." *Georgia Historical Quarterly* 54 (winter 1970): 577–584.

Wilkins, George Barratt, Jr. "The Commercial Rivalry between Charles Town and Savannah, 1732–1774." Master's thesis, Emory University, 1965.

Williams, Jack K. "Travel in Ante-Bellum Georgia as Recorded by English Visitors." *Georgia Historical Quarterly* 33 (September 1948): 158–174.

Williams, James A. "Savannah Silver and Silversmiths." *Antiques* 91 (March 1967): 347–349.

Wilson, Adelaide. *Historic and Picturesque Savannah.* Boston: Photogravure, 1889.

Wood, Betty. "Prisons, Workhouses, and the Control of Slave Labour in Low Country Georgia, 1763–1815." *Slavery and Abolition* 8 (1987): 247–271.

———. "Some Aspects of Female Resistance to Chattel Slavery in Low Country Georgia, 1763–1815." *Historical Journal* 30 (September 1987): 603–622.

———. "Thomas Stephens and the Introduction of Black Slavery in Georgia." *Georgia Historical Quarterly* 58 (spring 1974): 24–39.

———. "'Until He Shall Be Dead, Dead, Dead': The Judicial Treatment of Slaves in Eighteenth-Century Georgia." *Georgia Historical Quarterly* 71 (fall 1987): 377–398.

———. "'White Society' and the 'Informal Slave Economies of Lowcountry Georgia, c. 1763–1830.'" *Slavery and Abolition* 11 (1990): 313–331.

———. *Women's Work, Men's Work: The Informal Slave Economies of Lowcountry Georgia.* Athens: University of Georgia Press, 1995.

Wright, J. Leitch, Jr. *Anglo-Spanish Rivalry in North America.* Athens: University of Georgia Press, 1971.

Wyatt-Brown, Bertram. *Southern Honor: Ethics and Behavior in the Old South.* New York: Oxford University Press, 1982.

Wynne, Lewis N., and Guy Porcher Harrison. "'Plain Folk' Coping in the Confederacy: The Garrett-Asbell Letters." *Georgia Historical Quarterly* 72 (spring 1988): 102–118.

Yancey, Wanda. "In Savannah, First African Baptist Church Means *First.*" *American Visions* 4 (August, 1989): 42–43.

Young, Ann O'Quinn. "Thomas Causton." In *Dictionary of Georgia Biography,* ed. Kenneth Coleman and Charles S. Gurr, 181–182. Athens: University of Georgia Press, 1983.

Young, Jeffrey Robert. *Domesticating Slavery: The Master Class in Georgia and South Carolina, 1670–1837.* Chapel Hill: University of North Carolina, 1999.

Young, Rogers W. "The Construction of Fort Pulaski." *Georgia Historical Quarterly* 20 (March 1936): 41–51.

Index